3rd Edition

UNDERSTANDING COMPUTERS
IN A CHANGING SOCIETY

DEBORAH MORLEY

COURSE TECHNOLOGY
CENGAGE Learning™

Australia • Brazil • Japan • Korea • Mexico • Singapore • Spain • United Kingdom • United States

COURSE TECHNOLOGY
CENGAGE Learning™

Understanding Computers in a Changing Society, 3rd Edition
is published by Course Technology Cengage Learning

Executive Editor: Marie Lee

Senior Product Manager: Kathy Finnegan

Product Manager: Erik Herman

Associate Acquisition Editor: Brandi Henson

Associate Product Manager: Leigh Robbins

Marketing Manager: Ryan DeGrote

Marketing Specialist: Jennifer Hankin

Developmental Editor: Pam Conrad

Content Project Manager: Erin Dowler

Composition: GEX Publishing Services

Text and Cover Designer: Joel Sadagursky

© 2009 Course Technology, Cengage Learning

For product information and technology assistance, contact us at
Cengage Learning Customer & Sales Support, 1-800-354-9706

For permission to use material from this text or product, submit all requests online at **cengage.com/permissions**
Further permissions questions can be emailed to
permissionrequest@cengage.com

Student Edition ISBN 13: 978-0-324-59605-2

Student Edition ISBN-10: 0-324-59605-7

Course Technology
25 Thomson Place
Boston, Massachusetts 02210
USA

Cengage Learning is a leading provider of customized learning solutions with office locations around the globe, including Singapore, the United Kingdom, Australia, Mexico, Brazil, and Japan. Locate your local office at:
international.cengage.com/region

Cengage Learning products are represented in Canada by Nelson Education, Ltd.

Visit our corporate website at **cengage.com**

For your lifelong learning solutions, visit **course.cengage.com**

Purchase any of our products at your local college store or at our preferred online store **www.ichapters.com**

Printed in China
2 3 4 5 6 7 15 14 13 12 11 10 09 08

PREFACE

In today's computer-oriented society, computers and technology impact virtually everyone's life. *Understanding Computers in a Changing Society, 3rd Edition* (formerly *Computers and Technology in a Changing Society*) presents an integrated, well-balanced look at computers and technology, including the issues and concepts surrounding our constantly changing, computer-oriented society. This information will give students the understanding they need to succeed in today's world.

As computers and technology become more prevalent in our daily lives, it is increasingly important to understand not only their uses and benefits, but also the issues and risks that accompany their use. This unique textbook explores both aspects—the benefits and the risks—of computers and technology. It also explains in straightforward terms the basic computer concepts and terminology students will need to know in order to fully understand and discuss these important issues. The goal of this text is to provide readers with a solid knowledge of computer fundamentals, an understanding of the impact of our computer-oriented society, and a framework for using this knowledge effectively in their lives.

KEY FEATURES

Just like its previous editions, *Understanding Computers in a Changing Society, 3rd Edition* provides current and comprehensive coverage of important topics. Flexible organization and an engaging presentation combined with a variety of learning tools associated with each chapter help the student master important concepts. Numerous marginal notations direct students to the Understanding Computers in a Changing Society Web site where they can access **Online Videos**, **Podcasts**, and **Further Exploration** links. The Web site also includes **Interactive Activities**, **Testing Activities**, **Study Tools**, and **Additional Resources**.

Currency and Accuracy

The state-of-the-art content of this book and its Web site reflect the latest technologies, trends, and classroom needs. To ensure the content is as accurate and up to date as possible, more than 30 **Industry Expert Reviewers** provided feedback and suggestions for improvements to the content in their areas of expertise. Throughout the writing and production stages, enhancements were continually made to ensure that the final product is as current and accurate as possible.

Comprehensiveness and Depth

Accommodating a wide range of teaching preferences, *Understanding Computers in a Changing Society, 3rd Edition* provides comprehensive coverage of traditional topics while also covering relevant, up-to-the-minute new technologies and important societal issues, such as embedded computers, UMPCs, multi-core CPUs, ExpressCards, hybrid hard drives, solid-state drives, IMOD displays, LED and SED displays, 3D printers, Microsoft

Surface, mobile phone projectors, water cooling systems, Memory Spots, DataDots, and other new and emerging types of hardware; terascale computing, Windows SideShow, full disk encryption (FDE), self-encrypting hard drives, self-destructing hard drives, and other hardware technologies; virtualization, net neutrality, and other computing concepts; new software products and technologies, such as Windows Vista, Windows Speech Recognition, Software as a Service (SaaS), Microsoft Office 2007, and the Ribbon; new communications technologies, such as dual-mode mobile phones, WiMAX, mobile WiMAX, broadband over fiber (BoF), fiber to the premises (FTTP), WirelessHD, multimedia networking, wireless sensor networks, network access control (NAC) systems, and identity management; new and growing Internet applications, such as real-time search engines, Webinars, social networking sites, blogs, podcasts, mobile TV, video-on-demand (VOD), 3D virtual worlds, and online customized products; new security issues, such as Wi-Fi piggybacking, drive-by pharming, evil twins, spear phishing, cyberbullying, and mobile malware; and important new societal issues, such as data destruction, online age verification systems, virtual income taxation, server consolidation, and ENERGY STAR 4.0.

Readability

We remember more about a subject if it is presented in a straightforward way and made interesting and exciting. This book is written in a conversational, down-to-earth style—one designed to be accurate without being intimidating. Concepts are explained clearly and simply, without the use of overly technical terminology. More complex concepts are explained in an understandable manner and with realistic examples from everyday life.

Chapter Learning Tools

1. **Outline, Learning Objectives, and Overview:** For each chapter, an **Outline** of the major topics covered, a list of student **Learning Objectives**, and a **Chapter Overview** help instructors put the subject matter of the chapter in perspective and let students know what they will be reading about.

2. **Boldfaced Key Terms and Running Glossary:** Important terms appear in boldface type as they are introduced in the chapter. These terms are defined at the bottom of the page on which they appear and in the end-of-text glossary.

3. **Chapter Boxes:** In each chapter, a **Trend** box provides students with a look at current and upcoming developments in the world of computers; an **Inside the Industry** box provides insight into some of the practices that have made the computer industry unique and fascinating; a **How It Works** box explains in detail how a technology or product works; and a **Technology and You** box takes a look at how computers and technology are used in everyday life.

NEW 4. **Ask the Expert Boxes:** In each chapter, several **Ask the Expert** boxes feature a question about a computing concept, a trend, or how computers are used on the job or otherwise in the real world along with the response from an industry leader at a prominent company, including McDonald's, Jack in the Box, Microsoft, Google, SanDisk, Kingston, Seagate, The Linux Foundation, AMD, ACM, and Symantec.

5. **Marginal Tips:** TIP marginal elements feature time-saving tips or ways to avoid a common problem or terminology mistake, or present students with interesting additional information related to the chapter content.

6. **Illustrations and Photographs:** Instructive, current, full-color illustrations and photographs are used to illustrate important concepts. Figures and screenshots show the latest hardware and software and are annotated to convey important information.

TIP

If a legitimate application installed on your PC that needs the Internet can't get to the Internet, check your firewall settings—you may need to unblock that program.

NEW 7. **Online Video Marginal Element: Online Video** marginal elements direct students to the Understanding Computers in a Changing Society Web site to watch a short video (provided by Google, IBM, Symantec, and other companies) related to the topic in that section of the text.

NEW 8. **Podcast Marginal Elements: Podcast** marginal elements direct students to the Understanding Computers in a Changing Society Web site to download and listen to a podcast related to the chapter content.

9. **Summary and Key Terms:** The end-of-chapter material includes a concise, section-by-section **Summary** of the main points in the chapter. The chapter's Learning Objectives appear in the margin next to the relevant section of the summary so that students are better able to relate the Learning Objectives to the chapter material. Every boldfaced key term in the chapter also appears in boldface type in the summary.

10. **Review Activities and Projects:** End-of-chapter activities allow students to test themselves on what they have just read. A matching exercise of selected **Key Terms** helps students test their retention of the chapter material. A **Self-Quiz** (with the answers listed at the end of the book) consists of ten true-false and completion questions. Five additional easily graded matching and short-answer **Exercises** are included for instructors who would like to assign graded homework. A **Discussion Question** for each chapter provides a springboard to jump-start a classroom discussion; a **Balancing Act** project introduces a more complex topic for in-depth class discussions or student opinion papers. End-of-chapter **Projects** require students to extend their knowledge by doing research and activities beyond merely reading the book. Organized into nine types of projects (Hot Topics, Short Answer/Research, Hands On, Writing About Computers, Presentation/Demonstration, Group Discussion, Ethics in Action, Video Viewpoint, and Web Activities), the projects feature explicit instructions so that students can work through them without additional directions from instructors. Special marginal icons denote projects that require Internet access.

11. **Understanding Computers in a Changing Society Web Site:** Throughout each chapter, **Further Exploration** marginal elements direct students to the Understanding Computers in a Changing Society Web site where they can access collections of links to Web sites containing more in-depth information on a given topic from the text, as well as streaming videos and downloadable podcasts. At the end of every chapter, students are directed to the Understanding Computers in a Changing Society Web site to access a variety of other **Interactive Activities**, as well as **Testing Activities**, **Study Tools**, and **Additional Resources**.

References and Resources Guide

A **References and Resources Guide** at the end of the book brings together in one convenient location a collection of computer-related references and resources, including a **Computer History Timeline**, a **Guide to Buying a PC**, **A Closer Look at Numbering Systems** feature, and a **Coding Charts** feature.

NEW and Updated Expert Insight Features

In this exciting feature located at the end of each of the first seven chapters, industry experts provide students with personal insights on topics presented in the book, including their personal experiences with technology, key points to remember, and advice for the future. The experts, professionals from these major companies—**Nokia**, **Hewlett-Packard**, **Microsoft**, **Symantec**, **eBay**, **ACM/Google**, and **Dell**—provide a unique perspective on the book's content and how the topics discussed in the text impact their lives and their industry, what it means for the future, and more!

ONLINE VIDEO

Go to **www.course.com/uccs/ch4** to watch the "How to Protect Yourself Against Online Threats" video clip.

PODCAST

Go to **www.course.com/uccs/ch1** to download or listen to the "Is it Time for a New Computer?" podcast.

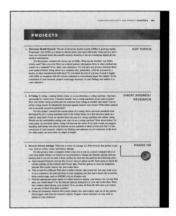

FURTHER EXPLORATION

Go to **www.course.com/uccs/ch3** for links to further information about podcasts.

Expanded Web Site Content

The **Understanding Computers in a Changing Society Web site** includes a wealth of information at your fingertips to help enhance the classroom experience and to help students master the material covered in the book. Some of the content featured on the site includes new and updated **Key Term Matching**, **Self-Quizzes**, **Exercises**, and **Practice Tests**; interactive activities, such as **Student Edition Labs**, **Video Viewpoint Projects**, **Crossword Puzzles**, **Podcasts**, **Online Videos**, and **Further Exploration** links; and many other resources, including **Online Study Guides**, **Online Summaries**, **Online Glossaries**, a **Web Guide**, and **Online References and Resources Guide** content.

Student and Instructor Support Materials

Understanding Computers in a Changing Society, 3rd Edition is available with a complete package of support materials for instructors and students. Included in the package are the Understanding Computers in a Changing Society Web site, Instructor Resources (available on CD and online), and SAM Computer Concepts.

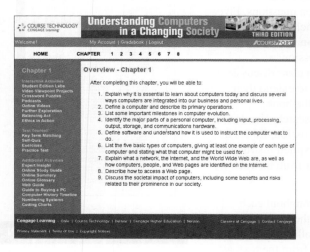

The Understanding Computers in a Changing Society Web Site

The Understanding Computers in a Changing Society Web site is located at **www.course.com/uccs** and provides media-rich support for each chapter of the book. The Web site includes the following:

▼ **Key Term Matching**—this feature allows students to test their knowledge of selected chapter key terms by matching the terms with their definitions.

▼ **Self-Quiz** and **Exercises**—these features allow students to test their retention of chapter concepts.

▼ **Practice Test**—this feature allow students to test how ready they are for upcoming exams.

▼ **Crossword Puzzles**—this feature incorporates the key terms from each chapter into an online interactive crossword puzzle.

▼ **Student Edition Lab**—this feature reinforces and expands the concepts covered in the chapters.

▼ **Balancing Act**—this feature presents the pros and cons of a technology-oriented issue, followed by discussion questions designed to promote class discussions or thoughtful opinion papers.

▼ **Ethics in Action Project**—this feature presents students with a current technology-related ethical issue and challenges them to form and express an opinion on the ethical ramifications of this issue.

▼ **Video Viewpoint Project**—this feature includes the complete **Video Viewpoint Project** associated with each chapter, as well as a link to watch the appropriate video.

▼ **Podcasts**—this feature includes downloadable podcasts related to chapter topics.

▼ **Online Videos**—this feature includes several streaming videos per chapter related to the topics in that chapter.

▼ **Further Exploration**—this feature includes links to additional information about content covered in each chapter.

▼ **Additional Resources**—this feature includes a wide range of additional resources, such as **Expert Insights**; an **Online Study Guide**, **Online Summary**, and **Online Glossary** for each chapter; a **Web Guide**, **Guide to Buying a PC**, and **Computer History Timeline**; and more information about **Numbering Systems** and **Coding Charts**.

Instructor Resources

Course Technology instructional resources and technology tools provide instructors with a wide range of tools that enhance teaching and learning. These tools can be accessed from the Instructor Resources CD or at www.course.com.

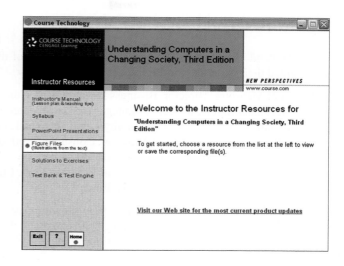

Electronic Instructor's Manual

The Instructor's Manual is written to provide instructors with practical suggestions for enhancing classroom presentations. For each chapter, the Instructor's Manual provides: **Lecture Notes**, **Teacher Tips**, **Quick Quizzes**, **Classroom Activities**, **Discussion Questions**, **Key Terms**, a **Chapter Quiz**, and more!

ExamView Test Bank

This textbook is accompanied by ExamView, a powerful testing software package that allows instructors to create and administer printed, computer (LAN-based), and Internet exams. ExamView includes over 800 questions that correspond to the topics covered in this text, enabling instructors to create exams mapping exactly to the content they cover. The computer-based and Internet testing components allow instructors to administer exams over the computer and also save time by grading each exam automatically.

PowerPoint Presentations

This book comes with **Microsoft PowerPoint presentations** for each chapter. These are included as a teaching aid for classroom presentation, to make available to students on a network for chapter review, or to be printed for classroom distribution. Instructors can customize these presentations to cover any additional topics they introduce to the class. **Figure Files** for all figures in the textbook are also on the Instructor Resource CD.

Online Content

We offer a full range of content for use with Blackboard learning platforms to simplify the use of *Understanding Computers in a Changing Society, 3rd Edition* in distance education settings. Contact your sales representative for more details.

Blackboard

SAM 2007

Add more flexibility to your course with SAM. SAM (Skills Assessment Manager) helps you energize your assignments by allowing students to train and test on important computer skills in an active, hands-on environment. By adding SAM to your curriculum, you can do the following:

▼ Reinforce your students' knowledge of key skills with hands-on application exercises.

▼ Allow your students to "learn by listening" with rich audio in their computer labs.

▼ Build computer concepts exams from a test bank of more than 50,000 questions.

▼ Schedule your students' assignments with powerful administrative tools.

▼ Track student exam grades and training progress using helpful reports by class or by student.

SAM features assessment, training, and project-grading solutions for skills in both Microsoft Office 2003 and Office 2007. Let SAM save you time in grading, while students get hands-on practice on valuable real-world skills.

ACKNOWLEDGEMENTS

We would like to extend a special thank you to all of the industry professionals who reviewed chapter content and provided their expertise for the **Expert Insight** features:

Vipul Mehrotra, Director, Business Development, Convergence, Nokia North America
John Janakiraman, Research Manager for Data Center Architecture, HP Labs
Graham Watson, Senior Community Lead, Technical Audience Global Marketing, Microsoft
Collin Davis, Development Manager, Consumer Product Solutions, Symantec Corporation
Jim Griffith, Dean of eBay Education, eBay
Stuart Feldman, President, ACM and Vice President, Engineering, Google
Frank Molsberry, Technologist, Dell Inc.

In addition, we are very grateful to the following past and present Industry Expert Reviewers for their technical reviews and helpful suggestions. We would also like to thank the following Educational Reviewers, who have helped to define and improve the quality of this text over the years.

Industry Expert Reviewers
Jason Taylor, Worldwide Director of Corporate Communications, MobiTV
Nicole Rodrigues, Public Relations Manager, MobiTV
Stephen Yeo, Worldwide Strategic Marketing Director, IGEL Technology
Bob Hirschfeld, Public Information Officer, Lawrence Livermore National Lab
Bryan Crum, Vice President of Communication, Omnilert, LLC
David Bondurant, MRAM Product Manager, Freescale Semiconductor, Inc.
Rick McGowan, Vice President & Senior Software Engineer, Unicode, Inc.
Margaret Lewis, Director of Commercial Solutions, AMD
Mark Tekunoff, Senior Technology Manager, Kingston Technology
Billy Rudock, Customer Service Staff Engineer, Seagate Technology
James M. DePuydt, Ph.D., Technology Director, Imation Corporation
Dan Bloom, Sr. PR Manager, SanDisk
Kevin Curtis, CTO, InPhase Technologies
Gail Levy, Director of Marketing, TabletKiosk
Novell Marketing
John McCreesh, Marketing Project Lead, OpenOffice.org
Jackson Dunlap, ESP Systems
Laura Abram, Director of Corporate Marketing, Dust Networks
Kevin Schader, Communications Director, ZigBee Alliance
Mauro Dresti, Linksys Product Marketing Manager
Lianne Caetano, Executive Director, WirelessHD, LLC
Brad Booth
Howard Frazier
Bob Grow
Michael McCormack
George Cravens, Technical Marketing, D-Link
Christiaan Stoudt, Founder, HomeNetworkHelp.Info
Douglas M. Winneg, President, Software Secure, Inc.
Frank Archambeault, Director of Network Services, Dartmouth College
Adam Goldstein, IT Security Engineer, Dartmouth College
Ellen Young, Manager of Consulting Services, Dartmouth College
Becky Waring, Executive Editor, JiWire.com
Ellen Craw, General Manager, Ilium Software
Michael Behr, Senior Architect, TIBCO
Joe McGlynn, Director of Product Management, CodeGear
John Nash, Vice President of Marketing, Visible Systems
Josh Shaul, Director of Technology Strategy, Application Security, Inc.
Jodi Florence, Marketing Director, IDology, Inc.
Dr. Maressa Hecht Orzack, Director, Computer Addiction Services

Industry Expert Reviewers–Previous Editions

Janice K. Mahon, Vice President of Technology Commercialization, Universal Display Corporation; Dr. Nhon Quach, Next Generation Processor Architect, AMD; Jos van Haaren, Department Head Storage Physics, Philips Research Laboratories; Terry O'Kelly, Technical Communications Manager, Memorex; Randy Culpepper, Texas Instruments RFID Systems; Aaron Newman, CTO and Co-Founder, Application Security Inc.; John Nash, Vice President of Marketing, Visible Systems; Dr. Maressa Hecht Orzack, Director, Computer Addiction Study Center; Alan Charlesworth, Staff Engineer, Sun Microsystems; Khaled A. Elamrawi, Senior Marketing Engineer, Intel Corporation; Timothy D. O'Brien, Senior Systems Engineer, Fujitsu Software; John Paulson, Manager, Product Communications, Seagate Technology; Omid Rahmat, Editor in Chief, Tom's Hardware Guide; Jeremy Bates, Multimedia Developer, R & L Multimedia Developers; Charles Hayes, Product Marketing Manager, SimpleTech, Inc.; Rick McGowan, Vice President & Senior Software Engineer, Unicode, Inc.; Russell Reynolds, Chief Operating Officer & Web Designer, R & L Multimedia Developers; Rob Stephens, Director, Technology Strategies, SAS; Dave Stow, Database Specialist, OSE Systems, Inc.

Educational Reviewers

Beverly Amer, Northern Arizona University; James Ambroise Jr., Southern University, Louisiana; Virginia Anderson, University of North Dakota; Robert Andree, Indiana University Northwest; Linda Armbruster, Rancho Santiago College; Michael Atherton, Mankato State University; Gary E. Baker, Marshalltown Community College; Richard Batt, Saint Louis Community College at Meremec; Luverne Bierle, Iowa Central Community College; Fariba Bolandhemat, Santa Monica College; Jerry Booher, Scottsdale Community College; Frederick W. Bounds, Georgia Perimeter College; James Bradley, University of Calgary; Curtis Bring, Moorhead State University; Brenda K. Britt, Fayetteville Technical Community College; Cathy Brotherton, Riverside Community College; Chris Brown, Bemidji State University; Janice Burke, South Suburban College; James Buxton, Tidewater Community College, Virginia; Gena Casas, Florida Community College, Jacksonville; Thomas Case, Georgia Southern University; John E. Castek, University of Wisconsin-La Crosse; Mario E. Cecchetti, Westmoreland County Community College; Jack W. Chandler, San Joaquin Delta College; Alan Charlesworth, Staff Engineer, Sun Microsystems; Jerry M. Chin, Southwest Missouri State University; Edward W. Christensen, Monmouth University; Carl Clavadetscher, California State Polytechnic University; Vernon Clodfelter, Rowan Technical College, North Carolina; Joann C. Cook, College of DuPage; Laura Cooper, College of the Mainland, Texas; Cynthia Corritore, University of Nebraska at Omaha; Sandra Cunningham, Ranger College; Marvin Daugherty, Indiana Vocational Technical College; Donald L. Davis, University of Mississippi; Garrace De Groot, University of Wyoming; Jackie Dennis, Prairie State College; Donald Dershem, Mountain View College; John DiElsi, Marcy College, New York; Mark Dishaw, Boston University; Eugene T. Dolan, University of the District of Columbia; Bennie Allen Dooley, Pasadena City College; Robert H. Dependahl Jr.; Santa Barbara City College; William Dorin, Indiana University Northwest; Mike Doroshow, Eastfield College; Jackie O. Duncan, Hopkinsville Community College; John Dunn, Palo Alto College; John W. Durham, Fort Hays State University; Hyun B. Eom, Middle Tennessee State University; Michael Feiler, Merritt College; Terry Felke, WR Harper College; J. Patrick Fenton, West Valley Community College; James H. Finger, University of South Carolina at Columbia; William C. Fink, Lewis and Clark Community College, Illinois; Ronald W. Fordonski, College of Du Page; Connie Morris Fox, West Virginia Institute of Technology; Paula S. Funkhouser, Truckee Meadows Community College; Janos T. Fustos, Metropolitan State; Gene Garza, University of Montevallo; Timothy Gottleber, North Lake College; Dwight Graham, Prairie State College; Wade Graves, Grayson County College; Kay H. Gray, Jacksonville State University; David W. Green, Nashville State Technical Institute, Tennessee; George P. Grill, University of North Carolina, Greensboro; John Groh, San Joaquin Delta College; Rosemary C. Gross, Creighton University; Dennis Guster, Saint Louis Community College at Meremec; Joe Hagarty, Raritan Valley Community College; Donald Hall, Manatee Community College; Jim Hanson, Austin Community College; Sallyann Z. Hanson, Mercer County Community College; L. D. Harber, Volunteer State Community College, Tennessee; Hank Hartman, Iowa State University; Richard Hatch, San Diego State University; Mary Lou Hawkins, Del Mar College; Ricci L. Heishman, Northern Virginia Community College; William Hightower, Elon College, North Carolina; Sharon A. Hill, Prince George's Community College, Maryland; Alyse Hollingsworth, Brevard College; Fred C. Homeyer, Angelo State University; Stanley P. Honacki, Moraine Valley Community College; L. Wayne Horn, Pensacola Junior College; J. William Howorth, Seneca College, Ontario, Canada; Mark W. Huber, East Carolina University; Peter L. Irwin, Richland College, Texas; John Jasma, Palo Alto College; Elizabeth Swoope Johnson, Louisiana State University; Jim Johnson, Valencia Community College; Mary T. Johnson, Mt. San Antonio College; Susan M. Jones, Southwest State University; Amardeep K. Kahlon, Austin Community College; Robert T. Keim, Arizona State University; Mary Louise Kelly, Palm Beach Community College; William R. Kenney, San Diego Mesa College; Richard Kerns, East Carolina University, North Carolina; Glenn Kersnick, Sinclair Community College, Ohio; Richard Kiger, Dallas Baptist University; Gordon C. Kimbell, Everett Community College, Washington; Robert Kirklin, Los Angeles Harbor Community College; Judith A.

Knapp, Indiana University Northwest; Mary Veronica Kolesar, Utah State University; James G. Kriz, Cuyahoga Community College, Ohio; Joan Krone, Denison University; Fran Kubicek, Kalamazoo Valley Community College; Rose M. Laird, Northern Virginia Community College; Robert Landrum, Jones Junior College; Shelly Langman, Bellevue Community College; James F. LaSalle, The University of Arizona; Chang-Yang Lin, Eastern Kentucky University; Linda J. Lindaman, Black Hawk College; Alden Lorents, Northern Arizona University; Paul M. Lou, Diablo Valley College; Deborah R. Ludford, Glendale Community College; Kent Lundin, Brigham Young University-Idaho; Barbara J. Maccarone, North Shore Community College; Wayne Madison, Clemson University, South Carolina; Donna L. Madsen, Kirkwood Community College; Randy Marak, Hill College; Gary Marks, Austin Community College, Texas; Kathryn A. Marold, Ph.D., Metropolitan State College of Denver; Cesar Marron, University of Wyoming; Ed Martin, Kingsborough Community College; Vickie McCullough, Palomar College; James W. McGuffee, Austin Community College; James McMahon, Community College of Rhode Island; William A. McMillan, Madonna University; Don B. Medley, California State Polytechnic University; John Melrose, University of Wisconsin—Eau Claire; Dixie Mercer, Kirkwood Community College; Mary Meredith, University of Southwestern Louisiana; Marilyn Meyer, Fresno City College; Carolyn H. Monroe, Baylor University; William J. Moon, Palm Beach Community College; Marilyn Moore, Purdue University; Marty Murray, Portland Community College; Don Nielsen, Golden West College; George Novotny, Ferris State University; Richard Okezie, Mesa Community College; Joseph D. Oldham, University of Kentucky; Dennis J. Olsen, Pikes Peak Community College; Bob Palank, Florissant Community College; James Payne, Kellogg Community College; Lisa B. Perez, San Joaquin Delta College; Savitha Pinnepalli, Louisiana State University; Delores Pusins, Hillsborough CC; Mike Rabaut, Hillsborough CC; Robert Ralph, Fayetteville Technical Institute, North Carolina; Herbert F. Rebhun, University of Houston-Downtown; Nicholas John Robak, Saint Joseph's University; Arthur E. Rowland, Shasta College; Kenneth R. Ruhrup, St. Petersburg Junior College; John F. Sanford, Philadelphia College of Textiles and Science; Kammy Sanghera, George Mason University; Carol A. Schwab, Webster University; Larry Schwartzman, Trident Technical College; Benito R. Serenil, South Seattle Community College; Allanagh Sewell, Southeastern Louisiana University; Tom Seymour, Minot State University; John J. Shuler, San Antonio College, Texas; Gayla Jo Slauson, Mesa State College; Harold Smith, Brigham Young University; Willard A. Smith, Tennessee State University; David Spaisman, Katherine Gibbs; Elizabeth Spooner, Holmes Community College; Timothy M. Stanford, City University; Alfred C. St. Onge, Springfield Technical Community College, Massachusetts; Michael L. Stratford, Charles County Community College, Maryland; Karen Studniarz, Kishwaukee College; Sandra Swanson, Lewis & Clark Community College; Tim Sylvester, Glendale Community College; Semih Tahaoglu, Southeastern Louisiana University; Jane J. Thompson, Solano Community College; Sue Traynor, Clarion University of Pennsylvania; William H. Trueheart, New Hampshire College; James D. Van Tassel, Mission College; James R. Walters, Pikes Peak Community College; Joyce V. Walton, Seneca College, Ontario, Canada; Diane B. Walz, University of Texas at San Antonio; Joseph Waters, Santa Rosa Junior College, California; Liang Chee Wee, University of Arizona; Merrill Wells, Red Rocks Community College; Fred J. Wilke, Saint Louis Community College; Charles M. Williams, Georgia State University; Roseanne Witkowski, Orange County Community College; David Womack, University of Texas, San Antonio; George Woodbury, College of the Sequoias; Nan Woodsome, Araphoe Community College; James D. Woolever, Cerritos College; Patricia Joann Wykoff, Western Michigan University; A. James Wynne, Virginia Commonwealth University; Robert D. Yearout, University of North Carolina at Asheville; Israel Yost, University of New Hampshire; and Vic Zamora, Mt. San Antonio College.

We would also like to thank the people on the Course team—their professionalism, attention to detail, and enormous enthusiasm make working with them a pleasure. In particular, we'd like to thank Marie Lee, Erik Herman, Erin Dowler, Brandi Henson, Leigh Robbins, Pam Conrad, and Jennifer Goguen McGrail for all their ideas, support, and tireless efforts during the design, writing, rewriting, and production of this book. Thanks to Brianna Hawes for managing the development of the Understanding Computers in a Changing Society Web site, and Ryan DeGrote and Jennifer Hankin for their efforts on marketing this text. We would also like to thank Joel Sadagursky for working on the new interior and cover design. Thanks also to Nicole Pinard.

We are also very appreciative of the numerous individuals and organizations that were kind enough to supply information and photographs for this text, the many organizations that generously allowed us to use their videos in conjunction with this text to add the new Online Video feature, and Christiaan Stoudt of HomeNetworkHelp.Info who kindly permitted us to incorporate his podcasts into this edition of the text.

We sincerely hope you find this book interesting, informative, and enjoyable to read. If you have any suggestions for improvement, or corrections that you'd like to be considered for future editions, please send them to deborah.morley@cengage.com.

Deborah Morley
Charles S. Parker

BRIEF CONTENTS

CONTENTS

TREND M-Commerce and U-Commerce:
Steps Toward a Cashless Society 63
HOW IT WORKS CPUs and Computer-
Generated Films 68
INSIDE THE INDUSTRY Data
Recovery Experts 78
TECHNOLOGY AND YOU Connecting
to a Wi-Fi Hotspot 86

 **Expert Insight on
Hardware** 98

Chapter 3 The Internet and World
Wide Web 100
Overview 101

INSIDE THE INDUSTRY Net
Neutrality 103
TREND Twittering 124
TECHNOLOGY AND YOU P2P Legal
Implications for College Students 135
HOW IT WORKS Podcasting 138

 **Expert Insight on
Software** 156

INSIDE THE INDUSTRY Identity Management (IDM) 171
TECHNOLOGY AND YOU E-Tokens on Campus 172
HOW IT WORKS Private Key Encryption 178
TREND Evil Twins 180

 Expert Insight on Networks and the Internet 208

Expert Insight on Computers and Society 322

3rd Edition

UNDERSTANDING COMPUTERS

IN A CHANGING SOCIETY

1
CHAPTER

Introduction to the World of Computers

OUTLINE

LEARNING OBJECTIVES

After completing this chapter, you will be able to do the following:

1. Explain why it is essential to learn about computers today and discuss several ways computers are integrated into our business and personal lives.

2. Define a computer and describe its primary operations.

3. List some important milestones in computer evolution.

4. Identify the major parts of a personal computer, including input, processing, output, storage, and communications hardware.

5. Define software and understand how it is used to instruct the computer what to do.

6. List the six basic types of computers, giving at least one example of each type of computer and stating what that computer might be used for.

7. Explain what a network, the Internet, and the World Wide Web are, as well as how computers, people, and Web pages are identified on the Internet.

8. Describe how to access a Web page.

9. Discuss the societal impact of computers, including some benefits and risks related to their prominence in our society.

OVERVIEW

Computers and other forms of technology impact our lives daily. We encounter computers in stores, restaurants, and other retail establishments. We use computers and the Internet regularly to obtain information, experience online entertainment, buy products and services, and communicate with others. Many of us carry a computer or mobile phone with us at all times so we can remain in touch with others on a continual basis and can access Internet information as we need it. It is even becoming more common to use these portable devices to pay for purchases, play online games with others, watch TV and movies, and much, much more. Businesses use computers to keep track of bank transactions, inventories, sales, and credit card purchases; control robots and other machines in factories; and provide business executives with the up-to-date information they need to make decisions. The government uses computers to support our nation's defense systems, for space exploration, for storing and organizing vital information about citizens, and other important tasks. In short, computers and computing technology are used in an endless number of ways.

Understanding Computers in a Changing Society is a guide to computers and related technology and their impact on our society. It will provide you with a comprehensive introduction to computer concepts and terminology. It will also help you develop an understanding of the potential impact of computers and related technology on our society through discussions of a variety of important issues surrounding computer use, such as security, privacy, ethics, and the environment.

Chapter 1 is designed to help you understand what computers are, how they work, and how people use them. It introduces the important terms and concepts that you will encounter throughout this text and in discussions about computers with others, as well as provides an overview of the history of computers. It also takes a brief look at how to use a computer to perform basic tasks and to access resources on the Internet and the World Wide Web, in order to provide you with the knowledge, skills, and tools you will need to complete the projects and online activities that accompany this textbook. The chapter closes with a look at the societal impact of computers; these and other topics related to computers and society are discussed in more detail in subsequent chapters of this text. ∎

PODCAST

Go to **www.course.com/uccs/ch1** to download or listen to the "Expert Insight on Personal Computers" podcast.

COMPUTERS IN YOUR LIFE

Computers today are used in virtually every aspect of most individuals' lives—at home, at school, at work, and while on the go. The next few sections take a look at some of the computer-related activities many individuals encounter every day.

Why Learn About Computers?

Fifty years ago, computers were used primarily by researchers and scientists. Today, computers are an integral part of our lives. Experts call this trend *pervasive computing*, in which few aspects of daily life remain untouched by computers and computing technology. With pervasive computing—also referred to as *ubiquitous computing*—computers are found virtually everywhere and computing technology is integrated into scores of devices to give those devices additional functions or to enable them to communicate with other devices on an on-going basis. Because of the prominence of computers in our society, it is important to understand what a computer is, a little about how a computer works, and the implications of living in a computer-oriented society.

Prior to about 1980, computers were large and expensive, and few people had access to them. Most computers used in organizations were equipped to do little more than carry out high-volume processing tasks, such as issuing bills and keeping track of product inventories. The average person did not need to know how to use a computer for his or her job, and it was uncommon to have a computer at home. Furthermore, the use of computers generally required a lot of technical knowledge. Because there were few good reasons or opportunities for learning how to use computers, the average person was unfamiliar with them.

Suddenly, in the early 1980s, things began to change. *Microcomputers*—inexpensive *personal computers* that you will read about later in this chapter—were invented and computer use increased dramatically. Today, more than 60% of all U.S. households include a personal computer, and most individuals use a computer of some sort or another on the job. Whether you become a teacher, attorney, doctor, salesperson, professional athlete, musician, executive, or skilled tradesperson, you will likely use a computer to obtain and evaluate information, to facilitate necessary on-the-job tasks, and to communicate with others. Today's computers are very useful tools for these purposes; they are also taking on new roles in our society, such as providing a means of entertainment and facilitating the tasks we need to accomplish in our day-to-day lives. In fact, computers and the traditional devices that we use every day—such as the telephone, television, stereo, and music player—have begun to *converge* into single units with multiple capabilities. As a result of this *convergence* trend (see Figure 1-1), the personal computer has moved beyond being primarily a productivity tool. Today, it is also a personal entertainment and communications hub that can be used to help individuals obtain information from the *Internet*, organize and access multimedia content, communicate with others, and more.

FIGURE 1-1
Convergence.
Today's computers typically take on the role of multiple devices.

HANDHELD DEVICES
Typically include the functions of a telephone, organizer, digital media player, gaming device, Web browser, and digital camera.

HOME COMPUTERS
Can often be used as a telephone, television, and stereo system, in addition to their regular computing functions.

Just as you can learn to drive a car without knowing much about car engines, you can learn to use a computer without understanding the technical details of how a computer works. However, a little knowledge gives you a big advantage. Knowing something about cars can help you to make wise purchases and save money on repairs. Likewise, knowing something about computers can help you buy the right one for your needs, get the most efficient use out of it, and have a much higher level of comfort and confidence along the way. Therefore, basic **computer literacy**—knowing about and understanding computers and their uses—is an essential skill today for everyone. The next few sections illustrate how computers are currently used by individuals.

Computers in the Home

Home computing has increased dramatically over the last few years as computers and Internet access have become less expensive and an increasing number of computer-related consumer activities have become available. Use of the Internet at home to look up

---

>**Computer literacy.** The knowledge and understanding of basic computer fundamentals.

information, exchange *e-mail* (electronic messages), shop, watch TV and videos, download music and movies, research products, pay bills and manage bank accounts, check news and weather, store and organize digital photos, play games, plan vacations, and so forth is now the norm for many individuals (see Figure 1-2). As computers, the Internet, television, *digital video recorders* (*DVRs*), and *gaming consoles* have converged, the computer is becoming a central part of home entertainment. And the ability to now make telephone calls over the Internet has resulted in an increasing number of individuals using a *dual-mode mobile phone* (a mobile phone that can make phone calls over both the Internet and a *cellular network*—a communications network used to place telephone calls via a *cellular phone*) as their only phone.

Home computing for work purposes is also increasing rapidly. Checking office e-mail from home or otherwise working at home in the evening is normal for many jobs. Working entirely from home, such as *telecommuting* for a company or working from home as a self-employed individual, is becoming more common as a result of fast Internet access and the wide use of e-mail, telephone calls, *faxing*, and other communications technologies that are regularly used for business communications. *Wireless networking* has added to the convenience of home computing, allowing the use of computers in virtually any location. For instance, e-mail can be answered from the backyard or living room, recipes can be looked up in the kitchen, and computer games can be played in the family room.

Computing technologies also make it possible to have *smart appliances*—traditional appliances with some type of built-in computer or communications technology. For instance, the smart oven shown in Figure 1-2 both refrigerates and cooks, and it can be controlled by the user via a telephone or the Internet. *Smart homes*—in which household tasks (such as watering the lawn, turning the air conditioning on or off, making coffee, monitoring the security of the home and grounds, and managing Internet access and home entertainment devices) are controlled by a main computer in the home—are expected to be the norm in less than a decade.

REFERENCE, PRODUCTIVITY, AND COMMUNICATIONS
Many individuals today have access to the Internet at home; retrieving information, obtaining news, managing digital photos, and exchanging e-mail are popular home computer activities.

ONLINE SHOPPING AND BANKING
Computers and the Internet have made online shopping and banking the norm for many individuals.

ENTERTAINMENT
Computers and gaming consoles are becoming a central hub for entertainment and digital media (photos, music, recorded TV, etc.) delivery.

Smart oven

The oven can be controlled remotely, such as from the office.

SMART APPLIANCES
Smart appliances (such as the smart oven shown here) are regular appliances with some type of built-in computer technology.

VOICE OVER IP (VOIP)
Making phone calls over the Internet, such as with the dual-mode phone shown here, is becoming common.

FIGURE 1-2
Computer use

at home.

Computers in Education

Today's youth could definitely be called the *computing generation*. Baby boomers may have been introduced to computers at college or on the job, and older Americans may never have used a computer until after retirement, if at all, but many of today's young people have been brought up with computing technology. From handheld gaming devices to computers at school and home, most children and teens today have been exposed to computers and related technology all their lives. Although the amount of computer use varies from school to school, students in elementary, middle, and high schools typically have access to computers either in the classroom or in a computer lab, and virtually all colleges have some sort of computing facility available for student use.

With the increased availability of computers and Internet access, the emphasis on computer use in K–12 schools has evolved from straight drill-and-practice programs to using the computer as an overall student-based learning tool. Today, students use multimedia programs to enhance learning; productivity software—such as *word processors* and *presentation software*—for creating papers and electronic presentations; and the Internet for research. Some middle and high schools even have *laptop programs* where students do their schoolwork both in and out of class on their own personal laptops or ones that the school provides (see Figure 1-3). K–12 teachers also typically use computers for a variety of tasks, such as creating lesson plans, researching topics, delivering classroom presentations, and submitting daily attendance information and other required school-related online tasks.

FIGURE 1-3
Computer use in education.

At colleges and universities, computer use is typically much more integrated into daily classroom life than in K–12 schools. Computers are commonly found in classrooms, computer labs, dorms, and libraries. And many college campuses today have *wireless hotspots* that allow students to use their PCs to connect wirelessly to the college network and the Internet from anywhere on campus. College students today are typically expected to use the Internet for research, as well as to prepare papers and classroom presentations and to access online course materials. In fact, some colleges require a computer for enrollment.

Most college instructors use computers to prepare handouts and exams, to prepare and deliver classroom presentations and lectures, and to create and maintain course *Web pages*. Many colleges also offer *distance learning*—an alternative to traditional classroom learning—in which students participate from their current location (via their computers and Internet connections) instead of physically going to class. With distance learning, students can do coursework and participate in class discussions from home, work, or

COMPUTER LABS AND CLASSROOMS
Many schools today have computers available in a lab or the library, as well as computers or Internet connections in classrooms for student use.

PRESENTATIONS
Using computers and projection equipment, instructors can incorporate electronic slide shows, online videos, and other interesting content into their classroom presentations.

CAMPUS WIRELESS HOTSPOTS
Many college students can access the Internet from anywhere on campus to do research, check e-mail, and more, via the campus hotspot.

DISTANCE LEARNING
With distance learning, students—such as these U.S. Navy sailors—can take classes from home or wherever they happen to be at the moment.

wherever they happen to be at the moment. Consequently, distance learning gives students greater flexibility to schedule class time around their personal, family, and work commitments. Distance learning also allows students, such as individuals located in very rural areas or stationed at military posts overseas, to take courses when they are not able to physically attend classes.

Computers in the Workplace

Although computers have been used in the workplace for years, their role is continually evolving. Originally used as a research tool for computer experts and scientists, and then as a productivity tool for office workers, the computer is used today by all types of employees in all types of businesses—including CEOs, retail store clerks, traveling sales professionals, artists and musicians, police officers, insurance adjusters, doctors and nurses, auto mechanics and repair personnel, and so forth. In essence, the computer has become a universal tool for on-the-job decision making, productivity, and communications (see Figure 1-4). It is also used extensively for access control at many organizations, such as *authentication systems* that allow individuals to enter the office building, punch in or out of work, or access the company network by providing the proper credentials or being authenticated via a fingerprint or hand scan, as shown in Figure 1-4 (authentication systems are discussed in detail in Chapter 4).

FURTHER EXPLORATION

Go to **www.course.com/uccs/ch1** for links to information about computer certification programs.

FIGURE 1-4
Computer use in the workplace.

DECISION-MAKING
Many individuals today use a computer to help them make on-the-job decisions.

PRODUCTIVITY
Many individuals today use a computer to perform on-the-job tasks efficiently and accurately.

COLLABORATION
Computers and the Internet enable individuals located in different places to hold meetings, collaborate on documents, and other important tasks.

OFFSITE COMMUNICATIONS
Handheld or wearable computers are often used by employees who need to record data or access remote data when they are out of the office.

CUSTOMER SERVICE
Service professionals frequently use computers to process orders and store customer signature authorizations.

WORK AUTHENTICATION SYSTEMS
Allow workers to punch in and out of work, access facilities, or other tasks that require authentication.

ASK THE EXPERT

Tony Onorati, Former Naval Aviator and Former Commanding Officer, Strike Fighter Weapons School Pacific, NAS Lemoore

What computer experience is needed to be a U.S. Navy pilot?

While no computer experience is necessarily required to enter flight school, failure to have a solid knowledge of the Windows operating system will put the candidate well behind his/her contemporaries when they finally do reach the fleet as a pilot. All the tactical planning tools for preflight preparation, navigation, ordnance delivery, and mission planning, as well as all aircraft specific publications, manuals, and training are all computer based. For the FA-18 Hornet, all mission data is created on the computer, copied to a mission computer card, and plugged into the jet where it is downloaded into the aircraft's computer for use in flight. Becoming a naval aviator without computer skills is like entering flight school without ever having flown before—it can be done but it places you well behind the power curve.

One of the fastest growing uses for workplace computing is in the service industry, in which service professionals—such as food servers, repair technicians, and delivery people—use *portable computers* to record and process customer orders, access needed information, and capture customer signatures for purchases, deliveries, and other provided services. Computers are also used extensively by military personnel for communications and navigational purposes, as well as to control missiles and other weapons, identify terrorists and other potential enemies, and perform other necessary tasks. To update their computer skills, when needed, employees in all lines of work today may take computer training classes or enroll in computer certification programs.

Computers on the Go

In addition to using computers in the home, at school, and in the workplace, most people encounter and use all types of computers in other aspects of day-to-day life (see Figure 1-5). Some individuals depend on computers and the Internet while traveling and either take a computer with them to use in conjunction with the wireless Internet access available at many locations (such as hotels, airports, restaurants, libraries, schools, and coffeehouses) around the world or use a computer available at one of these locations or at an *Internet café*—a business that provides computer and Internet access to individuals. Some of these locations charge for access; others offer free access as a courtesy to customers, such as the unlimited Internet access some hotels offer guests. It is also becoming the norm for individuals to carry Web-enabled mobile phones, *handheld computers*, or other portable devices with them on a regular basis to remain electronically in touch with others and to obtain stock quotes, driving directions, airline flight updates, movie times, news headlines, and other needed information while on the go. These devices are also increasingly being used to watch TV, download and listen to music, and perform other mobile entertainment options. For a look at the status of mobile TV today, see the Trend box.

On a day-to-day basis, many individuals encounter *consumer kiosks* (small self-service computer-based stations, such as ATM machines, bridal registries, and ticketing systems) that provide information or other services to the public) and *self-checkout systems* (which allow retail store customers to scan their purchases and pay for them without a salesclerk). An emerging payment option is the use of *m-commerce systems*—systems that allow individuals to pay for products and services via a mobile phone or other portable device. For instance, the m-commerce system shown in Figure 1-5 allows MasterCard customers to pay for purchases by tapping their mobile phone on the reader located in the retail store. Individuals may also need to use a consumer authentication system (such as swiping an ID card through a reader or passing a fingerprint or hand scan) to gain access to a local health club, theme park, or other membership-based facility; check out books from the local library; or other common consumer activity. *Global positioning system* (*GPS*) capabilities built into cars, computers, mobile phones, and other devices are increasingly being used by individuals to obtain driving directions and other navigational aids while traveling or hiking.

PORTABLE COMPUTERS
Many people today carry a portable PC with them at all times or when they travel in order to remain in touch with others and Internet resources.

CONSUMER KIOSKS
Electronic kiosks are widely available to view conference or gift registry information, print photographs, order products or services, and more.

SELF-CHECKOUT SYSTEMS
Allow individuals in retail stores to pay for purchases without assistance from an employee.

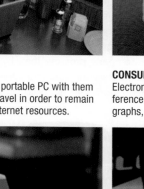

M-COMMERCE SYSTEMS
Allow individuals to pay for purchases using a mobile phone or other device.

CONSUMER AUTHENTICATION SYSTEMS
Allow access to facilities for authorized members only, such as for theme park annual pass holders, as shown here.

GPS APPLICATIONS
Computers and handheld devices with built-in GPS capabilities can be used for navigational purposes, such as to show users their exact geographical location or to plan the most efficient route to a destination.

WHAT IS A COMPUTER AND WHAT DOES IT DO?

FIGURE 1-5
Computer use while on the go.

A **computer** can be defined as a programmable, electronic device that accepts data, performs operations on that data, presents the results, and stores the data or results as needed. Being *programmable*, a computer will do whatever the instructions—called the *program*—tell it to do. The programs being used with a computer determine the tasks the computer is able to perform.

The four operations described in this definition are more technically referred to as *input*, *processing*, *output*, and *storage*. These four primary operations of a computer can be defined as follows:

▶ **Input**—entering data into the computer.

▶ **Processing**—performing operations on the data.

▶ **Output**—presenting the results.

▶ **Storage**—saving data, programs, or output for future use.

>**Computer.** A programmable, electronic device that accepts data input, performs processing operations on that data, and outputs and stores the results. >**Input.** The process of entering data into a computer; can also refer to the data itself. >**Processing.** Performing operations on data that has been input into a computer to convert that input to output. >**Output.** The process of presenting the results of processing; can also refer to the results themselves. >**Storage.** The operation of saving data, programs, or output for future use.

TREND

Mobile TV

The entertainment factor of mobile phones just went up a notch, a big notch. In addition to the games and Web access that smart phones already provide, a hot new application is *mobile TV* (see the accompanying figure). Live television programming delivered via mobile phones is now available in a number of countries, including the United States. One of the leaders in this area is *MobiTV*, which offers over 100 channels of news, music videos, comedies, and cartoons, including content from NBC, ABC News, FOX Sports, FOX News, The Oxygen Network, Telemundo Mobile, C-SPAN, and the Discovery Channel. The service costs less than $10 per month and is available through a number of wireless providers, including Sprint and AT&T.

A related alternative to live mobile TV is *mobile video-on-demand* (*mobile VOD*); that is, video clips that are delivered to a mobile phone on demand, whenever the user requests them. Mobile VOD typically includes short news clips, music videos, TV show updates, and more. Content is available 24/7 and the video clips are updated throughout the day in order to offer breaking news stories and up-to-date sports scores as they happen. Two examples of mobile video-on-demand providers are *GoTV* and Verizon's *VCAST* service. Some mobile TV providers—such as *MediaFLO* and MobiTV—offer both live and on-demand content.

Another option is a device or service that enables you to watch shows from your home TV system (such as live TV or shows recorded on a DVR, for instance). *Orb* is a free Web-based solution; *SlingPlayer Mobile* is a service designed for owners of the *Slingbox* (a *place-shifting* device that allows you to watch your live or recorded TV shows from a computer via the Internet). For instance, SlingPlayer Mobile allows you to view content on your mobile phone from your TV connection and DVR, as well as navigate program guides, program your DVR, and skip through commercials while watching recorded shows—just like you would at home.

Mobile TV use is growing rapidly. In fact, the ARC Advisory Group research company projects that, by 2008, 250 million consumers worldwide will be watching some form of mobile TV or video, generating more than $5 billion in annual revenues.

For example, let's assume that we have a computer that has been programmed to add two numbers. As shown in Figure 1-6, *input* occurs when data (in this example, the numbers 2 and 5) is entered into the computer; *processing* takes place when the computer program adds those two numbers; and *output* happens when the sum of 7 is displayed on the monitor. The *storage* operation occurs any time the data, program, or output is saved for future use.

For an additional example, let's look at a supermarket *barcode reader* to see how it fits this definition of a computer. First, the grocery item being purchased is passed over the barcode reader—*input*. Next, the description and price of the item are looked up—*processing*. Finally, the item description and price are displayed on the cash register and printed on the receipt—*output*—and the inventory, ordering, and sales records are updated—*storage*.

This progression of input, processing, output, and storage is sometimes referred to as the *IPOS cycle* or the *information processing cycle*. In addition to these four primary computer operations, today's computers typically also perform *communications* functions, such as sending or retrieving data via the Internet, updating information located in a shared

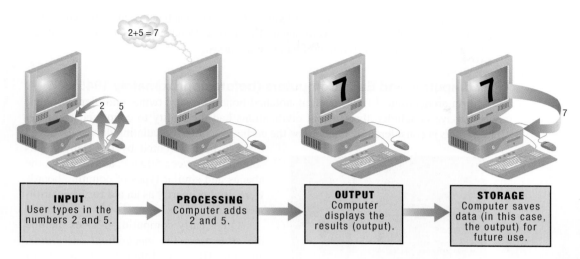

| **INPUT** User types in the numbers 2 and 5. | **PROCESSING** Computer adds 2 and 5. | **OUTPUT** Computer displays the results (output). | **STORAGE** Computer saves data (in this case, the output) for future use. |

FIGURE 1-6
The information processing cycle.

company database, or exchanging e-mail messages. Therefore, **communications**—technically an input or output operation, depending on which direction the information is going—is increasingly considered the fifth primary computer operation.

Data vs. Information

As just discussed, a user inputs **data** into a computer, and then the computer processes it. Almost any kind of fact or set of facts can become computer data—the words in a letter to a friend, the text and pictures in a book, the numbers in a monthly budget, a photograph, a song, or the facts stored in a set of employee records. Consequently, data can exist in many forms, such as to represent *text* (words consisting of standard alphabetic, numeric, and special characters), *graphics* (illustrations or photographs), *audio* (sound, such as music or voice), or *video* (live video or video clips). When data is processed into a meaningful form, it becomes **information**.

Information is frequently generated to answer some type of question. An individual might want to know, for example, how many of a firm's employees earn more than $100,000, how many seats are available on a particular flight from Los Angeles to San Francisco, or what Hank Aaron's lifetime home run total was. Of course, you don't need a computer system to process data into information. Anyone can go through an employee file and make a list of people earning a certain salary. Done by hand, this work would take a lot of time, especially for a company with thousands of employees. Computers, however, can perform such tasks almost instantly with accurate results.

Information processing (the conversion of data into information) is a vital activity today because the success of many businesses depends heavily on the wise use of information. Because better information often improves employee decisions and customer service, many companies today regard information as one of their most important assets and consider the creative use of information a key competitive strategy.

Computers Then and Now

The basic ideas of computing and calculating are very old, going back thousands of years. However, the computer in the form in which it is recognized today is a fairly recent invention. In fact, personal computers have only been around since the late 1970s. The history of computers is often referred to in terms of *generations*, with each new generation character-ized by a major technological development. The next sections summarize some early cal-culating devices and the different computer generations.

FIGURE 1-7
A brief look at computer generations.

Precomputers and Early Computers (before approximately 1945)

Based on archeological finds, such as notched bones, knotted twine, and hieroglyphics, experts have concluded that ancient civilizations had the ability to count and compute. The *abacus* is considered by many to be the earliest recorded calculating device. Believed to have been invented by the Babylonians sometime between 500 B.C. and 100 B.C., the abacus and similar types of counting boards were used primarily as an aid for basic arith-metic calculations.

Other early computing devices include the *slide rule*, the *mechanical calculator*, and Dr. Herman Hollerith's *Punch Card Tabulating Machine and Sorter*. This device (see Figure 1-7) was the first electro-mechanical machine that could read *punch cards*—special cards with holes punched in them to represent data. In the first success-ful case of an information processing sys-tem replacing a paper-and-pen-based system, Hollerith's machine was used to process the 1890 U.S. Census data. It was able to complete the task in two and a half years, instead of the decade it usually took to process the data manually. Hollerith's company eventually became *International Business Machines (IBM)*.

PRECOMPUTERS AND EARLY COMPUTERS
Dr. Herman Hollerith's Punch Card Tabulating Machine and Sorter is an example of an early computing device. It was used to process the 1890 U.S. Census in about one-quarter of the time usually required to tally the results by hand.

FIRST-GENERATION COMPUTERS
First-generation computers, such as ENIAC shown here, were large and bulky, used vacuum tubes, and had to be physically wired and reset to run programs.

SECOND-GENERATION COMPUTERS
Second-generation computers, such as the IBM 1401 mainframe shown here, used transistors instead of vacuum tubes so they were physically smaller, faster, and more reliable than earlier first-generation computers.

THIRD-GENERATION COMPUTERS
The integrated circuit marked the beginning of the third generation of computers. These chips allowed the introduction of smaller computers, such as the DEC PDP-8 shown here, which was the first commercially suc-cessful minicomputer.

FOURTH-GENERATION COMPUTERS
Fourth-generation computers, such as the original IBM PC shown here, are based on microprocessors. Most of today's computers fall into this category.

First-Generation Computers (approximately 1946–1957)

The first computers were enormous, often taking up entire rooms. They were powered by thousands of *vacuum tubes*—glass tubes that look similar to large, cylindrical light bulbs. Vacuum tubes needed replacing con-stantly, required a great deal of electricity, and generated a lot of heat. *First-generation computers* could solve only one problem at a time since they needed to be physically rewired with cables to be reprogrammed (see Figure 1-7), which typically took several days (sometimes even weeks) to complete and several more days to check before the computer could be used. Usually paper punch cards and paper tape were used for input, and output was printed on paper.

Two of the most significant examples of first-generation computers were *ENIAC* and *UNIVAC*. ENIAC, shown in Figure 1-7, was the world's first large-scale, general-purpose computer. Although it was not completed until 1946, ENIAC was developed during World War II to compute artillery-firing tables (the settings to be used when firing different weapons under various conditions) for the U.S. Army. Instead of the 40 hours required for a person to compute the optimal settings for a single set of conditions and a single gun using manual calculations, ENIAC could complete the same calculations in less than two minutes. UNIVAC, released in 1951, was initially built for the U.S. Census Bureau and was used to analyze votes in the 1952 U.S. presidential election. Interestingly, its correct prediction of an Eisenhower victory only 45 minutes after the polls closed was not publicly aired because the results were not trusted. Despite this initial mistrust of its capabilities, UNIVAC did go on to become the first computer to be mass produced for general commercial use.

Second-Generation Computers (approximately 1958–1963)

The second generation of computers began when the *transistor*—a small device made of semiconductor material that acts like a switch to open or close electronic circuits—started to replace the vacuum tube. Transistors allowed *second-generation computers* to be physically smaller, more powerful, cheaper, more energy-efficient, and more reliable than first-generation computers. Typically, programs and data were input on punch cards and magnetic tape, output was on punch cards and paper printouts, and magnetic tape and disks were used for storage (see Figure 1-7). *Programming languages* (such as *FORTRAN* and *COBOL*) were also developed and implemented during this generation.

Third-Generation Computers (approximately 1964–1970)

The replacement of the transistor with *integrated circuits* (*ICs*) marked the beginning of the third generation of computers. Integrated circuits incorporate many transistors and electronic circuits on a single tiny silicon *chip*, allowing *third-generation computers* to be even smaller and more reliable than computers in the earlier computer generations. Instead of punch cards and paper printouts, keyboards and monitors were introduced for input and output; magnetic disks were typically used for storage. An example of a third-generation computer is shown in Figure 1-7.

Fourth-Generation Computers (approximately 1971–present)

A technological breakthrough in the early 1970s made it possible to place an increasing number of transistors on a single chip. This led to the invention of the *microprocessor* in 1971, which ushered in the fourth generation of computers. In essence, a microprocessor contains the core processing capabilities of an entire computer on one single chip. The original IBM PC (see Figure 1-7) and Apple Macintosh®, and most of today's modern computers, fall into this category. *Fourth-generation computers* typically use a keyboard and mouse for input, a monitor and printer for output, and magnetic disks, flash memory media, and optical discs for storage. This generation also witnessed the development of *computer networks*, *wireless technologies*, and the *Internet*.

Fifth-Generation Computers (now and the future)

Although some people believe that the fifth generation of computers has not yet begun, most think it is in its infancy stage. *Fifth-generation computers* have no precise classification, since experts tend to disagree about the definition for this generation of computers. However, one common opinion is that fifth-generation computers will be based on *artificial intelligence*, allowing them to think, reason, and learn. Voice will likely be a primary means of input, and computers may be constructed differently than they are today, such as in the form of *optical computers* that process data using light instead of electrons, tiny computers that utilize *nanotechnology*, or as entire general-purpose computers built into desks, home appliances, and other everyday devices.

TIP

For a more detailed timeline regarding the development of computers, see the "Computer History Timeline" located in the References and Resources Guide at the end of this book.

FURTHER EXPLORATION

Go to **www.course.com/uccs/ch1** for links to information about the history of computers.

Hardware

The physical parts of a computer (the parts you can touch, as shown in Figure 1-8 and discussed next) are collectively referred to as **hardware**. The instructions or programs used with a computer—called *software*—are discussed in a later section.

Hardware components can be *internal* (located inside the main box or *system unit* of the computer) or *external* (located outside the system unit). External hardware components typically plug into connectors called *ports* located on the exterior of the system unit. There are hardware devices associated with each of the five computer operations previously discussed (input, processing, output, storage, and communications), as summarized in Figure 1-9. Both hardware and software are discussed in more detail in Chapter 2.

Input Devices

An *input device* is any piece of equipment that is used to input data into the computer. The most common input devices today are the *keyboard* and *mouse* (shown in Figure 1-8). Other possibilities include *scanners*, *touch screens*, *digital cameras*, *electronic pens*, *touch pads*, *fingerprint readers*, *joysticks*, and *microphones*. Input devices can connect via a wired or wireless connection.

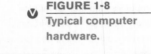

❤ **FIGURE 1-8**

Typical computer hardware.

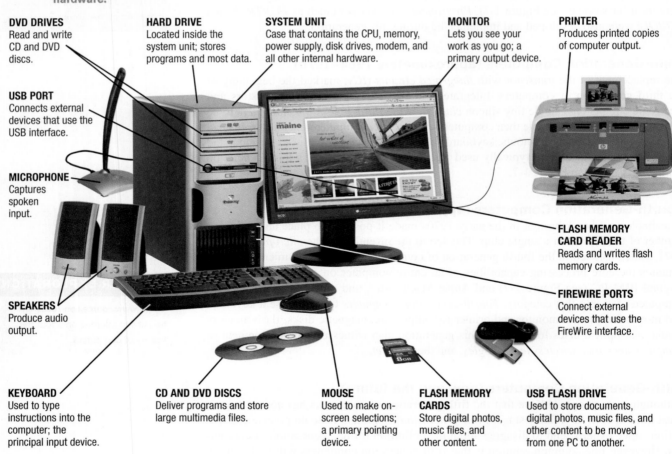

DVD DRIVES
Read and write CD and DVD discs.

HARD DRIVE
Located inside the system unit; stores programs and most data.

SYSTEM UNIT
Case that contains the CPU, memory, power supply, disk drives, modem, and all other internal hardware.

MONITOR
Lets you see your work as you go; a primary output device.

PRINTER
Produces printed copies of computer output.

USB PORT
Connects external devices that use the USB interface.

MICROPHONE
Captures spoken input.

SPEAKERS
Produce audio output.

KEYBOARD
Used to type instructions into the computer; the principal input device.

CD AND DVD DISCS
Deliver programs and store large multimedia files.

MOUSE
Used to make on-screen selections; a primary pointing device.

FLASH MEMORY CARDS
Store digital photos, music files, and other content.

FLASH MEMORY CARD READER
Reads and writes flash memory cards.

FIREWIRE PORTS
Connect external devices that use the FireWire interface.

USB FLASH DRIVE
Used to store documents, digital photos, music files, and other content to be moved from one PC to another.

>**Hardware.** The physical parts of a computer system, such as the keyboard, monitor, printer, and so forth.

Processing Devices

The main *processing device* for a computer is the *central processing unit* (*CPU*). The CPU is a *computer chip* located inside the system unit that performs the calculations and comparisons needed for processing; it also controls the computer's operations. For these reasons, the CPU is often considered the "brain" of the computer. Also involved in processing are various types of *memory*—additional chips located inside the system unit that the computer uses to temporarily store data and instructions while it is working with them.

Output Devices

An *output device* accepts processed data from the computer and presents the results to the user, most of the time on the computer screen (*monitor*), on paper (via a *printer*), or through a *speaker*. Other possible output devices include *headphones* and *headsets* (used to deliver audio output to a single user) and *data projectors* (used to project computer images onto a projection screen). Output devices can connect via a wired or wireless connection.

INPUT	OUTPUT
Keyboard	Monitor
Mouse	Printer
Microphone	Speakers
Scanner	Headphones and headsets
Digital camera	Data projector
Electronic pen	
Touch pad	**STORAGE**
Joystick	Hard drive
Fingerprint reader	Floppy disk
PROCESSING	Floppy disk drive
	CD/DVD disc
CPU	CD/DVD drive
	Flash memory card
COMMUNICATIONS	USB flash drive
Modem	Flash memory card reader
Network adapter	

 FIGURE 1-9
Common hardware listed by operation.

Storage Devices

Storage devices are used to store data on or access data from *storage media*, such as *floppy disks*, *CD discs*, *DVD discs*, or *flash memory cards*. The storage hardware featured in Figure 1-8 includes a *hard drive*, a *DVD drive*, a *flash memory card reader*, a *USB flash drive*, CD discs, DVD discs, and flash memory cards. Storage devices are used to save data, programs, or output for future use and can either be installed inside the computer, attached to the computer as an external device, or accessed remotely through a network or wireless connection.

Communications Devices

Communications devices allow users to communicate electronically with others and to access remote information via the Internet or a home, school, or company network. Communications hardware includes *modems* (used to connect a computer to the Internet) and *network adapters* (used to connect a computer to a computer network). A variety of modems and network adapters are available because there are different ways to connect to the Internet and computer networks. Communications hardware is discussed in more detail in Chapter 2; connecting to the Internet is covered in Chapter 3.

Software

The term **software** refers to the programs or instructions used to tell the computer hardware what to do. Software is generally purchased on a CD or DVD or downloaded from the Internet. In either case, once the program has been obtained, it needs to be *installed* on a computer before it can be used. An alternative is running programs directly from the Internet as *Web-based software* without installing them on your computer, as discussed in more detail in Chapter 2. With this option, the programs are accessed via Web pages.

Computers use two basic types of software: *system software* and *application software*. The differences between these types of software are discussed next.

>**Software.** The instructions, also called computer programs, that are used to tell a computer what it should do.

System Software

The programs that allow a computer to operate are collectively referred to as *system software*. The main system software is the **operating system**, which starts up the computer and controls its operation. Common operating system tasks include setting up new hardware, allowing users to run other software, and allowing users to manage the documents stored on their computers. Without an operating system, a computer cannot function. Common operating systems are *Windows*, *Mac OS*®, and *Linux*.

To use a computer, the user first turns on the power by pressing the power button, and then the computer begins to **boot**. During the *boot process*, part of the computer's operating system is loaded into memory, the computer does a quick diagnostic of itself, and then it launches any programs—such as an *antivirus* or *instant messaging* (*IM*) program—designated to run each time the PC starts up.

Once a computer has finished the boot process, it is ready to be used and waits for input from the user. The manner in which an operating system or any other type of program interacts with its users is known as its *user interface*. Older software programs used a text-based *command line interface*, which required the user to type precise instructions indicating exactly what the computer should do. Most programs today use a *graphical user interface* or *GUI* (pronounced "goo-ey"), which uses graphical objects (such as *icons* and *buttons*) that are selected with the mouse to tell the computer what to do. For instance, the **Windows desktop** (the user's basic workspace—the place where documents, folders, programs, and other objects are displayed when they are being used) contains a variety of objects, as shown in Figure 1-10 and discussed next.

TIP

Point to the clock located in the system tray at the right edge of the Windows taskbar to see the current date; click it to view a calendar or to adjust the date or time.

FIGURE 1-10
The Windows desktop.

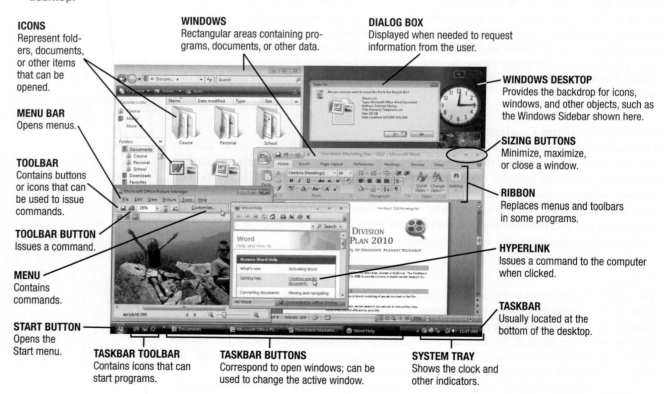

ICONS
Represent folders, documents, or other items that can be opened.

MENU BAR
Opens menus.

TOOLBAR
Contains buttons or icons that can be used to issue commands.

TOOLBAR BUTTON
Issues a command.

MENU
Contains commands.

START BUTTON
Opens the Start menu.

WINDOWS
Rectangular areas containing programs, documents, or other data.

DIALOG BOX
Displayed when needed to request information from the user.

WINDOWS DESKTOP
Provides the backdrop for icons, windows, and other objects, such as the Windows Sidebar shown here.

SIZING BUTTONS
Minimize, maximize, or close a window.

RIBBON
Replaces menus and toolbars in some programs.

HYPERLINK
Issues a command to the computer when clicked.

TASKBAR
Usually located at the bottom of the desktop.

TASKBAR TOOLBAR
Contains icons that can start programs.

TASKBAR BUTTONS
Correspond to open windows; can be used to change the active window.

SYSTEM TRAY
Shows the clock and other indicators.

>**Operating system.** A type of system software that enables a computer to operate and manage its resources and activities. >**Boot.** To start up a computer. >**Windows desktop.** The background work area displayed on the screen in Microsoft Windows. >**Window.** A rectangular area in which programs, documents, and other content are displayed. >**Icon.** A small graphical image that invokes some action when selected.

▶ **Windows**—rectangular areas in which programs, documents, and other content are displayed on the desktop.

▶ **Icons**—small pictures located on the desktop, a toolbar, or in a window that represent programs, folders, documents, or other elements that can be opened.

▶ **Menus**—text-based lists that appear at the top of many windows and can be used to issue commands to that program. Items contained on a menu either display another, more specific, menu; open a *dialog box* to prompt the user for more information; turn a feature on or off; or execute a command.

▶ **Toolbars**—sets of icons or buttons, called *toolbar buttons*, which can be clicked with the mouse to issue commands, such as to print a document.

▶ **Ribbon**—the new interface in *Microsoft Office 2007* that is used instead of traditional toolbars and menus to issue commands. The Ribbon contains *tabs*, which display *groups* of related commands.

▶ **Taskbar**—a bar located along the bottom of the desktop which houses the *Start button* at the left edge (used to open the *Start menu*—shown in Figure 1-11—which is used to launch programs), the *taskbar toolbar* and *taskbar buttons* in the center (used to launch programs and switch between open windows), and a clock and other indicators (such as a volume indicator and icons for programs that are running in the *background* and so are not listed on the taskbar, such as a security program and the *Windows Sidebar*) in the *system tray* at the far right edge.

▶ **Hyperlinks**—text or images (located on the desktop, a Web page, a program interface, or in a document) that are clicked to display more information; hyperlinks found on Web pages are discussed in more detail later in this chapter.

▶ **Sizing buttons**—small buttons located at the top-right corner of each window that are used to resize the window, such as to *maximize* (enlarge as big as possible), *minimize* (temporarily hide), *restore down* (return a maximized window to its previous size), or *close* (exit) it.

▶ **Dialog boxes**—small boxes displayed whenever additional input is needed from the user, such as to specify the desired options when printing or saving a document.

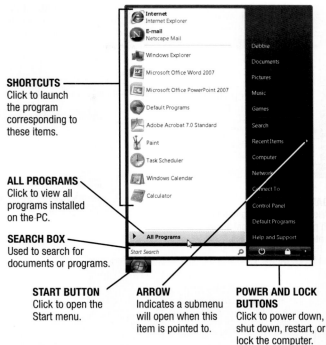

SHORTCUTS — Click to launch the program corresponding to these items.

ALL PROGRAMS — Click to view all programs installed on the PC.

SEARCH BOX — Used to search for documents or programs.

START BUTTON Click to open the Start menu.

ARROW Indicates a submenu will open when this item is pointed to.

POWER AND LOCK BUTTONS Click to power down, shut down, restart, or lock the computer.

FIGURE 1-11
The Windows Vista Start menu.

TIP

In Windows Vista, begin to type the name of a program in the Search box at the bottom of the Start menu to quickly launch that program.

TIP

Right-click a taskbar button to see commands associated with that task button, such as to minimize, maximize, restore, or close the window.

Application Software

Application software consists of programs designed to allow people to perform specific tasks or applications using a computer, such as creating letters (*word processing software*), preparing budgets (*spreadsheet software*), managing databases (*database software*), editing photographs (*image editing software*), viewing Web pages (*Web browsers*), recording or playing CDs (*multimedia software*), and exchanging e-mail (*e-mail programs*). Application software can be sold as individual stand-alone programs; related programs are sometimes bundled together into a *software suite*, such as the popular *Microsoft Office* software suite. Some examples of common types of application software are illustrated in Figure 1-12.

>**Menu.** A set of options (usually text-based) used to issue commands to the computer. >**Toolbar.** A set of icons used to issue commands to the computer. >**Ribbon.** A set of commands grouped by task and used in Office 2007 programs to issue commands to the computer. >**Taskbar.** The bar located at the bottom of the Windows desktop that contains the Start button, task buttons, and the system tray. >**Hyperlink.** Text or an image that is linked to a Web page or other type of document. >**Sizing button.** One of a group of small buttons located at the top-right corner of a window that are used to resize the window. >**Dialog box.** A window that requires the user to supply additional information. >**Application software.** Programs that enable users to perform specific tasks on a computer, such as writing a letter or playing a game.

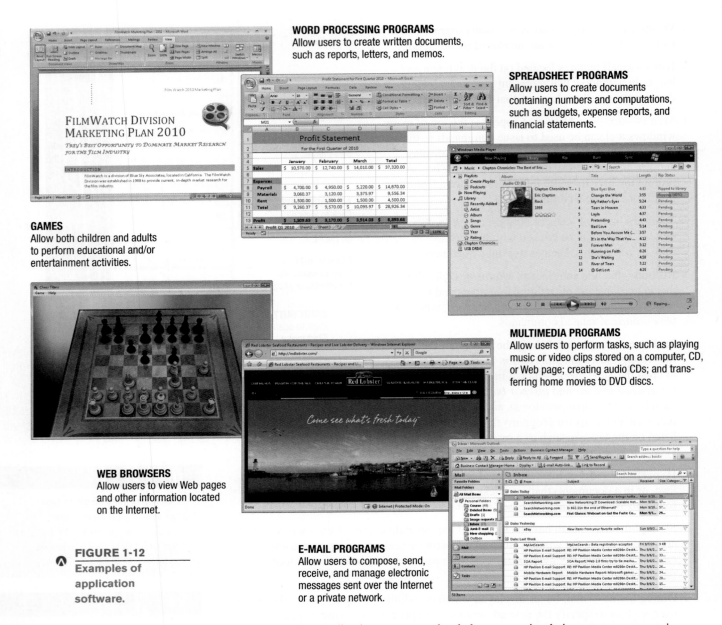

WORD PROCESSING PROGRAMS
Allow users to create written documents, such as reports, letters, and memos.

SPREADSHEET PROGRAMS
Allow users to create documents containing numbers and computations, such as budgets, expense reports, and financial statements.

GAMES
Allow both children and adults to perform educational and/or entertainment activities.

MULTIMEDIA PROGRAMS
Allow users to perform tasks, such as playing music or video clips stored on a computer, CD, or Web page; creating audio CDs; and transferring home movies to DVD discs.

WEB BROWSERS
Allow users to view Web pages and other information located on the Internet.

E-MAIL PROGRAMS
Allow users to compose, send, receive, and manage electronic messages sent over the Internet or a private network.

FIGURE 1-12
Examples of application software.

There are also application programs that help users write their own programs using a *programming language*—a set of commands written in a form that the computer system can understand. Programming languages come in many varieties—for example, *BASIC*, *Visual Basic*, *Pascal*, *COBOL*, *C++*, and *Java*. Some languages are traditional programming languages for developing applications; others are designed for use with Web pages or multimedia programming. For overall Web page development, *markup languages*—such as *Hypertext Markup Language* (*HTML*) and *Extensible Hypertext Markup Language* (*XHTML*)—can be used. Markup languages use text-based *tags* embedded into Web pages to indicate where and how the content of a Web page should be displayed. *Scripting languages* (such as *JavaScript* or *VBScript*) are often used to create interactive Web page elements.

Computer Users and Professionals

In addition to hardware, software, data, and *procedures* (the predetermined steps to be carried out in particular situations), a computer system includes *people*. The people involved in a computer system include both the people who make the computers work and those who use them.

Computer users, or *end users*, are the people who use a computer to obtain information. Anyone who uses a computer is a computer user, including an accountant electronically preparing a client's taxes, an office worker using a word processing program to create a letter, a supervisor using a computer to check and see whether manufacturing workers have met the day's quotas, a parent e-mailing his or her child's teacher, a college student analyzing science lab data, a child playing a computer game, and a person bidding at an *online auction* over the Internet.

Programmers, on the other hand, are computer professionals whose primary job responsibility is to write the programs that computers use. Although some computer users may do small amounts of programming to customize the software on their desktop computers, the distinction between a computer user and a programmer is based on the work that the person has been hired to do. In addition to programmers, organizations may employ other *computer professionals*. For instance, *systems analysts* design computer systems to be used within their companies. *Computer operations personnel*, in contrast, are responsible for the day-to-day operations of large computer systems. Computer operations personnel are also often employed to help train users or assist them with their desktop computers and to troubleshoot user-related problems.

COMPUTERS TO FIT EVERY NEED

The types of computers available today vary widely from the tiny computers embedded in consumer devices and appliances, to the pocket-sized computers and mobile phones that do a limited number of computing tasks, to the powerful and versatile *desktop computers* and *portable PCs* found in homes and businesses, to the superpowerful computers used to control the country's defense systems. Computers are generally classified in one of six categories, based on size, capability, and price.

ONLINE VIDEO

Go to **www.course.com/uccs/ch1** to watch the "Smart Car Technologies" video clip.

- ▶ *Embedded computers*—tiny computers embedded into products to perform specific functions or tasks for that product.

- ▶ *Mobile devices*—mobile phones and other communications devices with computing or Internet capabilities.

- ▶ *Personal computers*—conventional *desktop*, *notebook*, *tablet*, and *handheld computers*.

- ▶ *Midrange servers*—computers that host data and programs available to a small group of users.

- ▶ *Mainframe computers*—powerful computers used to host a large amount of data and programs available to a wide group of users.

- ▶ *Supercomputers*—extremely powerful computers used for complex computations and processing.

In practice, classifying a computer into one of these six categories is not always easy or straightforward. For example, some high-end personal computers are as powerful as midrange servers, and some personal computers today are nearly as small as a Web-enabled mobile phone or other mobile device. In addition, technology changes too fast to have precisely defined categories. Nevertheless, these six categories are commonly used to refer to groups of computers designed for similar purposes.

>**Computer user.** A person who uses a computer. >**Programmer.** A person whose primary job responsibility is to write, maintain, and test computer programs.

FIGURE 1-13

Most cars manufactured today include numerous embedded computers to add high-tech safety and convenience features.

FIGURE 1-14

A smart phone.

Embedded Computers

An **embedded computer** is a tiny computer embedded into a product designed to perform specific tasks or functions for that product. For example, computers are embedded into household appliances (such as dishwashers, microwaves, cooktops, washing machines, coffee makers, and so forth) to help those appliances perform their designated tasks. Other devices around the home—such as thermostats, answering machines, sewing machines, DVD players, televisions, and so forth— also often contain embedded computers. And cars increasingly use many types of embedded computers to assist with diagnostics, to notify the user of important conditions (such as an underinflated tire or an oil filter that needs changing), to control the use of the airbag and other safety devices, and to help the driver perform tasks. For instance, the car shown in Figure 1-13 uses embedded computers for all of these features plus many others including an *adaptive cruise control* (which uses a radar sensor to measure the distance between the front of the car and vehicles ahead of it and then automatically adjusts vehicle speed accordingly), a *Blind Spot Information System* (which uses cameras near the outside mirrors to detect vehicles that might be in a blind spot and alerts the driver), and a *Personal Car Communicator* (which allows the driver to check the security status of the car from a distance, unlock and start the car without a key, and tell if an intruder is in the car via a heartbeat sensor located inside the car). Embedded computers are designed for specific tasks and specific products and so cannot be used as general-purpose computers.

Mobile Devices

A **mobile device** is loosely defined as a very small device that has built-in computing or Internet capability. Mobile devices today are typically based on mobile phones; these devices are often referred to as **smart phones** (see Figure 1-14). Smart phones can be used to access the Web and e-mail wirelessly—as well as offer other capabilities, such as to take digital photos, play games, download and play music, watch TV shows, and access calendars, address books, and other personal productivity features—in addition to performing their regular telephone functions. Smart phones typically include easy navigation tools, such as control buttons or a touch screen, to locate and input the desired command. For text entry, most smart phones today come with some type of built-in keyboard; others use an onscreen keyboard instead that is touched with a finger or stylus to input data. There is an increasing amount of software available for smart phones; in fact, many come with the ability to view and edit documents stored in a common format, such as *Microsoft Office* documents. Because of this, the distinction between smart phones and *handheld computers* (fully functioning computers that are small enough to fit in the palm of your hand, as discussed shortly) is blurring.

Mobile devices based on wristwatches are called *smart watches*. Smart watches can download weather, sports scores, news headlines, and other content wirelessly from the Internet. Some can be used to transfer personal files, store and play music files, or store voice recordings. Others are designed to give directional information or record workout data, keep track of golf scores, monitor dive information, or other sports applications. Handheld gaming devices (such as the *Sony PSP* and the *Nintendo DS*) and portable digital media players (such as the *Zune* and *Sansa*) that include Internet capabilities can also be referred to as mobile devices. Smart watches, handheld gaming devices, and portable digital media players don't usually have a built-in keyboard and are controlled by the buttons located on the device. When text input is needed, these devices can typically display an

TECHNOLOGY AND YOU

High-Tech Workouts

Got an iPod®? You now have a personal trainer. Training *podcasts*–recorded digital files available in both audio and video versions–are on track to replace the workout video. Numerous trainers have a variety of workouts–from body sculpting to aerobics to meditation to boxing and more–available for download on their Web sites. Costs range from 99 cents to about $20 a workout, depending on the format (audio or video) and the length of the workout. Cheaper than a personal trainer, these podcasts allow individuals to work out more easily at home or on the road.

Another high-tech workout aid that is available from Nike and designed for runners contains a sensor that goes inside your running shoe and a receiver that plugs into your iPod. The sensor transmits data about your run–such as time, distance, or calories burned–to your iPod as you work out. A related mobile phone application uses the GPS capabilities of your mobile phone to collect data about your workout, such as duration, distance, speed, and altitude changes. Both of these applications allow

you to upload data to a Web site to create an online running logbook; the GPS application can even map your route using a Google satellite map.

onscreen keyboard. For a look at how *iPods* and other types of digital media players are being used as workout tools, see the Technology and You box.

While some mobile devices have a built-in hard drive, most use built-in flash memory or flash memory cards for storage. Mobile phones almost always run on rechargeable batteries and come with an adapter to allow them to be plugged into a power outlet to be recharged or to run off electricity when desired. Because of their typically small screen size and often crowded keyboards, today's mobile devices are most appropriate for individuals wanting constant e-mail and messaging ability—plus occasional updates on stock prices, weather, directions, or other timely information, as well as access to music and other multimedia content stored on the device or available online—rather than general Web browsing and computing. This is beginning to change, however, as mobile phones, mobile devices, and portable computers continue to converge, and wireless communications continue to improve and become faster. This has happened faster in some countries than in the United States. For instance, smart phones currently available in Japan can be used for videoconferencing, storing gym IDs and concert tickets in digital form, purchasing products, and even unlocking apartment doors.

Personal Computers

A **personal computer** (**PC**) or **microcomputer** is a small computer system designed to be used by one person at a time. PCs are small enough to fit on a desktop, inside a briefcase, or even inside a shirt pocket and are widely used in homes, small businesses, and large

ONLINE VIDEO

Go to **www.course.com/uccs/ch1** to watch the "Wireless O ROKR Sunglasses" video clip.

>**Personal computer (PC).** A type of computer based on a microprocessor and designed to be used by one person at a time; also called a **microcomputer**.

businesses alike. For instance, an individual might use a PC at home to play games, pay bills, prepare taxes, exchange e-mail, and access Web pages. A small business might use its PCs for a variety of computing tasks, including tracking merchandise, preparing correspondence, creating marketing material, billing customers, responding to customer e-mails, updating the company Web site, and completing routine accounting chores. A large business might use PCs for all these tasks, plus as an analysis tool for decision makers and other important applications. Office PCs are also commonly connected to a company *computer network* to provide access to company files, as well as to the company's Internet connection. Personal computers are available in a variety of sizes and configurations (sometimes called *form factors*), as discussed next.

Desktop PCs

Conventional PCs are often referred to as **desktop PCs** because the complete computer system (system unit, monitor, keyboard, mouse, and so forth) fits on or next to a desk (see Figure 1-15). The most common style of desktop PC today uses a *tower case*; that is, with a system unit that is designed to sit vertically, typically on the floor. Desktop PCs can also have a *desktop case* that is designed to be placed horizontally on a desk's surface, usually with the monitor sitting on top of the system unit, although it is more common today for desktop cases to be used with *mini PCs*—very tiny desktop PCs that sit on the desk next to the monitor. A third possibility is the *all-in-one* desktop PC case, which incorporates the monitor and system unit into a single piece of hardware (refer again to Figure 1-15).

Desktop PCs typically cost between $500 and $1,500 and usually conform to one of two standards: *PC-compatible* or *Macintosh* (one of each of these types of PCs is shown in Figure 1-15). PC-compatible computers (sometimes referred to as *Windows PCs* or *IBM-compatible PCs*) evolved from the original IBM PC—the first personal computer widely accepted for business use—and are the most common type of personal computer used today. In general, PC-compatible hardware and software are compatible with all brands of PC-compatible computers—such as those made by Dell, Hewlett-Packard, NEC, Acer, Lenovo, Fujitsu, and Gateway—and these computers typically run the Microsoft Windows operating system. Macintosh (*Mac®*) computers are made by Apple®, use the Mac OS operating system, and often use different hardware and software than PC-compatible computers. Although PC-compatible computers are by far the most widely used, the Mac is traditionally the computer of choice for artists, designers, and others who require advanced graphics capabilities. But because there are virtually no Macintosh-compatible computers on the market to help drive down the price, Macs tend to cost more than PC-compatible computers with comparable hardware. A user who is deciding between these two *platforms* must consider what the computer will be used for and if it needs to be compatible with any other PCs, such as a school or an office computer.

FIGURE 1-15
Desktop PCs.

TOWER CASE; PC-COMPATIBLE COMPUTER

ALL-IN-ONE CASE; MACINTOSH COMPUTER

>**Desktop PC.** A personal computer designed to fit on or next to a desk.

Portable PCs

Portable PCs are computers that are designed to be carried around easily, such as in a carrying case, briefcase, purse, or pocket, depending on their size. Portable computers are essential for many workers, such as salespeople who need to make presentations or take orders from clients off-site, agents who need to collect data at remote locations, and managers who need computing and communications resources as they travel. They are also used by many students and are increasingly being purchased as primary home computers. Portable PCs today almost always come with built-in communications capabilities, so the PCs can be easily connected to an office network or the Internet. Portable PCs are designed for users who need a fully functioning computer that they can take with them easily wherever they go. Like mobile devices, portable PCs almost always run on rechargeable batteries and come with an adapter to allow them to be plugged into a power outlet to be recharged; some can also run off electricity when desired.

Two types of portable PCs that are about the size of a standard paper notebook or ruled tablet are *notebook computers* and *tablet PCs*. A smaller alternative is the *handheld computer*. These types of portable computers are discussed next.

Notebook computers (also called **laptop computers**) are fully functioning computers that open to reveal a screen and keyboard. Most notebooks follow the traditional *clamshell* design in which the monitor is on the inside top half of the PC, and the keyboard and touch pad are on the inside bottom half, as shown in Figure 1-16. **Tablet PCs** can use either a *slate* or a *convertible tablet PC* design. Slate tablets include what looks like just the top half of a notebook PC. Typically slate tablets are not used with a keyboard; instead, an electronic pen is used to select objects and write electronically on the screen (the handwritten text can typically be converted to typed text, if desired). Convertible tablet PCs are essentially a combination of a notebook computer and a slate tablet PC. In its notebook format, a convertible tablet PC is used just the same as a notebook PC; that is, with keyboard and touch pad input. When the screen is rotated and then closed with the screen facing out, the device resembles a slate tablet PC, and pen or touch input is used. Although similar in capabilities to their desktop cousins, notebook computers and tablet PCs tend to cost a little more, have smaller screens, and use denser keyboard arrangements (if a keyboard exists). Both notebook computers and tablet PCs also tend to use alternative pointing devices (such as an electronic pen or a touch pad) instead of a mouse, although a mouse can be connected to the computer, if the computer has an available *mouse port* or *USB port*.

TIP

PCs that allow pen input—such as tablet PCs—are convenient in crowded situations, as well as in places where the clicking of a keyboard would be annoying to others.

▼ **FIGURE 1-16**
Notebook and tablet PCs.

NOTEBOOK COMPUTER

SLATE TABLET PC

CONVERTIBLE TABLET PC

> **Portable PC.** A small personal computer, such as a notebook, tablet, or handheld PC, designed to be carried around easily.
> **Notebook computer.** A fully functioning portable PC that opens to reveal a screen and keyboard; also called a **laptop computer**.
> **Tablet PC.** A portable PC about the size of a notebook that is designed to be used with an electronic pen.

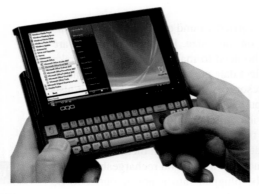

SMART PHONE CAPABILITIES
Some handheld computers can also perform the functions of a smart phone.

SLIDING KEYBOARDS
UMPCs typically have a sliding keyboard for easier input.

FIGURE 1-17
Handheld computers.

Handheld computers are about the size of a paperback book or pocket calculator (see Figure 1-17). Most handheld computers have a built-in keyboard or a *thumbpad*; some also accept input via digital pen or touch. Devices without a built-in keyboard can often be wirelessly connected to a portable keyboard when lengthy input is needed. Many handheld computers include a built-in digital camera and GPS capabilities. Increasingly, handheld computers can perform the functions of a smart phone (including Web browsing, messaging, electronic mail, and phone calls), as well as more general computing functions (including the ability to view and edit documents). While the computing ability of smart phones is growing rapidly, computers classified as handheld computers are generally fully functioning computers that just happen to be able to fit in the palm of your hand. For instance, recent handheld computers—referred to as **ultra mobile personal computers** (**UMPCs**)—run Windows and can run a wide variety of application programs (see Figure 1-17).

Like notebook and tablet PCs, most UMPCs include built-in wireless connectivity, digital cameras, microphones, flash memory card slots, and a variety of connectors; some include a built-in fingerprint scanner so they cannot be used by unauthorized individuals. UMPCs are optimized for mobility and tend to weigh two pounds or less, have a screen size of seven inches or less, have a *sliding keyboard* that can be exposed when it is needed, and support both touch and pen input. UMPCs usually have a built-in hard drive for storage, but no DVD drive so an external drive is typically required to use CDs and DVDs. Some UMPCs include the *Origami Experience* interface designed by Microsoft to provide easy access to books, movies, music, photos, games, and other content stored on the PC; to find, use, and share information faster and easier; and to input commands and data more easily. As the capabilities of handheld computers have improved—for instance, having sharp screens, adequate-sized hard drives, and decent keyboards, as well as being able to run Windows and Windows applications—they are becoming increasingly practical for day-to-day tasks. For some individuals, they are a feasible alternative to a notebook computer.

ASK THE EXPERT

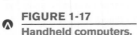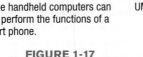

Martin Smekal, President and Founder, TabletKiosk

When would an individual want to use a tablet PC for his or her primary personal computer?

The tablet form factor is the most conducive and adaptable setup for mobile computing. The tablet PC has been embraced by mobile professionals who use pen and touch input in the field and may hook up the tablet PC to a docking station in the house or office to access traditional input modes of mouse and keyboard. A person can use a tablet PC to take notes and input information when standing and moving around, unlike a laptop which must be supported by a solid surface.

Overall, I don't think that the tablet PC will ever replace a keyboard and mouse set up for home computing, though with the right accessories (such as a docking station, keyboard, mouse, and monitor for use while in an office setting), the tablet PC provides the most flexibility for computing both in and out of the office.

>**Handheld computer.** A portable personal computer about the size of a paperback book or pocket calculator; some fully functioning handheld computers are called **ultra mobile personal computers (UMPCs)**.

For individuals who choose to use both a desktop and a portable computer, the ability to share information and *synchronize* data between the two computers is an important consideration. Most handheld computers come with *wireless networking* capabilities that allow the user to wirelessly send data from the portable PC to his or her primary PC or a special USB cable that can be used to connect the handheld computer to the desktop PC. Still others can store data on flash memory cards, which can then be inserted into a desktop PC's flash memory card reader to retrieve the data. And with some types of wireless net-

SYNCHING A HANDHELD AND NOTEBOOK PC
The photos stored on the handheld computer are being transferred (via Bluetooth wireless technology) to the notebook computer.

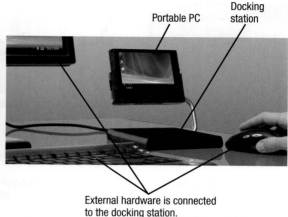

Portable PC   Docking station

External hardware is connected to the docking station.

DOCKING STATIONS
Once a portable PC is connected to a docking station, the monitor and other hardware connected to the docking station can be used.

FIGURE 1-18
Synching and docking a handheld PC.

working technology (for example, *Bluetooth*—a short range wireless networking standard often used to connect devices, such as a keyboard to a computer or a headset to a mobile phone), it is possible for portable and desktop PCs to be in communication with each other and to synchronize data whenever they are within a specific range (see Figure 1-18). Some Web-based services can even synch a handheld computer or mobile device to a desktop PC via the Internet on a continual basis so changes made to your schedule or contact list on your primary PC are automatically reflected on your portable PC or mobile device.

For users who prefer to use a portable PC as their primary PC but want the features of a desktop computer when working at home or in the office, a *docking station* can be used. Docking stations connect a portable PC (typically a notebook or tablet PC) to *peripheral devices*, such as a monitor, keyboard, mouse, and printer. The peripheral devices are always attached to the docking station, so as soon as the PC is connected to the docking station (via a special slot or connector), the hardware attached to the docking station (such as a keyboard, mouse, and printer) can be used and all output that would go to the portable PC's monitor is displayed on the monitor attached to the docking station (see Figure 1-18). Docking stations that are designed to raise the notebook PC's monitor to an appropriate height so it can be used instead of an external monitor are sometimes referred to as *notebook stands*.

FURTHER EXPLORATION

Go to www.course.com/uccs/ch1 for links to information about personal computers.

Thin Clients and Internet Appliances

Most personal computers today are sold as stand-alone, self-sufficient units that are equipped with all the necessary hardware and software needed to operate independently. In other words, they can perform input, processing, output, and storage without being connected to a network, although they can be networked if desired. In contrast, a device that must be connected to a network to perform processing or storage tasks is referred to as a *dumb terminal*. Somewhere between a PC and a dumb terminal are devices that may be able to perform a limited amount of independent processing but are designed to be used with a network. Two examples of these are *thin clients* and *Internet appliances*.

THIN CLIENT

SET-TOP BOX INTERNET APPLIANCE

PORTABLE INTERNET APPLIANCE

INTERNET-ENABLED GAMING CONSOLE

FIGURE 1-19
Thin clients and Internet appliances.

A **thin client**—also called a *network computer (NC)*—is designed to be used in conjunction with a company network. Instead of using local disk drives for storage, programs are accessed from and data is stored on the network server, although some thin clients have USB ports and so can store data locally on USB flash drives. And, while thin clients typically have a local CPU for basic tasks, the primary processing power is located on the network server. The main advantage of thin clients is lower cost (such as for overall hardware and software, PC maintenance, and power and cooling costs), increased security (since data is not stored locally), and easier maintenance (since all software is located on the server). Disadvantages include having limited or no local storage (although this is an advantage for companies with highly secure data that need to prevent data from leaving the facility) and not being able to function as a stand-alone computer when the network is not working. Thin clients are used by businesses to provide employees with access to network applications; they are also sometimes used to provide Internet access to the public. For instance, the thin client shown in Figure 1-19 is installed in a hotel in Boston, Massachusetts, and is used to provide guests with Internet access, hotel and conference information, room-to-room calling, and free phone calls via the Internet.

Network computers or other devices designed primarily for accessing Web pages and/or exchanging e-mail are called **Internet appliances** (sometimes also referred to as *Internet tablets* and *Internet media players*). These devices, some of which are shown in Figure 1-19, can take on a variety of configurations. Some are designed to be located in the home and either come with a monitor or take the form of a *set-top box* that connects to a TV, such as the *MSN TV 2 Internet Media Player* device shown in Figure 1-19. Other Internet appliances look like handheld computers but can only run a Web browser, e-mail program, and other specified applications (such as playing music or videos or viewing digital photos) and so cannot be used as general-purpose computers. Gaming consoles (such as the *Nintendo Wii* and *Sony PlayStation 3*) that can be used to view Internet content, in addition to their gaming abilities, can also be classified as Internet appliances when they are used to access the Internet.

Midrange Servers

A **midrange server**—also sometimes called a *minicomputer* or *midrange computer*—is a medium-sized computer used to host programs and data for a small network. Typically larger, more powerful, and more expensive than a desktop PC, a midrange server is usually located in a closet or other out-of-the-way place and can serve many users at one time. Users connect to the server through a network, using their desktop computer,

>**Thin client.** A PC designed to access a network for processing and data storage, instead of performing those tasks locally; also called a network computer (NC). >**Internet appliance.** A specialized network computer designed primarily for Internet access and/or e-mail exchange.
>**Midrange server.** A medium-sized computer used to host programs and data for a small network.

notebook PC, thin client, or a dumb terminal consisting of just a monitor and keyboard (see Figure 1-20). Midrange servers are often used in small- to medium-sized businesses, such as medical or dental offices, as well as in school computer labs.

Some midrange servers consist of a collection of individual *circuit boards* called *blades*; each blade contains the hardware necessary to provide the complete processing power of one PC. These servers—called *blade servers*—are much easier to expand and upgrade than traditional servers, have lower overall power and cooling costs, and are more secure. With some blade servers, the processing power of the blades is shared among users. With others, each user has his or her own individual blade, which functions as that individual's PC, but the blades are locked in a secure location instead of having that hardware located on each employee's desk. In either case, the thin client hardware designed specifically for user access to a blade server is sometimes called a *blade workstation*.

Mainframe Computers

A **mainframe computer** is a powerful computer used by many large organizations—such as hospitals, universities, large businesses, banks, and government offices—that need to manage large amounts of centralized data. Larger, more expensive, and more powerful than midrange servers, mainframes usually operate 24 hours a day, serving thousands of users connected to the mainframe via PCs, thin clients, or dumb terminals, in a manner similar to the way users connect to midrange servers. Mainframe computers are typically located in climate-controlled *data centers* and connected to the rest of the company computers via a network. During regular business hours, a mainframe runs multiple programs as needed to meet the different needs of its wide variety of users. At night, it commonly performs large processing tasks, such as payroll and billing. Today's mainframes are sometimes referred to as *high-end servers* or

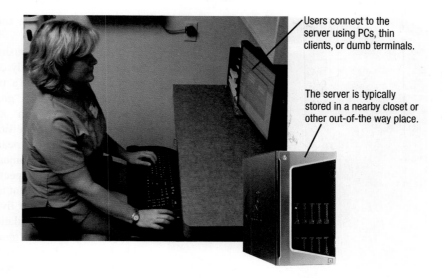

Users connect to the server using PCs, thin clients, or dumb terminals.

The server is typically stored in a nearby closet or other out-of-the-way place.

FIGURE 1-20
Midrange servers.

ASK THE EXPERT

Stephen Yeo, Worldwide Strategic Marketing Director, IGEL Technology

When would a business want to use thin clients instead of PCs?

Today's thin clients can be used to replace PCs wherever you have reliable, unbroken, network access. They come in a wide variety of form factors including traditional desktops, quad screens, LCD integrated units, and mobile wireless tablets. They can be used to access server-based Windows applications, mainframes, the Web, Java, and even VoIP telephony. Superior performance, security, manageability, and user experience make thin clients very popular with many organizations.

A business shouldn't use a thin client if the user has intermittent network access (such as an executive who travels a lot or an outside sales rep) or the programs being used require 3D moving graphics (such as gaming applications).

> **Mainframe computer.** A computer used in large organizations (such as hospitals, large businesses, and colleges) that need to manage large amounts of centralized data and run multiple programs simultaneously.

enterprise-class servers and usually cost at least several hundred thousand dollars each.

One issue facing businesses today is the high cost of electricity to power (and consequently cool) the mainframes, servers, and PCs in an organization. There is a movement among businesses and computer manufacturers alike to "green" up the data center; that is, to make the computers located in a business—particularly mainframes and servers—more energy efficient. For example, IBM has announced that it will consolidate the nearly 4,000 servers located in its data centers onto about 30 mainframes (one of the new mainframes is shown in Figure 1-21). IBM expects that this new environment will consume approximately 80 percent less energy than the current setup and expects significant savings over five years in energy, software, and system support costs. This consolidation is possible because of *virtualization*—the ability of a single mainframe to behave as hundreds or thousands of individual servers. For a closer look at virtualization, see the Inside the Industry box. *Green computing* and other environmental concerns are discussed in more detail in Chapter 7.

FIGURE 1-21
Mainframe computers.

Supercomputers

Some applications require extraordinary speed, accuracy, and processing capabilities—for example, sending astronauts into space, controlling missile guidance systems and satellites, forecasting the weather, exploring for oil, and assisting with some kinds of scientific research. **Supercomputers**—the most powerful and most expensive type of computer available—were developed to fill this need. Some relatively new supercomputing applications include hosting extremely complex Web sites and decision-support systems for corporate executives, as well as three-dimensional applications, such as 3D medical scans, image projections, and architectural modeling. Unlike mainframe computers, which typically run multiple applications simultaneously to serve a wide variety of users, supercomputers generally run one program at a time, as fast as possible.

FIGURE 1-22
The Blue Gene/L supercomputer.
Supercomputers are used for specialized situations in which immense processing speed is required.

Conventional supercomputers (see Figure 1-22) can cost several million dollars each. To reduce the cost, it has become more common to build less-expensive supercomputers by connecting hundreds of smaller computers—increasingly midrange servers running the Linux operating system—into a **supercomputing cluster** that acts as a single computer. The computers in the cluster usually contain several CPUs each and are dedicated to processing cluster applications. The resulting supercomputer is often referred to as a *massively parallel processor* (*MPP*) computer. For example, one of the fastest supercomputers in the world, IBM's *Blue Gene/L* (shown in Figure 1-22), contains 65,536 nodes containing two CPUs each for a combined total of 131,072 CPUs. This

BLUE GENE/L SUPERCOMPUTER
This supercomputer is installed at Lawrence Livermore National Laboratory.

BLUE GENE/L CIRCUIT BOARDS
Each rack holds several circuit boards; each circuit board contains four processors.

>**Supercomputer.** The fastest, most expensive, and most powerful type of computer. >**Supercomputing cluster.** A supercomputer comprised of numerous smaller computers connected together to act as a single computer.

INSIDE THE INDUSTRY

Virtualization

In general, the term "virtualization" refers to creating an environment whose appearance to end users is different from its physical structure. For instance, if an individual uses a computer to access an operating system and application software located on a server, but it appears to the user that he or she is working directly on his or her computer, that is virtualization. Typically, virtualization is used to create separate environments on a computer that, although physically located on the same computer, do not interact with each other. Often virtualization is used with servers—and, more recently, mainframes—to divide one physical computer into multiple isolated virtual environments. Each virtual environment typically contains an operating system and the necessary application software—this is called *server virtualization* (see the accompanying illustration). Virtualization can also be used on a single PC, such as to host different operating systems or types of software, or to create separate environments for testing software during development. While virtualization has existed for many years—IBM introduced software to create virtual environments on mainframe computers in 1972—it stopped being widely used in the 1980s. However, today's extensive computing demands have led to renewed interest in virtualization, and it is currently a hot computing trend.

The primary reason companies are turning toward server virtualization is efficiency. Traditionally, individual servers are allocated to particular applications or groups of users and are not used to full capacity—one estimate is about a 10% utilization of server capability compared with the 90% utilization common with mainframe computers. With virtualization, all applications for an organization are installed in virtual environments on one or more physical servers, enabling companies to fulfill their computing needs with fewer servers. This translates into reduced costs, as well as a server architecture that is easier to manage. Each virtual environment is self-contained and can be backed up individually, as well as moved to another physical server as needed.

While widespread *desktop virtualization* is a little further down the road, desktop virtualization is expected to enable servers to host an entire desktop environment for each user when it does become available. A user sees his or her own personal desktop when booting a device (typically a thin client or other device) using desktop virtualization, even though the processing hardware, operating system, and application programs are located on the shared server. The virtual desktops can be displayed wherever the user happens to be at the moment—such as in the office, at home, or on the road. Virtualization requires special software to create and manage the virtual environments, although processors with built-in virtualization hardware and operating systems that include virtualization features are beginning to become available and are expected to make virtualization easier to implement in the future. The concepts of virtualization are also beginning to be applied to other computing areas, such as networking and storage.

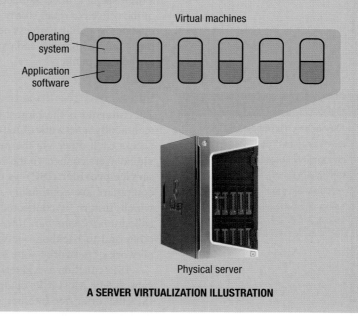

A SERVER VIRTUALIZATION ILLUSTRATION

supercomputing cluster, built for the U.S. Department of Energy, is installed at the Lawrence Livermore National Laboratory in California. It cost approximately $100 million, performs about 360 *teraflops* (trillions of *floating point operations per second*), runs the Linux operating system, and is used primarily to perform the computations needed to conduct nuclear weapons simulations to help ensure the safety, security, and reliability of the nation's nuclear weapon stockpile. Another supercomputer—named *Roadrunner*—in development at the Los Alamos National Laboratory that will also be used for nuclear weapon stockpile safety could be as fast as 1,000 teraflops (one *petaflop*) when fully installed—a speed that has not yet been sustained.

A concept related to cluster computing is *grid computing*—a growing trend of utilizing the unused processing power of a large number of computers—typically PCs—connected through the Internet to work together on a single task, on demand. For instance, consumers can volunteer their PCs to be used for scientific or medical research purposes and their PCs' processing power will be tapped (via the Internet) when needed by the research organization. New grid computing services are beginning to be offered to provide companies with immense processing power on demand, similar to the way electricity is delivered as it is needed. For instance, businesses can form a grid of their employees' PCs and sell that processing power during off-hours (whenever employees are not at work) to those who need it.

COMPUTER NETWORKS AND THE INTERNET

Many computers today are connected to a *computer network*. A **computer network** is a collection of hardware and other devices that are connected together so that users can share hardware, software, and data, as well as electronically communicate with each other. As shown in Figure 1-23, many networks use a *network server* to manage the data flowing through the network devices and the resources on a network. For example, a network server might control access to shared printers and other shared hardware, as well as to shared programs and data. The other computers on a network that access network resources through the network server are called *clients*.

Computer networks exist in many sizes and types. For instance, a home network might connect two computers inside a home to share a single printer and Internet connection, as well as to exchange files. A small office network of five or six computers might be used to enable workers to access the company database, communicate with other employees, share a high-speed printer, and access the Internet. A large corporate network might connect all of the offices or retail stores in the corporation, creating a network that spans several cities or states. A public wireless network—such as those available at some coffeehouses, restaurants, public libraries, and parks—might be used to provide Internet access to customers or the general public.

What Are the Internet and the World Wide Web?

The **Internet** is the largest and most well-known computer network in the world. It is technically a network of networks, since it consists of thousands of networks that can all access each other via the main *backbone* infrastructure of the Internet. Typically, individual users connect to the Internet by connecting to computers belonging to an **Internet service provider (ISP)**—a company that provides Internet access, usually for a fee. ISP computers are continually connected to a larger network, called a *regional network*, which, in turn, is connected to one of the major high-speed networks within a country, called a *backbone network*. Backbone networks within a country are connected to each other and to backbone networks in other countries. Together they form one enormous network of networks—the Internet.

ISPs function as a gateway or onramp to the Internet, providing Internet access to their subscribers. Most ISPs charge a monthly fee for Internet access, although there are some ISPs that offer free Internet access in exchange for onscreen advertising. If you connect to the Internet using a school or company network, the school or company acts as your ISP. If you connect using a smart phone or other type of mobile device, your wireless provider is usually your ISP. Home PC users typically use a national ISP (such as *SBC*, *America Online (AOL)*, *EarthLink*, *PeoplePC*, *Verizon*, *NetZero*, *Comcast*, or *Road Runner*) that provides Internet service to a large geographical area, or a local ISP that has a more limited service area. Tips for choosing and getting set up with an ISP are included in Chapter 3.

>**Computer network.** A collection of computers and other hardware devices that are connected together to share hardware, software, and data, as well as to communicate electronically with one another. >**Internet.** The largest and most well-known computer network, linking millions of computers all over the world. >**Internet service provider (ISP).** A business or other organization that provides Internet access to others, typically for a fee.

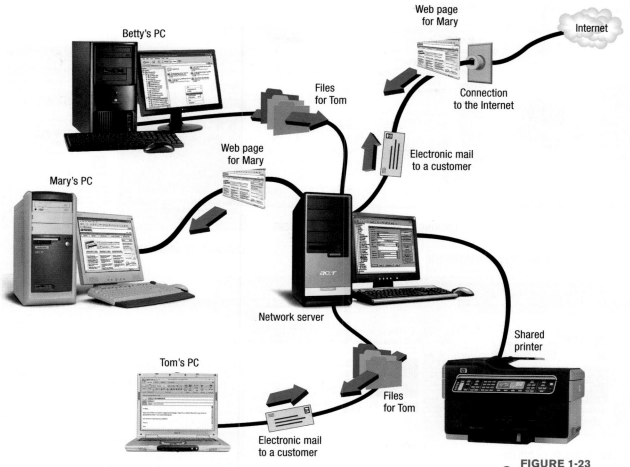

Betty's PC

Mary's PC

Web page
for Mary

Tom's PC

Electronic mail
to a customer

Files
for Tom

Web page
for Mary

Network server

Electronic mail
to a customer

Files
for Tom

Connection
to the Internet

Internet

Shared
printer

FIGURE 1-23
Example of a
computer network.

Millions of people and organizations all over the world are connected to the Internet. Two of the most common Internet activities today are exchanging e-mail and accessing the *World Wide Web* (*WWW*). While the term "Internet" refers to the physical structure of that network, the **World Wide Web** refers to one resource—a collection of documents called **Web pages**—available through the Internet. A group of Web pages belonging to one individual or company is called a **Web site**. Web page files are stored on computers (called **Web servers**) that are continually connected to the Internet; they can be accessed at any time by anyone with a computer (or other Web-enabled device) and an Internet connection. A wide variety of information is available via Web pages, such as news, weather, airline schedules, product information, government publications, music downloads, maps, telephone directories, movie trailers, and much, much more. You can also use Web pages to shop, bank, trade stock, and perform other types of online financial transactions, as well as to listen to music, play games, watch television shows, and perform other entertainment-oriented activities (see Figure 1-24). You can even use the Internet to research political issues and candidates, and—beginning in 2007—to submit video questions for U.S. Presidential debates. Web pages are viewed using a **Web browser**, such as *Internet Explorer*, *Netscape Navigator*, *Safari*, *Opera*, or *Firefox*.

FURTHER EXPLORATION

Go to **www.course.com/uccs/ch1**
for links to information about Web
browsers.

ACCESSING PRODUCT INFORMATION

LOOKING UP MAPS AND PHONE NUMBERS

LISTENING TO MUSIC AND WATCHING VIDEOS

SHOPPING AND PAYING BILLS ONLINE

READING NEWS

SENDING AND RECEIVING E-MAIL

FIGURE 1-24
Some common
Web activities.

Accessing a Network or the Internet

To access a computer network (such as a home network, company network, or the Internet), you need a modem or a network adapter that physically connects your computer to the network. Communications software (either built into your operating system or installed as a separate program) allows you to connect to and *log on* to the network, if needed, so that you can access network resources. Sometimes a *username*, *user ID*, or *login ID* and a password are required to log on to a network; if so, you will typically be asked to supply them each time you boot the computer. After providing the correct information, you will have access to network resources, and you can select the program you want to run.

To access the Internet, you must be connected to it. Many computers today are continually connected to the Internet (called a *direct* or *always-on connection*), in which the computer or other device being used to access the Internet is continually connected to the ISP's computer. With a direct connection, you only need to open your browser (using the desktop icon for your browser, the desktop icon for your ISP, or the appropriate Start menu item) to begin using the Internet. With a *dial-up connection*, the PC or device must dial up and connect to the ISP's computer via a telephone line when Internet access is needed. Most national dial-up ISPs include a desktop icon or Start menu item that opens your browser and dials your telephone together as a single step; smaller, regional dial-up ISPs may require you to open your browser and start the *dialing program* installed on your PC as two separate steps. You may also be asked to enter your username and password before being connected to the Internet; these will have been assigned or chosen during your ISP setup procedure. Once connected to the Internet, you can open a Web browser program and begin to view Web pages.

In order to request a Web page or other resource located on the Internet, you need to use its *Internet address*. **Internet addresses** are numerical or text-based addresses used to identify resources accessible through the Internet, such as computers, Web pages, and people. Each Internet address is unique and is assigned to one—and only one—person or thing. The most common types of Internet addresses are *IP addresses* and *domain names* (to identify computers); *URLs* (to identify Web pages); and *e-mail addresses* (to identify people).

IP Addresses and Domain Names

IP addresses and their corresponding **domain names** are used to identify computers available through the Internet. IP (short for *Internet Protocol*) addresses are numeric, such as *207.46.197.32*, and are commonly used by computers to refer to other computers. A computer that hosts information available through the Internet (such as a Web server hosting Web pages) usually has a unique text-based domain name (such as *microsoft.com*) that corresponds to the host computer's IP address to make it easier for people to remember the address to use to access that information. IP addresses and domain names are unique; that is, there cannot be two computers on the Internet using the exact same IP address or exact same domain name. To ensure this, specific IP addresses are allocated to each network to be used with the computers on that network, and there is a worldwide registration system for domain name registration. Domain names are typically registered on an annual basis; the required fee varies from registrar to registrar. When a domain name is registered, the IP address of the computer that will be hosting the Web site associated with that domain name is also registered; the Web site can either be accessed using its domain name or corresponding IP address. When a Web page is requested by domain name, the corresponding IP address is looked up using the central *domain name system* (*DNS*) and then the appropriate Web page is displayed.

Domain names typically identify who owns that computer and either the type of entity (such as a school, a commercial business, the government, or an individual person) or the computer's location. A period separates the different parts of a domain name. The rightmost part of the domain name (beginning with the rightmost period) identifies the type of the organization or its location and is called the *top-level domain* (*TLD*). There were seven original TLDs used in the United States (see Figure 1-25). Since then, over 240 additional two-letter *country code TLDs* have been created to represent countries or territories (*.us* for United States and *.jp* for Japan, for instance). Because of the high demand for domain names, new top-level domains are periodically proposed to *ICANN* (*Internet Corporation for Assigned Names and Numbers*), the nonprofit organization responsible for Internet IP address allocation and domain name management. Several

V FIGURE 1-25
Some top-level domains (TLDs).

ORIGINAL TLDS	INTENDED USE
.com	Commercial businesses
.edu	Educational institutions
.gov	Government organizations
.int	International treaty organizations
.mil	Military organizations
.net	Network providers and ISPs
.org	Noncommercial organizations

NEW TLDS	INTENDED USE
.aero	Aviation industry
.biz	Businesses
.coop	Coop organizations
.info	Resource sites
.jobs	Employment sites
.mobi	Sites optimized for mobile users
.museum	Museums
.name	Individuals
.pro	Licensed professionals
.travel	Travel-oriented sites

>**Internet address.** An address that identifies a computer, person, or Web page on the Internet, such as an IP address, domain name, or e-mail address. >**IP address.** A numeric Internet address used to uniquely identify a computer on the Internet. >**Domain name.** A text-based Internet address used to uniquely identify a computer on the Internet.

DOMAIN NAME	ORGANIZATION	TYPE/LOCATION OF ORGANIZATION
microsoft.com	Microsoft Corporation	Commercial business
stanford.edu	Stanford University	Educational institution
fbi.gov	Federal Bureau of Investigation	Government organization
navy.mil	United States Navy	Military organization
royal.gov.uk	The British Monarchy	Government organization in the United Kingdom

FIGURE 1-26
Examples of domain names.

new TLDs have been approved and implemented (the most common of these are listed in Figure 1-25); several additional TLDs are still under consideration.

Some TLDs—such as .gov, .edu, and .mil—are *restricted TLDs* and can only be registered by a qualifying organization; *unrestricted TLDs*—such as .com, .net, .biz, .name, and .us—can be registered by any person or type of organization. However, only the legitimate holder of a trademarked name (such as Microsoft) can use that trademarked name as a domain name (such as Microsoft.com). Some sample domain names are shown in Figure 1-26. Although many domain names consist solely of two parts, additional parts can be used to identify an organization more specifically, as in the last example in Figure 1-26. When this occurs, all of the pieces of the domain name are separated by periods.

Uniform Resource Locators (URLs)

Similar to the way an IP address or domain name uniquely identifies a computer on the Internet, a **uniform resource locator** (**URL**) uniquely identifies a Web page. URLs consist of information identifying the Web server hosting the Web page (typically the *computer name* assigned to that computer by the organization's system administrator to uniquely identify that computer within the organization's domain name), the name of any folders in which the Web page file is stored, and the Web page's filename. For example, looking at the URL for the Web page shown in Figure 1-27 from right to left, we can see that the Web page is called *index.html*, and that file is stored in a folder called *arthur* on a Web server in the *pbskids.org* domain.

Some characteristics of the URL shown in Figure 1-27 are common to most URLs. The letters *http* stand for *Hypertext Transfer Protocol*—the protocol typically used to display Web pages. Web pages are the most common Internet resource accessed with a Web browser. If a different type of Internet resource is requested, a different protocol indicator is used. For example, URLs beginning with *ftp://* use *File Transfer Protocol*—a protocol used to upload and download files—and URLs beginning with *https://* use *Secure Hypertext Transfer Protocol*—the protocol used to display *secure Web pages*; that is, Web pages that can safely be used to transmit sensitive information, such as credit card numbers. The file extensions *.html* and *.htm* both stand for Hypertext Markup Language— the language usually used to create

FIGURE 1-27
A Web page URL.

Web page URLs usually begin with the standard protocol identifier http://.

This part of the URL identifies the Web server hosting the Web page.

Next comes the folder(s) in which the Web page is stored, if necessary.

This is the Web page document that is to be retrieved and displayed.

http:// pbskids.org/ arthur/ index.html

Web pages, as previously discussed (Web pages written using XHTML also typically use the file extension .html). Other file extensions are possible, such as *.asp* (*Active Server Pages*), *.jsp* (*Java Server Pages*), and *.php* (for pages written in the *PHP scripting language*), which are commonly used with Web pages that are created dynamically based on user input.

E-Mail Addresses

To contact people using the Internet, you most often use their **e-mail addresses**. An e-mail address consists of a **username** (an identifying name), followed by the @ symbol, followed by the domain name for the computer that will be handling that person's e-mail (called a *mail server*). For example,

> jsmith@cengage.com
> maria_s@cengage.com
> sam.peterson@cengage.com

are the e-mail addresses assigned respectively to jsmith (John Smith), maria_s (Maria Sanchez), and sam.peterson (Sam Peterson), three hypothetical employees at Cengage Learning, the publisher of this textbook. Usernames are typically a combination of the person's first and last names and sometimes include periods, underscores, and numbers, but cannot include blank spaces. To ensure a unique e-mail address for everyone in the world, usernames must be unique within each domain name. So, even though there could be a *jsmith* at Cengage Learning using the e-mail address *jsmith@cengage.com* and a *jsmith* at Stanford University using the e-mail address *jsmith@stanford.edu*, the two e-mail addresses are unique. It is up to each organization with a registered domain name to ensure that one—and only one—exact same username is assigned under its domain. Using e-mail addresses to send e-mail messages is discussed later in this chapter; other forms of online communications—such as *instant messaging* (*IM*)—are covered in Chapter 3. For a look at how online communications are being used to help keep college students safe, see the How It Works box.

Pronouncing Internet Addresses

Because Internet addresses are frequently given verbally, it is important to know how to pronounce them. A few guidelines are listed next, and Figure 1-28 shows some examples of Internet addresses and their proper pronunciations.

▶ If a portion of the address forms a recognizable word or name, it is spoken; otherwise, it is spelled out.

▶ The @ sign is pronounced *at*.

▶ The period (.) is pronounced *dot*.

▶ The forward slash (/) is pronounced *slash*.

FIGURE 1-28
Pronouncing Internet addresses.

TYPE OF ADDRESS	SAMPLE ADDRESS	PRONUNCIATION
Domain name	berkeley.edu	berkeley dot e d u
URL	microsoft.com/windows/ie/default.asp	microsoft dot com slash windows slash i e slash default dot a s p
E-mail address	president@whitehouse.gov	president at whitehouse dot gov

---

>**E-mail address.** An Internet address consisting of a username and computer domain name that uniquely identifies a person on the Internet.
>**Username.** A name that uniquely identifies a user on a particular network.

HOW IT WORKS

Campus Emergency Notification Systems

Recent on-campus tragedies, such as the Virginia Tech shootings in 2007, have increased attention on ways organizations can quickly and effectively notify a large number of individuals. For instance, many colleges are implementing emergency notification systems to notify students, faculty, staff, and campus visitors of an emergency, severe weather condition, campus closure, or another important announcement.

With nearly all college students today having a mobile phone, sending emergency alerts via text message is a natural option for many colleges. To be able to send a text message to an entire campus typically requires the use of a company who specializes in this type of mass communications. One such company is Omnilert, which has systems installed in more than 300 colleges and universities around the country. With the Omnilert campus notification system—called *e2Campus*—the contact information of the students, faculty, and staff to be notified is entered into the system and then the individuals can be divided into groups, depending on the types of messages each individual should receive. When an alert needs to be sent, an administrator sends the message (via a mobile phone or PC) and it is distributed to the appropriate individuals (see the accompanying illustration).

While many colleges are opting for mobile phone notifications (via SMS text messages), alerts can also be simultaneously and automatically sent via virtually any voice or text communications medium, such as e-mail, RSS feeds, instant messaging (IM), computer desktop alerts, Web pages (such as the campus home page or Facebook page), phones, digital signage systems (such as signs in dorms and the student union), PA systems located around campus, and more. To facilitate systems such as these, some colleges—such as Montclair

State University in New Jersey—now require all undergraduate students to have a mobile phone. The phones are used to receive campus alerts as well as to access other useful features, such as tracking campus shuttle buses, participating in class polls, and accessing class assignments and grades. An additional safety feature is the ability to use the phones to activate a *Guardian* alert whenever a student feels unsafe on campus; Guardian alerts automatically send the student's physical location (determined via the phone's GPS coordinates) to the campus police so the student can be quickly located.

And the systems are working. For instance, when a masked student walked onto the St. John's University Queens, New York, campus with a rifle in late 2007, school officials alerted students via text messages within 18 minutes. This occurred just three weeks after the system was installed in response to the Virginia Tech shootings and underscores the importance of campus emergency notification systems today.

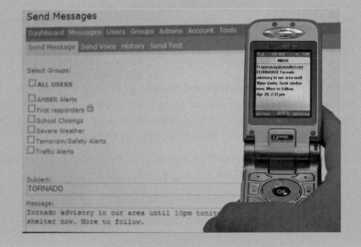

Surfing the Web

Once you have an Internet connection, you are ready to begin *surfing the Web*—that is, using a Web browser to view Web pages. In addition to being used to display Web pages, most Web browsers today can be used to perform other Internet tasks, such as downloading files, exchanging e-mail, accessing *discussion groups*, and participating in *chat sessions*. The ability to perform a variety of Internet tasks, either as part of the Web browser program itself or using a separate companion program that is opened automatically when needed, has made the Web browser a universal tool for exploring and using the Internet.

The first page that your Web browser displays when it is opened is your browser's starting page—or *home page*. Often this is the home page for the Web site belonging to your browser, school, or ISP. However, you can change your browser's home page to any page—such as a *search site* (a Web site that helps you find Web pages containing the information that you are seeking, as discussed shortly) or a news site—that you plan to visit regularly. The browser's *Options* or *Preferences* dialog box typically includes an

TIP

The *home page* for a Web site is the starting page of that particular site; the *home page* for your browser is the Web page designated as the first page you see each time the browser is opened.

option for changing the browser's home page. From your browser's home page, you can move to any Web page you desire, as discussed next.

Using URLs and Hyperlinks

To navigate to a new Web page for which you know the URL, type that URL in the browser's *Address bar* and press Enter (see Figure 1-29). You can either edit the existing URL or delete it and type a new one, but be sure to match the spelling, capitalization, and punctuation exactly. If you do not know the exact URL, you can type the URL for a *search site* to display the search site's home page and then use that site to search for the Web page, as discussed shortly.

Web pages are connected by *hyperlinks*, which can be graphics or text. When a hyperlink is clicked with the mouse, the Web page associated with that hyperlink is displayed (when you point to a hyperlink, the *status bar* displays the URL of the page that will load if the hyperlink is clicked, as shown in Figure 1-29). Text-based hyperlinks are often underlined, although hyperlinks may also be displayed in a different color than the rest of the text on the page or underlined only when the mouse points to them. To more easily identify hyperlinks, the mouse pointer typically changes to a pointing hand indicator when pointing to a hyperlink; the pointing hand indicates that the item being pointed to is, indeed, a hyperlink. When a hyperlink is clicked, the Web page associated with that hyperlink is displayed, regardless of whether the new page is located on the same Web server as the original page, or on a Web server in an entirely different state or country. In addition to Web pages, hyperlinks can also be linked to other types of files, such as to enable Web visitors to view or download images, listen to or download music files, view video clips, or download software programs.

The most commonly used Web browser is *Internet Explorer* (*IE*). As shown in Figure 1-29, the newest version of IE (*Internet Explorer 7* or *IE 7*) features *tabbed browsing* so you can have multiple Web pages open at the same time and switch between them by clicking the appropriate tab. It also has improved display and printing options, and new security features (such as not allowing the Address bar of any browser window to be hidden and notifying the user of potential security issues on a new *Security Status bar* next to the Address bar) to help protect users from malicious software attacks and *phishing scams* (these and other Internet security risks are discussed in detail in Chapter 4). In IE 7, to open a new tab, click the *New Tab* button to the right of the last tab; to change the display size, click the *Change Zoom Level* button at the bottom right corner of the browser window. In

FIGURE 1-29
Surfing the Web with IE7. URLs, hyperlinks, and favorites can be used to display Web pages.

TOOLBARS
Include Back, Favorites, Home, and Print buttons.

TABS
Click to open a new tab within this IE window.

USING FAVORITES
Click a name in the Favorites list to display the corresponding Web page.

USING URLS
Type a URL in the Address bar and press Enter to display the corresponding Web page.

USING HYPERLINKS
Point to a hyperlink to see the corresponding URL on the status bar; click the hyperlink to display that page.

STATUS BAR
Includes zoom options and security indicators.

any browser, you can use the Back button on the browser's toolbar to return to a previous page. To print the current Web page, click the browser's Print button or select *Print* from the browser's File menu.

Using Favorites and the History List

Virtually all browsers have a feature (usually called *Favorites* or *Bookmarks*) that you can use to save Web page URLs. This feature allows you to return to Web pages easily at a later time. To add the URL for the page you are currently viewing in IE 7 to your Favorites list, click the *Add to Favorites* button and then select the *Add to Favorites* option. Once the URL for a page is saved as a favorite, you can redisplay that page again by selecting its link from the Favorites list (refer again to Figure 1-29). Because a *Favorites list* can get large and unwieldy, you can delete outdated items from the list or move items into folders to keep them organized. In IE 7, you can create a favorite for an entire group of tabbed windows (by using the *Add Tab Group to Favorites* option on the Add to Favorites button) and then all of those tabs will be opened when the favorite is selected.

Most browsers also maintain a *History list*, which is a record of all Web pages visited in the last few weeks (how long a page stays in the History list depends on your browser settings). If you want to revisit a page you have been to recently that is not on your Favorites list, click the History button (if one is available on your browser), or look for a *History* option on the menu to display the History list, and then select the desired page.

Searching the Web

While casual surfing is a popular Web pastime, people often turn to the Internet to find specific types of information. When you know generally what you want but do not know which URL to use to find that information, one of your best options is to perform an *Internet search*. There are a number of special Web pages, called *search sites*, available to help you locate what you are looking for on the Internet. One of the most popular search sites—*Google*—is shown in Figure 1-30. Searching the Web is discussed in more detail in Chapter 3, but you typically type one or more *keywords* into the search box on a search site, and a list of links to Web pages matching your search criteria is displayed. There are also numerous *reference sites* available on the Web to look up addresses, phone numbers, ZIP codes, maps, and other information. To find a reference site, type the information you are looking for (such as "ZIP code lookup" or "topographical maps") in a search site's search box to see links to sites with that information.

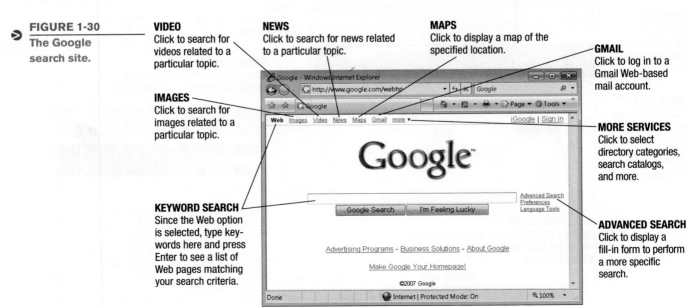

FIGURE 1-30
The Google search site.

VIDEO
Click to search for videos related to a particular topic.

NEWS
Click to search for news related to a particular topic.

MAPS
Click to display a map of the specified location.

GMAIL
Click to log in to a Gmail Web-based mail account.

IMAGES
Click to search for images related to a particular topic.

MORE SERVICES
Click to select directory categories, search catalogs, and more.

KEYWORD SEARCH
Since the Web option is selected, type keywords here and press Enter to see a list of Web pages matching your search criteria.

ADVANCED SEARCH
Click to display a fill-in form to perform a more specific search.

E-Mail

Electronic mail (more commonly called **e-mail**) is the process of exchanging electronic messages between computers over a network—usually the Internet. It is one of the most widely used Internet applications—Americans alone send billions of e-mail messages daily. If you are connected to the Internet (via a desktop computer, portable computer, or mobile device), then you can send an e-mail message to anyone who has an Internet e-mail address. As illustrated in Figure 1-31, e-mail messages typically travel from the sender's PC to his or her ISP's *mail server*, and then through the Internet to the mail server of the recipient's ISP. When the recipient logs on to the Internet and requests his or her e-mail, it is sent to the PC he or she is currently using. Because e-mail is stored for an individual on his or her ISP's mail server until it is requested, the sender and the receiver do not have to be online at the same time to exchange e-mail. In addition to text, e-mail messages can include attached files, such as photos and other documents. Some e-mail systems today allow for video transmission, as well—sometimes called *video e-mail*.

In order to send or receive e-mail, you can either use an *e-mail program* (such as *Netscape Mail*, *Microsoft Outlook Express*, *Microsoft Outlook*, or a proprietary mail program used by your ISP) or *Web-based e-mail*. When using an e-mail program, it needs to be set up with your name, e-mail address, incoming mail server, and outgoing mail server information. Once your e-mail program has been set up successfully, you do not need to specify this information again, unless you want to retrieve e-mail sent to a different e-mail account, you want to check your e-mail from a different PC, or you change ISPs. Some e-mail programs allow multiple e-mail accounts (such as both a personal and school account) to be set up at one time. Others support only one e-mail account at a time, so the settings must be changed to check a different e-mail account. When using a conventional e-mail program, messages are usually downloaded to the user's PC and are viewed using an e-mail program. The messages are stored on the user's PC unless they are deleted.

With Web-based e-mail, the user sends and views e-mail messages by loading the Web page of his or her Web mail provider and logging in. Web-based e-mail is offered by many ISPs, and free Web-based e-mail is available from some Web-based e-mail providers, such as *Hotmail, Yahoo! Mail, AOL Mail,* and *Google Gmail*. Web-based e-mail is more flexible than conventional e-mail, since a user's e-mail can be accessed from any computer with an Internet connection. The user does not have to change his or her e-mail settings in order to view e-mail messages from a different PC, and all e-mail messages in the user's Inbox can be viewed from any computer. However, Web-based e-mail is typically slower than conventional e-mail and users need to be careful not to exceed the capacity of their online mailbox, since e-mail messages are typically stored online, though some Web mail providers (such as Gmail) allow you to download copies of the messages to your computer, if desired.

FIGURE 1-31
How conventional e-mail works.

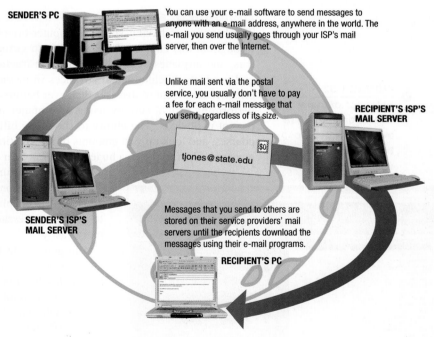

SENDER'S PC

You can use your e-mail software to send messages to anyone with an e-mail address, anywhere in the world. The e-mail you send usually goes through your ISP's mail server, then over the Internet.

Unlike mail sent via the postal service, you usually don't have to pay a fee for each e-mail message that you send, regardless of its size.

RECIPIENT'S ISP'S MAIL SERVER

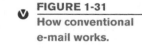

tjones@state.edu $0

SENDER'S ISP'S MAIL SERVER

Messages that you send to others are stored on their service providers' mail servers until the recipients download the messages using their e-mail programs.

RECIPIENT'S PC

>**Electronic mail (e-mail).** Electronic messages sent from one user to another over the Internet or other network.

Virtually all ISPs used with desktop and portable PCs include e-mail service in their monthly fee and do not charge additional fees for sending or receiving e-mail messages. However, some plans from wireless providers (such as those used with handheld computers and smart phones) include a limited number or size of e-mail messages that can be sent or received during a billing period; messages after that point result in additional fees.

COMPUTERS AND SOCIETY

The vast improvements in technology over the past decade have had a distinct impact on daily life, both at home and at work. Computers have become indispensable tools in our homes and businesses, and related technological advancements have changed the way our everyday items—cars, microwaves, coffee pots, toys, exercise bikes, telephones, televisions, and more—look and function. As computers and everyday devices become smarter, they tend to do their normal jobs faster, better, and more reliably than before, as well as take on additional functions. In addition to affecting individuals, computerization and advancing technologies have changed society as a whole. Without computers, banks would be overwhelmed by the job of tracking all the transactions they process, moon exploration and the space shuttle would still belong to science fiction, and scientific advances—such as DNA analysis and gene mapping—would be nonexistent. In addition, we as individuals are getting accustomed to the increased automation of everyday activities, such as shopping and banking, and we depend on having fast and easy access to information via the Internet and rapid communications via e-mail and instant messaging. In addition, many of us would not think about making a major purchase without first researching it online. In fact, it is surprising how fast the Internet and its resources have become an integral part of our society. But despite all its benefits, *cyberspace* has some risks. Some of the most important societal implications related to computers and the Internet are discussed next.

Benefits of a Computer-Oriented Society

The benefits of having such a computer-oriented society are numerous, as touched on throughout this chapter. The capability to virtually design, build, and test new buildings, cars, and airplanes before the actual construction begins helps professionals create safer end products. Technological advances in medicine allow for earlier diagnosis and more effective treatment of diseases than ever before. The benefit of beginning medical students performing virtual surgery using a computer instead of performing actual surgery on a patient is obvious. The ability to shop, pay bills, research products, participate in online courses, and look up vast amounts of information 24 hours a day, 7 days a week, 365 days a year via the Internet is a huge convenience. In addition, a computer-oriented society generates new opportunities. For example, technologies—such as speech recognition software and Braille input and output devices—enable physically or visually challenged individuals to perform necessary job tasks and communicate with others more easily.

In general, technology has also made a huge number of tasks in our lives go much faster. Instead of experiencing a long delay for a credit check, an applicant can get approved for a loan or credit card almost immediately. Documents and photographs can be e-mailed or faxed in mere moments, instead of taking at least a day to be physically mailed. You can watch your favorite TVs shows online (see Figure 1-32) or access current news at your convenience. And you can download information, programs, music files, and more on demand when you want or need them, instead of having to order them and then wait for delivery or physically going to a store to purchase the desired items.

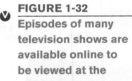

FIGURE 1-32
Episodes of many television shows are available online to be viewed at the user's convenience.

Risks of a Computer-Oriented Society

Although there are a great number of benefits from having a computer-oriented society and a *networked economy*, there are risks as well. A variety of problems have emerged in recent years, ranging from stress and health concerns, to the proliferation of *spam* (unsolicited e-mails) and *malware* (harmful programs that can be installed on your PC without your knowledge), to personal security and privacy issues, to legal and ethical dilemmas. Many of the security and privacy concerns stem from the fact that so much of our personal business takes place online—or at least ends up as data in a computer database somewhere—and the potential for misuse of this data is enormous. Another concern is that we may not have had time to consider all the repercussions of collecting such vast amounts of information. Some people worry about creating a "Big Brother" situation, in which the government or another organization is watching everything that we do. Although the accumulation and distribution of information is a necessary factor of our networked economy, it is one area of great concern to many individuals. And some Internet behavior, such as downloading music or movies from an unauthorized source or viewing pornography on a school or an office PC, can even get you arrested or fired.

Security Issues

One of the most common online security risks today is your PC becoming infected with a malware program, such as a *computer virus*—a malicious software program designed to change the way a computer operates. Malware often causes damage to the infected PC, such as erasing data or bogging down the computer so it does not function well; it can also be used to try to locate sensitive data on your PC (such as passwords or credit card numbers) and send it to the malware creator. Malware can be attached to a program (such as one downloaded from the Internet), as well as attached to, or contained within, an e-mail message. To help protect your computer, never open e-mail attachments from someone you do not know or that have an executable *file extension* (the last three letters in the filename preceded by a period), such as *.exe*, *.com*, or *.vbs*, without first checking with the sender to make sure the attachment is legitimate and be careful about what files you download from the Internet. It is also crucial to install an *antivirus program* on your PC and set it up to scan all e-mail messages, attachments, and files before they are downloaded to make sure they are virus-free, as well as to scan your entire PC periodically for viruses. If a virus or other type of malware is found in an e-mail message (see Figure 1-33), the antivirus program will delete the infected file before the message appears in your Inbox; if malware is found on your PC, the antivirus program will try to remove it.

Another growing security problem is *identity theft*—in which someone else uses your identity, typically to purchase goods or services. Identity theft can stem from personal information discovered from offline means—like discarded papers—or from information found online, stolen from an online database, or obtained via a malware program. *Phishing*—in which identity thieves send fraudulent e-mails to people masquerading as legitimate businesses to obtain social security numbers or other information needed for identity theft—is also a major security issue today. Common security concerns and precautions, such as protecting your PC from malware and protecting yourself from identity theft and phishing schemes, are discussed in more detail in Chapter 4.

ONLINE VIDEO

Go to **www.course.com/uccs/ch1** to watch the "Results from the Symantec Internet Security Threat Report" video clip.

FIGURE 1-33

Antivirus software. Antivirus software is crucial for protecting your PC from computer viruses.

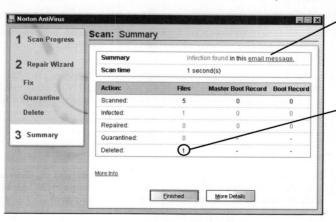

An infected e-mail message was detected as the message was being retrieved from the ISP's e-mail server.

The infected file was deleted before the message reached the user's Inbox, so the infected file was never stored on the user's PC and the PC was protected from the virus.

TIP

Use a *throw-away e-mail address* (a free e-mail address from Yahoo! Mail or another free e-mail provider that you can change easily) when shopping or signing up for free newsletters or sweepstakes. This will help protect your privacy and cut back on the amount of spam delivered to your regular e-mail account.

Privacy Issues

Some individuals view the potential risk to personal privacy as one of the most important issues regarding our networked society. As more and more data about our everyday activities is collected and stored in databases, our privacy is at risk because the potential for privacy violations increases. Today, data is collected about practically anything we buy online or offline, although offline purchases may not be associated with our identity unless we use a credit card or a membership or loyalty card. At issue is not that data is collected—with virtually all organizations using computers for recordkeeping, that is just going to happen—but rather how the collected data is used and how secure it is. Data collected by businesses may be used only by that company or, depending on the businesses' *privacy policy*, may be shared with others. Data shared with others often results in *spam*—unsolicited e-mails. Spam is an enormous problem for individuals and businesses today, and it is considered by many to be a violation of personal privacy. Privacy concerns and precautions are discussed in more detail in Chapter 5.

Differences in Online Communications

There is no doubt that e-mail, instant messaging, and other online communications methods have helped speed up both personal and business communications and have made them more efficient (no more telephone tag, for instance). As you spend more and more time communicating online, you will probably notice some differences between online communications methods (e-mail, chat, and discussion groups, for example) and traditional communications methods (such as telephone calls and written letters). In general, online communications tend to be much less formal. This may be because people usually compose e-mail messages quickly and just send them off, without taking the time to reread and consider their message content or check their spelling or grammar. However, you need to be careful not to be so casual—particularly in business—that your communications appear unprofessional or become too personal with people you do not know.

To help in that regard, a special etiquette—referred to as *netiquette*—has evolved to guide online behavior. A good rule of thumb is always to be polite and considerate of others and to refrain from offensive remarks. This holds true whether you are asking a question via a company's e-mail address, posting a discussion group message, or chatting with a friend. When the communication involves business, you should also be very careful with your grammar and spelling, to avoid embarrassing yourself. Some specific guidelines for what is considered to be proper online behavior are listed in Figure 1-34.

Another trend in online communications is the use of abbreviations and *emoticons*. Abbreviations or *acronyms*, such as BTW for "by the way," are commonly used to save time in all types of communications today. They are being used with increased frequency in text messaging and e-mail exchanged via wireless phones to speed up the text entry process. Emoticons—also sometimes called *smileys*—allow people to add an emotional tone to written online communications. Without these symbols, it is sometimes difficult to tell if the person is serious or joking, since you cannot see the individual's face or hear his or her tone of

FIGURE 1-34

Netiquette. Use these netiquette guidelines and common sense when communicating online.

RULE	EXPLANATION
Use descriptive subject lines	Use short, descriptive subject lines for e-mail messages and discussion group posts. For example, "Question regarding MP3 downloads" is much better than a vague title, such as "Question."
Don't shout	SHOUTING REFERS TO TYPING YOUR ENTIRE E-MAIL MESSAGE OR DISCUSSION GROUP POST USING CAPITAL LETTERS. Use capital letters only when it is grammatically correct to do so or for emphasizing a few words.
Watch what you say	Things that you say or write online can be interpreted as being sexist, racist, ethnocentric, xenophobic, or in just general bad taste. Also check spelling and grammar—typos look unprofessional and nobody likes wading through poorly written materials.
Avoid e-mail overload	Don't send *spam mail*, which is unsolicated bulk e-mail and the Internet equivalent of junk mail. The same goes for forwarding e-mail chain letters or every joke you run across to everyone in your address book.
Be cautious	Don't give out personal information—such as your real name, telephone number, or credit card information—to people you meet in a chat room or other online meeting place.

voice. Emoticons are illustrations of faces showing smiles, frowns, and other expressions that are created with keyboard symbols, such as the popular smile emoticon :-). With some programs, emoticons are changed into actual faces, such as ☺. While most people would agree that these abbreviations and symbols are fine to use with personal communications, they are not usually viewed as appropriate for formal business communications.

The Anonymity Factor

By their very nature, online communications lend themselves to *anonymity*. Since recipients usually do not hear senders' voices or see their handwriting, it is difficult to know for sure who the sender is. Particularly in discussion groups and chat rooms, where individuals use made-up names instead of real names, there is an anonymous feel to being online.

Being anonymous gives many individuals a sense of freedom, which makes them feel able to say or do anything online. This sense of true freedom of speech can be beneficial. For example, a reserved individual who might never complain about a poor product or service in person may feel comfortable lodging a complaint by e-mail. In political newsgroups or chat discussions, many people feel they can be completely honest about what they think and can introduce new ideas and points of view without inhibition. Anonymous e-mail is also a safe way for an employee to blow the whistle on a questionable business practice, or for an individual to tip off police to a crime or potential terrorist attack.

But, like all good things, online anonymity can be abused. Using the Internet as their shield, some people use rude comments, ridicule, profanity, and even slander to attack people, places, and things they do not like or agree with. Others may use multiple online identities (such as multiple usernames in a discussion group) to give the appearance of increased support for their points of view. Still others may use multiple identities to try to manipulate stock prices (by posting false information about a company to drive the price down, for instance), to get buyers to trust an online auction seller (by posting fictitious positive feedback about themselves), or to commit other illegal or unethical acts.

It is possible to hide your true identity while browsing or sending e-mail by removing personal information from your browser and e-mail program or by using a cloaking service, such as the *Anonymizer* service available for about $30 per year. But, in fact, even when personal information is removed, ISPs and the government may still be able to trace communications back to a particular computer when a crime has occurred, so it is difficult—perhaps impossible—to be completely anonymous online.

Information Integrity

The Web contains a vast amount of information on a wide variety of topics. While much of the information is factual, other information may be misleading, biased, or just plain wrong. As more and more people turn to the Web for information, it is crucial that they take the time to determine if the information they obtain and pass on to others is accurate. There have been numerous cases of information intended as a joke being restated on a Web site as fact, statements being quoted out of context (which changed the meaning from the original intent), and hoaxes circulated via e-mail. Consequently, use common sense when evaluating what you read online, and double-check information before passing it on to others.

One way to evaluate online content is by its source. If you obtain information from a news source that you trust, you should feel confident that the accuracy of its online information is close to that of its offline counterpart. For information about a particular product, go to the originating company. For government information, government Web sites have more objective information than Web sites that may have a bias.

> **TIP**
>
> To check if a story you hear about or receive via e-mail is a hoax or chain letter, try the *Hoaxbusters* site at hoaxbusters.ciac.org or the *Urban Legends Reference Pages* at snopes.com.

SUMMARY

COMPUTERS IN YOUR LIFE

Computers appear almost everywhere in today's world, and most people need to use a computer or a computerized device frequently on the job, at home, at school, or while on the go. **Computer literacy**, which is being familiar with basic computer concepts, helps individuals feel more comfortable using computers and is a necessary skill for everyone today.

Computers abound in today's homes, schools, workplaces, and other locations. Increasingly, students and employees need to use a computer for productivity or research. Individuals often use computers at home and/or carry portable computers or devices with them to remain in touch with others or to use Internet resources on a continual basis.

WHAT IS A COMPUTER AND WHAT DOES IT DO?

A **computer** is a *programmable* electronic device that accepts **input**; performs **processing** operations; **outputs** the results; and provides **storage** for data, programs, or output when needed. Most computers today also have **communications** capabilities. This progression of input, processing, output, and storage is sometimes called the *information processing cycle*.

Data is the raw, unorganized facts that are input into the computer to be processed. Data that the computer has processed into a useful form is called **information**. Data can exist in many forms, representing *text*, *graphics*, *audio*, and *video*.

One of the first calculating devices was the *abacus*. Early computing devices that predate today's computers include the *slide rule*, the *mechanical calculator*, and Dr. Herman Hollerith's *Punch Card Tabulating Machine and Sorter*. *First-generation computers*, such as *ENIAC* and *UNIVAC*, were powered by *vacuum tubes*; *second-generation computers* used *transistors*; and *third-generation computers* were possible because of the invention of the *integrated circuit (IC)*. Today's *fourth-generation computers* use *microprocessors* and are frequently connected to the *Internet* and other *networks*. Some people believe that *fifth-generation computers* will likely be based on *artificial intelligence*.

A computer is made up of **hardware** (the actual physical equipment that makes up the computer system) and **software** (the computer's programs). Common hardware components include the *keyboard* and *mouse* (*input devices*), the *CPU* and *memory* (*processing devices*), *monitors* and *printers* (*output devices*), and *storage devices* and *storage media* (such as *floppy disks*, *CDs*, and *flash memory cards*). Most computers today also include a *modem* or other type of *communications device* to allow users to connect to the Internet or other network.

All computers need *system software*, namely an **operating system** (usually *Windows*, *Mac OS*, or *Linux*), to function. The operating system assists with the **boot** process, and then controls the operation of the computer, such as to allow users to run other types of software and to manage their files. Most software programs today use a *graphical user interface (GUI)*, which typically displays information in **windows** on the **Windows desktop**. The Windows **taskbar** contains the *Start button*, *taskbar buttons* and *taskbar toolbars*, and the *system tray*. Common features found on windows include **menus**, **toolbars**, **icons**, **dialog boxes**, and **sizing buttons**. The **Ribbon** is a new interface used with *Microsoft Office 2007* programs. **Hyperlinks**, sometimes found in windows and documents, are clicked to display another document, Web page, or other information.

Application software consists of programs designed to allow people to perform specific tasks or applications, such as word processing, Web browsing, photo touch-up, and so on. Software programs are written using a *programming language*. Programs are written by **programmers**; **computer users** are the people who use the computer system.

COMPUTERS TO FIT EVERY NEED

Embedded computers are built into products to give them added functionality. **Mobile devices** are small devices with computing or Internet capabilities and are used by individuals to maintain communications with the office while on the road, as well as for quick checks of weather forecasts, flight information, and other Internet resources available for that particular device. A mobile device based on a mobile phone is called a **smart phone**.

Small computers used by individuals at home or work are called **personal computers** (**PCs**) or **microcomputers**. Most PCs today are either **desktop PCs** or **portable PCs** (**notebook computers**, **tablet PCs**, or **handheld computers**) and typically conform to either the *PC-compatible* or *Macintosh* standard. Tablet PCs come in both *slate* and *convertible* tablet *PC* formats; newer fully functioning handheld computers are called **ultra mobile personal computers** (**UMPCs**). **Thin clients** are designed solely to access a network; **Internet appliances** are designed specifically for accessing the Internet and e-mail.

Medium-sized computers, or **midrange servers**, are used in small- to medium-sized businesses to host data and programs that can be accessed by the company network. The powerful computers used by most large businesses and organizations to perform the information processing necessary for day-to-day operations are called **mainframe computers**. The very largest, most powerful computers, which typically run one application at a time, are classified as **supercomputers**. A supercomputer comprised of numerous smaller computers connected together to act as a single computer is called a **supercomputing cluster**.

Chapter Objective 6:
List the six basic types of computers, giving at least one example of each type of computer and stating what that computer might be used for.

COMPUTER NETWORKS AND THE INTERNET

Computer networks are used to connect individual computers and related devices so that users can share hardware, software, and data as well as communicate with one another. The **Internet** is a worldwide collection of networks. Typically, individual users connect to the Internet by connecting to computers belonging to an **Internet service provider** (**ISP**)—a company that provides Internet access, usually for a fee. One resource available through the Internet is the **World Wide Web**—an enormous collection of **Web pages** located on **Web servers**. The starting page for a **Web site** (a related group of Web pages) is called the *home page* for that site. Web pages are viewed with a **Web browser**, are connected with hyperlinks, and can be used to retrieve news and product information, download music and movies, play online games, shop, and access a host of other activities.

To access a computer network, you need some type of *modem* or *network adapter*. To access the Internet, an Internet service provider (ISP) is also used. **Internet addresses** are used to identify resources on the Internet and include numerical **IP addresses** and text-based **domain names** (used to identify computers), **uniform resource locators** or **URLs** (used to identify Web pages), and **e-mail addresses** (a combination of a **username** and domain name that is used to send an individual e-mail messages).

Web pages are displayed by clicking hyperlinks or by typing appropriate URLs in the browser's *Address bar*. *Search sites* can be used to locate Web pages matching certain criteria, and **electronic mail** (**e-mail**) is used to send electronic messages over the Internet.

Chapter Objective 7:
Explain what a network, the Internet, and the World Wide Web are, as well as how computers, people, and Web pages are identified on the Internet.

Chapter Objective 8:
Describe how to access a Web page.

COMPUTERS AND SOCIETY

Computers and devices based on related technology have become indispensable tools for modern life, making ordinary tasks easier and quicker than ever before and helping make today's worker more productive than ever before. However, there are many societal implications related to our heavy use of the Internet and the vast amount of information available through the Internet. Issues include privacy and security risks and concerns, the differences in online and offline communications, the anonymity factor, and the amount of unreliable information that can be found on the Internet.

Chapter Objective 9:
Discuss the societal impact of computers, including some benefits and risks related to their prominence in our society.

REVIEW ACTIVITIES

KEY TERM MATCHING

Instructions: Match each key term on the left with the definition on the right that best describes it.

a. computer

b. hardware

c. hyperlink

d. Internet

e. operating system

f. software

g. storage

h. supercomputer

i. uniform resource locator (URL)

j. Web site

1. _____ A collection of related Web pages usually belonging to an organization or individual.

2. _____ An Internet address, usually beginning with http://, that uniquely identifies a Web page.

3. _____ A programmable, electronic device that accepts data input, performs processing operations on that data, and outputs and stores the results.

4. _____ A type of system software that enables a computer to operate and manage its resources and activities.

5. _____ Text or an image located on a Web page or other document that is linked to a Web page or other type of document.

6. _____ The operation of saving data, programs, or output for future use.

7. _____ The fastest, most expensive, and most powerful type of computer.

8. _____ The instructions, also called computer programs, that are used to tell a computer what it should do.

9. _____ The largest and most well-known computer network, linking millions of computers all over the world.

10. _____ The physical parts of a computer system, such as the keyboard, monitor, printer, and so forth.

SELF-QUIZ

Instructions: Circle **T** if the statement is true, **F** if the statement is false, or write the best answer in the space provided. **Answers for the self-quiz are located in the References and Resources Guide at the end of the book.**

1. **T   F**   A mouse is one common input device.

2. **T   F**   Software includes all the physical equipment in a computer system.

3. **T   F**   A computer can run without an operating system if it has good application software.

4. **T   F**   One of the most common types of home computers is the midrange server.

5. **T   F**   An example of a domain name is *microsoft.com*.

6. _____ is the operation in which data is entered into the computer.

7. A(n) _____ PC can come in convertible or slate form.

8. Web pages are connected using _____, which can be either text or images.

9. Electronic messages sent over the Internet that can be retrieved by the recipient at his or her convenience are called _____.

10. Write the number of the term that best matches each of the following descriptions in the blank to the left of its description.

   a. _____ Allows access to resources located on the Internet.
   b. _____ Supervises the running of all other programs on the computer.
   c. _____ Helps prepare written documents, such as letters and reports.
   d. _____ Allows an individual to create application programs.

   1. Word processing program
   2. Operating system
   3. Programming language
   4. Web browser

1. For the following list of computer hardware devices, indicate the principal function of each device by writing the appropriate letter—I (input device), O (output device), S (storage device), P (processing device), or C (communications device)—in the space provided.

   a. CPU _____
   b. Monitor _____
   c. CD drive _____
   d. Keyboard _____
   e. Hard drive _____
   f. Modem _____
   g. Speakers _____
   h. DVD drive _____
   i. Microphone _____

2. Supply the missing words to complete the following statements.

   a. The starting page for a Web site is called the site's _____.

   b. For the e-mail address *jsmith@cengage.com*, *jsmith* is the _____ and *cengage.com* is the _____ name.

   c. The e-mail address pronounced *bill gee at microsoft dot com* is written _____.

   d. One of the most common online security risks today is a computer becoming infected with a(n) _____, which is a software program designed to change the way a computer operates without the permission or knowledge of the user and which often causes damage to the PC.

3. What is the difference between a desktop PC and an ultra mobile PC (UMPC)?

4. List two reasons why a business may choose to network its employees' computers.

5. If a computer manufacturer called Apex created a home page for the Web, what would its URL likely be? Also, supply an appropriate e-mail address for yourself, assuming that you are employed by that company.

The ubiquitous nature of mobile phones today brings tremendous convenience to our lives, but will misuse of new improvements to this technology result in the loss of that convenience? For instance, camera phones being used to take photos in changing rooms has resulted in a ban on camera phones in many fitness centers, park restrooms, and other similar facilities. Mobile phones being used to cheat on exams by taking photos of the exam to give to other students in a later class or to exchange answers during the test via text messaging has led to a ban on mobile phones in many classrooms during exam periods. Do you think these reactions to mobile phone misuse are justified? Is there another way to ensure the appropriate use of mobile phones without banning their use for all individuals? Should there be more stringent consequences for those who use technology for illegal or unethical purposes?

BALANCING ACT

NEW TECHNOLOGY: BENEFITS VS. RISK

As illustrated throughout this chapter, new technology adds convenience to our lives, helps many employees become more productive, and can increase the length and quality of our lives. So, is a new technological advancement always a good thing? Possibly not.

There is usually a positive side and a negative side to each new technological improvement. Agricultural advancements help farmers grow more food more economically, but many people are concerned that heavy pesticide use and genetic engineering of crops and animals are dangerous to their health. Nuclear energy generates a very clean source for power, but it also has the possibility of tremendous destruction. The Internet allows users to obtain information very quickly and efficiently and to communicate with others at their convenience, but it also permits unscrupulous individuals to locate private information about others and commit crimes in ways that are easier than any that existed before.

Before forming an opinion about a new technology or deciding whether or not to incorporate that technology into your home or workplace, it is worth taking the time to ask yourself a few questions. What benefits does this new advancement offer me? Does it bring any potential risks to my health, privacy, or security? If so, what can I do to minimize these risks? Is it compatible with any related existing technology I currently use? How will I need to change my current situation in order to take full advantage of the new technology? If I don't use this new technology, will I be at a disadvantage? If so, in what ways? Although chances are that, most of the time, you will decide new technology is a good thing and that the benefits outweigh the potential risks, it is always good to make an informed decision.

YOUR TURN

Think of a technology, product, or service that you use and like (such as PCs, mobile phones, online shopping, ATM machines, e-mail, digital cameras, USB flash drives, portable digital media players, digital video recorders (DVRs), or gaming consoles). Form an opinion about the benefits and risks of using this technology, product, or service. Consider the following when forming your opinion and be prepared to discuss your position (in class, via an online class discussion group, in a class chat room, or via a class blog) or to write a short paper expressing your opinion, depending on your instructor's directions.

- If this technology, product, or service did not exist, how would your life be different?

- What type of data about you, if any, is collected when you use this technology, product, or service? By whom? Should the government or other organizations be able to have access to this data?

- If the government decided that your selected technology, product, or service was too risky to be used, should the government be able to ban it? Are there any circumstances in which you believe the government has the right or obligation to ban a technology, product, or service? If so, what are they?

PROJECTS

1. **Mobile TV** As discussed in the Trend box, TV is one of the newest entertainment options available for mobile phones. From live TV to video clips to reruns of TV shows and movies, mobile TV is taking off.

   For this project, investigate the mobile TV options available today. Find at least two services and compare features, such as cost, compatibility, channels, and programming. Do your selected services offer live TV, video-on-demand, or both? If you have a mobile phone, are any of the services available through your mobile provider? Have you ever watched TV on a mobile phone? Would you want to? Why or why not? At the conclusion of your research, prepare a one-page summary of your findings and submit it to your instructor.

2. **Buying a New PC** New PCs are widely available directly from manufacturers, as well as in retail, computer, electronic, and warehouse stores. Some stores carry only standard configurations as set up by the manufacturers; others allow you to customize a system.

   For this project, assume that you are in the market for a new PC. Make a list of your hardware and software requirements (refer to the "Guide for Buying a PC" in the References and Resources Guide at the end of this book, if needed), being as specific as possible. By researching newspaper ads, manufacturer Web sites, and/or systems for sale at local stores, find three systems that meet your minimum requirements. Prepare a one-page comparison chart, listing each requirement and how each system meets or exceeds it. Also include any additional features each system has, and information regarding the brand, price, delivery time, shipping, sales tax, and warranty for each system. On your comparison sheet, mark the system that you would prefer to buy and write one paragraph explaining why. Turn in your comparison sheet and summary to your instructor, stapled to copies of the printed ads, specifications printed from Web sites, or other written documentation that you collected during this project.

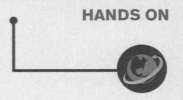

3. **The Internet** The Internet and World Wide Web are handy tools that can help you research topics covered in this textbook, complete many of the projects, and perform the online activities located on the textbook's Web site.

   For this project, find an Internet-enabled computer on your campus, at home, or at your public library and access the Understanding Computers Web site located at www.course.com/uccs. Once you are at the site, note the types of information and activities that are available to you as a student and select a few of them by using your mouse to click the hyperlinks—usually underlined or otherwise highlighted text or graphical buttons—corresponding to the options you want to explore. At the conclusion of this task, prepare a one-page summary describing the resources available through this textbook's Web site and submit it to your instructor.

WRITING ABOUT COMPUTERS

4. **Online Education** The amount of distance learning available through the Internet and World Wide Web has exploded in the last couple of years. A few years ago, it was possible to take an occasional course online—now, a college degree can be earned online.

For this project, look into the online education options available at your school and two other colleges or universities. Compare and contrast the programs in general, including whether or not the institution is accredited, the types of courses available online, whether or not an entire certificate or degree can be earned online, and the required fees. Next, select one online course and research it more closely. Find out how the course works in an online format, including whether or not any face-to-face class time is required, whether assignments and exams are submitted online, which software programs are required, and other course requirements. Summarize your findings in a two- to three-page paper. Be sure to include your opinion as to whether or not you would be interested in taking an online course and why.

PRESENTATION/ DEMONSTRATION

5. **E-Mail Options** If you have access to the Internet, you can exchange e-mail—including digital photos and other types of files—with any other person who has an e-mail address. This exchange can be accomplished using your computer or a PC available through your home, school, public library, or other location, provided that computer is connected to the Internet.

For this project, research what e-mail options are available to the students at your school through the school, as well as through free Web-based e-mail services, such as Windows Live, Hotmail, Yahoo! Mail, AOL Mail, or Google Gmail. Compare features, such as mailbox size and any limitations on attachments or storage space, of the available services. Select one free Web-based e-mail provider and sign up for an account. Send yourself one e-mail to experience the service and evaluate the features. Share your findings with the class in the form of a short presentation. The presentation should not exceed 10 minutes and should make use of one or more presentation aids, such as the chalkboard, handouts, overhead transparencies, or a computer-based slide presentation (your instructor may provide additional requirements). If possible, demonstrate the e-mail service you selected to the class. You may also be asked to submit a summary of the presentation to your instructor.

GROUP DISCUSSION

6. **Emotion Recognition Software** An emerging application is *emotion recognition software*, which tries to read people's emotions. An emotion recognition system uses a camera and software to analyze an individual's face and attempts to recognize his or her current emotion. The first expected application of such a system is for ATM machines, since they already have cameras installed. Possibilities include changing the advertising display, based on the customer's emotional response to displayed advertising, and enlarging the screen text if the customer appears to be squinting. It is not surprising that privacy advocates are concerned about the emotions of citizens being read in public locations without their consent. Proponents of the technology argue that it is no different than when human tellers or store clerks interpret customers' emotions and modify their treatment of the customer accordingly. Is this a worthy new technology or just a potential invasion of privacy? What are the pros and cons of such a system from a business point of view and from a customer point of view? Are there any safeguards that could be implemented to alleviate the disadvantages? What other potential uses for such a system might there be besides the ones mentioned in this project? Would you object to using an ATM machine with emotion-recognition capabilities?

For this project, form an opinion of the use of emotion recognition systems and be prepared to discuss your position (in class, via an online class discussion group, in a class chat room, or via a class blog, depending on your instructor's directions). You may also be asked to write a short paper expressing your opinion.

7. **Consumer Hacks** There have been many instances where individuals have hacked into consumer products—such as toys, mobile phones, gaming consoles, DVRs, and more—to alter their functionality. Some of these hacks (such as one that required an individual to break the encryption built into a robot in order to reprogram it to perform other activities) violate the *Digital Millennium Copyright Act*, which prohibits breaking technological controls placed on any copyrighted work. Do you think hacking into a product you own is ethical? Have you ever considered hacking into a product you own? If so, for what purpose? Do you think consumer hacks should be illegal if the hack requires breaking the product's encryption? If so, should the law apply to those individuals who break through a copy protection scheme only for their own use, or should the law apply just to those individuals who share the circumvention process with others? What about those individuals who try to break a copy protection or security technology just to prove it can be done? Should they be prosecuted, sued, or congratulated for exposing a weakness in the existing technology?

   For this project, form an opinion about the ethical ramifications of consumer hacks and be prepared to discuss your position (in class, via an online class discussion group, in a class chat room, or via a class blog, depending on your instructor's directions). You may also be asked to write a short paper expressing your opinion.

ETHICS IN ACTION

8. **Campaigning and the Web** From Web ads to YouTube videos to MySpace pages, the Web has become an important tool for political candidates. The accompanying video clip discusses the use of the Web in the 2008 Presidential race and shows some examples of Web content created by individuals to express their political opinions.

   Go to www.course.com/uccs/ch1 to watch the "Internet Plays Pivotal Role in Campaign '08" video clip. After watching the video, think about the impact of the Web on political campaigns. How does the ability to post videos of candidates (such as speeches and debates) affect campaigning in general? What about the ability of individuals and opposing political parties to post edited videos of campaign events, such as comments taken out of context or political blunders performed by an opponent? Should this be legal? Is it ethical? Does the extensive use of the Web by individuals and political candidates help or hurt campaigns? Should use of Web content by a candidate during a political campaign be regulated like TV air time? Has Web content ever impacted your decision in an election?

   Express your viewpoint: What is the impact of the Web on political campaigning?

   Use the video clip and the questions previously asked as a foundation for your response. Be prepared to discuss your position (in class, via an online class discussion group, in a class chat room, or via a class blog) or to write a short paper stating and supporting your viewpoint on the issue, depending on your instructor's direction. You may also be asked to do research and provide resources to support your point of view on this issue.

VIDEO VIEWPOINT

9. **Interactive Activities** Go to www.course.com/uccs/ch1 and work the interactive **Crossword Puzzle**, listen to the **Podcasts** and watch the **Online Videos** associated with this chapter, and explore the **Further Exploration** links. In addition, work the following interactive **Student Edition Labs**.
   - Using Windows
   - E-Mail
   - Word Processing
   - Spreadsheets
   - Databases
   - Presentation Software

   If you have a SAM user profile, you have access to even more interactive content. Log in to your SAM account and go to your assignments page to see what your instructor has assigned for this chapter.

WEB ACTIVITIES

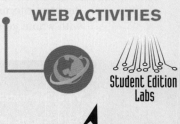

Student Edition Labs

10. **Test Yourself** Go to www.course.com/uccs/ch1 and review the **Online Study Guide** for Chapter 1, then test your knowledge of the terms and concepts in this chapter by completing the **Key Term Matching** exercise, the **Self-Quiz**, the **Exercises**, and the **Practice Test**.

EXPERT INSIGHT ON . . .
Personal Computers

NOKIA

A conversation with **VIPUL MEHROTRA**
Director, Business Development, Convergence, Nokia North America

My Background . . .

From an early age I was very interested in science (my dad is an Aeronautical Engineer). In undergraduate college I took Information Sciences Engineering as my field of study. I have been lucky to be able to work with computers, workstations, services, software, and networks right from the beginning of my career. I gained experience in the IT industry before I moved to the telecom industry which attracted me due to the immense growth potential of mobility and communication. After 10 years of work experience, I decided to take a year off and pursue my MBA at IMD, Switzerland, to further my skill set, before returning back to work at Nokia.

> **❝The power of mobility has transformed the way people live their lives, in addition to the way they communicate.❞**

It's Important to Know . . .

The different kinds of computers available today. Computers are rapidly evolving, and new technology (hardware and software) is surfacing faster than before. The next step in the PC/computer evolution is the personal multimedia computer or personal convergence device; i.e. your mobile phone. Chapter 1 gives students a clear understanding and a good starting point to navigate through the world of computers.

What the Internet can be used for. I think this is a key point because our society today revolves around the Internet eco-system and we are highly dependent on it. The Internet is rapidly going mobile, allowing you and me to take all of our connected applications (and services) always with us. Imagine the power of the Internet with you, wherever you are! Or the world in your hands!

The power of mobile devices. Mobile phone capabilities have expanded from just voice to video, music, imaging, navigation, online sharing, gaming, and many other exciting applications. Today a cellular phone can be built with a computer-like functionality to take pictures, play games, show maps and navigate routes, share information/media, read news, stream videos, and much more. The power of mobility has transformed the way people live their lives, in addition to the way they communicate. People are more connected to their friends and family, as well as to information, media, entertainment, etc., while they are mobile. The transition from wired Internet to the wireless Internet is happening now and is creating new experiences for all of us. Students should understand how they can use this power to their advantage, such as to become better informed, communicate more easily, and share information. Also keep in mind that with this anytime anywhere access to the Internet comes the responsibility of protecting your information and that of your friends and family. Be careful and judicious about how, where, and with whom you share personal information.

Vipul Mehrotra is currently the Director, Technology and Portfolio Management for Nokia North America. He is part of the Customer and Market Operations team engaged in technology marketing with key customers and the analysts, and portfolio analysis and development. In his 12 years working in this industry, he has worked for Nokia in the United States, Finland, and India. Vipul holds college degrees in both Engineering and Business.

. . . the mobile phone is becoming the one personal device with which one can communicate, share information, find places, transact, stream video and music, and so forth.

How I Use this Technology . . .

I regularly use computers to search for information, to read and write e-mail, to share pictures, to keep in touch with family and friends, to pay bills, etc. I use my personal mobile phone (Nokia N95) to be connected (via voice and text messaging) with my friends, family, and colleagues, as well as to read the news, exchange e-mail, share images, and download video clips. I also use my mobile phone as an alarm clock and calculator, and I use it to take pictures of my one year old daughter daily and send them via the phone to her grandparents. They love seeing her on a daily basis, thousands of miles away.

What the Future Holds . . .

Moore's Law states that the computing power of a chip doubles every 18 months. This has resulted in smaller and more powerful computing devices available every year. Computers will be faster, smaller, and full of rich media applications; will increasingly use wireless connections; and will become the main information and entertainment platform at home. As mobile phones are evolving to a voice device combined with connected rich mobile Internet services, the mobile phone is becoming the one personal device with which one can communicate, share information, find places, transact, stream video and music, and so forth. It will be the preferred device while on the go. Future evolution of mobile devices will see them interoperate with other devices at home—for example, streaming video from your mobile phone to your TV. Mobile video applications (such as live TV, video downloads, and video phone calls) have a lot of potential for the future as mobile devices and the communications infrastructure continue to become increasingly capable of handling such powerful applications/services. The mobile phone is becoming the fourth screen for entertainment (movie theatre, TV, PC, and now the mobile phone).

Computers in general have transformed our society and today we are a digital society. Mobile devices will transform the society further and our life will be increasingly mobile. The ability to be connected "whenever and wherever you are" will drive the creation of the Mobile Information Society. Students today should embrace mobility and use it for more than voice. They should use mobile Internet services to become a more informed person and to connect with other people and applications.

My Advice to Students . . .

Use technology to become a better informed person and use information to become a responsible person. Technology should be used to achieve your goals, improve your life, and improve the lives of others.

Discussion Question

Vipul Mehrotra views the mobile phone as the "personal" platform of choice for the future. Think about the tasks you use your mobile phone for and which ones you cannot. What changes need to be made in the future in order to perform all of these tasks on a mobile phone? Will they be primarily hardware or software changes? Is the mobile phone the computer of the future? Be prepared to discuss your position (in class, via an online class discussion group, in a class chat room, or via a class blog, depending on your instructor's directions). You may also be asked to write a short paper expressing your opinion.

>**For more information on Nokia and Nokia products, visit www.nokia.com.**

2 CHAPTER

A Closer Look at Hardware and Software

OUTLINE

LEARNING OBJECTIVES

After completing this chapter, you will be able to do the following:

1. Understand how data is represented to a computer.

2. Identify several types of input devices and explain their functions.

3. Explain the functions of the primary hardware components found inside the system unit, namely the motherboard, the CPU, and memory.

4. List several output devices and explain their functions.

5. Understand the difference between storage and memory, as well as between a storage device and a storage medium.

6. Name several types of storage systems and explain the circumstances under which they are typically used.

7. Describe the purpose of communications hardware.

8. Understand basic software concepts and commands.

OVERVIEW

When you hear the phrase "computer system," you probably picture hardware—a desktop or notebook computer, a printer, or maybe a smart phone. But a computer system involves more than just hardware. As you already know from Chapter 1, computers need software in order to function. It is the software that tells the hardware what to do and when to do it. Computers also need data input, which is used to begin the information processing cycle.

This chapter opens with a discussion of data and how it is represented to a computer. Next, we take a closer look at the hardware that makes up a computer system. Since it is not possible to mention all of the hardware products available today, a sampling of the most common hardware products used for input, processing, output, storage, and communications is described in this chapter. Although a complete discussion of software is also beyond the scope of this book, the chapter concludes with a brief look at some basic software concepts and operations.

The basic hardware and software concepts and terminology covered in this chapter are important for all computer users to understand. In addition, these concepts will provide you with a solid foundation for discussing the important societal issues featured throughout this text. While most of you reading this chapter will likely apply its contents to conventional personal computer systems—such as desktop and notebook computers—keep in mind that the principles and procedures discussed in this chapter apply to virtually all types of computers and related devices—from smart household appliances and mobile devices, to mainframe computers and supercomputers. ■

PODCAST

Go to **www.course.com/uccs/ch2** to download or listen to the "Expert Insight on Hardware" podcast.

DIGITAL DATA REPRESENTATION

Virtually all computers today—such as the embedded computers, mobile devices, microcomputers, midrange servers, mainframes, and supercomputers discussed in Chapter 1—are *digital computers*. Most digital computers are *binary computers*, which can understand only two states, usually thought of as *off* and *on* and represented by the digits 0 and 1. Consequently, all data processed by a binary computer must be in binary form (0s and 1s) for it to be processed and stored. Representing data in digital form so it can be used by a digital computer is called *digital data representation*. Fortunately, the computer takes care of translating input into the form needed by the computer being used and then, after processing, translates and outputs the resulting information into a form that can be understood by the user.

Bits and Bytes

The 0s and 1s used to represent data can be represented in a variety of ways, such as with an open or closed circuit, the absence or presence of an electronic charge, the absence or presence of a magnetic spot or depression on a storage medium, and so on. Regardless of their physical representations, these 0s and 1s are commonly referred to

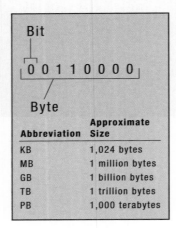

Abbreviation	Approximate Size
KB	1,024 bytes
MB	1 million bytes
GB	1 billion bytes
TB	1 trillion bytes
PB	1,000 terabytes

FIGURE 2-1

Bits and bytes.

Document size, storage capacity, and memory capacity are all measured in bytes.

FIGURE 2-2

Examples from the ASCII code.

CHARACTER	ASCII
0	00110000
1	00110001
2	00110010
3	00110011
4	00110100
5	00110101
A	01000001
B	01000010
C	01000011
D	01000100
E	01000101
F	01000110
+	00101011
!	00100001
#	00100011

as *bits*, a computing term derived from the phrase *binary digits*. A **bit** is the smallest unit of data that a binary computer can recognize, so the input you enter via a keyboard, the music stored on your digital media player, and the term paper and digital photos stored on your PC are all just groups of bits. Consequently, binary can be thought of as the computer's "native language."

A bit by itself typically represents only a fraction of a piece of data. Consequently, bits are usually grouped together to form letters and other characters, documents, program files, graphics files, and more. Eight bits grouped together are collectively referred to as a **byte**. It is important to be familiar with this concept because "byte" terminology is frequently used in a variety of computer contexts. For example, document size and storage capacity are measured in bytes, based on the amount of data that is contained in the document or that can be stored on the storage medium. In fact, the size of any item—such as a computer program, written document, digital photograph, or music file—stored on a storage medium is measured in bytes. Prefixes are commonly used with the term *byte* to represent larger amounts of data (see Figure 2-1). A **kilobyte** (**KB**) is equal to 1,024 bytes, but is usually thought of as approximately 1,000 bytes. A **megabyte** (**MB**) is about 1 million bytes, a **gigabyte** (**GB**) is about 1 billion bytes, a **terabyte** (**TB**) is about 1 trillion bytes, and a **petabyte** (**PB**) is about 1,000 terabytes (2^{50} bytes). Therefore, 5 KB is about 5,000 bytes, 10 MB is approximately 10 million bytes, and 2 TB is about 2 trillion bytes.

Numbering Systems and Coding Systems

A *numbering system* is a way of representing numbers. The numbering system we commonly use is called the *decimal numbering system* because it uses 10 symbols—the digits 0, 1, 2, 3, 4, 5, 6, 7, 8, and 9—to represent all possible numbers. Numbers greater than nine, such as 21 and 683, are represented using combinations of these 10 symbols. The **binary numbering system** uses only two symbols—the digits 0 and 1—to represent all possible numbers. Consequently, computers use the binary numbering system to represent numbers and perform math computations.

In both the decimal and binary numbering systems, the position of each digit determines the power, or exponent, to which the *base number* (10 for decimal or 2 for binary) is raised. In the decimal numbering system, going from right to left, the first position or column (the ones column) represents 10^0 or 1; the second position (the tens column) represents 10^1, or 10; the third position (the hundreds column) represents 10^2, or 100; and so forth. Therefore, although 101 represents "one hundred one" in the decimal number system, it equals "five" ($1 \times 2^2 + 0 \times 2^1 + 1 \times 2^0$ or 4 + 0 + 1 or 5) using the binary number system. For more information about numbering systems and some examples of converting between numbering systems, see the "A Look at Numbering Systems" section in the References and Resources Guide at the end of this book.

To represent text-based data, special fixed-length binary *coding systems*—namely, *ASCII* and *Unicode*—were developed. These codes represent all characters that can appear in text data, including numeric characters, alphabetic characters, and special characters such as the dollar sign ($) and period (.). **ASCII** (**American Standard Code for Information Interchange**) is the coding system traditionally used with PCs. It is a 7-digit code, although there are several different 8-bit *extended* versions of ASCII that include extra characters to represent non-English characters, graphics symbols, and mathematical symbols. The extended ASCII character sets represent each character as a unique combination of 8 bits (see Figure 2-2). One group of 8 bits (one byte) allows 256 (2^8) unique combinations. Therefore, an 8-bit code (like extended ASCII) can represent up to 256 characters.

Unlike ASCII, which is limited to only the Latin alphabet used with the English language, **Unicode** is a universal international coding standard designed to represent text-based data written in any ancient or modern language, including those with different alphabets, such as Chinese, Greek, Hebrew, Amharic, Tibetan, and Russian (see Figure 2-3). Unicode uniquely identifies each character using 0s and 1s, no matter which language, program, or computer platform is being used. It is a longer code—from 1 to 4 bytes (8 to 32 bits) per character—and can represent over one million characters, which is more than enough unique combinations to represent the standard characters in all the world's written languages, as well as thousands of mathematical and technical symbols, punctuation marks, and other symbols and signs. The biggest advantage of Unicode is that it can be used worldwide with consistent and unambiguous results. Unicode is quickly replacing ASCII as the primary text-coding system. For more examples of ASCII and Unicode, as well as the *EBCDIC* coding system used primarily with mainframe computers, see the "Coding Charts" section in the References and Resources Guide at the end of this book.

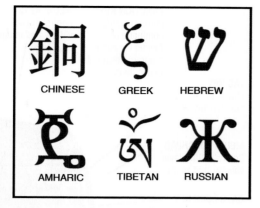

FIGURE 2-3
Unicode. Many characters, such as these, can be represented by Unicode but not by ASCII.

ONLINE VIDEO

Go to **www.course.com/uccs/ch2** to watch the "The Amazing Race 2007" video clip.

INPUT HARDWARE

As discussed in Chapter 1, *input* is the process of entering data into a computer. An **input device** is any piece of hardware that is used to perform data input. Traditional input devices include the *keyboard* and *mouse*, but there are also many other types of input devices in use today.

Keyboards

Most PCs today are designed to be used with a **keyboard**. Virtually all desktop PCs are used in conjunction with either a wired or wireless keyboard. *Wired keyboards* are connected via a cable to the computer's system unit (typically using a *USB port* or *keyboard port*); *wireless keyboards* are powered by batteries and send wireless signals to a receiver that is usually plugged into one of the computer's USB ports. Most desktop keyboards today contain standard alphanumeric keys along with a variety of special keys for specific purposes. A notebook PC usually has a keyboard that is smaller and contains fewer keys than a desktop PC keyboard, and the keys are typically placed closer together. Notebook computer users can also typically connect and use a conventional keyboard, when desired. Handheld PCs and mobile devices may include a keyboard or rely on other means of input instead. A handheld PC that contains two different keyboards is shown in Figure 2-4; a typical desktop keyboard is shown in Figure 2-5.

FIGURE 2-4
Handheld PC keyboards. This device features both a telephone keypad and a slide-out keyboard.

While many handheld PCs and mobile devices today have a built-in keyboard or *thumb pad* (a full keyboard that is designed to be pressed with just the thumbs), the order and layout of the keys may be different than a conventional keyboard and the keyboard layout may vary from device to device. For instance, the device shown in Figure 2-4 has a standard telephone keypad with multiple letters associated with each key, as well as a *slide-out keyboard* that can be used to more easily enter large quantities of text. If a device does not have a built-in keyboard, a *portable keyboard* can often be used for easier data entry. Portable keyboards designed for handheld PCs typically fold or roll up; the keyboard and PC are connected either physically via a connector on the keyboard or wirelessly via a wireless network connection. Portable computers that do not support a keyboard or thumb pad typically rely on *pen input* or *touch input* instead, as discussed shortly.

>**Unicode.** An international coding system for text-based data using any written language. >**Input device.** A piece of hardware that supplies input to a computer. >**Keyboard.** An input device containing numerous keys that can be used to input letters, numbers, and other symbols.

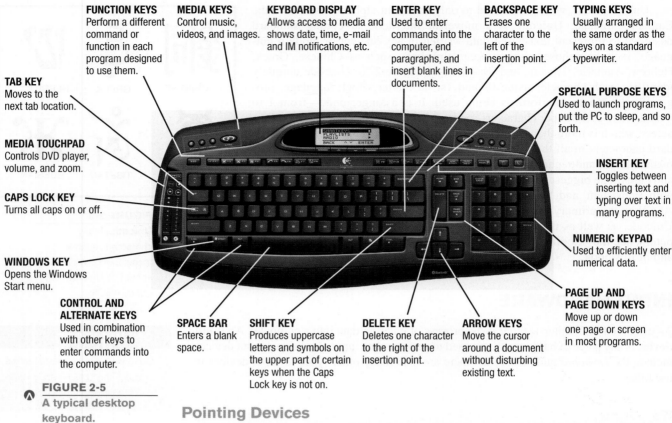

FUNCTION KEYS
Perform a different command or function in each program designed to use them.

MEDIA KEYS
Control music, videos, and images.

KEYBOARD DISPLAY
Allows access to media and shows date, time, e-mail and IM notifications, etc.

ENTER KEY
Used to enter commands into the computer, end paragraphs, and insert blank lines in documents.

BACKSPACE KEY
Erases one character to the left of the insertion point.

TYPING KEYS
Usually arranged in the same order as the keys on a standard typewriter.

TAB KEY
Moves to the next tab location.

SPECIAL PURPOSE KEYS
Used to launch programs, put the PC to sleep, and so forth.

MEDIA TOUCHPAD
Controls DVD player, volume, and zoom.

INSERT KEY
Toggles between inserting text and typing over text in many programs.

CAPS LOCK KEY
Turns all caps on or off.

NUMERIC KEYPAD
Used to efficiently enter numerical data.

WINDOWS KEY
Opens the Windows Start menu.

PAGE UP AND PAGE DOWN KEYS
Move up or down one page or screen in most programs.

CONTROL AND ALTERNATE KEYS
Used in combination with other keys to enter commands into the computer.

SPACE BAR
Enters a blank space.

SHIFT KEY
Produces uppercase letters and symbols on the upper part of certain keys when the Caps Lock key is not on.

DELETE KEY
Deletes one character to the right of the insertion point.

ARROW KEYS
Move the cursor around a document without disturbing existing text.

FIGURE 2-5
A typical desktop keyboard.

Pointing Devices

In addition to a keyboard, most PCs today have some type of **pointing device**. Unlike keyboards, which are used to enter characters at the *insertion point* (sometimes called the *cursor*) location, pointing devices are used to select and manipulate objects, to input certain types of data (such as handwritten data or edits to images), and to issue commands to the PC. The most common types of pointing devices include the *mouse*, *electronic pen*, and *touch screen*.

The Mouse

The **mouse** is the most common pointing device for a desktop PC. It typically rests on the desk or other flat surface close to the user's PC and is moved across the surface with the user's hand in the appropriate direction to point to and select objects on the screen. As it moves, an onscreen *mouse pointer*—usually an arrow—moves accordingly. Once the mouse pointer is pointing to the desired object on the screen, that object can be selected (usually by pressing a button on the pointing device) or otherwise manipulated. Older *mechanical mice* have a ball exposed on the bottom surface of the mouse to control the pointer movement. Most mice today are *optical mice* or *laser mice* that track movements with light. Mice are commonly used to start programs; open, move around, and edit documents; draw or edit images; and more. A list of common mouse commands is included in Figure 2-6. Similar to keyboards, mice today typically connect via a USB port, *mouse port*, or wireless connection. Conventional, wireless, and small travel mice can all be used with desktop, notebook, and tablet PCs, as desired, as long as an appropriate port is available.

>**Pointing device.** An input device that moves an onscreen pointer, such as an arrow, to allow the user to select objects on the screen.
>**Mouse.** A common pointing device that the user slides along a flat surface to move a pointer around the screen and clicks its buttons to make selections.

The Electronic Pen and the Stylus

Handheld PCs, tablet PCs, mobile devices, and other portable devices usually can accept *pen input*; that is, input by writing, drawing, or tapping on the screen with a pen-like device. Some PCs and devices use special **electronic pens** (also called *digital pens* and *tablet pens*) that contain computer circuitry and can be battery powered; others accept input via a small metal or plastic **stylus**. The idea behind pen-based input and *digital writing* in general is to make using a computer as convenient as writing with a pen, while adding the functionality that a computer can provide, such as converting pen-based input to editable, typed text or retrieving and editing digitally stored documents.

Although their capabilities depend on the type of computer and software being used, pen input can be used with a variety of computer types and devices (see Figure 2-7). Most often, pens are used with handheld or tablet PCs to input handwritten text and sketches, as well as to manipulate objects (such as to select an option from a menu, select text, or resize an image). They can also be used with desktop PCs that support pen input, and they are increasingly being used for photography, graphic design, animation, industrial design, document processing, and healthcare applications. Depending on the software being used, handwritten pen input can be stored as an image, stored as handwritten characters that can be recognized by the computer, or converted to editable, typed text.

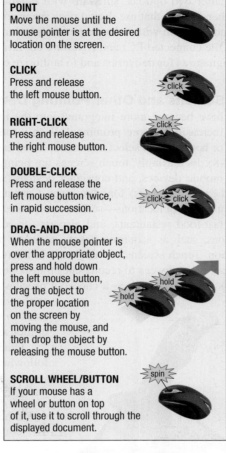

POINT
Move the mouse until the mouse pointer is at the desired location on the screen.

CLICK
Press and release the left mouse button.

RIGHT-CLICK
Press and release the right mouse button.

DOUBLE-CLICK
Press and release the left mouse button twice, in rapid succession.

DRAG-AND-DROP
When the mouse pointer is over the appropriate object, press and hold down the left mouse button, drag the object to the proper location on the screen by moving the mouse, and then drop the object by releasing the mouse button.

SCROLL WHEEL/BUTTON
If your mouse has a wheel or button on top of it, use it to scroll through the displayed document.

COMMON MOUSE OPERATIONS

A LASER MOUSE

Move the mouse to move the mouse pointer.

USING A MOUSE

FIGURE 2-6
Using a mouse.

FIGURE 2-7
Examples of digital pen use.

Stylus

HANDHELD PCS

GRAPHICS TABLETS

SIGNATURE CAPTURE DEVICES

>**Electronic pen.** An input device that is used to write electronically on the display screen; also called a **stylus** when made out of metal or plastic.

For the latter two options, software with *handwriting recognition* capabilities must be used. Other devices that use digital pens are *graphics tablets* (flat, touch-sensitive tablets used in conjunction with a digital pen to transfer input drawn or written on the graphics tablet to the connected PC) and *signature capture devices* (devices used to electronically record signatures for deliveries and to authorize credit card purchases).

Touch Screens and Other Pointing Devices

As PCs have become more integrated into the lives of consumers, **touch screens** have become increasingly more prominent. With a touch screen, the user touches the screen with his or her finger to select commands or otherwise provide input to the computer (see Figure 2-8). Increasingly, touch screens are being used with personal computers, mobile phones, mobile devices, and consumer devices (such as multimedia remote controls and handheld gaming devices) for easy input. Consumer kiosks containing touch screens are found in a variety of locations—such as retail stores, movie theaters, courthouses, conference centers, fast-food restaurants, and airports—to allow consumers to perform self-service applications, such as acquiring tickets, ordering products, self-checkout, and looking up information. Touch screens are also used in many *point-of-sale* (*POS*) *systems*—systems used by sales employees to record sales transaction data at the point where the product or service is purchased, such as a checkout or sales counter—and are useful for on-the-job applications (such as factory work) that require users to wear gloves, or where using a keyboard or mouse is otherwise impractical.

Other common pointing devices include the following (refer again to Figure 2-8):

▶ *Gaming devices*—*joysticks*, *gamepads*, *steering wheels*, *dance pads*, and other devices commonly used with computer games.

▶ *Control buttons and wheels*—used to select items and issue commands on many consumer devices today, such as portable digital media players, GPS devices, and handheld gaming devices.

▶ *Touch pads*—rectangular pads across which a fingertip or thumb slides to move the onscreen pointer; most often found on notebook PCs and other portable computers.

Scanners, Readers, and Digital Cameras

Some input devices are designed either to convert existing data to digital form or to capture data initially in digital form. Three of the most common types of these input devices—*scanners*, *readers*, and *digital cameras*—are discussed next.

▼ FIGURE 2-8
Examples of other common pointing devices.

TOUCH SCREENS
Used with many types of computers today.

JOYSTICKS
Used most often in computer games.

Click wheel

Center button

CONTROL BUTTONS AND WHEELS
Commonly found on portable digital media players and other consumer devices.

TOUCH PADS
Commonly found on notebook PCs and keyboards.

>**Touch screen.** A display device that is touched with the finger to issue commands or otherwise generate input to the connected device.

Scanners and Readers

There are various types of scanners and readers that can be used to capture data from a *source document* (a document containing data that already exists in physical form, such as an order form, photograph, invoice, check, or price label) and convert it into input that the computer can understand. Capturing data electronically from a source document can save a great deal of time and is much more accurate than inputting that data manually.

A **scanner**, more officially called an *optical scanner*, captures the image of a usually flat object (such as a printed document, photograph, or drawing) in digital form and then transfers that data to a PC. Typically, the entire document (including both text and images) is input as a single graphical image that can be resized, inserted into other documents, posted on a Web page, e-mailed to someone, printed, or otherwise treated like any other graphical image. The text in the image, however, cannot be edited unless *optical character recognition* (*OCR*) software is used in conjunction with the scanner to input the scanned text as individual text characters. Scanners are frequently used by individuals to input photographs and other personal documents into a digital format that a PC can understand. Businesses are increasingly using scanners to convert paper documents into electronic format for archival or document processing pur-

FLATBED SCANNERS
Used to input photos, sketches, slides, bound books, and other relatively flat documents into the computer.

PORTABLE BARCODE READERS
Used to read barcodes when portability is needed.

Portal RFID readers

RFID READERS
This portal RFID reader reads all of the RFID tags on a palette at one time, as it passes between the readers.

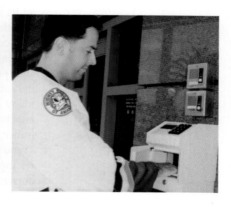

BIOMETRIC READERS
Often used for access control, such as to authenticate NHL Mighty Ducks players at their arena, as shown here.

poses. The most common type of scanner is the *flatbed scanner* (see Figure 2-9), which is designed to scan flat objects one page at a time. *Handheld scanners* are designed to capture text one line at a time, and they are useful for capturing short newspaper or magazine articles, as well as Web addresses, names, and telephone numbers. The quality of scanned images is indicated by *resolution*, which can be specified when an item is scanned or when the scanned image is modified using an *image editing program*. Common resolutions today are 300 dpi or 600 dpi for print-quality images and 96 dpi for Web page images.

A **barcode** is an *optical code* that represents data with bars of varying widths or heights. Barcodes are read with **barcode readers**. To read the data encoded in the barcode, light from the laser inside the barcode reader is reflected from the light spaces on the barcode (the dark bars absorb the light), and the barcode reader interprets the patterns of white space as the numbers or letters represented by the barcode. The data associated with that barcode—typically identifying data, such as data used to uniquely identify a product, shipped package, or other item—can then be retrieved. Two of the most familiar barcodes

FIGURE 2-9
Scanners and readers transform data from physical form into digital form.

FURTHER EXPLORATION

Go to **www.course.com/uccs/ch2** for links to further information about scanning documents and photographs.

>**Scanner.** An input device that reads printed text and graphics and transfers them to a computer in digital form. >**Barcode.** A machine-readable code that represents data as a set of bars. >**Barcode reader.** An input device that reads barcodes.

are *UPC* (*Universal Product Code*)—the barcode found on packaged goods in supermarkets and other retail stores—and *ISBN* (*International Standard Book Number*)—the type of barcode used with printed books. Businesses and organizations can also create and use custom barcodes to fulfill their unique needs. For instance, shipping organizations (such as FedEx, UPS, and the U.S. Postal Service) use custom barcodes to mark and track packages; hospitals use custom barcodes to match patients with their charts and medicines; libraries and video stores use custom barcodes for checking out and checking in materials, such as books and movies; researchers use custom barcodes to tag and track the migration habits of animals; and law enforcement agencies use custom barcodes to mark evidence. *Fixed barcode readers* are frequently used in point-of-sale (POS) systems; *portable barcode readers* (see Figure 2-9) are also available.

Radio frequency identification (*RFID*) is a technology that can store and transmit data located in *RFID tags*. **RFID tags** contain tiny chips and radio antennas and can be attached to objects, such as products, ID cards, assets, shipping containers, and more. The data in RFID tags is read by **RFID readers** and can be unique so that each item containing an RFID tag can be individually identified. Whenever an RFID-tagged item is within range of an RFID reader (from two inches to up to 300 feet or more, depending on the type of tags and the radio frequency being used), the tag's built-in antenna allows the information located within the RFID tag to be sent to the reader. Because RFID tags are read by radio waves (not by light like barcodes), the tags only need to be within range (not within line of sight) of a reader. This enables RFID readers to read the data stored in many RFID tags at the same time and read them through cardboard and other materials. RFID can be used for many different purposes, such as for tracking the movement of the items the tags are attached to, for tracking the movement of inventory pallets and shipping containers during transit, as a replacement for barcodes, and as part of an electronic payment system (see the Trend box). In addition, prescription drug companies and luxury goods manufacturers are testing the use of RFID tags to prevent theft and counterfeiting and the United States is currently debating the inclusion of RFID tags into U.S. passports and other types of identification systems. *Handheld RFID readers* look similar to handheld barcode readers; *portal RFID readers* (such as the one shown in Figure 2-9) can be used to read all the RFID tags inside a shipping box or palette when it passes through the portal.

Biometric readers (refer again to Figure 2-9) read *biometric data* (measurable biological characteristics, such as an individual's fingerprint, hand geometry, face, iris of the eye, or voice) in order to identify or authenticate individuals, as discussed in more detail in Chapter 4. Other types of readers include *optical mark readers* (*OMRs*), which input data from special forms to score or tally exams, questionnaires, ballots, and so forth; *optical character recognition* (*OCR*) *readers*, which are used to read *optical characters* printed on documents, such as invoices and utility bills; and *magnetic ink character recognition* (*MICR*) *readers*, which are used to read the MICR-encoded bank and account information on checks, in order to sort and process the checks.

Digital Cameras

Digital cameras work much like conventional film cameras, but instead of recording images on film they record them on a digital storage medium, such as a *flash memory card*, *digital tape cartridge*, built-in *hard drive*, or *DVD disc*. Digital cameras are usually designated either as *still* cameras (which take individual still photos) or *video* cameras (which capture moving video images), although many cameras today take both still images and video.

FURTHER EXPLORATION

Go to **www.course.com/uccs/ch2** for links to further information about digital cameras and digital photography.

>**RFID tag.** A device containing a tiny chip and a radio antenna that is attached to an object so it can be identified using RFID technology.
>**RFID reader.** A device used to read RFID tags. >**Biometric reader.** A device used to input biometric data. >**Digital camera.** An input device that takes pictures and records them as digital data (instead of film or videotaped) images.

TREND

M-Commerce and U-Commerce: Steps Toward a Cashless Society

M-commerce (*mobile commerce*) has finally arrived. In many areas of the United States and the world, you can buy fast food, pay for a cab, buy theater tickets, and more—all with your mobile phone. Although debit, credit, and check cards have helped to move us toward a cashless society, until recently it was difficult to buy a soda or pay for parking without cash. But many think the time for m-commerce has arrived, and several new options are becoming available. For instance, *PayPal* users can send money to others via mobile phones, and MobilRelay has a *Mobile Box Office* system that allows moviegoers to buy tickets for movies at specific theaters using their mobile phones (the "tickets" appear as a barcode that can be displayed on the mobile phone screen when needed for admittance). Many m-commerce services today are carried out via a mobile Web page or a text message. For instance, mobile PayPal users can send funds via either the mobile.paypal.com Web site or by sending a text message to PAYPAL containing the dollar amount and the phone number or e-mail address of the recipient. With an estimated $103 billion of "social money" exchanged each year for splitting dinner checks or cab fares or for reimbursing friends for purchases made, the market for m-commerce services designed for exchanging money between individuals is huge. And, since more people now carry a mobile phone than not, the mobile phone is a logical medium for these transactions.

An emerging m-commerce alternative is *Near Field Communication* (*NFC*) technology, which uses RFID to facilitate communication between devices, including payments between terminals and mobile phones (see the accompanying photo). NFC phones and terminals are on the market now, and Juniper Research predicts that the mobile phone will be the payment of choice for 50 million consumers worldwide by 2011. Some credit card companies—such as MasterCard—are strong proponents of m-commerce and allow cardholders to charge purchases at participating locations to their credit cards via their mobile phones. Vending machines are also increasingly going cashless—supporting only NFC, credit cards, and other electronic payment methods, instead of cash, particularly in locations where theft is an issue.

As e-commerce and m-commerce continue to evolve from "point of sale" to "point of convenience"—performing financial transactions wherever and whenever they need to occur—we are heading toward what some view as *u-commerce* (*universal commerce*). With u-commerce, transferring funds electronically via your PC, PDA, mobile phone, or other electronic device is expected to continue to get easier and easier. For instance, u-commerce can facilitate activities such as easily transferring funds to your secretary for your share of an office gift, paying for lunch and paying the taxi fare during the cab ride to a restaurant, or buying a movie or lottery ticket from a public kiosk at the mall. With u-commerce, these types of transactions can take place seamlessly regardless of the time of day, physical location, or currency and payment device being used.

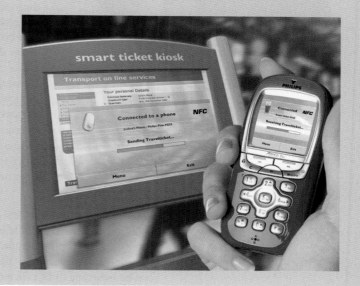

Digital still cameras are available in a wide variety of sizes and capabilities. For instance, relatively inexpensive (less than $100) point-and-shoot digital cameras are designed for everyday consumer use, more expensive professional digital cameras with removable lenses are designed for professional use, and most mobile phones and many other mobile devices today that include digital camera capabilities are designed for consumer convenience. The primary appeal of digital still cameras is that the images are immediately available for viewing or printing, instead of having to have the film developed

Virtually all digital cameras let you display and erase images.

Most cameras use removable storage media in addition to, or instead of, built-in storage.

DIGITAL STILL CAMERAS
Typically store photos on flash memory media.

DIGITAL CAMCORDERS
Typically store video on DVDs (as shown here), digital tape, or a built-in hard drive.

FIGURE 2-10
Digital cameras.

first. Digital still cameras typically use removable flash memory cards for storage (see Figure 2-10). The number of digital photos that can be stored at one time depends on the capacity of the storage medium being used and the resolution of the photos being taken (many cameras let you select the resolution to be used). At any time, photos stored on a digital camera can be transferred to a PC or printer, usually by removing the flash memory card and inserting it into the PC or printer, by connecting the camera to the PC via a cable, by attaching the camera to a special *camera docking station* attached to the printer or PC, or via a wireless connection between the printer and PC. Once the photos have been transferred to a PC, they can be retouched with image editing software, saved, printed, posted to a Web page, or burned onto a CD or DVD disc, just like any other digital image. The images on the storage medium can be deleted at any time to make room for more photos.

Digital video cameras include *digital camcorders* (such as the one shown in Figure 2-10) and small *PC video cameras*. Both types of digital video cameras are commonly used by individuals and businesses today to capture or transmit video images. Digital video cameras can also be used for identification purposes, such as in conjunction with face recognition technology to authorize access to a secure facility or computer resource, as discussed in more detail in Chapter 4. Digital camcorders are similar to conventional *analog* camcorders, but they store images on digital media—typically either on *mini digital video* (*DV*) *tape cartridges*, rewritable DVDs, or built-in hard drives. Once the video is recorded, it can be transferred to a PC, edited with software as needed, and saved to a DVD or other type of storage medium. It can also be *compressed* (made smaller), if needed, and then uploaded to video sharing sites, such as YouTube or Google Video. Some digital video cameras today can take high-definition (HD) video. PC video cameras—commonly called *PC cams*—are often built into computers, particularly notebook PCs; they are also available as stand-alone devices. PC cams are often used to transmit video images over the Internet, such as during a *videoconference* or *video phone call* to send images of the participants to each other or to serve as a live *Web cam* in order to broadcast images of interest to the general public via a Web page on a continual basis.

Other Input Devices

Other input devices include *microphones* or *headsets* (used for voice input, such as issuing commands to a computer, dictating documents, or recording spoken voice for a *podcast*—a recorded audio file that is distributed via the Internet—or other vocal application). Music can be input into a PC via a CD, a DVD, or a Web download. For original compositions, a *MIDI* (*musical instrument digital interface*) device, such as a *MIDI keyboard* that contains piano keys instead of, or in addition to, alphanumeric keys, can be used. Once music is input into the computer, it can be saved, modified, played, inserted into other programs, or burned to a CD or DVD. *Adaptive input devices* (designed for users with a physical disability) and *ergonomic input devices* (designed to lessen the physical impact of computer use) are discussed in detail in Chapter 7; types of emerging input devices are covered in Chapter 8.

PROCESSING HARDWARE AND OTHER HARDWARE INSIDE THE SYSTEM UNIT

The **system unit** is the main case of a computer. On a desktop PC, it often looks like a rectangular box, although other shapes and sizes are available, such as the all-in-one PC illustrated in Figure 1-15 in Chapter 1. The system unit for portable PCs and mobile devices is usually combined with the computer screen to form a single piece of hardware. The system unit contains *processing hardware*; namely a *motherboard*, one or more *CPUs*, and several types of *memory*. In addition, the system unit contains interfaces used to connect external *peripheral devices* (such as keyboards and printers) to the computer, storage devices to be used with that PC, a power supply, and cooling fans. The inside of a system unit for a typical desktop PC system is shown in Figure 2-11.

The Motherboard

A *circuit board* is a thin board containing *computer chips*—very small pieces of silicon or other semiconducting material—and other electronic components. The main circuit board inside the system unit is called the **motherboard** or *system board*. As shown in Figure 2-11, the motherboard has a variety of chips and boards attached to it; in fact, all devices used with a computer need to be connected in one way or another to the motherboard. To accomplish this, a variety of *ports*—special connectors exposed through the exterior of the system unit case—are either built into the motherboard or are created via an *expansion card* inserted into an *expansion slot* on the motherboard. These ports are used to connect *external* devices (such as monitors, keyboards, mice, and printers) to the PC.

FIGURE 2-11

Inside a typical system unit. The system unit houses the CPU, memory, and other important pieces of hardware.

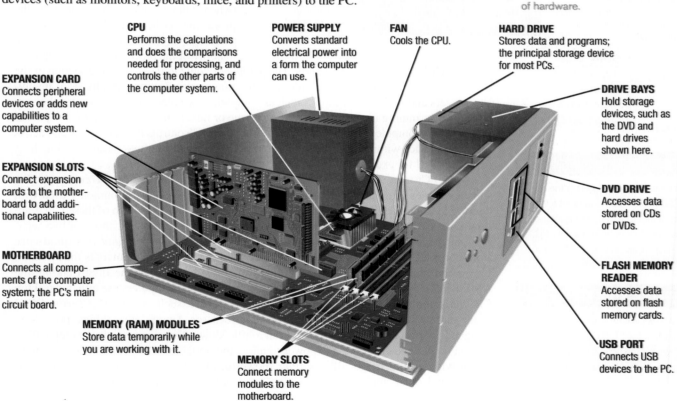

CPU
Performs the calculations and does the comparisons needed for processing, and controls the other parts of the computer system.

POWER SUPPLY
Converts standard electrical power into a form the computer can use.

FAN
Cools the CPU.

HARD DRIVE
Stores data and programs; the principal storage device for most PCs.

EXPANSION CARD
Connects peripheral devices or adds new capabilities to a computer system.

EXPANSION SLOTS
Connect expansion cards to the motherboard to add additional capabilities.

MOTHERBOARD
Connects all components of the computer system; the PC's main circuit board.

MEMORY (RAM) MODULES
Store data temporarily while you are working with it.

MEMORY SLOTS
Connect memory modules to the motherboard.

DRIVE BAYS
Hold storage devices, such as the DVD and hard drives shown here.

DVD DRIVE
Accesses data stored on CDs or DVDs.

FLASH MEMORY READER
Accesses data stored on flash memory cards.

USB PORT
Connects USB devices to the PC.

>**System unit.** The main box of a computer that houses the CPU, motherboard, memory, and other devices. >**Motherboard.** The main circuit board of a computer, located inside the system unit, to which all computer system components connect.

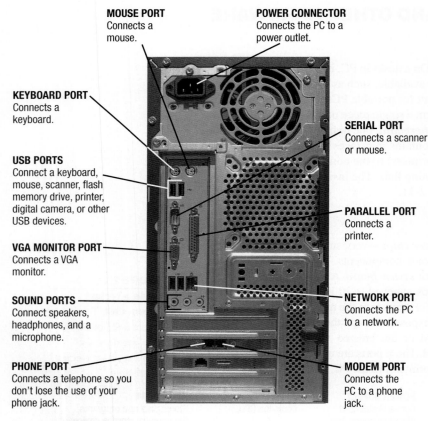

MOUSE PORT
Connects a mouse.

POWER CONNECTOR
Connects the PC to a power outlet.

KEYBOARD PORT
Connects a keyboard.

USB PORTS
Connect a keyboard, mouse, scanner, flash memory drive, printer, digital camera, or other USB devices.

VGA MONITOR PORT
Connects a VGA monitor.

SOUND PORTS
Connect speakers, headphones, and a microphone.

PHONE PORT
Connects a telephone so you don't lose the use of your phone jack.

SERIAL PORT
Connects a scanner or mouse.

PARALLEL PORT
Connects a printer.

NETWORK PORT
Connects the PC to a network.

MODEM PORT
Connects the PC to a phone jack.

FIGURE 2-12
Ports are used to connect external devices to the motherboard.

The most common ports for a desktop PC are shown in Figure 2-12. Notebook and handheld PCs often have some of these ports (such as USB ports and network ports). In addition, many notebook computers contain an *ExpressCard slot* designed for the *ExpressCard modules* often used for notebook PC expansion; handheld PCs often have an *SD slot* that can be used with the *Secure Digital* (*SD*) type flash memory media discussed later in this chapter, as well as with peripheral devices (such as barcode readers and GPS receivers) adhering to the *Secure Digital Input/Output* (*SDIO*) standard.

The Central Processing Unit (CPU)

The **central processing unit** (**CPU**) consists of a variety of circuitry and components which are packaged together and connected directly to the motherboard. The CPU—also called the **microprocessor** (when talking about PCs) or just the **processor** (when speaking in general terms for any computer)—does the vast majority of the processing for a computer.

The CPU has two principal parts. The *arithmetic/logic unit* (*ALU*) is the section of the CPU that performs arithmetic (addition, subtraction, multiplication, and division) involving integers and logical operations (such as comparing two pieces of data to see if they are equal or determining if a specific condition is true or false). In other words, it is the part of the CPU that computes. The *control unit* coordinates and controls the operations and activities taking place within the CPU, such as retrieving data and instructions and passing them on to the ALU for execution.

Most PCs today use CPUs manufactured by *Intel* or *Advanced Micro Devices* (*AMD*); some examples of their processors are shown in Figure 2-13. CPUs commonly used with desktop PCs include the Intel *Core 2 Duo* and AMD *Athlon 64 X2*. Both of these CPUs are **dual-core CPUs** (CPUs that contain the processing components—or *cores*—of two separate, independent processors on a single CPU). The Intel *Core 2 Quad* is a **quad-core** (four-core) **CPU**; AMD's quad-core CPU designed for desktop computers is the *Phenom*. Lower-end home PCs may use an Intel single-core CPU, such as the Intel *Celeron*, the AMD *Athlon 64*, or the AMD *Sempron*. Typically, portable computers use either a desktop CPU or a similar processor designed for portable PC use, such as the AMD *Turion 64 X2* or the mobile version of the Intel Core 2 Duo processor. Among other things, processors designed for portable PC use typically run a little slower than comparable desktop CPUs, but run cooler and consume less power to allow the portable PCs to run longer on battery power without a recharge. *Workstations* (powerful PCs designed for users running engineering and other applications requiring extra processing capabilities) and servers use

Four cores

Level 2 cache memory

INTEL CORE 2 QUAD
(quad-core)

FIGURE 2-13
CPUs. Most CPUs today use multiple cores.

AMD ATHLON 64 X2
(dual-core)

more powerful processors, such as the Intel *Xeon* or *Itanium 2*, the AMD *Opteron*, the IBM *POWER5*, or the Sun *UltraSPARC* processors. Most server processors are available in dual-core and/or quad-core versions.

Until recently, most CPUs designed for desktop PCs had only a single core; a common way to increase the amount of processing performed by these CPUs was to increase the speed of the CPUs. Because heat constraints are making it progressively more difficult to continue to increase the speed of a CPU, the trend today is to include multiple cores in a CPU to increase the amount of processing the CPU can do. These *multi-core CPUs* (such as dual-core and quad-core CPUs) allow computers to work simultaneously on more than one task at a time, such as burning a DVD while surfing the Web. Another benefit of multi-core CPUs is that they typically experience fewer heat problems than single-core CPUs because each core typically runs slower than a single-core CPU, although the total processing power of the multi-core CPU is greater. One measurement of the *processing speed* for a CPU is *CPU clock speed*, which is rated in *megahertz (MHz)* or *gigahertz (GHz)*. A higher CPU clock speed means that more instructions can be processed per second than the same CPU with a lower CPU clock speed. For instance, a Core 2 Duo processor running at 3.0 GHz would be faster than a Core 2 Duo running at 2.4 GHz, if all other components remain the same. Although CPU clock speed is an important factor in computer performance, other factors (such as the number of cores, the amount of memory, and the speed of external storage devices) greatly affect the overall processing speed of the computer. As a result, computers today are beginning to be classified less by CPU clock speed and more by the computer's overall processing speed or performance. For a look at the CPUs and processing power required for creating computer-generated movies, see the How It Works box.

ASK THE EXPERT

AMD

Margaret Lewis, Director of Commercial Solutions, AMD

What types of performance improvements will the average user notice going from a single-core PC to a dual-core PC?

Today, average consumers demand more power and better performance from their PCs than ever before, and as multi-threaded applications spread from the enterprise market to consumer devices, single-core machines may not be up to these demands. This illustrates the need for multi-core based PCs as they can deliver significantly increased performance over single-core chips. Dual-core technology, such as the AMD Athlon™ 64 X2 dual-core processor, offers improved efficiency and up to 80% increased performance over single-core processors on certain applications. For end users this means an increase in response and performance when running multiple applications simultaneously, such as burning a CD or running firewall software in the background while banking online. In addition, AMD Dual-Core Opteron™ processors are strategically equipped to run new generations of multi-threaded software leading to performance benefits in data center environments.

HOW IT WORKS

CPUs and Computer-Generated Films

Today's *computer-generated* (CG) films are continually pushing the envelope when it comes to visual effects. To support the development of CG films, an enormous amount of processing power is required. For instance, creating the *Shrek the Third* animated film (see the accompanying figure) required more than 150 workstations powered by AMD Opteron dual-core processors to provide the DreamWorks animation artists with the computing power necessary to render incredibly detailed characters, props, and environments. The CG development process involves creating thousands of drawings, paintings, and models of the characters and environments used in the story. Each character is represented by a digital 3D model that can be manipulated on the computer to make the character move, change its expressions, and be synchronized with the voice performances given by the actor playing that character. Digital sets also need to be built and then dressed with furniture and other props, and digital costumes need to be created for each character. Effects and lighting are then added to each scene to make the scene look as realistic as possible, and the necessary sound effects and music are created.

When all of the elements for a scene (sets, colors, characters, movement, lighting, etc.) have been created, that scene is ready to be *rendered*. The rendering process combines these elements frame by frame into the finished film. Rendering requires an immense amount of processing power and time and is usually accomplished by a collection of servers (called a *renderfarm*) dedicated to that purpose. For instance, the renderfarm used for *Shrek the Third* consisted of servers containing two dual-core Opteron processors (for a total of four cores each) and 8 GB of RAM each. All in all, nearly 4,000 processors were dedicated to rendering *Shrek the Third* and the rendering process required more than 20 million render hours—four times as many as the original *Shrek* movie.

Rendering the film *Shrek the Third* required nearly 20 million hours of processing time.

TIP

In addition to computers, CPUs are increasingly being incorporated into other devices, such as mobile phones, digital media players, gaming consoles, cars, and more.

FURTHER EXPLORATION

Go to **www.course.com/uccs/ch2** for links to further information about CPUs.

Memory

Memory refers to chip-based storage. When the term "memory" is used alone, it refers to chip-based storage used by the computer—usually the amount of the computer's main memory (called **random access memory** or **RAM**), which is located inside the system unit. In contrast, "storage" refers to the amount of long-term storage available to a PC—usually in the form of the PC's hard drive or removable storage media, such as CDs, DVDs, flash memory cards, and USB flash drives, all discussed later in this chapter. RAM is used to store the essential parts of the operating system while the computer is running, as well as the programs and data that the computer is currently using. RAM is **volatile**, which means its content is lost when the computer is shut off. Data in RAM is also deleted when it is no longer needed, such as when the program using that data is closed. If you want to retrieve a document at a later time, you need to save the document on a storage medium before closing it. There are several forms of *nonvolatile RAM* (*NVRAM*) under development that may be a possibility for the future; this and other types of emerging processing hardware are discussed in more detail in Chapter 8.

>**RAM (random access memory).** Chips connected to the motherboard that provide a temporary location for the computer to hold data and program instructions while they are needed. >**Volatile.** Describes a medium whose content is erased when the power is shut off.

Like the CPU, RAM consists of circuits etched onto chips. These chips are arranged onto circuit boards called *memory modules* (see Figure 2-14) which, in turn, are plugged into the motherboard. RAM capacity is measured in bytes and most notebook and desktop PCs sold today have at least 512 MB of RAM. It is important for a PC to have enough RAM to run the necessary applications (minimum RAM requirements are almost always stated on a software program's packaging), as well as to work efficiently (more RAM allows more programs to be opened at one time).

In addition to RAM, computer users should be aware of four other types of computer memory. Two of these—*cache memory* and *registers*—are volatile like RAM; the other two—*read-only memory* (*ROM*) and *flash memory*—are *nonvolatile*.

Cache memory is a special group of very fast memory chips located on or close to the CPU. Cache memory is used to speed up processing by storing the data and instructions that may be needed next by the CPU in handy locations. Cache memory today is usually *internal cache* (built right into the CPU chip). In the past, some cache memory was *external cache* (located close to, but not inside, the CPU) but that is less common today because the continued miniaturization of CPU components allows for more room inside the CPU. Cache memory level numbers indicate the order in which the various caches are accessed by the CPU when it requires new data or instructions. *Level 1* (*L1*) *cache* (which is the fastest type of cache but typically holds less data than other levels of cache) is checked first, followed by *Level 2* (*L2*) *cache*, followed by *Level 3* (*L3*) *cache* if it exists. If the data or instructions are not found in cache memory, the computer looks for them in RAM, which is slower than cache memory. If the data or instructions cannot be found in RAM, then they are retrieved from the hard drive—an even slower operation. Typically more cache memory results in faster processing.

Registers are another type of high-speed memory built into the CPU. Registers are used by the CPU to temporarily store data and intermediary results during processing. Registers are the fastest type of memory used by the CPU, even faster than Level 1 cache. Generally, the more data a register can contain at one time, the faster the CPU performs.

ROM (**read-only memory**) consists of nonvolatile chips that permanently store data or programs. Like RAM, these chips are attached to the motherboard inside the system unit, and the data or programs are retrieved by the computer when they are needed. An important difference, however, is that you can neither write over the data or programs in ROM chips (which is the reason ROM chips are called *read-only*), nor destroy their contents when you shut off the computer's power. ROM is used for storing permanent instructions used by a PC—referred to as *firmware*—but is now increasingly being replaced with *flash memory*, as discussed next, for any data that may need to be updated during the life of the PC.

Flash memory is a type of nonvolatile memory into which data can be stored and retrieved. Flash memory chips have begun to replace ROM for storing system information, such as a PC's *BIOS* or *basic input/output system*—the sequence of instructions the PC follows during the boot process. By storing this information in flash memory instead of in ROM, the BIOS information can be updated as needed. Similarly, firmware for PCs and other devices (such as mobile phones, networking hardware, and more) are now typically stored in flash memory embedded in the device so the firmware can be updated over the life of the product. In addition to built-in flash memory chips that are used only by the computer, PCs and other devices can include built-in flash memory chips designed to be used by the user for storage purposes, as discussed shortly.

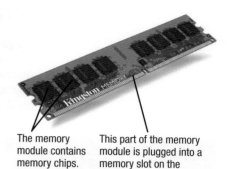

The memory module contains memory chips.

This part of the memory module is plugged into a memory slot on the motherboard.

FIGURE 2-14
A RAM memory module.

>**Cache memory.** A group of fast memory chips located on or near the CPU to help speed up processing. >**Register.** High-speed memory built into the CPU that temporarily stores data during processing. >**Read-only memory (ROM).** Nonvolatile chips located on the motherboard into which data or programs have been permanently stored. >**Flash memory.** A type of nonvolatile memory that can be erased and reprogrammed; commonly implemented in the form of sticks or cards.

OUTPUT HARDWARE

Output hardware consists of all the devices that are used to produce the results of processing—usually, output is displayed on a computer screen, printed on paper, or presented as audio output. Hardware devices that produce output are called **output devices**. The most common output devices are discussed next; types of emerging output devices are discussed in Chapter 8.

Display Devices

FIGURE 2-15
Consumer products, such as the handheld gaming device shown here, often have a display screen.

A **display device**—the most common form of output device—presents output visually on some type of screen. The display device for a desktop PC is more formally called a **monitor**. With all-in-one PCs, notebook computers, handheld PCs, and other types of computers for which the screen is built into the unit, the term **display screen** is often used instead. In addition to being used with computers, display screens are also built into a variety of devices, such as mobile phones, portable digital media players, handheld gaming devices (see Figure 2-15), and other consumer products. A *data projector* is a display device that projects computer output onto a wall or projection screen for a large group presentation.

The traditional type of monitor for a desktop PC is the *CRT monitor*. CRTs use *cathode-ray tube* technology to display images; as a result they are large, bulky, and heavy like conventional televisions. While CRTs are still used with computers, the use of thinner and lighter *flat-panel displays* (such as the one shown with the tower computer in Figure 1-15 in Chapter 1) are becoming the norm. Flat-panel displays form images by manipulating electronically charged chemicals or gases sandwiched between thin panes of glass or other transparent material. Flat-panel displays are used on portable computers and mobile devices, and with the majority of desktop PCs purchased today. They are also increasingly being used on television sets. Flat-panel displays have the advantage of taking up less desk space and consuming less power than CRTs, although the images displayed on a flat-panel display sometimes cannot be seen clearly when viewed from certain angles.

Regardless of the technology used, the screen of a display device is divided into a fine grid of small areas or dots called **pixels** (from the phrase *picture element*). *A pixel is* the smallest colorable area in an electronic image. The number of pixels used on a display screen determines the *screen resolution*, which affects the amount of information that can be displayed on the screen at one time. When a high resolution is selected, such as 1,280 pixels horizontally by 1,024 pixels vertically (written as 1,280 × 1,024 and read as *1280 by 1024*), more information can fit on the screen, but everything will be displayed smaller than with a lower resolution, such as 800 × 600 or 1,024 × 768 (see Figure 2-16). The screen resolution on many computers today can be changed by users to match their preferences and the software being used (on Windows PCs, display options are changed using the *Control Panel*). Very high-resolution monitors are available for special applications, such as viewing digital X-rays.

Display devices today are typically *color displays*, which form colors by mixing combinations of three colors—red, green, and blue—although *monochrome displays* are also still used sometimes. Screen size is usually measured diagonally from corner to corner, in a manner similar to the way TV screens are measured. Some monitors today support high-definition images, such as *HDTV*, and some monitors support touch screen input.

ONLINE VIDEO

Go to **www.course.com/uccs/ch2** to watch the "IBM, the Mayo Clinic, and Medical Imaging" video clip.

>**Output device.** A piece of hardware that presents the results of processing in a form the user can understand. >**Display device.** An output device that contains a viewing screen. >**Monitor.** A display device for a desktop PC. >**Display screen.** A display device built into a notebook computer, handheld PC, or other device. >**Pixel.** The smallest colorable area in an electronic image, such as a scanned document, digital photograph, or image displayed on a display screen.

800 × 600

1,024 × 768

1,280 × 1,024

FIGURE 2-16

Screen resolution. A higher screen resolution (measured in pixels) displays everything smaller than a lower screen resolution.

Printers

Instead of the temporary, ever-changing soft copy output that a monitor produces, **printers** produce *hard copy*; that is, a permanent copy of the output on paper. Most desktop PCs are connected to a printer; portable PCs can use printers as well. Printers designed to be connected to a single computer are referred to as *personal printers*; *network printers* are designed to be shared by multiple users via a network.

Printers produce images through either impact or nonimpact technologies. *Impact printers*, like old ribbon typewriters, have a print mechanism that actually strikes the paper to transfer ink to the paper. Most printers today are *nonimpact printers*, meaning they form images without the print mechanism actually touching the paper. Impact printers, such as the older *dot-matrix printers*, are primarily used today for producing multipart forms, such as invoices, packing slips, and credit card receipts. Nonimpact printers usually produce higher-quality images and are much quieter than impact printers. Both impact and nonimpact printers form images with dots, similar to the way monitors display images using pixels. Because of this, printers are very versatile and can print text in virtually any size, as well as print photos and other graphical images.

Printers can be *color printers* or *black-and-white printers*, printer quality is measured in *dots per ink* (*dpi*), and printer speed is measured in *pages per minute* (*ppm*). The two most common types of printers today are *laser printers* and *ink-jet printers*, both of which are nonimpact printers.

Laser Printers

Laser printers are the standard for business documents and come in both personal and network styles. To print a document, the laser printer first uses a laser beam to charge the appropriate locations on a drum to form the page's image, and then *toner powder* (powdered ink) is released from a *toner cartridge* and sticks to the drum. The toner is then transferred to a piece of paper when the paper is rolled over the drum, and a heating unit fuses the toner powder to the paper to permanently form the image (see Figure 2-17). Laser printers are available in both color and black-and-white versions, print one entire page at a time, and are typically faster and have better quality output than *ink-jet printers*, discussed next. Common print resolutions for laser printers are between 600 and 2,400 dpi; speeds for personal laser printers range from about 15 to 30 ppm. Black-and-white laser printers start at about $100; color laser printers start at about $300.

TIP

Printers that offer more than just printing capabilities (such as printing, copying, scanning, and faxing) are referred to as *multifunction devices* (*MFD*) or *all-in-ones*.

TIP

To save money, consider buying *recharged* (refilled) toner cartridges when your laser printer cartridge runs out of toner powder. Recharged cartridges typically cost about one-third less than new cartridges and last at least as long.

>**Printer.** An output device that produces output on paper. >**Laser printer.** An output device that uses toner powder and technology similar to that of a photocopier to produce images on paper.

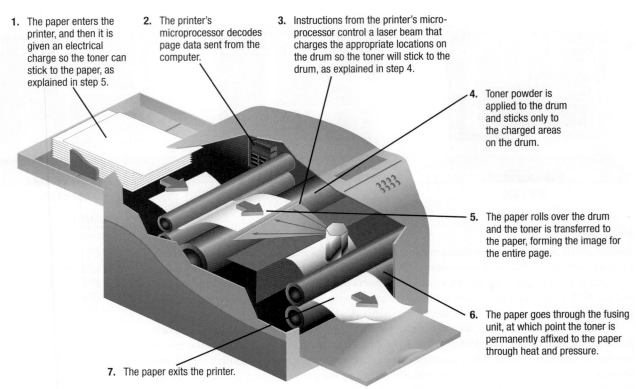

1. The paper enters the printer, and then it is given an electrical charge so the toner can stick to the paper, as explained in step 5.

2. The printer's microprocessor decodes page data sent from the computer.

3. Instructions from the printer's microprocessor control a laser beam that charges the appropriate locations on the drum so the toner will stick to the drum, as explained in step 4.

4. Toner powder is applied to the drum and sticks only to the charged areas on the drum.

5. The paper rolls over the drum and the toner is transferred to the paper, forming the image for the entire page.

6. The paper goes through the fusing unit, at which point the toner is permanently affixed to the paper through heat and pressure.

7. The paper exits the printer.

FIGURE 2-17
How laser printers work.

Ink-Jet Printers

Ink-jet printers form images by spraying tiny drops of liquid ink onto the page, one printed line at a time (see Figure 2-18). Some printers print with one single-sized ink droplet; others print using different-sized ink droplets and using multiple nozzles or varying electrical charges for more precise printing. Because they are relatively inexpensive, have good-quality output, and usually can print in color, ink-jet printers are typically the printer of choice for home use. With the use of special photo paper, *photo-quality ink-jet printers* can also print photograph quality digital photos. At around $100 for a simple home printer, ink-jet printers are affordable, although the cost of the replaceable ink cartridges can add up, especially if you do a lot of color printing.

Special-Purpose Printers

Although printers can typically print on a variety of media, such as sheets of labels, envelopes, transparencies, photo paper, and even fabric, some printers are designed for a particular purpose. For instance, *photo printers* are color printers specifically designed to print photographs (refer again to Figure 2-18); *barcode printers* enable businesses and other organizations to print custom barcodes on price tags, shipping labels, and other documents for identification or pricing purposes; *portable printers* are small, lightweight printers that can be used on the go, such as with a notebook computer, handheld PC, or smart phone; *plotters* and *wide-format ink-jet printers* are designed to produce charts, drawings, maps, blueprints, advertising banners, and other large documents; and *3D printers* form output in layers using plastic powder and other materials during a series of passes to build a 3D version of the desired output.

> **Ink-jet printer.** An output device that sprays droplets of ink to produce images on paper.

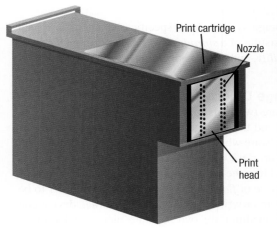

Print cartridge

Nozzle

Print head

CONVENTIONAL INK-JET PRINTER

Photos can be previewed and edited here.

Flash memory media can be inserted here.

INK-JET PHOTO PRINTER

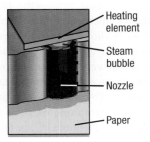

Heating element

Steam bubble

Nozzle

Paper

1. A heating element makes the ink boil, which causes a steam bubble to form.

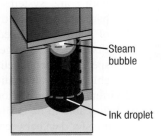

Steam bubble

Ink droplet

2. As the bubble expands, it pushes ink through the nozzle.

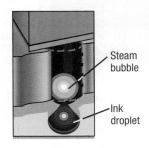

Steam bubble

Ink droplet

3. The pressure of the bubble forces an ink droplet to be ejected onto the paper. When the steam bubble collapses, more ink is pulled into the print head, so it is ready for the next steam bubble.

HOW INK-JET PRINTERS WORK
Color ink-jet printers create colors by mixing different combinations of four colors of ink—magenta, cyan, yellow, and black. The different colors can be in one or multiple cartridges. Each cartridge is made up of 300 or more tiny ink-filled firing chambers, each attached to a nozzle smaller than a human hair. To print images, the appropriate color ink is ejected through the appropriate nozzle.

FIGURE 2-18
How ink-jet printers work.

Other Output Devices

Other types of output devices include **speakers**, such as the speakers often connected to or built into a computer to produce audio output from programs, digital music, or Web content. *Headphones* can be used with speakers so the sound will not disturb others (such as in a school computer lab or public library). *Headsets* are headphones with a built-in microphone and are often used for dictating to the PC, as well as for making telephone calls using a PC; wireless headsets are commonly used in conjunction with mobile phones. Even smaller than headphones are the *earphones* and *earbuds* often used with portable digital media players, handheld gaming devices, and other mobile devices.

STORAGE HARDWARE

Unlike RAM, which is volatile and holds data only temporarily, *storage systems* are nonvolatile and are used anytime you want to save a document for future use. The basic characteristics of storage systems are discussed first, followed by a look at the most common types of storage systems.

>**Speakers.** Output devices that produce sound.

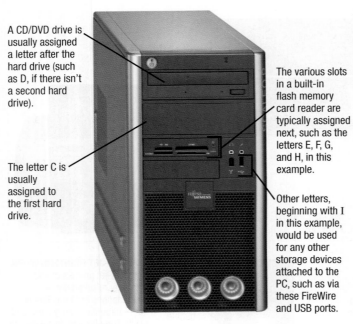

A CD/DVD drive is usually assigned a letter after the hard drive (such as D, if there isn't a second hard drive).

The various slots in a built-in flash memory card reader are typically assigned next, such as the letters E, F, G, and H, in this example.

The letter C is usually assigned to the first hard drive.

Other letters, beginning with I in this example, would be used for any other storage devices attached to the PC, such as via these FireWire and USB ports.

FIGURE 2-19

Storage device identifiers. To keep track of storage devices in an unambiguous way, the computer system assigns letters of the alphabet or names to each of them.

Storage System Characteristics

All storage systems have specific characteristics, such as consisting of a *storage device* and a *storage medium*, *portability*, and the type of storage technology used.

Storage Devices and Storage Media

There are two parts to any storage system: the **storage device** and the **storage medium**. A storage medium is the hardware where data is actually stored (for example, a *CD* or *flash memory card*); a storage medium is inserted into the corresponding storage device (such as a *CD drive* or *flash memory card reader*) in order to be read from or written to. Usually the storage device and storage medium are two separate pieces of hardware (that is, the storage medium is *removable*), although with some systems—such as a *hard drive*—the two parts are permanently sealed together to form one piece of hardware (called a *fixed-media* storage system). Fixed-media storage systems generally provide higher speed and better reliability at a lower cost than removable-media alternatives, but removable-media storage systems have the advantages of virtually unlimited storage capacity (by purchasing more of the proper storage medium), being able to be easily transported from one location to another (to share data with others, transfer data between a work PC and a home PC, or take digital photos to a photo store, for instance), and being able to be moved to a secure area (such as for backup purposes or to protect sensitive data).

Storage devices can be *internal* (located inside the system unit), *external* (plugged into an external port on the system unit), or *remote* (located on another computer, such as a network server). Regardless of how storage devices are connected to a computer, letters of the alphabet and/or names are typically assigned to each storage device so that the user can identify each device easily when it needs to be used (see Figure 2-19).

Magnetic Disks vs. Optical Discs

Data is stored *magnetically* or *optically* on most storage media. With magnetic storage systems, such as hard drives, data is stored magnetically, which means the data (0s and 1s) is represented using different magnetic alignments. The magnetic alignment can be changed, so the data on a hard drive can be deleted and overwritten as needed. Optical storage media (such as CDs and DVDs) store data optically using laser beams. On some optical media, the laser burns permanent marks into the surface of the medium so the data cannot be erased or rewritten. With *rewritable* optical media, the laser changes the reflectivity of the medium but does not permanently alter the disc surface so that the reflectivity of the medium can be changed again. Consequently, the data stored on the disc can be deleted and overwritten.

Some storage systems use a combination of magnetic and optical technology. Others use a different technology altogether, such as *flash memory storage systems* that represent data using *electrons*. Some of the most widely used storage systems are discussed in the next few sections.

> **Storage device.** A piece of hardware, such as a DVD drive, into which a storage medium is inserted to be read from or written to.
> **Storage medium.** The part of a storage system where data is stored, such as a DVD disc.

Magnetic Disk Systems

Speedy access to data, relatively low cost, and the ability to erase and rewrite data make **magnetic disk systems** one of the primary storage systems used with today's computers. With magnetic storage systems, data is written by *read/write heads*, which magnetize particles a certain way on the medium's surface to represent the data's 0s and 1s. The particles retain their magnetic orientation until the orientation is changed again, so data can be stored, rewritten to the disk, and deleted as needed. The most common type of magnetic disk is the *hard disk*; another type of magnetic disk is the *floppy disk*.

Floppy Disks and Drives

PCs have traditionally been set up to use a **floppy disk**—sometimes called a *diskette* or *disk*—to meet removable storage needs (see Figure 2-20). Floppy disks are written to and read by **floppy disk drives** (commonly called *floppy drives*). Because floppy drives are relatively slow and the capacity of floppy disks is very small compared to newer removable storage media, the floppy drive is commonly viewed as a *legacy drive* and many manufacturers are no longer automatically including one as part of their computer systems (although one can often be added as an option). However, understanding how a floppy disk works will help you to understand in general how magnetic disks work.

A floppy disk consists of a round piece of flexible plastic (hence the name "floppy disk") coated with a magnetizable substance. The disk is protected by a square, rugged plastic cover. To use a floppy disk, it must first be inserted into a floppy drive. When it is completely inserted, the disk clicks into place and the *metal shutter* that covers an opening in the plastic cover is moved aside to expose the surface of the disk. The surface of a floppy disk is organized into circular rings, called *tracks*, and pie-shaped groups of *sectors*. On most PC systems, the smallest storage area on a disk is a *cluster*—one or more sectors (see Figure 2-21). Tracks, sectors, and clusters are numbered by the computer so it can keep track of where data is stored. The PC uses a *file system* to record where each document (called a *file*) is physically stored and what *filename* the user has assigned to it. When the user requests a document (always by filename), the computer uses its file system to retrieve it. Since a cluster is the smallest addressable area on a disk, everything stored on a disk always takes up at least one cluster of space on the disk.

When the floppy disk in the floppy drive needs to be accessed, the drive begins to rotate the disk within its plastic cover. The drive's read/write head can *read* (retrieve) data from or *write* (store) data to the surface of the disk while the disk is spinning. The read/write heads move in and out over the surface of the disk, allowing the read/write heads access to all tracks on that disk. Floppy disks in use today measure 3.5 inches in diameter and can store 1.44 MB of data, which is sufficient to store about 500 pages of double-spaced text or one or two digital photos, depending on the photo settings used. Music files, large numbers of digital photos, and documents containing images usually require a higher-capacity removable storage media—such as a CD, a DVD, or one of the many types of flash memory media available today; these storage media are discussed shortly.

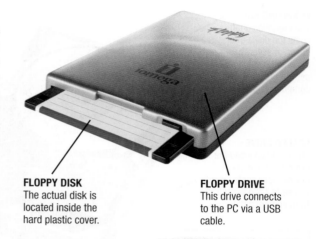

FLOPPY DISK
The actual disk is located inside the hard plastic cover.

FLOPPY DRIVE
This drive connects to the PC via a USB cable.

FIGURE 2-20
A floppy disk and drive.

FIGURE 2-21
Magnetic disks are organized into tracks, sectors, and clusters.

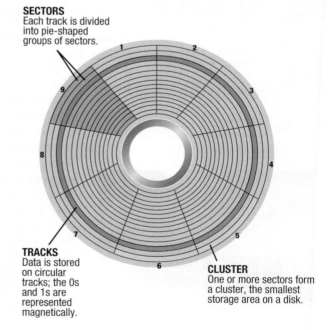

SECTORS
Each track is divided into pie-shaped groups of sectors.

TRACKS
Data is stored on circular tracks; the 0s and 1s are represented magnetically.

CLUSTER
One or more sectors form a cluster, the smallest storage area on a disk.

>**Magnetic disk system.** A type of storage system that uses flexible plastic or rigid metal disks onto which data is recorded magnetically.
>**Floppy disk.** A low-capacity, removable magnetic disk made of flexible plastic permanently sealed inside a hard plastic cover. >**Floppy disk drive.** A storage device that reads from and writes to floppy disks.

MOUNTING SHAFT
The mounting shaft spins the disks at a speed of several thousand revolutions per minute while the computer is turned on.

SEALED DRIVE
The hard disks and the drive mechanism are hermetically sealed inside a case to keep them free from contamination.

READ/WRITE HEADS
There is a read/write head for each disk surface. On most systems, the heads are positioned on the same track and sector on each disk so they can move in and out together.

HARD DISKS
There are usually several hard disk surfaces on which to store data. Most hard drives store data on both sides of each disk.

ACCESS MECHANISM
The access mechanism moves the read/write heads in and out together between the hard disk surfaces to access required data.

INSIDE A 3.5-INCH HARD DRIVE

2.5-INCH HARD DRIVE LOCATED INSIDE A NOTEBOOK PC

 FIGURE 2-22
Hard drives.

FIGURE 2-23
This portable hard drive holds 250 GB.

Hard Disk Drives (HDDs)

With the exception of computers designed to use only network storage devices (such as network computers and some Internet appliances), virtually all PCs come with a **hard disk drive (HDD)**, also commonly referred to as a **hard drive**, that is used to store most programs and data. Similar to floppy drives, hard drives store data magnetically; they use read/write heads to store and retrieve data; and their disks are organized into tracks, sectors, and clusters. However, the disks used with a hard drive are made out of metal and are permanently sealed (along with the read/write heads and an *access mechanism*) inside the hard drive to avoid contamination and to enable the disks to spin faster. Desktop hard drives typically use 3.5-inch hard disks and notebook hard drives typically use 2.5-inch hard disks (see Figure 2-22). The tiny hard drives embedded into some portable digital media players, mobile phones, and other mobile devices typically use 1.5-inch hard disks or smaller. Regardless of the size, one hard drive usually contains a stack of several hard disks; if so, there is a read/write head for each disk surface (top and bottom), as illustrated in Figure 2-22.

Internal hard drives are permanently located inside the system unit and are not designed to be removed, unless they need to be repaired or replaced. Virtually all PCs have at least one internal hard drive that is used to store programs and data; the hard drives for desktop PCs today typically hold at least 250 GB. *External hard drives* can be used to transport a large amount of data from one PC to another (by moving the entire drive to another PC) or for additional storage. *Portable hard drives* (see Figure 2-23) are physically smaller than a typical external hard drive, usually have a smaller storage capacity (from 40 GB to 250 GB is common), and are often powered via the PC so they do not require an external power adapter. Very portable hard drives designed to be carried around easily (such as in a pocket) are sometimes referred to as *pocket hard drives*. Most external, portable, and pocket hard drives connect to the PC via a USB connection; some have the option of connecting via a *FireWire connection*—a high-speed universal connection similar to USB, but less widely used.

>**Hard disk drive (HDD).** A storage system consisting of one or more metal magnetic disks permanently sealed with an access mechanism inside its drive. Also called a **hard drive**.

It is important to realize that a hard drive's read/write heads never touch the surface of the hard disks at any time, even during reading and writing. If the read/write heads do touch the surface—for example, if the PC is bumped while the hard drive is spinning or a foreign object gets onto the surface of a disk, a *head crash* occurs, which may do permanent damage to the hard drive. When hard drives containing critical data become damaged, *data recovery firms* may be able to help out, as discussed in the Inside the Industry box.

FURTHER EXPLORATION

Go to **www.course.com/uccs/ch2** for links to further information about hard drives.

Optical Disc Systems

Data stored on **optical discs** (such as **CDs**, **DVDs**, and **Blu-ray Discs (BDs)**) is read *optically*—using laser beams—instead of magnetically, like floppy and hard disks. Optical discs are thin circular discs made out of molded *polycarbonate substrates*—essentially a type of very strong plastic. Data can be stored on one or both sides of an optical disc, depending on the disc design, and some types of discs use multiple recording layers on each side of the disc to increase capacity. To keep data organized, optical discs are divided into tracks and sectors like magnetic disks but use a single grooved spiral track beginning at the center of the disc (see Figure 2-24), instead of a series of concentric tracks. Data is written to an optical disc by stamping or molding the surface of the disc (for *read-only* discs like movie, music, and software CDs and DVDs) or by changing the reflectivity of the disc with a laser (for *recordable* or *rewritable* discs that can be written to by the user. In either case, the disc is read with a laser. The computer interprets the reflection of the laser off the disc surface as 1s and 0s.

To accomplish this with molded or stamped optical discs, tiny depressions (when viewed from the top side of the disc) or bumps (when viewed from the bottom) are created on the disc's surface. These bumps are called *pits*; the areas on the disc that are not changed are called *lands*. Although many people think that each individual pit and land represents a 1 or 0, that is not completely accurate—it is the transition between a pit and land that represents a 1. When the disc is read, the amount of laser light reflected back from the disc changes when the laser reaches a transition between a pit and a land. When the drive detects a transition, it is interpreted as a 1; no transition for a specific period of time indicates a 0.

With a CD or DVD that is recorded using a CD or DVD drive, the recording laser beam changes the reflectivity of the appropriate microscopic areas on the disc to represent the data stored

FIGURE 2-24
How recorded optical discs work.

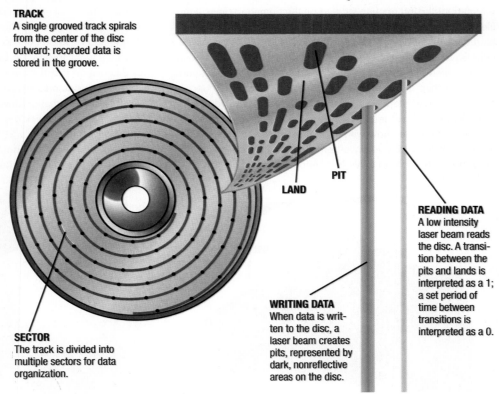

TRACK
A single grooved track spirals from the center of the disc outward; recorded data is stored in the groove.

PIT

LAND

READING DATA
A low intensity laser beam reads the disc. A transition between the pits and lands is interpreted as a 1; a set period of time between transitions is interpreted as a 0.

WRITING DATA
When data is written to the disc, a laser beam creates pits, represented by dark, nonreflective areas on the disc.

SECTOR
The track is divided into multiple sectors for data organization.

>**Optical disc.** A type of storage medium read from and written to using a laser beam. >**CD.** An optical disc with a typical storage capacity of 650 MB; common formats include CD-ROM, CD-R, and CD-RW discs. >**DVD.** An optical disc with a typical storage capacity of 4.7 GB or 8.5 GB; common formats include DVD-ROM, DVD-R, DVD+R, DVD-RW, and DVD+RW. >**Blu-ray Disc (BD).** A type of high-capacity optical disc with a storage capacity of 25 GB or 50 GB that is designed for high-definition content.

INSIDE THE INDUSTRY

Data Recovery Experts

It happens far more often than most people imagine. A hard drive quits working the day before a big report is due, a laptop is dropped in the parking lot and then run over by a car, or a business burns down taking the PC containing the only copy of the company records with it. If the data on the drive was recently backed up, the data can be installed on a new drive with just a little expense and a short delay. When critical data located on a potentially destroyed hard drive is not backed up, it is time to seek help from a professional data recovery expert.

Data recovery firms, such as DriveSavers in California, specialize in recovering data from severely damaged storage media (see the accompanying photos). The damaged drives are taken apart in a *clean room* (a sealed room similar to the ones in which computer chips are manufactured) and temporarily repaired as needed in order to copy all of the data (bit by bit) from the drive onto a server. The copied data is then used to reconstruct the information located on the damaged drive. If the file directory is not recovered, engineers try to match the jumbled data to file types in order to reconstruct the original files. DriveSavers clients have included Barbara Mandrell, whose musical director's hard drive containing several months of work and more than 1,200 orchestra charts needed for a concert nine days away stopped working; the executive producer of "The Simpsons," whose computer crashed taking scripts for 12 episodes of the show with it; an individual whose notebook PC was trapped for two days beneath a sunken cruise ship in the Amazon River; a MacWorld attendee whose notebook PC

containing a sales presentation due in two days was run over and crushed by a shuttle bus; and a Fortune 500 company, which lost all its financial data and stockholder information when its server went down. In all five cases, DriveSavers was able to recover all of the lost data.

In addition to these dramatic examples, data recovery firms are also frequently used when hard drives and other storage media just stop functioning. In fact, DriveSavers estimates that 75% of its business is due to malfunctioning devices. And with the vast amounts of digital data (such as digital photos, music, home videos, school papers, and more) that the average person stores today, data recovery firms, in addition to being used by businesses, are increasingly being used by individuals to recover personal data.

Data recovery firms stress the importance of backing up data. According to Scott Gaidano, president of DriveSavers, "The first thing we tell people is back up, back up, back up. It's amazing how many people don't back up." It is also important to make sure the backup procedure is working. For instance, the Fortune 500 company mentioned previously performed regular backups and kept the backup media in a fire-resistant safe, but when they went to use the backup after their server crashed, they discovered that the backup media were all blank.

Because potentially losing all the data on a drive can be so stressful and traumatic, DriveSavers has its own data-crisis counselor, a former suicide hotline worker. Fortunately for their clients, DriveSavers has a 90% recovery rate. The services of data recovery experts are not cheap, but when the lost data is irreplaceable, they are a bargain.

Data recovery. All the data located on the hard drive of this computer (left) that was virtually destroyed in a fire was recovered by data recovery experts in less than 24 hours. Recovery takes place in a clean room (right).

STANDARD 120 MM (4.7 INCH) SIZED DISC

MINI 80 MM (3.1 INCH) SIZED DISC

CUSTOM SHAPED BUSINESS CARD DISC

there—dark, nonreflective areas are pits; reflective areas are lands, as illustrated in Figure 2-24—but the transition between a pit and a land still represents a 1 and no transition for a specific distance along the track represents a 0. Conventional CD discs use *infrared* lasers and conventional DVDs use *red* lasers. To store even more data on the same size disc, the newest high-capacity *high-definition DVDs* (such as Blu-ray Discs) use *blue-violet lasers*, which can store data more compactly on a disc.

Standard-sized optical discs are 120-mm (approximately 4.57-inch) discs (see Figure 2-25). There are also smaller 80-mm (approximately 3-inch) *mini CDs* and *mini DVDs*. In addition, optical discs can be made into a variety of sizes and shapes—such as a heart, triangle, irregular shape, or the hockey-rink shape commonly used with *business card CDs*—because the track starts at the center of the disc and the track just stops when it reaches the outer edge of the disc. Standard-sized CD discs hold either 650 MB or 700 MB, standard-sized DVD discs usually hold 4.7 GB (*single-layer discs*) or 8.5 GB (*dual-layer discs*), and high-definition DVDs hold up to 50 GB, depending on the format and number of layers being used. A dual-layer disc (also called a *double-layer disc*) stores data in two layers on a single side of the disc, so the capacity is approximately doubled. A *double-sided disc* also doubles the capacity, but the disc must be turned over to access the second side. Double-sided discs are most often used with movies and other prerecorded content, such as storing a *widescreen version* of a movie on one side and a *standard version* on the other. Discs can be both dual-layer and double-sided.

> **FIGURE 2-25**
> **Optical disc sizes.**
> Optical discs can be made in a variety of shapes and sizes, such as the regular size, mini, and business card CDs shown here.

Read-Only Discs: CD-ROM, DVD-ROM, and BD-ROM Discs

CD-ROM (*compact disc read-only memory*) discs and *DVD-ROM* (*digital versatile disc read-only memory*) discs are *read-only optical discs* and come prerecorded with commercial products, such as software programs, clip art and other types of graphics collections, and product demos. For high-definition content, *read-only Blu-ray Discs* (*BD-ROM discs*) can be used. The data on a read-only disc cannot be erased, changed, or added to, since the pits that are molded into the surface of the disc when the disc is produced are permanent. CD-ROM and DVD-ROM discs are designed to be read by *CD-ROM* and *DVD-ROM drives*, respectively. CD-ROM drives can usually read both data and audio CDs; DVD-ROM drives can typically read data and audio CDs, DVD-ROM discs, and DVD movies. BD discs are read by *BD drives*; drives that can read all or most optical formats (such as CDs, DVDs, and BDs) are sometimes referred to as *hybrid drives*.

Recordable Discs: CD-R, DVD-R, DVD+R, and BD-R Discs

Recordable optical discs can be written to, but the discs cannot be erased and reused. Recordable CDs are referred to as *CD-R discs*. Single-layer recordable DVDs are either *DVD-R discs* or *DVD+R discs*, depending on the standard being used. The newest recordable DVDs

FURTHER EXPLORATION

Go to **www.course.com/uccs/ch2** for links to further information about DVD technology.

(*DVD-R DL and DVD+R DL discs*) are dual-layer discs, so they have a capacity of 8.5 GB. Recordable BD discs (referred to as *BD-R discs*) are also available. Recordable optical discs are written to using an appropriate optical drive, such as a *CD-R drive* for CD-R discs or a *DVD-R drive* for DVD-R discs, although optical drives are usually *downward-compatible*, meaning that they can be used with lower formats, such as using a DVD-R drive to burn a CD-R disc.

Recordable CDs are commonly used for backing up files, sending large files to others, and creating custom music CDs (for example, from music files legally downloaded from the Internet or from songs on CDs the user owns). DVD-Rs can be used for similar purposes when more storage space is needed, such as for large backups and for storing home movies, digital photos, and other multimedia files. BD-R discs can be used when an even greater amount of storage is needed, such as extra large backups or high-definition multimedia files.

Rewritable Discs: CD-RW, DVD-RW, DVD+RW, and BD-RE Discs

Rewritable optical discs can be written to, erased, and overwritten just like magnetic disks. The most common types of rewritable optical media are *CD-RW*, *DVD-RW*, *DVD+RW*, and *BD-RE discs*. CD-RW discs can be written to using a *CD-RW drive* and can be read by most CD and DVD drives. DVD-RW and DVD+RW discs are recorded using a *DVD-RW* or *DVD+RW drive*, respectively, and can be read by most DVD drives. BD-RE discs are recorded and read by *rewritable Blu-ray Disc drives* (see Figure 2-26). The capacities of rewritable discs are the same as their read-only and recordable counterparts.

It is important to realize that recordable and rewritable DVDs have not yet reached—and may never reach—a single standard, so there are competing formats that are not necessarily compatible with each other. Luckily, most DVD drives today support more than one format. But it is important for users to purchase the type of optical media that is compatible with their drives.

FIGURE 2-26
Blu-ray Disc rewritable drive.
This drive can record data on CD, DVD, and BD recordable and rewritable discs, as well as read all CD, DVD, and BD formats.

Flash Memory Systems

Unlike magnetic and optical storage systems, **flash memory storage systems** have no moving parts; instead, data is stored as electrical charges on *flash memory media*. Because they have no moving parts, flash memory storage systems are not subject to mechanical failures like hard drive and optical disc systems, and, therefore, are more resistant to shock and vibration. They also consume less power and make no noise. In addition, flash memory media is very small and so is especially appropriate for use with digital cameras, portable digital media players, handheld PCs, notebook computers, mobile phones, and other types of portable devices, as well as for transporting data from one place to another. Flash memory media is rewritable and has a longer expected life than magnetic media, though it is typically more expensive per MB.

Today, flash memory is most often found in the form of *flash memory cards*, *USB flash drives*, *solid-state drives*, and *hybrid hard drives*, as discussed next and illustrated in Figure 2-27. In addition, flash memory chips are also embedded directly into a variety of consumer products—such as portable digital media players, digital cameras, handheld gaming devices, GPS devices, mobiles phones, and even sunglasses and wristwatches—to provide built-in data storage.

FURTHER EXPLORATION

Go to **www.course.com/uccs/ch2** for links to further information about removable storage media and other portable storage systems.

>**Flash memory storage system.** A storage system that uses flash memory media.

Flash Memory Cards

A **flash memory card** is a small card containing one or more flash memory chips, a controller chip, other electrical components, and metal contacts to connect the card to the device or reader with which it is being used. Flash memory cards are the most common type of storage media for handheld PCs, digital cameras, portable digital media players, mobile phones, and other types of mobile devices. They can also be used with desktop and notebook computers, such as to transfer data to the PC from another device. For convenience, most computers and many mobile devices today contain a built-in *flash memory card reader* that can read from and write to at least one type of flash memory media; the type of media your devices can accept will determine the type of flash memory cards you need to use. When an appropriate reader is not built into the device, an external flash memory card reader (that

EMBEDDED FLASH MEMORY
These sunglasses contain a built-in MP3 player with 1 GB of embedded flash memory for storing MP3 files.

Flash memory card

FLASH MEMORY CARDS AND READERS
Flash memory cards are often used to store data for a digital camera or other device; that data can be transferred to a PC via a flash memory card reader.

USB FLASH DRIVES
USB flash drives are often used to store data and transfer files from one PC to another.

SOLID-STATE DRIVES
This solid-state drive fits into an ExpressCard slot and holds 32 GB of data.

typically connects via a USB port) can often be used. Flash memory cards come in a variety of formats, such as *CompactFlash (CF)*, *Secure Digital (SD)*, *Secure Digital High Capacity (SDHC)*, *MultiMedia Card (MMC)*, *xD Picture Card (xD)*, *Memory Stick (MS)*, and *SmartMedia (SM)*. The capacity of flash memory cards is continually growing and is up to about 4 GB for standard cards and 16 GB for high-capacity cards, with 32 GB SDHC cards expected in the near future.

FIGURE 2-27
Flash memory systems. Flash memory is used in a variety of storage systems today.

USB Flash Drives

USB flash drives (sometimes called *USB flash memory drives*, *thumb drives*, or *jump drives*) consist of flash memory media integrated into a self-contained unit that uses a USB interface and, consequently, connects to a PC or other device via a standard USB port. USB flash drives do not contain batteries and so are active only when plugged into a USB port, since their power is provided through the USB interface. They are designed to be very portable and are small enough to fit in a pocket or to be carried on a keychain. USB flash drives are available in a wide range of sizes, colors, and appearances—including drives designed to be worn as a wristband (such as the one shown in Figure 2-27), as well as drives with clips to attach to backpacks, drives built into necklaces, and drives built into wristwatches—in order to appeal to a wide variety of users. To read from or write to a USB flash

TIP

To avoid data loss when you are finished using a USB flash drive on a Windows PC, first double-click the *Safely Remove Hardware icon* in the system tray, and then stop the drive before removing it from the USB port.

>**Flash memory card.** A small, rectangular flash memory media, such as a CompactFlash (CF) or a Secure Digital (SD) card.
>**USB flash drive.** A small storage device that plugs into a PC's USB port and contains flash memory media.

MAGNETIC HARD DRIVE
This drive contains 2 hard disks and 4 read/write heads that operate similar to a conventional hard drive.

FLASH MEMORY DISK CACHE
This drive uses 256 MB of flash memory disk cache to duplicate data as it is stored on the hard disks so the data can be accessed when hard disks are not spinning.

FIGURE 2-28
Hybrid hard drives (HHDs). HHDs combine a magnetic hard drive with a large flash memory cache for increased performance.

drive, the user plugs it into a USB port. The capacity of USB flash drives today typically ranges from 512 MB to 16 GB.

Solid-State Drives (SSDs) and Hybrid Hard Drives (HHDs)

A relatively new option is the use of *solid-state drives* (*SSDs*)—hard drives that use flash memory instead of spinning platters and magnetic technology—as a replacement for conventional hard drives. Although previously too expensive for all but specialty applications, prices of solid-state drives (also sometimes called *flash memory hard drives*) have fallen significantly over the past few years. Solid-state drives are smaller and faster than conventional hard drives, use less power, and are less susceptible to physical damage, making them especially appropriate for portable computers. Another alternative to the conventional hard drive is the *hybrid hard drive* (*HHD*)—a magnetic hard drive that contains flash memory in addition to magnetic disks (see Figure 2-28) to increase performance while reducing the amount of power required and the amount of heat generated. Data to be written to the hard drive can be *cached* (temporarily stored) in flash memory so the magnetic disks don't have to be accessed as often, saving wear-and-tear on the disks, as well as extending battery life in notebook PCs and other portable devices.

Other Types of Storage Systems

Two additional types of storage systems that are frequently used are *remote storage systems* and *smart cards*. Types of emerging storage systems are discussed in Chapter 8.

Remote Storage Systems

Remote storage refers to using a storage device that is not connected directly to the user's PC system; instead, the device is accessed through a local network or through the Internet. Using remote storage works in much the same way as using *local storage* (the storage devices and media that are directly attached to the user's PC)—the user just selects the appropriate remote storage device (such as a hard drive or folder on a computer accessed via a network, as shown in Figure 2-29), and then stores data on or retrieves data from it. When the remote device is accessed through a local network, it is referred to as *network storage*; the term *online storage* typically refers to storage accessed via the Internet. An example of an online storage site is also shown in Figure 2-29.

>**Remote storage.** A storage device that is not directly part of the PC being used, such as network storage or online storage.

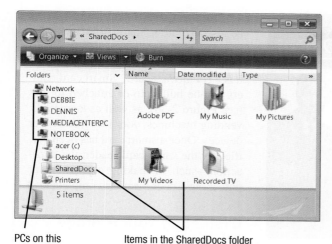

NETWORK STORAGE
Shared folders on network computers appear and are accessed similar to local folders.

SECURE ONLINE STORAGE
This site is designed to securely store files for backup or to be shared with others. After logging on, users can upload, download, or delete files, as well as designate who is allowed to access files.

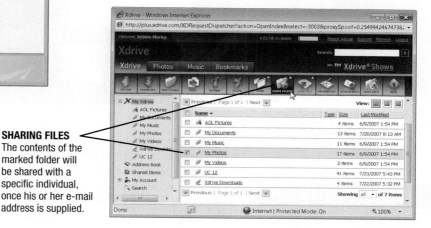

PCs on this network.

Items in the SharedDocs folder on the PC called NOTEBOOK.

SHARING FILES
The contents of the marked folder will be shared with a specific individual, once his or her e-mail address is supplied.

Individuals and businesses can use remote storage for a variety of purposes. For instance, the additional PCs on a home network and online storage sites can be used to back up files in case of a fire or other disaster, and online storage sites can be used by individuals who want to share personal files—such as digital photographs—through the Internet. They can also be used as a place to store content you want to access while on the go. Although some online storage sites allow access to anyone, most require users to log on with usernames and passwords to limit access to authorized individuals.

FIGURE 2-29
Remote storage systems.

Smart Cards

A **smart card** is a credit card-sized piece of plastic that contains computer circuitry and components—typically a processor, memory, and storage. Smart cards today store a relatively small amount of data (typically 64 KB or less) that can be used for payment or identification purposes. For example, a smart card can store a prepaid amount of *digital cash*, which can be used for purchases at a smart card-enabled vending machine or PC that contains a *smart card reader*—the amount of cash available on the card is reduced each time the card is used. Smart cards are also commonly used worldwide for national and student ID cards; credit and debit cards; and cards that store loyalty system information (frequent flyer points, for example), identification data for accessing facilities or computer networks, or an individual's medical history and health insurance information for fast treatment and hospital admission in an emergency. Although these applications have used conventional *magnetic stripe* technology in the past, the processor integrated into a smart card can perform computations—such as to authenticate the card and *encrypt* the data on the card to protect its integrity and secure it against unauthorized access—and data can be added to the card or modified on the card as needed.

>**Smart card.** A credit card-sized piece of plastic containing a chip and other circuitry into which data can be stored.

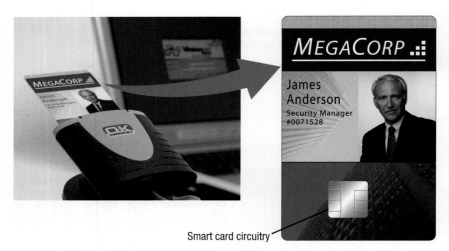

△ FIGURE 2-30
Smart cards.

TIP

Virtually all computer users today need at least one USB port in order to connect external hard drives, USB flash drives, and other storage hardware. If your PC doesn't have one, you can add one by installing a USB expansion card.

ONLINE VIDEO

Go to **www.course.com/uccs/ch2** to watch the "What is Bluetooth?" video clip.

To use a smart card, it must either be inserted into a smart card reader (if it is the type of card that requires contact) or placed close to a smart card reader (if it is a *contactless* card). Smart card readers can be built into or attached to PCs (see Figure 2-30), as well as keyboards, vending machines, door locks, and other devices. Once a smart card has been verified by the smart card reader, the transaction—such as making a purchase or unlocking a door—can be completed.

Evaluating Your Storage Alternatives

Storage alternatives are often compared by weighing a number of product characteristics and cost factors. Some of these product characteristics include speed, compatibility, storage capacity, convenience, and the portability of the media. Keep in mind that each storage alternative normally involves trade-offs. For instance, most systems with removable media are slower than those with fixed media, and external drives are typically slower than internal ones. Although cost is a factor when comparing similar devices, it is often not the most compelling reason to choose a particular technology. For instance, although USB flash drives are relatively expensive per GB, many users find them essential for transferring files between work and home or for taking presentations or other files with them as they travel. For drives that use a USB interface, the type of USB port being used is also significant. For instance, storage devices that connect via the original *USB 1.0* port transfer data at up to 1.5 MB per second; *USB 2.0* devices are about 40 times faster, and devices conforming to the emerging *USB 3.0* standard will be even faster.

COMMUNICATIONS HARDWARE

Most computers today include *communications hardware* to enable the user to communicate with others over a network or the Internet. The type of **communications device** used depends on the device being used (desktop PC, notebook computer, or mobile phone, for instance), as well as the *communication standard* (such as *Ethernet* for wired networks, *Wi-Fi* for wireless networks, *Bluetooth* for short-range wireless connections, or a *cellular standard* for a mobile phone) being used. Common communications devices include *network adapters*, *modems*, *cabling*, and other networking hardware as discussed next; emerging communications standards and devices are covered in Chapter 8.

Network Adapters and Modems

A **network adapter**, also called a *network interface card* (*NIC*) when it is in the form of an expansion card, is used to connect a PC to a network. The type of network adapter used depends on the type of network and communications medium being used. For instance, to connect a PC to an Ethernet network, an Ethernet network adapter is used; to connect a PC to a Wi-Fi network, a Wi-Fi network adapter is used (for a look at how to connect to a

---

>**Communications device.** A piece of hardware that allows one device to communicate with other devices via a network or the Internet.
>**Network adapter.** A network interface, such as an expansion card or external network adapter.

Wi-Fi hotspot, see the Technology and You box). Network adapters are typically available as *internal adapters* that connect directly to the motherboard, *USB adapters* that connect to the PC via a USB port, and *ExpressCard adapters* that connect via an ExpressCard slot (see Figure 2-31 for some examples of network adapters).

Modem is the term used for a device that connects a computer to another computer or to a network (typically, the Internet) over telephone lines. There are a number of different types of modems in use today, each matching a particular type of Internet connection, such as *conventional dial-up*, *cable*, *fixed wireless*, and *DSL* (the types of Internet services that utilize these modems are discussed in detail in Chapter 3). Similar to network adapters, modems are available in both internal and external versions and in a variety of formats (see the external cable modem shown in Figure 2-31), although not all types of modems may be available in all formats.

Other Networking Hardware

To connect the devices on a network together, typically a central device is needed. This device can be a *hub*, *switch*, or *router* for wired networks; networks designed for wireless users typically use a *wireless access point* or *wireless router* instead (a Wi-Fi wireless access point is shown in Figure 2-31). To increase the range of a network, *repeaters*, *range extenders*, and *antennas* can be used. To connect the wired devices to the network, *cabling* (typically *twisted-pair*, *coaxial cable*, or *fiber-optic cable*) is used.

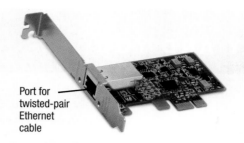

Port for twisted-pair Ethernet cable

INTERNAL ETHERNET ADAPTER FOR DESKTOP PC

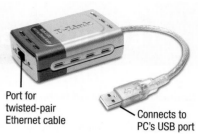

Port for twisted-pair Ethernet cable

Connects to PC's USB port

USB ETHERNET ADAPTER FOR DESKTOP OR NOTEBOOK PC

EXPRESSCARD WI-FI ADAPTER FOR NOTEBOOK PC

Connects to PC's USB port

USB WI-FI ADAPTER FOR DESKTOP OR NOTEBOOK PC

Incoming coaxial cable from cable provider and either a USB or an Ethernet cable going to the PC connect to the back of the modem.

CABLE MODEM

A modem typically connects to the back of this device so users can connect wirelessly to the Internet via this device.

WI-FI WIRELESS ACCESS POINT

FIGURE 2-31
Common types of communications hardware.

SOFTWARE BASICS

As discussed in Chapter 1, all computers need an operating system (such as Windows, Linux, or Mac OS) in order to function. The operating system is used to boot the computer, control its operation, and allow users to run application software—the programs used to perform specific tasks on the computer. Although features and capabilities vary from program to program, most software programs today use similar basic features and operations.

>**Modem.** A communications device that enables digital computers to connect to other computers or to a network (typically the Internet) via telephone lines.

TECHNOLOGY AND YOU

Connecting to a Wi-Fi Hotspot

To connect to a free Wi-Fi hotspot, all you need is a device (such as a notebook computer) with a Wi-Fi adapter installed and enabled (some notebook computers have a switch located on the case to turn off wireless networking and some power settings disable it—check these things if you can't connect using the following steps). On a Windows PC that has a Wi-Fi adapter installed, there is an icon in the system tray representing the available wireless networks. When you are within range of a Wi-Fi hotspot, click this icon and choose "View Available Wireless Networks" to see all of the Wi-Fi access points in the area (see the accompanying illustration). If there is more than one hotspot listed on the Wireless Network Connection list, select the appropriate one and then click the Connect button. For free hotspots that are in range, you should be connected shortly and can then open your browser and perform Internet activities. For secured networks, you will be asked to supply the appropriate passphrase before you can connect to the Internet via that hotspot, as discussed in more detail in Chapter 4. For most fee-based hotspots (and some free ones, as well, such as networks at a hotel or conference center designed for paying customers), you will see a logon screen and will need to obtain an appropriate username and password from a hotspot representative and enter that information via the logon screen before

being connected. Security issues related to public hotspot use are discussed in more detail in Chapter 4.

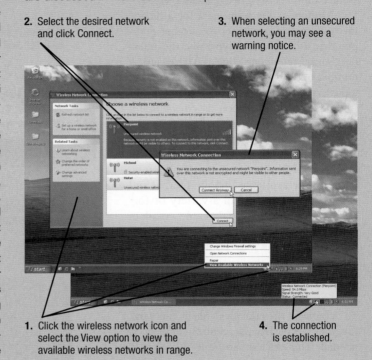

2. Select the desired network and click Connect.

3. When selecting an unsecured network, you may see a warning notice.

1. Click the wireless network icon and select the View option to view the available wireless networks in range.

4. The connection is established.

While covering how to use specific software programs is beyond the scope of this book, an understanding of basic software concepts and operations is an important part of becoming familiar with computers. An overview of booting a computer, using the Windows user interface, and some common types of software applications was included in Chapter 1. Other important software basics—including software ownership rights, installation options, common software commands, and the concept of *file management*—are discussed in the remainder of this chapter.

Software Ownership Rights

The *ownership rights* of a software program specify the allowable use of the program. After a software program is developed, the developer holds the ownership rights for that program. Whether or not the program can be sold, shared with others, or otherwise distributed is up to that developer, typically an individual or an organization. When a software program is purchased, the buyer is not actually buying the software. Instead, the buyer is acquiring a **software license** that permits him or her to use the software. This license specifies the conditions under which a buyer can use the software, such as whether or not it may be shared with others and the number of computers on which it may be installed

FURTHER EXPLORATION

Go to **www.course.com/uccs/ch2** for links to further information about wired and wireless communications media.

>**Software license.** An agreement, either included in a software package or displayed on the screen during installation, that specifies the conditions under which a buyer of the program can use it.

(many software licenses permit the software to be installed on just one PC). In addition to being included in printed form inside the packaging of most software programs, the licensing agreement is usually displayed and must be agreed to by the end user at the beginning of the software installation process.

There are four basic categories of software: *commercial software* (software that is developed and sold for a profit), *shareware* (software that is distributed on the honor system), *freeware* (software that is given away free of charge), and *public domain software* (software that is not copyrighted). In addition, software that falls into any of these four categories can also be *open source software*— programs whose source code is available to the general public. An open source program can be copyrighted, but individuals and businesses are allowed to modify the program and redistribute it—the only restrictions are that changes must be shared with the open source community and the original copyright notice must remain intact.

ASK THE EXPERT

Dave Weick, Senior Vice President, Chief Information Officer, McDonald's Corporation

How has the emergence of Wi-Fi affected companies such as McDonald's?

The emergence of Wi-Fi has fueled our customers' expectations of having immediate access to information. Our customers and employees love the convenience and relevance of McDonald's "hotspots." Through wireless connectivity, Wi-Fi is creating a more modern and relevant experience for our customers. The ability to conveniently check e-mail or download music or games can be a deciding factor in choosing a place to eat—a trend we don't see ending anytime soon.

TIP
Ownership rights for original creative works are referred to as *copyrights* and are discussed in more detail in Chapter 6.

Installed vs. Web-Based Software

Software also differs in how it is accessed by the end user. It can be *installed software* that is installed on and run from the end user's PC, or it can be *Web-based software* that is accessed by the end user over the Internet. Installed software is the most common type of software at the present time and is either purchased in physical form (such as in a shrink-wrapped box containing a CD or DVD, license agreement, and user's manual) or downloaded from the Internet. Web-based software is delivered on demand via the Web to wherever the user is at the moment, provided he or she has an Internet connection (and has paid to use the software, if a payment is required). Also referred to as *Software as a Service (SaaS)*, the use of Web-based software is growing rapidly. One advantage of Web-based software over installed software is that the programs and your documents can be accessed from any PC with an Internet connection regardless of the type of PC or operating system used; some can also be accessed via a mobile phone, portable digital media player, or other type of mobile devices. Some potential disadvantages are that online applications tend to run more slowly than applications stored on a local hard drive, many online applications have a limit on the file size of the documents you create, the cost may eventually exceed the cost of buying a similar shrink-wrapped package, and you cannot access the program and your documents when the server on which they reside goes down or when you are in a location with no Internet access, such as on a plane or in a remote area.

ONLINE VIDEO
Go to **www.course.com/uccs/ch2** to watch the "Google Docs in Plain English" video clip.

Common Software Commands

Application programs today have a number of concepts and commands in common. For example, many programs allow you to create a new document (such as a letter, drawing, house plan, or greeting card) and then *save* it. To reopen the document at a later time, you use the *open* command; to print the document, you use the *print* command. One of the greatest advantages of using software instead of paper and pencil to create documents is that you can make changes without erasing or recreating the entire document because the document is created in RAM and then saved on a storage medium, instead of it being created directly on paper. Consequently, the document can be retrieved, modified, saved, and

FURTHER EXPLORATION

Go to **www.course.com/uccs/ch2**
for links to further information about
application software resources.

printed as many times as needed. Many programs also include tools to help you as you create documents, such as a *spelling and grammar check* feature to locate and help you correct possible spelling and grammar errors in your documents, and a *styles* feature that allows you to apply a common format to a series of documents or a group of similar headings within a single document.

Toolbars, Menus, Keyboard Shortcuts, and the Ribbon

Most commands in an application software program are issued through *menus*, *keyboard shortcuts*, or buttons located on a *toolbar* or *Ribbon*. The *menu bar* appears at the top of many windows and contains text-based lists (menus), which provide access to commands that can be selected to perform actions in that program. Many programs also have toolbars—sets of *icons* or *command buttons* that are clicked with the mouse to issue commands. *Keyboard shortcuts* are commands issued with the keyboard that correspond to command buttons. Typically, keyboard shortcuts are key combinations that use the Ctrl or Alt keys, the function keys, and/or the alphanumeric keys on the keyboard. For instance, the keyboard shortcut *Ctrl+S* is issued by holding down the Ctrl key and pressing the S key and typically issues the Save command.

The **Ribbon** is a new feature of **Microsoft Office 2007** (a popular *office software suite* consisting of *Microsoft Word*, *Excel*, *PowerPoint*, and other programs). The Ribbon (see Figure 2-32) consists of *tabs*, which contain *groups* of related commands for the program being used. Most programs have a *Home tab* that contains the most frequently used commands in that program, and additional *contextual tabs* are displayed as needed, depending on the action being taken. For instance, selecting a picture or other graphic in Microsoft Word displays the *Picture Tools tab* that contains commands related to a picture, such as to crop, resize, rotate, or recolor the picture. Clicking a command button either carries out that command or displays a *gallery* of choices from which the user can select the desired action, such as a list of bulleted list styles, font sizes, margin settings, paper sizes, and so forth. In addition to the Ribbon, Office 2007 programs include a *Mini toolbar* that appears whenever text is selected and contains commands that can be used to quickly change the appearance of that text (such as changing its color or size) and a *Quick Access Toolbar* that provides easy access to frequently used commands. Office 2007 programs also include a new *Microsoft Office Button* that replaces the File menu used in previous versions of Office and contains commands commonly used with documents, such as to open, save, print, send, and publish them.

FIGURE 2-32
The Microsoft Office 2007 Ribbon.

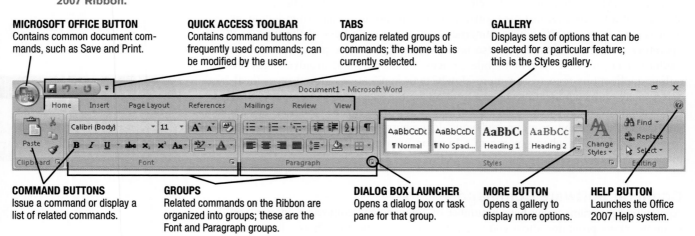

MICROSOFT OFFICE BUTTON
Contains common document commands, such as Save and Print.

QUICK ACCESS TOOLBAR
Contains command buttons for frequently used commands; can be modified by the user.

TABS
Organize related groups of commands; the Home tab is currently selected.

GALLERY
Displays sets of options that can be selected for a particular feature; this is the Styles gallery.

COMMAND BUTTONS
Issue a command or display a list of related commands.

GROUPS
Related commands on the Ribbon are organized into groups; these are the Font and Paragraph groups.

DIALOG BOX LAUNCHER
Opens a dialog box or task pane for that group.

MORE BUTTON
Opens a gallery to display more options.

HELP BUTTON
Launches the Office 2007 Help system.

>**Ribbon.** A set of commands grouped by task and used in Office 2007 programs to issue commands to the computer. >**Microsoft Office 2007.**
The current version of one of the most widely used office software suites.

Editing a Document

Editing a document refers to changing the content of the document, such as adding or deleting text. Most application software programs that allow text editing display an insertion point at the current location in the document; that is, where the next change will be made to that document. To insert text, just start typing and the text will appear at the insertion point location. To delete text, press the Delete key to delete one character to the right of the insertion point; press the Backspace key to delete one character to the left of the insertion point. If the insertion point is not in the proper location for the edit, it must be moved (by using the arrow keys on the keyboard or by pointing and clicking with the mouse) to the appropriate location in the document. To select an object or block of text, click the object or drag the mouse over the text. Usually, once an object or some text is selected, it can be manipulated, such as to be moved, deleted, copied, or *formatted*.

Formatting a Document

While editing changes the actual content of a document, *formatting* changes the appearance of the document. Common types of formatting include changing the *font face*, *font size*, *font style*, and *font color* of text; changing the *line spacing* or *margins* of a document; adding *page numbers*; and adding *shading* or *borders*. A font face or *typeface* is a named collection of text characters that share a common design, such as Calibri or Times New Roman. The characters in a font face are usually available in a wide variety of font sizes, which are measured in *points*. All the characters in a particular font face and font size are referred to as a *font*; for example, 11-point Calibri is a font. *Font style* refers to formatting that adds additional features to the text, such as bold, italic, or underline, and *font color* refers to the color of the text. Default fonts are installed on a PC with the operating system and some application programs; additional fonts can be purchased and added by the user.

Working with Files and Folders

It is important for software users to understand the concepts of *files* and *folders* and be able to work with them quickly and efficiently. Anything (such as a program, letter, digital photograph, or song) stored on a storage medium is called a **file**. When the item is first stored on a storage medium the user gives the file a name, called a **filename**; the user specifies that filename whenever he or she wants to open the file again. To keep files organized, related documents are often stored in **folders** located on the storage medium. For example, one folder might contain memos to business associates while another might hold budgets (see Figure 2-33). To further organize files, you can create *subfolders* within a folder. For instance, you might create a subfolder within the *Budgets* subfolder for each fiscal year. In Figure 2-33, both *Budgets* and *Memos* are subfolders inside the *Documents* folder and the *Budgets* subfolder contains two additional subfolders.

File management programs (such as *Windows Explorer*) allow you to perform file management tasks, such as looking to see which files are stored on a storage medium, as well as copying, moving, deleting, and renaming folders and files. For instance, you can see the folders and files stored on your hard drive, USB flash drive, or any other storage medium by clicking the appropriate letter or name for that medium in the Windows Explorer window, and you can copy a file or folder by selecting the desired item, issuing the *Copy* command (such as by pressing Ctrl+C), displaying the location where you want the copy to go, and then issuing the *Paste* command (such as by pressing Ctrl+V). You can delete an item by selecting it and pressing the Delete key on the keyboard.

FIGURE 2-33
Organizing data.
Folders are used to organize related items on a storage medium.

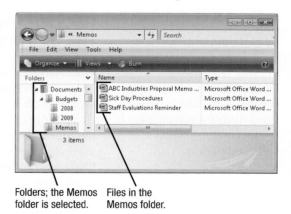

Folders; the Memos folder is selected.   Files in the Memos folder.

>**File.** Something stored on a storage medium, such as a program, document, or image. >**Filename.** A name given to a file by the user that is used to retrieve the file at a later time. >**Folder.** A named place on a storage medium into which files can be stored to keep the files stored on that medium organized.

SUMMARY

DIGITAL DATA REPRESENTATION

Chapter Objective 1:
Understand how data is represented to a computer.

Data must be represented appropriately (using 0s and 1s) in order to be used by a computer. A single 0 or 1 is called a **bit**; 8 bits together is referred to as a **byte**. A kilobyte (**KB**) equals 1,024 bytes, a **megabyte** (**MB**) is about 1 million bytes, a **gigabyte** (**GB**) is about 1 billion bytes, a **terabyte** (**TB**) is about 1 trillion bytes, and a **petabyte** (**PB**) is about 1,000 terabytes. To represent numbers and do mathematical operations, computers use the **binary numbering system**; for representing characters, coding systems, such as **ASCII** (**American Standard Code for Information Interchange**) and **Unicode**, are used.

INPUT HARDWARE

Chapter Objective 2:
Identify several types of input devices and explain their functions.

An **input device** is any piece of hardware that is used to input data into a computer. Two of the most common input devices are the **keyboard** and **mouse**. While a keyboard is designed to enter input by pressing keys, a mouse is a **pointing device** that is used to select objects and commands on the screen. Another common pointing device is the **electronic pen** (also called a **stylus** or *digital pen*), which is used with computers and other devices to input handwritten data and select options. **Touch screens** are touched with the finger to select commands or provide input. Other pointing devices include *graphics tablets*, *gaming devices*, *control buttons and wheels*, and *touch pads*.

To input data that already exists, a **scanner** (either *flatbed* or *handheld*) can be used. When used with *optical character recognition* (*OCR*) software, the computer system recognizes scanned text characters and stores them digitally so they can be manipulated by the computer. If not, the scanned data is input as an image. Other types of scanners or readers include **barcode readers** (used to read **barcodes** on consumer products and other objects), **RFID readers** (used to read **RFID tags**), and **biometric readers** (used to read *biometric data* belonging to an individual). **Digital cameras** (both *still* and *video cameras*) are used to capture images in digital form and record images on some type of digital storage medium. *Microphones*, *headsets*, and *MIDI* devices can be used for input, as well.

PROCESSING HARDWARE AND OTHER HARDWARE INSIDE THE SYSTEM UNIT

Chapter Objective 3:
Explain the functions of the primary hardware components found inside the system unit, namely the motherboard, the CPU, and memory.

Processing hardware is located inside the **system unit**, along with other important components. The **motherboard** or *system board* is the main *circuit board* for a PC. All hardware used with a computer must be connected to the motherboard, either directly or via a *port*. Every PC has at least one **central processing unit** (**CPU**)—also called a **processor** or a **microprocessor** when referring to PCs—attached to its motherboard that performs the processing for the computer. CPUs today are often *multi-core CPUs*, such as **dual-core** (two cores) and **quad-core** (four cores) **CPUs**. The term *memory* is usually used to refer to **random access memory** (**RAM**)—groups of chips that are also attached to the motherboard and provide temporary storage for the PC to use. RAM is **volatile**, so all data in RAM is erased when the power to the computer goes off. Other types of memory used by the PC include **cache memory**, **registers**, **read-only memory** (**ROM**), and **flash memory**.

OUTPUT HARDWARE

Output devices present the result of processing to the user, usually in the form of a **display device**—also called a **monitor** or a **display screen**—or a **printer**. The common types of monitors are *CRTs* and *flat-panel displays*. Monitors form images using **pixels**, and the number of pixels used to display an image determines the *screen resolution*.

Printers produce *hard copy* output. The most widely-used printers are **laser printers** (the standard for business documents) and **ink-jet printers** (used in homes and for inexpensive color printouts). Specialty printers, such as *photo printers*, *barcode printers*, and *portable printers* are also available. Other output devices include **speakers** and *headphones*.

Chapter Objective 4:
List several output devices and explain their functions.

STORAGE HARDWARE

Storage systems make it possible to save programs, data, and processing results for later use. All storage systems involve a **storage medium** (which holds the data) and a **storage device** (which reads from and writes to the medium). Data is stored either *magnetically* or *optically* on most storage media. Storage devices can be *internal*, *external*, or *remote* and are typically assigned letters by the computer that are used to identify the drive.

Magnetic disk systems include **floppy disks/floppy disk drives** and **hard disk drives** (also called **HDDs** or **hard drives**). Hard drives are used to store most programs and data. Magnetic disks are divided into *tracks*, *sectors*, and *clusters* so the computer can keep track of where each file is stored. Hard drives can be *internal*, *external*, or *portable*.

Optical discs (such as **CDs**, **DVDs**, and **Blu-ray Discs** (**BDs**)) store data using laser beams, and they store data much more densely than magnetic disks. Optical discs can be *read-only, recordable,* or *rewritable*. The capacity of an optical disc depends on the type and physical size of the disc, as well as how many recording sides and layers are being used.

Flash memory storage systems have no moving parts. **Flash memory cards** are commonly used with a variety of devices, and come in many formats. **USB flash drives** are a convenient method of transferring files between computers. *Solid-state drives* contain flash memory media instead of magnetic disks; *hybrid hard drives* (*HHDs*) contain both magnetic and flash memory media. Other storage possibilities include **remote storage** (storage accessed through the Internet or other network) and **smart cards** (that contain small amounts of data, such as digital cash or personal data, for a variety of purposes).

Chapter Objective 5:
Understand the difference between storage and memory, as well as between a storage device and a storage medium.

Chapter Objective 6:
Name several types of storage systems and explain the circumstances under which they are typically used.

COMMUNICATIONS HARDWARE

Communications devices, such as **network adapters** and **modems**, enable users to communicate with others over a network or the Internet. Other networking hardware (such as *hubs*, *routers*, *wireless access points*, and *cabling*) is used to connect the devices on a network; *repeaters*, *range extenders*, and *antennas* can be used to extend the range of a network.

Chapter Objective 7:
Describe the purpose of communications hardware.

SOFTWARE BASICS

A program's **software license** explains its *ownership rights*; that is the allowable use of the program. Most software today is *commercial*, *shareware*, *freeware*, or *public domain* and can be either *installed software* or *Web-based software*. *Editing* refers to making changes to the content of a document; *formatting* refers to changing its appearance. To issue commands to a software program, interface tools such as *menus*, *keyboard shortcuts*, *toolbar buttons*, and the **Ribbon** (used in the **Microsoft Office 2007**) are typically used. Anything stored on a storage medium (such as a document, program, image, etc.) is called a **file** and is given an identifying **filename** by the user. To keep files organized, related documents can be stored inside **folders**. Users can open, copy, move, and delete files and folders.

Chapter Objective 8:
Understand basic software concepts and commands.

REVIEW ACTIVITIES

KEY TERM MATCHING

Instructions: Match each key term on the left with the definition on the right that best describes it.

a. byte

b. central processing unit (CPU)

c. file

d. keyboard

e. laser printer

f. modem

g. motherboard

h. optical disc

i. software license

j. USB flash drive

1. _____ A communications device that enables digital computers to connect to other computers or to a network (typically the Internet) via telephone lines.

2. _____ A group of 8 bits.

3. _____ An agreement, either included in a software package or displayed on the screen during installation, that specifies the conditions under which a buyer of the program can use it.

4. _____ A small storage device that plugs into a PC's USB port and contains flash memory media.

5. _____ A type of storage medium read from and written to using a laser beam.

6. _____ An input device containing numerous keys that can be used to input letters, numbers, and other symbols.

7. _____ An output device that uses toner powder and technology similar to that of a photocopier to produce images on paper.

8. _____ Something stored on a storage medium, such as a program, document, or image.

9. _____ The chip located inside the system unit of a computer that performs the processing for a computer; also called a processor.

10. _____ The main circuit board of a computer, located inside the system unit, to which all computer system components connect.

SELF-QUIZ

Instructions: Circle **T** if the statement is true, **F** if the statement is false, or write the best answer in the space provided. **Answers for the self-quiz are located in the References and Resources Guide at the end of the book.**

1. **T** **F** A storage medium that can hold 256 GB can hold about 256 million characters.

2. **T** **F** A mouse is an example of a pointing device.

3. **T** **F** Most digital cameras store photos on conventional floppy disks.

4. **T** **F** An ink-jet printer normally produces a better image than a laser printer.

5. **T** **F** Changing the font size in a document is an example of a formatting operation.

6. A(n) _____ can be used to convert flat printed documents, such as a drawing or photograph, into digital form.

7. A CPU with four separate processing cores is referred to as a(n) _____ CPU.

8. A hybrid hard drive includes _____ media, in addition to magnetic media.

9. Files can be stored inside _____ to keep them organized.

10. Match each input device to its appropriate application, and write the corresponding number in the blank to the left of the application.

a. _____ Gaming
b. _____ Secure facilities access
c. _____ Consumer kiosk
d. _____ Text-based data entry
e. _____ Tracking goods

1. RFID tag
2. Biometric reader
3. Joystick
4. Keyboard
5. Touch screen

EXERCISES

1. Number the following terms from 1 to 6 to indicate their size from smallest to largest.

a. _____ Petabyte   b. _____ Kilobyte   c. _____ Byte
d. _____ Terabyte   e. _____ Gigabyte   f. _____ Megabyte

2. For the following list of hardware devices, write the appropriate abbreviation (I, P, O, S, or C) in the space provided to indicate whether each device is used for input (I), output (O), processing (P), storage (S), or communications (C).

a. _____ Biometric reader   f. _____ Digital camera
b. _____ Hub   g. _____ USB flash drive
c. _____ Speaker   h. _____ Microphone
d. _____ Photo printer   i. _____ Hard disk drive (HDD)
e. _____ Memory   j. _____ Network adapter

3. Supply the missing words to complete the following statements.

a. The smallest piece of data that can be represented by a computer (0 or 1) is called a(n) _____ .

b. _____ is an international coding system for text-based data using any written language.

c. A(n) _____ optical disc can hold either 25 GB or 50 GB and is designed for high-definition content, such as movies.

4. List one personal or business application that you believe is more appropriate for a dot-matrix printer, instead of another type of printer, and explain why.

5. Which types of storage media would be appropriate for someone who needed to exchange large (5 MB to 75 MB) files with another person? List at least three different types, stating why each might be the most appropriate under specific conditions.

DISCUSSION QUESTION

The choice of an appropriate input device for a product is often based on both the type of device being used and the target market for that device. For instance, a device targeted to college students and one targeted to older individuals may use different input methods. Suppose that you are developing an Internet appliance being marketed to senior citizens. What type of hardware would you select as the primary input device? Why? What are the advantages and disadvantages of your selected input device? How could the disadvantages be minimized?

BALANCING ACT

OPEN SOURCE SOFTWARE: WILL IT PROMOTE OR HINDER SOFTWARE DEVELOPMENT?

As mentioned in the chapter, open source software is software for which the actual program code (also called the *source code*) is made available free of charge to the general public. The growing number of open source products—such as the *Linux operating system* and *Apache Web server*, two of the most famous examples—are reviewed and improved by independent programmers who update the software at no charge for fun, notoriety, or programming practice. Proponents of open source software believe that if programmers who are not concerned with financial gain work on an open source program, they will produce a more useful and error-free product much faster than the traditional commercial software development process. Programs based on open source code are often available for free or for a nominal fee (compared to the price of similar commercial software) for documentation and support. Commercial versions of open source programs are also available. For instance, Linux is available in both commercial and free versions.

The use of open source software has been growing steadily. Over the past years, for instance, Linux has grown from an operating system used primarily by computer techies who disliked Microsoft to a widely accepted operating system with strong support from mainstream companies, such as IBM, HP, Dell, and Novell. For instance, many large companies, including Charles Schwab & Co, use Linux to run their data centers; the city of Munich, Germany has switched to Linux; and several large cities in Brazil are running only Linux software. One reason individuals and organizations are switching to Linux and other open source software is cost. Typically, using the Linux operating system and a free or low-cost office suite, Web browser program, and e-mail program can enable a business to work competitively while at the same time saving several hundreds of dollars per computer user. Other reasons some companies are moving to Linux include dissatisfaction with Microsoft products, the need for only a limited number of specialized applications (such as retail store computers that are set up to do a limited number of tasks), and the ability to modify the software to customize it for particular applications or to correct problems as they arise.

If open source use continues to grow as expected, it will impact software as we know if today. Will the growth force existing commercial software companies to streamline their development process in order to cut costs to better compete with open source products? Or will they feel the need to produce products that are better and more reliable than open source competitors? Or will commercial software companies simply go out of business?

YOUR TURN

Give some thought to the potential impact on the software industry in the next few years if the open source software trend continues and form an opinion on this issue. Consider the following when forming your opinion and be prepared to discuss your position (in class, via an online class discussion group, in a class chat room, or via a class blog) or to write a short paper expressing your opinion, depending on your instructor's directions.

- Do you think open source software will have a positive or negative impact on the quality of software? Why or why not?
- Would commercial software manufacturers be justified in raising prices to make up for revenue lost to open source competitors? Do you think that strategy would be effective?
- Would you prefer to use open source software or commercial software? Why?
- Products based on open source code can be sold as commercial products after they have been modified. Is that fair to commercial software vendors? Why or why not?

PROJECTS

1. **Natural Input** As pen and voice input technologies continue to improve, these types of more natural input methods are increasingly being supported by software programs.

   For this project, research either pen input or voice input and its use in conjunction with application software. How frequently is it used today with desktop computers? Select one office application program (such as a word processor or spreadsheet program) and determine what hardware or software is needed to use your selected method of input. What are the advantages of your selected method of input? The disadvantages? Would you prefer to use a keyboard and mouse or your selected method of input with this program? Explain. At the conclusion of your research, prepare a one- to two-page summary of your findings and submit it to your instructor.

HOT TOPICS

2. **Adding Memory** Adding additional RAM to a PC is one of the most common computer upgrades. Before purchasing additional memory, however, it is important to make sure that the purchased memory is compatible with the PC.

   For this project, select a computer (such as your own PC, a school PC, or a PC at a local store) and then determine (by looking at the PC or asking an appropriate individual—such as a lab aide in the school computer lab or a salesperson at the local store) the following: manufacturer and model number, CPU, current amount of memory, total memory slots, and the number of available memory slots. (If you look inside the PC, be sure to unplug the power cord first and do not touch any components inside the system unit.) Once you have the necessary information, call a local store or use your information and a memory supplier's Web site to determine the appropriate type of memory needed for your selected PC. What choices do you have in terms of capacity and configuration? Can you add just one memory module, or do you have to add memory in pairs? Can you keep the old memory modules, or do they have to be removed? At the conclusion of your research, prepare a one-page summary of your findings and submit it to your instructor.

**SHORT ANSWER/
RESEARCH**

3. **File Practice** As discussed in the chapter, file management programs, such as Windows Explorer, can be used to perform file management tasks.

   For this project, obtain a removable storage medium (such as a floppy disk or USB flash drive) appropriate for a computer you have access to and perform the following tasks.
   a. Open the file management program and select the icon representing the storage medium you are using to display its content. Are there any files on the storage medium? How much room is available on the storage medium?
   b. Open any word processing program available on your PC (such as Word or Notepad). Create a new document consisting of just your name, then save the document onto your storage medium (be sure to change the save location to the appropriate drive and use an appropriate filename). In the file management program, view the content of your storage medium to see the new document. What is the file size and how much room is now left on your storage medium?
   c. Prepare a short summary of your work to submit to your instructor, listing the software programs and storage medium used, the name and size of the file, and the amount of space left on your storage medium once the file was stored on it.
   d. Return to your file management program and delete the file from your storage medium.

HANDS ON

WRITING ABOUT COMPUTERS

4. Unwired Home networks—particularly wireless home networks—are becoming very common today.

For this project, suppose that you have a home desktop computer and are planning to buy a notebook computer to use at home, as well as on the go, and you would like to network the two PCs wirelessly. Determine the hardware you will need to accomplish this. Create a labeled sketch of the network and a list of the hardware you would need to acquire. Next, research the approximate cost of the hardware to determine the overall cost of the network. Does the cost seem reasonable for the benefits? Would you want to network your home PCs in this manner? Would you need any additional hardware if you wanted to also use a printer with both PCs? What security precautions, if any, would you need to implement? At the conclusion of your research, prepare a short essay (not more than two pages in length) explaining the issues involved with creating a wireless network and submit it to your instructor, along with your sketch and list of hardware.

PRESENTATION/ DEMONSTRATION

5. Flash Cards There are a wide variety of flash memory cards available today and they can be used with a variety of devices.

For this project, research the various uses for flash memory cards today. Find at least two examples of flash memory products in each of the following three categories: user storage, software, and an interface for a peripheral device. Share your findings with the class in the form of a short presentation, including the products that you found and their specifications, as well as your opinion regarding the flash card market in the future. Be sure to include any current or potential application you find in your research in addition to the three categories listed here. The presentation should not exceed 10 minutes and should make use of one or more presentation aids, such as the chalkboard, handouts, overhead transparencies, or a computer-based slide presentation (your instructor may provide additional requirements). You may also be asked to submit a summary of the presentation to your instructor.

GROUP DISCUSSION

6. Biometrics and Personal Privacy Biometric input devices, such as fingerprint readers and iris scanners, are increasingly being used for security purposes, such as to clock in and out of work, or to obtain access to locked facilities, a computer, or a computer network. Other uses of biometric technology are more voluntary, such as expedited airport-screening programs used by some frequent travelers and the fingerprint payment systems used at some retail stores. While viewed as a time-saving tool by some, other individuals may object to their biometric characteristics being stored in a database for this purpose. Is convenience worth compromising some personal privacy? What about national security? Would you be willing to sign up for a voluntary program, such as an airport-screening system or a fingerprint payment system, that relies on biometric data? Would you work at a job that required you to use a biometric input device on a regular basis? Do you think a national ID card containing hard-to-forge biometric data could help prevent terrorist attacks, such as the September 11, 2001 attacks? If so, do you think most Americans would support its use?

For this project, form an opinion of the use of biometric input devices and any potential impact their use may have on personal privacy. Be sure to consider the questions mentioned in the previous paragraph and be prepared to discuss your position (in class, via an online class discussion group, in a class chat room, or via a class blog, depending on your instructor's directions). You may also be asked to write a short paper expressing your opinion.

7. **Lost and Found** Portable computers, mobile phones, USB flash drives, and other portable devices are lost all the time today. They can be dropped out of a pocket or bag, inadvertently left on a table, and so forth. If the owner has identifying information (name, phone number, or e-mail address, for instance) printed on the device, the individual who finds the device can attempt to return it to the owner. But what if there is no identifying information clearly visible on the device? Should the finder look at the contents of the device to try to determine the owner? If the device is lost in a location where there is a responsible party (such as an airplane or a restaurant) the finder can turn over the device to that authority (such as a flight attendant or manager), but is it ethical for the responsible party to look at the contents in order to identify the owner? If you lost a device, would you want someone to look at the contents to try to determine your identity? Why or why not? Is looking at the contents on a found device ever ethical? Should it be illegal?

For this project, form an opinion about the ethical ramifications of lost devices and be prepared to discuss your position (in class, via an online class discussion group, in a class chat room, or via a class blog, depending on your instructor's directions). You may also be asked to write a short paper expressing your opinion.

ETHICS IN ACTION

8. **Internet Intrusions** The high numbers of unsecured wireless home and business networks in existence today can results in more than just someone borrowing your Internet connection. As discussed in the accompanying video clip, it can allow individuals access to your personal information, as well as carry out Internet activities that appear to be performed by you.

Go to www.course.com/uccs/ch2 to watch the "Internet Intrusions Could Lead to I.D. Theft" video clip. After watching the video, think about the impact of leaving your wireless network unsecured. In addition to the risk of having your personal information stolen (and perhaps used in identity theft or other illegal activities), you also risk being framed for illegal activities by hackers performing activities using your Internet connection. If you leave your wireless network unsecured, should you be held responsible for any activities performed via that connection? Should networking hardware manufacturers be required to enable encryption and other security measures on networking hardware by default? Who is responsible for preventing crimes carried out via wireless networks? Should using someone else's Internet connection via his or her unsecured network be illegal, regardless of the activities performed?

Express your viewpoint: What is the impact of unsecured wireless networks on our society today?

Use the video clip and the questions previously asked as a foundation for your response. Be prepared to discuss your position (in class, via an online class discussion group, in a class chat room, or via a class blog) or to write a short paper stating and supporting your viewpoint on the issue, depending on your instructor's direction. You may also be asked to do research and provide resources to support your point of view on this issue.

VIDEO VIEWPOINT

9. **Interactive Activities** Go to www.course.com/uccs/ch2 and work the interactive **Crossword Puzzle**, listen to the **Podcasts** and watch the **Online Videos** associated with this chapter, and explore the **Further Exploration** links. In addition, work the following interactive **Student Edition Labs**.

- Binary Numbers
- Peripheral Devices
- Understanding the Motherboard
- Managing Files and Folders
- Using Input Devices

If you have a SAM user profile, you have access to even more interactive content. Log in to your SAM account and go to your assignments page to see what your instructor has assigned for this chapter.

WEB ACTIVITIES

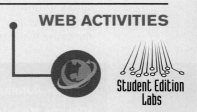

Student Edition Labs

10. **Test Yourself** Go to www.course.com/uccs/ch2 and review the **Online Study Guide** for Chapter 2, then test your knowledge of the terms and concepts in this chapter by completing the **Key Term Matching** exercise, the **Self-Quiz**, the **Exercises**, and the **Practice Test**.

My Background . . .

I studied engineering since I have always enjoyed solving problems. I got fascinated by the creativity in building electronic/computing devices and pursued graduate studies in computer science to prepare for a career in this field. I now lead a team researching how the next generation of servers must be architected and managed. My primary responsibility is to create a future where the architecture and management of servers enable a range of applications (e.g., digital movie rendering, searching the Web, and voice-over-IP) to be performed much more reliably, efficiently, and easily.

> **"Students in all fields should become computer-literate and keep abreast of developments in the field of computing."**

It's Important to Know . . .

Basic computer concepts. Whether it is a laptop, iPod, or digital camera, the hardware components are essentially the same: processors that execute instructions provided by the programmer; storage such as disks or flash memory which maintain all permanent data; memory and caches which temporarily store instructions and data close to the processor; and peripherals, such as wireless interfaces and displays, to interact with the user and the environment. All computer users should be aware of these concepts.

Computer designers are focused on building products that are environmentally-responsible and easy-to-use for non-technical people these days. Their designs increasingly focus on non-performance objectives such as lowering energy consumption, improving reliability, and improving usability. The industry is also envisioning new ways of using processors to improve the way we live. Computers can be embedded in medicines for health applications, in the environment for ecological applications, and so on.

Computing appliances must be able to interact with each other. For instance, a PDA must be able to communicate with a PC. So, computer hardware and software vendors must actively develop standards in every aspect of computing so that computers can work together. Creating standards while simultaneously building unique products is an important business challenge for the computer industry.

How I Use this Technology . . .

I use my computers at home to interact with family and friends (e.g., through e-mail and VoIP phone calls), to follow news, to shop and pay bills, to work from home, and to maintain my personal content (e.g., photos and financial documents). I maintain a wireless network which allows me to roam around the house while still being connected to the Internet through my broadband provider. I use my cell phone

John Janakiraman is currently the Research Manager for the Data Center Architecture group at HP Labs. He is leading research on the architecture and management of the server infrastructure in data centers, where his team is researching virtualization and automation techniques to improve the efficiency, reliability, and manageability of data centers. He and his team have developed many technologies that have influenced HP products, industry standards, and open-source community projects. John has a Ph.D. in Computer Science.

Advances in computer hardware will enable pervasive wireless connectivity, permit more of the human experience to be captured in digital form, and provide richer entertainment.

almost like a Swiss army knife—to take impromptu photos and videos of my family and share them with others, to exchange e-mail, to keep track of time and raise reminders/alarms, etc. I use a photo-quality printer to print photos and other documents. Like other individuals, I also invisibly use computers integrated into devices, such as in cars and in the garden sprinkler system.

What the Future Holds . . .

Computer hardware will decrease in cost while becoming more powerful, compact, and energy-efficient. Advances in computer hardware will enable pervasive wireless connectivity, permit more of the human experience to be captured in digital form, and provide richer entertainment. Computers will get woven, invisibly in many cases, into many more aspects of life, such as in maintaining a healthy lifestyle, education, the environment, and government services.

Future advances in hardware technology and their decreasing costs can have a beneficial impact on society in many ways, such as to improve the quality of personal life, improve economic opportunity in developing regions, and improve environment management. Technology also imposes some societal responsibilities, such as the appropriate handling of used computer parts (e.g., recycling) so that they do not contaminate the environment.

My Advice to Students . . .

A career in the intersection between technology and some other field (as diverse as, for example, medicine, library management, or geology) can give you an edge. Getting real-world experience through internships in related jobs is also key. To rise to a position of leadership, solid verbal and written communication skills and the ability to influence people's thinking are also critical.

Students in all fields should become computer-literate and keep abreast of developments in the field of computing. This knowledge can enable them to use computing to advance their field by conceiving new solutions and tools. It will also equip them to reason about the risks and rewards of specific computing applications and to influence the development of governance policies.

Discussion Question

John Janakiraman views the appropriate handling of used computer parts so that they do not contaminate the environment as one of the responsibilities involved with the use of technology. Think about all of the computing refuse you create—such as old printouts, depleted toner cartridges, broken hardware, and so forth. What do you feel is your responsibility for making sure this refuse is disposed of properly? Does the manufacturer share any of that responsibility? Some states—such as California—charge a recycling fee on some hardware, such as computer monitors, to help pay for the cost of properly disposing of that hardware. Do you agree with this trend? What should individuals be required to do to help alleviate the computing refuse problem? Is there a long-term solution to this problem? Be prepared to discuss your position (in class, via an online class discussion group, in a class chat room, or via a class blog, depending on your instructor's directions). You may also be asked to write a short paper expressing your opinion.

>**For more information on HP, visit www.hp.com. For more information on HP Labs, visit www.hpl.hp.com. Some good industry association references are www.acm.org and www.ieee.org.**

3
CHAPTER

The Internet and World Wide Web

OUTLINE

LEARNING OBJECTIVES

After completing this chapter, you will be able to do the following:

1. Discuss how the Internet evolved and what it is like today.

2. Identify the various types of individuals, companies, and organizations involved in the Internet community and explain their purposes.

3. Describe device and connection options for connecting to the Internet, as well as some considerations to keep in mind when selecting an ISP.

4. Understand how to effectively search for information on the Internet and how to properly cite Internet resources.

5. List several useful things that can be done using the Internet, in addition to basic Web browsing and e-mail.

6. Discuss censorship and privacy, and how they are related to Internet use.

OVERVIEW

It is hard to believe that before 1990 few people outside the computer industry and academia had ever heard of the Internet, and even fewer had used it. Why? Because the hardware, software, and communications tools needed to unleash the power of the Internet as we know it today were not available then. In fact, it is only recently that technology has evolved enough to allow multimedia applications—such as downloading music and movies, watching TV and videos online, and playing multimedia interactive games—to become everyday activities. Today, the Internet and the World Wide Web are household words, and in many ways they have redefined how people think about computers and communications.

Despite the popularity of the Internet, however, many users cannot answer some important basic questions about it. What makes up the Internet? Is it the same thing as the World Wide Web? How did the Internet begin, and where is it heading? What types of tools are available to help people make optimal use of the Internet? How can the Internet be used to find specific information? This chapter addresses these types of questions and more.

Chapter 3 begins with a discussion of the evolution of the Internet, from the late 1960s to the present, followed by a look at the many individuals, companies, and organizations that make up the Internet community. Next, the chapter covers different options for connecting to the Internet, including types of Internet access devices, Internet connections, and ISPs available today. Then, it is on to one of the most important Internet skills you should acquire—efficient Internet searching. To help you appreciate the wide spectrum of resources and activities available through the Internet, we also take a brief look at some of the most common applications available via the Internet. The final sections of the chapter discuss a few of the important societal issues that apply to Internet use. ∎

PODCAST

Go to **www.course.com/uccs/ch3** to download or listen to the "Expert Insight on Software" podcast.

EVOLUTION OF THE INTERNET

The **Internet** is a worldwide collection of separate, but interconnected, networks that are used daily by millions of people to obtain information, disseminate information, access entertainment, or communicate with others. Just as the shipping industry has simplified transportation by providing standard containers for carrying all sorts of merchandise via air, rail, highway, and sea, the Internet furnishes a standard way of sending messages and information across virtually any type of computer platform and transmission media. While *Internet* has become a household word only during the past two decades or so, it has actually operated in one form or another for much longer than that.

>**Internet.** The largest and most well-known computer network, linking millions of computers all over the world.

From ARPANET to Internet2

The roots of the Internet began with an experimental project called *ARPANET*. The Internet we know today is the result of the evolution of ARPANET and the creation of the *World Wide Web*. For a look at a new issue surrounding the Internet—*net neutrality*—see the Inside the Industry box.

ARPANET

ARPANET was created in 1969 by the U.S. Department of Defense *Advanced Research Projects Agency (ARPA)*. One objective of the ARPANET project was to create a computer network that would allow researchers located in different places to communicate with each other. Another objective was to build a computer network capable of sending or receiving data over a variety of paths to ensure that network communications could continue even if part of the network was destroyed, such as in a nuclear attack or by a natural disaster.

Initially, ARPANET connected four supercomputers. As it grew during its first few years, ARPANET enabled researchers at a few dozen academic institutions to communicate with each other and with government agencies on topics of mutual interest. However, with the highly controversial Vietnam War in full swing, e-mail sent via ARPANET began to include not only legitimate research discussions, but also heated debates about United States involvement in Southeast Asia. Students were granted access to ARPANET, and then other unintended uses—such as playing computer games—began.

As the project grew during the next decade, hundreds of college and university networks were connected to ARPANET. These local area networks consisted of a mixture of PC-compatible computers, Apple Macintosh computers, and workstations running a variety of operating systems. Over the years, protocols were developed for tying this mix of computers and networks together, for transferring data over the network, and for ensuring that data was transferred intact. Other networks soon connected to ARPANET, and this *internet*—or network of networks—eventually evolved into the present day *Internet*.

The Internet infrastructure today can be used for a variety of purposes, such as researching topics of interest; exchanging e-mail and instant messages; participating in discussion groups, chat sessions, and videoconferences; making telephone calls; downloading software, music, and movies; purchasing goods and services; watching online TV and video; getting a wide variety of news and information; accessing computers remotely; and sharing files with others. One of the most widely used Internet resources is the *World Wide Web*.

The World Wide Web

In its early years, the Internet was used primarily by the government, scientists, and educational institutions. Despite its popularity in academia and with government researchers, the Internet went virtually unnoticed by the general public and the business community for over two decades because it required a computer and it was hard to use (see the left image in Figure 3-1). As always, however, technology improved and new applications quickly followed. First, communications hardware improved, and then computers gained speed and better graphics capabilities. Then, in 1989, a researcher named *Tim Berners-Lee* proposed the idea of the **World Wide Web** while working at *CERN* (a physics laboratory in Europe). He envisioned the World Wide Web as a way to organize information in the form of pages linked together through selectable text or images (today's hyperlinks) on the screen. Although the introduction of Web pages did not replace all other Internet resources (such as e-mail and collections of downloadable files), it became a popular way for researchers to provide written information to others.

>**ARPANET.** The predecessor of the Internet, named after the Advanced Research Projects Agency (ARPA), which sponsored its development.
>**World Wide Web.** The collection of Web pages available through the Internet.

INSIDE THE INDUSTRY

Net Neutrality

The term "net neutrality" refers to the equality of data as it is transferred over the Internet. That is, whether the data is a video clip, podcast, Web page, or phone call, and whether the data is coming from your house or Microsoft headquarters, the data is treated the same. This equal treatment of data allows a level playing field for all individuals and businesses that have content on the Web. In other words, everyone has the same potential audience as everyone else. The concept isn't new—it's the way the Internet and World Wide Web were developed—but what is new is that some telecommunications and cable companies have indicated that they want to provide higher speeds over their infrastructure for large companies that can afford to pay premium prices for that privilege. Since telecomm and cable companies provide the vast majority of high-speed Internet to consumers, this premium pricing plan would essentially separate the Internet into two paths: a free lane and an express, premium lane.

Critics argue that startup companies like *YouTube* would never have gotten the audiences they have today if their content—in the case of YouTube, videos—ran slower than competitors. Critics also argue that allowing net neutrality to end would bring an end to the Internet innovations that we see now. They also fear that ending net neutrality would lead to telecomm and cable companies blocking selected traffic—such as blocking VoIP or video services from competing companies. Proponents argue that network operators need a reasonable opportunity to recoup the cost of their infrastructure. Legislation has been proposed to preserve net neutrality, but some experts believe that legislating against something that hasn't happened yet isn't necessary. Nevertheless, there are a variety of organizations (one example is shown in the accompanying figure) committed to ensuring net neutrality remains a reality.

Things really got rolling with the arrival of the *graphical user interface*. In 1993, a group of professors and students at the University of Illinois *National Center for Supercomputing Applications* (*NCSA*) released *Mosaic*, the first graphically based Web browser. Mosaic used a graphical user interface and allowed Web pages to include graphical images in addition to text. Soon after, use of the World Wide Web began to increase dramatically because the graphical interface and graphical Web pages made using the World Wide Web both easier and more fun than in the past. Today's Web pages are a true multimedia experience (see the right image in Figure 3-1). They can contain text, graphics, animation, sound, video, and three-dimensional virtual reality objects.

Although the Web is only part of the Internet, it is by far one of the most popular and one of the fastest-growing

FIGURE 3-1

Using the Internet: Back in the "old days" versus now.

EARLY 1990s
Even at the beginning of the 1990s, using the Internet for most people meant learning how to work with a cryptic sequence of commands. Virtually all information was text-based.

TODAY
Today's Web organizes much of the Internet's content into easy-to-read pages that can contain text, graphics, animation, and more. Instead of typing cryptic commands to access information, users click hyperlinks.

ASK THE EXPERT

Carmen Bolanos, Co-Founder, NuNomad Ventures

Is it possible for a recent college graduate to become a "nu nomad"—an individual who works via the Internet while traveling and living abroad—without first having a conventional job?

I think the challenges of becoming a Nu Nomad would be the same for college graduates as they would be for anyone. The biggest challenge is finding the career that will allow you to work completely remotely. If you can find that sort of career, then a college grad can be a Nu Nomad as well as anyone else. In fact, college age students have an advantage because they can take courses in preparation for such a career and embark on it before they are burdened with mortgages or debts, or have family obligations. At that point, it can be more complicated to adopt a nomadic lifestyle.

However, a recent college graduate with no track record will need stronger communication skills than usual in order to be able to effectively communicate with employers (and prospective employers) virtually and will need to be open to net internships where they may be working for free or for a stipend.

parts. As interest in the Internet grew, companies began looking for ways to make it more accessible to customers, to make the user interface needed to access the Internet more functional, and to make more services available. Today, most companies regard their use of the Internet and their World Wide Web presence as indispensable competitive business tools. Many individuals view the Internet, and especially the Web, as a vital research, communications, and entertainment medium.

One remarkable characteristic of both the Internet and World Wide Web is that they are not owned by any person or business, and no single person, business, or organization is in charge. Web pages are developed by individuals and organizations, and they are hosted on Web servers owned by individuals, schools, businesses, or other entities. PCs and other devices used to access the Internet typically belong to individuals, organizations, or public facilities. Each network connected to the Internet is owned and managed individually by that network's administrator, and the primary infrastructure that makes up the *Internet backbone* is typically owned by telecommunications companies, such as telephone and cable companies. So, while individual components of the Internet are owned by individuals and organizations, the Internet as a whole has no owner or network administrator. The closest the Internet comes to having a governing body is the group of organizations—such as the *Internet Society* (*ISOC*), *Internet Corporation for Assigned Names and Numbers* (*ICANN*), and the *World Wide Web Consortium* (*W3C*)—committed to overseeing it. These organizations are involved with issues such as establishing the protocols used on the Internet, making recommendations for changes, and encouraging cooperation between and coordinating communications among the networks connected to the Internet.

Internet2

The next significant improvements to the Internet infrastructure might be a result of *Internet2*, a consortium of over 200 universities working together with industry and the government. Internet2 was created to develop and implement advanced Internet applications and technologies, which may lead to improvements for tomorrow's Internet. A new faster Internet2 network with an overall speed of 100 Gbps was recently implemented in order to better serve the evolving needs of the research and education community. However, one of the primary goals of the Internet2 project is to ensure that new network services and applications are quickly applied to the broader Internet community, not just to the Internet2 participants. Although Internet2 is a separate physical network from the Internet, it is important to realize that Internet2 does not refer to a new network that will eventually replace the Internet—it is simply a research and development project geared toward developing technology to ensure that the Internet in the future can handle tomorrow's applications. For that reason, much of Internet2 research is focused on speed. For instance, the *Internet2 Land Speed Record* is an ongoing contest for the highest-bandwidth end-to-end network. The current record is an average speed of 9.08 Gbps sustained for about 30 minutes in order to transfer 585 GB of data across about 20,000 miles of network.

The Internet Community Today

The Internet community today consists of individuals, businesses, and a variety of organizations located throughout the world. Virtually anyone with a computer or other Web-enabled device can be part of the Internet, either as a user or as a supplier of information or services. Most members of the Internet community fall into one or more of the following groups.

Users

Users are people who use the Internet to retrieve content or perform online activities, such as to look up a telephone number, read the day's news headlines or top stories, browse through an online catalog, make an online purchase, download a music file, watch an online video, make a phone call, or send an e-mail message. According to the Pew Internet & American Life Project, nearly 75% of the United States population are Internet users, using the Internet at work, home, school, or another location. Free Internet access at libraries, school, and other public locations, as well as the availability of low-cost PCs and low-cost or free Internet access in many areas today, has helped Internet use begin to approach the popularity and widespread use of telephones and TVs.

Internet Service Providers (ISPs)

Internet service providers (ISPs) are businesses or other organizations that provide Internet access to others, typically for a fee. As shown in Figure 3-2, a variety of communications and media companies—such as conventional and wireless telephone companies, as well as cable and satellite providers—offer Internet service over their respective media. In addition, a variety of other ISPs provide services over existing communications media. Some ISPs, such as Road Runner and America Online, provide service nationwide; others provide service to a more limited geographical area. In either case, ISPs are the onramp to the Internet, providing their subscribers with access to the World Wide Web, e-mail, and other Internet resources. In addition to Internet access, some ISPs provide proprietary online services available only to their subscribers. A later section of this chapter covers ISPs in more detail, including factors to consider when selecting an ISP.

COMMUNICATIONS COMPANIES

CABLE AND SATELLITE COMPANIES

REGIONAL AND NATIONAL ISPS

FIGURE 3-2
ISPs today include a variety of communications companies, in addition to regional and national ISPs.

Internet Content Providers

Internet content providers supply the information that is available through the Internet. Internet content providers can be commercial businesses, nonprofit organizations, educational institutions, individuals, and more. Some examples of Internet content providers are listed next.

- ► A photographer who posts samples of her best work on a Web page.

- ► A political action group that sponsors an online forum for discussions about topics that interest its members.

- ► An individual who publishes his opinion on various subjects to an online journal or *blog*.

>**Internet service provider (ISP).** A business or other organization that provides Internet access to others, typically for a fee. >**Internet content provider.** A person or an organization that provides Internet content.

▶ A software company that creates a Web site to provide product information and software downloads.

▶ A national newspaper that maintains an online site to provide up-to-the-minute news, feature stories, and video clips.

▶ A television network that develops a site for its TV shows, including episode summaries and links to watch past episodes online.

▶ A music publisher that creates a site to provide song demos and to sell downloads of its artists' songs and albums.

▶ A film student who releases her original short movie to be viewed on the Web.

Application Service Providers (ASPs) and Web Services

Application service providers (**ASPs**) are companies that manage and distribute software-based services to customers over the Internet. Instead of providing access to the Internet like ISPs do, ASPs provide access to software applications via the Internet. In essence, ASPs rent access to software programs to companies or individuals—typically, customers pay a monthly or yearly fee to use each application. The advantages to using an ASP over buying software outright include less up-front cost and the ability to try out a software program without potentially wasting money purchasing software that might not fit the customer's needs. In addition, all users see the most up-to-date software each time they use the application, since the software is located on the ASP's server and can be updated as needed. Free or low-cost technical support and training may also be available from the ASP which, combined with the fact that the software is not installed on user PCs, may result in a computer support savings for the customer utilizing the ASP service.

FIGURE 3-3

Web services.

Once downloaded and installed, this Web service allows users to send documents to a FedEx Kinko's location from within their software programs.

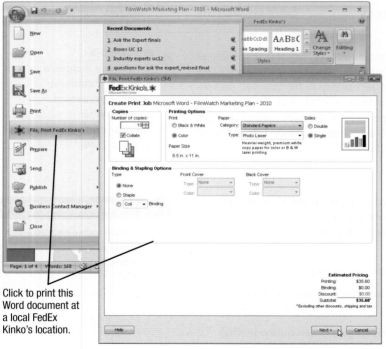

Click to print this Word document at a local FedEx Kinko's location.

Common ASP applications for businesses include office suites, collaboration and communications software, accounting programs, and e-commerce software. Some industry experts—such as the CEOs of Sun Microsystems and Microsoft—predict that within a relatively short period of time, software purchasing as we know it today will not exist. Instead, they believe software will be delivered as a service, and the option to purchase software outright might not exist.

One type of self-contained business application designed to work over the Internet or a company network is a **Web service**. Web services can be added to Web pages to provide specific services for end users. For example, Web services can be used to facilitate communications between suppliers and customers or to provide a service via a Web site that was otherwise not feasible (such as the inclusion of mapping information on a Web site or in a Web application using Microsoft's MapPoint .NET Web service). Web services can also add functionality to the end user via the Internet, such as the *File, Print FedEx Kinko's* (see Figure 3-3) Web service that

---

>**Application service provider (ASP).** A company that manages and distributes software-based services over the Internet. >**Web service.** A self-contained business application that operates over the Internet.

allows users to send documents to a FedEx Kinko's location to be printed and then either shipped or held for pickup using just their application's Print menu. Web services themselves do not have a user interface—they are simply a standardized way of allowing different applications and computers to share data and processes via a network. To do this, Web services use specific standards for transferring data so that they can work together with other Web services and be used with many different computer systems. A company that provides Web services is sometimes referred to as a *Web services provider*.

Infrastructure Companies

Infrastructure companies are the enterprises that own or operate the paths or "roadways" along which Internet data travels, such as the Internet backbone and the communications networks connected to it. Examples of infrastructure companies include conventional and wireless telephone companies, cable companies, and satellite Internet providers.

Hardware and Software Companies

A wide variety of hardware and software companies make and distribute the products used with the Internet and Internet activities. For example, companies that create or sell the software used in conjunction with the Internet (such as Web browsers, e-mail programs, e-commerce and multimedia software, and Web development tools) fall into this category. So, too, do the companies that make the hardware (modems, cables, routers, servers, PCs, and smart phones, for instance) that is used in conjunction with the Internet.

The Government and Other Organizations

Many organizations influence the Internet and its uses. Governments have the most visible impact; their laws can limit both the information made available via Web servers located in a particular country, as well as access to the Internet for individuals residing in that country. For example, in France it is illegal to sell items or post online content related to racist groups or activities and in China tight controls are imposed on what information is published on Web servers located in China, as well as on the information available to its citizens. In the United States, anything illegal offline (illegal drugs, child pornography, and so forth) is illegal online. In addition, rulings—such as the 1968 *Carterfone Decision* (that allowed companies other than AT&T to utilize the AT&T infrastructure), the 1996 *Telecommunications Act* (that deregulated the entire communications industry so that telephone companies, cable TV and satellite operators, and firms in other segments of the industry were free to enter each other's markets), and the recent ruling by the U.S. Supreme Court that cable companies will not have to share their infrastructure with competing Internet service providers—have had a large impact on the communications industry in general. Under consideration now by the Federal Communications Commission (FCC) is a petition to apply the Carterfone Decision to wireless networks to allow open access to wireless networks. In addition to making these types of decisions, the FCC also greatly influences the communications industry through its ability to allocate the radio frequencies used with wireless networks, radio and TV broadcasts, mobile phones, and other wireless applications, and to implement policies and regulations related to interstate and international communications via radio, television, wire, satellite, and cable. The ability of the government to block potential mergers between communications companies and to break apart companies based on antitrust law to prevent new monopolies also impacts the Internet and communications industry.

Key Internet organizations are responsible for many aspects of the Internet. For example, the *Internet Society* (*ISOC*) provides leadership in addressing issues that confront the future of the Internet. It also oversees the groups responsible for Internet infrastructure standards, such as determining the protocols that can be used and how Internet addresses are constructed. *ICANN* (*Internet Corporation for Assigned Names and Numbers*) is charged with responsibilities such as IP address allocation and domain name management. The *World Wide Web Consortium* (*W3C*) is a group of over 450 organizations dedicated to developing new protocols and specifications to promote the evolution of the Web and to ensure its interoperability. In addition, many colleges and universities support Internet research and manage blocks of the Internet's resources.

Myths About the Internet

Because the Internet is so unique in the history of the world—and its content and applications keep evolving—several widespread myths about it have surfaced.

Myth 1: The Internet Is Free

This myth stems from the fact that there has traditionally been no cost associated with online content—such as news and product information—or e-mail exchange, other than what the Internet users pay their ISPs for Internet access. And many people—such as students, employees, and consumers who opt for free Internet service or use free access available at public libraries or other public locations—pay nothing for Internet access. Yet it should also be obvious that someone, somewhere, has to pay to keep the Internet up and running.

Businesses, schools, public libraries, and most home users pay Internet service providers flat monthly fees to connect to the Internet; businesses, schools, libraries, and other large organizations might have to lease high-capacity communications lines (such as from a telephone company) to support their high level of Internet traffic. Mobile users that want to access Internet content typically pay hotspot providers or mobile phone providers for Internet access. ISPs, phone companies, cable companies, and other organizations that own part of the Internet infrastructure pay to keep their respective physical parts of the Internet running smoothly. ISPs also pay software and hardware companies for the resources they need to support their subscribers. Eventually, most of these costs are passed along to end users through ISP fees. ISPs that offer free Internet access typically obtain revenue by selling onscreen ads that display on the screen when the service is being used.

Another reason that the idea the Internet is free is a myth is the growing trend of subscription or per-use fees to access resources—such as journal or newspaper articles, music, movies, and games—via the Internet. For some content, such as viewing online articles, the fees are relatively small, and many companies are working on ways to make the processing of small fees (sometimes called *micropayments*) practical, such as allowing individuals to buy virtual money via a credit card and then spend that money as needed (such as ten cents to read a Web article) on participating Web sites. In lieu of a mandatory fee, some sites request donations for use of the site (see Figure 3-4). Many experts expect the use of fee-based Internet content to continue to grow at a rapid pace.

Myth 2: Someone Controls the Internet

The popularity of conspiracy theories in past years has contributed to the spread of this myth. In fact, as already discussed, no single group or organization controls the Internet. Governments in each country have the power to regulate the content and use of the Internet within their borders, as allowed by their laws. However, legislators often face serious obstacles getting legislation passed into law—let alone getting it enforced. Making governmental control even harder is the "bombproof" design of the Internet itself. If a government tries to block access to or from a specific country, for example, users can establish links between the two countries through a third country.

**V FIGURE 3-4
Fee-based Web content.** Both required fees and requested donations for accessing Web content are becoming common.

REQUIRED FEE
A subscription is required to view articles on this site.

REQUESTED DONATION
A donation is requested for using this site.

Myth 3: The Internet and World Wide Web Are Identical

Since you can now use a Web browser to access most of the Internet's resources, many people think the Internet and the Web are the same thing. Even though in everyday use many people use the terms *Internet* and *Web* interchangeably, they are not the same thing. Technically, the Internet is the physical network, and the Web is the collection of Web pages accessible over the Internet. A majority of Internet activities today take place via Web pages, but there are Internet resources other than the Web. For instance, *FTP (File Transfer Protocol)* is a protocol different from the HTTP protocol used to view Web pages. FTP is a common means of uploading files to or downloading files from an *FTP server*—a server set up by a business specifically to host files others might need to access. FTP access can be open to anyone (such as to allow the general public to download software updates or trial programs) or it can be password protected (such as to allow only authorized employees or partners access to company files). While FTP can be performed via a Web browser (by using the *ftp://* protocol indicator instead of *http://* followed by the name of the FTP server), it is more often performed using a stand-alone *FTP program*, such as the one shown in Figure 3-5.

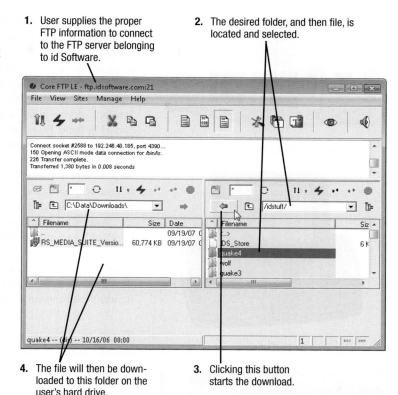

1. User supplies the proper FTP information to connect to the FTP server belonging to id Software.

2. The desired folder, and then file, is located and selected.

4. The file will then be downloaded to this folder on the user's hard drive.

3. Clicking this button starts the download.

FIGURE 3-5

FTP. An FTP program, such as the one shown here, can be used to upload or download files to or from an FTP server.

GETTING SET UP TO USE THE INTERNET

Getting set up to use the Internet typically involves three decisions—determining the type of device you will use to access the Internet, selecting the type of connection desired, and deciding on the Internet service provider to be used. Once these determinations have been made, your computer can be set up to access the Internet.

Type of Device

The Internet today can be accessed using a variety of devices. The type of device used depends on a combination of factors, such as the devices available to you, if you need access just at home or while on the go, and what types of Internet content you want to access. Some possible devices are shown in Figure 3-6 and discussed next.

Desktop, Notebook, or Tablet PCs

Most users who have access to a desktop (see Figure 3-6), notebook, or tablet PC at home, work, or school will use it to access the Internet. One advantage of using PCs for Internet access is that they have large screens and can be connected to high-speed Internet connections. They also can be used to view or otherwise access virtually any Web page content, such as graphics, animation, music files, games, and video clips. In addition, they usually have a large hard drive and are connected to a printer so Web pages, e-mail messages, and downloaded files can be easily saved and/or printed.

Internet Appliances, Mobile Devices, and Gaming Devices

Internet appliances (devices that are designed specifically for accessing the Internet) are sometimes used in homes that do not have a PC. These devices are typically very easy to

DESKTOP, NOTEBOOK, OR TABLET PC

MOBILE DEVICE

GAMING CONSOLE

FIGURE 3-6
A variety of devices can be used to access the Internet.

FIGURE 3-7
Length of time to download a 1.5 GB movie using different home Internet options.

use and can access Web pages, e-mail, or both. Sometimes these devices incorporate other features, such as the ability to display live TV shows or play DVDs, and often take the form of an all-in-one device (designed to be located in a kitchen or other central location) or a set-top box (designed to be located near a living room TV). Most Internet appliances today have built-in storage and can be connected to a printer. Some require you to subscribe to a specific Internet service plan, in addition to purchasing the hardware.

Handheld PCs and mobile phones are also increasingly being used to view Web page content, exchange e-mail and instant messages, and download music and other online content. In fact, mobile Web use—or *wireless Web*, as it is frequently called—is one of the fastest growing uses of the Internet today. Some devices, such as the one shown in Figure 3-6, include a keyboard for easier data entry; others utilize pen or touch input instead.

Another option is using a gaming device (such as a gaming console or handheld gaming device) to access Web content, in addition to using that device to play games. For instance, the Sony PlayStation 3 (see Figure 3-6), Sony PSP, and Nintendo Wii all have built-in Web browsing capabilities, and the Nintendo DS has an optional *DS Browser* game cartridge that can be used to add Web browsing capabilities to that device.

Type of Connection and Internet Access

In order to use the Internet, your computer needs to be connected to it. Typically, this occurs by connecting your PC to another computer (usually belonging to an ISP, your school, or your employer) that is connected continually to the Internet. There are a variety of wired and wireless ways to connect to another computer. Some Internet connections are *dial-up connections*, meaning your PC dials up and connects to your ISP's computer only when needed. Other Internet connections are *direct* or *always-on connections*, meaning your computer is connected to your ISP whenever your computer is on. Direct Internet connections are typically *broadband* connections; that is, high-speed connections that allow more than one signal to be transferred over the transmission medium at one time. Therefore, direct Internet connections are much faster than dial-up connections. In theory, they can be up to 1,000 times faster than a dial-up connection, but actual speeds at the present time are closer to 25 to 150 times faster. This discrepancy is due to factors such as the speed of the device being used, the condition of the transmission media being used, and the amount of traffic currently using the same transmission medium and Web server.

Although dial-up Internet is still used in some homes, home broadband use is growing rapidly. More than half of all home Internet connections are now broadband connections, and that percentage is expected to climb to 75% by 2010. As applications requiring high-speed connections are continuing to grow in popularity, broadband Internet speeds are becoming more necessary. For instance, high-definition television, video-on-demand (VOD), and other multimedia applications (discussed shortly) all benefit from fast broadband connections (see Figure 3-7).

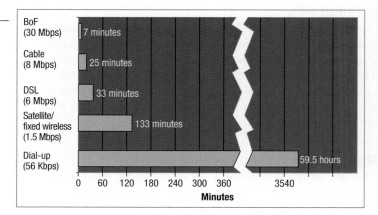

	Minutes
BoF (30 Mbps)	7 minutes
Cable (8 Mbps)	25 minutes
DSL (6 Mbps)	33 minutes
Satellite/fixed wireless (1.5 Mbps)	133 minutes
Dial-up (56 Kbps)	59.5 hours

0 60 120 180 240 300 360   3540
Minutes

TYPE OF INTERNET CONNECTION	DIAL-UP?	ALWAYS ON?	AVAILABILITY	APPROXIMATE MAXIMUM SPEED *	APPROXIMATE MONTHLY PRICE
Conventional dial-up	Yes	No	Anywhere there is telephone service	56 Kbps	Free–$20
Cable	No	Yes	Virtually anywhere cable TV service is available	6–8 Mbps	$40–55
DSL	No	Yes	Within 3 miles of a switching station that supports DSL	768 Kbps–6 Mbps	$15–35
Satellite	No	Yes	Anywhere there is a clear view to the southern sky and where a satellite dish can be mounted and receive a signal	512 Kbps–1.5 Mbps	$50–80
Fixed wireless	No	Yes	Mainly urban areas where service is available	768 Kbps–1.5 Mbps	$30–50
Broadband over fiber (BoF)	No	Yes	Anywhere fiber has been installed to the building	5–40 Mbps	$40–180
Mobile wireless	No	Yes	Anywhere cellular phone service is available	14.4 Kbps–4 Mbps	Varies greatly

* Download speed; most connections have slower upload speeds.

The basic types of Internet connections are discussed next, and the most common types of Internet connections used by individuals are summarized in Figure 3-8. Many providers today offer bundles (such as cable TV and Internet service, or telephone and Internet service) to lower an individual's overall total cost for the services.

FIGURE 3-8
Typical home Internet connection options.

Dial-Up Connections

Dial-up connections usually work over standard telephone lines. To connect to the Internet, your computer dials its modem and connects to a modem attached to a computer belonging to your ISP. While you are connected to your ISP, your PC can access Internet resources. To end your Internet session, you disconnect from your ISP. One advantage of a dial-up connection is security. Since you are not continually connected to the Internet, it is much less likely that anyone (such as a *hacker*, as discussed in Chapter 4) will gain access to your computer via the Internet, either to access the data located on your PC or, more commonly, to use your computer in some type of illegal or unethical manner.

However, dial-up connections are typically much slower than other types of connections. Another disadvantage of using a dial-up connection is the inconvenience of having to instruct your PC to dial up your ISP every time you want to check your e-mail or view a Web page. Also, your telephone line will be tied up while you are accessing the Internet, unless you have a second phone line or use an Internet call-waiting or call-forwarding service to notify you about incoming telephone calls while you are connected to the Internet. These services are generally set up to allow the person to leave a short message; some systems give you a short window of time to disconnect from the Internet and pick up the

>**Dial-up connection.** A type of Internet connection in which the PC or other device must dial up and connect to a service provider's computer via telephone lines before being connected to the Internet.

telephone call, if desired. The two most common forms of dial-up Internet service are *conventional dial-up* and *ISDN*.

Conventional Dial-Up

Conventional dial-up Internet access uses a *conventional dial-up modem* connected to a standard telephone jack with regular twisted-pair telephone cabling. Conventional dial-up Internet service is commonly used with home PCs and Internet appliances; it can also be used with notebook PCs or other portable devices, provided the device has a conventional dial-up modem. Conventional dial-up Internet access ranges from free to about $20 per month. Advantages include inexpensive hardware, ease of setup and use, and widespread availability. The primary disadvantage is slow connection speed.

Conventional dial-up connects to the Internet at a maximum of 56 *Kbps* (thousands of bits per second), although some ISPs offer what they call *high-speed dial-up access*. Even though the connection speed is still a maximum of 56 Kbps, high-speed dial-up uses *caching*—saving Web page content on your PC—so the pages that you view often can load faster. Users who visit pages that change frequently or that need to load completely from the Web server each time they are viewed (such as pages containing news, stock quotes, and other timely information) may not see much of an increase in speed over conventional dial-up service.

ISDN

ISDN (integrated services digital network) Internet access also transfers data over ordinary telephone lines, but it is faster than conventional dial-up. It typically uses two phone lines to transfer data up to 128 Kbps—over twice as fast as conventional dial-up—and the telephone and the Internet can be used at the same time, although Internet speeds might decline during telephone calls. At about $60 per month, ISDN is fairly pricey, considering the speed is still significantly slower than many *direct connections* with similar costs, as discussed next. ISDN requires an *ISDN modem* and is used primarily by businesses.

Direct Connections

Unlike dial-up connections that connect to your ISP only when you need to access the Internet, **direct connections** (also called *always-on connections*) keep you continually connected to your provider and, therefore, continually connected to the Internet whenever your computer or other device being used to access the Internet is on. With a direct connection, you access the Internet simply by opening a Web browser program, such as Internet Explorer, Netscape Navigator, or Firefox. Direct Internet connections are commonly used in homes and offices. In addition, they are often available at hotels, libraries, and other public locations for use by individuals. Users can connect to direct Internet connections via either wired or wireless media.

Because direct connections keep your computer connected to the Internet at all times (as long as your PC is powered up), it is important to protect your computer from unauthorized access or hackers. Consequently, all home and office PCs with a direct Internet connection should use a *firewall* program. Firewall programs block access to a PC from outside computers and enable each user to specify which programs on his or her PC are allowed to have access to the Internet. Firewalls, as well as other network and Internet security precautions, are discussed in more detail in Chapter 4.

The most significant characteristics of the most common types of direct Internet connections are discussed next. Additional alternatives—such as the emerging *broadband over power lines* (*BPL*) standard discussed in Chapter 8, which allows people to connect to the Internet through their power outlets—will likely be available in the future.

>**Conventional dial-up Internet access.** Dial-up Internet access via a conventional dial-up modem and standard telephone lines. >**ISDN (integrated services digital network) Internet access.** Dial-up Internet access that is faster than conventional dial-up, but still uses standard telephone lines. >**Direct connection.** An always-on type of Internet connection in which the PC or other device is continually connected to the Internet.

T1 Lines

T1 lines are high-speed (about 1.5 *Mbps*—millions of bits per second) dedicated lines that schools and large businesses often lease from the telephone company or an Internet service provider to provide a fast, direct connection to the Internet for the PCs on their networks. Very large businesses might choose to lease a faster *T3 line* (which transmits data at speeds up to about 30 Mbps), but these lines are more commonly used for Internet backbone connections and connections from ISPs to the Internet.

Cable

Cable Internet access is the most widely used type of home broadband connection, with over 60% of the home broadband market. Cable connections are very fast (up to 8 Mbps) and are available wherever cable TV access is available, provided the local cable provider supports Internet access. Consequently, cable Internet is not widely available in rural areas. Cable Internet service requires a *cable modem* and costs about $50 per month just for Internet access; cable TV and other services are optional and require an additional fee.

DSL

DSL (Digital Subscriber Line) Internet access provides fast transmissions over telephone lines and uses a technology that does not tie up your telephone line. DSL requires a *DSL modem* and is available only to users who are relatively close (within three miles) to a telephone switching station and who have telephone lines capable of handling DSL. DSL speeds are about half or less of cable speeds and the speed of the connection degrades as the distance between the modem and the switching station gets closer and closer to the three-mile limit. Consequently, DSL is typically only available in urban areas and is not as common as cable Internet. Download speeds are typically between 3 and 6 Mbps and the cost is around $35 per month.

Satellite

Satellite Internet access is slower and more expensive than cable or DSL access, but it is often the only broadband option for rural areas. In addition to a *satellite modem*, it requires a *transceiver satellite dish* mounted outside the home or building to receive and transmit data to and from the satellites being used. Installation requires an unobstructed view of the southern sky (to have a clear line of sight between the transceiver and appropriate satellite), and performance might degrade or stop altogether during very heavy rain or snowstorms. Typical cost is about $65 per month for speeds up to 1.5 Mbps.

Fixed Wireless

Fixed wireless Internet access is similar to satellite Internet in that it requires a modem and sometimes an outside-mounted transceiver, but it uses radio transmission towers instead of satellites. Fixed wireless has traditionally been available only in large metropolitan areas, although a new option is emerging that uses existing cell phone towers as radio towers to transmit fixed wireless signals, which allows the service to extend to more rural areas. Some fixed wireless companies are also using *WiMAX* technology to extend the range of their networks. Cost for service is about $35 per month for speeds up to 1.5 Mbps.

Broadband over Fiber (BoF)

A new alternative for homes and businesses today in areas where there is fiber optic cabling available all the way to the building is generically called **broadband over fiber (BoF)** or **fiber-to-the-premises (FTTP),** with other names being used by individual providers, such as Verizon's *fiber optic service (FiOS)*. These fiber optic networks are most often installed by the telephone company to upgrade their overall infrastructure, though some cities are creating fiber optic *MANs (metropolitan area networks)* that include connections to

TIP

If you have a direct Internet connection, leave your e-mail program open to retrieve your e-mail on a continual basis.

TIP

WiMAX and other emerging networking options are discussed in more detail in Chapter 8.

>**T1 line.** A leased high-speed dedicated line used to provide fast, direct Internet access. >**Cable Internet access.** Fast, direct Internet access via cable TV lines. >**DSL (Digital Subscriber Line) Internet access.** Fast, direct Internet access via standard telephone lines. >**Satellite Internet access.** Fast, direct Internet access via the airwaves using a satellite dish and satellite modem. >**Fixed wireless Internet access.** Fast, direct Internet access available in some areas via the airwaves and a radio transceiver. >**Broadband over fiber (BoF).** Very fast, direct Internet access via fiber optic networks; also referred to as **fiber-to-the-premises (FTTP)**.

businesses and homes to provide very fast broadband Internet services. Where available, download speeds for BoF service typically range between 5 Mbps and 30 Mbps, with costs ranging from $40 to $180. BoF requires a special networking terminal installed at the building. Typically, this terminal is connected to a router and then PCs can be connected easily to the router without special hardware (using just an appropriate Ethernet or Wi-Fi network adapter). BoF is also used to deliver telephone and HDTV service.

Mobile Wireless

Mobile wireless (sometimes called *wireless Web*) **Internet access** is most commonly used with handheld PCs, smart phones, and other mobile devices to keep them connected to the Internet, even as you carry them from place to place. These devices are connected typically through a wireless network and wireless provider (sometimes called a *WISP* or *wireless Internet service provider*) using a *wireless modem* or built-in Internet connectivity. The speed of mobile wireless depends on the cellular standard being used—today's *third-generation (3G)* mobile phones typically transfer data at rates between 128 Kbps and 2 Mbps. Costs for mobile wireless Internet access vary widely, with some packages including unlimited Internet, some charging by the number of minutes of Internet use, and some charging by the amount of data transferred. A typical cost for unlimited mobile wireless Internet is about $50 per month.

Hotspots

Both free and fee-based wireless Internet are widely available at **hotspots**—public locations with a direct Internet connection that allow users to connect wirelessly to that Internet connection. Examples include the Internet service available at many Starbucks coffeehouses and a number of McDonald's restaurants; wireless access points at hotels, airports, and other locations frequented by business travelers; and free hotspots located in the vicinity of some larger metropolitan area libraries, subway stations, parks, and other public locations (see Figure 3-9). Many businesses are also setting up hotspots within the corporate headquarters for use by employees in their offices, as well as by employees and guests in conference rooms, waiting rooms, lunchrooms, and other onsite locations. Users typically connect to hotspots via a Wi-Fi connection, although other options—such as the faster WiMAX, discussed in Chapter 8—might soon be an option for some locations.

Selecting an ISP and Setting Up Your PC

Once the type of Internet access to be used is determined, the final steps to getting connected to the Internet are selecting an ISP and setting up your system.

▼ FIGURE 3-9

Hotspots. Hotspots are used to wirelessly connect to the Internet via an Internet connection belonging to a business, city, school, or other organization.

COFFEEHOUSES
Typically fee-based.

HOTELS
Often free for guests.

PUBLIC AREAS
Usually free for residents and visitors, such as at this location in Seattle.

CORPORATE MEETING ROOMS
Usually free for employees and visitors.

>**Mobile wireless Internet access.** Internet access via a wireless communications network, such as the ones used with cellular phones.
>**Hotspot.** A location that provides wireless Internet access to the public.

AREA	QUESTIONS TO ASK
Services	Can I use the browser of my choice?
	Does the e-mail service support attachments, spam filtering, and multiple mailboxes?
	How many e-mail addresses can I have?
	What is the size limit on incoming and outgoing e-mail messages and attachments?
	Do I have a choice between conventional and Web-based e-mail?
	Is there dial-up service that I can use when I'm away from home (for broadband connections)?
	Are there any special member features or benefits?
	Is space available for posting a personal Web site or personal photos?
Speed	How fast are the maximum and usual downstream (ISP to my PC) speeds?
	How fast are the maximum and usual upstream (my PC to ISP) speeds?
	How much does the service slow down under adverse conditions, such as high traffic or poor weather?
	If it's a dial-up connection, how often should I expect to get a busy signal? (A customer-to-modem ratio of about 10:1 or less is optimal.)
Support	Is 24/7 telephone technical support available?
	Is any technical support available through a Web site, such as e-mail support or an online knowledge base?
	What is the response time to answer my phone calls or e-mails when I have a problem?
	Is there ever a charge for technical support?
Cost	What is the monthly cost for the service? Is it lower if I prepay a few months in advance?
	If it's a dial-up connection, is there a local access telephone number to avoid long-distance charges?
	Are there services that can be added or deleted (such as number of e-mail addresses or Web page hosting) to increase or decrease the monthly cost?
	Is there a set-up fee? If so, can it be waived with a 6-month or 12-month agreement?
	What is the cost of any additional hardware needed, such as modem or transceiver? Can the fee be waived with a long-term service agreement?
	Are there any other services (conventional or wireless telephone service, or cable or satellite TV, for instance) available from this provider that I have or want and that can be combined with Internet access for a lower total cost?

FIGURE 3-10

Choosing an ISP.
Some questions to ask
before making your
final selection.

Selecting an ISP

The type of device used (such as a desktop PC or handheld PC), the type of Internet connection and service desired (such as conventional dial-up or cable), and your geographical location (such as metropolitan or rural) will likely determine your ISP choices. The pricing and services available through any two ISPs might differ somewhat. For example, some ISPs simply provide you with an onramp to the Internet; others might include additional content or services, such as instant messaging, music management, Web site hosting, personal online photo galleries, Web site filtering, spam filtering, virus protection, and a personalized starting page. The questions listed in Figure 3-10 can help you understand the factors you need to consider when choosing an ISP.

Setting Up Your PC

The specific steps for setting up your PC to use your new Internet connection depend on the type of device, the type of connection, and the ISP you have chosen to use. Some types of Internet connections, such as satellite and broadband over fiber, require professional installation, after which you will be online; with other types, you can install the necessary hardware (typically an exterior modem or set-top box for a broadband connection or an internal or USB modem for a conventional dial-up connection) and then run any needed installation software to set up your system to use the ISP you selected. Typically, this setup process includes selecting a username (used to log on to some Internet connections and for your e-mail address), local access telephone numbers (for dial-up connections only), and a payment method.

After one PC is successfully connected to the Internet, you may need to add additional hardware to connect other PCs that you would like to use to access the Internet. To share a broadband connection, you can connect other PCs to the modem if the modem contains a built-in switch. Typically, this is done via *Ethernet cabling*, such as a twisted-pair cable with an *RJ-45 connector*. If the modem also functions as a wireless router, you can connect other PCs via a Wi-Fi connection. If the modem does not include switching or wireless routing capabilities, you will need to connect a switch, hub, or router to the modem (typically via an Ethernet cable), and then you can connect the additional PCs to that device. To share a dial-up connection, the computer that will connect to the Internet is set up as a host computer. Once the other PCs are networked successfully to the host computer, the Internet connection can be shared whenever the host PC is connected to the Internet. Typically, this is performed via Windows *Internet Connection Sharing* (*ICS*) software.

SEARCHING THE INTERNET

Most people who use the Internet turn to it to find specific information. For instance, you might want to find out the lowest price of the latest *Pirates of the Caribbean* DVD, the flights available from Los Angeles to New York on a particular day, a recipe for clam chowder, the weather forecast for the upcoming weekend, the text of Martin Luther King Jr.'s "I Have a Dream" speech, or a map of hiking trails in the Grand Tetons. The Internet provides access to a vast array of interesting and useful information, but that information is useless if you cannot find it when you need it. Consequently, one of the most important skills an Internet user can acquire today is how to successfully search for and locate information on the Internet. Basic Internet searching was introduced in Chapter 1, but understanding the various types of search sites available and how they work, as well as some key searching strategies, can help you save time by performing more successful Internet searches. These topics are discussed next.

Search Sites

Search sites (see Figure 3-11) are Web sites designed specifically to help you find information on the Web. Most search sites use a **search engine**—a software program—in conjunction with a huge database of information about Web pages to help visitors find Web pages that contain the information they are seeking. Search site databases are updated on a regular basis (Google estimates that its entire index is updated about once per month), typically with small, automated programs (often called *spiders* or *webcrawlers*) that use the hyperlinks located on Web pages to jump continually from page to page. At each Web page, the program records important data about the page—such as its URL, page title, and keywords that appear frequently on the page, as well as the keywords and descriptive information added to the page's code by the Web page author when the page was created—into the database. This information is used by the search site to find Web pages that match a search request. Spider programs can be tremendously fast, visiting millions of pages per day. Search site databases also obtain information when people who create Web sites submit URLs and keywords to them through an option on the search site. Some search sites also use human editors to manually classify the Web pages according to content. The size of the search database varies with each particular search site, but typically includes several billion Web pages—Google has over 10 billion entries alone.

>**Search site.** A Web site designed to help users search for Web pages that match specified keywords or selected categories.
>**Search engine.** A software program used by a search site to retrieve matching Web pages from a search database.

As searching becomes more and more important, new search alternatives are being developed. One emerging possibility is *real-time search engines* that search the Web live, instead of relying on a search site database. One such service—called *MyLiveSearch*—was in beta testing at the time of this writing. Another emerging search site—*ChaCha Search*—uses human guides that you can chat with via the ChaCha Search page if you can't find the information you are looking for. ChaCha Search is expected to be expanded to mobile phone users (via a toll-free telephone number) in the near future. Google and Yahoo! searching is already available to mobile phone users via text message. To use either service, you text *Googl* (*46645*) or *Yahoo* (*92466*) followed by a search phrase and send the message, and then you receive your search results as a text message (text messaging rates apply).

To begin a search using a search site, type the URL for the desired search site—such as Yahoo.com, Google.com, AltaVista.com, Excite.com, or Ask.com—in the Address bar of your browser. Search sites usually allow one or both of the two most common types of search operations: *keyword searches* and *directory searches*.

1. Type a URL or use an appropriate favorite to display a search site.

2. Type keywords in the box provided to perform a keyword search (or select appropriate categories for a directory search instead).

3. Click the hyperlink of a Web page shown in the search results to display that page.

FIGURE 3-11
Using a search site.
Many search sites allow you to search by keyword, directory, or both.

Keyword Search

The most common type of Internet search is the **keyword search**. To perform a keyword search, enter appropriate **keywords** (one or more key terms) describing what you are looking for in the search box and press Enter. The site's search engine then uses those keywords to return a list of Web pages (called *hits*) that match your search criteria; you can view one of these Web pages by clicking the appropriate hyperlink (see Figure 3-11). Search sites differ in how close a match between the specified search criteria and a Web page has to be before a link to that page is displayed, so the number of hits from one search site to another may vary. To reduce the number of hits displayed, good search strategies (discussed shortly) can be used. Search sites also differ with respect to the order in which the hits are displayed. Some sites list the most popular sites (usually judged by the number of Web pages that link to it); others list Web pages belonging to organizations that pay a fee to receive a higher rank (typically called *sponsored links*) first.

The keyword search is the most commonly used search type and is used on other types of search sites, in addition to conventional search sites like the Google search site shown in Figure 3-11. For instance, as shown in Figure 3-12, keyword search boxes are often found on *metasearch sites* (sites that search multiple search sites and consolidate the results) and *natural language search sites* (sites that are designed to be used with search criteria in full

>**Keyword search.** A type of Internet search in which keywords are typed in a search box to locate information on the Internet.
>**Keyword.** A word typed in a search box on a search site or other Web page to locate information related to that keyword.

Search box   Search box   Search box

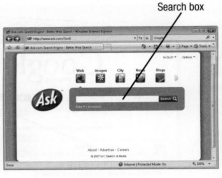

METASEARCH SITE
Allows users to search by keyword and displays hits from several different search sites.

NATURAL LANGUAGE SITE
Allows users to search by using natural language sentences.

WEB SITE SEARCH
Allows users to search the Web site to find products and other information located on the site.

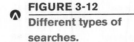 **FIGURE 3-12**
Different types of searches.

sentence form), as well as on many business Web sites in order to allow visitors to find information (such as items for sale via the site or support documents for a purchased product) located on those sites.

Directory Search

An alternate type of Internet search available on some search sites is the **directory search**, which uses a list of categories displayed on the screen (refer again to Figure 3-11). Directories are usually a good choice if you want information about a particular category but do not have a very specific subject in mind. A directory also uses a database, but one that is typically screened by a human editor, so it is much smaller, although often more accurate. For example, a spider program might classify a Web page about computer chips under the keyword "chips" together with information about potato chips, but a human editor would not categorize those two "chips" concepts together.

To use a directory located on a search site, click the category that best matches what you are looking for. A list of more specific subcategories for the main category that you selected is then displayed, along with a list of matching Web pages. To reach more specific subcategories and matching Web pages, keep selecting categories. Whenever the name of an appropriate Web page appears in the list of matching Web pages, click its hyperlink to display that page.

Search Site Tools

Many search sites contain a variety of tools that can be used to search for specific types of information. For instance, many search sites include links next to the search box that allow you to search for items other than Web pages, such as music files, videos, images, maps, news articles, products for sale—even files on your computer. Google is one of the most versatile search sites at the present time and is continually adding new search options. In addition to the options just listed, Google allows for a variety of special searches in its search box to find other useful information, such as to quickly track a shipped package, look up a telephone number, or make a calculation or conversion. Some examples of search tools that can be performed using the Google search box are listed in Figure 3-13. Some searches show the results automatically; others display a link that you can click to show the requested information.

>**Directory search.** A type of Internet search in which categories are selected to locate information on the Internet.

FUNCTION	EXPLANATION
Calculator	Enter a mathematical expression or a specific conversion to see the result.
Currency converter	Enter an amount and desired currency type to see the corresponding value.
Dictionary	Enter the term *define* followed by a term to view definitions for that term from online sources.
Flight information	Enter an airline and a flight number to see status information about that flight.
Movie showtimes	Enter the term *movie* followed by a ZIP code to view movies showing in that area.
Number search	Enter a UPS, FedEx, or USPS tracking number, an area code, or a UPC code to view the associated information.
Phonebook	Enter a last name followed by a city and a state or a ZIP code (or enter a first name or initial and last name followed by a state or an area code) to look up that person's address and phone number.
Reverse phonebook	Enter a telephone number to look up the person or business associated with that number.
Stock quotes	Enter one or more stock ticker symbols to retrieve stock quotes.
Street maps	Enter an address to find a map to that location.
Travel conditions	Enter an airport code followed by the term *airport* to view current conditions at that airport.
Weather	Enter the term *weather* followed by a city name or ZIP code to view the weather for that location.
Yellow pages	Enter a type of business and city name or ZIP code to view businesses in that local area.

EXAMPLES:

`weather san francisco` [Search]

Weather for **San Francisco, CA**

75°F
Clear
Wind: N at 7 mph
Humidity: 53%

Thu — 78° | 50°
Fri — 66° | 54°
Sat — 63° | 52°

`10 miles in feet` [Search]

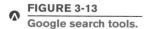 **10 miles = 52 800 feet**

FIGURE 3-13
Google search tools.

Search Strategies

There are a variety of strategies that can be employed to help whittle down a list of hits to a more manageable number (some searches can return billions of Web pages). Some search strategies can be employed regardless of the search site being used; others are available only on certain sites. Some of the most useful search strategies are discussed next.

Using Phrases

One of the most straightforward ways to improve the quality of the hits returned is to use *phrase searching*—essentially typing more than one keyword in a keyword search. Most search engines automatically list the hits that include all the keywords first, followed by hits matching most of the keywords, continuing down to hits that fit only one of the keywords. To force this type of sorting, virtually all search engines allow you to use some type of character—often quotation marks—to indicate that you want to search for all the keywords. Because search options vary from site to site, it is best to look for a search tips link on the search site you are using; the search tips should explain the options available for that particular site. Examples of the results based on different search phrases to find Web pages about hand signals used with dogs and conducted at two search sites are listed in Figure 3-14. Notice that while the last two searches shown in Figure 3-14 both returned relevant Web pages, the number of Web pages found varied dramatically.

SEARCH PHRASE USED	SEARCH SITE	NUMBER OF PAGES FOUND	TITLE OF FIRST TWO NONSPONSORED PAGES FOUND*
dogs	Google	68,200,000	Dogs & Puppies – Next Day Pets Dog – Wikipedia, the free encyclopedia
	Yahoo!	252,000,000	American Kennel Club (AKC) Animal Planet's Dog Guide
hand signals	Google	3,890,000	Military Hand Signals Bicycle Safety – Hand Signals
	Yahoo!	24,000,000	Waterskiing/Wakeboarding Hand Communications and Signals Hand Signals
dog hand signals	Google	394,000	DDEAF Training Hand Signals Border Collies Rescue: Universal Commands
	Yahoo!	3,250,000	LongLiveYourDog.com – Guides – Teaching Hand Signals DDEAF Training Hand Signs
"dog hand signals"	Google	1,600	DDEAF Training Hand Signals Video: How to Teach Your Dog Hand Signals
	Yahoo!	213	DDEAF Training Hand Signs D for Dog – Deaf Dog Hand Signals

*Highlighted entries indicate Web pages about dog hand signals.

FIGURE 3-14
Examples of phrase searching. Using different search phrases and different search sites can dramatically change the search results.

Using Boolean Operators

To further specify exactly what you want a search engine to find, *Boolean operators*—most commonly AND, OR, and NOT—can often be used in keyword searches. For example, if you want a search engine to find all documents that cover *both* the Intel and AMD microprocessor manufacturers, you can use the search phrase *Intel AND AMD* if the search engine supports Boolean operators. If, instead, you want documents that discuss *either* (or both) of these companies, the search phrase *Intel OR AMD* can be used. On the other hand, if you want documents about microprocessors that are cataloged with no mention of Intel, *microprocessors NOT Intel* can be used. Just as with other operators, the rules for using Boolean operators might vary from search site to search site—check the search tips for the search site that you are using to see if that site supports Boolean operators. Some sites include an *Advanced Search* option that helps you specify Boolean conditions and other advanced search techniques; other sites use the characters + for AND and – for NOT.

Using Multiple Search Sites

Most users have a favorite search site that they are most comfortable using. However, as illustrated in Figure 3-14, different search sites can return surprisingly different results. It is important to realize that sometimes a different search site might perform better than the one you use regularly. If you are searching for something and are not making any progress with one search site, then try another search site.

TIP

When searching, be efficient—if an appropriate Web page is not included among the first page or two of hits, redo the search using more specific criteria or a different search strategy.

Using Appropriate Keywords, Synonyms, Variant Word Forms, and Wildcards

When choosing the keywords to be used with a search site, it is important to select words that represent the key concept you are searching for. Unless you are using a natural language site, do not include any extraneous words, such as "the," "a," and "in," unless those words are part of a specific phrase you are searching for. For example, if you want to find out about bed and breakfasts located in the town of Leavenworth, Washington, a keyword phrase, such as *Leavenworth Washington bed and breakfast*, should return appropriate results.

If your initial search did not produce the results you were hoping for, you can try *synonyms*—words that have meanings similar to other words. For example, you could replace *bed and breakfast* with *hotel* or *lodging*. To use synonyms in addition to the original keywords, Boolean operators can be used, such as the search phrase *"bed and breakfast" OR "hotel" OR "lodging" AND Leavenworth AND Washington*. *Variant*—or alternate— word forms are another possibility. Try to think of a different spelling or form of your key- words, if your search still does not work as desired. For example, *bed and breakfast* could be replaced or supplemented with the variants *bed & breakfast* and *B&B*, and *hand signal* and *hand signaling* are variant word forms for the *hand signals* keywords used in Figure 3-14. Using alternative spellings is a form of this strategy, as well.

Another strategy that is sometimes used with keywords is the *wildcard* approach. A wildcard is a special symbol that is used in conjunction with a part of a word to specify the pattern of the terms you want to search for. For instance, the asterisk wildcard (*) is used to represent any number of letters at the asterisk location, so on many sites searching for *hand sign** would search for *hand sign*, *hand signal*, *hand signals*, *hand signaling*, and any other keywords that fit this specific pattern.

Using Field Searches

A more advanced search strategy that can be used when basic searching is not producing the desired results is *field searching*—a search limited to a particular search characteristic (or *field*), such as the page title, URL, page text, top-level domain, or Web site. When a field search is performed, only the Web pages that match the specified field criteria are dis- played (see Figure 3-15 for some examples of field searching). Many, but not all, search engines support some type of field searching. Check the search tips for the particular search site you are using to see if it has that option.

FIELD TYPE	EXAMPLE	EXPLANATION
Title	title:"tax tips"	Searches for Web pages containing the words "tax tips" in the page title.
URL	url:taxtips	Searches for Web pages containing "taxtips" in the page URL.
Text	text:"tax tips"	Searches for Web pages containing "tax tips" in the text of the page.
Domain	domain:gov	Searches for Web pages located on government Web servers with a domain that ends in .gov.
Site	forms site:irs.gov	Searches for Web pages associated with the keyword "forms" that are located only on the irs.gov Web site.
Combination	title:"tax tips" domain:gov	Searches for Web pages containing "tax tips" in the page title located on government Web servers with a domain that ends in .gov.

FIGURE 3-15
Field searching.
Field searches limit search results to just those pages that match specific field criteria, in addition to any specified search criteria.

Evaluating Search Results

Once a list of Web sites is returned as a result of a search, it is time to evaluate the sites to determine their quality and potential for meeting your needs. Two questions to ask yourself before clicking a link for a matching page are as follows:

▶ Does the title and listed description sound appropriate for the information you are seeking?

▶ Is the URL from an appropriate company or organization? For example, if you want technical specifications about a particular product, you might want to start with information on the manufacturer's Web site. If you are looking for government pub- lications, stick with government Web sites.

GUIDELINE	EXPLANATION
Evaluate the source.	Information from the company or organization in question is generally more reliable than information found on an individuals Web site. Government and educational institutions are usually good sources for historical or research data. If you clicked a link on a Web page to open a document, double-check the URL to make sure you still know what organization the page is from—it may be located on a completely different Web site than the page from which it was accessed.
Evaluate the author.	Does the author have the appropriate qualifications for the information in question? Does he or she have a bias, or is the information supposed to be objective?
Check the timeliness of the information.	Web page content may be updated regularly or posted once and forgotten. Always look for the publication date on online newspaper and magazine articles; check for a "last updated" date on pages containing other types of information you'd like to use.
Verify the information.	When you will be using Web-based information in a report, paper, Web page, or other document in which accuracy is important, try to locate the same information from other reputable Web sources to verify the accuracy of the information you plan to use.

FIGURE 3-16

Evaluating search results. Before using information obtained from a Web page, use the following criteria to evaluate its accuracy and appropriateness.

FURTHER EXPLORATION

Go to **www.course.com/uccs/ch3** for links to further information about citing online references.

FIGURE 3-17

Web citation examples.

After an appropriate Web page is found, the evaluation process is still not complete. If you are using the information on the page for something other than idle curiosity, you want to be sure the information can be trusted. Some general guidelines are listed in Figure 3-16.

Citing Internet Resources

According to the online version of the Merriam-Webster Dictionary, the term *plagiarize* means "to steal and pass off the ideas or words of another as one's own" or to "use another's production without crediting the source." To avoid plagiarizing Web page content, you need to credit Web page sources—as well as any other Internet resources—when you use them in papers, on Web pages, or in other documents.

The guidelines for citing Web page content are similar to those for written material. In general, the author, date of publication, and article or Web page title are listed along with a "Retrieved" statement listing the date the article was retrieved from the Internet and the appropriate URL of the Web page used. Some citation examples based on the guidelines obtained from the *American Psychological Association (APA)* Web site are shown in Figure 3-17. If in doubt when preparing a research paper, check with your instructor as to the style manual (such as APA, *Modern Language Association (MLA)*, or *Chicago Manual of Style*) he or she prefers you to follow and refer to that guide for direction.

TYPE OF RESOURCE	CITATION EXAMPLE
Web page article (magazine)	Louderback, Jim (2007, June 26). Beware of Botnets. *PC Magazine.* Retrieved June 14, 2007, from http://www.pcmag.com/article2/0,1895,2138720,00.asp.
Web page article (journal)	Veronica, Ann (2007, June). Electronic Health Records. *American Journal of Nursing,* 107 no. 6. Retrieved June 14, 2007, from http://www.nursingcenter.com/library/JournalArticle.asp?Article_ID=718430.
Web page article (not appearing in a periodical)	Wong, May (2007, June 11). Apple extends Web browser to Windows. MSNBC. Retrieved June 14, 2007, from http://msnbc.msn.com/id/19175417.
Web page content (not an article)	*Biography of Ronald Reagan.* (n.d). Retrieved August 1, 2007 from http://www.whitehouse.gov/history/presidents/rr40.html.
E-mail (cited in text, not reference list)	Maria Rodriquez (personal communication, March 28, 2008).

BEYOND BROWSING AND E-MAIL

In addition to basic browsing and e-mail, there are a host of other activities that can take place via the Internet. Some of the most common of these Web-based applications are discussed next.

Instant Messaging (IM), Voice over Internet Protocol (VoIP), and Other Types of Online Communications

Many types of online communications methods exist. E-mail was discussed in Chapter 1. Some of the most common other types of online communications are discussed next. For a look at one new option—*twittering*—see the Trend box.

Instant Messaging (IM)

Instant messaging (IM) allows you to exchange real-time messages easily with people on your *buddy list*—a list of individuals (such as family, friends, and business associates) that you specify. Popular instant messaging services include *AOL Instant Messenger (AIM)*, *MSN Messenger*, *Windows Live Messenger*, *Yahoo! Messenger*, *iChat®*, and the new *Microsoft Office Communicator 2007*. Because there is no single IM standard at the present time, you and your buddies must use the same (or compatible) instant messaging systems in order to exchange instant messages. IMs can be sent via PCs, as well as via mobile phones and mobile devices. Originally a popular communications method among friends, IM has also become a valuable business tool. In fact, the Radicati Group predicts that over 10 billion work-related messages will be sent via IM each day by 2010.

To send an IM via a PC, you need to have an IM program installed and running on your PC and you need to be signed in, or you need to open the Web site for a *Web-based IM service* and sign in. In either case, you can then send an IM (typically a short typed message) to one of your *buddies* that is currently online and signed in to his or her IM program); the IM immediately appears on your buddy's computer, as shown in Figure 3-18. Some IM programs can also be configured to send IMs as text messages to mobile phones and most IM programs include other options in addition to typed IMs, such as sending a photo or file, starting a voice or video conversation, playing an online game, and viewing news headlines or weather forecasts. Another option offered by some IM programs is to send *offline IMs*; that is, IMs that are sent to buddies who are currently offline (the IMs are delivered the next time the buddy signs in).

> **Instant messaging (IM).** A way of exchanging real-time typed messages with other individuals.

TREND

Twittering

Twittering is a new way of staying in touch and keeping up with friends no matter where you are or what you're doing. This free service allows members to post short (up to 140 character) updates (called *tweets*) about what they are doing at any moment. The updates can be sent via text message, IM, or e-mail and are posted to the member's Twitter.com page, as well as sent to the mobile phones belonging to friends, if designated by the member (standard text messaging rates apply when a mobile phone is used to send or receive tweets). As shown in the accompanying screen shot, the updates also briefly appear on the *Public Timeline* of the Twitter.com site, unless a user opts to keep his or her updates private. Members can also send tweets via their Facebook pages.

The idea behind Twitter is to allow individuals an easy way of staying in constant touch with their friends and family. Members join via the Twitter Web site and can then invite friends to join. Since Twitter also works via mobile phone, members can "twitter" whenever the mood strikes.

Because IM programs display the status of your buddies (such as if they are online, if they have chosen to change their status to "Busy" or "In a meeting," or some other indicator identifying what they are currently doing), IM is an example of an application that uses *presence technology*—technology that enables one computing device to locate or identify the current status of another device. Presence technology is increasingly being integrated into devices and applications and is discussed in more detail in Chapter 5.

FIGURE 3-18
How instant messaging (IM) works.

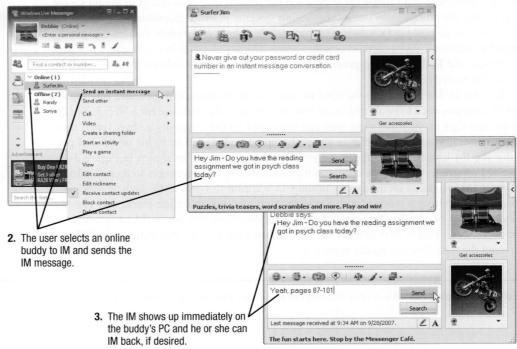

1. The user signs in to the IM program in order to send or receive messages.

2. The user selects an online buddy to IM and sends the IM message.

3. The IM shows up immediately on the buddy's PC and he or she can IM back, if desired.

Voice over Internet Protocol (VoIP)

Internet telephony is the original industry term for the process of placing telephone calls over the Internet. In its early stages, Internet telephony took place either from one PC to another (using a headset or the PC's speakers and microphone instead of a telephone) or from one PC to the recipient's telephone, depending on the setup. Today, the standard term for placing telephone calls over any type of data network (including the Internet, as well as a LAN, WAN, or other type of data network) is **Voice over Internet Protocol** (**VoIP**) and it can take many forms.

At its simplest level, VoIP calls can take place from PC to PC, such as by starting a voice conversation with an online buddy using an IM program or using the *Skype* or *Gizmo* service to call another Skype or Gizmo user (see Figure 3-19) using a headset or microphone connected to the PC. PC to PC calls are generally free, but calls can be received from or made to conventional or mobile phones for a small fee, as low as one cent per minute.

VoIP can also be performed via a Wi-Fi connection (sometimes called *Voice over Wi-Fi*). Individuals can place VoIP calls via a portable PC using a Wi-Fi hotspot or a home Wi-Fi connection; there are also mobile phones that can be used for VoIP, such as the dual-mode phones discussed in Chapter 1. There are also specific *VoIP phones* available for certain VoIP services, such as the phones that are designed to allow Skype users to place calls to other Skype users without using a PC. Vonage offers an additional option—using the *V-Phone* USB flash device (shown in Figure 3-19) to make VoIP calls from any computer with a broadband Internet connection. The V-Phone allows the user to access all of his or her VoIP information (such as phone number, contact list, call history, voice mail, and onscreen dialer) from any PC to which the device is connected, without installing any software because all of the needed information is located on the V-Phone device.

More permanent VoIP setups are designed to replace conventional *landline phones* in homes and businesses. They typically require a broadband Internet connection and a *VoIP phone adapter* (also called an *Internet phone adapter*) that goes between a conventional phone and a broadband router, as shown in Figure 3-19. Special *VoIP-enabled routers* are also available that connect directly to the broadband modem and function both as a VoIP phone adapter and a broadband router. VoIP phone adapters and routers are typically designed for a specific VoIP service. With these more permanent VoIP setups, most users switching from landline phone service can keep their existing telephone number.

ONLINE VIDEO

Go to **www.course.com/uccs/ch3** to watch the "Installing and Using VoIP" video clip.

FIGURE 3-19
Voice over IP (VoIP).

PC-TO-PC CALLS
A special program (such as Gizmo shown here) or an IM program can be used to make voice calls from one PC to another.

CALLS WHILE ON THE GO
The V-Phone shown here can be used with any PC with a broadband connection to make VoIP calls to any phone.

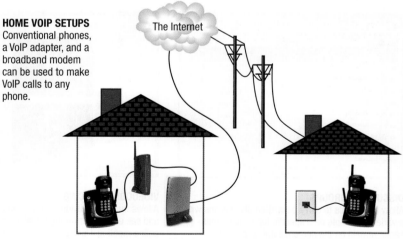

HOME VOIP SETUPS
Conventional phones, a VoIP adapter, and a broadband modem can be used to make VoIP calls to any phone.

The Internet

1. A conventional phone is plugged into a VoIP adapter, which is connected to a broadband modem.

2. Calls coming from the VoIP phone travel over the Internet to the recipient.

>**Voice over Internet Protocol (VoIP).** The process of placing telephone calls via the Internet.

TIP

VoIP is also called *digital phone*, *broadband phone*, or *Internet phone service*. The ability to deliver communications (phone calls, e-mail, messages, etc.) to an individual via a central location and independent of the access device being used is referred to as *unified communications*.

VoIP is one of the fastest growing communications applications today and is available from most major communications companies, as well as VoIP companies, such as Skype and Vonage. While problems—such as dropped or poor quality calls, telephone number transfer problems, and hidden fees—are common complaints about some VoIP providers, VoIP growth shows no signs of slowing down. VoIP use by businesses is growing as companies realize the advantages of routing voice data over their data networks (such as cost savings and increased capabilities). There are also a number of VoIP packages available for home use and the biggest advantage is cost savings, such as unlimited local and long-distance calls for as little as $25 per month or cable and VoIP services bundled together for $50 per month. One of the biggest disadvantages of VoIP at the present time is that it does not function during a power outage or if your Internet connection goes down. In addition, calls to 911 might not be identified with your home address, depending on your VoIP service and how it was set up. To solve this problem, the FCC modified *enhanced 911* (*e911*) regulations (that require mobile phone providers to use location detection capabilities to enable 911 operators to determine the location of mobile phone 911 callers) to include VoIP calls. Under these rules, 911 calls placed via VoIP will display the caller's telephone number and, in many cases, their location. To accomplish this, most VoIP companies require consumers to supply, during the sign up process, the address where the fixed VoIP system is used.

Discussion Groups

Discussion groups (also called *message boards*, *newsgroups*, or *online forums*) facilitate written discussions between people on specific subjects, such as TV shows, computers, movies, gardening, music, photography, hobbies, and politics. When a participant posts a message, it is displayed for anyone accessing the message board to read and respond to. Messages are usually organized by topics (called *threads*). Participants can post new messages in response to an existing message and stay within that thread, or they can post discussion group messages that start new threads. Many discussion groups can be accessed with just a Web browser, as in Figure 3-20; others require a *newsreader* (a special program for handling newsgroup messages that is often incorporated into e-mail programs).

FIGURE 3-20
Other types of online communications.

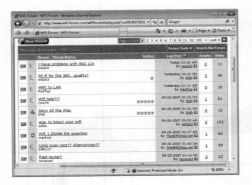

DISCUSSION GROUPS
Allow individuals to carry on written discussions with a variety of people on a specific topic; since messages remain on the site once they are posted, users don't need to be online at the same time to participate.

VIDEOCONFERENCING
Allows multiple individuals to talk with and see each other during a real-time online meeting. Used both by individuals and businesses.

BLOGS
Allow individuals to post entries to an online personal journal.

>**Discussion group.** A type of Internet communications that enables individuals to post messages on a particular topic for others to read and respond to.

Participants in discussion groups do not have to be online at the same time because messages can be posted and responded to at each participant's convenience.

Chat Rooms

A **chat room** is an Internet service that allows multiple users to *chat* (exchange real-time typed messages) at one time. Unlike e-mail and discussion groups, chat rooms require participants to be online at the same time. Like discussion groups, chat rooms are typically set up for specific topics. While most chat rooms are open to anyone, an individual can set up a private chat room that can be accessed only by users (typically family, friends, or coworkers) who know the proper password.

Videoconferences and Webinars

Videoconferencing (also called *teleconferencing* or *Web conferencing*) refers to the use of computers, video cameras, microphones, and other communications technologies to conduct face-to-face meetings among people in different locations over the Internet. Small videoconferences can take place using the participants' PCs, as in Figure 3-20; large group videoconferences might require a more sophisticated setup, such as a dedicated videoconferencing room. Videoconferencing can also take place today via smart phones and other mobile devices.

Videoconferences are nearly always two-way, with all users sending and receiving video. PC videoconferencing can be used both by businesses and individuals; personal applications include allowing grandparents to see their grandchildren during a phone call and enabling soldiers and family members to stay in touch while the soldier is deployed. Some uses for one-way Internet videoconferencing include allowing parents to watch live video of their children in childcare or at school throughout the day, and monitoring homes and offices for intruders and other problems. **Webinars** (Web seminars) are similar to PC videoconferences, but typically have a designated presenter and an audience. Although interaction with the audience is usually included (such as question and answer sessions), a Webinar is typically more one-way than a videoconference.

Blogs

A **blog**—also called a *Web log*—is a Web page that contains short, frequently updated entries in chronological order, typically by an individual as a means of expression or communication (see Figure 3-20). In essence, a blog is an online personal journal accessible to the public that is typically created by and updated by one individual. Blogs are written by a wide variety of individuals—including ordinary people, as well as celebrities, writers, students, and experts on particular subjects—and can be used to post personal commentary, research updates, comments on current events, political opinions, celebrity gossip, travel diaries, and more. An increasing trend is for companies to use blogs to raise their external visibility by blogging about issues that might interest their current or prospective customers. Some companies also use intranet blogs to facilitate communications with employees. Some blogs are set up to have multiple authors, such as a group of employees collaborating on a project or all the students in a particular writing class.

With their increased use and audiences, bloggers and the *blogosphere* (the complete collection of blogs on the Internet) are beginning to have increasing influence on businesses and politicians today. Some popular bloggers have huge audiences, so the impact of blogging is more influential than in the past. As a result of the increasing influence of blogs, there are news services available that monitor blogs—some watch around

> **TIP**
>
> There are numerous online blog search engines and directories—such as Technorati.com—to help you find blogs that meet your interests.

> **Chat room.** A type of Internet communications that allows multiple users to exchange written messages in real time. > **Videoconferencing.** The use of computers, video cameras, microphones, and other communications technologies to conduct face-to-face meetings over the Internet. > **Webinar.** A seminar presented via the Web. > **Blog.** A Web page that contains short, frequently updated entries in chronological order, typically by just one individual; also called a Web log.

100,000 blogs each day—and relay any new blog articles that mention specified company names, brands, people, competitors, or other selected criteria to the subscriber. These services are designed to help businesses and other organizations identify interest in a competitor's products or services, potential problems with an existing product or service, and new issues related to their products that they might not be aware of. There are even Web sites set up to pay bloggers for blogging about certain products. Although some believe that commercializing blogging will corrupt the blogsphere, others view it as a natural evolution to word-of-mouth advertising.

Blogs are usually created and published to the Web using *blogging software* available on blogging sites, such as Blogger.com. Blogs are also frequently published on school, business, and personal Web sites. Blogs are usually updated frequently, and entries can be posted via PCs, e-mail, and mobile devices. Entries can contain text, photos, and voice updates stored as *MP3* files. Blogs that contain video clips are sometimes referred to as *vlogs*.

Social Networking

A **social networking site** can be loosely defined as a site that creates a community of individuals with common interests. Some examples are *MySpace* and *Facebook* (see Figure 3-21) that allow users to post information about themselves for others to read; *Meetup.com* that connects people with common hobbies and interests; video sharing sites like *YouTube*; photo sharing sites like *Flickr* and *Fotki*; the *Digg* collaborative news community (which allows members to submit and vote on news articles, and the articles with the most "diggs" get promoted to the home page of the Digg site); and *del.icio.us* (a social bookmarking site that allows users to create bookmarks, as well as search and view bookmarks made by other members). Social networking sites are part of a group of Web-based applications and services referred to as *Web 2.0* applications. Although there is no precise definition, Web 2.0 generally refers to Web-based applications and services that let people collaborate and share information online. Other Web 2.0 applications include Software as a Service (SaaS) and blogs, as well as *wikis*, *podcasts*, and *RSS feeds* (discussed shortly).

Originally, social networking sites were used by individuals to connect with existing friends and make new ones. Today, however, they are also used by businesspeople, political candidates, up and coming musicians, families, and more. For instance, the *LinkedIn* business social networking site shown in Figure 3-21 can be used for recruiting new employees and finding new jobs, building sales and finding new clients, and locating possible investors. MySpace and YouTube are often used by political candidates, emerging musicians, and other individuals interested in publicity and increasing name recognition. In the 2008 U.S. Presidential race, for instance, all major candidates had a MySpace page and

ASK THE EXPERT

THROW THE FIGHT

Ryan Baustert, Guitarist, Throw the Fight

What impact has the Internet and social networking sites had on your band's success?

The Internet has had a major impact on us. The best marketing is when the distance between artist and audience is short and direct. Due to sites like MySpace, Purevolume, and Last.fm, we are able to stay better connected and interact with our fans on a more personal level. We can also gauge how our music is received by peoples' reactions and comments online.

It's much easier to promote shows, tours, and album releases, as well. We also book and confirm 90% of all our shows via MySpace. The majority of venues and promoters utilize the site, so it just makes it that much easier.

>**Social networking site.** A Web site that creates a community of individuals with common interests.

PERSONAL PROFILING SITES

Allow individuals to post information about themselves, link pages with friends, exchange messages, and so forth.

PHOTO SHARING SITES

Allow individuals to upload photos to share with others.

BUSINESS NETWORKING SITES

Help businesspeople find business contacts, potential new employees and clients, dinner and traveling partners during business trips, and so forth.

FAMILY NETWORKING SITES

Help families communicate via shared calendars, shopping lists, task lists, posted messages, and more.

FIGURE 3-21

Social networking sites. A variety of social networking sites are available to meet different needs.

the presidential debates held during 2007 featured questions submitted in video form via YouTube. Children are increasingly using child-oriented social networking sites that work similarly to MySpace, but that have safeguards in place to prevent certain personal information from being posted, to monitor language, and so forth. And parents can use family social networking sites such as *Cozi Central* to send their children reminder messages and to access a shared family calendar (sometimes color-coded by family member, as in Figure 3-21), online shopping and tasks lists, and more.

As the use of social networking sites continues to grow, adults and children should be cautious about revealing too much personal information via these sites, both for personal safety reasons and to prevent the information from being used in personalized, targeted *spear phishing* attacks, discussed in Chapter 4. And adults should also take a close look at their online posts and photos and remove anything that might be potentially embarrassing if viewed by current or future employers, a future mate, or other people important to them.

Online Shopping and Investing

Online shopping and *online investing* are examples of *e-commerce*—online financial transactions. It is very common today to order products, buy and sell stock, pay bills, and manage financial accounts online. In fact, Forrester Research predicts that U.S. online sales will reach approximately $331 billion (about 13% of all retail sales) by 2010.

Since *online fraud*, *credit card fraud*, and *identity theft* (a situation in which someone gains enough personal information to pose as another person) are continuing to grow at a rapid pace, it is important to be cautious when participating in online financial activities. To protect yourself, use a credit card whenever possible when purchasing goods or services online so that any fraudulent activities can be disputed, but be sure to enter your credit card number only on a secure Web page. To identify a secure Web page, look for a URL that begins with *https* instead of *http*, a locked padlock or a complete—unbroken—key on your Web browser screen, or some other indication that a *secure Web page* is being used. Secure Web pages should also be used to enter other types of sensitive information (such as a bank account number or any information that you would not want anyone else to see), and financial accounts should be protected with *strong user passwords* that are changed frequently. Some of the most common consumer e-commerce activities are illustrated in Figure 3-22 and discussed next. Internet security and passwords are discussed in detail in Chapter 4.

FURTHER EXPLORATION

Go to **www.course.com/uccs/ch3** for links to further information about online shopping precautions.

Online Shopping

With **online shopping**, products and services are purchased online. These can be physical products (like clothing, books, DVDs, shoes, furniture, and more), as well as electronic products (such as downloadable software, movies, music, and books). Airline tickets, hotel reservations, insurance policies, and other items can also be purchased online. Typically, shoppers locate the items they would like to purchase on an online shopping site (one example is shown in Figure 3-22), and then they add those items to their online *shopping carts* or *shopping bags*; the site's *checkout* process—including supplying the necessary billing and shipping information—is used to complete the sale. Most online purchases are paid for using a credit card, although other alternatives—such as using an *online payment account* like *PayPal*, sending in a check or money order, or paying with a preloaded *smart card* or *electronic gift card*—are sometimes available. After the payment is processed, the item is either shipped to the customer (if it is a physical product), or the customer is given instructions on how to download it (if it is a software program, electronic book or article, music, movie rental, or some other product in electronic form).

>**Online shopping.** Buying products or services over the Internet.

ONLINE SHOPPING
Allows you to purchase goods and services online. As items are selected, they are moved to an online shopping cart or bag.

ONLINE AUCTION
Allows you to bid on goods for sale by other individuals; the highest bidder purchases the item.

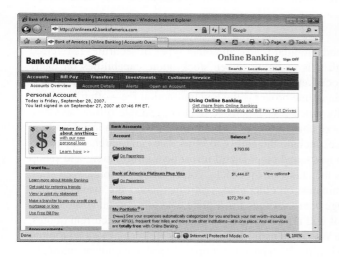

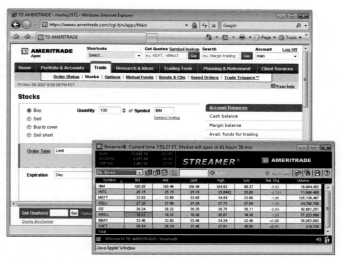

ONLINE BANKING
Allows you to check your account balances, make electronic payments, view your transaction history, and more.

ONLINE INVESTING
Allows you to buy and sell stocks, view your portfolio, get real-time quotes, and more.

Online Auctions

Online auctions are the most common way to buy items online from other individuals. Sellers list items for sale on an auction site (such as eBay) by paying a small listing fee, entering a description of the item, posting a picture if available, and identifying a length of time that the auction should run. Sellers can specify a starting bid amount (that bidders see), as well as a minimum selling price (that bidders do not see) that must be met in order for there to be a winning bidder. Individuals can enter bids on auction items (see Figure 3-22) until the end of the auction. For convenience, most auction sites allow bidders to enter a maximum bid amount for a particular auction, and the auction site will automatically bid for

FIGURE 3-22
Common e-commerce activities.

>**Online auction.** An online activity for which bids are placed for items, and the highest bidder purchases the item.

TIP

The data on Web pages—such as on an online auction page—is typically not updated automatically once it is displayed on your screen. To get updated information—such as the current bid for an auction and auction time remaining—use your browser's Refresh or Reload button to redisplay the page.

that person (using the minimum bid increment for that item) whenever the bidder is outbid, until the amount reaches that bidder's maximum bid. At the time the auction closes, the person with the highest bid is declared the successful bidder (provided the minimum selling price was met, if one was established) and then arranges payment for and delivery of the item directly with the seller. The seller also pays a percentage of the sale price as a commission to the auction site.

Online Banking

Many banks today offer **online banking** as a free service to their customers. With online banking, activities such as reviewing account activity, transferring funds between accounts, and looking up credit card balances and activities can all be performed online (see Figure 3-22). Other common online banking tools include online account reconciliation tools and the ability to pay bills electronically. Typically, individuals can send electronic payments to individuals and businesses, and automatic payments can be set up for recurring expenses, such as for credit card payments and utility bills. An emerging option is the ability to make electronic deposits of physical checks by properly endorsing and then scanning both sides of the check and transferring that information electronically to the bank via the bank's secure Web site. Online banking is continually growing—according to the Pew Internet & American Life Project, close to half of all U.S. adults now bank online.

Online Investing

Buying and selling of stocks, bonds, mutual funds, and other types of securities is referred to as **online investing**. Although it is common to see stock quote capabilities on many search and news sites, trading stocks and other securities usually requires an *online broker*. The biggest advantage to using an online broker is the low transaction fee—often just $5 to $15 per trade, which is generally much less expensive than comparable offline services. Online investing is also much more convenient for those investors who do a lot of trading. Common online investing services include the ability to order sales and purchases; access performance histories, corporate news, and other useful investment information; and set up an *online portfolio* that displays the status of the stocks you specify. On some Web sites, stock price data is delayed 20 minutes; on other sites, real-time quotes are available. It is important to realize that Web page data—such as stock price data—is current at the time it is retrieved via a Web page, but it will not be updated (and you will not see current quotes, for instance) until you reload the Web page using your browser's Refresh or Reload toolbar button. An exception to this rule is if the Web page is set up to refresh the content automatically for you on a regular basis. For example, the portfolio shown in Figure 3-22 uses a *Java applet*—a small program built into a Web page—to redisplay updated data continuously.

Online Entertainment

There are an ever-growing number of ways to use the Web for entertainment purposes, such as listening to music, watching TV and videos, and playing online games (see Figure 3-23). Some applications can be accessed with virtually any type of Internet connection; others are only practical with a broadband connection.

Online Music

Online music is perhaps one of the hottest Web-based entertainment activities today. Two of the most widely used possibilities are listening to online radio broadcasts and

---

>**Online banking.** Performing banking activities over the Internet. >**Online investing.** Buying and selling stocks or other types of investments over the Internet. >**Online music.** Music played or obtained via the Internet.

downloading music. Online radio is broadcast from *online radio stations*, also called *Internet radio stations*. To listen to an Internet radio station, you open the radio station's Web page in your browser and click an appropriate hyperlink. A *media player program* usually opens automatically, and you begin to hear the broadcast. Many common media players (such as *Windows Media Player* and *RealPlayer*) are available free of charge and include tools to help you not only listen to radio stations but also organize both your online and offline music.

To purchase music online, *online music stores* (such as the iTunes Music Store®, Napster, RealPlayer Music Store, Wal-Mart Music Downloads, and Yahoo! Music) allow you to download music singles and albums in digital format legally. Some online music stores are stand-alone services; others are integrated into a media player program so that songs can be purchased, played, organized, and transferred to a CD or portable music player all from the same program. Still other online music services—such as Real's Rhapsody subscription service—are designed for unlimited access to an enormous collection of online music that can be listened to on demand for a set fee (typically about $10 per month). Music can also be downloaded to mobile phones and portable digital media players, via a mobile wireless or Wi-Fi connection. Market research firm Strategy Analytics expects mobile music to be a $9 billion business by 2010.

ONLINE MUSIC
Many radio stations today allow you to listen to radio broadcasts live, as well as to other music-oriented content that can be accessed on demand.

ONLINE TV
Full episodes of many TV shows today are available to watch online on demand via the TV network Web site.

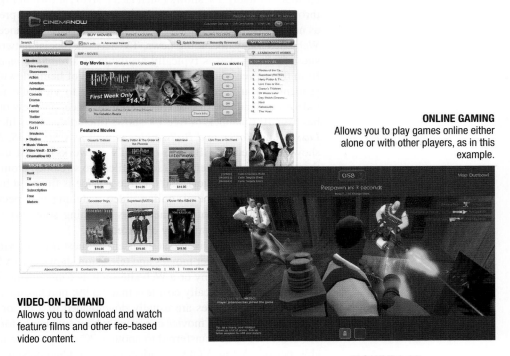

ONLINE GAMING
Allows you to play games online either alone or with other players, as in this example.

VIDEO-ON-DEMAND
Allows you to download and watch feature films and other fee-based video content.

FIGURE 3-23
Common online entertainment activities; some are free, others are fee-based.

To avoid copyright violations, all legal downloaded music is available either as free downloads (sometimes found on sites featuring new artists, for example) or for purchase (typically 99 cents per song, part of which is used for royalties owed to the artist or record company). Once downloaded, music files can be played from your PC's hard drive using a media player program installed on your PC. Provided the download agreement did not preclude it, music files can also be copied to a CD to create a custom music CD or transferred to a portable digital media player, such as an iPod.

Another alternative for downloading music is via **peer-to-peer (P2P) file sharing**—sharing files directly between users from one PC to another via the Internet instead of from a Web server. P2P music sharing began with the original *Napster* many years ago. Instead of storing music files on the Napster server, files downloaded using the Napster service were downloaded from one Napster user's PC to another Napster user's PC—from one peer to another. However, most exchanges at the time violated copyright restrictions and a flood of lawsuits from the music industry eventually shut down Napster and other P2P sites that were being used to exchange copyright-protected content illegally. Today, there are legal P2P sites available (including the new Napster) to enable music and other digital content to be purchased and shared legally, with artists and record labels being paid appropriately for all music shared via the site. For a closer look at P2P services and the possible impact of P2P file sharing on college students, see the Technology and You box.

Online TV, Online Videos, and Video-On-Demand (VOD)

Another very popular type of online entertainment is online access to television shows, movies, and other types of video. Television content delivered over the Internet is sometimes referred to as *IPTV (Internet Protocol Television)*. Live online TV is fairly limited at the present time, although there are some Web sites that provide live video feeds, such as the interactive Web sites that accompany television shows like *Big Brother*. However, episodes of many TV shows (such as *Survivor*, shown in Figure 3-23) are available online through the television network Web site. Other types of prerecorded video content (such as news clips, movie trailers, and music videos, for instance) are found on many types of Web sites today, including news, TV network, social networking, business, and personal sites. Online video is typically available as *streaming media*, in which the video plays from the server when it is requested, instead of being downloaded to the user's PC. Consequently, you need access to the Web site to view the video. Many streaming online videos are available free of charge. For instance, one new online video provider—*Joost*—has over 100 channels of free TV shows (including oldies like *Charlie's Angels*, *Babylon 5*, *Lassie*, and *Rocky and Bullwinkle*, as well as *CSI*, *NCIS*, *NUMB3RS*, and other current shows provided by CBS and other TV networks). Joost uses P2P technology to deliver these TV shows on demand (so the files are streamed from other members' PCs, instead of from a central server), and the free service is financed by only three commercial minutes per hour. In general, online video watching is expected to continue to grow with approximately 85% of Internet users watching some type of video via the Internet by 2011, according to a study by eMarketer.

Video content delivered at the user's request is called **video-on-demand (VOD)**. With VOD, individuals order movies and television shows via a VOD provider (such as the individuals' cable company or a Web site such as *CinemaNow*, *iTunes*, *Movielink*, or *Amazon Unbox*). Rentals typically cost less than $3.99; purchasing a movie costs around $9.99. In either case, the movies are usually downloaded to a PC or DVR and are played using a media player. Rented movies can usually be viewed only for a limited time; some services allow movies to be transferred to another PC or a portable media player during the allowable period. A few VOD providers (such as CinemaNow, shown in Figure 3-23) offer movies in DVD quality and allow purchased movies to be burned to a DVD. VOD has the convenience of users not having to leave their houses to pick up or return movies and getting movies faster than services that rent DVDs via regular mail. However, movies from some VOD providers may not be high-enough quality to play well on a large-screen monitor or TV and they typically take at least an hour to download. One new P2P-based VOD service—*VUDU*—overcomes this time limitation by continually downloading the newest

---

>**Peer-to-peer (P2P) file sharing.** The process of sharing resources directly between users via the Internet. >**Video-on-demand (VOD).** The process of downloading movies and televisions shows, on demand, via the Internet.

TECHNOLOGY AND YOU

P2P Legal Implications for College Students

Since P2P file sharing began, many individuals—often high school and college students—have been illegally exchanging copyrighted music files via P2P networks. Although the original file sharing services that facilitated the illegal exchange of copyrighted music and movies were eventually shut down, P2P file sharing continues. To fight back, the recording industry is taking legal action against individuals suspected of illegally exchanging music files via P2P services and has filed over 26,000 lawsuits since 2003. One focus by the Recording Industry Association of America (RIAA) is on college students. In 2007 alone, the RIAA sent nearly 4,000 letters to college students identified as significant copyright violators directing them to pay a settlement fee (typically from $2,000 to $3,500) for allegedly sharing copyrighted music or face a lawsuit. According to the RIAA, this type of file sharing is "an emerging epidemic of music theft." If an individual is tried and found guilty of copyright infringement, the fines are steep—up to $150,000 per instance. For instance, the first P2P lawsuit to come to trial ended in late 2007 and the Minnesota woman charged was found guilty of sharing copyrighted material online and ordered to pay six record companies a total of $222,000.

In addition to the personal liability for students, high amounts of P2P file exchanges also impact colleges—both by making the college vulnerable to industry lawsuits and by slowing down network performance. To protect themselves, some colleges are installing specialty filtering software to block unauthorized P2P file exchanges. Another solution offered by Dell and the new legal Napster is to use Dell servers located on campus to store the entire Napster collection and then legally distribute that music to students for a small fee. Since downloads only need to be transmitted over the college network and not the Internet, student downloads of music files via the Napster service and its local cache of music has minimal impact on a college's network bandwidth. At most colleges using the

Dell/Napster service, a flat fee for the service is passed on to all students—typically around $3 per month instead of the normal $9.95 per month that Napster charges—and then all students have unlimited access to the Napster collection (see the accompanying screen shot).

Despite these efforts, the risk of prosecution, and the risk of accidentally downloading *spyware* (discussed later in this chapter), a computer virus, or a corrupted file when downloading a file from another person's PC, illegal file sharing continues. However, as more P2P users understand the risks, legal implications, and ethical implications involved with illegal P2P file sharing, they will likely consider it worth their while to pay the roughly $1 per song for music downloads from a legitimate site instead of obtaining the song illegally. And with consumers beginning to want quality, efficiency, and safety, in addition to value, legal digital media distribution is expected to eventually become the norm.

and most popular films to the VUDU set-top box in order to have at least the beginning of any movie you might want to watch downloaded and ready to go. When you want to rent a movie, the opening starts playing while the VUDU box simultaneously downloads pieces of the rest of the movie from other VUDU boxes spread around the country. As long as your Internet connection doesn't go down, the movie will play without any interruption.

In addition to being used with home computers and televisions, VOD is also available for mobile phones and other types of mobile devices, as discussed in the Chapter 1 Trend box. New hardware receivers, such as *Apple TV* (which allows iTunes users to view content on a TV) and the *digital media receivers* used to deliver multimedia content to PCs, TVs, and other devices over a home network, will also help VOD and other types of online video services continue to grow and evolve.

FURTHER EXPLORATION

Go to **www.course.com/uccs/ch3** for links to further information about the Napster controversy and other related peer-to-peer file sharing issues.

FIGURE 3-24
News and reference sites.

Online Gaming

Online gaming refers to games played over the Internet. Many sites—especially children's Web sites—include games for visitors to play. There are also sites whose sole purpose is hosting games that can be played online. Some of the games are designed to be played alone or with just one other person. Others, called *online multiplayer* games, are designed to be played online against many other online gamers. Online multiplayer games (such as Hearts, Doom, EverQuest, Final Fantasy XI, and City of Heroes) are especially popular in countries, such as South Korea, that have high levels of both high-speed Internet connections and Internet use in general. Gaming consoles (such as the PlayStation 3 and Xbox 360) and portable gaming devices (such as the Sony PSP and Nintendo DS Lite) that have built-in Internet connectivity can also be used for online gaming. Online gaming is also associated quite often with *Internet addiction*—the inability to stop using the Internet or to prevent extensive use of the Internet from interfering with other aspects of one's life. Internet addiction is a growing concern and is discussed in more detail in Chapter 7.

Online News, Reference, and Information

There is an abundance of news and other important information available through the Internet. The following sections discuss some of the most widely-used news, reference, and information resources.

News and Reference Sites

News organizations, such as television networks, newspapers, and magazines, nearly always have Web sites (see one example in Figure 3-24) that are updated on a continual basis to post current news articles and videos, as well as online versions of the articles contained in their offline (paper-based) publications. Similar to a conventional newspaper or magazine, news sites commonly contain local, U.S., and world news, as well as sports, entertainment, health, travel, weather, and other news topics. Many news sites also have searchable archives to look for past articles, although some require a fee to view back articles. Once articles are displayed, they can typically be saved, printed, or sent to other individuals via e-mail or IM. News radio programs that are broadcast over the Internet are also available.

Reference sites are designed to provide users access to specific types of useful information. For example, reference sites can be used to generate maps, check the weather forecast, look up the value of a home, or provide access to encyclopedias, dictionaries, ZIP code directories, and telephone directories. To find an appropriate reference site, type the information you are seeking (such as *ZIP code lookup* or *topographical map*) as keywords in a search site. Some reference sites, such as the MapQuest site shown in Figure 3-24, allow you to send data (such as maps and driving directions) from the Web site to your mobile phone. Additional mobile reference tools are available through some wireless providers.

NEWS SITES
News organizations typically update their sites several times per day to provide access to the most current news and information.

REFERENCE SITES
Reference Web sites provide access to specific types of useful information, such as the maps and driving directions available via this Web site.

>**Online gaming.** Playing games over the Internet.

Portal Pages, RSS Feeds, Podcasts, and Widgets

Portal Web pages are Web pages designed to be selected as a browser's home page and visited on a regular basis. Portal pages typically include search capabilities, news headlines, weather, and other useful content, and can usually be customized by users to display their requested content (see Figure 3-25). Once the portal page is customized, each time the user visits the portal page, the specified information is displayed. Popular portals include My Yahoo!, iGoogle, My MSN, and AOL.com.

RSS (**Really Simple Syndication**) is an online news tool designed for facilitating the delivery of news articles, *podcasts*, and other content regularly published to a Web site. Provided the content has an associated *RSS feed*, individuals can *subscribe* to that feed (typically by copying the RSS URL to an *RSS reader* or to a portal page) to have new content delivered to them as it becomes available (refer again to the portal page in Figure 3-25). Many different types of Web sites today offer RSS feeds, but some of the most common are for national, sports, finance, technical, or entertainment news. Because RSS feeds are based on *XML* (*Extensible Markup Language*), they are flexible and can be delivered to a wide variety of devices. For example, in addition to PCs, RSS feeds today can be delivered to mobile phones and other mobile devices. Some companies are even replacing e-mail with RSS for employee and customer notifications—for instance, one Web site uses RSS to alert subscribers to new coupons and another uses RSS to notify subscribers of new computer virus threats. In the future, expect to see RSS feeds delivered to televisions—perhaps even to watches, refrigerators, and other display devices.

Podcasts are another news tool often available via Web sites. A podcast is a recorded audio or video file (typically, an MP3 file for an audio podcast or an *MP4* file for a video podcast) that is available via the Internet. The term "podcast" is derived from the iPod digital music player (the first widely used device for playing digital audio files), although podcasts today can be listened to using a desktop PC, portable PC, or smart phone, in addition to an iPod or other type of portable digital media player. Podcasts are often created as a series of files that are uploaded on a regular basis, similar to updating a blog. Podcasts can be downloaded manually from a Web site (such as the podcasts available for download via the Web site that accompanies this textbook), or they can be downloaded automatically via an RSS feed, if that option is available. Video podcasts are sometimes referred to as *vodcasts* or *vidcasts*. For a look at how to create an audio podcast, see the How It Works box.

News headlines can also be delivered via *widgets*—small programs (also called *gadgets*) that can be displayed on portal pages, computer desktops, dashboards, and other objects. For instance, news widgets typically display headlines and clicking a headline displays that news story. Windows Vista includes a number of gadgets (such as to display a calendar, a clock, weather information, a news ticker, or traffic maps) that that can be added to the Windows desktop.

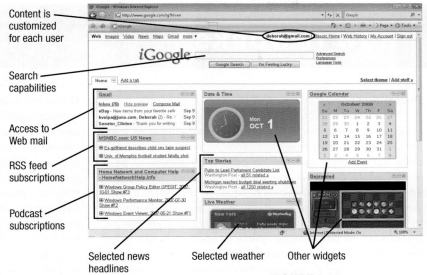

Content is customized for each user

Search capabilities

Access to Web mail

RSS feed subscriptions

Podcast subscriptions

Selected news headlines

Selected weather

Other widgets

FIGURE 3-25

Portal pages. Portal pages contain customized news and information, including headlines, weather, RSS feeds, podcasts, and widgets.

FURTHER EXPLORATION

Go to **www.course.com/uccs/ch3** for links to further information about podcasts.

>**Portal.** A Web page designed to be designated as a browser home page; typically can be customized to display personalized content. >**RSS (Really Simple Syndication).** An XML-based format designed for sharing content published to a Web site. >**Podcast.** A recorded audio or video file that is available over the Internet.

HOW IT WORKS

Podcasting

Podcasting enables individuals to create self-published, inexpensive Internet radio broadcasts, such as to share their knowledge, express their opinions on particular subjects, or as a means to share original poems, songs, or short stories with interested individuals. Originally created and distributed by individuals, podcasts are now also being created and distributed by businesses. Some commercial radio stations are making portions of their broadcasts available via podcasts, and a growing number of news sites and corporate sites now have regular podcasts available. In fact, some view podcasts as the new and improved radio since it is an easy way to listen to your favorite radio broadcasts on your own schedule.

To create a podcast, you need a microphone or headset connected to your PC and audio capture software, such as the free *Audacity* program shown in the accompanying illustration. You can then record your podcast content and save it. You can also import additional audio files to mix in with your recorded content and otherwise edit the podcast as needed, such as arranging the order of the tracks, fading opening or closing segments in or out, editing out sneezes or long stretches of silence, adding sound effects, and so forth.

Once the podcast is finished, it needs to be saved; typically the MP3 format is used (the Audacity program shown in the accompanying illustration requires you to download the free *LAME* MP3 encoder in order to save files in the MP3 format).

During the save process, you should add *ID3 tags* to include important details about your show, such as the title of the show, your name, your URL, a copyright notice, and any other desired information. The ID3 information is displayed when the podcast is played and is also used to help your podcast be organized and located easily by podcasting software and directories. You then can upload the podcast file to the Web. If you use a podcast hosting site (such as the free hosting site shown in the accompanying illustration), you may just need to upload the file and the site will take care of placing it on a Web page and creating the download link. If you are hosting the podcast on your own site or would like individuals to be able subscribe to your podcast via an RSS feed, you will have additional steps to perform, such as creating the download link on the appropriate Web page or creating a *podcast feed*—an RSS file that contains the information needed for users to subscribe to your podcast. RSS files can be created in a text-editing program like Windows Notepad and saved with an *.rss* file extension. There are also Web sites that can generate a podcast feed for you and the ability to create a podcast feed is included in some podcast editing programs. To be safe, you should test your download link or podcast feed (there are free *RSS validators* designed for this purpose) to make sure it downloads properly. Once your podcast is ready to go, you can submit a link to the podcast to podcast directories, such as Podcast Alley, so people can find and download it.

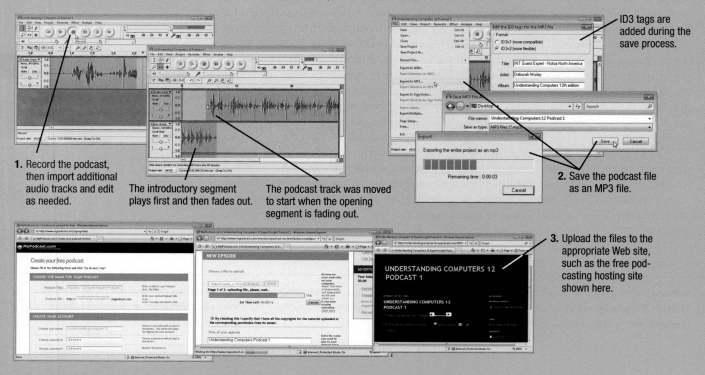

1. Record the podcast, then import additional audio tracks and edit as needed.

The introductory segment plays first and then fades out.

The podcast track was moved to start when the opening segment is fading out.

ID3 tags are added during the save process.

2. Save the podcast file as an MP3 file.

3. Upload the files to the appropriate Web site, such as the free podcasting hosting site shown here.

Product, Corporate, and Government Information

The Web is a very useful tool for locating product and corporate information. Before buying an item online (or in a conventional *brick-and-mortar store*, for that matter), many people research product options online. Manufacturer and retailer Web sites, such as the one in Figure 3-26, often include product specifications, instruction manuals, and other useful information. For investors and consumers, a variety of corporate information is available online, both from the company Web site and from sites, such as Hoover's Online, that offer free or fee-based corporate information.

Government information is also widely available on the Internet. Most state and federal agencies have Web sites to provide information to citizens, such as government publications, archived documents, forms, and legislative bills. You can also perform tasks, such as downloading tax forms and filing your tax returns online. In addition, many cities, counties, and states allow you to pay your car registration, register to vote, view property tax information, or update your driver's license online, as well.

PRODUCT INFORMATION
Businesses often include product specifications, instruction manuals, and other types of product information on their Web sites.

CORPORATE INFORMATION
Businesses often list company information on their Web sites.

GOVERNMENT INFORMATION
Local, state, and federal Web sites contain a variety of useful information and e-services.

FIGURE 3-26
Product, corporate, and government information.

FIGURE 3-27
The UC Web site.

Online Education and Writing

Online education—using the Internet to facilitate learning—is a rapidly growing Internet application. The Internet can be used to deliver part or all of any educational class or program, such as through *Web-based training* (*WBT*) and *distance learning*; it can also be used to supplement or support traditional education, such as with *online testing* and *online writing*. In addition, many high school and college courses use Web content—such as online syllabi, schedules, chat rooms, discussion boards, study guides, podcasts, and tutorials—as required or suggested supplements. For example, similar to the Web site for the Understanding Computers Comprehensive textbook (see Figure 3-27), the Web site that supplements this book contains an online study guide, online quizzes, online hands-on labs, Web links, downloadable podcasts, streaming videos, and other online resources for students taking a course that uses this textbook. The next few sections take a look at some of the most widely used online education applications.

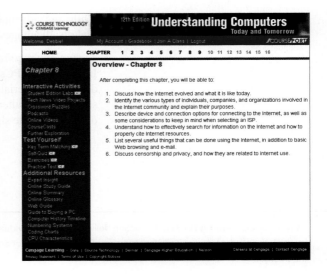

Web-Based Training and Distance Learning

There are more opportunities for online learning today than ever before. Both businesses and schools are utilizing **Web-based training (WBT)**—instruction delivered via the Web—for employee training or course materials, and millions of people take classes via **distance learning** each year. With distance learning, students take classes from a location, such as from home or work, which is different from the one where the delivery of instruction takes place. Distance learning (also called *online learning* and *e-learning*) is available through many high schools, colleges, and universities; it is also used for corporate education and training. Distance learning can be used for training employees in just one task or new skill, as well as for an entire college course or degree program. Typically the majority of distance learning coursework is completed over the Internet via class Web pages, discussion groups, chat rooms, and e-mail, although schools might require some in-person contact, such as sessions for orientation and testing. Distance learning classes often utilize Web-based training components.

Web-based training and distance learning are typically experienced individually and at the user's own pace. Online content for Web-based training components is frequently customized for each individual user, according to his or her mastery of the material already completed. Online content and activities (such as exercises, exams, and animations) are accessed in real time, just as other Web pages are. Some advantages of Web-based training and distance learning include the following:

▶ *Self-paced instruction*. Students can usually work at their own pace and at their convenience, at any time of the day or night.

▶ *Flexible location*. Web-based training can be accessed from home, while traveling, or from any location in which the student has access to a computer with an Internet connection.

▶ *Up-to-date material*. Since all instructional material is hosted on a Web server, it can be updated whenever necessary. Once content is updated, all users see the newest version of the instructional material the next time they access the Web site.

▶ *Immediate feedback and customized content*. Web-based training components can provide immediate feedback for online activities. It can display supplemental material for any problem areas that are identified based on the user's responses. It can also require mastery of material before the student is allowed to move on to the next test or assignment, and it can jump students to more advanced topics as appropriate. This flexibility can result in highly customized content, based on a student's progress and abilities.

While the advantages of Web-based training and distance learning are numerous, potential disadvantages include the following:

▶ *Technology requirements and problems*. Users must have access to a computer and the Internet. Slow PCs or Internet connections can be frustrating for students as they try to download materials or participate in online discussions. Technological problems—such as a computer crashing or a Web server becoming inaccessibile on an exam day—can create significant problems for students and instructors.

>**Web-based training (WBT).** Instruction delivered on an individual basis via the World Wide Web. >**Distance learning.** A learning environment in which the student is physically located away from the instructor and other students; commonly, instruction and communications take place via the Internet.

▶ *Anonymity.* Because students are in remote locations, it can be difficult to ensure that the student registered for the class is the actual student participating in online discussions and online exams. This concern and some possible solutions are discussed shortly.

▶ *Lack of face-to-face contact.* Many educators view the interactive exchange of ideas as a very important part of the educational experience. Although interactivity can take place online via chat rooms and discussion groups, the lack of face-to-face contact—which allows students to see, ask questions of, or have discussions with other students and their instructor in person—is cited as a disadvantage by some educators.

Online Testing

In both distance learning and traditional classes, *online testing*—which allows students to take tests via the Internet—is a growing trend. Both objective tests (such as those containing multiple choice or true/false questions) and performance-based exams (such as those given in computer classes to test student mastery of software applications) can be administered and taken online. For instance, there are *SAM* (*Skills Assessment Manager*) tests available for use in conjunction with this textbook to test both Office software skills and computer concepts. Typically online tests are graded automatically, freeing up instructor time for other activities, as well as providing fast feedback to the students.

One challenge for online testing is ensuring that an online test is taken by the appropriate individual in an authorized manner. Some distance learning programs require students to physically go to a testing center to take the test or find an acceptable test proctor (such as clergy or a commanding officer). Other options are using smart cards, fingerprint scans, and other means to authenticate students taking an online exam. For instance, one new solution is the *Securexam Remote Proctor* system shown in Figure 3-28. This system uses a device that first authenticates the individual taking the test via a fingerprint scan, and then captures real-time audio and video during the exam. The Securexam software also locks down the PC so that it cannot be used for any purpose not allowed during the test (such as performing an Internet search), and flags any suspicious behavior (such as significant noises or movements) in the recording so that the instructor can review those portions of the recording to see if any unauthorized behavior (such as leaving the room or making a telephone call) occurred during the testing period. The device's camera points to a reflective ball which allows it to capture a full 360-degree image of the room, and the recording is uploaded to a server so it can be viewed by the instructor from his or her location. The system is currently being used at a number of schools, including Troy University in Alabama which has over 10,000 online students. Students who plan to take online tests must purchase the device (it costs approximately $150), then they are allowed to take online exams from their remote locations.

FIGURE 3-28
Secure online testing.

1. The device authenticates the individual via a fingerprint scan before the exam can begin.

2. The device captures real-time audio and video during the exam.

3. The computer is locked down during the exam so it can only be used for authorized activities.

Online Writing

In addition to blogs (discussed earlier in this chapter), online writing applications used in an educational context today include *wikis* and *e-portfolios* (*electronic portfolios*). Students might also publish original written material online via personal Web pages.

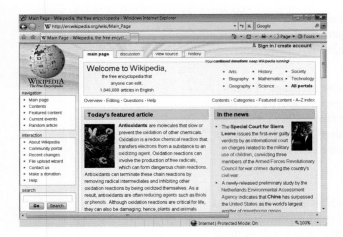

FIGURE 3-29

Wikis. Wikis, such as the Wikipedia collaborative online encyclopedia shown here, can be edited by any authorized individual.

A **wiki**, (named for the Hawaiian phrase *wiki wiki* meaning *quick*) is a way of creating and editing collaborative Web pages quickly and easily. Similar to a blog, the content on a wiki page can be edited and republished to the Web just by pressing a Save or Submit button. However, the entire wiki page is edited to create a new updated page, unlike a blog contribution which is added to the existing content and does not modify the previous blog content. In a nutshell, blogs are designed primarily for one-way running communications, while wikis are intended to be modified by others. In an educational setting, wikis can be used to create and access an easy-to-use shared workspace, such as one used by students or faculty who are collaborating on a group or class project. They can also be used to create and publish Web pages for class projects or presentations. To protect the content of a wiki from sabotage, editing privileges can be password protected. One of the largest wikis is *Wikipedia* (see Figure 3-29), a free online encyclopedia that contains over eight million articles written in 250 languages, is updated by more than 75,000 active contributors, and is visited by hundreds of thousands of individuals each day. While most Wikipedia pages can be edited by any registered user, some are protected and can only be edited by certain members or by administrators. A new online writing experience occurred in 2007, when Penguin Books launched the first ever wiki-based novel called "A Million Penguins." Over the course of the six-week contribution period, more than 1,500 authors collaborated on the novel which ended up being over 1,000 pages in length.

An **e-portfolio**, also called an *electronic portfolio* or *Webfolio*, is a collection of an individual's work accessible through a Web site. Today's e-portfolios are typically linked to a collection of student-related information, such as résumés, papers, projects, and other original works. Some e-portfolios are used for a single course; others are designed to be used and updated throughout a student's educational career, culminating in a comprehensive collection of information that can be used as a job-hunting tool.

CENSORSHIP AND PRIVACY ISSUES

There are many important societal issues related to the Internet. One—network and Internet security—will be covered in Chapter 4. Two other important issues—*censorship* and *privacy*—are discussed next, in the context of Internet use. Other societal issues and how they relate to computer use in general are discussed in further detail in Chapters 5, 6, and 7.

Censorship

The issue of Internet censorship affects all countries that have Internet access. In some countries, Internet content is filtered by the government, typically to hinder the spread of information from political opposition groups, to filter out subjects deemed offensive, or to block information from sites that could endanger national security. Increasingly, some countries are also blocking information from leaving the country, such as via blogs and personal Web pages. In at least two instances, such as during the recent protests in Burma (also known as Myanmar), the government completely shut down Internet access to and from the country to stop the flow of information.

>**Wiki.** A collaborative Web page that is designed to be edited and republished by a variety of individuals. >**E-portfolio.** A collection of an individual's work accessible through a Web site.

In the United States, the First Amendment to the U.S. Constitution guarantees a citizen's right to free speech. This protection allows people to say or show things to others without fear of arrest. People must observe some limits to free speech, of course, such as the prohibition of obscenity over the public airwaves and of child pornography. But how does the right to free speech relate to alleged patently offensive or indecent materials available over the Internet where they might be observed by children and the public at large? There have been some attempts in the United States and other countries at Internet content regulation—what some would view as *censorship*—in recent years, but the courts have had difficulty defining what is "patently offensive" and "indecent" as well as finding a fair balance between protection and censorship. For example, the *Communications Decency Act* was signed into law in 1996 and made it a criminal offense to distribute patently indecent or offensive material online. Although intended to protect children from being exposed to inappropriate Web content, the Supreme Court, in 1997, declared this law unconstitutional on the basis of free speech. A second attempt at Internet censorship was the *Child Online Protection Act of 1998* (*COPA*). COPA imposed severe criminal and civil penalties on individuals who put material deemed harmful to minors on the Web. The law was immediately challenged and never enforced and, in 2007, was overruled as a federal court determined that Internet filters are far more effective than COPA at protecting children from inappropriate material on the Web.

Internet filtering is the act of blocking access to particular Web pages or types of Web pages. It can be used on home computers (for instance, by individuals to protect themselves from material they would view as offensive or by parents to protect their children from material they feel is inappropriate for their children). It is also commonly used by employers to keep non-work-related material off company PCs, by some ISPs and search sites to block access to potentially objectionable materials, and by many schools and libraries to control the Web content that children are able to view. Available through browser and operating system settings, as well as through stand-alone programs, Internet filtering typically restricts access to Web pages that contain specified keywords or that exceed a rating for potentially offensive categories, such as language, nudity, sex, or violence. One limitation with this procedure, however, is that the description of each site and how the categories apply to its content are provided voluntarily by the content provider, not by an independent rating organization. Typically, a password is required to change the filter settings to prevent them from being changed by an unauthorized individual, such as a child or an employee. As shown in Figure 3-30, Internet Explorer's *Content Advisor* can be used to filter the Web sites displayed for all users of a particular computer (though blocked Web sites can be viewed if the user knows the appropriate password) and *Parental Controls* can be used to set restrictions for individual users, such as the Web sites that can be viewed, whether or not the user can download files, and so forth.

An ongoing debate has been whether or not public computers should use Internet filtering. Filtering advocates want to protect children at public locations (such as libraries and schools) from accessing adult-oriented material. Individuals and organizations against Internet filtering at libraries and schools believe that filtering violates the patrons' and students' First Amendment rights to free speech. The *Child Internet Protection Act* (*CIPA*) that went into effect in 2001 required public libraries and schools to use Internet filtering to block Internet access to certain materials in order to receive public funds. Although intended to protect children, it was fought strenuously by free speech advocacy groups and some library associations and was ruled unconstitutional by a federal court in 2002. In a 6 to 3 ruling in 2003, however, the Supreme Court reversed the lower court decision and ruled that the law was constitutional because the need for libraries to prevent

>**Internet filtering.** Using a software program or browser option to block access to particular Web pages or types of Web pages.

minors from accessing obscene materials outweighs the free speech rights of library patrons and Web site publishers. However, the Court also modified the law to require the library to remove the filter at a patron's request.

Web Browsing Privacy

Privacy, as it relates to the Internet, encompasses what information about individuals is available, how it is used, and by whom. As more and more transactions and daily activities are being performed online, there is the potential for vast amounts of private information to be collected and distributed without the individual's knowledge or permission. Therefore, it is understandable that public concern regarding privacy and the Internet is on the rise. Although privacy will be discussed in more detail in

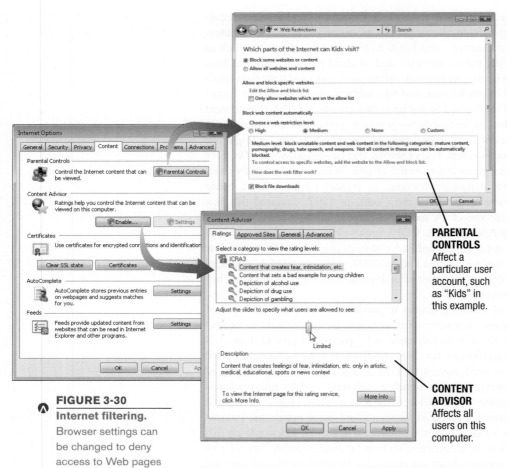

PARENTAL CONTROLS
Affect a particular user account, such as "Kids" in this example.

CONTENT ADVISOR
Affects all users on this computer.

Ⓐ **FIGURE 3-30**
Internet filtering.
Browser settings can be changed to deny access to Web pages with objectionable content.

Chapter 5, a few issues that are of special concern to Internet users regarding Web browsing privacy and e-mail privacy are discussed in the next few sections.

Cookies

Many Web pages today use **cookies**—small text files that are stored on your hard drive by a Web server, typically the one associated with the Web page being viewed—to identify return visitors and their preferences. While some individuals view all cookies as a potentially dangerous invasion of privacy, the use of cookies can provide some benefits to consumers. For example, cookies can enable a Web site to remember preferences for customized Web site content (such as displaying customized content on a portal page, such as the one shown Figure 3-25), as well as to retrieve a shopping cart containing items selected during a previous session. Some Web sites use cookies to keep track of which pages on their Web sites each person has visited, in order to recommend products on return visits that match that person's interests.

Cookies are relatively safe from a privacy standpoint. Web sites can read only their own cookie files; they cannot read other cookie files on your PC or any other data on your computer, for that matter. A cookie file might, however, record the pages viewed on the site associated with the cookie, the amount of time spent on pages with similar content, and other factors used to target third-party advertisements. For instance, if you spend a lot of

> **Cookie.** A small file stored on a user's hard drive by a Web server; commonly used to identify personal preferences and settings for that user.

time checking airline prices on a travel site, you might start seeing ads for hotels, rental cars, airfare, and other travel-oriented goods and services displayed on the pages of your travel site—and many of the ads will be from third-party organizations with which the site has an advertising relationship.

The information stored in a cookie file typically includes the name of the cookie, its expiration date, the domain that the cookie belongs to, and either selected personal information that you have entered while visiting the Web site or an ID number assigned by the Web site that allows the Web site's server to retrieve your information from its database. Such a database can contain two types of information: *personally identifiable information* (*PII*) and *non-personally identifiable information* (*Non-PII*). Personally identifiable information is connected with a specific user's identity—such as his or her name, address, and credit card number provided to the site—and is typically given during the process of ordering goods or services. Non-personally identifiable information is anonymous data—such as which product pages were viewed or which advertisements located on the site were clicked—that is not directly associated with the visitor's name or another personally identifiable characteristic. Cookies are stored on the computer's hard drive and can be looked at, if desired—although sometimes deciphering the information contained in a cookie file is difficult. Figure 3-31 shows how to see the cookie files stored on your PC when using Internet Explorer to browse the Web.

Browser privacy settings can be changed to specify which type of cookies (if any) are allowed to be used, such as permitting the use of regular cookies, but not *third-party cookies* (cookies placed by companies, such as advertising firms who have placed ads on that page) or cookies using personally identifiable information (see Figure 3-32). Turning off cookies entirely might make some features—such as a shopping cart—on some Web sites

ONLINE VIDEO

Go to **www.course.com/uccs/ch3** to watch the "Google Search Privacy: Plain and Simple" video clip.

FIGURE 3-31

Viewing cookies in Internet Explorer.

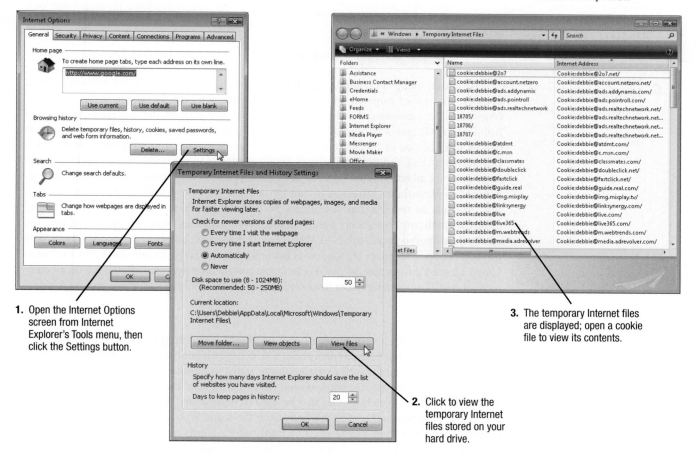

1. Open the Internet Options screen from Internet Explorer's Tools menu, then click the Settings button.

2. Click to view the temporary Internet files stored on your hard drive.

3. The temporary Internet files are displayed; open a cookie file to view its contents.

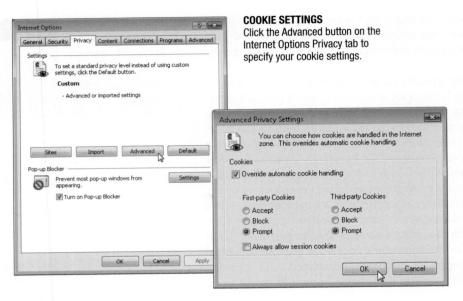

COOKIE SETTINGS
Click the Advanced button on the Internet Options Privacy tab to specify your cookie settings.

COOKIE PROMPTS
After selecting the "Prompt" option, you will be prompted to accept or reject cookies as they are encountered.

Web sites requesting cookie use

FIGURE 3-32
Browser cookie management. The desired cookie settings can be specified in the browser settings.

inoperable. The *Medium High* privacy option in Internet Explorer is a widely used setting since it allows the use of regular cookies but blocks third-party cookies that use personally identifiable information without explicit permission. Both Internet Explorer and Netscape Navigator users who want more control over their cookies can choose to accept or decline cookies as they are encountered. Although this option interrupts your Web surfing frequently, it is interesting to see the cookies generated from each individual Web site. For example, the two cookie prompts shown in the bottom of Figure 3-32 were generated while visiting the BestBuy.com Web site. Although one cookie request is from the BestBuy.com Web site directly, the other is a third-party cookie from an online marketing company. Another alternative for controlling cookies is to delete the cookie files stored on your hard drive periodically, either by using an option available through your Web browser or by deleting the temporary Internet files from your hard drive using the Internet Explorer option or your file management program.

Although many individuals are slowly becoming more comfortable with the use of cookies, the use of targeted ads based on Web site activities is raising some consumer objections. In response, the advertising industry has formed the *Network Advertising Initiative (NAI)* and is hoping that voluntary compliance with online marketing standards can be used in lieu of legislation. The NAI works in conjunction with the Federal Trade Commission (FTC) to develop privacy standards for NAI members, which include many large Internet advertising companies. These standards detail under what conditions non-personally identifiable information can be merged with personally identifiable information, as well as require that consumers be given the choice to opt out from receiving advertisements from members based on their Web activities (you can opt out of targeted ads by NAI members via the NAI Web site). However, as consumer concerns about Web privacy continue to grow, legislation is becoming more likely. In late 2003, the European Union adopted privacy regulations on electronic communications, including a ban on all commercial e-mail unless a recipient has asked for it, and set strict rules for the use of cookies.

Web Bugs

A *Web bug* is usually a very small (often 1 pixel by 1 pixel) image on a Web page that contains code designed to transmit data about a Web page visitor back to the Web page's server. Web bugs are commonly used to gather usage statistics about a Web site, such as the number of visitors to the site, the most visited pages on the site, the time of each visit, and the Web browser used. Web bugs can also be used to retrieve and relay data stored in a cookie file, if the Web bug and cookie are both from the same Web site or advertising company. Consequently, Web bugs can be used by third-party advertising companies to compile data about individuals and are used extensively by Internet advertising companies.

Although Web bugs can be normal images that are set up to transfer information, as well as be displayed on the Web page, most Web bug images are tiny and match the color of the Web page's background, so they are invisible to the naked eye. This is perhaps the biggest objection to Web bugs—since they are not visible, users typically are not aware of this potential invasion of privacy. Cookie management software can prevent the use of cookies by Web bugs, and some can hinder the use of Web bugs by suppressing all images of a specified dimension, such as all images that are 1 pixel by 1 pixel, although this also suppresses small invisible images used for spacing and alignment.

Spyware and Adware

Spyware is the term used for any software program that is installed without the user's knowledge and that secretly gathers information about the user and transmits it through his or her Internet connection—typically, to advertisers but sometimes to criminals. Just as with cookies and Web bugs, the information gathered by the spyware software is usually not associated with a person's identity. Instead, it is typically used to provide advertisers with information to be used for marketing purposes, such as to help select advertisements to display on each person's PC. Like Web bugs, people are not normally aware when spyware is being used. Instead of being embedded into a Web page like a Web bug, however, spyware programs are installed—without the user's knowledge—on the user's computer. Spyware programs are usually installed secretly at the same time another program is installed, such as a program downloaded from a Web site or a P2P service. Spyware can also be used by unscrupulous individuals to retrieve personal data stored on your PC and is discussed in more detail in Chapter 4.

A related type of software is *adware*—free or low-cost software that is supported by onscreen advertising. Many free programs that can be downloaded from the Internet, such as the free version of the *NetZero* e-mail program, include some type of adware, which results in onscreen advertising. The difference between spyware and adware is that adware typically does not gather information and relay it to others via the Internet (although it can), and it is not installed without the user's consent. Adware might, however, be installed without the user's direct knowledge, since many users do not read licensing agreements before clicking OK to install a new program. When this occurs with a program that contains adware, the adware components are installed without the user's direct knowledge.

Both spyware and adware can be annoying and use up valuable system resources. In addition, privacy advocates object to spyware because it secretly collects and transmits data about individuals to others, and it can bog down a user's Internet connection without the user's knowledge. *Firewall programs* can protect against spyware programs transmitting information over your Internet connection, since firewalls typically control outgoing computer traffic as well as incoming traffic and will notify the user of any unauthorized transmissions. *Antispyware programs* can detect and remove spyware programs. *Firewalls* and *antispyware programs* are discussed in more detail in Chapter 4.

E-Mail Privacy

Many people mistakenly believe that the e-mail they send and receive is private and will never be read by anyone other than the intended recipient. Since it is transmitted over public media, however, only *encrypted* (electronically scrambled) e-mail can be transmitted safely, as discussed in Chapter 4. Although unlikely to happen to your personal e-mail, *nonencrypted* e-mail can be intercepted and read by someone else. Consequently, from a privacy standpoint, a nonencrypted e-mail message should be viewed more like a postcard than a letter (see Figure 3-33).

It is also important to realize that your employer and your ISP have access to the e-mail you send through those organizations, such as to scan incoming e-mail for spam filtering and virus protection, as well as for employee monitoring purposes. Businesses and ISPs typically also *archive* (keep copies of) e-mail messages that travel through their servers and are required to comply with subpoenas from law enforcement agencies for archived e-mail messages.

FIGURE 3-33

You cannot assume e-mail messages are private, unless they are encrypted.

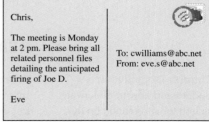

Chris,

The meeting is Monday at 2 pm. Please bring all related personnel files detailing the anticipated firing of Joe D.

Eve

To: cwilliams@abc.net
From: eve.s@abc.net

REGULAR (NONENCRYPTED E-MAIL) = POSTCARD

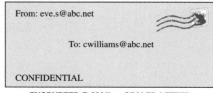

From: eve.s@abc.net

To: cwilliams@abc.net

CONFIDENTIAL

ENCRYPTED E-MAIL = SEALED LETTER

SUMMARY

EVOLUTION OF THE INTERNET

Chapter Objective 1:
Discuss how the Internet evolved and what it is like today.

The origin of the **Internet**—a worldwide collection of interconnected networks that is accessed by millions of people daily—dates back to the late 1960s. At its start and throughout its early years, the Internet was called **ARPANET**. It was not until the development of graphical user interfaces and the **World Wide Web** that public interest in the Internet began to soar. Most companies have Web sites today and consider the Web to be an indispensable business tool. While the Web is a very important and widely used Internet resource, it is not the only one. Over the years, *protocols* have been developed to download files, send e-mail messages, and other tasks, in addition to using Web pages. Today, the term *Internet* has become a household word and, in many ways, has redefined how people think about computers and communications. The next significant improvement to the Internet infrastructure may be the result of projects such as *Internet2*.

Chapter Objective 2:
Identify the various types of individuals, companies, and organizations involved in the Internet community and explain their purposes.

The Internet community is made up of individual *users*; companies, such as **Internet service providers** (**ISPs**), **Internet content providers**, **application service providers** (**ASPs**), *infrastructure companies*, and a variety of software and hardware companies; the government; and other organizations. Virtually anyone with a computer with communications capability can be part of the Internet, either as a user or supplier of information or services. **Web services** are self-contained business functions that operate over the Internet.

Because the Internet is so unique in the history of the world—and it remains a relatively new phenomenon—several widespread myths about it have surfaced. Three such myths are that the Internet is free, that it is controlled by some central body, and that it is synonymous with the World Wide Web.

GETTING SET UP TO USE THE INTERNET

Chapter Objective 3:
Describe device and connection options for connecting to the Internet, as well as some considerations to keep in mind when selecting an ISP.

When preparing to become connected to the Internet, you need to decide which type of device (PC, Internet appliance, or mobile device) to use, which type of connection—**dial-up connection** (**conventional dial-up** or **ISDN** (**integrated services digital network**) **Internet access**) or **direct connection** (through a **T1 line**, **cable**, **DSL** (**Digital Subscriber Line**), **satellite**, **fixed wireless**, **mobile wireless**, or **broadband over fiber** (**BoF**)—also called **fiber-to-the-premises** (**FTTP**)—**Internet access**, or via a **hotspot**)—to use, and which specific Internet service provider to use. Once all these decisions are made, you can acquire the proper hardware and software and set up your system for Internet access.

SEARCHING THE INTERNET

Chapter Objective 4:
Understand how to effectively search for information on the Internet and how to properly cite Internet resources.

Search sites—Web sites that enable users to search for and find information on the Internet—typically locate pages using a **keyword search** (in which the user specifies **keywords** for the desired information) or a **directory search** (in which the user selects categories corresponding to the desired information). Both types of searches use a *search database* that contains information about pages on the Web and a **search engine** to retrieve the list of matching Web pages from the database. Search site databases are generally maintained by automated *spider* programs; directory databases are typically maintained by human editors. *Metasearch engines* use multiple search engines, some search sites are *natural language* sites, and many search sites use a combination of search options.

There are a variety of search strategies that can be used, including typing phrases instead of single keywords; using *Boolean operators*; trying the search at multiple search sites; and using *synonyms*, *variant word forms*, *wildcards*, and *field searches*. Once a list of links to Web pages matching the search criteria is displayed, the hits need to be evaluated for their relevancy. If the information found on a Web page is used in a paper, report, or other original document, the source should be credited appropriately.

BEYOND BROWSING AND E-MAIL

The Internet can be used for many different types of activities in addition to basic Web browsing and e-mail exchange. Other common types of online communications tools include **discussion groups** (where people post messages on a particular topic for others to read and respond to), **chat rooms** (online locations where multiple users can carry on real-time typed conversations), **instant messaging** (**IM**) (a form of private chat in which messages are sent in real time to online *buddies*), **videoconferencing** (real-time meetings taking place online using video cameras and microphones for participants to see and hear each other), **Webinars** (seminars presented over the Web), **blogs** (Web pages that contain short regularly-updated entries), and **Voice over Internet Protocol** (**VoIP**), which refers to making voice telephone calls over the Internet. **Social networking sites** are Web sites that are designed for creating a community of users.

Common Web activities for individuals include a variety of consumer *e-commerce* activities, such as **online shopping**, **online auctions**, **online banking**, and **online investing**. When performing any type of financial transaction over the Internet, it is very important to use only *secure* Web pages.

Online entertainment applications include downloading *MP3* files and other types of **online music**, *interactive TV* and **video-on-demand** (**VOD**), and **online gaming**. **Peer-to-peer** (**P2P**) **file sharing** is also commonly used to exchange entertainment media. A wide variety of news, reference, government, product, and corporate information is available via the Web as well. News, reference, and search tools are commonly found on **portal** Web pages; **RSS** (**Really Simple Syndication**) feeds can be used to deliver current news, **podcasts**, and other Web content to individuals as it becomes available. **Web-based training** (**WBT**), **distance learning**, *online testing*, **wikis**, and **e-portfolios** are commonly used *online education* applications.

CENSORSHIP AND PRIVACY ISSUES

Among the most important societal issues relating to the Internet are censorship and *privacy*. Web content is not censored as a whole, but **Internet filtering** can be used by parents, employers, educators, and anyone wishing to prevent access to sites they deem objectionable on computers for which they have control. *Privacy* is a big concern for individuals, particularly as it relates to their Web activity. **Cookies** are typically used by Web sites to save customized settings for that site and can also be used for advertising purposes. Other items of possible concern are *Web bugs* and *spyware*. Unless an e-mail message is *encrypted*, it should not be assumed to be completely private.

Chapter Objective 5:
List several useful things that can be done using the Internet, in addition to basic Web browsing and e-mail.

Chapter Objective 6:
Discuss censorship and privacy, and how they are related to Internet use.

REVIEW ACTIVITIES

KEY TERM MATCHING

Instructions: Match each key term on the left with the definition on the right that best describes it.

a. cookie

b. dial-up connection

c. direct connection

d. distance learning

e. Internet

f. keyword

g. podcast

h. search engine

i. video-on-demand (VOD)

j. World Wide Web

1. _____ A learning environment in which the student is physically located away from the instructor and other students; commonly, instruction and communications take place via the Internet.

2. _____ An always-on type of Internet connection in which the PC or other device is continually connected to the Internet.

3. _____ A small file stored on a user's hard drive by a Web server; commonly used to identify personal preferences and settings for that user.

4. _____ A software program used by a search site to retrieve matching Web pages from a search database.

5. _____ A type of Internet connection in which the PC or other device must dial up and connect to a service provider's computer via telephone lines before being connected to the Internet.

6. _____ A recorded audio or video file that is available over the Internet.

7. _____ A word typed in a search box on a search site to locate information on the Internet.

8. _____ The collection of Web pages available through the Internet.

9. _____ The largest and most well-known computer network, linking millions of computers all over the world.

10. _____ The process of downloading movies and televisions shows, on demand, via the Internet.

SELF-QUIZ

Instructions: Circle **T** if the statement is true, **F** if the statement is false, or write the best answer in the space provided. **Answers for the self-quiz are located in the References and Resources Guide at the end of the book.**

1. **T   F**   When the Internet was first developed, it was called Mosaic.

2. **T   F**   On the Internet, an *access provider* and a *content provider* are essentially the same thing.

3. **T   F**   With a direct connection, you need only open your browser to start your Internet session.

4. **T   F**   A hotspot is used to provide Internet access to individuals via a wireless connection.

5. **T   F**   With peer-to-peer (P2P) file sharing, individuals upload files to a central server, and then others can download them from that server.

6. _____ is a type of always-on broadband Internet service that transmits data over standard telephone lines.

7. With a(n) _____ search, keywords are typed into the search box; with a(n) _____ search, users select categories to find matching Web pages.

8. _____ is a form of private chat set up to allow users to easily and quickly exchange real-time typed messages with the individuals they specify.

9. With a(n) _____, people bid on products over the Internet, and the highest bidder purchases the item.

10. Match each Internet application with its possible situation and write the corresponding number in the blank to the left of each situation.

a. _____ To communicate with a friend in a different state.
b. _____ To rent a movie without leaving your home.
c. _____ To pay only as much as you specify for an item purchased through the Internet.
d. _____ To pay a bill without writing a check.
e. _____ To develop new business contacts.
f. _____ To find Web pages containing information about growing your own Bonsai trees.

1. Online banking   3. Online auction   5. Video-on-demand (VOD)
2. E-mail   4. Internet searching   6. Social networking site

---

1. Match each type of Internet access with its description and write the corresponding number in the blank to the left of each description.

a. _____ A fast type of Internet access via standard phone lines; does not tie up your phone.
b. _____ The most widely used type of home broadband connection; does not use standard phone lines.
c. _____ Provides access to the Internet via a very fast fiber optic network.
d. _____ Provides wireless Internet access to a handheld PC or mobile device.
e. _____ Requires a transceiver and a clear view of the southern sky.
f. _____ Accesses the Internet via standard phone lines and ties up your phone; the maximum speed is 56 Kbps.

1. Conventional dial-up   3. DSL   5. Satellite
2. BoF   4. Cable   6. Mobile wireless

2. What would each of the following searches look for?

a. hot AND dogs _____
b. snorkel* _____
c. text:"Internet privacy" domain:gov _____

3. List three different sets of keywords that could be used to search for information on how to maintain a trumpet.

4. Explain the difference between a blog, a wiki, and a podcast.

5. List one advantage and one disadvantage of the use of Web site cookies.

Although slow to embrace new technology, courtrooms today are becoming high-tech. For example, videoconferencing systems that allow defendants and witnesses to participate in proceedings from remote locations are becoming more common. Allowing defendants to participate via teleconferencing from the jail facility saves travel time and expense, as well as eliminates any risk of flight. Remote testimony from witnesses can save both time and money. But could having defendants and witnesses participate remotely affect the jury's perspective? If the videoconference takes place via the Internet, can it be assured that proceedings are confidential? Do you think the benefits of these systems outweigh any potential disadvantages? Can you think of other "virtual" courtroom applications or tools that might be a reality in the future? Do you think they should become a reality?

BALANCING ACT

REAL SELF VS. VIRTUAL SELF

The term *virtual* is commonly used to describe a situation or activity that is merely conceptual, instead of having a physical reality, and is often applied to computer activities. For example, a *virtual tour* of a museum allows you to view 3D images of the museum and "walk" through its exhibits; a *virtual mall* is a collection of shopping Web sites that is organized graphically using a mall/store structure; and a *virtual vacation* is a getaway taken completely online, such as by touring a virtual reality (VR) version of a vacation destination or by sending your *avatar* (an online representation of yourself used in virtual worlds or online multiplayer games to move through the game, express emotions, and so forth) on a vacation in Second Life or another virtual world.

The very nature of online communications fosters anonymity. When participating in chat sessions and exchanging e-mail, an individual's physical characteristics (such as age, gender, race, and appearance) are not visible. Instead, individuals can project any image of themselves that they wish to present, either by what they say or by the avatars they choose to use to portray themselves online. In other words, when they are online, individuals are free to create a *virtual self* that may not necessarily be representative of who they really are. Sometimes this is harmless. Sometimes this is even beneficial, allowing individuals to be judged online solely by their ideas, not their physical appearance. At other times, such as when child molesters masquerade as young people to lure youngsters to meet with them face-to-face, it can be downright dangerous and criminal.

YOUR TURN

Give some thought to how an individual's virtual self can differ from his or her real self, and form an opinion regarding the use of a virtual self. Consider the following when forming your opinion and be prepared to discuss your position (in class, via an online class discussion group, in a class chat room, or via a class blog) or to write a short paper expressing your opinion, depending on your instructor's directions.

- Under what circumstances might a person consider giving false or misleading information (such as regarding his or her age, gender, appearance, education, areas of expertise, and so forth) online? Do you feel that it would be ethical under any of these circumstances? Why or why not?

- Should chat room and virtual community participants be required to submit their real identities to the person or organization hosting the chat room or community before being allowed to participate? Why or why not?

- What role should the government take in online communications? Should the government be allowed to monitor online communications and have access to a participant's real identity? If so, under what circumstances?

- In 1996, the first virtual wedding between two actual individuals was held in an Internet virtual world with the bride, groom, and guests represented by avatars. What is your opinion about "virtualizing" these types of important events?

PROJECTS

1. **Blogs** A blog is a Web page that serves as a publicly accessible personal journal for an individual. In the past, publishing a blog was complicated; today, *blog tools* make it much easier.

   For this project, investigate blogs. By searching a news site or using a search site, find at least two blogs and review them. What types of information is the user sharing? Why do you think he or she prefers to put this information on the Web instead of in a private written journal? Did the blogs you found belong to a private individual, a well-known person, or an individual representing an organization? Would you want to have your own blog? Why or why not? Do you think blog use will continue to grow? Why or why not? At the conclusion of your research, prepare a one-page summary of your findings and submit it to your instructor.

   HOT TOPICS

2. **Online Travel Planning** Planning and booking travel arrangements online is a very popular Internet activity today and there are a number of sites that can be used.

   For this project, review two popular travel sites, such as Expedia.com and Travelocity.com, to see what services they offer and how easy it is to locate the information needed to plan and book a flight via those sites. Select a destination and use one of the sites to obtain a quote for a particular flight on a particular day. Next, go to the Web site for the airline of the flight and use the site to obtain a quote for the same flight. Is there a difference in price or flight availability? Could you make a reservation online through both sites? Would you feel comfortable booking an entire vacation yourself online, or are there services that a travel agent could provide that you feel would be beneficial? Do you think these sites are most appropriate for making business travel plans or vacation plans, or are they suited to either? At the conclusion of your research, prepare a one-page summary of your findings and submit it to your instructor.

   SHORT ANSWER/ RESEARCH

3. **Web Searching** Search sites can be used to find Web pages containing specific information, and there are strategies that can be used to make Web searching an efficient and useful experience.

   For this project, go to the Google search site and perform the following searches, then submit your results and printouts to your instructor. (Note: Some of the answers will vary from student to student.)

   a. Search for *rules*. How many pages were found? What is the name of the first page in the list of hits? Next, search for *backgammon rules*. How many pages were found? Use the hits to find a picture of how a backgammon board is initially set up, then, print that page.

   b. Go to Advanced Search option. Use the form fields to perform a search for Web pages that contain all of the words *hiking trails Sierras*, do not contain the word *horse*, and have the domain *.gov*. After the hits are displayed, record the actual search phrase that is listed in the search box along with the name and URL of the first page displayed in the list of hits.

   c. Search to find a recipe for Buffalo Chicken Wings; a map of where your house, apartment or dorm is located; and the ZIP code for 200 N. Elm Street, Hinsdale, IL and print the pages containing this information.

   HANDS ON

WRITING ABOUT COMPUTERS

4. Online Job Hunting There are a number of Web sites that contain useful job-hunting tools, such as job searching, the ability to post an online résumé, and job-hunting tips.

For this project, visit two career-oriented Web sites, such as Monster.com or CareerBuilder.com, and review the types of information and services available from the perspective of both a job seeker and an employer. Are there fees for any of the services? If you post a résumé, is it available for anyone to see? Are the sites useful from an employer's perspective? Would you use either of these sites? List any advantages and disadvantages you can think of for using one of these sites to find a new job. Submit your findings and opinions to your instructor in the form of a short paper, not more than two pages in length.

PRESENTATION/ DEMONSTRATION

5. Wi-Fi Hotspots There are an increasing number of public locations offering Wi-Fi hotspots available for public use.

For this project, find one location in your local area that offers public Wi-Fi access and either visit the location or call the provider on the phone to find out the how the hotspot works, in terms of fees and access. Is there a fee to use the hotspot? If so, do you have to subscribe on a regular basis, or can you pay only when you want to use the hotspot? Where and how is payment made? Do you need any special software to access the hotspot? Do you need to be assigned a username or key (such as a *WEP*, *WPA*, or *WPA 2* key) before you can use the service? Share your findings and opinions with the class in the form of a short presentation. The presentation should not exceed 10 minutes and should make use of one or more presentation aids, such as the chalkboard, handouts, overhead transparencies, or a computer-based slide presentation (your instructor may provide additional requirements). You may also be asked to submit a summary of the presentation to your instructor.

GROUP DISCUSSION

6. Rural Broadband Citizens who live in rural areas typically have less access to broadband Internet than those in more highly populated areas. There are differing opinions regarding the importance of broadband Internet for everyone and whose responsibility it is to provide it. If a region has only 56 Kbps dial-up service, does that really put it at a disadvantage? Is the *digital divide* more about separating those who have access to technology, such as the Internet, and those who do not, or is it about the quality of that technology? What about the government's role—should it provide the necessary infrastructure to ensure an appropriate level of Internet access to all U.S. citizens? If not, how will the digital divide within the United States be eliminated? Will it ever be eliminated?

For this project, form an opinion of the necessity of broadband Internet and the role of the government (if any) in providing broadband Internet access to its citizens and be prepared to discuss your position (in class, via an online class discussion group, in a class chat room, or via a class blog, depending on your instructor's directions). You may also be asked to write a short paper expressing your opinion.

7. **Internet Sales Tax** Based on a 1992 Supreme Court decision regarding mail order sales tax collection, online purchases in the U.S. have not been subject to sales tax, unless the buyer lives in the same state where the merchant maintains a physical presence. With an increasing percentage of potential state sales tax revenue not being collected as the result of online shopping, however, many state and local governments want that law to change, and a national online sales tax plan—called the *Streamlined Sales Tax Project* (*SSTP*)—has been in development since 2000. Some online merchants now voluntarily collect sales tax, and mandatory sales tax collection on online purchases is a possibility for the future. This issue brings up ethical decisions for both businesses and individuals. Should a business collect sales tax, even if it isn't required to by law? Consumers who live in a state that collects sales tax are technically required to pay a "use" tax to the state when an Internet retailer doesn't collect sales tax. Ethically, how careful should individuals be with respect to keeping track of online purchases for tax purposes?

   For this project, form an opinion about Internet sales tax collection and the ethical implications for businesses and consumers. Be prepared to discuss your position (in class, via an online class discussion group, in a class chat room, or via a class blog, depending on your instructor's directions). You may also be asked to write a short paper expressing your opinion.

ETHICS IN ACTION

8. **File-Sharing Risks** By design, P2P users have to access the content of other users' hard drives. The accompanying video clip discusses the risks associated with P2P use.

   Go to www.course.com/uccs/ch3 to watch the "File Sharers May Risk Identity Theft" video clip. After watching the video, think about the impact of P2P sites. How does the ability of others to access the content of your hard drive if you choose to use a P2P file sharing service impact your personal privacy? If you have ever used a P2P service, did you limit the folders other P2P users were allowed to access? Did you realize you had that option? Should P2P software be set up to prevent sharing files until the user selects the locations to be shared? Why or why not? There have been cases where sensitive data stored on corporate and government computers has been exposed via P2P file sharing services. What measures should businesses and the government take to ensure that these types of breaches do not occur? If private information is stolen from a P2P user's hard drive via a P2P service and then used in identity theft, should the P2P site be held responsible? Why or why not?

   Express your viewpoint: What is the impact of P2P services on personal privacy and security?

   Use the video clip and the questions previously asked as a foundation for your response. Be prepared to discuss your position (in class, via an online class discussion group, in a class chat room, or via a class blog) or to write a short paper stating and supporting your viewpoint on the issue, depending on your instructor's direction. You may also be asked to do research and provide resources to support your point of view on this issue.

VIDEO VIEWPOINT

9. **Interactive Activities** Go to www.course.com/uccs/ch3 and work the interactive **Crossword Puzzle**, listen to the **Podcasts** and watch the **Online Videos** associated with this chapter, and explore the **Further Exploration** links. In addition, work the following interactive **Student Edition Labs**.

   - Networking Basics
   - Getting the Most Out of the Internet
   - Connecting to the Internet
   - E-Commerce

   If you have a SAM user profile, you have access to even more interactive content. Log in to your SAM account and go to your assignments page to see what your instructor has assigned for this chapter.

WEB ACTIVITIES

Student Edition Labs

10. **Test Yourself** Go to www.course.com/uccs/ch3 and review the **Online Study Guide** for Chapter 3, then test your knowledge of the terms and concepts in this chapter by completing the **Key Term Matching** exercise, the **Self-Quiz**, the **Exercises**, and the **Practice Test**.

EXPERT INSIGHT ON . . .
Software

A conversation with GRAHAM WATSON
Senior Community Lead, Technical Audience Global Marketing, Microsoft

My Background . . .

I actually got started with computers at school when I discovered I could either take a lesson where I played with a computer terminal or one involving cross-country running in winter! I quickly worked out that the computer was more fun! I'm now part of the Technical Audience Global Marketing Group at Microsoft. My specific responsibilities include making sure that the IT Professional and Developer User Groups around the world—representing over four million people—have the connection they need with Microsoft.

> **"... everyone needs to know how to at least send an e-mail and create, edit, and print a document."**

It's Important to Know . . .

About computer systems. No matter how directly you will be involved with computer systems in your career, everyone will need to know enough about systems to be able to make appropriate decisions as to how to use technology to help them in their work and daily lives in general. For example, everyone needs to know how to at least send an e-mail and create, edit, and print a document. Think about the business tasks you need to complete each day, and make sure you can efficiently use the right tools on your computer to help you work more effectively.

The impact of Windows Vista. One of the biggest impacts on society that Windows Vista will have is enhanced security for users. One problem with the connectivity that computers provide is that it can also provide thieves and other miscreants with access to you. Windows Vista is the most secure mass market operating system, and its use will improve resilience against the most common forms of attack.

How IT affects your chosen career. It is important to understand the business impact and future trends within the IT space and how it can affect your chosen career. For example, think about the way the retail sales industry has changed over the past ten years. Depending on your chosen career, computer power, graphics, communications capabilities, or mobility may be particularly important to you. You will also need to keep abreast of the latest trends and understand the benefits, costs, effort, risks, and details of how to implement solutions to business problems successfully, taking into account the needs of the customer and the user.

How I Use this Technology . . .

There are two main areas where computers affect me personally. The first one is the most obvious—it provides me with highly enjoyable employment! It's interesting, though, how my current role is more

Graham Watson is a Senior Community Lead in the Technical Audience Group Marketing Team at Microsoft. He has worked for Microsoft for 14 years, initially as an enterprise infrastructure consultant. Prior to his current position, he worked as a computer operator and a support engineer. In all, he has over 30 years of experience working with computer systems, networks, and other computer-related areas. Graham has a Bachelor of Arts degree in Computer Studies and, along with his client, had the honor of sending the first ever production e-mail from Microsoft Exchange. He runs a blog at blogs.technet.com/grahamtwatson.

> ## One of the biggest impacts on society that Windows Vista will have is enhanced security for users.

related to computers as a social tool, given my responsibilities toward technical communities. The second one is the same as for many people—my family and friends are all connected, and I often communicate with my wife and children via e-mail or IM. I also do most of my shopping via the Internet—I think I got most of my Christmas shopping done last year without leaving my desk. It's hard to imagine how I would live my life without Windows Vista!

What the Future Holds . . .

Connectivity is probably the biggest thing—not just between people, but also between parts of computer applications. Web services will continue to grow in importance, and Windows Vista, together with .NET 3.0, will further enable the ability to quickly develop applications by "stitching together" services obtained from a variety of companies and building on them to fulfill specific needs. Mobility is another interesting area—as computers become smaller, more powerful, and more connected, additional opportunities open up. On one hand, we are finding some devices becoming more general purpose (for example, your cell phone may also take pictures and play music), but at the same time there is an opposite movement toward more dedicated devices which work better. Some people just want a simple-to-use cell phone.

I expect that the software we know today will continue to evolve and get more sophisticated but simpler to use—for example, Microsoft Office continues to improve on its ability to very easily create professional documents. There will probably be at least one "left field" innovation—something that will be obvious once it's taken off, but almost unnoticed until that time. Examples of this from the last few years include digital video recorders, such as TiVo (or Windows Media Center Edition) and Voice over IP. Possibilities for the future include intelligent search (imagine being able to ask your computer almost any question in the same way you would ask a friend, and get a single, correct answer) and improved connectivity between computers and devices (imagine phoning friends and arranging to meet them, and then automatically getting directions given to you by your car, meetings set up and moved, flights booked, etc.).

My Advice to Students . . .

Use technology to become a better informed person and use the information gained to become a responsible person. Technology should be used as an enabler to achieve your goals, improve your life, and improve the lives of others.

Discussion Question

Graham Watson believes that every employee needs to know at least how to send an e-mail and how to create, edit, and print a document. Think about the jobs available today. Are there any that may not require computer skills? If so, would computer skills give that employee an advantage, even if it's not required? Should companies be required to teach any necessary computer skills or is it reasonable to require basic computer skills for any job today? Be prepared to discuss your position (in class, via an online class discussion group, in a class chat room, or via a class blog, depending on your instructor's directions). You may also be asked to write a short paper expressing your opinion.

>**For more information on Microsoft, visit www.microsoft.com. For interesting IT-related information, visit www.technet.com and www.msdn.com. To set up a personalized browser home page, visit www.live.com. To check if your PC is Vista ready, go to www.microsoft.com/windowsvista/getready.**

4

CHAPTER

Network and Internet Security

OUTLINE

LEARNING OBJECTIVES

**After completing this chapter, you will be able to do the
following:**

1. Explain why computer users should be concerned about
network and Internet security.

2. List several examples of unauthorized access, unauthorized
use, and computer sabotage.

3. Explain how access control systems, firewalls, antivirus
software, and encryption protect against unauthorized
access, unauthorized use, and computer sabotage.

4. Discuss online theft, identity theft, Internet scams,
spoofing, phishing, and other types of dot cons.

5. Detail steps an individual can take to protect against online
theft, identity theft, Internet scams, spoofing, phishing, and
other types of dot cons.

6. Identify personal safety risks associated with Internet use.

7. List steps individuals can take to safeguard their personal
safety when using the Internet.

8. Name several laws related to network and Internet security.

OVERVIEW

Networks and the Internet help users finish many tasks quickly and efficiently and add convenience to many people's lives. However, there is a downside, as well. As more and more personal and business data is stored on computer networks, the risks and consequences of unauthorized computer access, theft, fraud, and other types of computer crime increase; so do the chances of data loss due to crime or employee errors. Some online activities can even put your personal safety at risk, if you are not careful.

This chapter looks at a variety of security concerns stemming from the use of computer networks in our society, including topics such as unauthorized access and use, computer viruses and other types of sabotage, and online theft and fraud. Safeguards for each of these concerns are also covered, with an explanation of precautions that can be taken to reduce the risk of experiencing problems related to these security concerns. Personal safety issues related to the Internet are also discussed, and the chapter closes with a look at legislation related to network and Internet security. ∎

PODCAST

Go to **www.course.com/uccs/ch4** to download or listen to the "Expert Insight on Networks and the Internet" podcast.

WHY BE CONCERNED ABOUT NETWORK AND INTERNET SECURITY?

From a *computer virus* making your PC function abnormally, to a *hacker* using your personal information to make fraudulent purchases, to someone harassing you online in a discussion group, a variety of security concerns related to computer networks and the Internet exist. Many Internet security concerns today can be categorized as **computer crimes**. Computer crime—sometimes referred to as *cybercrime*—includes any illegal act involving a computer. Many computer crimes involve breaking through the security of a network; others include theft of financial assets or information. Still other computer crimes involve manipulating data (such as grades or account information) for personal advantage, or acts of sabotage (such as releasing a computer virus or shutting down a Web server). Regardless of its form, cybercrime is an important security concern today, and cybercrime is a multibillion dollar business that is often performed by seasoned criminals.

All computer users should be aware of the security concerns surrounding computer network and Internet use, including the risks and the associated consequences, and they should take appropriate precautions. In some cases, such as when a *spyware program* changes your browser's home page, the consequence may be just an annoyance. In other cases, such as when someone steals your identity and purchases items using your name and credit card number, the consequences are much more serious. And with the growing use of Web 2.0 applications (such as social networking sites) at home and at work, as well as an increase in the number of individuals working from home or otherwise accessing a company network remotely, Internet security has never been more important. The most common types of

---

>**Computer crime.** Any illegal act involving a computer.

security concerns related to network and Internet use, along with some precautions that users can take to reduce the risks associated with these concerns, are discussed throughout the remainder of this chapter.

UNAUTHORIZED ACCESS, UNAUTHORIZED USE, AND COMPUTER SABOTAGE

Unauthorized access occurs whenever an individual gains access to a computer, network, file, or other resource without permission. **Unauthorized use** involves using a computer resource for unauthorized activities. Unauthorized use can occur even if the user is authorized to access that computer or network but is not authorized for that particular activity. For instance, while a student may be authorized to access the Internet via a campus computer lab, some use—such as viewing pornography—would likely be deemed off-limits. If so, viewing that content from a school computer would be considered unauthorized use. For employees of some companies, checking personal e-mail at work might be classified as unauthorized use. So, likely, would be employees viewing other employees' personnel files located on the company server, unless that act was part of their job responsibilities.

FIGURE 4-1
A sample code of conduct.

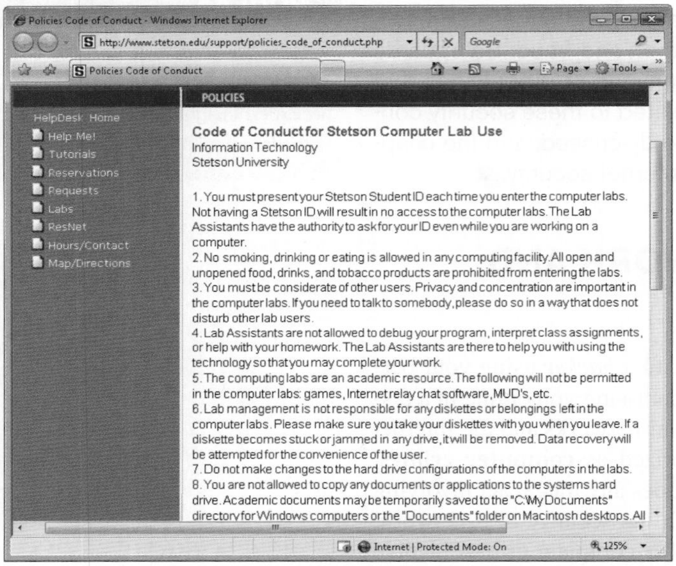

Unauthorized access and many types of unauthorized use are criminal offenses in the United States and many other countries and can be committed by both *insiders* (people who work for the company against which the crime is committed) and *outsiders* (people who do not work for that company). Whether or not a specific act constitutes unauthorized use or is illegal depends on the circumstances, as well as the specific company or institution involved. To explain acceptable computer use to their employees, students, or other users, many organizations and educational institutions publish guidelines for behavior, often called *codes of conduct* (see Figure 4-1). Codes of conduct typically address prohibited activities, such as installing personal software on the network, violating copyright laws, causing harm to the PC and network, and snooping in other people's files.

Hacking

Hacking refers to the act of breaking into another computer system. The person doing the hacking is called a *hacker*. By definition, hacking involves unauthorized access and is illegal. An exception is authorized hacking, such as *professional hacking* that takes place at the request of an organization to test the security of its system. Unless authorized, hacking in the United States and many other countries is a crime and is being vigorously prosecuted.

Often, the motivation for hacking is to steal data, sabotage a computer system, or perform some other type of illegal act. In particular, the theft of consumer data (such as credit card numbers and cardholder information) has dramatically increased over the past several years. For instance, the largest reported consumer data breach to date—the theft of over 45 million credit card and debit card numbers from The TJX Companies—was discovered

---

>**Unauthorized access.** Gaining access to a computer, network, file, or other resource without permission. >**Unauthorized use.** Using a computer resource for unapproved activities. >**Hacking.** Using a computer to break into another computer system.

and reported in 2007. Another growing trend is to hack into a PC and "hijack" it for use in an illegal or unethical act, such as generating spam or hosting pornographic Web sites. Hackers are also increasingly aiming attacks at very specific individuals, such as product designers and other individuals who have access to valuable corporate data, as well as VoIP phone calls to eavesdrop on business conversations. Other driving forces for some hackers are to prove their computer expertise, to expand their knowledge, or to bring attention to a social cause.

In addition to the threat toward individuals and businesses, hacking is considered a very serious threat to our nation's security. With the increased number of computers and systems connected to the Internet, the abilities of hackers continually improving, and the increased availability of sets of tools (sometimes called *rootkits*) that allow hackers to access a system, some experts believe the risk of *cyberterrorism*—in which terrorists launch attacks via the Internet—has increased significantly. Current concerns include attacks against the computers controlling vital systems, such as the nation's power grids, banks, and water filtration facilities, as well as computers related to national defense.

While the general public tends to use the term *hacker* to refer to any type of computer break-in regardless of what activities take place after the security breach, many hackers differentiate between types of hacking. For instance, individuals that perform

ASK THE EXPERT

Moshe Vardi, Rice University, Co-Chair of the ACM Globalization and Offshoring of Software Taskforce

Is there a national security risk as a result of software development being outsourced to other countries?

Offshoring magnifies existing risks and creates new and often poorly understood threats. When businesses offshore work, they increase not only their own business-related risks (e.g., intellectual property theft), but also risks to national security and to individuals' privacy. While it is unlikely these risks will deter the growth of offshoring, businesses and nations should employ strategies to mitigate them. Businesses have a clear incentive to manage these new risks to suit their own interests, but nations and individuals often have little awareness of the exposures created. For example, many commercial off-the-shelf (COTS) systems are developed offshore, making it extremely difficult for buyers to understand all of the source and application code in the systems. This creates the possibility that a hostile nation or nongovernmental hostile agent (such as a terrorist or criminal) can compromise these systems. Individuals are also often exposed to loss of privacy or identity theft due to the number of business processes being offshored today and managed under much less restrictive laws than in most developed countries.

authorized hacks are sometimes referred to as *white hat hackers* to distinguish them from *black hat hackers* who break the law, and some hackers prefer the term *cracker* when referring to individuals who break into systems to be destructive or for material gain. Hackers that break into telephone systems (often VoIP systems today) to make phone calls at someone else's expense are sometimes referred to as *phreakers*.

Wi-Fi Hacking

While in the past hacking took place primarily via telephone lines or the Internet, it is common today for hackers to also gain access to a computer via a wireless network. It is easier to hack into a wireless network than a wired network because it is possible to gain access just by being within range (about 100 to 300 feet, depending on the Wi-Fi standard being used) of a wireless access point, unless the access point is sufficiently protected. For instance, in 2004 two men hacked into the Wi-Fi network belonging to a Lowe's Home Improvement store in Michigan; they used the network to access the computer systems located at other stores and modify the software used to process credit card transactions in order to store the numbers for later retrieval. Although the men stole several customer credit card numbers, they were discovered before their plan was fully executed. The men were charged with violating the *Computer Fraud and Abuse Act*—the main federal law regarding computer crime—and were both sentenced to several years in prison.

Although security features are built into Wi-Fi hardware, they are typically not turned on by default. As a result, many wireless networks belonging to businesses and individuals—some estimates put the number as high as 70% of all Wi-Fi networks—are left unsecured (Wi-Fi security is discussed shortly). This leaves the transmissions sent by individuals, the company, and customers (such as individuals using a hotspot's Wi-Fi service or hotel guests using the hotel's complimentary Wi-Fi Internet access) open to interception.

War Driving and Wi-Fi Piggybacking

Accessing someone else's Wi-Fi network to gain free access to the Internet is called **war driving** or **Wi-Fi piggybacking**. War driving involves driving around neighborhoods in a car with a portable computer and appropriate software looking for unsecured Wi-Fi networks, either out of curiosity or looking for a network to "borrow." The term "Wi-Fi piggybacking" refers to accessing someone else's unsecured Wi-Fi connection from your current location (such as in your home, outside a hotspot location, or near a local business). Both war driving and Wi-Fi piggybacking are ethically—if not legally—questionable acts and can lead to illegal behavior. For instance, the two men that hacked into the Lowe's wireless network originally found the network during a war drive and—six months later—developed the plan to steal credit card numbers. War driving and Wi-Fi piggybacking can also have security risks, both for the war driver and the owner of the Wi-Fi network that is being used. For instance, both the war driver and the owner risk the introduction of computer viruses (either intentionally or unintentionally) and unauthorized access of the data located on their PCs; Wi-Fi owners may also experience reduced performance or even the cancellation of the Internet service for violating their ISP's acceptable use policy.

Laws in some countries, such as the U.K., are clear that using a Wi-Fi connection without authorization is illegal (for example, one London resident was arrested in 2007 for connecting to an unsecured Wi-Fi network while standing outside the network owner's home). In the United States, federal law isn't as clear, although some states have made using a Wi-Fi connection without permission illegal. For instance, it is a felony in Michigan and a man was found guilty, fined, and sentenced to community service in 2007 for using the free Wi-Fi service offered to customers at a local café from his parked car located on the street outside the café to check his e-mail on a regular basis. There are products designed to help mobile users locate Wi-Fi networks and some Web sites can display public Wi-Fi hotspot locations on maps of any specified geographical area (see Figure 4-2); however, these services are intended to help individuals locate authorized hotspots.

Advocates of war driving state that, unless individuals or businesses protect their access points, they are welcoming others to use them. Critics compare that logic to the case of an unlocked front door—you cannot legally enter a home just because the front door is unlocked. Although some wireless network owners do leave their access points unsecured on purpose and some communities are creating a collection of wireless access points to provide wireless Internet access to everyone in that community, it is difficult—if not impossible—to tell if an unsecured network was left that way intentionally, unless connecting to the wireless network displays a welcome screen stating that it is a free hotspot. Some feel the

FIGURE 4-2

Locating accessible Wi-Fi networks.

Some online mapping services list the Wi-Fi hotspots for a particular geographic area.

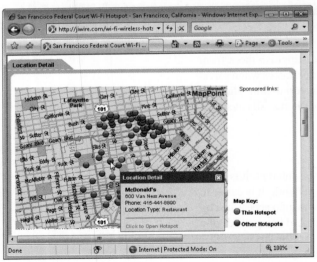

---

ethical distinction of using an unsecured wireless network is determined by the amount of use, believing that it is acceptable to borrow someone's Internet connection to do a quick e-mail check or Google search, but that continually using a neighbor's Internet connection to avoid paying for your own is crossing over the line. Others feel that allowing outsiders to share an Internet connection is acceptable use, as long as the owner does not charge the outsider for that access. Still others believe that an Internet connection is intended for use only by the subscriber and that sharing it with others is unfair to the subscriber's ISP. This issue is beginning to be addressed by the courts and ISPs, and some answers regarding the legality of war driving and Internet connection sharing will likely be forthcoming in the near future. However, the ethical questions surrounding this issue may take longer to resolve.

Interception of Communications

To gain access to data stored on a particular computer, criminals can attempt to hack directly into that computer—sometimes in person, but more often via the Internet. It is also possible to gain unauthorized access to data, files, e-mail messages, VoIP calls, and other content being sent over the Internet, instead of accessing the computer on which that data is stored. For instance, unsecured messages, files, logon information, and more sent over a wireless network (such as at a public hotspot or over a home Wi-Fi network)—can be captured by anyone within range using software designed for that purpose. Once intercepted, the data can be used for unintended or fraudulent purposes.

Although it is unlikely that anyone would be interested in intercepting personal e-mail sent to friends and relatives, proprietary corporate information and sensitive personal information (such as credit card, bank account, or brokerage account information, as well as Web site logon information) is at risk if it is sent over the Internet—or over a wireless home or corporate network—unsecured. The increased use of wireless networks, as well as the increased use of wireless connections to transmit data via mobile phones, handheld PCs, and other portable devices, has opened up new opportunities for data interception. For instance, the data on mobile devices with Bluetooth capabilities enabled can be accessed by other Bluetooth devices that are within range.

> **TIP**
>
> When using a public hotspot, be aware that data sent wirelessly to the hotspot can be intercepted and read, unless that data is *encrypted*.

Computer Sabotage

Computer sabotage—acts of malicious destruction to a computer or computer resource—is another common type of computer crime today. Computer sabotage can take several forms, including launching a *computer virus* or a *denial of service attack*, altering the content of a Web site, or changing data or programs located on a computer. A common tool used during computer sabotage is a *botnet*. Computer sabotage is illegal in the United States, and acts of sabotage are estimated to cost individuals and organizations billions of dollars per year, primarily for labor costs related to correcting the problems caused by the sabotage, lost productivity, and lost sales.

Botnets

A PC that is controlled by a hacker or other computer criminal is referred to as a **bot** or *zombie PC*; a group of bots that are controlled by one individual and can work together in a coordinated fashion is called a **botnet**. Botnets are a major security threat since criminals (called *botherders*) are increasingly creating botnets to use for computer sabotage. For instance, botherders often sell their botnet services to send spam and launch Internet attacks on their clients' behalf, as well as use them to steal identity information, credit card

---

>**Computer sabotage.** An act of malicious destruction to a computer or computer resource. >**Bot.** A computer that is controlled by a hacker or other computer criminal. >**Botnet.** A group of bots that are controlled by one individual.

numbers, passwords, corporate secrets, and other sensitive data. For instance, one botnet discovered in 2007 used software installed on its bot PCs to find e-commerce applications with security flaws and then steal credit card data to be used for fraudulent purposes. According to the FBI, an estimated one million U.S. computers are currently part of a botnet; consequently, botnets are a growing threat to national security, the national information infrastructure, and the economy. An ironic twist is that there are so many security threats in existence today that botherders are increasingly protecting their bots from other less-sophisticated attacks in order to prevent the legitimate owners of the bot PCs from suspecting their computers might be compromised and installing security software. Botnets are often used today to spread *malware* and to launch *denial of service (DOS) attacks*, discussed next.

Computer Viruses and Other Types of Malware

Malware is a generic term that refers to any type of malicious software. Malware programs are intentionally written to perform destructive acts. One type of malware is the **computer virus**—a software program that is installed without the permission or knowledge of the computer user, that is designed to alter the way a computer operates, and that can replicate itself to infect any new media it has access to. Computer viruses are often embedded into program or data files (often games, videos, and music files downloaded from Web pages or shared via a P2P service) and are spread whenever the infected file is downloaded from the Internet or another network, is transferred to a new computer via an infected removable storage medium, or is e-mailed to another computer (see Figure 4-3). Viruses can also be installed when a recipient clicks a link in an e-mail message, often in an unsolicited e-mail message (called *spam*, as discussed in Chapter 5) that resembles a legitimate e-mail message containing links, such as an electronic greeting card e-mail that contains a link to view the card. When the link is clicked, the malware is installed. Malware can also be spread through links in instant messages. Regardless of how it is obtained, once a copy of the infected file reaches a new computer it typically embeds itself into program, data, or system files on the new PC and remains there, affecting that PC according to its programmed instructions, until it is discovered and removed.

Another common form of malware is the **computer worm**. Like a computer virus, a computer worm is a malicious program designed to cause damage. Unlike a computer virus, however, a computer worm does not infect other computer files to replicate itself; instead, it spreads by creating copies of its code and sending those copies to other computers via a network. Often, the worm is sent as an e-mail attachment to other computers. Usually after the infected e-mail attachment is opened by an individual, the worm inflicts its damage, and then automatically sends copies of itself to other computers via the Internet or a private network, typically using addresses in the e-mail address book located on the newly infected PC. When those e-mail messages and their attachments are opened, the

---

>**Malware.** Any type of malicious software. >**Computer virus.** A software program installed without the user's knowledge and designed to alter the way a computer operates or to cause harm to the computer system. >**Computer worm.** A malicious program designed to spread rapidly to a large number of computers by sending copies of itself to other computers.

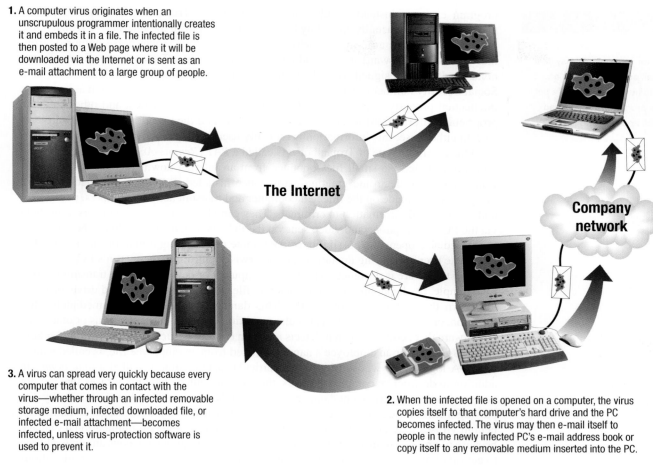

1. A computer virus originates when an unscrupulous programmer intentionally creates it and embeds it in a file. The infected file is then posted to a Web page where it will be downloaded via the Internet or is sent as an e-mail attachment to a large group of people.

The Internet

Company network

3. A virus can spread very quickly because every computer that comes in contact with the virus—whether through an infected removable storage medium, infected downloaded file, or infected e-mail attachment—becomes infected, unless virus-protection software is used to prevent it.

2. When the infected file is opened on a computer, the virus copies itself to that computer's hard drive and the PC becomes infected. The virus may then e-mail itself to people in the newly infected PC's e-mail address book or copy itself to any removable medium inserted into the PC.

FIGURE 4-3
How a computer virus or other type of malicious software might spread.

new computers become infected and the cycle continues. Some newer worms do not require any action by the users (such as opening an e-mail attachment) to infect their PCs. Instead, the worm scans the Internet looking for computers that are vulnerable to that particular worm and sends a copy of itself to those PCs to infect them. Other worms just require the user to view the e-mail message, in order to infect the PC.

Because of its distribution method, a worm can spread very rapidly. For instance, the *Mydoom* worm (released in 2004) spread so rapidly that, at one point, one out of every 10 e-mails contained the worm. And some worms are specifically written to take advantage of newly discovered *security holes* (vulnerabilities) in operating systems and e-mail programs. Worms and other types of malware that are designed to take advantage of a security hole and are released at a time when no *security patch* to correct the problem is available are referred to as *zero-day attacks*. Unfortunately, as malware writing tools become more sophisticated, zero-day attacks are becoming more common.

A **Trojan horse** is a type of malware that masquerades as something else—usually an application program (such as what appears to be a game or utility program), although some recent Trojan horses are masquerading as normal ongoing activities (such as the Windows Update service) to try to trick unsuspecting users into approving the download of the Trojan horse file. When the seemingly legitimate program is run, the destructive

>**Trojan horse.** A malicious program that masquerades as something else.

program executes instead. Unlike viruses and worms, Trojan horses cannot replicate themselves and are usually spread by being downloaded from the Internet. A Trojan horse may also be sent as an e-mail attachment, either from the Trojan horse author or from individuals who forward it, not realizing the program is a Trojan horse. Some Trojan horses today are designed to find sensitive information about an individual (such as a Social Security number or a bank account number) or about a company (such as corporate intellectual property like mechanical designs, electronic schematics, and other valuable proprietary information) located on an infected PC and then send it to the malware creator. In either case, this information is typically used in illegal activities.

One emerging type of Trojan horse is called a *RAT* (*Remote-Access Trojan*). RATs are typically installed via small files obtained from an Internet download, such as free software, games, or electronic greeting cards. Once installed, RATs are designed to record every keystroke made on the infected computer and transmit account numbers, passwords, and other related information to criminals. They can also capture voice conversations held via the PC's microphone and video sent via the PC's Web cam. The ability to be remotely-controlled also opens the possibility of the remote user sending e-mail posing as the PC's legitimate user, modifying documents, or otherwise controlling the victim's PC.

Most malware is designed to harm the computers or devices they are transmitted to—for example, by damaging programs, deleting files, erasing the entire hard drive, or slowing down the performance of the PC. This damage can take place immediately after infection, or it can begin when a particular condition is met. A computer virus or other type of malware that activates when it detects a certain condition, such as when a particular keystroke is pressed or an employee's name is deleted from an employee file, is called a *logic bomb*. A logic bomb whose trigger is a particular date or time is called a *time bomb*. In addition to destructive computer viruses, there are so-called "benign" viruses that are not designed to do any permanent damage, but instead they make their presence known by displaying a text or video message, or by playing a musical or audio message. Even though benign viruses may not cause any lasting harm (although some do unintentional damage because of programming errors), they are annoying, can require enormous amounts of time to get rid of and to fix any problems created by the virus, and can disrupt communications for the organizations involved.

In addition to PCs, malware also can infect mobile phones, portable digital media players, printers, and other devices that contain computing hardware and software. In fact, some GPS devices and portable digital media players (including some video iPods) shipped recently had malware already installed on them. Mobile phones with Bluetooth capabilities in particular are vulnerable since they can be infected via a Bluetooth connection just by being within range (about 30 feet) of a carrier. Some malware is designed to crash the phone's operating system; other malware is designed to be a nuisance by changing icons or otherwise making the device more difficult to use. And some are money-oriented, such as malware designed to steal credit card data located on the mobile phone. It is also possible that a mobile phone virus can be transferred to other devices, such as by copying itself to the phone's flash memory card so that any PC into which that flash memory card is inserted will become infected. Similarly, it is possible that malware located on a mobile device could be introduced to a company network, if that device is used to access corporate e-mail or other applications through the company server. According to IBM, more malware directed to mobile phones and other devices—such as cars—that contain embedded computers is expected in the near future, as those devices continue to incorporate more computer software components and, consequently, become more vulnerable to malware. However, the lack of a universal operating system for these devices at the present time limits the scope of infection for *mobile viruses*.

Writing a computer virus or other type of malware or even posting the malware code on the Internet is not illegal, but it is considered highly unethical and irresponsible behavior. Distributing malware, on the other hand, is illegal, and virus writers who release their malware are being vigorously prosecuted. For instance, a Minnesota teenager was facing three years in jail and a $250,000 fine for creating and unleashing a variant of the

MSBlaster worm that infected nearly 50,000 computers and caused over a million dollars worth of damage, according to federal investigators. In 2005, the teenager pled guilty to the crime and was sentenced to 18 months in prison and 225 hours of community service.

Malware can be very costly in terms of the labor costs associated with removing the viruses and correcting any resulting damage, as well as the cost of lost productivity of employees. While *antivirus software* and other security programs have improved, malware was still listed as the second most expensive type of computer crime in the 2007 *Computer Crime and Security Survey* performed by the Computer Security Institute and the FBI.

In addition to being used to disable computers, malware is also increasingly being used to gain access to individuals' PCs. For instance, the *Storm Worm* released in 2007 is designed to take control of people's PCs in order to hijack them for spam distribution and to perform *denial of service (DoS)* attacks (which are discussed next). The Storm Worm botnet is estimated to contain between one and 10 million computers around the world.

FURTHER EXPLORATION

Go to **www.course.com/uccs/ch4** for links to further information about computer viruses and virus detection.

Denial of Service (DoS) Attacks

A **denial of service (DoS) attack** is an act of sabotage that attempts to flood a network server or Web server with so many requests for action that it shuts down or simply cannot handle legitimate requests any longer, causing legitimate users to be denied service. For example, a hacker might set up one or more computers to continually *ping* a server (contact it with a request to send a responding ping back) with a false return address or to continually request nonexistent information. If enough useless traffic is generated, the server has no resources left to deal with legitimate requests (see Figure 4-4).

During the past few years, many DoS attacks have occurred. One recent example is the DoS attack that shut down the electronic ticketing system used by the Colorado Rockies baseball team 10 minutes after tickets went on sale for the 2007 World Series games. Many DoS attacks today utilize multiple computers (referred to as a *distributed denial of service attack* or *DDoS attack*). To perform DDoS attacks, hackers typically create a botnet that participates in the attacks without the owners' knowledge. Because home PCs increasingly are using always-on connections but tend to be less protected than school and business PCs, hackers are increasingly targeting home PCs to use in botnets for DDoSs and other attacks. Another trend is to use malware to launch a DoS attack. Denial of service attacks can be very costly in terms of business lost (such as when an e-commerce site is shut down), as

FIGURE 4-4
How a denial of service (DoS) attack might work.

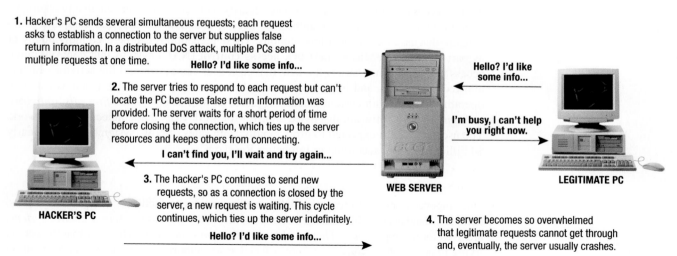

1. Hacker's PC sends several simultaneous requests; each request asks to establish a connection to the server but supplies false return information. In a distributed DoS attack, multiple PCs send multiple requests at one time.

Hello? I'd like some info...

Hello? I'd like some info...

2. The server tries to respond to each request but can't locate the PC because false return information was provided. The server waits for a short period of time before closing the connection, which ties up the server resources and keeps others from connecting.

I'm busy, I can't help you right now.

I can't find you, I'll wait and try again...

3. The hacker's PC continues to send new requests, so as a connection is closed by the server, a new request is waiting. This cycle continues, which ties up the server indefinitely.

WEB SERVER

LEGITIMATE PC

HACKER'S PC

Hello? I'd like some info...

4. The server becomes so overwhelmed that legitimate requests cannot get through and, eventually, the server usually crashes.

>**Denial of service (DoS) attack.** An act of sabotage that attempts to flood a network server or a Web server with so much activity that it is unable to function.

well as the time and expense required to bring the site back online. Networks that use VoIP are particularly vulnerable to DoS attacks since the real-time nature of VoIP calls means their quality is immediately affected when a DoS attack slows down the network.

Data or Program Alteration

Another type of computer sabotage occurs when a hacker breaches a computer system in order to delete data, change data, modify programs, or otherwise alter the data and programs located there. For example, a student might try to hack into the school database to change his or her grade, a hacker might change a program located on a company server in order to steal money or information, or a disgruntled or former employee might perform a vengeful act, such as altering programs so they work incorrectly, deleting customer records or other critical data, or randomly changing data in a company's database. Like other forms of computer sabotage, data and program alteration is illegal. And it is increasingly being prosecuted. For instance, five former California State University, Fresno students were charged in 2007 with conspiracy, identity theft, unauthorized computer access, and fraud for changing grades while they were attending that college, and, at the time of this writing, a former manager of a San Diego health clinic was facing up to 10 years in prison after being convicted of hacking into the clinic's computers and deleting software and a variety of data, such as appointment schedules, patient histories, diagnoses, and treatment plans. Another type of data alteration is *Web site defacement*—defacing or otherwise changing Web sites without permission. A form of *cybervandalism*, Web site defacement is performed by individuals with a grudge, as well by as hackers who want to draw attention to themselves or to a specific political cause. Fortunately, as businesses have continued to increase security measures to protect their servers against unauthorized access, Web site defacements—particularly in the United States—have become less common.

PROTECTING AGAINST UNAUTHORIZED ACCESS, UNAUTHORIZED USE, AND COMPUTER SABOTAGE

A number of security risks can be reduced by carefully controlling access to an organization's facilities and computer network to ensure that only authorized individuals are granted access, and by using appropriate security software and other sensible precautions. Specific precautions against unauthorized access, unauthorized use, and computer sabotage are discussed in the next few sections. These precautions can be used individually or as part of a comprehensive **network access control (NAC) system** that controls initial access to the system, restricts the data that each user can access and the activities each is allowed to perform, and implements and enforces security procedures (such as using an operating system with current patches in place, as well as up-to-date *firewalls*, *antivirus*, and *antispyware* software, discussed shortly) for all devices that connect to the network. The use of NACs is expected to grow rapidly, with sales of NAC systems reaching nearly $4 billion by 2008, according to Infonetics Research.

Access Control Systems

One important security precaution is controlling access to facilities, computer networks, company databases, individual Web site accounts, and other assets. *Access control systems* are used for these purposes. They can be *identification systems*, which verify that the person trying to access the facility or system is listed as an authorized user, and/or *authentication*

>**Network access control (NAC) system.** A comprehensive system that controls the initial access to a computer system.

systems, which determine whether or not the person attempting access is actually who he or she claims to be. The three most common types of access control systems are discussed next, followed by a discussion of additional considerations for controlling access to wireless networks.

Possessed Knowledge Access Systems

A **possessed knowledge access system** is an identification system that requires the individual requesting access to provide information that only the authorized user is supposed to know. *Usernames, passwords, PINs, passcodes,* and *cognitive authentication systems* fall into this category.

Passwords, the most commonly used type of possessed knowledge, are secret words or character combinations associated with an individual. They are often used in conjunction with a *username* (typically a variation of the person's first and/or last names or the individual's e-mail address) and are entered when requested. While usernames and e-mail addresses are not considered to be secret, passwords are and, for security purposes, typically appear as asterisks or dots so they cannot be viewed as they are being entered (see Figure 4-5). Username/password combinations can be used to restrict access to a facility or, more commonly, to a network, computer, Web site, router, wireless access point, or other computing resource. For example, a company or institution might require an authorized user to supply one password to access a corporate or school computer network, and then use a different password to access drives, folders, or documents containing sensitive or confidential information on that same network. For some applications (such as ATM machines), a *PIN* or *personal identification number—* a secret combination of numeric digits selected by the user—is used instead of a password. Numeric passwords are also referred to *passcodes*.

It is important to select secure passwords and change them frequently. One of the biggest disadvantages of password-only systems is that passwords can be forgotten; another is that passwords can be guessed or deciphered by a hacker's PC easily if secure password selection strategies are not applied. For example, many hackers are able to access networks or databases because the system administrator passwords for those resources are still the default passwords (the ones assigned during manufacturing) and so are commonly known. As illustrated by this example, any individual possessing the proper password will be granted access to the system because the system recognizes the password, regardless of whether or not the person using the password is the authorized user.

The best passwords are *strong passwords*. Strong passwords are at least eight characters long; use a combination of letters, numbers, and symbols; and do not form words found in the dictionary or that match the username. Some additional strategies for selecting secure passwords are listed in Figure 4-6. For an even higher level of security, some systems use passwords that are automatically generated when the user is ready to access the system. For instance, some secure Web sites use *security token* devices that generate a new passcode every 30 or 60 seconds. To successfully log on to the site, the user needs to enter that passcode while it is being displayed. A similar system for credit cards and access cards is starting to become available. These cards generate and display a one-time passcode when the user presses a button on the card (see Figure 4-7). To log on to the system (such as an online banking site or a company network) or to make an online purchase using the card, the user needs to enter the passcode displayed on the card. Entering a passcode correctly verifies that the individual has the card in his or her possession at the time the transaction is made; software verifies that the entered passcode is associated with the card being used.

FIGURE 4-5
Passwords.
Passwords are used to log on to PCs, networks, Web sites, and other computing resources.

>**Possessed knowledge access system.** An access control system that uses information only the individual should know to identify that individual. >**Password.** A secret combination of characters used to gain access to a computer, computer network, or other resource.

PASSWORD STRATEGIES

Make the password at least eight characters, if allowed by the application. A four- or five-character password can be cracked by a computer program in less than one minute. A ten-character password, in contrast, has about 3,700 trillion possible character permutations and could take a regular computer decades to crack.

Choose an unusual sequence of characters to create a password that will not be in a dictionary—for instance, mix numbers and special characters with abbreviations or unusual words you will remember. The password should be one that you can remember, yet one that does not conform to a pattern a computer can readily figure out.

To help you remember strong passwords used to protect sensitive data, consider using a *passphrase* that you can remember and using corresponding letters and symbols (such as the first letter of each word) for your password. For instance, the passphrase "My son John is five years older than my daughter Abby" could help you remember the strong password "Msji5yotMd@".

Do not use your name, your kids' or pets' names, your address, your birthdate, or any other public information as your password.

Do not keep a written copy of the password in your desk or taped to your monitor. If you need to write down your password, create a password-protected file on your PC that contains all your passwords so you can look them up as needed.

Use a different password for your highly sensitive activities (such as online banking or stock trading) than for Web sites that remember your settings or profile (such as online news, auction, shopping, or bookstore sites). Computers storing passwords used on nonsensitive Web sites are usually easier for hackers to break into than those storing passwords used on high-security sites; and if a hacker determines your password on a low-security site, he or she can use it on an account containing sensitive data if you use the same password on both accounts.

Change your passwords frequently.

FIGURE 4-6
Strategies for creating secure passwords.

A growing trend is the use of *cognitive authentication systems* instead of, or in conjunction with, usernames and passwords. Cognitive authentication uses information that an individual should know or can easily remember. Some systems use information that can be found in public databases (such as the user's city of birth, first elementary school attended, or amount of home mortgage); others use answers previously supplied by the individual (such as details of a favorite trip or the name of the individual's childhood best friend). The cognitive authentication system shown in Figure 4-7 takes a different approach. Each user is assigned or selects a series of faces (called *passfaces*); to log on, the individual needs to correctly select their passfaces out of a group of displayed faces.

Passwords, usernames, PINs, and cognitive authentication systems are often used in conjunction with each other, as well as with *possessed object access systems* and *biometric access systems* (which are discussed shortly). Using two different methods to authenticate a user is called *two-factor authentication*. Typically the methods used are some type of possessed knowledge (something you know) along with either a *possessed object* (something you have) or a *biometric* feature (something you are). Two-factor authentication—also called *strong authentication*—adds another level of security to an access control system, since hackers are much less likely to be able to gain access to two different types of required factors. Two-factor authentication systems are common in many countries and use is growing in the United States. In fact, a federal guideline that went into effect in 2007 calls on banks, credit unions, and other financial institutions to replace single-factor authentication systems (typically username/password systems) with systems using two-factor authentication.

For a look at an emerging trend for access control—*identity management*—see the Inside the Industry box.

FIGURE 4-7
New possessed knowledge systems.

Current passcode

AUTOGENERATED PASSCODES
To log on or finalize any other secure transaction, the user must enter the passcode generated by the card.

PASSFACES
To log on, the user must recognize and select his or her assigned passfaces.

INSIDE THE INDUSTRY

Identity Management (IDM)

With many companies having multiple systems that require employees to provide usernames and passwords to access, as well as the heightened concerns regarding security and privacy today, *identity management* (*IDM*) is a hot topic. In an information system (IS) context, IDM usually refers to identifying users and managing access to enterprise systems. Often in these work environments, a user must sign on to a number of different systems using a different username and password for each system. One solution to having multiple usernames and passwords is *single sign-on* (*SSO*)–a single ID and password used to grant each individual the appropriate rights to all of the systems in the company that he or she is allowed to access. SSO vastly reduces the number of password resets a company has to perform due to forgotten passwords since users have to remember only a single username and password. For better security, two-factor authentication (such as requiring both a password and a smart card, as in the accompanying photo, or requiring a password in conjunction with some type of biometric authentication) and periodic required password changes can be used.

Another aspect of IDM is *automated user provisioning*. Automated user provisioning immensely reduces the amount of time required and work involved in managing user accounts as employees are hired, transferred, promoted, and leave the company. IDM also supports a company's ability to comply with federal regulations, such as the *Sarbanes-Oxley Act* (*SOX*) and the *Health Insurance Portability and Accountability Act* (*HIPAA*), that include provisions about securing the systems containing sensitive data. The goal of developing and implementing an IDM strategy is to improve efficiencies through automation, while improving security and limiting privacy liabilities.

Possessed Object Access Systems

Possessed object access systems use physical objects for identification purposes and are frequently used to control access to facilities and computer systems. Common types of possessed objects are smart cards, RFID-encoded badges, and magnetic cards that are swiped through or placed close to a reader to be read (see Figure 4-8). Increasingly, *USB security keys* or *e-tokens*—flash memory drives that are inserted into a PC to grant access to a network, to supply Web site usernames and passwords, or to provide other security features—are also being used. For a closer look at how e-tokens are being used to secure computers at one college campus, see the Technology and You box.

One disadvantage of using possessed objects is that the object can be lost or, like passwords, can be used by an unauthorized individual. This latter disadvantage can be overcome by requiring the user to supply a password or be authenticated by a fingerprint or other type of *biometric* data in order to use the possessed object. For example, some smart card readers and some USB security tokens contain *fingerprint readers* (discussed in more detail shortly) to authenticate that the person using the possessed object is the authorized individual. As mentioned earlier, two-factor authentication is much more secure than security procedures involving only one factor.

 FIGURE 4-8

Possessed objects, such as the smart card being used here, help protect against unauthorized access.

>**Possessed object access system.** An access control system that uses physical objects an individual has in his or her possession to identify that individual.

TECHNOLOGY AND YOU

E-Tokens on Campus

E-tokens have arrived on campus at Dartmouth College in New Hampshire. Instead of just using usernames and passwords, sensitive data and applications on the campus network are beginning to be protected by e-tokens—special USB keys that are used to authenticate individuals for network and application access. The e-tokens contain a digital certificate associated with the individual using the e-token. In addition to being used to identify the individual so he or she can have access to network and application resources, the e-token can be used by the individual to digitally sign e-mail and other electronic documents and to encrypt both documents and data transmission.

To use the e-token (shown in the accompanying photograph), the individual first connects it to his or her computer (via a USB port), and then the individual supplies his or her e-token password. The two levels of authentication (the actual e-token and the e-token password) provide a more secure way to verify users trying to access network applications than the traditional username/password approach. At Dartmouth, the e-tokens are currently used to gain access to the secure wireless network and to applications on the Dartmouth network, such as student grades and administrative and personal data, as well as to academic programs, such as Blackboard applications.

Biometric Access Systems

Biometrics is the study of identifying individuals using measurable, unique physiological or behavioral characteristics. **Biometric access systems** typically identify users by a particular unique biological characteristic (such as a fingerprint, hand, face, or *iris*—the colored portion surrounding the pupil of the eye), although personal traits are used in some systems. For instance, some systems today use *keystroke dynamics* to recognize an individual's unique typing pattern to authenticate the user as he or she types in his or her username and password; other systems identify an individual via his or her voice, signature, or gait. Because the means of access (usually a part of the body) cannot typically be used by anyone other than the authorized individual, biometric access systems can perform both identification and authentication.

Biometric access systems typically use a *biometric reader* (such as a *fingerprint reader* or *hand geometry reader*) or a digital camera in conjunction with software and a database to match the supplied biometric data with the biometric data previously stored in the database to identify and authenticate an individual. To speed up the process, many biometric access systems require users to identify themselves first (such as with a username, PIN, magnetic card, or smart card), and then the system uses that identifying information to verify that the supplied biometric data matches the identified person. In general, biometric access systems are very accurate. In fact, the odds of two different individuals having identical irises is 1 in 10^{78} and the statistical probability of two different irises being declared a match are 1 in 1.2 million—even identical twins (who have the same DNA

>**Biometric access system.** An access control system that uses one unique physical characteristic of an individual (such as a fingerprint, face, or voice) to authenticate that individual.

structure) have different fingerprints and irises. Systems based on biological characteristics (such as a person's iris, hand geometry, face, or fingerprint) tend to be more accurate than those based on a personal trait (such as an individual's voice or a written signature) because biological traits do not change, unlike physical traits that might change (such as an individual's voice, which might be affected by a cold, or a written signature, which might be affected by a broken wrist). For increased accuracy and/or flexibility (depending on whether or not multiple biometric characteristics are required), some biometric access systems use a combination of biometric features (such as a face and a fingerprint)—called *fusion biometrics* or *multi-modal biometrics*.

The primary disadvantages of biometric access systems in general are that much of the hardware and software is expensive, and the data used for authentication (such as a fingerprint or an iris image) cannot be reset if it is compromised. In addition, fingerprint and hand geometry systems typically require contact with the reader device and lighting may affect the results of face and iris recognition systems. However, biometric access systems are very accurate and offer a great deal of convenience since biometric characteristics cannot be lost

FINGERPRINT RECOGNITION SYSTEM
Typically used to protect access to office PCs, to automatically supply Web site passwords on home PCs, to pay for products or services, and to access resources such as Welfare benefits.

HAND GEOMETRY SYSTEM
Typically used to control access to facilities (such as government offices, prisons, and military facilities) and to punch in and out of work.

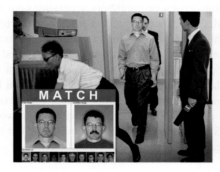

FACE RECOGNITION SYSTEM
Typically used to control access to highly secure areas, as well as to identify individuals for law enforcement purposes.

IRIS RECOGNITION SYSTEM
Typically used to control access to highly secure areas and by the military; also beginning to be used to authenticate ATM users and other consumers.

(like an access card), cannot be forgotten (like a password), and don't have to be pulled out of a briefcase or pocket (like an access card or other type of possessed object). Consequently, biometric access systems are increasingly being used to control access to secure facilities (such as corporate headquarters and prisons), log users on to computer systems and secure Web sites (by using an external reader or one built into the PC), punch employees in and out of work, and confirm consumers' identities at ATM machines and check-cashing services. Biometric readers are increasingly being built into notebook PCs, handheld computers, and other devices to prevent unauthorized use of those devices, as well as to be used to authenticate online purchases and other financial transactions performed via those devices. Biometrics is also an important component of government identification systems and border control systems in many countries, such as to identify citizens, travelers, criminal suspects, potential terrorists, and so forth. In the United States, for instance, fingerprints are required to obtain a driver's license in many states, as well as for U.S. Visas, and *face recognition systems* (biometric systems that use cameras and a database of photos to attempt to identify individuals as they walk by the camera) are used in many airports and other public locations to help identify known terrorists and criminal suspects. In addition, a number of databases containing biometric data are used by law enforcement agencies and the U.S. military, and biometric identification systems are used extensively by law enforcement agencies and the military in areas of conflict. For instance, they are being used in Iraq to identify members of the Iraqi police and military, prisoners, prison guards, authorized gun owners, citizens, contract employees, known criminals, and criminal suspects.

Some examples of the most commonly used types of biometric access and identification systems are shown in Figure 4-9.

FIGURE 4-9

Types of biometric access and identification systems.

Controlling Access to Wireless Networks

As already discussed, wireless networks—such as Wi-Fi networks—are less secure, in general, than wired networks. There are Wi-Fi security procedures, however, that can be used to protect against unauthorized use of a wireless network and to *encrypt* data sent over the network so that it is unreadable if intercepted. The original Wi-Fi security standard was *WEP* (*Wired Equivalent Privacy*). WEP is now considered insecure and has been replaced with the more secure *WPA* (*Wi-Fi Protected Access*) and the even more secure *WPA2* standards. However, Wi-Fi security features only work if they are enabled. Most Wi-Fi hardware today is shipped with the security features switched off, and many network owners never enable them, leaving those networks unsecured.

To protect against unauthorized access, Wi-Fi network owners should secure their networks by changing the router or access point settings to enable one of the encryption standards and to assign a *network key* or *passphrase* (essentially a password) that must be supplied in order to access the secured network. In addition, the name of the network (called the *SSID*) can be hidden from view by turning off the SSID broadcast feature. While hiding the network name will not deter serious hackers, it may reduce the number of casual war drivers or neighbors accessing your network. These changes are all typically made using the router or access point *configuration utility*, which is usually accessed by typing the IP address assigned to that device (such as 192.168.0.1) in a Web browser window (see Figure 4-10). To prevent unauthorized individuals from changing the router or access point settings, it is extremely important that the administrator password used to access the configuration utility is changed from its default setting, since the default passwords are freely available. Once the network is secured, users who want to connect to that network need to either select or supply the network SSID name (depending on whether or not the SSID is being broadcast) and then enter the network key assigned to that network (refer again to Figure 4-10).

FIGURE 4-10
Securing and accessing a Wi-Fi network.

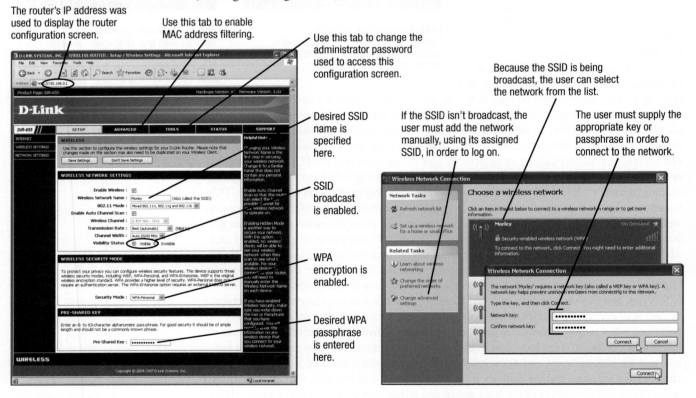

The router's IP address was used to display the router configuration screen.

Use this tab to enable MAC address filtering.

Use this tab to change the administrator password used to access this configuration screen.

Because the SSID is being broadcast, the user can select the network from the list.

Desired SSID name is specified here.

If the SSID isn't broadcast, the user must add the network manually, using its assigned SSID, in order to log on.

The user must supply the appropriate key or passphrase in order to connect to the network.

SSID broadcast is enabled.

WPA encryption is enabled.

Desired WPA passphrase is entered here.

SECURITY SETTINGS
Owners of wireless networks should use their router configuration utility (such as the one shown here) to change the security settings of their wireless network.

ACCESSING THE NETWORK
To access a secure network, the appropriate passphrase must be supplied.

For additional security, *MAC* (*Media Access Control*) *address filtering* can be used. A *MAC address* is a unique identifying 12-digit hexadecimal number assigned to a network adapter by the manufacturer. A MAC address is usually written in six groups of two digits, separated by a colon or hyphen (such as 11:11:11:22:22:22) where the first three sets of digits are the ID number of the manufacturer and the second three sets are the serial number assigned to the adapter by the manufacturer. When MAC address filtering is enabled, the MAC addresses of all devices that are allowed to connect to the network are entered into the router or access point configuration utility. When a device attempts to connect to the network, the router or access point compares the device's MAC address with the list of allowable addresses, and the devices not on the list are denied access. While MAC addresses can be "spoofed" by hackers changing the MAC addresses of their devices to match an authorized MAC address (once the hacker determines those addresses) and so should not be considered an alternative to using WPA or WPA2 encryption, MAC address filtering does add another layer of protection against attacks. Many routers also allow you to designate access control times; that is, times when no one can access the router, such as when you are away from home or during the night. If you don't need the full range of the wireless signal to reach your needed locations in your home, you can also change the strength of the wireless signal (such as to medium or low) to prevent anyone outside your home from accessing your network. These settings are also performed using the router configuration utility.

Firewalls, Encryption, and Virtual Private Networks (VPNs)

In addition to the access control systems just discussed, there are a number of other tools that can be used to prevent access to an individual computer or to prevent data being sent from a computer from being intercepted (or intercepted in an understandable form) during transit. These tools—*firewalls*, *encryption*, and *virtual private networks* (*VPNs*)—are discussed next. While most of the time these security tools are implemented by installing individual software programs, they can also be implemented via a *security appliance*—a piece of hardware containing a set of preinstalled security software that connects to a network to secure it.

FIGURE 4-11

A personal firewall program. The firewall is on, so only authorized traffic can access the PC.

Firewalls

A **firewall** is a security system that essentially creates a wall between a computer or network and the Internet in order to protect against unauthorized access. Firewalls are typically two-way, so they check all incoming (from the Internet to the computer or the network) and outgoing (from the computer or the network to the Internet) traffic and only allow authorized traffic to pass through the firewall. *Personal firewalls* are typically software-based systems that are geared toward protecting home PCs from hackers attempting to access those computers through their Internet connections. Hackers who gain access to home PCs can access the information on them (such as passwords stored on the hard drive), as well as use those computers in denial of service attacks and other illegal activities. Consequently, all PCs with direct (always-on) Internet connections (such as DSL, cable, or satellite Internet access) should use a firewall (PCs using dial-up Internet access are relatively safe from hackers). Personal firewalls can be stand-alone programs (such as the free *ZoneAlarm* program); they are also built into many operating systems (such as the *Windows Firewall* program shown in Figure 4-11). Many

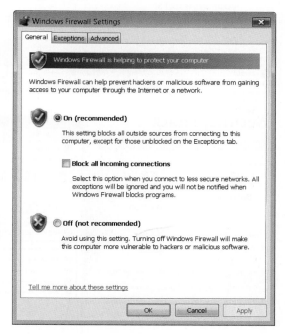

> **Firewall.** A collection of hardware and/or software intended to protect a computer or computer network from unauthorized access.

routers, modems, and other pieces of networking hardware also include built-in firewalls to help secure the networks with which they are used. Firewalls designed to protect business networks may be software-based, hardware-based, or a combination of the two. They can typically be used both to prevent network access by hackers and other outsiders, and to control employee Internet access.

Firewalls work by closing down all external *communications port addresses*—the electronic connections that allow a PC to communicate with other computers—to unauthorized computers and programs. While business firewalls are set up by the network administrator and those settings cannot typically be changed by end users, the settings for personal firewalls can be changed, such as to choose to be notified when an application program on the PC is trying to access the Internet, to specify the programs that are allowed to access the Internet, or to temporarily block all incoming connections. In addition to protecting your PC from outside access, firewall programs also protect against inside attacks from computer viruses and other malicious programs that may have slipped through your virus protection. If communications port addresses are not blocked by a firewall, malware programs can open the ports and send data from your PC to a hacker at the hacker's request.

Another type of security system increasingly being used by businesses today that is somewhat related to a firewall is an *intrusion prevention system* (*IPS*). Whereas a firewall tries to block unauthorized traffic, an IPS continuously monitors and analyzes the traffic allowed by the firewall to try to detect possible attacks as they are occurring. If an attack is in progress, IPS software can immediately block it. Intrusion protection and firewalls are often included with other security software tools (such as *antivirus software*, discussed shortly) in a complete *security suite*. In addition, Web browsers and operating systems can help prevent programs from being installed on a PC without the user specifically authorizing them. For instance, in Internet Explorer, users can disable *ActiveX*—a Microsoft technology that allows Web sites and e-mail attachments to run executable programs on users' PCs—to prevent programs from being run on their PCs without permission. Windows Vista's *User Accounts* feature also offers some protection. For example, beginning to install a program typically prompts the user to verify the action (using an administrative password, if he or she is not logged on as an administrator) before the program can be installed; this feature can be disabled by an administrator, if desired.

After installing firewall and other security software, individuals and businesses should test their systems for remaining vulnerabilities. Individuals may wish to use online security tests—such as the *Symantec Security Check* shown in Figure 4-12 or the tests at Gibson Research's *Shields Up* site to check their PCs; businesses may wish to hire an outside consultant to perform a comprehensive security assessment.

FIGURE 4-12
Online security scans can check your system for vulnerabilities.

1. Click to run security scan.

2. No threats were found.

Encryption

Encryption is a way of temporarily converting data into a form, known as a *cipher*, which is unreadable until it is *decrypted* (unscrambled) in order to protect that data from being viewed by unauthorized people. As previously discussed, secure Wi-Fi networks use encryption to secure data that is transferred over the network. **Secure Web pages** use encryption so that sensitive data (such as credit card numbers) sent via the Web page is protected as it travels over the Internet. The most common security protocols used with secure Web pages are *Secure Sockets Layer* (*SSL*) and *Extended Validation Secure Sockets Layer* (*EV SSL*). The URL for Web pages using either form of SSL begins with *https:* instead of *http:*.

Other types of data that are sent over the Internet—such as e-mail messages, IMs, VoIP calls, and attached files—can also be secured using encryption so their content is unreadable or otherwise undecipherable if they are intercepted during transit or if the files are otherwise obtained by an unauthorized individual (such as if a PC or device containing sensitive files is lost or stolen). Some Internet services (such as Skype VoIP calls and *HushMail* Web-based e-mail) use built-in encryption. Individual files can also be encrypted before they are stored on a hard drive so they will be unreadable if opened by an unauthorized person. Encryption is often implemented using a third-party encryption program, such as *Pretty Good Privacy* (*PGP*) for files and e-mail messages or *SimpLite* for instant messages. Encryption options are also built into some operating systems, such as Windows Vista and Max OS X. The manner in which the data is encrypted depends on the *encryption algorithm*—such as *Blowfish* or *Advanced Encryption Standard* (*AES*)—being used. There are also special USB flash drives that are designed to encrypt the files on a PC—to decrypt those files, the USB flash drive must be reinserted in the PC's USB port. *Self-encrypting hard drives* (in which all data is automatically encrypted, as discussed in Chapter 5) are also available and are most often used with portable PC hard drives so the data will be unreadable if the PC is stolen. Businesses are increasingly turning to encryption to prevent data loss, if a data breach should occur.

The two most common types of encryption are *private key encryption* and *public key encryption*. **Private key encryption**, also called *symmetric key encryption*, uses a single secret *private key* to both encrypt and decrypt the file or message. It is often used to encrypt files stored on an individual's PC, since the individual who selects the private key is likely the only one who will need to access those files. Private key encryption can also be used to securely send files to others, provided both the sender and recipient agree on the private key (essentially a secret password) that will be used to access the file. For a look at how private key encryption works, see the How It Works box.

Public key encryption, also called *asymmetric key encryption*, utilizes two encryption keys to encrypt and decrypt documents. Specifically, public key encryption uses a pair of keys (a *public key* and a *private key*) that has been assigned to a particular individual—each key is a very long number that is mathematically related to the other key. An individual's public key is not secret and is available for anyone to use, but a private key is used only by the individual to whom it was assigned. Documents or messages encrypted with a public key can only be decrypted with the matching private key.

Public/private key pairs are either generated by the encryption program being used or are obtained through a *Certificate Authority*, such as VeriSign or Thawte (Certificate Authorities are discussed in more detail in a later section). Once obtained, encryption keys are stored in your browser, e-mail program, and any other program with which they will be used—this is typically done automatically for you with key pairs obtained via the Internet. Obtaining a business public/private key pair usually requires a fee, but free key pairs for personal use are available through some Certificate Authorities. Some encryption programs (such as freeware versions of PGP) are also available without charge for personal use.

>**Encryption.** A method of scrambling e-mail or files to make them unreadable if they are intercepted by an unauthorized user. >**Secure Web page.** A Web page that uses encryption to protect information transmitted via that Web page. >**Private key encryption.** A type of encryption that uses a single key to encrypt and decrypt the file or message. >**Public key encryption.** A type of encryption that uses key pairs to encrypt and decrypt the file or message.

HOW IT WORKS

Private Key Encryption

Stand-alone private key encryption programs can be used to encrypt individual files or an entire hard drive. Private key encryption is also incorporated into a variety of programs—such as Microsoft Office, the WinZip file compression program, and Adobe Acrobat (the program used to create PDF files)—to encrypt documents created in those programs so that they can be stored in an encrypted form on a storage medium. The accompanying illustration shows how to encrypt a Microsoft Word 2007 document. Once the file is encrypted, the password assigned to that file must be entered to open the original file or any copies of the file, such as those sent via e-mail. To send a privately encrypted file to another individual, the sender uses the agreed-upon private key (password) to encrypt the file, and the recipient uses that same private key (password) to decrypt and open the file. If the proper private key is not supplied, the file will not open.

In addition to, or instead of, encrypting a file, a user can password-protect a document to control who is able to modify the file. Although password-protecting a document is not the same as encrypting a file, it can help avoid unintended modifications of a file. To password-protect a document in Word 2007, you select the Tools option in the Save As dialog box and choose *General Options*, and then supply the desired modification password (encryption can be enabled using this dialog box as well, if desired). When a password-protected document is opened, the user must supply the appropriate password to open the file as an editable file; he or she can also choose not to supply the password and view a read-only version of that file that cannot be saved using the same filename as the original file.

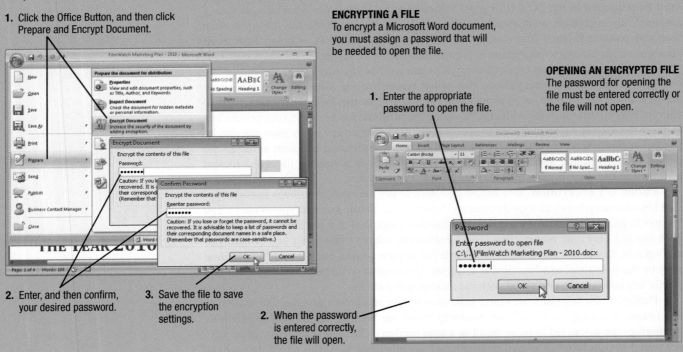

1. Click the Office Button, and then click Prepare and Encrypt Document.

2. Enter, and then confirm, your desired password.

3. Save the file to save the encryption settings.

ENCRYPTING A FILE
To encrypt a Microsoft Word document, you must assign a password that will be needed to open the file.

1. Enter the appropriate password to open the file.

OPENING AN ENCRYPTED FILE
The password for opening the file must be entered correctly or the file will not open.

2. When the password is entered correctly, the file will open.

To send someone an encrypted e-mail message or file using public key encryption, you need his or her public key. If that person has previously sent you his or her public key (such as via an e-mail message), it was likely stored by your e-mail program in your address book or contacts list, or by your encryption program in a special *key ring* feature used by that program. In either case, that public key is available whenever you want to send that person an encrypted document. If you do not already have the public key belonging to the individual to whom you wish to send an encrypted e-mail or file, you will need to request it from that individual. Once the recipient's public key has been used to encrypt the file or e-mail message and that document is received, the recipient's private key decrypts the encrypted contents (see Figure 4-13).

To avoid the need to obtain the recipient's public key before sending that person an encrypted e-mail, *Web-based encrypted e-mail* can be used. Web-based encrypted e-mail works similarly to regular Web-based e-mail (in which e-mail is composed and viewed on a Web page belonging to the Web-based e-mail service), but Web-based encrypted e-mail systems use secure Web servers to host the Web pages that are used to compose and read e-mail messages. With some Web-based encrypted e-mail systems, the recipient is notified via his or her regular e-mail address that an encrypted e-mail message is wait-

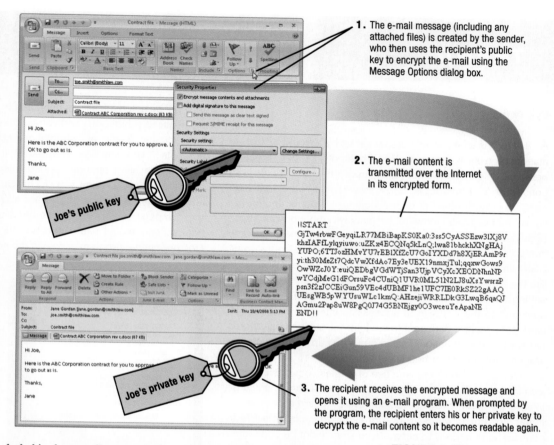

1. The e-mail message (including any attached files) is created by the sender, who then uses the recipient's public key to encrypt the e-mail using the Message Options dialog box.

2. The e-mail content is transmitted over the Internet in its encrypted form.

3. The recipient receives the encrypted message and opens it using an e-mail program. When prompted by the program, the recipient enters his or her private key to decrypt the e-mail content so it becomes readable again.

FIGURE 4-13
Using public key encryption to secure an e-mail message.

ing, and, using the link included in the e-mail message, the recipient can view the message on a secure Web page. With this type of system, often only the sender is required to have an account through the Web-based encrypted e-mail service. Other Web-based encrypted e-mail systems—such as the popular free *HushMail* service—require both the sender and recipient to have accounts through that system. Since all e-mail sent through the service is automatically encrypted, users just log on to the HushMail Web page and provide their passwords when requested in order to decrypt and view any encrypted e-mail messages sent to their HushMail e-mail addresses.

There are various strengths of encryption available; the stronger the encryption, the more difficult it is to crack. Older 40-bit encryption (which can only use keys that are 40 bits or 5 characters long) is considered *weak encryption*. Stronger encryption is available today—such as *strong 128-bit encryption* (which uses 16-character keys) and *military-strength 2,048-bit encryption* (which uses 256-character keys)—although not without some objections from law enforcement agencies and the government. According to the government, terrorists routinely use encryption methods to communicate. Current commercial encryption programs are so strong that cracking them can take government agencies days or even weeks and typically requires the use of a supercomputer. The government views this as unacceptable because terrorists often use encryption and government and law enforcement agencies need access to terrorist communications to protect our national security. To avoid a situation in which documents from criminals cannot be decrypted by these agencies in a timely manner, the government has long proposed a *key escrow system*, in which independent third-party escrow companies would hold copies of all private keys, and those copies could be used for law enforcement and national security purposes when such use is authorized by a court order. Civil liberties groups, on the other hand, have vowed to fight a key escrow or similar system, calling it an invasion of personal privacy. At the present time, this issue is still being debated and no solution has been reached.

FURTHER EXPLORATION

Go to **www.course.com/uccs/ch4** for links to further information about encryption.

TREND

Evil Twins

An *evil twin* is a fake Wi-Fi hotspot set up by a would-be thief to masquerade as a legitimate Wi-Fi hotspot in order to gather personal or corporate information from other individuals who connect to that hotspot because they think it is the legitimate one. Typically, the thief selects a legitimate hotspot and moves within range, uses software to discover the network name (SSID) and radio frequency being used by the legitimate hotspot, and then broadcasts his or her hotspot using the same SSID as the legitimate one. To the end user, the evil twin looks like the legitimate hotspot because it uses the same SSID and settings as the "good twin" it is impersonating. If an end user connects to the evil twin to access the Internet, the thief can intercept sensitive data sent to the Internet, such as passwords or credit card information. That information can then be used for *identity theft* and other fraudulent activities.

Because of the increased use of wireless devices in public locations and the availability of software enabling a would-be thief to set up an evil twin hotspot, evil twins are an increasing threat. To protect yourself, do not allow your portable PC to connect automatically to hotspots so you cannot be connected to an evil twin hotspot inadvertently (some evil twins are able to disrupt the legitimate hotspot and disconnect users in hopes

they will be automatically reconnected to the evil twin instead of the legitimate hotspot), and refrain from performing sensitive transactions (such as shopping and banking) at public hotspots. If you only view Web pages via a public hotspot that you don't mind a stranger seeing, there is little an evil twin attacker can do to harm you. To be safe while using a public hotspot, businesspeople should use a VPN when connecting to the company server; individuals needing to perform sensitive transactions should use a personal VPN, such as the *JiWire Hotspot Helper* program shown in the accompanying figure.

A personal VPN.

Virtual Private Networks (VPNs)

While e-mail and file encryption can be used to transfer individual messages and files securely over the Internet, a **virtual private network** (**VPN**) can be used when a continuous secure channel is needed. A VPN provides a secure private tunnel from the user's computer through the Internet (including all needed servers and wireless access points) and is most often used to provide remote employees with secure access to a company network. VPNs use encryption and other security mechanisms to ensure that only authorized users can access the network and that the data cannot be intercepted during transit. Since it uses a public infrastructure instead of an expensive private physical network, a VPN can provide a secure environment over a large geographical area at a manageable cost.

VPNs are also used by both businesses and individuals at public Wi-Fi hotspots to prevent data interception when connecting to the Internet via the hotspot. While businesspeople will typically use a VPN set up by their companies, individuals can create *personal VPNs* using software designed for that purpose. This software automatically encrypts all inbound and outbound Internet traffic, including Web pages, e-mail messages, IMs, VoIP calls, and so forth, and also acts as a personal firewall. Using a personal VPN at a public hotspot can help avoid falling victim to a growing trend—*evil twin* Wi-Fi access points, as discussed in the Trend box.

>**Virtual private network (VPN).** A private, secure path over the Internet that provides authorized users a secure means of accessing a private network via the Internet.

Antivirus and Other Security Software

To protect against becoming infected with a computer virus or other type of malware, all PCs, mobile phones, and other devices used to access the Internet or a company network in both homes and offices should have **antivirus software** installed. Antivirus software is designed to run continuously whenever the computer is on to perform *real-time monitoring* of the computer and incoming e-mail messages, instant messages, and downloaded files to prevent any malicious applications from executing; it can also be set up to run a complete scan of the entire PC on a regular basis. Ideally, antivirus software on business PCs should also automatically scan any devices as soon as they are connected to a USB port in order to guard against infections from a USB flash drive, portable digital media player, or other USB device. Antivirus software helps prevent malware from being installed on your PC since it deletes or quarantines any suspicious e-mail attachments or downloaded files as they arrive; full system scans (see Figure 4-14) can detect and remove any viruses or worms that did find their way onto your PC.

New viruses and other types of malware are released all the time (according to McAfee Security, a manufacturer of antivirus and security software, there were over 180,000 known viruses and other threats in existence in late 2007, and research firm IDC estimates that 450 new viruses and other types of malware are released each day), so it is vital to keep your antivirus program up to date. Antivirus programs are usually set up to download new *virus definitions* automatically from their associated Web site on a regular basis, as often as several times per day—a very important precaution. Most antivirus programs come with a year of access to free updates; users should purchase additional years after that to continue to be protected. Schools and businesses should also ensure that students and employees connecting to the campus or company network with personal PCs are using up-to-date antivirus software so they will not infect the network with malware inadvertently. Some colleges now require new students to go through a *quarantine process*, in which students are not granted access to the college network until they complete a security process that checks their PCs for security threats, updates their operating systems, and installs antivirus software. Some additional virus-prevention strategies are listed in Figure 4-15.

Many antivirus programs today scan for other threats in addition to malware, such as bots, *spyware*, and possible *phishing attacks* (discussed shortly). They are also commonly

ONLINE VIDEO

Go to **www.course.com/uccs/ch4** to watch the "How to Protect Yourself Against Online Threats" video clip.

FIGURE 4-14
Antivirus software.
Antivirus programs, such as this one, are used to detect and remove malware infections.

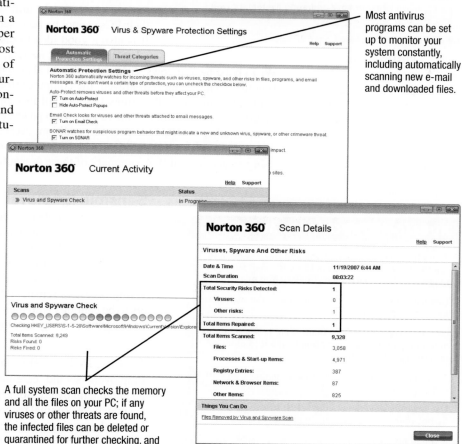

Most antivirus programs can be set up to monitor your system constantly, including automatically scanning new e-mail and downloaded files.

A full system scan checks the memory and all the files on your PC; if any viruses or other threats are found, the infected files can be deleted or quarantined for further checking, and any damaged files can be repaired.

>**Antivirus software.** Software used to detect and eliminate computer viruses and other types of malware.

VIRUS PREVENTION STRATEGIES

Use antivirus software to check incoming e-mail messages and files, and download updated virus definitions on a regular basis.

Limit the sharing of disks, flash memory cards, USB flash drives, and other removable storage media with others.

Only download files from reputable sites.

Only open e-mail attachments that come from people you know and that do not have an executable file extension (such as .exe, .com, .bat, or .vbs); double-check with the sender before opening an unexpected, but seemingly legitimate, attachment.

For any downloaded file you are unsure of, upload it to a Web site (such as VirusTotal.com) that tests files for viruses before you open them.

Keep the preview window of your e-mail program closed so you will not view messages until you determine that they are safe to view.

Regularly download and install the latest security patches available for your operating system, browser, and e-mail programs.

Avoid downloading files from P2P sites.

FIGURE 4-15

Sensible precautions can help protect against computer virus infections.

FIGURE 4-16

Sensible precautions for public hotspot users.

PUBLIC HOTSPOT PRECAUTIONS

Turn off automatic connections and pay attention to the list of available hotspots to try to make sure you connect to legitimate access points (not evil twins).

Use antivirus software and make sure your operating system is up to date.

Use a personal firewall to control the traffic going to and from your PC and temporarily use it to block all incoming connections.

Only enter passwords, credit card numbers, and other data on secure Web pages.

Use a virtual private network (VPN) to secure all activity between your PC and the Internet.

If you're not using a VPN, encrypt all sensitive files before transferring or e-mailing them.

If you're not using a VPN, avoid online shopping, banking, and other sensitive transactions.

Turn off file sharing so others can't access the files on your hard drive.

Turn off Bluetooth and Wi-Fi when you are not using them.

integrated with a firewall and other security components into a complete security suite. In addition, some ISPs offer antivirus protection to their subscribers. Typically, ISP antivirus software scans all incoming e-mail messages at the mail server level to filter out messages containing a virus. If a message containing a virus is detected, it is usually deleted and the recipient is notified that the message contained a virus and was deleted. Another type of program, which is currently in development and which is designed to protect against viruses sent via e-mail, is an *e-mail authentication system*. E-mail authentication systems are designed to tell recipients exactly where e-mail messages come from to help them determine which messages are safe to open and which might contain malware.

Additional Public Hotspot Precautions

Individuals need to take sufficient precautions when using a public Wi-Fi hotspot to avoid data (both on their PC and being sent over the Internet) from being compromised. In addition to the precautions already discussed (such as using up-to-date antivirus and firewall software, secure Web pages, VPNs, and file encryption), hotspot users should turn off file sharing so the files located on their PCs cannot be accessed if someone gains access to their PCs. It is also a good idea to disable Wi-Fi and Bluetooth capabilities when they are not needed, such as when working offline near a Wi-Fi hotspot. Windows Vista users should also make sure *Network Discovery* is disabled (via the Control Panel) to prevent the computer from being seen on the wireless network. And changing firewall settings to block all incoming connections is another good safeguard (you should still be able to view Web pages, exchange e-mail and IM messages, and conduct other normal activities). In addition, users should turn off automatic connections and disable *ad hoc* capabilities (which can allow one PC to connect to another without using an access point). A summary of these precautions are listed in Figure 4-16.

Sensible Employee Precautions

A significant number of business security breaches—over 60%, according to a recent University of Washington study—are the responsibility of insiders. Sometimes the employee deliberately performs the act; other times the employee makes a mistake, such as losing a portable PC or storage medium, or inadvertently providing access to sensitive data. Consequently, it pays for employers to be cautious with their employees. Some suggestions to avoid security breaches by employees are listed next.

Screen Potential New Hires Carefully

Employers should carefully investigate the background of all potential employees. Some people falsify résumés to get jobs. Others may have criminal records or currently be charged with a crime. One embarrassing mistake made by Rutgers University was to hire David Smith, the author of the *Melissa* virus, as a computer technician when he was out on bail following the arrest for that crime.

Watch for Disgruntled Employees and Ex-Employees

The type of employee who is most likely to commit a computer crime is one who has recently been terminated or passed over for a promotion, or one who has some reason to want to "get even" with the organization. Limiting access for each employee to only the resources needed for his or her job and monitoring any attempts to access off-limit resources can help prevent some types of sabotage. According to a 2005 *Insider Threat Study* by the U.S. Secret Service National Threat Assessment Center (NTAC) and the Software Engineering Institute's Computer Emergency Response Team (CERT), 57% of the insiders who sabotaged their companies were perceived as disgruntled employees and, in 92% of the cases, an event or series of events (such as a dispute with another employee or a demotion) triggered the incident. In the majority (nearly 60%) of the cases, the sabotage took place after the employee left the company and about half of the ex-employees had been fired. Consequently, it is vital that whenever an employee leaves the company for any reason, all access to the system for that individual (username, password, e-mail address, and so forth) should be removed immediately. For employees with high levels of system access, simultaneously removing access while the termination is taking place is even better. Waiting even a few minutes can be too late, since just-fired employees have been known to barricade themselves in their office immediately after being terminated in order to change passwords, sabotage records, and perform other malicious acts. Some wait slightly longer, such as one salesman at a

ASK THE EXPERT

 Marian Merritt, Internet Safety Advocate, Symantec Corporation

What is the single most important thing computer users should do to protect themselves from online threats?

The single most important step to protect computer users from online threats is to make sure their Internet security solution is current and up-to-date. There are several all-in-one security solutions available, such as Symantec's Norton 360, which combine PC security, antiphishing capabilities, backup, and tuneup technologies.

It's also pivotal to maintain a healthy wariness when receiving online communications. Do not click on links in suspicious e-mails or instant messages (IMs). These links will often direct you to sites that will ask you to reveal passwords, PINs, or other confidential data. Genuine organizations or institutions do not send such e-mails, nor do they ask for confidential data (like your Social Security number) for ordinary business transactions. If you're unsure whether or not an e-mail is legitimate, type the URL directly in your browser or call the institution to confirm they sent you that e-mail. Finally, do not open attachments in e-mails of questionable origin, since they may contain viruses.

New York staffing company who allegedly accessed the company computer system the evening after being fired and deleted all e-mail belonging to his boss. He was charged in federal court with one count of unauthorized access to a computer and intentionally causing more than $5,000 in damage.

Develop Policies and Controls

All companies should develop policies and controls regarding security matters. As a start, employees should be granted the least amount of access to the company network that they need to perform their job, in order to limit the damage that can be caused by employee error or a malicious security breach—a principle referred to as *The Principle of Least Privilege*. Employees should be educated about the seriousness and consequences of computer crime, and they should be taught what to do when they suspect a computer crime has been committed. Policies such as shredding sensitive documents that are no longer needed, immediately removing access for any employee who leaves the company, and separating employee functions as much as possible are all wise precautions. Employees should also be instructed about proper computer and e-mail usage policies—such as whether or not downloading and installing software on company PCs is allowed, whether or not employees are responsible for updating their PCs, and how to avoid opening attachments containing malware—to avoid inadvertently creating a security problem.

Some businesses and government organizations are using a technique called *inoculation*—essentially, trying to trick their employees with *spear phishing* and other schemes that result in downloading malware or revealing sensitive information, as discussed shortly, in order to see which employees take the bait and then educate them about how to avoid these types of traps in the future. Policies for removing computers and storage media containing sensitive data from the premises should also be implemented and enforced.

Employees who work from home or otherwise access the company network via the Internet also need to be educated about security policies for remote access and the proper precautions that need to be taken, such as using up-to-date designated security software, using only encrypted storage devices (such as self-encrypting USB flash drives) when transporting documents between work and home, and not installing peer-to-peer (P2P) software on PCs containing company documents. Data is increasingly being exposed through the use of P2P networks, primarily on computers used by telecommuting workers and outside contractors. For instance, a security breach of Social Security numbers and other personal data belonging to about 17,000 current and former Pfizer workers in 2007 occurred after an employee installed unauthorized P2P software on a company notebook PC provided for use at her home. Before the leak was discovered, data on about 15,700 of the workers was copied via the P2P service.

FIGURE 4-17

Data-leakage prevention software can control which devices can be connected to an employee's PC.

Use Data-Leakage Prevention and Enterprise Rights-Management Software

To prevent employees from intentionally or accidentally sending confidential data to others, *data-leakage prevention systems* can be used. These systems are available as software and/or hardware systems, and have a range of capabilities, but the overall goal is to prevent sensitive data from exposure. For instance, some systems control which devices (such as USB flash drives and portable digital media players) can be connected to an employee's PC (see Figure 4-17) in order to prevent sensitive data from being taken home inadvertently or intentionally. Other data-leakage prevention systems—sometimes also called *outbound-content monitoring systems*—scan all outgoing communications (e-mail, transferred files, instant messages, and so forth) for documents containing Social Security numbers, intellectual property, and other confidential information. Some can also continually scan network devices to locate sensitive data in documents stored on PCs to ensure that sensitive files are not on the PC of an employee who should not have access to them. For even stronger protection of confidential company documents, *enterprise rights-management software*, which encrypts confidential documents and limits functions such as printing, editing, and copying the data to only authorized users with the appropriate password, can be used.

Ask Business Partners to Review their Security

In this networked economy, many organizations provide some access to internal resources for business partners. If those external companies are lax with their security measures, however, attacks through the business partners' computers (such as via an employee or hacker) are possible. Consequently, businesses should make sure that their business partners maintain adequate security policies and controls. Regulations—such as the *Sarbanes-Oxley Act of 2002*—increasingly require businesses to ensure that adequate controls are in place to preserve the integrity of financial reports. This includes outside companies—such as business partners and *outsourcing companies* (outside vendors used for specific business tasks)—if they have access to sensitive corporate data.

ONLINE THEFT, FRAUD, AND OTHER DOT CONS

A booming area of computer crime involves online fraud, theft, scams, and related activities collectively referred to as **dot cons**. In fact, the *Internet Crime Complaint Center (IC3)*, a joint venture of the FBI and the National White Collar Crime Center that receives cybercrime complaints from consumers and reports them to the appropriate law enforcement agency, received its one millionth complaint in mid-2007. Common types of dot cons include theft of data, information, and other resources; *identity theft*; *online auction fraud*; and *Internet offer scams*, *spoofing*, *phishing*, *spear phishing*, and *pharming*.

Theft of Data, Information, and Other Resources

Data theft or *information theft*—the theft of data or information usually located on a computer—can be committed by stealing an actual PC (as discussed in more detail in Chapter 5); it can also take place over the Internet or a network after a hacker gains unauthorized access to a computer system. Common types of stolen data and information include customer data and proprietary corporate information. Recently, there have been numerous examples of personal data stolen via computers. For instance, hackers stole more than 45 million customer credit card and debit card numbers stored on TJX Companies servers; hackers stole personal data associated with 800,000 UCLA staff members and current, former, and prospective students; attackers used a Trojan horse to steal the contact information of more than 1.6 million users of the Monster.com online job search service; and a worker at a Fidelity National Information Services subsidiary stole 8.5 million customer records containing credit card numbers, bank account information, and other personal data. Stolen personal data is often used to commit *credit card fraud*, *identity theft*, *phishing schemes*, and other crimes.

Money is another resource that can be stolen via a computer. Company insiders sometimes steal money by altering company programs to transfer small amounts of money—for example, a few cents' worth of bank account interest—from a very large number of transactions to an account controlled by the thief. This type of crime is sometimes called *salami shaving*. Victims of salami-shaving schemes generally are unaware that their funds have been accessed because the amount taken from each individual is very small. However, added together, the amounts can be substantial. Another example of monetary theft performed via computers involves hackers electronically transferring money illegally from online bank accounts, traditional bank accounts, credit card accounts, or accounts at online payment services, such as *PayPal*. For instance, $449,000 belonging to the city of Carson, California was stolen in 2007 via an unauthorized online banking transaction after a Trojan horse was installed on the city treasurer's notebook computer to give the thieves access to the username and password needed to transfer the funds from the city's bank account. In the biggest case of Internet fraud to date, Russian criminals used Trojan horses to steal more than $1.2 million from customers of a Swedish bank. The bank's online customers were targeted with spam asking them to download an antispam program. The computers of the customers who downloaded the program were infected by a Trojan horse that activated when the customers tried to log on to their online bank accounts, and then captured the access information needed to transfer money from that account.

Identity Theft

Identity theft occurs when someone obtains enough information about a person (such as name, date of birth, Social Security number, address, phone number, and credit card

ONLINE VIDEO

Go to **www.course.com/uccs/ch4** to watch the "Online Gaming Threats" video clip.

>**Dot con.** A fraud or scam carried out through the Internet. >**Identity theft.** Using someone else's identity to purchase goods or services, obtain new credit cards or bank loans, or otherwise illegally masquerade as that individual.

1. The thief obtains information about an individual (such as his or her name, address, Social Security number, or credit card number) from discarded mail, employee records, credit card transactions, Web server files, or some other method.

2. The thief uses the information to make online purchases, open new credit card accounts, sign up for a service, buy or rent property, and more—all in the victim's name. Often, the thief changes the address on the account to delay the victim's discovery of the theft.

3. The victim eventually finds out, usually by being denied credit or by being contacted about overdue bills generated by the thief. Although victims can file reports and complaints, cancel accounts, and dispute unauthorized charges, clearing their names after identity theft is time-consuming and can be very difficult and frustrating.

FIGURE 4-18
How identity theft works.

numbers) to be able to masquerade as that person for a variety of activities—usually to buy products or services in that person's name (see Figure 4-18). Typically, identity theft begins with obtaining a person's name and Social Security number, often from a discarded or stolen document (such as a credit card application or rental application), from information obtained via the Internet (such as from an unsecured document intercepted during transit or a résumé posted online), or from information located on a computer (such as on a stolen PC, hacked server, or information sent from a PC via a computer virus or spyware program installed on that PC). Once the thief finds that individual's home address (either from the same source or by using a telephone book or an Internet search), he or she usually has enough information to order a copy of the individual's birth certificate over the phone, to obtain a "replacement" driver's license, and to open credit or bank accounts in the victim's name. Assuming the thief requests a change of address for these new accounts after they are opened, it may take quite some time—often until a company or collections agency contacts the victim about overdue bills—for the victim to become aware that his or her identity has been stolen. Although identity theft often takes place via a computer today, information used in identity theft can be gathered from trash dumpsters, mailboxes, and other locations. It can also be obtained by *skimming* (stealing credit card or debit card numbers by using a special device attached to ATM machines or credit card readers that reads and stores the card numbers to be retrieved by the thief at a later time) or via *social engineering* (pretending—typically via phone or e-mail—to be a bank officer, potential employer, or other trusted individual in order to get the potential victim to supply personal information). In 1998, the federal government passed the *Identity Theft and Assumption Deterrence Act*, which made identity theft a federal crime.

Unfortunately, identity theft is a very real danger to individuals today. According to the Federal Trade Commission (FTC), approximately 9 million Americans have their identity stolen each year, and it is estimated that identity theft cost businesses and consumers approximately $50 billion in 2007. Identity theft can be extremely distressing for victims, can take years to straighten out, and can be very expensive. Some victims, such as Michelle Brown, believe that they will always be dealing with their "alter reality" to some extent. For a year and a half, an identity thief used Brown's identity to obtain over $50,000 in goods and services, to rent properties—even to engage in drug trafficking. Although the culprit was arrested and convicted eventually for other criminal acts, she continued to use Brown's identity and was even booked into jail using Brown's stolen identity. As a final insult after the culprit was in prison, the real Michelle Brown was detained by U.S. customs agents when returning from a trip to Mexico because of the criminal record of the identity thief. Brown states that she has not traveled out of the country since, fearing an arrest or some other serious problem resulting from the theft of her identity, and estimates she has spent over 500 hours trying to correct all the problems related to the identity theft.

Online Auction Fraud

Online auction fraud (sometimes called *Internet auction fraud*) occurs when an online auction buyer pays for merchandise that is never delivered, or that is delivered but it is not as represented. Online auction fraud is an increasing risk for online auction bidders. According to the Internet Crime Complaint Center, online auction fraud accounted for about 45% of all reported Internet fraud cases in 2006 for an average loss of around $600.

Like other types of fraud, online auction fraud is illegal, but the criminals are often difficult to stop, as well as to identify and prosecute. As is the case in many types of Internet cons, prosecution is difficult because multiple jurisdictions are usually involved. In addition, some online auction fraud victims pay by personal check or money order and know very little about the seller's identity. Although most online auction sites have policies that suspend sellers with a certain number of complaints lodged against them, it is very easy for those sellers to come back using a new e-mail address and identity.

Internet Offer Scams, Spoofing, Phishing, Spear Phishing, and Pharming

There are a number of ways criminals try to steal money from Internet users. Some of the most common types of Internet scams are discussed next.

Internet Offer Scams

Internet offer scams include a wide range of scams available through Web sites or unsolicited e-mails. The anonymity of the Internet makes it very easy for con artists to appear to be almost anyone they want to be, including a charitable organization or a reputable-looking business. Common types of scams include loan scams, work-at-home cons, pyramid schemes, bogus credit card offers and prize promotions, and fraudulent business opportunities and franchises. These offers typically try to sell potential victims nonexistent services or worthless information, or they try to convince potential victims to voluntarily supply their credit card details and other personal information that are then used for fraudulent purposes. Some scammers use hacking as a means of obtaining a list of e-mail addresses for potential targets for a scam (such as stealing contact information from sites related to investing for a stock market scam) to increase the odds of a potential victim falling for the scam.

One ongoing Internet scam is the *Nigerian letter fraud* scheme, in which an e-mail message appearing to come from the Nigerian government promises the potential victim a share of a substantial amount of money in exchange for the use of the victim's bank account to supposedly facilitate a wire transfer (but the victim's account is emptied instead) and/or up-front cash to pay for nonexistent fees (that is kept by the con artist with nothing given in return). The theme of these scams (sometimes called *419 scams* after the number of the relevant section of Nigerian criminal law code) sometimes changes to fit current events like the war in Iraq or the Katrina hurricane, but the scams always involve a so-called fortune that is inaccessible to the con artist without the potential victims' help and the victims always lose money when they pay fees or provide bank account information in the hope of sharing in the wealth. Despite the fact that this scam is well known,

>**Online auction fraud.** When an item purchased through an online auction is never delivered after payment, or the item is not as specified by the seller.

people are still falling for this con and with heavy losses—at $5,100, the Nigerian letter fraud scam had the highest average dollar loss per individual for 2006 complaints, according to a report issued by the IC3.

Other schemes involve con artists who solicit donations after disasters and other tragic events, but who keep the donations instead of giving them to any charitable organization. For instance, immediately after Hurricane Katrina hit the United States in August 2005, a number of fraudulent Web sites appeared that were designed to take advantage of people's sympathy for the hurricane victims by soliciting donations supposedly meant for Katrina victims, but these donations were diverted into private accounts instead. In fact, more than 2,500 Katrina- or storm-related domain names were registered—over 450 with the word "Katrina" in them—right after the hurricane. Although some were sites set up to really help victims or solicit legitimate donations, the FBI reports that over 60% of the 2,000 sites it has reviewed that claim to offer aid to Katrina victims are registered to people outside the United States and so are likely to be fraudulent.

Another common scam involves setting up a pornographic site that requires a valid credit card, supposedly to prove that the visitor is of the required age (such as over 18), but which is then used for credit card fraud. A new type of scam involves posting fake job listings on job search sites to elicit personal information (such as Social Security numbers) from job seekers. An even more recent twist is to hire individuals through online job sites for seemingly legitimate positions involving money handling (such as bookkeeping or accounting positions), but then use those individuals—often without their knowledge—as legitimate-looking go-betweens to facilitate Internet auction scams and other monetary scams.

Spoofing, Phishing, Spear Phishing, and Pharming

Some Internet scams involve **spoofing**—making it appear that an e-mail or a Web site originates from somewhere other than its actual source. One of the most common uses of spoofing is **phishing** (pronounced "fishing"). Phishing is the use of an e-mail message or other communication that appears to be generated by America Online, eBay, PayPal, Citibank, or another well-known legitimate organization, but that is really sent by a criminal. A phishing e-mail typically looks legitimate, but it contains a link in the e-mail that goes to the phisher's Web site, not the legitimate business, when the link is clicked—an act called *Web site spoofing*. Phishing e-mails are sent to a wide group of individuals and typically include an urgent message stating that the individual's credit card or account information needs to be updated and requesting that the recipient of the e-mail click the link provided in the e-mail in order to keep the account active (see Figure 4-19). If the victim clicks the link and supplies the requested information, the criminal gains access to all information—such as account numbers, credit card numbers, and passwords—provided by the victim via the spoofed Web page. Phishing attempts can also occur today via IM and fake messages sent via eBay or MySpace, in addition to via e-mail.

FIGURE 4-19

Phishing. Phishing schemes use legitimate-looking e-mails to trick users into providing private information.

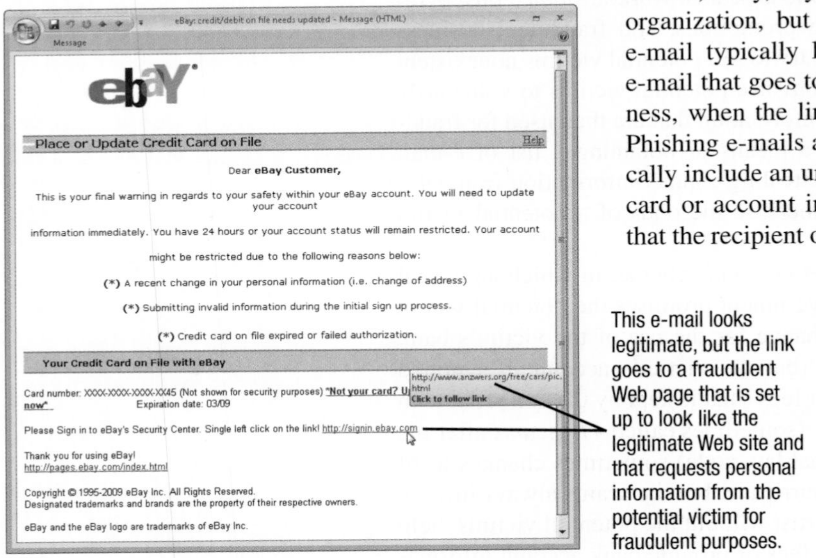

This e-mail looks legitimate, but the link goes to a fraudulent Web page that is set up to look like the legitimate Web site and that requests personal information from the potential victim for fraudulent purposes.

When creating a phishing scheme, the criminal typically uses a copy of the legitimate Web page (sometimes the spoofed Web site even contains some live links to selected Web pages of the legitimate site in order to appear more legitimate) and a secure connection between the victim and the criminal's server (so the Web page looks secure with an *https:* in the Web browser's Address bar). The domain name of the legitimate company (such as *ebay* for an eBay phishing page) is also often used in the URL of the phishing link to make it appear more legitimate. And, because spoofed sites usually look and respond like a legitimate site, victims often supply the requested information without realizing they are on a spoofed site. Other phishing sites use a technique called *typosquatting*—setting up fake sites with addresses slightly different than legitimate sites (such as www.amazon.com to catch shoppers intending to reach the Amazon.com Web site located at www.amazon.com) in hopes customers making that typo will not notice and will use the fake site they arrive at it.

Another recent trend is the use of more targeted, personalized phishing schemes, known as **spear phishing**. Spear phishing e-mails are directly targeted to a specific individual and typically appear to come from an organization or person that the targeted individual has an association with. They also often include personalized information (such as the potential victim's name) to make them seem even more legitimate. Several recent spear phishing attacks were targeted at users of social networking sites like MySpace since the personal information (name, age, hobbies, friends list, favorite music, and so forth) typically included on these sites makes them a good resource for spear phishers. Some of these attacks used spoofed logon pages to obtain an individual's logon information and password. Since many individuals use the same logon information for a variety of sites, once a scammer has a valid username/password combination, he or she can try it on a variety of sites in order to buy products, send money via PayPal, and perform other types of financial transactions posing as the victim, if he or she is able to successfully log on as that individual. Another spear phishing attack aimed at MySpace users this past year brought potential victims to a fake music download site, in hopes of capturing credit card information when the victims entered it on the fake site in the processing of downloading music.

Spear phishers also target employees of selected organizations by posing as someone within the company, such as a human resources or technical support employee. These spear phishing e-mails often request confidential information (such as logon IDs and passwords) or direct the employee to click a link to reset his or her password. The goal for corporate spear phishing attacks is usually to steal intellectual property, such as software source code, design documents, or schematics. Corporate spear phishing attacks can also be used to steal money, as in the case of the Supervalu grocery chain which was conned into depositing more than $10 million in 2007 into two fraudulent bank accounts after it received two fraudulent e-mails appearing to come from two approved suppliers and instructing future payments to be sent to the new bank accounts listed in the e-mail. Both phishing and spear phishing e-mail messages and Web sites are now more professional-looking than in the past, and the response rate has increased accordingly—current estimates are a 3 to 5% response rate for conventional phishing schemes and as high as 80% for spear phishing schemes.

The number of Web sites used for phishing schemes has skyrocketed recently—the number of unique new sites discovered per month by the Anti-Phishing Working Group increased by nearly 500% from April 2006 to April 2007. One explanation for the recent increase is the availability of phishing-creation kits sold by hackers that enable criminals to set up convincing phishing sites containing layouts and images from the legitimate site with very little effort.

>**Spear phishing.** A personalized phishing scheme targeted at an individual.

Another related scam is **pharming**—the use of spoofed domain names to obtain personal information to be used in fraudulent activities. With pharming, the criminal hacks into a *DNS server*—a computer that translates URLs into the appropriate IP addresses needed to display the Web page corresponding to that URL—in order to reroute traffic intended for a commonly used Web site to a spoofed Web site set up by the pharmer. Although pharming can take place at one of the 13 *root DNS servers* (the DNS servers used in conjunction with the Internet), the hacking more often takes place at a *company DNS server* (which is used to route Web page requests received by a company to the appropriate company server). For instance, a company may have several different Web servers set up to process requests received via its Web page URLs, and the company DNS server routes individual requests to an available Web server via that Web server's IP address. After hacking into a DNS server, the pharmer changes the IP addresses used in conjunction with a particular company URL (called *DNS poisoning*) so that Web page requests for that company Web page made via that legitimate URL are routed (via the company's poisoned DNS server) to a phony spoofed Web page located on the pharmer's Web server. So, even though a user types the proper URL for a Web page in his or her browser, the spoofed page is displayed instead. Since spoofed sites are set up to look like the legitimate sites, the user typically does not notice any difference, and any information sent via that site is captured by the pharmer. To avoid suspicion, some pharming schemes capture the user's account name and password as it is entered the first time on the spoofed site, and then display a password error message. The spoofed site then sends the user back to the legitimate site where he or she is able to log on to the legitimate site, thinking he or she must have just mistyped the password the first time. But, by then, the pharmer has already captured the victim's username and password and can use that information to gain access to the victim's account.

Pharming can also be carried out via *drive-by pharming*. The goal is still to redirect victims to spoofed sites, but the pharmer accomplishes this by changing the DNS server designated in the victim's router or access point settings to a DNS server that the pharmer has set up to direct victims to the spoofed versions of common Web sites. Typically, the DNS settings are changed when a Web page that includes malicious JavaScript code is viewed on a computer connected to a network in which the default administrator password for the router or access point has not been changed—the code logs into the router using the default password and changes the DNS settings to the pharmer's DNS server.

Spyware

Spyware is the term used for any software program that is installed without the user's knowledge and that secretly gathers information about the user and transmits it through his or her Internet connection. The obtained information can be directed to advertisers; it can also be used in conjunction with phishing schemes to transmit passwords and other sensitive data to a phisher. When used in a phishing scheme, clicking a link in the phishing e-mail installs the spyware on the victim's computer, and it will remain there until it is detected and removed. Spyware programs can be installed secretly at the same time another program—such as a program downloaded from a Web site or a P2P service—is installed. Spyware can also be installed via an instant message, or it can be installed automatically during a visit to a Web site (sometimes called a *drive-by download* because the installation requires no action on the part of the Web site visitor other than visiting the site), if the user's browser security settings do not prevent the installation.

Unfortunately, spyware use is on the rise and can affect the performance of a PC (such as slowing it down or causing it to work improperly), in addition to its potential security risks. In fact, a Consumer Reports survey estimates that spyware infections prompted

850,000 U.S. households to replace their computers during the first half of 2007. And the problem will likely become worse before it gets any better. Some spyware programs—sometimes referred to as *stealthware*—are getting more aggressive, such as delivering ads regardless of the activity you are doing on your PC, changing your browser home page or otherwise resetting your browser settings (referred to as *browser hijacking*), and performing other annoying actions. The worst spyware programs rewrite your computer's main instructions—such as the *Windows Registry*—to change your browser settings back to the hijacked settings each time you reboot your PC, undoing any changes you may have made to your browser settings.

PROTECTING AGAINST ONLINE THEFT, FRAUD, AND OTHER DOT CONS

Businesses and consumers can both help to prevent some types of online theft—businesses by using good security measures to protect the data stored on their computers, and consumers by only sending sensitive information via secure servers. Various other techniques (as discussed next) can help protect against identity theft, online auction fraud, and other types of dot cons. With any of these cons, it is important to act quickly if you think you have been a victim; for instance, you should work with your local law enforcement agency, credit card companies, and the three major consumer credit bureaus (*Equifax*, *Experian*, and *TransUnion*) to close any accessed or fraudulent accounts, place fraud alerts on your credit report, and take other actions to prevent additional fraudulent activity while the fraud is being investigated.

Arrests and prosecutions by law enforcement agencies may also help cut down on cybercrimes. Prosecution of online scammers has been increasing and sentences are not light. For instance, one man—the first person convicted by a jury under the *CAN-SPAM Act of 2003* for operating a phishing scheme—was sentenced in mid-2007 to 70 months in federal prison and ordered to pay over one million dollars to his victims.

Protecting Against Identity Theft

In a nutshell, the best protection against identity theft is to protect your identifying information. Do not give out personal information—especially your Social Security number or mother's maiden name—unless it is absolutely necessary. In addition, before revealing any personal information to a new organization, find out how it will be used and if it will be shared with other organizations. Also, never give out sensitive personal information to anyone who requests it over the phone or by e-mail. Most businesses that need bank account information, passwords, or credit card numbers already have all the information they need and will not call or e-mail a request for more information. If additional information is needed, it will almost always be requested in writing. To help prevent individuals from inadvertently giving out potentially private data via the Internet, some security programs include a component that monitors for personal information being read via or sent across a network and notifies the individual.

To prevent someone from using the preapproved credit card offers and other documents containing personal information that frequently arrive in the mail, shred them before throwing them in the trash. To prevent the theft of outgoing mail containing sensitive information, don't place it in your mailbox—mail it at the post office or in a USPS drop box. When working online, never click a link on a third-party site or in an e-mail message to go to an online shopping or banking site, or any site that uses passwords or contains sensitive data—always type the URL instead. Some additional tips for minimizing your risk of identity theft are listed in Figure 4-20.

PODCAST

Go to **www.course.com/uccs/ch4** to download or listen to the "Identity Theft and Fraud Prevention" podcast.

TIPS FOR AVOIDING IDENTITY THEFT

Protect your Social Security number—give it out only when necessary.

Be careful with your physical mail and trash—shred all documents containing sensitive data.

Secure your computer—update your operating system and use up-to-date security (antivirus, antispyware, firewall, etc.) software.

Be cautious—NEVER click on a link in an e-mail message or respond to a too-good-to-be-true offer.

Use strong passwords for your PC and online accounts.

Verify sources before sharing sensitive information—never respond to e-mail or phone requests for sensitive information.

Be vigilant while on the go—safeguard your wallet, mobile phone, and portable PC.

Watch your bills and monitor your credit reports—react immediately if you suspect fraudulent activity.

Use security software or browser features that warn you if you try to view a known phishing site.

FIGURE 4-20
Tips to reduce your risk of identity theft.

TIP

Some homeowner's and rental policies include coverage for financial losses resulting from identity theft; stand-alone identity theft insurance is also available.

To catch instances of credit card fraud or identity theft early, it is a good idea to keep a close eye on your credit card bills and credit history. Make sure your bills come in every month (some thieves will change your mailing address to delay detection), and read credit card statements carefully to look for unauthorized charges. Be sure to follow up on any calls you get from creditors, instead of assuming it is just a mistake. Most security experts also recommend ordering a full credit history on yourself a few times a year to check for accounts listed in your name that you did not open and any other problems. The *Fair and Accurate Credit Transactions Act* (*FACTA*), enacted in December 2003, enables all Americans to get a free copy of their credit report, upon request, each year from the three major consumer credit bureaus. Ideally, you should request one every four months to regularly monitor your credit. These reports contain information about inquiries related to new accounts requested in your name, as well as any delinquent balances or other negative reports.

One of the easiest ways to get a free copy of your credit report is using a Web site such as AnnualCreditReport.com. These sites use secure Web pages and first typically ask your state and then ask you to supply identifying information, such as name, date of birth, and Social Security number. After verifying that the information displayed is your correct information, you will need to correctly answer one or more questions about your credit that only you should know the answer to, such as the county in which you have a mortgage, your approximate monthly mortgage payment, and so forth. After verification, you will be provided with a link to view your report online. The report can also be printed.

The questions used to obtain an online credit report are a type of cognitive authentication. As discussed earlier in this chapter, cognitive authentication uses obscure questions gathered from online databases and other sources to verify the identity of individuals requesting online transactions. These questions—such as "What is the make and model of your oldest child's car?" or "In what city was your first elementary school,"—are intended to be easy for the individual to answer but difficult for hackers to guess the correct answer. These types of questions are sometimes called "out of wallet" questions, since the answers are typically not carried in a wallet, and are increasingly being used by banks and credit companies to protect against criminals accessing bank accounts and other sensitive online accounts. Some banks—such as Bank of America—are also paying more attention to users' habits to look for patterns that vary from the norm, such as accessing accounts online at an hour unusual for that individual or a higher than normal level of online purchases. If the banks suspect the account may be compromised, they contact the owner for verification. Bank of America and some other financial institutions have also added an additional step in their logon process—displaying an image or word preselected by the user and stored on the bank's server—to prove to the user that the site being viewed is the legitimate (not a phishing) site. In addition, if the system does not recognize the computer that the user is using to log on to the system, the user is required to go through a comprehensive authentication process to enroll that computer into the system.

Protecting Against Other Dot Cons

The best protection against Internet offer scams and other dot cons is common sense. Be extremely cautious of any unsolicited e-mail messages you receive and realize that if an offer sounds too good to be true, it probably is. When dealing with individuals online through auctions and other person-to-person activities, it makes sense to be cautious. Before bidding on an auction item, check out the feedback rating of the seller to see comments written by other auction sellers and buyers (see Figure 4-21). Whenever possible,

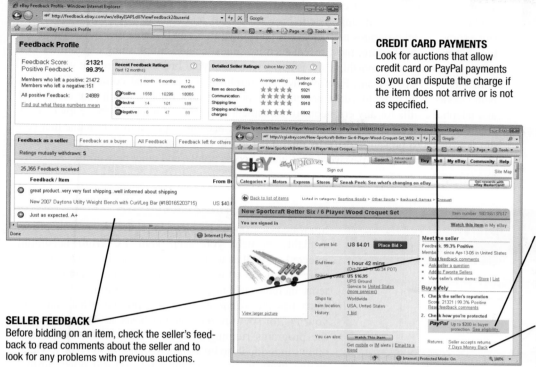

CREDIT CARD PAYMENTS
Look for auctions that allow credit card or PayPal payments so you can dispute the charge if the item does not arrive or is not as specified.

BUYER PROTECTION PLAN
Auction items on eBay are typically covered for $200 when the payment is made via PayPal.

SELLER FEEDBACK
Before bidding on an item, check the seller's feedback to read comments about the seller and to look for any problems with previous auctions.

RETURNS
Some sellers will allow you to return the item if you are not satisfied.

FIGURE 4-21
Smart online auction buying.

FIGURE 4-22
Tips for spotting phishing e-mail messages.

pay for auctions and other online purchases using a credit card or an online payment service (such as PayPal) that accepts credit card payments so you can dispute the transaction through your credit card company, if needed. Using an online payment service that bills the charge to your credit card, instead of allowing the seller to charge your credit card, also keeps your credit card information private. In addition, some auction sites and online payment services offer free buyer protection against undelivered items or auction items that are significantly different from their description provided in the auction information. For instance, most eBay purchases paid for via PayPal have at least $200 of buyer protection coverage at no additional cost. For expensive items, consider using an *escrow service*, which allows you to ensure that the merchandise is as specified before your payment is released to the seller.

To avoid spoofing and phishing schemes, never respond to e-mail requests for updated credit card information. Some tips for identifying phishing e-mails are shown in Figure 4-22. Remember that spear phishing schemes may include personalized information (such as your name)—do not let that fool you into thinking the phishing e-mail is legitimate. If you think an unsolicited e-mail message requesting information from you may be legitimate—if, for instance, the credit card you used to automatically pay for your Internet connection or other ongoing service is about to expire and the e-mail message asks you to update your credit card information—type the URL for that site in your browser (not necessarily the URL shown in the e-mail message) to load the legitimate site before updating your

A PHISHING E-MAIL OFTEN . . .

Tries to scare you into responding by sounding urgent, including a warning that your account will be cancelled if you do not respond, or telling you that you have been a victim of fraud.

Asks you to provide personal information, such as your bank account number, an account password, credit card number, PIN number, mother's maiden name, or Social Security number.

Contains links that do not go where the link text says it will go (point to a hyperlink in the e-mail message to view the URL for that link).

Uses legitimate logos from the company the phisher is posing as.

Appears to come from a known organization, but one you may not have an association with.

Appears to be text or text and images but is actually a single image; it has been created that way to avoid being caught in a *spam filter* (a program that sorts e-mail based on legitimate e-mail and suspected spam) since spam filters cannot read text that is part of an image in an e-mail message.

Contains spelling or grammatical errors.

FURTHER EXPLORATION

Go to **www.course.com/uccs/ch4** for links to further information about how to prevent and deal with identity theft and online auction fraud.

account information. *Never* click a link in an e-mail message to update your information. And make sure your operating system, browser, e-mail, and security software are up to date since some e-mail programs mark possible phishing e-mails and disable their links unless the user overrides this feature; most recent security suites include antiphishing capabilities that notify you if a possible phishing site is being viewed in your browser; and recent versions of both Internet Explorer and Firefox have an antiphishing feature that compares Web sites being loaded with those in a database of known phishing sites. Finally, watch your credit card and telephone bills for any erroneous or fraudulent charges, and request a free copy of your credit report at least once per year to watch for new accounts opened in your name that you did not open. To prevent a drive-by pharming attack, all businesses and individuals should change the administrator password for routers, access points, and other networking hardware to a strong password.

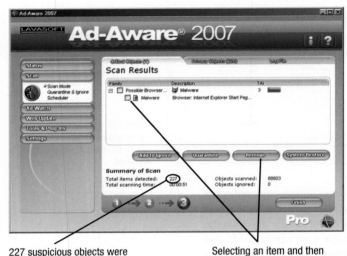

227 suspicious objects were found; 1 was classified as a critical object.

Selecting an item and then clicking Remove will remove that item from your PC.

FIGURE 4-23
Antispyware software is used to detect and remove spyware programs.

Protecting Against Spyware

Spyware is a growing problem, but there are several options available to help you keep your PC from becoming infected, as well as to help you detect and remove any spyware that makes its way onto your PC. Many operating systems include built-in precautions. For instance, Windows Vista has the *Windows Defender* program that can scan your PC for spyware on a regular basis, as well as monitor the programs running on your PC. Windows Vista also allows individuals to be assigned *Standard Accounts*, which enable users to run programs and perform other normal tasks, but requires permission (and may require an administrator password) to install programs, change security settings, and other administrator tasks. Browser security settings can also often be used to prevent programs from being installed without the user specifically authorizing them. In addition, many security programs—including Norton Internet Security and McAfee Internet Security—scan for spyware and other common threats. If a user's security software does not include *antispyware* capabilities, a stand-alone antispyware program, such as *Spybot Search & Destroy* and *Ad-Aware* (see Figure 4-23), can be used to detect spyware programs (as well as other items, such as adware and cookies, that may involve privacy risks) already installed on your PC. These programs typically both identify and allow you to remove any risky components found. Users can do their part by being cautious about the types of programs they download from the Internet, reading software license agreements before installing new software, and keeping operating systems and browsers up to date since some spyware authors take advantage of security holes in popular browsers, such as Internet Explorer. Consequently, using a less common browser—such as Opera or Mozilla's Firefox—can also help to reduce your risk.

Using Digital Signatures and Digital Certificates

While encryption is used to ensure that a document cannot be intercepted in a form that can be understood or altered during transmission, the purpose of *digital signatures* and *digital certificates* is to authenticate and guarantee the identity of a person or Web site.

A **digital signature** is a type of *electronic signature* that is used to verify the identity of the sender of a document. Unlike other types of electronic signatures (such as signed documents

---

>**Digital signature.** A unique digital code that can be attached to a file or an e-mail message to verify the identity of the sender and guarantee the file or message has not been changed since it was signed.

that are faxed to the recipient or credit card signatures captured by a signature capture device at a retail store, for instance), digital signatures use encryption to authenticate the sender of an electronic document. Digital signatures typically use the same public key encryption that is used with encrypted files, but the sender's private key is used to sign the document instead of his or her public key. The sender's private key and the document being signed are used together to generate the actual digital signature (a unique digital code); consequently, the signature is different with each signed document. When a digitally signed document is received, the recipient's PC uses the sender's public key to verify the digital signature. Since the document is signed with the sender's private key (that only the sender should know) and the digital signature will be deemed invalid if even one character of the document is changed after it is signed, digital signatures guarantee that the document was sent by a specific individual and that it was not tampered with after it was signed. Digitally-signed documents typically have some sort of indicator or button that can be clicked to display a verification of who signed the document. Digital signatures can be applied to both encrypted and nonencrypted files and messages.

Since the passing of the *Electronic Signatures in Global and National Commerce Act*, which then-President Clinton signed in 2000 with a digital signature, electronic signatures are as legally binding as handwritten signatures for e-commerce transactions. Designed to facilitate consumer transactions, this law enables people and businesses to buy insurance, get a mortgage, open a brokerage account, or finalize other transactions that require a signed authorization, without waiting for physical documents to be mailed back and forth. Although not widely used by individuals, digital signatures are increasingly being used by businesses and the government and are expected to become extremely important as contracts and other legal documents begin to be exchanged more commonly over the Internet. Digital signatures may also be used in the *e-mail authentication* systems currently in development (such as the *DomainKeys* system being adopted by Yahoo!, eBay, and PayPal) that are designed to authenticate e-mail messages sent from companies, in order to better detect phishing schemes.

In order to add a digital signature to an e-mail message or file, a **digital certificate** is needed. Digital certificates are obtained from a *Certificate Authority* and typically contain the name of the person, organization, or Web site being certified along with a certificate serial number, an expiration date, and a pair of keys (one public, one private) that can be used with both digital signatures and encryption. The Certificate Authority guarantees that individuals or organizations granted digital certificates are, in fact, who they claim to be, usually only after verifying their identity with a financial institution or through some other authentication procedure. Certificates issued to businesses and individuals are typically installed in their browser, e-mail program, and any third-party encryption program so that the certificate information is available for use whenever a file or e-mail message needs to be digitally signed or encrypted. Some application programs—such as Microsoft Word— include the option to add a digital signature to documents created in that program, using your digital certificate.

In addition to being used by individuals to sign and encrypt files and e-mail messages, digital certificates are also used in conjunction with secure Web sites to guarantee that Web pages are secure and actually belong to the stated organization (so users can know for sure who their credit card number or other sensitive data is really being sent to). Secure Web sites can obtain a normal *SSL digital certificate* or a newer *Extended Validation (EV) SSL digital certificate*. The EV SSL digital certificate was developed to provide consumers with a higher level of trust while online and requires businesses to complete a very thorough application process using reputable third-party sources to verify that the company has the right to use the Web site domain name in question and that the individual requesting the certificate is authorized to do so. EV SSL certificates work like conventional SSL

>**Digital certificate.** A group of electronic data, such as encryption key pairs and a digital signature, that can be used to verify the identity of a person or organization.

POSSIBLE CERTIFICATE PROBLEMS
IE 7 displays a warning when a Web site that may have a
certificate problem is about to be displayed.

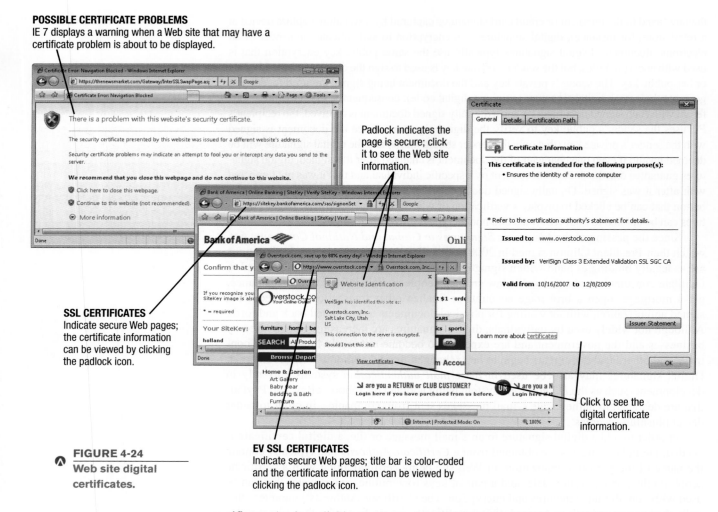

FIGURE 4-24
**Web site digital
certificates.**

SSL CERTIFICATES
Indicate secure Web pages;
the certificate information
can be viewed by clicking
the padlock icon.

Padlock indicates the
page is secure; click
it to see the Web site
information.

Click to see the
digital certificate
information.

EV SSL CERTIFICATES
Indicate secure Web pages; title bar is color-coded
and the certificate information can be viewed by
clicking the padlock icon.

certificates (and so clicking on the secure Web page icon in a browser displays that site's certificate), but they also display additional information when the Web site is viewed in an EV-compliant browser, such as Internet Explorer 7. For instance, IE 7 recolors the Address bar green and displays the name of the organization associated with the Web site and the Certificate Authority used in the Security Status bar, as shown in Figure 4-24. As also shown in this figure, some browsers (such as IE 7) display a warning if there is a possible problem with the certificate of a requested site. In order to view that site, the user needs to specifically confirm that he or she wants to view the site even though the recommendation is not to view it.

With the increased risk of Internet-related fraud today, it is expected that banks and other financial institutions may soon begin to issue free digital certificates to customers in order to authenticate both the customer and the bank's Web site each time the customer visits the site, to help protect against phishing, identity theft, and other types of dot cons.

FURTHER EXPLORATION

Go to **www.course.com/uccs/ch4**
for links to further information about
digital signatures and digital
certificates.

PERSONAL SAFETY ISSUES

In addition to being expensive and inconvenient, cybercrime can also be physically dangerous. Although most of us may not ordinarily view using the Internet as a potentially dangerous activity, cases of physical harm due to Internet activity do happen. For example, children and teenagers have become the victims of pedophiles who arranged face-to-face meetings by using information gathered via e-mail, discussion groups, or chat rooms. There are also a growing number of *e-bullying* incidents, in which children are being threatened by classmates via e-mail, Web site posts, or text messages. Adults have fallen for unscrupulous or dangerous individuals who misrepresented themselves online; they have also been victims of *cyberstalking*. In addition, the availability of personal information online has made it more difficult for individuals to hide from people who may want to do them harm, such as abused women trying to hide from their abusive husbands.

Cyberbullying and Cyberstalking

Bullying an individual via the Internet—such as through e-mail, a social networking site, a blog, or other online communications method—is referred to as **cyberbullying**. Cyberbullying often affects young people today. In fact, according to a recent report by the Pew Internet and American Life Project, about one-third of all teenagers say they have been bullied through the Internet. For instance, there have been cases of students hacking into other students' pages on MySpace or another social networking site and changing the content to harass the other student, and in one tragic instance a 13-year-old girl hanged herself after the mother of one of the girl's classmates arranged to have a MySpace profile created for a nonexistent teenage boy in order to gain the girl's confidence and determine what the girl was saying about the classmate, and then cruelly ended the friendship.

Repeated threats, cyberbullying, or other harassment carried out online is referred to as **cyberstalking**. Cyberstalkers often find their victims online—for instance, someone in a chat room who makes a comment or has a screen name that the cyberstalker does not like. Other examples of cyberstalking include employers who are stalked online by ex-employees who were fired or otherwise left their position under adverse conditions, and bloggers who are harassed and threatened with violence or murder because of their blogging activities. Cyberstalking typically begins with online harassment—such as sending harassing or threatening e-mail messages or unwanted files to the victim, posting inappropriate messages in chat rooms about the victim, posing as the victim in order to sign the victim up for pornographic or otherwise offensive e-mail newsletters, and publicizing the victim's home address and telephone number. It can also lead to offline stalking and possibly physical harm—in at least one case, it led to the death of the victim. Although there is no one exact definition of cyberstalking, the generally accepted definition covers any harassing online activity that would cause a reasonable person to experience fear or some sense of dread or threat. There are as yet no specific federal laws against cyberstalking, but all states have made it illegal, and some federal laws do apply if the online actions include computer fraud or another type of crime, suggest a threat of personal injury, or involve sending obscene e-mail messages. It has been estimated that about 500,000 people stalk someone online each year. Most cyberstalkers are not caught, however, due in part to the anonymity of the Internet, which assists cyberstalkers in concealing their true identities.

Online Pornography

A variety of controversial and potentially objectionable material is available on the Internet. Many parents are concerned about the vast amount of pornography available online. Although there have been attempts to ban this type of material from the Internet, they have not been successful. For example, the *Communications Decency Act*, signed into law in 1996—which made it a criminal offense to distribute patently indecent or offensive material online—was ruled unconstitutional in 1997 by the U.S. Supreme Court. However, like its printed counterpart, online pornography involving minors is illegal. Because of the strong link they believe exists between child pornography and child molestation, many experts are very concerned about the amount of child pornography that can be found and distributed via the Internet. They also believe that the Internet makes it easier for sexual

---

>**Cyberbullying.** Bullying an individual via the Internet. >**Cyberstalking.** Repeated threats or harassing behavior via e-mail or another Internet communications method.

predators to act out, such as by striking up "friendships" with children in chat rooms and convincing them to meet them in real life. And this can have devastating consequences, as it did for a 13-year-old girl from Connecticut who was strangled to death in 2002 by a 25-year-old man she met originally in an online chat room and eventually in person. Although the man confessed, he maintains that the strangling was accidental. The man was sentenced in late 2003 to a total of 40 years in prison for state and federal charges relating to the incident.

PROTECTING AGAINST CYBERSTALKING AND OTHER PERSONAL SAFETY CONCERNS

There is no surefire way to protect against cyberstalking and other online dangers completely, but some common-sense precautions can reduce the chance of becoming involved in a serious personal safety problem due to online activities.

Safety Tips for Adults

It is wise to be cautious and discreet in chat rooms, discussion groups, and other online locations where individuals communicate with strangers. To protect yourself against cyberstalking and other types of online harassment, use gender-neutral, nonprovocative identifying names, such as *jsmith*, instead of *janesmith* or *iamcute*. Do not reveal personal information—such as your real name, address, or telephone number—to people you meet in a chat room. Although they may feel like new friends, they are strangers and you have no idea who they really are or what they are like in real life. In addition, do not respond to any insults or other harassing comments you may receive online. You may also wish to request that your personal information be removed from online directories—especially those associated with your e-mail address or other online identifier.

Safety Tips for Children

Most experts agree that the best way to protect children from online dangers is to stay in close touch with them as they explore the Internet. To be able to check up on their online activities quickly, it is a good idea to have children—including teenagers—use a PC in a family room or other public location, instead of their bedroom, and they should be told which activities are allowed, which types of Web sites are off-limits, and why. In addition, it should be made clear that they are never to reveal personal information about themselves online without a parent's permission. They should also be instructed to tell a parent (or teacher if at school) if an individual ever requests personal information or a personal meeting, or threatens or otherwise harasses the child, via any type of online communications medium.

NETWORK AND INTERNET SECURITY LEGISLATION

Although new legislation is passed periodically to address new types of computer crimes, it is difficult for the legal system to keep pace with the rate at which technology changes. In addition, there are both domestic and international jurisdictional issues because many computer crimes affect businesses and individuals located in geographic areas other than the one in which the computer criminal is located, and hackers can make it appear that activity is coming from a different location than it really is. Nevertheless, computer crime legislation continues to be proposed and computer crimes are being prosecuted. A list of selected federal laws concerning network and Internet security is shown in Figure 4-25. Additional legislation regarding spyware, phishing, and identity theft is under consideration and may become law in the future. For instance, two bills under consideration at the time of this writing were the *Internet Spyware (I-SPY) Prevention Act of 2007* (which imposes criminal penalties for planting certain types of malicious software onto a computer) and the *Cyber-Security Enhancement Act of 2007* (which broadens penalties for botnet attacks and other crimes).

DATE	LAW AND DESCRIPTION
2004	**Identity Theft Penalty Enhancement Act** Adds extra years to prison sentences for criminals who use identity theft (including the use of stolen credit card numbers) to commit other crimes, including credit card fraud and terrorism.
2003	**Fair and Accurate Credit Transactions Act (FACTA)** Amends the Fair Credit Reporting Act (FCRA) to require, among other things, that the three nationwide consumer reporting agencies (Equifax, Experian, and TransUnion) provide to consumers, upon request, a free copy of their credit report once every 12 months.
2003	**PROTECT Act** Includes provisions to prohibit virtual child pornography.
2003	**Health Insurance Portability and Accountability Act (HIPAA)** Includes a Security Rule that sets minimum security standards to protect health information stored electronically.
2002	**Homeland Security Act** Includes provisions to combat cyberterrorism, including protecting ISPs against lawsuits from customers for revealing private information to law enforcement agencies.
2002	**Sarbanes-Oxley Act** Requires archiving a variety of electronic records and protecting the integrity of corporate financial data.
2001	**USA Patriot Act (USAPA)** Grants federal authorities expanded surveillance and intelligence-gathering powers, such as broadening the ability of federal agents to obtain the real identity of Internet users, intercept e-mail and other types of Internet communications, follow online activity of suspects, expand their wiretapping authority, and more.
1998	**Identity Theft and Assumption Deterrence Act of 1998** Makes it a federal crime to knowingly use someone else's means of identification, such as name, Social Security number, or credit card, to commit any unlawful activity.
1997	**No Electronic Theft (NET) Act** Expands computer piracy laws to include distribution of copyrighted materials over the Internet.
1996	**National Information Infrastructure Protection Act** Amends the Computer Fraud and Abuse Act of 1984 to punish information theft crossing state lines and crack down on network trespassing.
1994	**Computer Abuse Amendments Act** Amends the Computer Fraud and Abuse Act of 1984 to include computer viruses and other harmful code.
1986	**Computer Fraud and Abuse Act of 1986** Amends the 1984 law to include federally regulated financial institutions.
1984	**Computer Fraud and Abuse Act of 1984** Makes it a crime to break into computers owned by the federal government. This act has been regularly amended over the years as technology has changed.

FIGURE 4-25
Computer network and Internet security legislation.

SUMMARY

WHY BE CONCERNED ABOUT NETWORK AND INTERNET SECURITY?

Chapter Objective 1:
Explain why computer users should be concerned about network and Internet security.

There are a number of important security concerns related to computers and the Internet. Many of these are **computer crimes**. Because computers and networks are so widespread, there is unprecedented opportunity for criminals and other individuals to commit acts that are not in the public interest. All computer users should be aware of the risks of using networks and the Internet so they can take appropriate precautions.

UNAUTHORIZED ACCESS, UNAUTHORIZED USE, AND COMPUTER SABOTAGE

Chapter Objective 2:
List several examples of unauthorized access, unauthorized use, and computer sabotage.

Two important risks related to computer networks and the Internet are **unauthorized access** and **unauthorized use**. **Hacking** is the term used for using a computer to break into a computer system. Hacking can take place via the Internet or via a wireless network. **War driving** (also called **Wi-Fi piggybacking**) is the act of looking for unsecured Wi-Fi networks to access without authorization. Data can be intercepted as it is transmitted over the Internet or a wireless network.

Computer sabotage includes **malware** (**computer viruses**, **computer worms**, **Trojan horses**, and other programs designed to cause harm to computer systems), **denial of service (DoS) attacks** (attempts to shut down a network or Web server by flooding it with more requests than it can handle), data and program alteration, and *cybervandalism*. It can be performed by **bot** PCs in a **botnet**.

PROTECTING AGAINST UNAUTHORIZED ACCESS, UNAUTHORIZED USE, AND COMPUTER SABOTAGE

Chapter Objective 3:
Explain how access control systems, firewalls, antivirus software, and encryption protect against unauthorized access, unauthorized use, and computer sabotage.

There are many options for protecting a network against unauthorized access and use. For instance, comprehensive **network access control (NAC) systems** can be used. Specifically, *access control systems* used to control access to a computer, network, facility, or other resource include **possessed knowledge access systems** that use **passwords** or other types of possessed knowledge; **possessed object access systems** that use physical objects, such as badges and cards; and **biometric access systems** that identify users by a particular unique biological characteristic, such as a fingerprint, a hand, a face, or an iris. To be effective, passwords should be *strong passwords*; *two-factor authentication systems* that use multiple control factors are more effective than single-factor systems.

To protect wireless networks, security features should be enabled. **Firewalls** protect against unauthorized access; **antivirus software** protects against malware. Keeping your operating system, Web browser, and e-mail programs up to date, such as by installing security patches as soon as they become available, is another good precaution.

Sensitive transactions should be performed only on **secure Web pages**; sensitive files and e-mails should be secured with **encryption**. The two most common types of encryption are **public key encryption** (in which a private key and matching public key are used) and **private key encryption** (in which only a private key is used). *Web-based encryption* is also available. The strength of an encryption method is measured by the length of its keys, such as *weak* (40-bit) *encryption*, *strong 128-bit*, and *military-strength 2,048-bit encryption*. A **virtual private network** (**VPN**) can be used to provide a secure remote connection to a company network. Employers should take appropriate precautions with current and former employees.

ONLINE THEFT, FRAUD, AND OTHER DOT CONS

There are a variety of types of theft, fraud, and scams related to the Internet—collectively referred to as **dot cons**—that all Internet users should be aware of. Data, information, or money can be stolen from individuals and businesses. Sometimes this occurs in conjunction with **identity theft**, in which an individual poses as another individual. **Online auction fraud**, *Internet offer scams*, **spoofing**, **phishing**, **spear phishing**, and **pharming** are other common possibilities. **Spyware** programs can also be used to gather sensitive information about individuals, as well as to deliver ads and other possibly annoying content to Internet users.

Chapter Objective 4:
Discuss online theft, identity theft, Internet scams, spoofing, phishing, and other types of dot cons.

PROTECTING AGAINST ONLINE THEFT, FRAUD, AND OTHER DOT CONS

To protect against identity theft, individuals should guard their personal information carefully. To check for identity theft, watch your bills and credit history. When interacting with other individuals online or buying from an online auction, it is wise to be conservative and use a credit card whenever possible. To avoid other types of dot cons, be very wary of responding to unsolicited offers and e-mails, and steer clear of offers that seem too good to be true. Never click a link in an e-mail message to update your personal information. To verify the sender of a document, **digital signatures** can be used. Digital signatures are obtained as part of a **digital certificate** acquired through a *Certification Authority* (*CA*) after the applicant's identity is verified. Digital certificates can also be used to verify the identity of secure Web pages, and the keys included in the certificate can be used for sending encrypted files to others. *Antispyware* programs can help detect and remove spyware installed on your PC.

Chapter Objective 5:
Detail steps an individual can take to protect against online theft, identity theft, Internet scams, spoofing, phishing, and other types of dot cons.

PERSONAL SAFETY ISSUES

There are also personal safety risks for both adults and children stemming from Internet use. **Cyberbullying** and **cyberstalking**—online harassment that frightens or threatens the victim—is more common in recent years, even though most states have passed laws against it. *E-bullying* is a growing risk for children, as is the potential exposure to online pornography and other materials inappropriate for children.

Chapter Objective 6:
Identify personal safety risks associated with Internet use.

PROTECTING AGAINST CYBERSTALKING AND OTHER PERSONAL SAFETY CONCERNS

To protect their personal safety, adults and children should be cautious in online communications. They should be wary of revealing any personal information or meeting online acquaintances in person. To protect children, parents should keep a close watch on their children's online activities, and they should never reveal personal information to others online without a parent's consent.

Chapter Objective 7:
List steps individuals can take to safeguard their personal safety when using the Internet.

NETWORK AND INTERNET SECURITY LEGISLATION

Although the rapid growth of the Internet and jurisdictional issues have contributed to the lack of network and Internet security legislation, some important pieces of legislation are in place, such as the *USA Patriot Act*, *Identity Theft and Assumption Act*, and *Computer Fraud and Abuse Act*.

Chapter Objective 8:
Name several laws related to network and Internet security.

REVIEW ACTIVITIES

KEY TERM MATCHING

Instructions: Match each key term on the left with the definition on the right that best describes it.

a. computer virus

b. denial of service (DoS) attack

c. dot con

d. encryption

e. firewall

f. hacking

g. identity theft

h. password

i. spoofing

j. spyware

1. _____ A collection of hardware and/or software intended to protect a computer or computer network from unauthorized access.

2. _____ A fraud or scam carried out through the Internet.

3. _____ A method of scrambling e-mail or files to make them unreadable if they are intercepted by an unauthorized user.

4. _____ A secret combination of characters used to gain access to a computer, computer network, or other resource.

5. _____ A software program installed without the user's knowledge that secretly collects information and sends it to an outside party via the user's Internet connection.

6. _____ A software program installed without the user's knowledge and designed to alter the way a computer operates or to cause harm to the computer system.

7. _____ An act of sabotage that attempts to flood a network server or a Web server with so much activity that it is unable to function.

8. _____ Making it appear that an e-mail or a Web site originates from somewhere other than where it really does; typically used with dot cons.

9. _____ Using a computer to break into another computer system.

10. _____ Using someone else's identity to purchase goods or services, obtain new credit cards or bank loans, or otherwise illegally masquerade as that individual.

SELF-QUIZ

Instructions: Circle **T** if the statement is true, **F** if the statement is false, or write the best answer in the space provided. **Answers for the self-quiz are located in the References and Resources Guide at the end of the book.**

1. **T F** A computer virus can only be transferred to another computer via a storage medium.

2. **T F** An access control system that uses passwords is a possessed knowledge access system.

3. **T F** Spyware is a malicious program that masquerades as something else.

4. **T F** Secure Web pages use encryption to securely transfer data sent via those pages.

5. **T F** Cyberstalking is the use of spoofed e-mail messages to gain credit card numbers and other personal data to be used for fraudulent purposes.

6. Driving around looking for a Wi-Fi network to access is referred to as _____.

7. _____ access control systems use some type of unique physical characteristic of a person to grant or deny access to that individual.

8. A(n) _____ protects a computer or network from unauthorized access by closing down external communications port addresses to unauthorized programs or requests.

9. A(n) _____ is a unique digital code that can be attached to a file or an e-mail message to verify the identity of the sender and guarantee the file or message has not been changed.

10. Match each type of computer crime with its description and write the corresponding number in the blank to the left of each description.

    a. _____ A person working for the Motor Vehicle Division deletes a friend's speeding ticket from a database.

    b. _____ An individual attaches a harmful file to an e-mail message that will automatically send itself to the first 10 people in the recipient's e-mail address book.

    c. _____ An individual does not like someone's comment in a chat room and begins to send that individual harassing e-mail messages.

    d. _____ An individual sells the same item to 10 individuals via an online auction site.

    e. _____ A person creates and sends an e-mail message that looks like it belongs to a legitimate company but contains a link to a fraudulent Web site instead.

    f. _____ A person accesses a computer belonging to the IRS without authorization.

1. Online auction fraud	**3.** Computer sabotage	**5.** Phishing
2. Hacking	**4.** Data or program alteration	**6.** Cyberbullying

---

1. Write the appropriate letter in the blank to the left of each term to indicate whether it is related to unauthorized access (U), computer sabotage (C), online theft or fraud (O), or personal safety (P).

    a. _____ Cyberstalking   **d.** _____ Time bomb   **g.** _____ Malware

    b. _____ Phishing   **e.** _____ War driving   **h.** _____ Spoofing

    c. _____ Cybervandalism   **f.** _____ DoS attack   **i.** _____ Hacking

2. Is the password *john1* a good password? Why or why not? If not, suggest a better password.

3. Supply the missing words to complete the following statements.

    a. With an encrypted e-mail message, the recipient's _____ key is used to encrypt the message, and the recipient's _____ key is used to decrypt the message.

    b. With a digital signature, the sender's _____ key is used to sign the document, and the sender's _____ key is used to validate the signature.

4. To secure files on your PC so they are unreadable to a hacker who might gain access to your PC, what type of encryption (public key or private key) would be the most appropriate? Explain.

5. List two precautions that individuals can take when setting up a wireless home router or access point to prevent unauthorized access.

According to security experts, new variants of several worms released in past years contain more than just the virus code—they contain messages taunting other virus writers and code to remove competing malware from the PCs they infect. For instance, the Netsky worm includes code to remove the Mydoom and Bagle worms from PCs that the Netsky worm infects, and the latest variant of the Bozori worm removes competing worms, like Zotob, from the PCs it infects. The goal seems to be not only to gain control of an increasing number of infected machines—a type of "bot war" to build the biggest botnet—but also to one-up rivals. Some virus writers may just want to obtain notoriety, but another more alarming possibility is that an increasing percentage of virus writers are interested in gaining control of PCs for monetary gain—such as through identity theft and other fraudulent activities. And the increased use of spam to spread viruses just makes the entire situation worse. If this trend continues, do you think it will affect how hackers and other computer criminals will be viewed? Will they become cult heroes or be viewed as dangerous criminals? Will continuing to increase prosecution of these individuals help or hurt the situation?

BALANCING ACT

SECURITY VS. PERSONAL FREEDOM

There are some basic types of security we all depend on. We expect the military to protect us from invasions or attacks from other countries, we depend on our local police to keep our towns safe, and we expect our employers to provide a safe workplace. As the level of potential danger in our lives increases, it tends to limit our own personal freedom. For example, many citizens of large cities avoid walking the streets alone at night, even though they have the right to do so, and many Americans avoid traveling to the Middle East, South America, and other locations thought to be dangerous for Americans at the present time. Ironically, security measures established to protect us sometimes tend to limit our personal freedom as well—for example, having to submit to personal and baggage searches before boarding an airplane or having to show identification to gain admittance to your workplace. Most citizens are willing to give up some level of personal freedom in order to protect their personal safety, but the difficulty is determining the balance—how much loss of freedom is worth a certain level of additional security?

It is not surprising that the answer to this question varies from person to person. Some individuals are willing to trade some personal freedom and privacy for convenience, such as the frequent travelers who sign up for expedited airport screening programs. After submitting to a background check and entering personal data and a biometric characteristic into a computer database, these programs allow the travelers to speed past the security checks required of other passengers. Other individuals, however, may not be so willing to compromise their personal privacy and personal freedom, and might view these types of systems as a step toward restricted freedom and loss of personal privacy. Still others may believe that adequate security is possible without any loss of personal freedom.

YOUR TURN

Give some thought to the statements made in the preceding paragraphs regarding finding a balance between security and personal freedom, and form an opinion on this issue. Consider the following when forming your opinion and be prepared to discuss your position (in class, via an online class discussion group, in a class chat room, or via a class blog) or to write a short paper expressing your opinion, depending on your instructor's directions.

- Do you think it is necessary to sacrifice some degree of personal freedom in order to improve national security? Why or why not?

- Do you think a national ID card (such as a hard-to-forge national driver's license containing a fingerprint or other biometric data or the REAL ID state driver's licenses and identification cards mandated by the REAL ID Act) could help prevent terrorist attacks, such as the 9/11 attacks? Do you think Americans would support its use?

- There has been an increased use of video surveillance and face recognition systems in public locations to try to identify terrorists or known criminals so they can be apprehended. While some privacy advocates strongly object, law enforcement views these systems as necessary tools. What is your opinion?

- As we get further and further from the 9/11 attacks and other acts of terrorism, do you think there will be a decrease in public support for fingerprint scans at airports, national ID cards, public video surveillance systems, and other security methods we have now or that may be introduced in the future to help identify possible terrorist and possible terrorist attacks? Why or why not?

PROJECTS

---

1. **Phishing and Identity Theft** As discussed in the chapter, phishing is one way criminals obtain the information (such as an individual's name, address, Social Security number, and so forth) needed to perform identity theft.

   For this project, research the current status of phishing and identity theft. Identify any new phishing variations that have emerged, as well as any new means criminals are using to obtain the information needed for identity theft. Is identity theft still on the rise? Have any identity theft rings (organized, coordinated identity theft activities) been discovered recently? Are there any new precautions consumers can use to protect against identity theft? At the conclusion of your research, prepare a one-page summary of your findings and submit it to your instructor.

HOT TOPICS

---

2. **New Viruses** Unfortunately, new computer viruses and other types of malware are released all the time.

   For this project, locate an example of a current virus or worm (most security companies, such as Symantec and McAfee, list the most recent security threats on their Web sites) and answer the following questions: When was it introduced? What did it do? How was it spread? How many computers were affected? Is there an estimated cost associated with it? Is it still in existence? At the conclusion of your research, prepare a one-page summary of your findings and submit it to your instructor.

SHORT ANSWER/ RESEARCH

---

3. **Virus Check** There are several Web sites that include a free virus check, as well as other types of diagnostic software.

   For this project, go to the home page for a company that makes antivirus software (such as symantec.com or mcafee.com) and choose the option to run a free virus check (sometimes called a security check). NOTE: The programs may require temporarily downloading a small program or an ActiveX component. If you are unable to perform this task on a school PC, ask your instructor for alternate instructions. If the check takes more than 10 minutes and there is an option to limit the check to a particular drive and folder, redo the check just scanning part of the hard drive (such as the Documents folder) to save time. After the virus scan is completed, print the page displaying the result. Did the program find any viruses or other security threats? If so, did it recommend any particular course of action to remove the virus or otherwise deal with the security threats that were found? At the conclusion of this task, submit your printout with any additional comments about your experience to your instructor.

HANDS ON

WRITING ABOUT COMPUTERS

4. **Hacktivism** *Hacktivism* can be defined as the act of hacking into a computer system for a politically or socially motivated purpose. While some view *hacktivists* no differently than they view other hackers, hacktivists contend that they break into systems in order to bring attention to political or social causes.

    For this project, find an example of a recent act of hacktivism and research it. What site was hacked and what appeared to be the primary motive for the hack? Were the hackers identified? Is so, were they found guilty of a crime? Form an opinion about hacktivism in general, such as whether or not this is a valid method of bringing attention to specific causes, and whether or not hacktivists should be treated any differently when caught than other types of hackers are treated. Submit this project to your instructor in the form of a short paper, not more than two pages in length.

PRESENTATION/ DEMONSTRATION

5. **Virus Hoaxes** In addition to the valid reports about new viruses found in the news and on antivirus software Web sites, reports of viruses that turn out to be hoaxes abound on the Internet. In addition to being an annoyance, virus hoaxes waste time and computing resources. In addition, they may eventually lead some users to routinely ignore all virus warning messages, leaving them vulnerable to a genuine, destructive virus.

    For this project, visit at least two Web sites that identify virus hoaxes, such as the Symantec and McAfee Web sites and the government Hoaxbusters site, currently found at hoaxbusters.ciac.org. Explore the sites to find information about recent virus hoaxes, as well as general guidelines for identifying virus hoaxes and other types of online hoaxes. Share your findings with the class in the form of a short presentation. The presentation should not exceed 10 minutes and should make use of one or more presentation aids, such as the chalkboard, handouts, overhead transparencies, or a computer-based slide presentation (your instructor may provide additional requirements). You may also be asked to submit a summary of the presentation to your instructor.

GROUP DISCUSSION

6. **Homeless Hacker** Hackers who try to gain access to business and government computers and networks are a growing problem. Some hackers do it for monetary gain; others supposedly do it to bring attention to system vulnerabilities or other, purportedly more noble, purposes. One example of a business and government network hacker is Adrian Lamo, a freelance security consultant who is known for his transient lifestyle and hacking into secure computer systems without authorization, looking for their security holes and essentially performing unauthorized vulnerability assessments. What are the implications of this type of hack? Does it expose the data located on those networks to greater danger, or does it result in tightened security and, ultimately, a more secure system? Should these hackers be treated differently than hackers who break into systems to steal data or other resources? Are there varying degrees of criminal hacking, or is a hack just a hack, regardless of the motivation? In 2004, Lamo was indicted and pled guilty to breaking into a database at the New York Times containing employee records for op-ed columnists. He was sentenced to serve two years probation and to pay $65,000 in restitution. Does his conviction change your opinion about so-called "harmless hacking"?

    For this project, form an opinion of the impact of hackers breaching the security of business and government computers and networks and be prepared to discuss your position (in class, via an online class discussion group, in a class chat room, or via a class blog, depending on your instructor's directions). You may also be asked to write a short paper expressing your opinion.

7. **Teaching Computer Viruses** Some college computer classes include instruction on writing computer viruses. At one university, precautions include only allowing fourth year students to take the course, not having a network connection in the classroom, and prohibiting the removal of storage media from the classroom. <u>Do you think these precautions are sufficient</u>? <u>Should virus-coding be allowed as part of a computer degree curriculum</u>? Some believe that students need to know how viruses work in order to be able to develop antivirus software; however, the antivirus industry disagrees, and most antivirus professionals were never virus writers. <u>Is it ethical for colleges to teach computer virus writing</u>? Is it ethical for students to take such a course? Will including <u>teaching illegal and unethical acts in college classes help to legitimize the behavior in society</u>? Would you feel comfortable taking such a course? Why or why not?

    For this project, form an opinion about the inclusion of virus-writing instruction in college classes, the ethical responsibility colleges and students have with respect to this issue, and the potential impact on society and the computer industry. Be prepared to discuss your position (in class, via an online class discussion group, in a class chat room, or via a class blog, depending on your instructor's directions). You may also be asked to write a short paper expressing your opinion.

ETHICS IN ACTION

8. **Worldwide Hacking Wars** The design of the Internet allows easy communications between countries, but it can also open up global hacking opportunities. The accompanying video clip discusses the possibility of cyberattacks between countries and governments.

    Go to www.course.com/uccs/ch4 to watch the "Worldwide Hacking War May Be Underway" video clip. After watching the video, think about the impact of cyberattacks on national security and on relations between countries. If hackers in one country attack businesses and governments in another country, could it be considered an act of war? Should a country be held responsible for the actions individual citizens may take against other countries? Why or why not? Should international cyberattacks be regulated by NATO and other international organizations? Is a cyberattack on a country equivalent to a physical attack? Could World War III take place entirely in cyberspace? Why or why not?

    Express your viewpoint: What is the impact of cyberattacks on national security and on international relations?

    Use the video clip and the questions previously asked as a foundation for your response. Be prepared to discuss your position (in class, via an online class discussion group, in a class chat room, or via a class blog) or to write a short paper stating and supporting your viewpoint on the issue, depending on your instructor's direction. You may also be asked to do research and provide resources to support your point of view on this issue.

VIDEO VIEWPOINT

9. **Interactive Activities** Go to www.course.com/uccs/ch4 and work the interactive **Crossword Puzzle**, listen to the **Podcasts** and watch the **Online Videos** associated with this chapter, and explore the **Further Exploration** links. In addition, work the following interactive **Student Edition Labs**.

- Wireless Networking
- Advanced Databases
- Keeping Your Computer Virus Free
- Careers and Technology

    If you have a SAM user profile, you have access to even more interactive content. Log in to your SAM account and go to your assignments page to see what your instructor has assigned for this chapter.

10. **Test Yourself** Go to www.course.com/uccs/ch4 and review the **Online Study Guide** for Chapter 4, then test your knowledge of the terms and concepts in this chapter by completing the **Key Term Matching** exercise, the **Self-Quiz**, the **Exercises**, and the **Practice Test**.

WEB ACTIVITIES

Student Edition Labs

SAM

EXPERT INSIGHT ON . . .
Networks and the Internet

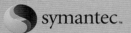 symantec.

A conversation with **COLLIN DAVIS**
Development Manager, Consumer Product Solutions, Symantec Corporation

My Background . . .

I have been working in the computer security industry for seven years. I started in 2001 as a Software Development Intern while studying at UCLA. After earning my Bachelor's degree in computer science from the University of California, Los Angeles Henry Samueli School of Engineering, I joined Symantec as an engineer on the Norton AntiVirus product team and worked with the team to develop and ship six iterations of that product. While I now work on various products in the Norton consumer product line, my primary focus is on Norton 360, Symantec's all-in-one security solution.

> **❝It is critical that you keep your security products up to date to stay protected from the latest threats.❞**

It's Important to Know . . .

To use a layered security system. A layered security system consists of multiple layers of protection to guard against intrusions and other threats. You should use a secure gateway or wireless router and advanced firewall and antivirus technologies. You should also ensure that all your passwords are secure and change them often.

That you need to stay up to date. The threat landscape is constantly changing. It is critical that you keep your security products up to date to stay protected from the latest threats. It's fairly easy for computer users to do this since most products download updates automatically or notify you when you need to download a new version. Don't ignore these notifications.

To think before you act. The online world is no different from the real one. If a link seems suspicious, proceed with caution before clicking it or seek information and services elsewhere.

How I Use this Technology . . .

I use this technology every day in my personal life. The more and more "connected" my data and applications become, the more important it becomes to secure them. Every time I connect to the Internet to send an e-mail, bank online, or view family photos, I am using the networking and Internet technologies discussed in this module to make the connection and I am using the security technologies listed in this module to ensure my private data is protected. I don't always see these technologies as they do their job (this is a good thing!), but the fact that they are there gives me the confidence to take advantage of all the other great technologies being offered today.

Collin Davis is a Development Manager in the Consumer Product Solutions Group at Symantec Corporation. He has worked for Symantec for seven years, initially as a Software Development Intern while in college. He has over 10 years of experience working with computer systems, networks, and other computer-related areas. Collin has a Bachelor of Science degree in Computer Science from the UCLA Henry Samueli School of Engineering.

> ## The hackers out there aren't in it for just notoriety anymore; they want your money–or worse, your identity.

What the Future Holds . . .

Our lives are becoming increasingly more and more dependent on technology. We store our documents and photos online. We work online and even date and form social networks online. All of this introduces increased privacy and security concerns that we must be aware of. It's important to be aware of what data is stored online and to use appropriate protection measures to secure that information.

One of the biggest Internet-related risks today is that threats have evolved to exploit people for financial gain. The hackers out there aren't in it for just notoriety anymore; they want your money—or worse, your identity. People need to be particularly cautious about whom they give their personal information (like credit card and Social Security numbers) to online. Everyone should check their bank and credit card statements often to monitor for fraudulent charges and change their passwords frequently.

In the future, we can expect to see businesses moving toward delivering an even more connected online experience. Personal computers are moving back toward their past role as simple "terminals" that provide a connection to the Internet where a wide array of data and applications are hosted. The line between what is stored and run from your local computer and what is "online" is being blurred. One impact of our online and local content becoming more interconnected is that we will be able to access our own personalized application experience from anywhere in the world, with many different types of devices. Wherever we are, our experience will remain consistent, according to our preferences and our content. However, security will remain essential. If people cannot trust that their information is secure and protected, they will be unable to take advantage of all the exciting services and benefits being offered today.

My Advice to Students . . .

Be curious—explore every facet of a technology that interests you. Try to learn everything about its inner workings but don't lose sight of the big picture. If you're interested in a career in a particular field, get an internship. There is no better way to learn something than to do it.

Discussion Question

Collin Davis stresses the importance of people trusting that their information is secure and protected. Think about the systems that contain personal data about you. How would you feel if those systems were breached and your information was stolen? Does your viewpoint change if the information was monetary (such as credit card information) versus private information (such as grades or health information)? What security precautions, if any, do you think should be imposed by laws? Are organizations that hold your personal data morally responsible for going beyond the minimum requirements? What types of security measures would you implement to protect these systems? Be prepared to discuss your position (in class, via an online class discussion group, in a class chat room, or via a class blog, depending on your instructor's directions). You may also be asked to write a short paper expressing your opinion.

>For more information on Symantec, visit www.symantec.com. To view the latest Symantec Internet Security Threat Report results, go to www.symantec.com/business/theme.jsp?themeid=threatreport.

5
CHAPTER

Computer Security and Privacy

OUTLINE

LEARNING OBJECTIVES

After completing this chapter, you will be able to do the following:

1. Explain why all computer users should be concerned about computer security.

2. List some risks associated with hardware loss, hardware damage, and system failure, and understand ways to safeguard a PC against these risks.

3. Define software piracy and digital counterfeiting and explain how they may be prevented.

4. Explain what information privacy is and why computer users should be concerned about it.

5. Describe some privacy concerns regarding databases, electronic profiling, spam, and telemarketing, and identify ways individuals can protect their privacy.

6. Discuss several types of electronic surveillance and monitoring and list ways individuals can protect their privacy.

7. Discuss the status of computer security and privacy legislation.

OVERVIEW

The increasing use of computers in our society today has many advantages. It also, however, opens up new possibilities for problems (such as data loss due to a system malfunction or a disaster), as well as new opportunities for computer crime (such as hardware theft, software piracy, and digital counterfeiting). In addition, our networked society has raised a number of privacy concerns. Although we can appreciate that sometimes selected people or organizations have a legitimate need for some types of personal information, whenever information is provided to others there is always the danger that the information will be misused. Facts may be taken out of context and used to draw distorted conclusions. Private information may end up being distributed to others without one's consent or knowledge. And with the vast amount of information that is contained in databases accessible via the Internet today, privacy is an enormous concern for both individuals and businesses.

Chapter 4 discussed security risks related to network and Internet use. This chapter takes a look at some of the other computer-related security concerns, as well as the most pressing computer-related privacy concerns facing us today. First, we explore security concerns, including hardware loss and damage, and the safeguards that can be used to reduce the risk of a problem occurring due to these concerns. Then, software piracy and digital counterfeiting are discussed, along with the steps that are being taken to reduce the occurrence of these computer crimes. Privacy topics come next, including various possible risks to personal privacy and precautions that can be taken to safeguard one's privacy. The chapter closes with a summary of legislation related to computer security and privacy. ■

PODCAST

Go to **www.course.com/uccs/ch5** to download or listen to the "Expert Insight on Web-Based Multimedia and E-Commerce" podcast.

WHY BE CONCERNED ABOUT COMPUTER SECURITY?

From having your PC stolen, to losing a term paper because the storage medium on which your paper was stored became unreadable, to losing your mobile phone containing your entire contact list, to running the risk of buying pirated or digitally counterfeited products via an online auction, there are a number of security concerns surrounding computers and related technology that all individuals should be concerned about. The most common network and Internet security risks and computer crimes were discussed in Chapter 4. The remaining common computer security concerns, along with some precautions that users can take to reduce the risks of problems occurring due to those security concerns, are discussed in the next few sections.

HARDWARE LOSS, HARDWARE DAMAGE, AND SYSTEM FAILURE

Hardware loss can occur when a portable PC, USB flash drive, mobile device, or other piece of hardware is stolen or is lost by the owner. Hardware loss, as well as other security issues, can also result from hardware damage (both intentional and accidental) and *system failure*.

Hardware Loss

One of the most obvious types of hardware loss is **hardware theft**, which occurs when hardware is stolen from an individual or from a business, school, or other organization. Computers, printers, and other computer hardware can be stolen during a break-in; notebook computers and mobile devices are also frequently stolen from cars, as well as from restaurants, airports, hotels, and other public locations. Although security experts stress that the vast majority of hardware theft is done for the value of the hardware itself, executives and government employees may be targeted for computer theft for the information contained on their PCs. In fact, *C-level attacks* (attacks aimed at C-level executives, such as CEOs and CIOs) are rapidly growing as executives are increasingly using e-mail and storing documents on their PCs, as well as traveling more with PCs and other digital devices. And even if the data on a PC is not the primary reason for a theft, any sensitive data stored on the stolen PC is at risk of being exposed or used for fraudulent purposes, and this is happening at unprecedented levels today. A significant number of data breaches in the last few years have occurred via notebook computer theft. One of the largest breaches occurred in 2006 when a U.S. Veteran's Administration employee took a notebook computer containing the names, Social Security numbers, and birthdates of 26.5 million U.S. veterans home, and then the notebook was stolen in a home burglary. In addition, nearly 500 Internal Revenue Service laptops—many likely containing unencrypted personal information of taxpayers—were lost or stolen over a period of 30 months, according to a report released in 2007. And 160 laptops belonging to the FBI were lost or stolen over a recent 44 month period of time, and it is not known publically how many contained classified or sensitive data. All of these thefts raise important privacy concerns.

In addition to hardware theft, hardware loss can occur when hardware is being transported in luggage or in a package that is lost by an airline or shipping company, or when an individual misplaces or otherwise loses a piece of hardware. With the vast amount of portable hardware devices that individuals carry with them today (such as portable PCs, mobile phones, and USB flash drives), this type of hardware loss is a growing concern. While lost hardware may be covered by insurance and the data stored on that device may not be used in a fraudulent manner, having to replace the hardware and restore the data—or, worse yet, losing the data entirely if it was not backed up—is still a huge inconvenience.

Hardware Damage

PCs consist of sensitive electronic devices and delicate components that can be damaged easily. Power fluctuations, heat, dust, and static can all damage computer hardware. Dropping a computer or a piece of hardware will often break it; spilling a

ASK THE EXPERT

Debra Jensen, Vice President and Chief Information Officer, Jack in the Box Inc.

If the computers or software supporting the order-entry system in one of your restaurants fails, can the restaurant still process orders?

Yes. The entry of orders is a critical function in our restaurants. The Point of Purchase system (POS) has built-in redundancy by design. If the main POS server fails, the individual registers used by the order takers continue to function and allow for the entry of the orders. To the customer, the experience will be transparent, with the exception of the use of gift cards, which cannot be processed during the outage. Once the server is back up, the registers reattach automatically and "catch up" on the transactions that were processed in offline mode. Of course, if the cause of the failure is power, then neither the computer systems nor the cooking processes will work.

>**Hardware theft.** The theft of computer hardware.

drink on a keyboard or other hardware component will also likely cause some damage. In addition to accidental damage, burglars, vandals, disgruntled employees, and other individuals sometimes intentionally damage the computers and other hardware they have access to.

System Failure and Other Disasters

Although many of us may prefer not to think about it, **system failure**—the complete malfunction of a computer system—and other types of computer-related disasters do happen. From accidentally deleting a file to having your computer just stop working, computer problems can be a huge inconvenience, as well as cost you a great deal of time and money. When the system contains your personal documents and data, it is a problem; when it contains the only copy of your company records or controls a vital system—such as a nuclear power plant—it can be a disaster.

System failure can occur because of a hardware problem, software problem, or computer virus. It can also occur because of a natural disaster (such as a tornado, fire, flood, or hurricane), sabotage, or a terrorist attack. The terrorist attack on the New York City World Trade Center Twin Towers on September 11, 2001, illustrated this all too clearly. When the Twin Towers collapsed, nearly 3,000 people were killed and hundreds of offices—over 13 million square feet of office space—were completely destroyed; another 7 million square feet of office space was damaged (see Figure 5-1). In addition to the devastating human loss, the offices located in the WTC lost their computer systems—including all the equipment, records, and data stored at that location. The ramifications of these system failures and the corresponding data loss were felt around the world by all the businesses and people connected directly or indirectly to these organizations.

FIGURE 5-1
System destruction.
The 9/11 attacks killed nearly 3,000 people and destroyed hundreds of business offices, including critical cables located in this Verizon office adjacent to Ground Zero.

Protecting Against Hardware Loss, Hardware Damage, and System Failure

To protect against hardware loss, hardware damage, and system failure, a number of precautions can be taken, as discussed next.

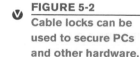

FIGURE 5-2
Cable locks can be used to secure PCs and other hardware.

Door and Computer Equipment Locks

Simple deterrents, such as locked doors and equipment, can go a long way in preventing computer theft. In addition to securing facilities with door locks, alarm systems, and other access control methods (such as the biometric access systems discussed in Chapter 4), *cable locks* (see Figure 5-2) are often used to secure computers and other semipermanent equipment in most schools and many businesses. Cable locks connect the computer to a table or other object that is difficult to move. These locks can also be used to secure portable computers, external hard drives, and other portable pieces of hardware, and they are increasingly being

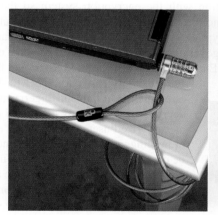

NOTEBOOK PCS
This cable lock connects via a security slot built into the notebook PC.

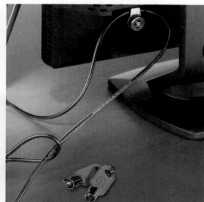

DESKTOP PCS AND MONITORS
This cable lock connects via a cable anchor attached to the back of the monitor.

>**System failure.** The complete malfunction of a computer system.

used by college students to secure their portable PCs to guard against theft when their computers are not in use. To facilitate using a computer lock, nearly all notebook and desktop computers today come with a *security slot*—a small opening built into the system unit case designed for computer locks. If a computer slot is not available, *cable anchors* (which attach to a piece of hardware using industrial strength adhesive and which contain a connector through which the cable lock can be passed—refer again to Figure 5-2) can be used. Computer locks are available in both key and combination versions.

In addition to securing computers, it is also extremely important for businesses to ensure that employees follow security protocols (such as signing in and out portable hard drives, USB flash drives, and other storage media, if required); use only company-approved USB devices with their company PCs; and use designated security software, do not use P2P services, and follow other important security precautions when using a home PC for work.

Encryption and Self-Encrypting Hard Drives

To ensure the data on a stolen or lost PC cannot be read by an unauthorized individual, *encryption* can be used. Encrypting individual files was discussed in Chapter 4. To protect an entire hard drive, it is now becoming more common to use **full disk encryption** (**FDE**). FDE systems encrypt everything stored on the drive (the operating system, application programs, data, temporary files, and so forth) automatically. This occurs without any user interaction, so users don't have to remember to encrypt sensitive documents. For additional security, the encryption is usually always turned on and cannot be turned off by the user. To access a drive that uses FDE (often referred to as a **self-encrypting hard drive**), a username and password or biometric characteristic is needed, typically before the computer containing the drive will boot. For additional security, some self-encrypting hard drives have encryption technology built into the hardware itself to ensure the data stored on the hard drive cannot be accessed, even if the drive is removed from its original computer. While self-encrypting hard drives are most commonly used with portable computers (in fact, the U.S. federal government is in the process of implementing FDE on all government owned notebook PCs and mobile devices), their use is beginning to be expanded to desktop computers and servers. Because FDE requires no user input and the user has no say in which files are encrypted (since all files are encrypted automatically), these systems provide an easy way to ensure all data is protected, provided strong passwords are used in conjunction with the encryption system so the system cannot be easily hacked. As FDE technology continues to improve to reduce any additional disk access time required by the encryption system, use of self-encrypting hard drives is expected to grow past corporate and government use to individuals' personal computers.

Encryption can also be used to protect the data stored on removable media, such as flash memory cards and USB flash memory drives; typically, a biometric feature (such as a built-in fingerprint reader, as shown in Figure 5-3) is used to decrypt the data. Many encrypted devices allow multiple users to be registered as authorized users (by assigning each individual a password or registering his or her fingerprint image, for instance), as well as allow a portion of the device to be designated as unencrypted for nonsensitive documents, if desired. To protect against data losses, avoid the time and expense involved with notifying individuals that their personal information was contained on a lost or stolen device (as required by law in over half of the states in the U.S.), and guard against possible lawsuits and damage to the company reputation resulting from a data breach, many businesses today are requiring encryption for all desktop PCs, portable PCs, portable storage devices, and smart phones issued to employees.

▼ **FIGURE 5-3**

Encrypted media. The data on this encrypted USB flash drive cannot be accessed until the user is authenticated via a fingerprint scan.

>**Full disk encryption (FDE).** A technology that encrypts everything stored on a storage medium automatically, without any user interaction.
>**Self-encrypting hard drive.** A hard drive that uses full disk encryption (FDE).

HOW IT WORKS

Self-Destructing Devices

When a business or an individual is less concerned about recovering a stolen device than they are about ensuring the data located on the PC is not compromised, devices that self-destruct upon command are a viable option. Available as part of some computer tracking software programs (such as the one shown in the accompanying illustration) and mobile phone utility programs, *kill switch* capabilities destroy the data on a device (typically by overwriting preselected files multiple times, rendering them unreadable) when instructed. If the kill switch is built into a computer tracking system, the kill switch is typically activated (if the customer requests it) when the device is reported as stolen. The device then erases all the data on the PC whenever it next connects to the Internet or when another predesignated remote trigger is activated (such as a certain number of unsuccessful logon attempts). Kill switch capabilities built into a mobile phone utility can be activated by the user sending the device a text message containing his or her kill switch password—when the device receives the message, all data stored on the device is erased.

Kill switch technology is also beginning to be built into hard drives. For instance, hard drives with Enscone Data's *Dead on Demand* technology contain a small canister filled with a corrosive chemical that completely destroys the drive when the drive is tampered with or when one of up to 17 remote triggers specified by the owner is activated. The self-destruction process does not damage the computer—only the hard drive—and the command to self-destruct can be activated even if the drive is removed from the computer. Not quite *Mission Impossible*, but when hardware containing sensitive data is stolen—which could impact an individual's personal privacy or a business's legal liability, reputation, and bottom line—kill switch technology could save the day.

Computer Tracking Software and Antitheft Tools

Some software tools are not designed to prevent hardware from being stolen; instead, they are designed to aid in its recovery. This can be beneficial since, according to FBI statistics, the recovery rate of a stolen or lost PC is normally about 2% or 3%. One software tool that can be used to help increase the chance of a stolen or lost PC being recovered is *computer tracking software*. Computer tracking software—sometimes called *stealth tracking software*—sends identifying information (such as ownership information and the location of the computer) when the PC is connected to the Internet. Typically, this occurs on a regular basis (such as once per day), as long as a computer is not reported as stolen or lost. Once a computer is reported as stolen or lost to the computer tracking software company, however, the computer is instructed to report its current location on a more frequent, regular basis (such as every 15 minutes), in order to generate information to be provided to law enforcement agencies to help them recover the computer. Some software can even take video or photos of whoever is using the stolen PC (if the PC has a built-in video camera like many notebook computers have today) to help identify and prosecute the thief. Because any sign that the software is running on the PC or is sending information via the Internet is hidden from the user, the thief is usually not aware that a computer tracking system is installed on the PC. These systems (the software and the support from the computer tracking software company) cost between $30 and $50 per year.

A new alternative for protecting the data on a portable computer if it is stolen is using a *kill switch*—technology that causes the device to self-destruct, as discussed in the How It Works box.

FURTHER EXPLORATION

Go to **www.course.com/uccs/ch5** for links to further information about protecting your PC from theft or damage.

TREND

DataDotDNA: A High Tech ID System

Would you like a cheap, easy way to identify your PC, iPod, bike, or other expensive personal item? Well, *DataDotDNA* might be the answer.

Based on the concept of hiding secret codes in tiny elements of a document or image, DataDotDNA consists of tiny discs made from a polyester substrate that are about the size of a grain of sand. These discs have text etched onto them using a sophisticated laser process. The text can be a vehicle identification number (VIN) for DataDotDNA placed on a new car by the manufacturer, or a unique PIN number for DataDotDNA to be placed on a personal or business asset (see the accompanying illustration). DataDotDNA is applied using a special adhesive that shows up under any UV blacklight. Once a single DataDot is located, the data contained inside can be read using a magnifying reader. Warning labels can be used to deter theft and, if a DataDotDNA-marked object is stolen and recovered, law enforcement agents can look up PIN numbers in the DataDotDNA database to trace ownership of the object. Because they are so small, DataDots can be applied to numerous locations on an object—both obvious and hidden—to make it very difficult for a thief to locate

and remove every tiny DataDot on an object. In fact, when used in new car production, up to 10,000 DataDots are sprayed on the chassis and other parts of the car.

There are DataDotDNA product solutions for many types of assets and they can provide relatively cheap peace of mind to individuals who own a variety of expensive electronic devices.

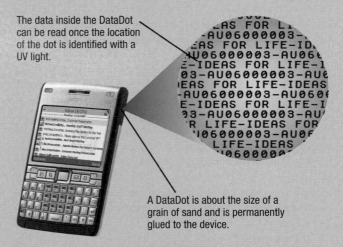

The data inside the DataDot can be read once the location of the dot is identified with a UV light.

A DataDot is about the size of a grain of sand and is permanently glued to the device.

DataDotDNA can be used to identify PCs and other electronic devices.

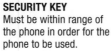

FIGURE 5-4
Locking mobile phones.

SECURITY KEY
Must be within range of the phone in order for the phone to be used.

To make sure no one can walk away with a PC, *laptop alarm software* that emits a very loud screech if the PC is unplugged or shut down without the owner's permission can be used. Another antitheft tool is the use of *tamper evident labels* on hardware and other expensive assets. These labels usually identify the owner of the asset and are designed to be permanently attached to the asset. If someone (typically a thief) tries to remove a label, it changes its appearance to indicate that it has been tampered with. For instance, some labels change the text printed on the label and others have a printed message hidden underneath the label that is etched into the surface of the computer and is exposed when the label is removed. Both of these features are designed to bring attention to the fact that the item the original label was attached to is likely stolen. For a look at another alternative for adding identification data to your PCs, mobile phones, and other electronic devices, see the Trend box.

Additional Precautions for Mobile Devices

With an increasing amount of personal data being stored on mobile phones and other mobile devices today, as well as the ability of some mobile phones to be used to make purchases and unlock doors, security features that guard against the unauthorized use of mobile devices are growing increasingly more important. There is tracking software (similar to the computer tracking systems just discussed) available for mobile phones and other types of devices that are frequently lost or stolen (such as portable digital media players and USB flash drives) to help aid in the recovery of those devices. However, the mobile phone shown in Figure 5-4 takes a different approach. Available in Japan, this phone is one of several types that comes with a *security key*—a small device that connects wirelessly to the phone and locks the phone if the distance between the phone and security key exceeds a prespecified distance. The phone shown in Figure 5-4 is designed for children and so it has a wrist strap security key; security keys for phones designed for adults are typically about the size of a movie ticket stub and are intended to be kept in a bag or pocket. The idea behind this type of *locking phone* system is to prevent the phone from being used if it is lost or stolen (if the owner loses the security key, he or she can enter a password to unlock the phone). The phone shown in Figure 5-4 can also send a voice or text message (which includes the location of the phone) to predesignated individuals if the child presses an alarm button on the phone or if the phone remains out of range of the security key for more than five minutes.

While on the go, the best antitheft measure is common sense; for example, you should never leave a portable PC or mobile device unattended in a public location (always keep a hand, finger, or other body part in contact with the device so it cannot be stolen without you noticing when you are distracted for a moment and glance away), and you should either take your PC with you or lock it in the hotel safe when you leave your hotel room for the day. Labeling your portable PC (and other portable hardware that you take with you on the go) with your contact information in case a lost or stolen item is recovered is another sensible precaution. Figure 5-5 lists some common sense precautions for keeping portable PCs and mobile devices safe while on the road. One additional possibility for protecting business data while on the road is using a thin client portable PC that has no hard drive, such as the *SafeBook* PC. These PCs look like ordinary notebook PCs, but since all programs and data are stored on the company server and accessed via the Internet through a Wi-Fi, Ethernet, or 3G wireless connection, there is no data to be compromised on the PC if it is stolen.

Proper Hardware Care

Proper care of hardware can help to prevent serious damage to a computer system, including the data that is stored on it. The most obvious precaution is not to physically harm your hardware, such as by dropping a portable PC, knocking a piece of hardware off a desk, or jostling a system unit. For users who need a more durable system, **ruggedized PCs** are available (see Figure 5-6). These computers—typically portable PCs—are designed to

PRECAUTIONS TO PREVENT DATA LOSS

Install and use encryption, antivirus, antispyware, and firewall software.

Use only secure Wi-Fi connections and disable Wi-Fi and Bluetooth when they are not needed.

Never leave usernames, passwords, or other data attached to your PC or inside its carrying case.

Use a plain carrying case to make a portable PC less conspicuous.

Keep an eye on your devices at all times, especially when going through airport security.

Avoid setting your devices on the floor or leaving them in your hotel room; use a cable lock to secure the device to a desk or other object whenever this is unavoidable.

Back up the data stored on the device regularly.

Consider installing tracking or kill switch software.

FIGURE 5-5
Common sense precautions for portable PC and mobile device users.

FIGURE 5-6
Ruggedized PCs. Semirugged PCs are designed to withstand more abuse than conventional PCs; fully rugged PCs are even more durable.

SEMIRUGGED NOTEBOOK PCS   FULLY RUGGED HANDHELD PCS

FULLY RUGGED NOTEBOOK PCS

>**Ruggedized PC.** A computer—typically a portable PC—that is designed to withstand much more physical abuse than a conventional PC.

ONLINE VIDEO

Go to **www.course.com/uccs/ch5** to watch the "The DriveSavers Data Recovery Service" video clip.

withstand much more physical abuse than conventional PCs and range from *semirugged* to *ultrarugged PCs*. For instance, semirugged PCs typically have a more durable case and are spill-resistant. Rugged and ultrarugged PCs go a few steps further—they are designed to withstand drops of three feet or more onto concrete, extreme temperature ranges, wet conditions, and use while being bounced around over rough terrain in a vehicle. Ruggedized PCs are most often used by individuals who work out of the office, such as field workers, construction workers, outdoor technicians, military personnel, and so forth. There are also rugged cases available for some mobile devices, such as water-resistant cases available for some BlackBerry devices that allow the device's screen, keypad, and buttons to be used while protecting the device from rain and dust damage.

To protect hardware from damage due to power fluctuations, it is important for all users to use a **surge suppressor** with a PC whenever it is plugged into a power outlet. When electrical power spikes occur, the surge suppressor prevents them from harming your system. For desktop PCs, surge suppressors should be used with all of the powered components in the computer system (such as the system unit, monitor, printer, and scanner); surge suppressors designed for notebook PCs are typically smaller than those designed for desktop systems, with only room to connect one device (see Figure 5-7). There are surge suppressors designed for business and industrial use, as well.

For users who want their computers to remain powered up when the electricity goes off, **uninterruptible power supply** (**UPS**) units containing a built-in battery that provides continuous power to a PC and other connected components when the electricity goes out are available (see Figure 5-7). The length of time that a UPS can power a system depends on the type and number of devices connected to the UPS, the power capacity of the UPS device (typically measured in watts), and the age of the battery (most UPS batteries last only 3 to 5 years before they need to be replaced). Most UPS devices also protect against power fluctuations. UPSs designed for use by individuals usually provide power for a few minutes to keep the system powered up during a short power blip, as well as to allow the user to save open documents and shut down the PC properly if the electricity remains off. Industrial-level UPSs typically run for a significantly longer amount of time (such as a few hours), but not long enough to power a facility during an extended power outage, such as those that happen periodically in some parts of the U.S. due to winter storms, summer rotating blackouts, and other factors. Facilities that cannot afford to be without power (such as hospitals, nuclear power plants, and business data centers) should also have a generator to provide more long-term power to the facility when needed.

Dust, heat, static, and moisture can also be dangerous to a PC, so be sure you do not place your PC equipment in direct sunlight or in a dusty area. Small handheld vacuums made for electrical equipment can be used periodically to remove the dust from the keyboard and from inside the system unit, but be very careful when vacuuming inside the system unit. Also, be sure the system unit has plenty of ventilation, especially around the fan vents. To help reduce

FIGURE 5-7
Surge suppressors and uninterruptible power supplies (UPSs).

SURGE SUPPRESSOR FOR NOTEBOOK PCS

SURGE SUPPRESSOR FOR DESKTOP PCS

UPS FOR HOME PCS

UPS FOR SERVERS

>**Surge suppressor.** A device that protects a computer system from damage due to electrical fluctuations. >**Uninterruptible power supply (UPS).** A device containing a built-in battery that provides continuous power to a PC and other connected components when the electricity goes out.

the amount of dust that gets drawn into the fan vents, raise your desktop PC several inches off the floor. You should also avoid placing a notebook PC on a soft surface, such as a couch or blanket, to help prevent overheating. To prevent static electricity from damaging the inside of your PC when installing a new expansion card or other internal device, turn off the power to the PC and unplug the power cord from the PC before removing the cover from the system unit. You should also discharge the static electricity from your fingertips by touching the outside of the power supply module inside the system unit before touching any other components. Unless your PC is ruggedized, do not use it in the rain (see Figure 5-8) or in other adverse conditions. Be careful with mobile phones and other mobile devices when you are near water (such as a fountain, lake, or large puddle), so that they do not get dropped into or fall into the water.

Both internal and external magnetic hard drives also need to be protected against jostling or other excess motion that can result in a *head crash*, which occurs when a hard drive's read/write heads actually touch the surface of a hard disk. Unless a notebook computer contains a flash memory (solid-state) hard drive, it is a good idea to turn off the computer, hibernate it, or put it into standby mode before moving it since notebook magnetic hard drives are more vulnerable to damage while they are spinning. In addition, storage media—such as flash memory cards, hard drives, CDs, and

⋀ **FIGURE 5-8**
Proper hardware care. Unless your PC is ruggedized, keep it out of the rain and other adverse conditions.

DVDs—are all sensitive storage media that work well over time, as long as appropriate care is used. To avoid data loss, don't remove a flash memory card when it is being accessed and use the *Safely Remove Hardware* icon in the system tray on a Windows PC to stop a USB flash drive or USB hard drive before unplugging it. In addition, keep CDs and DVDs in their protective *jewel cases* and handle them carefully to prevent fingerprints and scratches on the data sides of the discs (usually the bottom, unprinted side on a single-sided disc). *Screen protectors* (thin plastic film that covers the display screen of a mobile phone or mobile device) can be used to prevent scratches on the displays of pen-based devices. For more tips on how to protect your PC, see the Technology and You box.

Backups and Disaster Recovery Plans

Creating a *backup* means making a duplicate copy of important files so that when a problem occurs, you can restore those files using the backup copy. Businesses should make backups of at least all new data on a regular basis (such as once per day); individuals should make backups of important documents as they are created and consider making backups of all data periodically. Depending on where important data is stored, backups can be performed on PCs, servers, mobile phones, and other mobile devices. For an even higher level of security

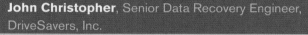

ASK THE EXPERT

John Christopher, Senior Data Recovery Engineer, DriveSavers, Inc.

Of the hard drives sent to you for recovery, what is the most common type of problem you see and is there a way that problem can be prevented?

We often receive hard drives that have severe media damage. That means that the read/write heads have come in contact with the platters and scraped off portions of the surface and data. This often occurs because the hard drive was left powered on after the problem occurred. The platters inside a drive spin at high speed, so a great deal of damage can occur in a very short period of time as the heads bounce around and create more debris. Eventually the damage becomes too great for even a professional data recovery company to overcome.

The best rule of thumb to prevent the loss of critical data is to back up religiously and to verify that the backup is really backing up the critical files. In addition, if a hard drive exhibits any sign of failure including unusual noises (repetitive clicking, grinding, etc.) and the data is irreplaceable and has not been backed up recently, the best solution is to immediately shut down the computer and then seek the assistance of a professional data recovery company like DriveSavers.

TECHNOLOGY AND YOU

Protecting Your PC

All computer users should take specific actions to protect their PCs. In this world of viruses, worms, hackers, spyware, and "buggy" (error-prone) software, it pays to be cautious. Although safeguards have been covered in detail throughout this book, some specific precautionary steps all computer users should follow are summarized in this box.

Step 1: Protect your hardware.
Be sure to plug all components of your computer system (such as the system unit, monitor, printer, scanner, and powered sub-woofer) into a surge suppressor. Be careful not to bump or move the computer when it is on. Do not spill food or drink onto the keyboard or any other piece of hardware. Store your flash memory cards and CDs properly. If you ever need to work inside the system unit, turn off the PC, unplug it, and ground yourself by touching the power supply before touching any other component inside the system unit. When taking a portable PC on the road, do not ever leave it unattended, and be careful not to drop or lose it.

Step 2: Install and use security software.
Install a good antivirus program and set it up to scan your system on an ongoing basis, including checking all files and e-mail messages before they are downloaded to your PC. To detect the newest viruses and types of malware, keep your antivirus program up-to-date (have it automatically check for and install updates) and use a personal two-way firewall program to protect your PC from unauthorized access via the Internet, as well as to detect any attempts by spyware to send data from your PC to another party. For additional protection if you have a home network, enable file sharing only for files and folders that really need to be accessed by other users. To check or change your global file sharing settings in Windows Vista, open the Network and Sharing Center from the Control Panel; it is best to turn off File Sharing, Public Folder Sharing, and Media Sharing, if they are not needed. Run an antispyware program—such as *Ad-Aware* or *Spybot Search & Destroy*—on a regular basis to detect and remove spyware.

Step 3: Back up regularly.
Once you have a new PC set up with all programs installed and the menus and other settings the way you like them, create a full backup so the PC can be restored to that configuration in case of a major problem with your computer or hard drive. Be sure also to back up your data files on a regular basis. Depending on how important your documents are, you may want to back up all of your data every night, or copy each document to a removable storage medium after each major revision. If keeping your e-mail is important to you, you should also back up the folder containing your e-mail, such as the *Outlook.pst* file used to store

Microsoft Outlook mail. To facilitate data backup, keep your data organized using folders (such as storing all data files in a main folder called "Data"). For an even higher level of security, install a second hard drive just for data. That way, if your main hard drive ever becomes unstable and needs to be reformatted or replaced, your data drive will remain untouched. Backups should be stored in a different location than your PC, such as in a different building or in a fire-resistant safe. An easy way to accomplish this is to use an online backup service or upload your backup files to an online storage service.

Step 4: Update your operating system, browser, and e-mail program regularly.
Most companies that produce operating systems, Web browsers, or e-mail programs regularly post updates and *patches*—small programs that take care of software-specific problems, or *bugs*, such as security holes—on their Web sites on a regular basis. Some programs include an option within the program to check online for updates; for other programs, you will need to go to each manufacturer's Web site directly to check for any critical or recommended updates. For any programs—such as Windows and most antivirus and firewall programs—that have the option to check for updates automatically, enable that option. Windows Vista users can check their current security settings using the Windows Security Center, available through the Control Panel and shown in the accompanying illustration.

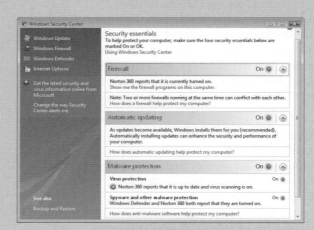

For optimal protection, all security essentials should be enabled.

Step 5: Test your system for vulnerabilities.
There are several free tests available through Web sites to see if your PC's ports are accessible to hackers or if your PC is infected with a virus or spyware. These tests, such as the one on the Symantec Web site shown in Figure 4-12 in Chapter 4, should be run to check for any remaining vulnerabilities once you believe your antivirus software, firewall, and any other protective components you are using are set up correctly.

than a scheduled backup, *continuous data protection (CDP)* can be used. A CDP backup system (most often used with company servers) records data changes on a continual basis so that data can be recovered from any point in time, even just a few minutes ago, when needed with no data loss. And recovery can be as fast as five minutes after a failure. Although expensive, it is one of the best ways to ensure that company data is protected. Data to be backed up includes e-mail and instant messages located on PCs, servers, mobile phones, and other mobile devices, in addition to business data, to adhere to the growing requirements for *e-discovery* of electronic documents. In fact, the size of the e-mail archiving market alone in 2011 is expected to be $1.4 billion, according to research firm IDC.

Backup media needs to be secured so that it will be intact when it is needed. If stored in-house, backup media should be placed in a fire-resistant safe. Even better is to store backup media in a different physical location. For instance, many businesses today use third-party *data storage companies* that store the business's backup media at a secure remote location; the backups can be returned to the company whenever they are needed. To secure the data on the backup media during transit and storage, the data should be encrypted. *Online backup services* can provide regular or continuous backup services for a business via the Internet, so physically transporting backup media to a new location is not an issue.

To supplement backup procedures, businesses and other organizations should have a **disaster recovery plan** (also sometimes called a *business continuity plan*)—a plan that spells out what the organization will do to prepare for and recover from a disruptive event, such as a fire, natural disaster, terrorist attack, power outage, or computer failure. Disaster recovery plans should include information such as who will be in charge immediately after the disaster has occurred, what alternate facilities and equipment can be used, where backup media is located, the priority of getting each operation back online, disaster insurance coverage information, emergency communications methods, and so forth. If a *hot site*—an alternate location equipped with the computers, cabling, desks, and other equipment necessary to keep a business's operations going—is to be used following a major disaster, it should be set up ahead of time, and information about the hot site should be included in the disaster recovery plan. Businesses that cannot afford to be without e-mail service should also consider making arrangements with an *emergency mail system provider* to act as a temporary mail server if and when the company mail server becomes unavailable. Copies of a disaster recovery plan should be located off-site, such as at an appropriate employee's house or at the office of an associated organization located in a different city. It is important to realize that disaster recovery planning isn't just for large businesses. In fact, disasters such as a fire or computer malfunction can cause a small company to go out of business if its data is not backed up. Measures as straightforward as backing up data daily and storing the backups in a fire-resistant safe at the owner's house with a plan regarding how that data can be quickly reinstated on a new system or otherwise used for business continuity can go a long way in protecting a small business.

The importance of a good disaster recovery plan was made obvious following the collapse of the World Trade Center Twin Towers in 2001. Minutes after the first airplane hit the towers, corporate executives, disaster recovery firms, and backup storage companies began arranging for employees and backup data to be moved to alternate sites. Employees at the data storage company Recall Corporation spent the day of the attack gathering backup tapes belonging to clients located in and near the attacks, using barcode scanners to locate the needed 30,000 tapes out of the 2 million in their secure storage facility. Bond trader Cantor Fitzgerald, which lost 700 employees and all the equipment and data located

> **TIP**
>
> Backup procedures, such as making copies of important documents and storing them in a safe location, also apply to important nonelectronic documents in your life, such as birth certificates, tax returns, passports, and so forth.

> **TIP**
>
> For an extra level of security for data that you want to archive for a long period of time, use at least two common file formats (such as JPEG and TIF for image files and Word's DOCX format and HTML or XML for text files) for the best chance that one of the formats will still be usable with PCs in the future. Also, be sure to make multiple copies of each backup medium.

> **Disaster recovery plan.** A written plan that describes the steps a company will take following the occurrence of a disaster.

in its WTC offices, relocated to a prearranged hot site where employees received backup tapes the day after the attack, and it was able to begin trading the next morning. Although Cantor Fitzgerald—like the other organizations and businesses located in the WTC—suffered enormous human loss, good disaster recovery planning enabled Cantor Fitzgerald to completely restore the records containing client accounts and portfolios, avoiding an additional economic disaster related to this tragedy.

SOFTWARE PIRACY AND DIGITAL COUNTERFEITING

Instead of stealing an existing computer program, object, or other valuable that belongs to someone else, *software piracy* and *digital counterfeiting* involve creating duplicates of these items, and then selling them or using them as authentic items.

TIP

The piracy of and ethical use of digital music and movies is discussed in detail in Chapter 6.

Software Piracy

Software piracy, the unauthorized copying of a computer program, is illegal in the United States and many other—but not all—countries. Because of the ease with which computers can create exact copies of a software program, software piracy is a widespread problem. According to a 2007 report from the *Business Software Alliance* (*BSA*)—an organization formed by a number of the world's leading software developers that has antipiracy programs in 65 countries worldwide—approximately 35% of all business application software globally (and about 21% of all business application software in the United States) is installed illegally. In more than half the countries studied, the software piracy rate exceeded 60%; in five countries, it was over 90%. The report estimates that the monetary loss due to software piracy during 2006 was approximately $40 billion worldwide.

FIGURE 5-9
An end-user license agreement (EULA).
An EULA specifies the number of PCs on which the software can be installed and other restrictions for use.

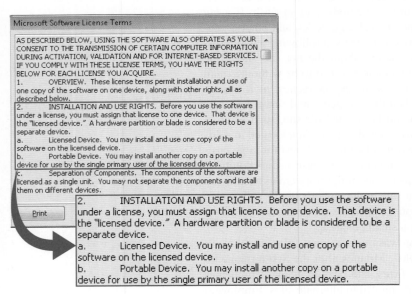

Software piracy can take many forms, including individuals making illegal copies of programs to give to friends, businesses installing software on more computers than permitted in the program's *end-user license agreement* (see Figure 5-9), PC sellers installing unlicensed copies of software on PCs sold to consumers, and large-scale operations in which the software and its packaging are illegally duplicated and then sold as supposedly legitimate products. Pirated software—as well as pirated music CDs and movie DVDs—are commonly offered for sale at online auctions. They can also be downloaded from some Web sites and peer-to-peer file sharing services. Creating and distributing pirated copies of any type of *intellectual property* (such as software, music, and movies) is illegal. Intellectual property is discussed in more detail in Chapter 6.

Digital Counterfeiting

The availability of high-quality, full-color imaging products (such as scanners, color printers, and color copiers) has made **digital counterfeiting**—creating counterfeit copies of items (such as currency and other printed resources) using computers and other types of digital equipment—easier and less costly than the offset printing process used before digital equipment became available. The U.S. Secret Service estimates that more than 50% of all counterfeit money today is produced digitally—up from 1% in 1996.

With digital counterfeiting, the bill (or other item to be counterfeited) is scanned into a computer and then printed, or it is color-copied. In addition to counterfeiting currency, some criminals choose to create fake business checks or printed collectibles, such as baseball cards or celebrity autographs. Other common digital counterfeiting activities include creating fake identification papers, such as corporate IDs, driver's licenses, passports, and visas (see Figure 5-10), although it is expected that this type of counterfeiting will decrease as more and more identification documents include RFID technology and other features that make these documents more difficult to counterfeit, as discussed shortly.

FIGURE 5-10

Digital counterfeiting.
Documents commonly counterfeited include currency, credit cards, driver's licenses, passports, and checks.

Counterfeiting is illegal in the United States and is taken very seriously. For creating or knowingly circulating counterfeit currency, for instance, offenders can face up to 15 years in prison for each offense. Counterfeiting of U.S. currency and other documents is a growing problem both in the United States and in other countries. Close to half of all counterfeit currency is seized before it goes into circulation—over 75% is seized outside the U.S. Although the majority of counterfeit currency is produced by serious criminals—such as organized crimes, gangs, and terrorist organizations—the Secret Service has seen a dramatic increase in counterfeiting among high school and college students. This is attributed primarily to the ease of creating counterfeit bills—although not necessarily high-quality counterfeit bills—with digital technology. Because the paper used with real U.S. currency is very expensive and cannot legally be made by paper mills for any other purpose and because bills contain a number of other characteristics that are difficult to reproduce accurately, as discussed in more detail shortly, the majority of the counterfeit money made by amateurs is easily detectable.

Protecting Against Software Piracy and Digital Counterfeiting

Software piracy and digital counterfeiting affect more than just big businesses and the government. Because software pirates cost software developers a great deal of money, these companies have to charge higher prices and have less money available for research and development, which hurts law-abiding consumers. Some tools currently being used to curb software piracy and digital counterfeiting are discussed next.

Education, Holograms, and Other Antipiracy Tools

One noteworthy tool the software industry is using in an attempt to prevent software piracy is education. By educating businesses and consumers about the legal use of software and the possible negative consequences associated with breaking antipiracy laws, the industry hopes to reduce the known use of illegal software significantly. Paired with this, the industry is continually working to strengthen antipiracy laws and adapt them to fit new technology, such as broadband Internet and rewritable DVDs. Many software companies now have the option to download software via the Internet, which gives consumers a legal option for obtaining software that is as fast and convenient as downloading a pirated version.

To make it more difficult for criminals to pass pirated copies of software off as legitimate copies, *holograms*—printed text or images that change their appearance when the items containing the holograms are tilted or looked at from a different angle—are commonly used on packaged software CDs and DVDs, as well as on stickers located on new PCs containing preinstalled software. Because holograms are difficult to duplicate, end users can feel confident that the software package they are buying or was installed on the PC they received is authentic if the hologram works correctly.

Requiring a unique activation code—such as during a mandatory online product registration—before the software can be used or before certain key features of the program are unlocked is another antipiracy tool. However, there is some controversy about some activation processes, such as the *Windows Genuine Advantage* (*WGA*) system used to ensure that Windows installations are legal. Originally, the system was set up to give users who install Windows Vista 30 days to activate their installation, either online or by phone using the product key that comes with the product. If Vista wasn't activated within that time period, the system would change to "reduced functionality mode." In this mode, people are able to use a Web browser for one hour only until being logged off and some key features of Vista—such as *Aero*, the new visual graphical user interface—are disabled. In addition, before being allowed to download software from Microsoft's Web site (such as templates for Microsoft Office or gadgets for the Vista Sidebar), users must run through an operating system validation process and they cannot download the resources if their operating system is deemed invalid. The goal is to make pirated software unusable enough so that individuals who illegally install a copy of Vista on their PC will buy a license. However, a glitch in Microsoft's authentication server in 2007 caused WGA to lose its ability to tell a legitimate copy of Windows from an unauthorized copy and, for 19 hours, thousands of legitimate Windows users were treated as if their software was pirated. Although that problem was corrected, many companies have been hesitant to upgrade to Vista company-wide because of activation problems. In response to this, Microsoft is removing the disabling features of the WGA process in the first update to Vista due out in 2008 and is replacing it with popup window notifications instead.

Some software manufacturers have launched extensive public relations campaigns—such as including information on their Web sites, in product information, and in advertisements—to inform consumers of how these types of antipiracy precautions work and why they are needed. Other antipiracy techniques used by software companies include watching online auction sites and requesting the removal of suspicious items, and buying pirated copies of software via Web sites and then filing lawsuits against the sellers. The increase in prosecution of consumers for illegally selling or sharing software (and other types of digital content, such as music and movies) may also help reduce some types of piracy and encourage individuals to obtain legal copies of these products. In 2007 alone, for instance, *Operation Fastlink* (a major Department of Justice initiative to combat online piracy worldwide that is credited with removing more than $50 million worth of illegally copied software, games, movies, and music from illicit distribution channels) netted its 50th conviction; several individuals were convicted and sentenced to prison for selling pirated software on eBay; and Symantec was awarded $21 million in damages in late 2007 against a large network of distributors selling counterfeit Symantec software.

Digital Counterfeiting Prevention

To prevent the counterfeiting of U.S. currency, the Treasury Department releases new currency designs every 7 to 10 years. These new designs (such as the new $5 bill released in 2008 and shown in Figure 5-11) contain features (such as

FIGURE 5-11
Anticounterfeiting measures used with U.S. currency.

MICROPRINTING
Extremely small print that is very difficult to reproduce appears in three different locations on the front of the bill (in the left and right borders, at the top of the shield on the Great Seal, and in between the columns of the shield), though it is hard to see without a magnifying glass.

SECURITY THREAD
A plastic security thread embedded in the paper contains the letters "USA" followed by the number "5"; it can be seen when the bill is held up to the light and glows blue when placed in front of an ultraviolet light.

COLORS
Harder to match colors, such as shades of yellow and purple, have been added to some details.

WATERMARKS
Watermark images containing the number "5" located to the right and left of the portrait are incorporated into the paper itself and are visible when the bill is held up to the light (not visible in this photograph).

microprinting, *watermarks*, and *a security thread*) that make the new currency much more difficult to duplicate than older currency. Because the watermarks and security thread are embedded into the paper, counterfeiters are unable to duplicate those features when creating counterfeit bills either from scratch or by bleaching the ink out of existing lower-denomination bills and reprinting them with higher denominations. Consequently, counterfeit copies of bills using the new designs are easy to detect just by holding them up to the light and looking for the proper watermark or security thread. In addition, digital imaging equipment (such as color copiers and scanners) is equipped with technologies that can be used to track currency and other counterfeit items created with those devices. For example, many color copiers print invisible codes on copied documents, making counterfeit money copied on those machines traceable. This type of technology is also thought to be incorporated into many scanners. In fact, printer and scanner manufacturer Canon has revealed that it has been incorporating anti-counterfeiting technologies into its products since 1992, but the company is prohibited by the government from disclosing any information about those technologies.

Prevention measures for the counterfeiting of other types of documents—such as checks and identification cards—include using holograms, RFID tags, *digital watermarks*, and other difficult-to-reproduce content. As discussed in more detail in Chapter 6, a digital watermark is a subtle alteration that is not noticeable when the work is viewed or played but that can be read using special software to authenticate the item. Finally, educating consumers about how the appearance of fake products differs from that of authentic products is a vital step in the ongoing battle against counterfeiting.

WHY BE CONCERNED ABOUT INFORMATION PRIVACY?

Privacy is usually defined as the state of being concealed or free from unauthorized intrusion. The term **information privacy** refers to the rights of individuals and companies to control how information about them is collected and used. The problem of how to protect personal privacy—that is, how to keep personal information private—existed long before computers entered the picture. For example, sealing wax and unique signet rings were used centuries ago to seal letters, wills, and other personal documents to guard against their content being revealed to unauthorized individuals, as well as to alert the recipient if such an intrusion occurred while the document was in transit. But today's computers, with their ability to store and manipulate unprecedented quantities of data in a very short amount of time, combined with the fact that databases containing our personal information can be accessed and shared via the Internet, have added a new twist to the issue of personal privacy.

As discussed in Chapters 3 and 4, one concern of many individuals is the privacy of their Web site activities and e-mail messages. Cookies, Web bugs, and spyware are all possible privacy risks; e-mail can be read if intercepted by another individual during transit unless it is encrypted. For businesses and employees, there is the additional issue of whether or not Web activities, e-mail, and instant messages sent through a company network are private, and businesses need to make sure they comply with privacy laws regarding the protection and the security of the private information they store on their servers. Recently, there have been an unprecedented number of high-profile data breaches. In fact, the Privacy Rights Clearinghouse lists over 300 incidents of lost or stolen personal data, compromising a total of nearly 120 million records containing personal data, in 2007 alone. Some of the losses were due to hacking or hardware (particularly notebook computer) theft; others were losses due to

TIP

To help visually-impaired individuals distinguish one bill from another, the new $5 bill includes the denomination of the bill in extra large print and high-contrast purple ink on the back of the bill.

ONLINE VIDEO

Go to **www.course.com/uccs/ch5** to watch the "New Currency Design and Counterfeiting" video clip.

PODCAST

Go to **www.course.com/uccs/ch5** to download or listen to the "Safe and Simple File and Printer Sharing" podcast.

>**Privacy.** The state of being concealed or free from unauthorized intrusion. >**Information privacy.** The rights of individuals and companies to control how information about them is collected and used.

ASK THE EXPERT

epic.org **Lillie Coney**, Associate Director, Electronic Privacy Information Center

What is the biggest Internet-related privacy risk for individuals today?

The biggest Internet-related privacy risk for individuals is the rapid consolidation of personal information based on online activity. Service suppliers offer individuals a user-friendly interface and include privacy statements or policies. However, the online experience allows the collection of unlimited amounts of personal information, such as search engine requests and the Web sites visited. In 2006, AOL inadvertently proved how vulnerable the privacy of users is when it posted over 650,000 users' search queries on the Internet. Although AOL believed that the identities of its users were protected because they were identified only by user number, a New York Times reporter was able to identify a user based on her search history.

The race to monetize Internet activities also leaves the privacy of users in a vulnerable position because of the lack of regulation and government oversight. Furthermore, Internet privacy protection is undermined when online service providers promote anti-privacy proposals as privacy protection.

carelessness with papers or storage media containing Social Security numbers or other sensitive data. For instance, computers and storage media containing sensitive information were sold or lost; CDs and papers containing sensitive information were found in recycling containers, trash dumpsters, and other public locations; backup tapes and documents containing sensitive information were lost during transit; and documents containing sensitive information were posted online with that information intact, or were faxed or e-mailed to the wrong recipient.

In addition to the loss of hardware, a damaged reputation, and the expense and trouble of notifying customers of a data breach (as required by law in over half the states in the United States), businesses with data breaches also need to be concerned about legal ramifications. To address these issues, a growing trend in businesses today is to appoint a *chief privacy officer* (*CPO*). CPOs are responsible for ensuring privacy laws are complied with, identifying the data in a company that needs to be protected, developing policies to protect that data, and responding to any incidents that occur. Another issue that must be dealt with by CPOs is the changing definition of what information is regarded as personal and, therefore, needs to be safeguarded. For instance, the head of the European Union's group of data privacy regulators announced in early 2008 that IP addresses should be regarded as personal information. If that view becomes widespread or integrated into privacy laws, it will have major implications on search sites and other businesses that store the IP address of individuals using online services.

All individuals today should also be familiar with privacy issues related to databases, *spam*, and other marketing activities, as well as those related to *electronic surveillance* and *electronic monitoring*. These issues, along with precautions that can be taken to safeguard information privacy, are discussed throughout the remainder of this chapter.

DATABASES, ELECTRONIC PROFILING, SPAM, AND OTHER MARKETING ACTIVITIES

There are marketing activities that can be considered privacy risks or, at least, a potential invasion of privacy. These include *databases*, *electronic profiling*, and *spam*.

Databases and Electronic Profiling

Information about individuals can be located in many different databases. For example, most educational institutions maintain databases containing student information, most organizations have an employee database for employee information, and most physicians and health insurance providers maintain databases containing individuals' medical information. If these databases are adequately protected from hackers and other unauthorized individuals and the data is not transported on a portable PC or other device that may be vulnerable to loss or theft, these databases are not of significant concern to consumers because the information can rarely be shared without the individuals' permission. However, data in these types of databases has been breached quite often in the past, so these databases, along with two other types of databases—*marketing databases* and *government databases*—that are typically associated with a higher risk of personal privacy violations and are discussed next, are of growing concern to privacy advocates.

Marketing databases contain data about people, such as where they live and what products they buy. This information is used for marketing purposes, such as sending advertisements that fit each individual's interests (via regular mail or e-mail) or trying to sign people up over the phone for some type of service. Virtually anytime you provide information about yourself online or offline—for example, when you subscribe to a magazine, fill out a sweepstakes entry or product registration card, or buy a product or service using a credit card—there is a good chance that information will find its way into a marketing database.

Marketing databases are also beginning to be used in conjunction with Web activities, such as participating in social networks and some personalized search services. For instance, the data stored on Facebook, MySpace, and other social networking sites can be gathered and used for advertising purposes by marketing companies, and the activities or users of personalized search services (where users log in to use the service) can be tracked and that data used for marketing purposes. There has been some objection to several of these possible privacy risks. For instance, Sears came under fire in early 2008 for two issues affecting individuals' privacy. First, its My SHC Community social network includes tracking software that can be used to track participants' Web activities, such as recording all Web sites visited and information in the headers of all e-mail messages received. Secondly, its Manage My Home community portal includes a feature called "Find Your Products" designed to enable participants to look up past purchases. However, the site allows anyone with basic information about an individual (such as name, address, and telephone number) to look up that individual's purchase history. Another example is Facebook, which met with significant objection to its *Beacon* advertising service. Beacon, introduced in late 2007, was designed to track members' Web purchases and other Web activities on more than 40 partner sites and share those purchases and activities with the users' Facebook friends (one user discovered that his Facebook friends had been notified that he had bought an engagement ring before he had even proposed). In response to user complaints, Facebook changed the service to work only on an *opt-in* basis, where it would only be enabled at a member's request. And Google, with its vast array of services that collect enormous amounts of data about individuals, has faced criticism over a number of issues. For instance, *Google Reader* shares tags about what users have read with those individuals' *Google Talk* contacts; the cameras used to capture the 360-degree street views in Google Maps are high-resolution enough to see the faces of individuals and the license plate numbers captured in the photographs; and documents, search histories, and e-mail messages are stored by Google for users of its Google Apps, Google Personalized Search, and Gmail services. And with Google attempting to purchase online advertising giant DoubleClick (the purchase was still pending at the time of this writing), privacy advocates are concerned about what might happen when Google's vast amount of data is combined with the tracking capabilities of DoubleClick cookies, if the merger is approved.

Information about individuals is also available in **government databases**. Some information, such as Social Security earnings and income tax returns, is confidential and should only be seen by authorized individuals. Other information—such as birth records, marriage certificates, and divorce information, as well as property purchases, assessments,

ONLINE VIDEO

Go to **www.course.com/uccs/ch5** to watch the "Google Search Privacy: Personalized Search" video clip.

>**Marketing database.** A collection of data about people that is stored in a large database and used for marketing purposes. >**Government database.** A collection of data about people that is collected and maintained by the government.

liens, and tax values—is available to the public, including to the marketing companies that specialize in creating marketing databases. One emerging government database application is the creation of a *national ID system* (mandated by the *Real ID Act* that was passed in 2005) that will link state databases containing data about all citizens; all state driver's licenses and other identification cards will be required to include a barcode or other machine-readable technology that can be used in conjunction with the database. Although scheduled to be implemented by mid-2008 (2009 for states that are granted an extension), many states are opposing the law and it is unclear what the outcome will be.

FIGURE 5-12

A variety of searchable databases containing personal information are available via the Internet.

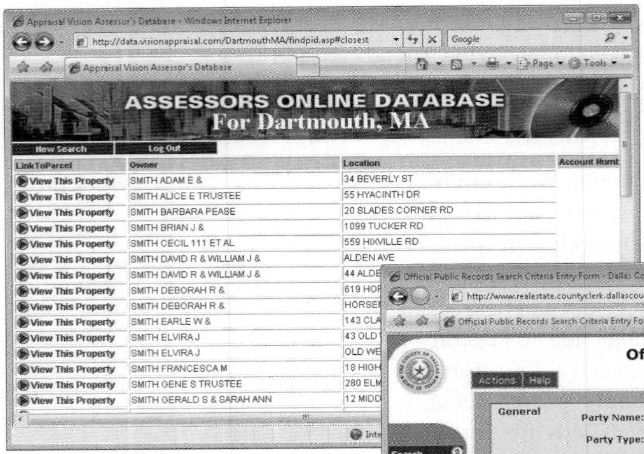

In the past, the data about any one individual was stored in a variety of separate locations, such as at different government agencies, individual retail stores, the person's bank and credit card companies, and so forth. Because it would be extremely time-consuming to locate all the information about one person from all these different places, there was a fairly high level of information privacy. Today, however, most of an individual's data is stored on computers that can communicate with each other via the Internet, which means accessing personal information about someone is much easier than it used to be. For example, a variety of information about individuals is available for free through the Internet; there are also paid services that can perform online database searches for you (see Figure 5-12). Although often this ability to search online databases is an advantage—such as running background checks on potential employees or looking up a misplaced phone number—it does raise privacy concerns. In response to the increased occurrence of identity theft, some local governments have removed birth and death information from their available online database records.

Collecting in-depth information about an

PROPERTY VALUE SEARCH
Some states permit searches for property located in that state, such as the Massachusetts database shown here that allows searches by address or owner name and displays the owner's name, address, and a link to additional information including property value.

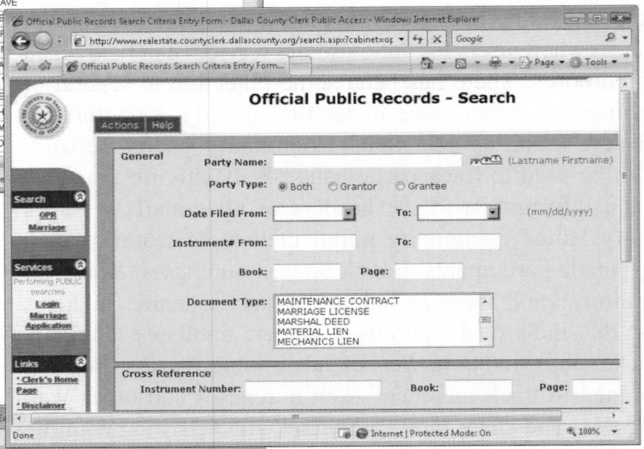

VITAL RECORDS SEARCH
Some counties and states allow searches for documents related to marriages, divorces, births, legal judgments, deeds, liens, powers of attorney, and so forth.

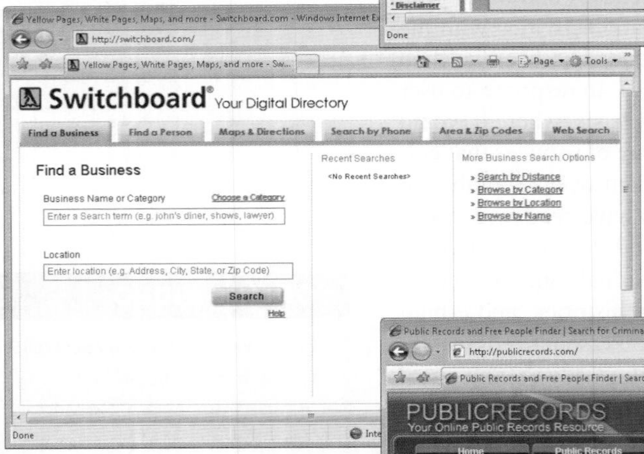

ADDRESS NUMBER AND PHONE NUMBER SEARCH
Any information listed in a U.S. telephone book can be found using this site. You can search either by name or telephone number to view the available information.

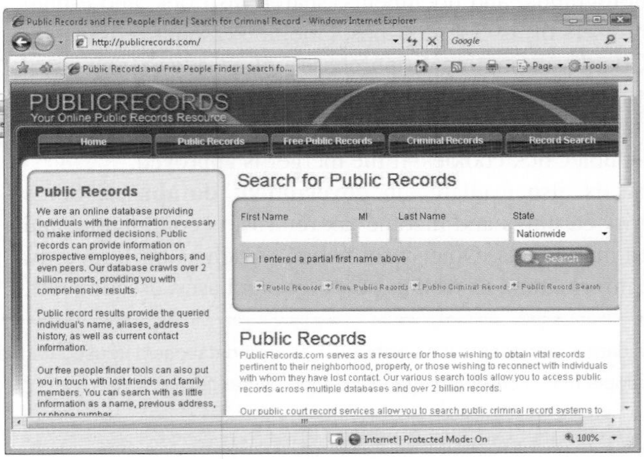

PAID PUBLIC RECORDS SEARCH
A number of sites offer a variety of public records searches, such as for criminal records or court records, to the public for a fee.

When you make an electronic transaction, information about who you are and what you buy is recorded, usually in a database.

Databases containing the identities of people and what they buy are sold to marketing companies.

The marketing companies add the new data to their marketing databases; they can then reorganize the data in ways that might be valuable to other companies.

The marketing companies create lists of individuals matching the specific needs of companies; the companies buy the lists for their own marketing purposes.

FIGURE 5-13
How electronic profiling might work.

individual is known as **electronic profiling**. Marketing companies use data acquired from a variety of sources—such as from product and service purchases that provide personally identifiable information, as well as from public information, such as property values, vehicle registrations, births, marriages, and deaths—to create electronic profiles of individuals. Electronic profiles generally provide specific information and can include an individual's name, current and previous addresses, telephone number, marital status, number and age of children, spending habits, and product preferences. The information contained in electronic profiles is then sold to companies upon request to be used for marketing purposes (see Figure 5-13). For example, one company might request a list of all individuals in a particular state whose street addresses are considered to be in an affluent area and who buy baby products. Another company might request a list of all SUV owners in a particular city

FIGURE 5-14
Privacy policies.
Web site privacy policies explain how your personal information might be used.

who have not purchased a car in five years. Still another company may want a list of business travelers who frequently fly to the East Coast.

Many Web sites have a **privacy policy** (see Figure 5-14) that discloses how the personal information you provide while visiting that Web site or while completing a product registration will be used. As long as their actions do not violate their privacy policy, it is legal for businesses to sell the personal data that they collect. There are some problems with privacy policies, however, such as the fact that they are sometimes difficult to decipher and the reality that most people do not take the time to read them before using a site. In addition, many businesses periodically change their privacy policies without warning, requiring consumers to reread privacy policies frequently or risk their personal information being used in a manner that they did not agree to when the information was

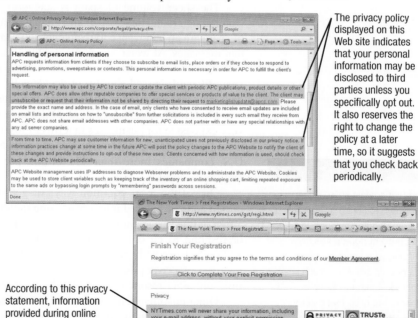

The privacy policy displayed on this Web site indicates that your personal information may be disclosed to third parties unless you specifically opt out. It also reserves the right to change the policy at a later time, so it suggests that you check back periodically.

According to this privacy statement, information provided during online registration will not be shared with others without your consent.

>**Electronic profiling.** Using electronic means to collect a variety of in-depth information about an individual, such as name, address, income, and buying habits. >**Privacy policy.** A policy, commonly posted on a company's Web site, that explains how personal information provided to that company will be used.

FIGURE 5-15

Spam. Users should be very wary of responding to unsolicited e-mail messages.

initially provided. Some companies notify customers by e-mail when their privacy policies change but, more commonly, they expect customers to check the current policy periodically and notify the business if any new actions are objectionable.

Spam and Other Marketing Activities

Spam refers to unsolicited e-mail sent to a large group of individuals at one time. The electronic equivalent of junk mail (see Figure 5-15), spam is most often used to sell products or services to individuals. Spam is also used in phishing schemes and is sent frequently via botnets, as discussed in Chapter 4. A great deal of spam involves health-related products (such as medicine or weight loss systems), counterfeit products (such as watches and medicine), pornography, and new—and often fraudulent—business opportunities and stock deals. Spam can also be generated by individuals forwarding e-mail messages they receive (such as jokes, recipes, or notices of possible new privacy or health concerns) to everyone in their address books. In addition to spam, most individuals receive marketing e-mails either from companies they directly provided with their e-mail addresses or from other companies that acquired their e-mail addresses from a third-party to whom that information was provided (such as from a partner site or via a purchased mailing list). While these latter types of marketing e-mail messages do not technically fit the definition of spam since they were permission-based, many individuals consider them to be spam. Spam can also be sent via IM (called *spim*), to mobile phones (called *mobile phone spam* or *SMS spam*), and to fax machines.

The sheer volume of spam is staggering today. For instance, e-mail security vendor Commtouch found that 96% of all e-mail messages in 2007 were spam. At best, large volumes of spam are an annoyance to recipients and can slow down a mail server's delivery of important messages. At worst, spam can disable a mail network completely, or it can cause recipients to miss or lose important e-mail messages because those messages have been caught in a *spam filter* (discussed shortly) or accidentally deleted by the recipient while he or she was deleting a large number of spam e-mail messages.

Most Internet users spend several minutes each day dealing with spam, making spam very expensive for businesses in terms of lost productivity, consumption of communication bandwidth, and drain of technical support. Nucleus Research estimates that spam costs U.S. companies more than $71 billion per year in lost productivity alone—$712 per employee annually.

One of the most common ways of getting on a spam mailing list is by having your e-mail address entered into a marketing database, which can happen when you sign up for a free online service or use your e-mail address to register a product, place an online order, or respond to an online or e-mail offer. Spammers also use software to gather e-mail addresses from Web pages and discussion group posts. Many individuals view spam as an invasion of privacy because it arrives on computers without permission and costs them time and other resources (bandwidth, mailbox space, and hard drive space, for instance).

Other unsolicited marketing activities that can be viewed as privacy violations because of their intrusion factor include *pop-up ads*, *pop-under ads*, and *telemarketing*. Pop-up and pop-under ads are Web-based advertisements that show up in a separate browser window when you are surfing the Web, typically generated by viewing a particular Web page. As

>**Spam.** Unsolicited, bulk e-mail sent over the Internet.

their names suggest, pop-up ads initially appear on top of all other browser windows, and pop-under ads appear beneath all other browser windows (and so may not be noticed until a later time). *Telemarketing*—a marketing activity that most individuals encounter on a regular basis—consists of unsolicited offers made via the telephone. Unlike pop-up and pop-under ads, which are typically displayed in response to a Web page just displayed, most telemarketing targets individuals based on the data contained in a marketing database, compiled from both offline and online activities.

Most types of spam are legal, but there are increased requirements now in order for it to be legal. For instance, the *CAN-SPAM Act of 2003* enacted requirements (such as using truthful subject lines and honoring remove requests) for spammers and other bulk e-mailers. While the CAN-SPAM Act has not reduced the amount of spam circulated today, it has increased the number of spammers prosecuted for sending spam. Several spammers have been convicted and sent to prison in recent years and more are awaiting trial. In early 2008, for example, 11 individuals (one of which authorities estimate is responsible for sending tens of millions of spam messages each day) were indicted as part of an alleged spam-based *pump-and-dump* scheme that primarily sent spam related to Chinese penny stocks owned by the spammers to drive up the price of those stocks, and then the spammers sold their stock in those companies for a profit. Investigators charge that the defendants used a botnet and other illegal methods to send the spam, as well as to trick recipients into opening and acting on advertisements contained in the spam. If convicted, the spammers face up to 20 years in prison plus a large fine. The CAN-SPAM Act also applies to spim, and the first federal charge of spimming took place in 2005 against an 18-year-old man who allegedly sent more than 1.5 million automated spim instant messages advertising pornography and mortgages. In addition to the CAN-SPAM Act violations, the man is being charged with intending to extort and cause damage to the IM hosting service, and he faces up to 18 years in federal prison if convicted.

TIP

To register a phone number in the National Do Not Call Registry, go to www.donotcall.gov.

Protecting the Privacy of Personal Information

There are a number of precautions that can be taken to protect the privacy of personal information. Safeguarding your e-mail address and other personal information is a good start. You can also surf anonymously, *opt out* of some marketing activities, and use filters and other tools to limit your exposure to spam and onscreen ads. Businesses need to take adequate measures to protect the privacy of information stored on their servers and storage media. These precautions are discussed next.

Safeguard Your E-Mail Address

Protecting your e-mail address is one of the best ways to avoid spam. One way to accomplish this is to use one private e-mail address for family, friends, colleagues, and other trusted sources. For online shopping, signing up for free offers, discussion groups, product registration, and other activities that typically lead to junk e-mail, use a *disposable* or **throw-away e-mail address**—such as a second address obtained from your ISP or a free e-mail address from Yahoo! Mail, AOL Mail, Windows Live Hotmail, or Google's Gmail (see Figure 5-16). Although you will want to check your alternate e-mail address periodically (to check for online shopping receipts or shipping notifications, for instance), this method can prevent a great deal of spam from getting to your regular e-mail account. Another advantage of using a throw-away

FIGURE 5-16

Gmail. Free Web mail services like Gmail can be used for throw-away e-mail addresses, in addition to regular e-mail addresses.

>**Throw-away e-mail address.** An e-mail address used only for nonessential purposes and activities that may result in spam; the address can be disposed of and replaced if spam becomes a problem.

e-mail address for only noncritical applications is that you can quit using it and get a new one if spam begins to get overwhelming or too annoying. If you only need an e-mail address to receive a confirmation (such as for signing up for a sweepstakes or registering for a free online service), use a very temporary e-mail address, such as the ones available through *10 Minute Mail* that are valid for only 10 minutes. Some ISPs, such as EarthLink, also provide disposable anonymous e-mail addresses to their subscribers. E-mail messages sent to a subscriber's anonymous address are forwarded to the subscriber's account until the disposable address is deleted by the subscriber. Consequently, individuals can easily change disposable addresses when they pick up spam or are otherwise no longer needed. There are also *anonymous e-mail services* (such as the one provided by Anonymizer's *Nyms* product) that allow users to create and delete anonymous e-mail addresses; messages sent to the anonymous e-mail addresses are forwarded to the user's specified e-mail account. These services typically cost about $20 per year.

To comply with truth-in-advertising laws, an *unsubscribe* e-mail address included in an unsolicited e-mail must be a working address. If you receive a marketing e-mail from a reputable source, you may be able to unsubscribe by clicking the supplied link or otherwise following the unsubscribe instructions. Since spam from less-legitimate sources often has unsubscribe links that do not work or that are present only to verify that your e-mail address is genuine—a very valuable piece of information for future use—many privacy experts recommend never replying to or trying to unsubscribe from any spam.

Be Cautious of Revealing Personal Information

In addition to protecting your real e-mail address, protecting your personal information is a critical step toward safeguarding your privacy. Consequently, it makes sense to be cautious about revealing your private information to anyone. Privacy tips for safeguarding personal information include the following:

► Read a Web site's privacy policy (if one exists) before providing any personal information. Look for a phrase saying that the company will not share your information with other companies under any circumstances. If the Web site reserves the right to share your information if the company is sold or unless you specifically notify them otherwise, it is best to assume that any information you provide will eventually be shared with others—do not use the site if that is unacceptable to you.

► Consider using privacy software, such as the free *Privacy Bird* program, created by AT&T. This program works in conjunction with your browser to notify you (by changing the appearance of its icon on the browser's title bar, as shown in Figure 5-17) if the Web sites you view meet your specified privacy criteria (such as how your health, financial, purchasing, contact, or other types of personal information will be used). The program makes its determination by comparing your specified criteria with the site's privacy information, which is based on the *Platform for Privacy Preferences* (P3P)—a set of privacy policy standards developed by the World Wide Web Consortium (W3C).

► Do not supply personal information online to people you meet in chat rooms. Although they may seem like close friends, it is important to realize that you do not know for sure who they are or what they are like in real life.

► Avoid putting too many personal details about yourself on your Web site or on a social networking site. If you would like to post photographs or other personal documents on a Web site for faraway friends and family members to see, consider using a photo sharing site that allows you to restrict access to your photos (such as *Flickr*, *Snapfish*, or *Fotki*).

FIGURE 5-17

Privacy bird icons. The Privacy Bird icon is displayed on the browser title bar and changes its appearance to notify the user if the Web site being viewed matches his or her privacy specifications.

— A sleeping gray bird indicates that Privacy Bird has been disabled.

— A yellow bird indicates that the site's privacy information cannot be accessed.

— A green bird indicates that the site's privacy information matches the user's specifications. A red X indicates that the site contains images or other content without a privacy policy associated with them or that don't match the user's specifications.

— An angry red bird indicates that the site's privacy information conflicts with the user's specifications.

► Beware of Web sites offering prizes or the chance to earn free merchandise in exchange for your personal information. Chances are good that the information will be sold to direct marketers, which will likely result in additional spam. If you choose to sign up for services from these Web sites, use your throw-away e-mail address.

► Consider using an *anonymous Web surfing* program, such as Anonymizer's *Anonymous Surfing* program (see Figure 5-18). This program, available for about $30 per year, hides the user's personal information as he or she browses the Web so it is not revealed and the user's activities cannot be tracked by marketers. All requests for Web pages go through the Anonymizer secure servers so that the user's IP address, Web surfing history, and other personal information is protected (Web sites see the IP address of the Anonymizer server instead of the individual's IP address and IP addresses are rotated daily for additional privacy protection).

► Just because a Web site or registration form asks for personal information, that does not mean you have to give it. Supply only the required information (these fields are often marked with an asterisk or are colored differently than nonrequired fields—if not, you can try leaving fields blank and see if the form will still be accepted). If you are asked for more personal information than you are comfortable providing, look for an alternate product or Web site. As a rule of thumb, do not provide an e-mail address (or else use a throw-away address) if you do not want to receive offers or other e-mail from that company.

► If you are using a public computer (such as at a school, a library, or an Internet café, be sure to remove any personal information and settings stored on the PC. If you logged into a Web mail service or e-commerce site, be sure to log out before you leave. In the browser you were using, you will also want to delete the browser's *cache* (copies of frequently visited Web pages that are stored on the hard drive to speed up browsing), cookies, saved Web form data, and any other temporary Internet files that might contain information about you or your Web activity (see Figure 5-19 for a look at how to accomplish this using Internet Explorer). To avoid any deleted data from being recovered, you should run the Windows Disk Cleanup program on the hard drive, making sure that the options for Temporary Internet Files and the Recycle Bin are selected during the Disk Cleanup process.

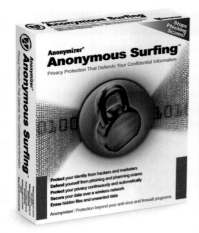

FIGURE 5-18
Anonymous surfing software can be used to protect your privacy online.

FIGURE 5-19
Privacy at public computers. Be sure to delete all traces of your personal settings and online activities.

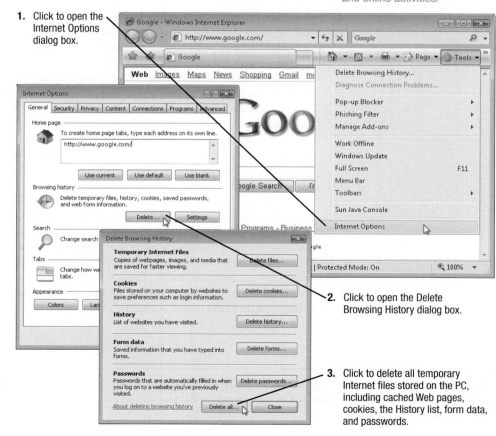

1. Click to open the Internet Options dialog box.

2. Click to open the Delete Browsing History dialog box.

3. Click to delete all temporary Internet files stored on the PC, including cached Web pages, cookies, the History list, form data, and passwords.

TIP

Don't forget that once you post content on a Web site or send it via e-mail, you cannot control how long it will "live" in digital form. Be very careful about the personal information you post and send to avoid it embarrassing you or otherwise creating problems for you in the future.

Use Filters and Opt Out

Keeping your personal information—particularly e-mail address, mailing address, and telephone number—as private as possible can help to reduce spam and other direct marketing activities. Some ISPs automatically block all e-mail messages originating from known or suspected spammers so those e-mail messages never reach the individuals' mailboxes; other ISPs flag suspicious e-mail messages as possible spam, based on their content or subject line, to warn individuals that those messages may contain spam. To deal with spam that makes it to your PC, you can use an **e-mail filter**—a tool for automatically sorting your incoming e-mail messages. E-mail filters used to capture spam are called **spam filters**. In addition, most e-mail programs are set up to identify possible spam and either flag it or move it to a Spam or Junk E-mail folder. To customize spam filtering, individuals can change the settings used in their e-mail program to detect spam, create their own e-mail filters in their e-mail program, or use third-party filtering software; they can also sometimes enable or disable ISP spam filtering for their e-mail accounts. In addition, many spam filters are designed to "learn" what each user views as spam based on the user identifying (usually via a *Report Spam* button in the Inbox or a *Not Spam* button in the Spam folder) e-mail messages that were classified incorrectly by the spam filter so those messages will be classified correctly for that user in the future. Businesses can set up spam filters in-house, but they are increasingly turning to dedicated *antispam appliances* to filter out spam as it arrives without increasing the load on the company e-mail server.

E-mail filters typically route messages automatically into particular folders based on stated criteria. For example, you could specify that e-mail messages with keywords frequently used in spam subject lines, such as *free, porn, opportunity, last chance, weight, pharmacy*, and similar terms, be routed into a folder named Possible Spam, and you could specify that all e-mail messages from your boss's e-mail address be routed into an Urgent folder. Filtering can help you find important messages in your Inbox by preventing it from becoming cluttered with spam, but you need to remember to periodically check the Possible Spam or Junk E-mail folder to locate any e-mail messages mistakenly filed there—especially before you permanently delete those messages. Changing the spam settings and creating a new e-mail filter in Microsoft Outlook is shown in Figure 5-20.

You can also choose to **opt out** as a way to reduce the amount of spam you receive and other direct marketing activities you encounter. *Opting out* refers to following a predesignated procedure to remove yourself from marketing lists, or otherwise preventing your personal information from being obtained by or shared with others. By opting out, you instruct companies you do business with (such as your bank, insurance company, investment company, or online store) not to share your personal information with third parties. You can also opt out of being contacted by direct marketing companies (such as by phone or regular mail) and online marketing companies.

To opt out from a particular company or direct marketing association, you can contact them directly (such as by phone, e-mail, Web-based form, or letter)—many organizations include opt-out instructions in the privacy policies posted on their Web sites. For Web sites that use registered accounts for repeat visitors, opt-out options are sometimes included in your personal settings and can be activated by modifying your personal settings for that site. Opt-out instructions for financial institutions and credit card companies are often included in the disclosure statements that are periodically mailed to customers; they can also often be found on the company's Web site.

>**E-mail filter.** A tool that automatically sorts your incoming e-mail messages based on specific criteria. >**Spam filter.** An e-mail filter used to redirect spam from a user's Inbox. >**Opt out.** To request that you be removed from marketing activities or that your information not be shared with other companies.

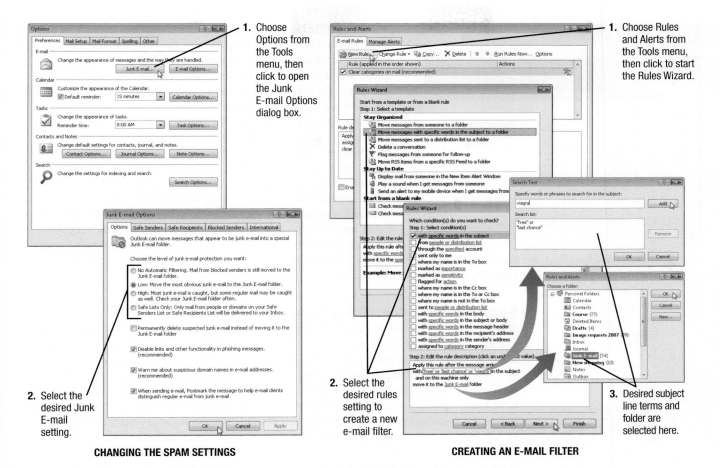

1. Choose Options from the Tools menu, then click to open the Junk E-mail Options dialog box.

2. Select the desired Junk E-mail setting.

CHANGING THE SPAM SETTINGS

1. Choose Rules and Alerts from the Tools menu, then click to start the Rules Wizard.

2. Select the desired rules setting to create a new e-mail filter.

3. Desired subject line terms and folder are selected here.

CREATING AN E-MAIL FILTER

To assist consumers with the opt-out process, there are a number of Web sites, such as the Center for Democracy and Technology and the PrivacyRightsNow! Web sites, which provide opt-out tools for consumers. For example, some sites help visitors create opt-out letters that can be sent to the companies in order to opt out. For online marketing activities, organizations—such as the *Network Advertising Initiative* (*NAI*)—have tools on their Web sites to help consumers opt out of online targeted ads (see Figure 5-21). Typically, this process replaces an advertiser's marketing cookie with an *opt-out cookie*. The opt-out cookie prevents any more marketing cookies belonging to that particular advertiser from being placed on the user's hard drive as long as the opt-out cookie is present (usually until the user deletes the opt-out cookie file, either intentionally or unintentionally).

At the present time, opting-out procedures are confusing and time-consuming, and they do not always work well. Consequently, some privacy groups are pushing to change to an *opt-in* process, in which individuals would need to **opt in** to a particular marketing activity before companies can collect or share any personal data (as is the case in the European Union). Until there is a change in legislation in the United States, however, the general practice in the U.S. business community is to use your information as allowed for by each privacy policy unless you specifically opt out.

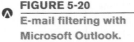
FIGURE 5-20
E-mail filtering with Microsoft Outlook.

FURTHER EXPLORATION

Go to **www.course.com/uccs/ch5** for links to further information about protecting your privacy online.

>**Opt in.** To request that you be included in marketing activities or that your information be shared with other companies.

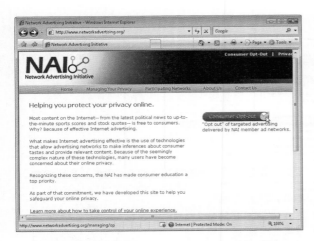

One of the biggest advancements in consumer privacy in the United States is the implementation of the *National Do Not Call Registry* in October 2003. Within three months of adding your telephone numbers (including home, business, and mobile phones) to the registry via the Internet or telephone, telemarketers can no longer call you, unless you have an established business relationship with them. The Do Not Call Registry also covers unsolicited calls—including spam—sent to mobile phones. It is possible that some day there will be similar legislation for PC-based spam. In fact, the CAN-SPAM Act of 2003 laid the groundwork for the creation of a federal *Do Not E-Mail Registry*. However, many insiders view such a registry as impractical and see *e-mail authentication systems*—systems that mark e-mail from authenticated senders (typically determined by major companies registering their mail server IP addresses which are then compared with e-mail addresses as they arrive) as legitimate, as opposed to spam filters that mark suspected spam—as a better alternative.

FIGURE 5-21

Opting out. Web sites, such as the NAI site shown here, can help you opt out of marketing activities.

FIGURE 5-22

Media disposal. When disposing of CDs, DVDs, and other storage media, the media should be shredded to ensure the information on the media is destroyed.

Secure Servers Containing Personal Information

Any business that stores personal information about employees, customers, or other individuals must take adequate security measures to protect the privacy of that information. There are some federal privacy laws already in place, and, in response to the number of privacy breaches occurring recently, additional federal legislation is under consideration, such as to require that businesses notify all individuals whose private information may have been exposed (which has already been enacted as state law in the majority of U.S. states). As discussed in Chapter 4, secure servers and encryption can protect the data stored on a server; firewalls and access systems can protect against unauthorized access. To prevent personal information from intentionally or inadvertently being sent via e-mail, organizations can use e-mail encryption systems that automatically encrypt e-mail messages containing certain keywords. For instance, some hospitals use encryption systems that scan all outgoing e-mail messages and attachments and then automatically encrypt all messages that appear to contain patient-identifiable information, such as a Social Security number, medical record number, patient name, or medical term like "cancer." Recipients of these encrypted e-mail messages receive a link to a secure Web site set up to deliver the hospital's encrypted e-mail messages. After being authenticated, they can view their e-mail messages. Similar systems are used by banks and other businesses.

Properly Dispose of Hardware and Outdated Data

A final consideration for protecting the privacy of personal information is protecting the information located on hardware to be disposed of, such as old backup media, used CDs, obsolete PCs, discarded mobile phones, and so forth. CDs, DVDs, and other media containing sensitive data should be shredded (see Figure 5-22), and the hard drives of computers to be disposed of that contain personal information should be *wiped* clean—overwritten several times using special *disk-wiping* or *disk-erasing* software—as a minimum before they are sold or recycled. Unlike the data on a drive that has merely been erased or even reformatted (which can still be recovered), data on a properly wiped drive is very difficult or impossible to recover. Wiping is typically viewed as an acceptable precaution for deleting hard drives and media belonging to individuals, as well as for media to be reused within an organization. However, for business media containing sensitive data that will not be reused or that will leave the company (such as to be sold or recycled), businesses should consider physically destroying the media, such as

INSIDE THE INDUSTRY

Data Killers

With the vast amount of personal, sensitive, and classified data stored on hard drives today, disposing of those devices or removing the data from those devices so they can be reused is an important issue for both businesses and individuals today. Individuals often give away or sell old computers, but those hard drives routinely contain sensitive data. Businesses may not sell old computer equipment quite as often as individuals do, but businesses do encounter the problem of how to properly dispose of old hard drives containing sensitive data, or how to properly delete the data stored on still-usable hard drives so they can be used by another employee.

Data destruction ranges from *purging* the data (such as wiping the drive clean or *degaussing* (demagnetizing) the drive so the data cannot be restored) to physically destroying the drive. The level of destruction needed depends on the type of data being deleted and where the hardware will go next. For instance, purging might be appropriate for personal hard drives being sold and for business hard drives that will be reused within the company, but all business hard drives that will no longer be used within the company and that contain sensitive data should be physically destroyed.

While data destruction can be performed in-house, there are *data destruction services* designed for this purpose. Such services typically can purge, degauss, or shred hard drives and other media, depending on the customer's preference. Once a

hard drive has been shredded (see the accompanying photo), it is virtually impossible for any data to be recovered from the pieces. However, for extra security, drives containing extremely sensitive data can be degaussed and then shredded. To ensure drives are not lost or compromised in transit, most data destruction companies offer secure transportation to the destruction facility using tamper proof locked cases, and will provide signed and dated Certificates of Purging or Certificates of Destruction, when requested. Some even offer destruction on site, if the customer desires. Purged hard drives are returned to the customer; shredded hard drives are typically recycled.

---

by shredding or melting the hardware. To help with this process, *data destruction services* can be used, as discussed in the Inside the Industry box. To ensure that all hardware containing business data is properly disposed of, it is important for all businesses today to develop and implement a policy (often called a *media sanitization* or *data destruction policy*) for destroying data that is no longer needed.

ONLINE VIDEO

Go to **www.course.com/uccs/ch5** to watch the "Proper Hardware Disposal" video clip.

ELECTRONIC SURVEILLANCE AND MONITORING

There are many ways electronic tools can be used to watch individuals, listen in on their conversations, or monitor their activities. Some of these tools—such as devices used by individuals to eavesdrop on wireless telephone conversations—are not legal. Other products and technologies, such as the GPS devices that are built into some cars so they can be located if they are stolen or the monitoring ankle bracelets used for offenders sentenced to house arrest, are used solely for law enforcement purposes. Still other electronic tools, such as *computer monitoring software*, *video surveillance* equipment, and *presence technology*, discussed next, can often be used legally by individuals, by businesses in conjunction with *employee monitoring*, and by law enforcement agencies.

Computer Monitoring Software

Computer monitoring software is used specifically for the purpose of recording keystrokes, logging the programs or Web sites accessed, or otherwise monitoring someone's computer activity. These programs are typically marketed toward parents (to check on their children's online activities), spouses (to determine if a spouse is having an affair, viewing pornography, or participating in other activities that are unacceptable to the other spouse), law enforcement agencies (to collect evidence against suspected criminals), or employers (to ensure employees are using company computers and time only for work-related or otherwise approved activities). Computer monitoring programs can keep a log of all computer keystrokes performed on a PC, record the activities taking place (such as the amount of time spent on each Web site and using each installed software program) on certain PCs, display or take screen shots of a user's desktop at any given time, or provide a summary of activities for a group of individual PCs (see Figure 5-23). Some computer monitoring software includes the ability to block access to certain Web sites or Internet activities (such as instant messaging), as well as to block access to the Internet in general for specific individuals or during specific time periods (such as a parent blocking all Internet access on school days until a predesignated time or an employer blocking access to certain popular non-work-related Web sites, except during the lunch hour).

Although it is legal to use computer monitoring software on your own computer or on the computers of your employees, installing it on other PCs without the owners' knowledge to monitor their computer activity is usually illegal. A growing illegal use of computer monitoring software is the use of a *keystroke-logging system*—typically software but also implemented via a small piece of hardware that is installed between the system unit and the keyboard of a computer—by hackers to record all keystrokes performed on the PC in order to capture usernames, passwords, and other sensitive data entered into the PC via the keyboard. Keystroke-logging-software can be installed on an individual's PC via malware, or it can be installed on public computers in person if the proper precautions are not taken. For instance, in 2008, a Colombian man pled guilty to installing keystroke-logging software on computers located in hotel business centers and Internet cafés around the world; the software collected

FIGURE 5-23
Computer monitoring software.

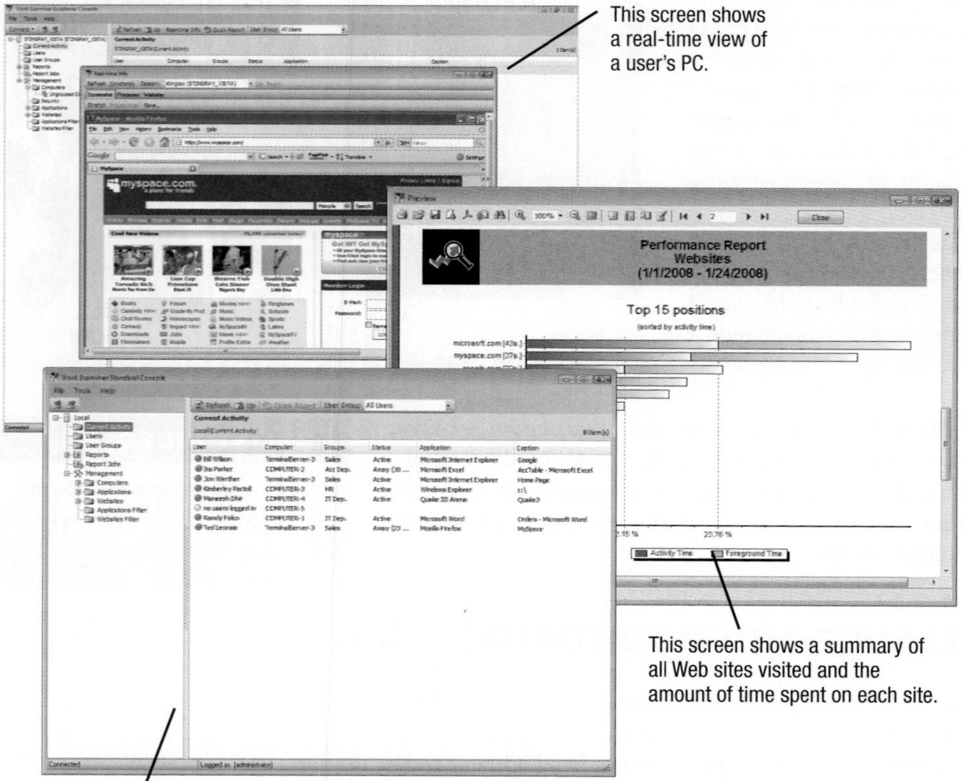

This screen shows a real-time view of a user's PC.

This screen shows a summary of all Web sites visited and the amount of time spent on each site.

This screen shows the current activity (including program and document being used) of all employees.

---

the personal information he needed to access the bank, payroll, brokerage, and other financial accounts of over 600 individuals. He had been arrested and indicted on 16 counts for the computer fraud scheme at the time of this writing, but had yet been tried.

In addition to computer monitoring products designed for individuals and businesses, there are also computer monitoring programs available for use only by law enforcement and other government agencies. Like wiretapping, electronic monitoring of computer activity requires a court order or similar authorization to be legal (although the *USA Patriot Act* does allow the FBI to conduct a limited form of Internet surveillance first, such as to capture e-mail addresses or IP addresses used with traffic going into or coming from a suspect's PC). Several years ago, before computer monitoring software was widely available, the FBI developed a special monitoring program called *Carnivore* to intercept e-mail and Web activity from individuals suspected of criminal activity. In 2005, however, the Carnivore program was officially retired and replaced with commercial computer monitoring software. With proper authorization and cooperation from a suspect's ISP, law enforcement agencies can use computer monitoring software to intercept files and e-mail messages sent to or from a suspect's PC. If the documents are encrypted, keystroke-logging software can be used to record e-mail messages and documents before they are encrypted, as well as to record the encryption keys used with messages and files.

Video Surveillance

The idea of **video surveillance** is nothing new. For years now, closed-circuit security cameras have been monitoring activities in retail stores, banks, office buildings, and other privately owned facilities that are open to the public. In recent years, video surveillance has been expanded in many cities in the United States and other countries to public locations (such as streets, parks, airports, sporting arenas, subway systems, and so forth) for law enforcement purposes. These cameras are typically located outside and attached to or built into fixtures like lamp posts (see Figure 5-24) or attached to buildings. Video surveillance cameras are also increasingly being installed in schools in the United States and other countries to enable administrators to monitor both teacher and student activities and to have a record of incidents as they occur. A snapshot of a live video feed from a camera installed inside a computer lab at a university in New York is shown in Figure 5-24.

Often used in conjunction with face recognition technology, public video surveillance systems are used to try to identify known terrorists and other criminals, to identify criminals whose crimes are caught on tape, and to prevent crimes from occurring. Video surveillance data is proving to be valuable to police for catching terrorists and other types of criminals and is routinely used to

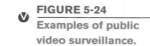

FIGURE 5-24
Examples of public video surveillance.

OUTDOOR SURVEILLANCE
Many cameras placed in public locations are designed to blend into their surroundings to be less intrusive, such as the camera inside this light fixture on a Washington, D.C. street.

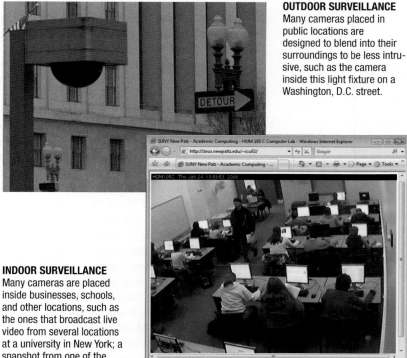

INDOOR SURVEILLANCE
Many cameras are placed inside businesses, schools, and other locations, such as the ones that broadcast live video from several locations at a university in New York; a snapshot from one of the video cameras is shown here.

>**Video surveillance.** The use of video cameras to monitor activities of individuals, such as employees or individuals in public locations, for work-related or crime-prevention purposes.

identify the individuals and cars used in attacks. Worldwide, Britain is the leader in video surveillance usage, with over four million video surveillance cameras installed in public locations—it is estimated that the average London resident can expect to be caught on camera about 300 times a day. A new installation in New York City, scheduled to be completed in 2009, is expected to rival London's system. Named the *Lower Manhattan Security Initiative*, this system will secure a 1.7-square mile area that includes the New York Stock Exchange and the site of the former World Trade Center. It will contain 3,000 video surveillance cameras and over 100 wireless license-plate readers and will be monitored around the clock by a team of police officers and private security specialists. Software will be used to alert personnel of suspicious activity and video will be discarded if it contains no incidents.

Privacy advocates object to the use of video surveillance and face recognition technology in public locations, primarily based on concerns regarding how the video captured by these systems will be used. In one instance in China in 2008, for example, a three-minute segment of a subway surveillance video showing a young couple hugging and kissing on a subway platform was uploaded to YouTube and other Web sites and attracted thousands of hits. The embarrassed couple is planning to sue the subway operator for the privacy breach. Privacy advocates also have doubts about the usefulness of these systems in protecting society against terrorism and object to the fact that, unlike private security video which is typically only viewed after a crime has occurred, the images from many public video cameras are watched all the time. In addition, networks of police video cameras that feed into a central operations center allow the observation of innocent people and activities on a massive scale. However, law enforcement agencies contend that face recognition systems and public video surveillance are no different than the many private video surveillance systems in place today in a wide variety of public locations, such as in retail stores and banks. They view this technology as just one more tool to be used to protect the public, similar to scanning luggage at the airport. Privacy advocates fear being under perpetual police surveillance and the eventual expansion of these security surveillance systems, such as using them to look for "deadbeat dads" or for other applications not vital for national security.

How accepting the public will be about being in a perpetual digital lineup—while at the grocery store, pumping gas, or playing in a park, for instance—remains to be seen. But individuals appear to be getting used to video surveillance cameras and other security measures that can impact privacy. While 60% of the respondents to a recent MSNBC.com survey said they feel their privacy is slipping away and it bothers them, only a small amount of Americans (7%, according to a recent survey by the Ponemon Institute) are changing their behavior in an effort to preserve their privacy.

A related privacy concern is the inclusion of digital camera capabilities in most mobile phones (nearly 83% of all mobile phones sold in the first half of 2007, according to one estimate) today. Although camera functions are included for personal enjoyment and convenience and are increasingly being used to help law enforcement (such as being used by citizens to take photos of crimes as they are being committed), some fear that the ubiquitous nature of mobile phones, combined with the inability to easily tell that a mobile phone is being used to take a photo, will lead to increased privacy violations. In fact, some athletic clubs have banned mobile phones entirely to protect the privacy of their members while working out and in the dressing rooms. Many YMCAs, city parks and recreation departments, and other recreational facilities have banned camera phone use in locker rooms and restrooms to protect the privacy of both children and adults. Camera phones are also being banned by some schools to prevent cheating, by many courthouses to prevent witness or jury intimidation, and by many research and production facilities to prevent corporate espionage. Legally speaking, people typically have few rights to privacy in public places, but many believe that new technology—such as camera phones—will require the law to reconsider and redefine what is considered to be a public place and where citizens can expect to retain particular aspects of personal privacy.

Employee Monitoring

Employee monitoring refers to companies recording or observing the actions of employees while on the job. With today's technology, employee monitoring is very easy to perform, and much of it can be done through the use of computers. Common employee monitoring activities include screening telephone calls, reviewing e-mail, and tracking computer and Internet usage; with the growing inclusion of video cameras into computers and monitors today, employee monitoring via these cameras may become more prominent in the near future. Although many employees feel that being watched at work is an invasion of their personal privacy, it is legal and very common in the United States. According to the American Management Association (AMA), the vast majority (nearly 78%) of all U.S. companies uses some type of electronic surveillance with their employees, 65% of the companies had disciplined employees for misuse of e-mail or the Internet at work, and 27% had fired an employee for that reason. Typically, the main reason is to monitor Internet usage for legal liability, but monitoring employee productivity is another common reason. A 2006 study by Salary.com and America Online revealed that for 52% of U.S. workers, Web surfing is the top time waster. Referred to as *wilfing* (for "What Was I Looking For?"), aimless Web browsing is a big culprit. In fact, a study in the United Kingdom found that workers lost an average of two full days of work per month due to wilfing—and some researchers view that number as being on the low side. Typically, computer and Internet usage is monitored using computer monitoring software, discussed in a previous section.

For monitoring the physical locations of employees, video cameras (such as video surveillance cameras or PC video cameras) can be used, but another possibility is the use of **proximity cards**. A proximity card is similar to the magnetic stripe ID cards frequently used to grant access to facilities or computer systems, but it has built-in smart card or RFID capabilities (see Figure 5-25) to give it additional functionality. For monitoring purposes, proximity cards can identify, on a continual basis, the location of each employee wearing one—an application that some privacy advocates feel crosses the line between valid employee monitoring and an invasion of privacy. Other less controversial uses for proximity cards include facilitating access to a building or computer network, automatically locking an employee's PC when he or she gets a certain distance away from it (to eliminate the problem of nosy coworkers), and automatically unlocking the PC when the employee returns (to eliminate the need for passwords). Other types of employee monitoring systems designed for tracking an employee's location are GPS-based systems, such as systems that track an employee (such as a repair worker or other employee who regularly works out of the office) via his or her mobile phone or those that notify the employer if the employee's company vehicle exits a prescribed work area.

Although some employees may view workplace monitoring as an invasion of their personal privacy, employers have several valid reasons for monitoring employee activities, such as security concerns, productivity measurement, legal compliance, and legal liability. For example, management has a responsibility to the company (and to its stockholders, for publicly held corporations) to make sure employees do the jobs that they are being paid to do. If any employees are spending too much time away from their desks chatting with other employees, answering their personal e-mail, or placing bids at online auctions, the company has the right to know and the responsibility to stop that misuse of company time and resources. For example, there have been many instances of employees viewing pornography, downloading pirated movies or music, watching live sports video feeds—even running

The proximity card is worn by an employee for continuous access and monitoring purposes.

Smart card circuitry

FIGURE 5-25
Proximity cards.
Proximity cards with smart card capabilities can be used for facility access, PC access, and employee monitoring.

their own businesses—on company time and computers. In addition, the company needs to protect itself against lost business (due to employee incompetence or poor client skills, for example) and lawsuits (such as from employees when offensive e-mail messages are circulated within the office or when an employee includes statements that defame another business or reveal private information in a company blog). In addition, government regulations—such as the *Sarbanes-Oxley Act*, which requires publicly traded companies to keep track of which employees look at sensitive documents—may require it. However, some employees object to being monitored, such as the protest by New York City cab drivers in 2007 in response to the plan to upgrade NYC cabs with a GPS tracking system.

Even though employee monitoring systems can be expensive—from \$20,000 for small companies to hundreds of thousands of dollars for larger firms, according to some estimates—many companies view the cost as insignificant compared to the risk of a potential multimillion-dollar lawsuit. It is becoming increasingly common for U.S. firms to face sexual harassment and/or racial discrimination claims stemming from employee e-mail and Internet use. And lawsuits can be costly—Chevron was once ordered to pay female employees \$2.2 million to settle a sexual harassment lawsuit stemming from inappropriate e-mail sent by male employees.

To reduce cost and objections from employees, some businesses have found employee training and education to be an effective and cost-efficient alternative to continuous monitoring. Others use statistical-analysis software to detect unusual patterns in data collected about employee computer usage, and then use the reports to investigate only the employees and situations indicated as possible problems. Regardless of the techniques used, it is wise for businesses to inform employees about their monitoring practices (including what activities may be monitored and how long records of that monitoring will be archived), although they are not required by law in the U.S. at the current time to do so. However, bills have been introduced in several states in the United States that would prohibit employee monitoring without employee notification and some countries—such as in the European Union—are much more limiting with respect to the types of employee monitoring that can be performed without active notification. And legislation has been implemented or is being considered in several states to prevent employers from implanting employees with RFID chips without the employee's consent, to prevent implanted chips from being required for monitoring purposes, security access, or other work-related functions.

Presence Technology

Presence technology refers to the ability of one computing device (such as a desktop PC, handheld computer, or smart phone) on a network (such as the Internet) to locate and identify another device on the same network and determine its status. It can be used to tell when someone on the network is using his or her computer or mobile phone, as well as where that device is physically located at any given time. It can also indicate the individual's availability for communications; that is, whether or not the individual is able and willing to take a call or respond to an IM at the present time. For example, when an employee at a company using presence technology (sometimes called *presence management* in a business context) has a question that needs answering, he or she can check the directory displayed on his or her PC or mobile phone to see which team members are available, regardless of where those team members are physically located. The employee can then call a team member or send an instant message. Presence technology is also expected to eventually be used on company Web pages so that visitors—usually potential or current customers—can see which salespeople, service representatives, or other contacts are currently available. Another possible

---

>**Presence technology.** Technology that enables one computing device (such as a desktop PC, handheld computer, or smart phone) to locate and identify the current status of another device on the same network.

application is including dynamic presence buttons in e-mail messages—the presence button would display one message (such as "I'm online") if the sender is online at the time the e-mail message is read, and a different message (such as "I'm offline") if the sender is not online at that time.

Presence technology today can be implemented via software, as well as by GPS or RFID technology. For instance, IM software indicates the current status of each buddy on an individual's contact list, and presence technology is also used with contact lists found in e-mail programs and mobile phone services (see Figure 5-26). Presence technology capabilities are also integrated into Microsoft Office 2007 in conjunction with collaborative *Document Workspaces* stored on a company server, and they are available via stand-alone programs. The GPS capabilities built into mobile phones can be used to determine the location of that phone and this presence information is frequently used by law enforcement.

While some aspects of presence technology are useful and intriguing, such as being able to tell that a loved one's flight arrived safely when you notice that his or her mobile phone is on again, knowing if a friend or colleague is available for a telephone call before dialing the number, or identifying the location of your children at any point in time, privacy advocates are concerned about the use of this technology for targeting ads and information to individuals based on their current physical location (such as close to a particular restaurant at lunchtime) and other activities that they view as potential privacy violations. In fact, a bill under consideration in California at the time of this writing would ban public schools from using RFID cards or badges to take attendance or monitor students' locations on campus.

Online—can send and receive phone calls and IMs. Away—busy, but can send and receive phone calls and IMs. Offline—cannot send or receive phone calls or IMs.

FIGURE 5-26
Presence technology.
Presence icons indicate the status of individual contacts.

Protecting Personal and Workplace Privacy

There are not many options for protecting yourself against computer monitoring by your employer or the government or against video surveillance systems, but businesses should take the necessary security measures (such as protecting the company network from hackers, monitoring for intrusions, and using security software) to ensure that employee activities are not being monitored by a hacker or other unauthorized individual. Individuals should also secure their home PCs to protect against keystroke logging or other computer monitoring software that may be inadvertently installed via an electronic greeting card, game, or other downloaded file, and that is designed to provide a hacker with account numbers, passwords, and other sensitive data that could be used in identity theft or other fraudulent activities. *Antispyware software*, such as the programs discussed in Chapter 4 and the example shown in Figure 5-27, can be used to detect and remove some types of illegal computer monitoring software.

FIGURE 5-27
Antispy software.
Antispy software can detect and remove illegally installed computer monitoring software.

The Employer's Responsibilities

To protect the personal privacy of their employees and customers, businesses and organizations have a responsibility to keep private information about their employees, the company, and their customers safe. Strong security measures, such as firewalls and access-prevention methods for both computer data and facilities, can help to protect against unauthorized access by hackers. Businesses and organizations should take precautions against both intentional and accidental breaches of privacy by employees. Finally, businesses and organizations have the responsibility to monitor their employees' activities to ensure workers are productive. In general, businesses must maintain a safe and productive workplace environment and protect the privacy of their customers and employees, while at the same time avoid leaving the company vulnerable to lawsuits.

To inform employees of what personal activities (if any) are allowed during company time or on company equipment, the company policies regarding company communications (such as e-mail messages and blog postings) and what employee activities (such as Web surfing, e-mail, telephone calls, and downloading files to an office PC) may be monitored, all businesses should have an *employee policy*. Employee policies are usually included in an employee handbook or posted on the company intranet.

The Employee's Responsibilities

Employees have the responsibility to read a company's employee policy when initially hired and to review it periodically to ensure that they understand the policy and do not violate any company rules while working for that organization. In addition, since at-work activities may legally be monitored by an employer, it is wise—from a privacy standpoint—to avoid personal activities at work entirely. From reading your organization's employee policy, you can determine if any personal activities are allowed at all (such as checking your personal e-mail on your lunch hour), but it is safer to perform personal activities at home, regardless. Be especially careful with any activity, such as sending a joke via e-mail to a coworker, that might be interpreted as harassment. For personal phone calls, use your mobile phone or an outside pay phone during your lunch hour or rest break.

COMPUTER SECURITY AND PRIVACY LEGISLATION

The high level of concern regarding computer security and personal privacy has led state and federal legislators to pass a variety of laws since the 1970s. Internet privacy is viewed as one of the top policy issues facing Congress today, and numerous bills have been proposed in the last several years regarding spam, telemarketing, spyware, online profiling, and other very important privacy issues, but Congress has had difficulty passing new legislation. There are several reasons for this. For instance, it is difficult for the legal system to keep pace with the rate at which technology changes, and there are jurisdictional issues domestically and internationally, since many computer crimes affect businesses and individuals located in geographic areas other than the one in which the computer criminal is located. In addition, privacy is difficult to define and there is a struggle to balance freedom of speech with the right to privacy. Another issue is weighing legislation versus voluntary methods. For instance, the *Child Online Protection Act* (*COPA*) has been highly controversial since it was passed in 1998, and, in fact, it has never been implemented. This legislation prohibited making pornography or any other content deemed harmful to minors available to minors via the Internet and carried a $50,000 fine. In mid-2004, the issue reached the U.S. Supreme Court for the third time, and the court ruled that a lower court was correct to block the law from taking effect because it likely violates the First Amendment. The case was sent back to a lower court for a trial to determine if Internet filtering and other related technologies provide sufficient protection for minors (that is, are they effective at keeping the material in question out of the hands of children) while allowing adults to view and buy material that is legal for them.

A list of selected federal laws related to computer security and privacy are shown in Figure 5-28. In response to the number of recent data security breaches, several new pieces of legislation have recently been introduced—such as the proposed *Personal Data Privacy and Security Act of 2007*—to help consumers better protect the privacy of their personal information and to enhance criminal penalties for security breaches and misuse of personally identifiable information. At the time of this writing, however, none had been signed into law.

FURTHER EXPLORATION

Go to **www.course.com/uccs/ch5** for links to further information about computer security and privacy legislation.

DATE	LAW AND DESCRIPTION
2006	**U.S. SAFE WEB Act of 2006** Grants additional authority to the FTC to help protect consumers from spam, spyware, and Internet fraud and deception.
2005	**Real ID Act** Establishes national standards for state-issued driver's licenses and identification cards.
2005	**Junk Fax Prevention Act** Requires unsolicited faxes to have a highly-visible opt-out notice.
2003	**CAN-SPAM Act** Implements regulations for unsolicited e-mail messages and lays the groundwork for a federal Do Not E-Mail Registry.
2003	**Do Not Call Implementation Act** Amends the Telephone Consumer Protection Act to implement the National Do Not Call Registry.
2003	**Health Insurance Portability and Accountability Act (HIPAA)** Includes a Security Rule that sets minimum security standards to protect health information stored electronically.
2002	**Sarbanes-Oxley Act** Requires archiving a variety of electronic records and protecting the integrity of corporate financial data.
2001	**USA Patriot Act (USAPA)** Grants federal authorities expanded surveillance and intelligence-gathering powers, such as broadening the ability of federal agents to obtain the real identity of Internet users and intercept e-mail and other types of Internet communications.
1999	**Financial Modernization (Gramm-Leach-Bliley) Act** Extends the ability of banks, securities firms and insurance companies to share consumers' non-public personal information, but requires them to notify consumers and give them the opportunity to opt-out before disclosing any information.
1998	**Child Online Protection Act (COPA)** Prohibits online pornography and other content deemed harmful to minors; has been blocked by the Supreme Court.
1998	**Children's Online Privacy Protection Act (COPPA)** Regulates how Web sites can collect information from minors and communicate with them.
1998	**Telephone Anti-Spamming Amendments Act** Applies restrictions to unsolicited, bulk commercial e-mail.
1996	**National Information Infrastructure Protection Act** Amends the Computer Fraud and Abuse Act of 1984 to punish information theft crossing state lines and crack down on network trespassing.
1992	**Cable Act** Extends the Cable Communications Policy Act to include companies that sell wireless services.
1991	**Telephone Consumer Protection Act** Requires telemarketing companies to respect the rights of people who do not want to be called.
1988	**Computer Matching and Privacy Protection Act** Limits the use of government data in determining federal-benefit recipients.
1988	**Video Privacy Protection Act** Limits disclosure of customer information by video-rental companies.
1986	**Computer Fraud and Abuse Act of 1986** Amends the 1984 law to include federally regulated financial institutions.
1986	**Electronic Communications Privacy Act** Extends traditional privacy protections governing postal delivery and telephone services to include e-mail, cellular phones, and voice mail.
1984	**Cable Communications Policy Act** Limits disclosure of customer records by cable TV companies.
1984	**Computer Fraud and Abuse Act of 1984** Makes it a crime to break into computers owned by the federal government.
1974	**Education Privacy Act** Stipulates that, in both public and private schools that receive any federal funding, individuals have the right to keep the schools from releasing such information as grades and evaluations of behavior.
1974	**Privacy Act** Stipulates that the collection of data by federal agencies must have a legitimate purpose.
1970	**Fair Credit Reporting Act** Prevents private organizations from unfairly denying credit and provides individuals the right to inspect their credit records.
1970	**Freedom of Information Act** Gives individuals the right to inspect data concerning them that is stored by the federal government.

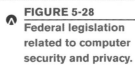

FIGURE 5-28

Federal legislation related to computer security and privacy.

SUMMARY

WHY BE CONCERNED ABOUT COMPUTER SECURITY?

Chapter Objective 1:
Explain why all computer users should be concerned about computer security.

There are a number of important security concerns related to computers, such as having your PC stolen, losing data, and running the risk of buying pirated or digitally counterfeited products via an online auction. All computer users should be aware of the possible security risks and they should know about the safeguards they can implement to prevent security problems since these problems can cost them time and money, as well as be an inconvenience.

HARDWARE LOSS, HARDWARE DAMAGE, AND SYSTEM FAILURE

Chapter Objective 2:
List some risks associated with hardware loss, hardware damage, and system failure, and understand ways to safeguard a PC against these risks.

Hardware loss (perhaps as a result of **hardware theft** or lost hardware), hardware damage (both intentional and unintentional), and **system failure** are important concerns. System failure can occur because of a hardware problem, as well as the result of a natural or man-made disaster. To protect against hardware theft, door and equipment locks can be used. To protect against accidental hardware damage, **surge suppressors**, **uninterruptible power supplies** (**UPSs**), proper storage media care, and precautions against excess dust, heat, and static are important. **Ruggedized PCs** can be used when necessary. To protect against data loss, backups are essential for both individuals and businesses—most businesses should also develop a **disaster recovery plan** for natural and man-made disasters. Encryption can be used to protect individual files and the content of data stored on a storage medium. **Full disk encryption** (**FDE**) and **self-encrypting hard drives** can be used to automatically encrypt all the content located on a hard drive.

SOFTWARE PIRACY AND DIGITAL COUNTERFEITING

Chapter Objective 3:
Define software piracy and digital counterfeiting and explain how they may be prevented.

Software piracy (the unauthorized copying of a computer program) and **digital counterfeiting** (creating fake copies of currency and other resources) are illegal in the United States. They cost manufacturers billions of dollars each year, and some of these costs are passed on to law-abiding consumers. Various tools, such as consumer education, holograms, and software activation procedures, can be used to prevent software piracy. Many businesses are also aggressively pursuing pirates in court in an attempt to reduce piracy. The government has various methods in place to prevent digital counterfeiting of currency, such as using difficult-to-reproduce materials and features like *security threads* and *watermarks*.

WHY BE CONCERNED ABOUT INFORMATION PRIVACY?

Chapter Objective 4:
Explain what information privacy is and why computer users should be concerned about it.

There are a number of important **privacy** concerns related to computers and the Internet. For instance, **information privacy** refers to the rights of individuals and companies to control how information about them is collected and used. Privacy issues affect the lives of everyone and common concerns include the privacy of Web site activities and e-mail messages, as well as the high number of security breaches on systems that contain personal information. Businesses need to be concerned with protecting the privacy of the personal information they keep, because data breaches are costly, and can result in lawsuits and damaged reputations.

DATABASES, ELECTRONIC PROFILING, SPAM, AND OTHER MARKETING ACTIVITIES

The extensive use of **marketing databases** and **government databases** brings concern to both privacy organizations and individuals. Information in marketing databases is frequently sold to companies and other organizations; information in some government databases is available to the public. Some database information can be retrieved via the Web. **Electronic profiling** is the collection of diverse information about an individual. An organization's **privacy policy** addresses how any personal information submitted to that company will be used. Another privacy issue individuals need to be concerned about centers on the vast amount of **spam** (unsolicited bulk e-mail) that occurs today.

Protecting your e-mail address is one of the best ways to avoid spam. A **throw-away e-mail address** can be used for any activities that may result in spam; then your permanent personal e-mail address can be used only for those communications that should not result in spam. Before providing any personal information via a Web page, it is a good idea to review the Web site's privacy policy to see if the information will be shared with other organizations. Consider whether or not the Web site is requesting too much personal information, and only provide the required data. Do not provide personal details in chat rooms and personal Web sites. Unless you do not mind spam or are using a throw-away e-mail address, avoid completing online forms, such as to enter sweepstakes.

E-mail filters can be used to manage an individual's e-mail; specifically **spam filters** are used to identify possible spam. To reduce the amount of spam, junk mail, online ads, and telemarketing calls received, an individual can **opt out**. It's possible that more marketing activities in the future will require individuals to **opt in** in order to participate. Individuals and businesses should be cautious when disposing of old hardware, such as hard drives and CDs, that contain sensitive data. Minimally, hard drives should be *wiped* clean; CDs, DVDs, and other media to be disposed of should be shredded.

Chapter Objective 5:
Describe some privacy concerns regarding databases, electronic profiling, spam, and telemarketing, and identify ways individuals can protect their privacy.

ELECTRONIC SURVEILLANCE AND MONITORING

Computer monitoring software that can record an individual's computer use is viewed as a privacy violation by some, as is the increased use of **video surveillance** in public locations. Although it is allowed by law, some employees view **employee monitoring** (such as monitoring computer use, telephone calls, and an individual's location using **proximity cards** or video surveillance) as an invasion of their privacy. **Presence technology**—the ability of one computer on a network to know the status and location of another computer on that network—allows users of computers, mobile phones, and other communications devices to determine the availability of other individuals before contacting them.

To protect the privacy of employees and customers, businesses have a responsibility to keep private information about their employees, the company, and their customers safe. Firewalls, password-protected files, and encryption can help secure this information. Businesses have the responsibility to monitor employee activities in order to ensure that employees are performing the jobs they are being paid to do, are not causing lost business, and are not leaving the company open to lawsuits. To inform employees of allowable activities, an *employee policy* or code of conduct should be developed and distributed to employees. For the highest level of privacy while at the workplace, employees should perform only work-related activities on the job.

Chapter Objective 6:
Discuss several types of electronic surveillance and monitoring and list ways individuals can protect their privacy.

COMPUTER SECURITY AND PRIVACY LEGISLATION

Although computer security and privacy are viewed as extremely important issues, legislating these issues is difficult due to ongoing changes in technology, jurisdictional issues, and varying opinions. Some legislation related to computer security has been enacted; new legislation is being considered on a regular basis.

Chapter Objective 7:
Discuss the status of computer security and privacy legislation.

REVIEW ACTIVITIES

KEY TERM MATCHING

Instructions: Match each key term on the left with the definition on the right that best describes it.

a. digital counterfeiting

b. disaster recovery plan

c. full disk encryption (FDE)

d. information privacy

e. presence technology

f. proximity card

g. software piracy

h. surge suppressor

i. system failure

j. uninterruptible power supply (UPS)

1. _____ A device containing a built-in battery that provides continuous power to a PC and other connected components when the electricity goes out.

2. _____ A device that protects a computer system from damage due to electrical fluctuations.

3. _____ A written plan that describes the steps a company will take following the occurrence of a disaster.

4. _____ An identification card with built-in smart card capabilities; used for access purposes, as well as for location monitoring.

5. _____ Technology that enables one computing device (such as a desktop PC, handheld computer, or smart phone) to locate and identify the current status of another device on the same network.

6. _____ The complete malfunction of a computer system.

7. _____ The rights of individuals and companies to control how information about them is collected and used.

8. _____ A technology that encrypts everything stored on a storage medium automatically, without any user interaction.

9. _____ The unauthorized copying of a computer program.

10. _____ The use of computers or other types of digital equipment to make illegal copies of currency, checks, collectibles, and other items.

SELF-QUIZ

Instructions: Circle **T** if the statement is true, **F** if the statement is false, or write the best answer in the space provided. **Answers for the self-quiz are located in the References and Resources Guide at the end of the book.**

1. **T F** As long as a business owns one legal copy of a software program, it can install that program on as many computers as desired without fear of retribution.

2. **T F** Electronic profiling is the act of using electronic means to collect a variety of in-depth information about an individual, such as name, address, income, and buying habits.

3. **T F** Encryption can be used for privacy purposes in addition to security purposes.

4. **T F** One way of safeguarding your e-mail address is to use a single e-mail address for all Internet activity, including personal communications, online shopping, and completing online surveys.

5. **T F** Very few major U.S. companies monitor the online activities of their employees.

6. A(n) _____ plan can help a business get operational again following a fire, act of sabotage, or similar disaster.

7. Color copying money is an example of _____.

8. An e-mail _____ can be used to route suspected spam automatically into a separate e-mail folder.

9. If you _____, you are requesting that you be removed from marketing activities or that your information not be shared with other companies; if you _____, you are requesting to participate.

10. Match each precaution with the security risk it is designed to protect against and write the corresponding number in the blank to the left of each security risk.

a. _____ Digital counterfeiting
b. _____ Hardware theft
c. _____ Privacy breach
d. _____ System damage
e. _____ Software piracy

1. Hologram
2. Encryption
3. Surge suppressor
4. Security thread
5. Cable lock

1. Match each privacy risk with its related term and write the corresponding number in the blank to the left of each term.

a. _____ Throw-away e-mail address
b. _____ Do Not Call Registry
c. _____ Proximity card
d. _____ Riding public transportation

1. Employee monitoring
2. Video surveillance
3. Telemarketing
4. Spam

2. Supply the missing words to complete the following statements.

a. A(n) _____ card can be used to determine the physical location of an employee, as well as grant the employee access to a facility, network, or computer.

b. _____ refers to the ability to locate the current status of an individual via a network.

3. List two precautions that can be taken while traveling with a portable PC to guard against its theft.

4. Explain the purpose of an uninterruptible power supply (UPS) and how it differs in function from a surge suppressor.

5. Think of one computer-related security or privacy risk you have encountered recently. Describe the risk and list at least one precaution that could be taken to minimize that risk.

According to a study by the Missouri School of Journalism at Columbia's University of Missouri, many Internet users are willing to accept spam in return for a discount on their ISP bill, and the study found that the users paying the highest rates for Internet access were more willing to trade spam for monetary savings. With the amount of spam-blocking taking place at the ISP level and the proliferation of third-party software to block spam, pop-up ads, and other forms of onscreen marketing, it makes one wonder what the long-term effect will be on online advertising and the Web in general. If these types of marketing techniques eventually become unprofitable, will free Web content begin to disappear? Is paying Internet users to receive spam or other types of advertisements a viable option? Would you be willing to pay higher rates for Internet access or pay for an increasing amount of Web content if you were guaranteed an ad-free and spam-free environment? Just as with television, some amount of advertising is typically necessary in order to support free content. What do you think is the optimal balance for the Web?

BALANCING ACT

PERSONAL PRIVACY VS. THE GOVERNMENT'S RIGHT TO KNOW

It has been several years since Sun Microsystems' co-founder and CEO Scott McNealy delivered his famous statement about consumer privacy: "You have zero privacy anyway. Get over it." Since then, as more and more of our personal data has become centralized and shared at an astounding rate, the privacy debate has escalated. What amount of personal privacy should individuals demand today? Have we given up some right to privacy by using the Internet and other tools that have added convenience to our lives? And, more importantly in this time of national insecurity, will giving the government access to more data about us as individuals really help to protect us and the country as a whole?

Most people would go along with the statement that the government needs some information about us to do its job. Certain agencies need to know where we live, how much money we make, and if we have a criminal record. But does the government need to know where we shop, what Web sites we visit, and what we say in our personal e-mail messages? Some individuals might believe that the government has the right to know anything about us if it helps to prevent crime and terrorism in order to provide a safer society in which to live. Others might believe that trading privacy for an additional sense of security is unacceptable.

Accepting the fact that data about individuals is going to be collected and stored on computers today, some privacy advocates want us to think about protecting specific types of data (such as social security numbers) that can be used to harm individuals (such as through identity theft), rather than trying to protect all personal data. For example, most individuals probably would not object to some personal information—such as their listed telephone numbers—being available over the Internet. However, many probably would object to their medical records becoming public knowledge.

YOUR TURN

Give some thought to the balance between personal privacy and the government's right to know and form an opinion on this issue. Consider the following when forming your opinion and be prepared to discuss your position (in class, via an online class discussion group, in a class chat room, or via a class blog) or to write a short paper expressing your opinion, depending on your instructor's directions.

- Do you think the level of personal privacy that most individuals view as essential has shifted in the last few years? Why or why not?

- Should the government be given access to all information it feels is needed to protect its citizens? To protect the country? Is there any personal information that you believe should be able to remain private no matter what? What about your phone records, e-mail exchanges, and Web-surfing activities? If you are not being investigated for a crime, should the government be able to access this information if it believes it is in the interest of national security or can prevent a crime?

- The technology now exists to implant a microchip under an individual's skin so that his or her personal data, such as identity and medical history, can be obtained by emergency room or law enforcement personnel using a special scanner. What is your opinion about this technology? Do you view it as a possible replacement for identification cards, such as driver's licenses and medical ID cards? What if consumer applications (such as being able to unlock your house or log on to your computer) or safety applications (such as ensuring only company airline pilots use the controls of an aircraft) were added? Would that change your opinion of this technology? Why or why not?

PROJECTS

1. **Electronic Health Records** The use of electronic health records (EHRs) is growing rapidly. Proponents view EHRs as a means to deliver better care more efficiently. Some privacy advocates are concerned about the possible security breaches of servers containing digital private medical information.

   For this project, research the current use of EHRs. What are the benefits? Are EHRs widely used? Have you ever filled out a digital patient information form or other medical document via a computer? If so, share your experience. Do you have any privacy concerns about your medical history being stored on a computer that, potentially, could be accessed by a hacker or other unauthorized individual? Do you think the risk of a privacy breach is higher with EHRs as compared with the records contained in conventional paper file folders? At the conclusion of your research, prepare a one-page summary of your findings and submit it to your instructor.

HOT TOPICS

2. **E-Voting** E-voting—casting ballots online or via an electronic e-voting machine—has been surrounded by controversy. Concerns include: Are e-voting machines secure and accurate? How will online voting systems prevent someone from voting as another individual? Can an online voting system be adequately protected against hackers and viruses? With either method, can an accurate recount be performed?

   For this project, research the current status of e-voting. Have universal standards been developed for all e-voting machines used in the United States or is that decision made on a state-by-state basis? Form an opinion about the use of e-voting machines and online voting. Would you be comfortable casting your vote via an e-voting machine? How about online? At some point, do you think online voting will become the norm? If so, how would you suggest handling individuals who have no Internet access available to them on Election Day? At the conclusion of your research, submit your findings and opinions to your instructor in the form of a short paper, no more than two pages in length.

SHORT ANSWER/ RESEARCH

3. **Browser Privacy Settings** There are a variety of settings in a Web browser that pertain to privacy, such as cookie, cache, and history settings.

   For this project, find a computer (either your own or one in a school computer lab or at your local public library) on which you are permitted to change the Internet options (ask permission first if you are not sure if these actions are allowed) and perform the following tasks:

   a. Open Internet Explorer and use the *Internet Options* option on the Tools menu to check the current settings on the General and Privacy tabs. Find the options to clear the temporary Internet files (cache, history list, and cookie files).

   b. Visit at least five different Web sites to build a history and cookie list. You may want to go to an e-commerce site and add items to your shopping cart (but don't check out) or personalize a portal page, such as MSNBC.com or iGoogle.com.

   c. Find the appropriate menu option or toolbar button to display your history list. Are the Web sites you visited listed? Use the Internet Options dialog box to view the cookie files. Were new cookies added during your session? If so, are they all from the Web sites you visited, or are any of them third-party cookies?

   d. Delete all temporary Internet files (cache, history list, and cookie), sign out of any personalized pages, and close the browser window. Prepare a short summary of your work to submit to your instructor.

HANDS ON

WRITING ABOUT COMPUTERS

4. Fourth Amendment   The Fourth Amendment to the U.S. Constitution is frequently mentioned in the privacy debate.

   For this project, locate the text of the Fourth Amendment and analyze it. Does it address personal privacy? If you think so, which part of the amendment applies to personal privacy? If you do not think it addresses privacy, why do you think this amendment is quoted so often in proprivacy arguments? Next, find at least two articles (either in print or online) in which the Fourth Amendment is mentioned in relation to personal privacy. In what context is the Fourth Amendment used in the articles? Do you agree with the stated opinions? Why or why not? Do you believe the Fourth Amendment guarantees all Americans privacy? Submit your findings and opinions to your instructor in the form of a short paper, not more than two pages in length.

PRESENTATION/ DEMONSTRATION

5. Privacy Policy Flip-Flops   Although a company's privacy policy may look acceptable when you read it before submitting personal information to that company, there is no guarantee that the policy will not be changed.

   For this project, locate three different privacy policies on Web sites, analyze them, and compare them. Do the policies specify what personal information might be shared and with whom? Do the organizations reserve the right to change their policies at a later time without notice? If so, will they try to notify consumers? Do any of the policies allow for any sharing of data to third-party organizations? If so, is the data personally identifiable, and can customers opt out? Form an opinion regarding a company's right to change its privacy policy and the impact such a change may have on customer loyalty. Share your findings with the class in the form of a short presentation. The presentation should not exceed 10 minutes and should make use of one or more presentation aids, such as the chalkboard, handouts, overhead transparencies, or a computer-based slide presentation (your instructor may provide additional requirements). You may also be asked to submit a summary of the presentation to your instructor.

GROUP DISCUSSION

6. Security Camera Networks   As discussed in the chapter, live surveillance cameras are being used at an increasing number of public locations. Some view this as a valid crime prevention tool; others think it is an invasion of privacy. Does the government have the responsibility to use every means possible to protect the country and its citizens? Or do citizens have the right not to be watched in public? One objection stated about these systems is "It's not the same as a cop on the corner. This is a cop on every corner." What if it were a live police officer at each video camera location instead of a camera? Would that be more acceptable from a privacy standpoint? If people do not plan to commit criminal acts in public, should they be concerned that law enforcement personnel may see them?

   For this project, form an opinion about the impact of public video surveillance on our society and who should have the final say regarding how (or if) it will be used. Be prepared to discuss your position (in class, via an online class discussion group, in a class chat room, or via a class blog, depending on your instructor's directions). You may also be asked to write a short paper expressing your opinion.

7. **Gossip Sites** A recent trend on college campuses today is the use of campus gossip sites, where students can post campus related news, rumors, and basic gossip. These sites were originally set up to promote free speech and to allow participants to publish comments anonymously without repercussions from school administrators, professors, and other officials. However, they are now being used to post vicious comments about others. What do you think of campus gossip sites? Is it ethical to post a rumor about another individual on these sites? How would you feel if you read a posting about yourself on a gossip site? School administrators cannot regulate the content since the sites are not sponsored or run by the college, and federal law prohibits Web hosts from being liable for the content posted by its users. Is this ethical? What if a posting leads to a criminal act, such as a rape, murder, or suicide? Who, if anyone, should be held responsible?

     For this project, form an opinion about the ethical ramifications of gossip Web sites and be prepared to discuss your position (in class, via an online class discussion group, in a class chat room, or via a class blog, depending on your instructor's directions). You may also be asked to write a short paper expressing your opinion.

ETHICS IN ACTION

8. **Google Maps and Privacy** While many individuals find the new Street View feature available for many cities in Google Maps useful and interesting, it raises privacy concerns for others. Currently available for about 50 cities in the United States, Street View allows users to see 360-degree photographs of cities from any street or intersection they select. Included in the photographs is whatever content (including cars and people) that happened to be visible when the photographs were taken. The accompanying video clip discusses Google's Street View and some of the privacy concerns that have arisen due to this feature.

     Go to www.course.com/uccs/ch5 to watch the "Google 'Street View' Raises Privacy Concerns" video clip. After watching the video, think about the impact of posting images of public locations on the Web. Is this an invasion of privacy for the individuals photographed? The high quality of many of the photographs allows individuals to be identified by their appearance and cars by their license plate numbers. Does this impact your opinion? What if an individual is photographed in a possibly compromising moment, such as passing in front of an adult bookstore? Is it ethical for Google to use photographs in which individuals are personally identifiable? How would you feel if your image appeared on a Google map?

     Express your viewpoint: What is the impact of using photographs of public locations on reference Web sites like Google Maps?

     Use the video clip and the questions previously asked as a foundation for your response. Be prepared to discuss your position (in class, via an online class discussion group, in a class chat room, or via a class blog) or to write a short paper stating and supporting your viewpoint on the issue, depending on your instructor's direction. You may also be asked to do research and provide resources to support your point of view on this issue.

VIDEO VIEWPOINT

9. **Interactive Activities** Go to www.course.com/uccs/ch5 and work the interactive **Crossword Puzzle**, listen to the **Podcasts** and watch the **Online Videos** associated with this chapter, and explore the **Further Exploration** links. In addition, work the following interactive **Student Edition Labs**.

   - Backing up Your Computer
   - Maintaining a Hard Drive
   - Protecting Your Privacy Online

     If you have a SAM user profile, you have access to even more interactive content. Log in to your SAM account and go to your assignments page to see what your instructor has assigned for this chapter.

WEB ACTIVITIES

10. **Test Yourself** Go to www.course.com/uccs/ch5 and review the **Online Study Guide** for Chapter 5, then test your knowledge of the terms and concepts in this chapter by completing the **Key Term Matching** exercise, the **Self-Quiz**, the **Exercises**, and the **Practice Test**.

My Background . . .

My current position at eBay—Dean of eBay Education—is unique, slightly unorthodox, and best understood in the context of my history with the company. I was originally a user on eBay in the very early days (1996) and spent a lot of time assisting other buyers and sellers on eBay's one chat board. My posts came to the attention of eBay founder Pierre Omidyar who offered me a job as eBay's first customer support rep. I continued to be an active member of the eBay community along with my new duties at the time, which included assisting and teaching buyers, sellers, and eBay employees how to use eBay. Over time, I also became an eBay spokesperson, lead instructor of our eBay University program, author of the *Official eBay Bible* (now in its third edition), and host of eBay Radio.

The skills that proved to be most critical during my eleven-year tenure at eBay (and I should say I am still refining them) besides the obvious knowledge of the eBay Web site, our policies, and the basics of business would be diplomacy, empathy, civility, and a strong sense of self-deprecating humor.

It's Important to Know . . .

The basic principles behind successful e-commerce are no different than those behind traditional offline commerce. For example, the most valuable asset for any business, online or offline, is the customer. This is especially true for e-commerce where the competition for customers is fierce. Although the technologies and transaction experience for the Web and for traditional retail are markedly different, the standard, tried-and-true business basics (such as business planning, inventory procurement and management, and marketing) are as crucial to e-commerce as they are to traditional business.

The importance of an easy-to-use, well-designed, and appealing Web site. All of the inventory in the world is for naught if the buyer cannot search through it and purchase it with ease.

Online commerce technologies are constantly changing. What is cutting edge today will soon be passé. Anyone who makes his or her living online absolutely must stay on top of all online marketplace technology advances and adopt and implement as necessary. Consumers in general—and online consumers in particular—are much more business and technology savvy than they were a mere 5 years ago. Demanding consumers will have little or no patience for online businesses that do not provide the best possible shopping experience.

> **"All of the inventory in the world is for naught if the buyer cannot search through it and purchase it with ease."**

Jim Griffith, aka "Griff," is the Dean of eBay Education, a roving eBay ambassador, an eBay spokesperson, the host of eBay Radio, and the author of *The Official eBay Bible*. An enthusiastic eBay buyer and seller since 1996, Griff spends nearly all his waking hours teaching others how to use eBay effectively, safely, and profitably, and spreading the word about eBay across print, radio, and TV. Griff has worked for eBay for 11 years.

Demanding consumers will have little or no patience for online businesses that do not provide the best possible shopping experience.

How I Use this Technology . . .

Besides working for eBay, I am an avid consumer and seller online. I make at least one online purchase a day and I always have a selection of items up for sale (on eBay). My online e-commerce activity along with my job of instructing and assisting buyers and sellers to navigate and utilize eBay and PayPal requires an extensive working knowledge of and familiarity with our own Web sites (eBay and PayPal).

What the Future Holds . . .

The Internet revolution has in many ways changed the nature of human commerce forever. The most important impact of the Internet revolution has been the empowerment of the consumer. Never before has the buyer had so much control over the direction of the marketplace. This will only increase as time goes on, and the businesses that acknowledge this new reality and plan accordingly are the ones that will survive and thrive.

In the future, more brick-and-mortar business owners will adopt the Internet as a primary or secondary channel for their businesses. In addition, more small businesses will start up solely on the Internet as the cost of entry into the online marketplace continues to drop and the gap in the costs of starting an online and offline business continues to grow. This will lead to even more choices for the online consumer, who will continue to exert increasing service demands and pricing pressure on online sellers.

However, as the Internet becomes more a part of our day to day lives, the idea of the Internet as a unique environment will start to disappear, especially as access to the Internet becomes cheaper and more widespread (for example, embedded in appliances, cell phones, media devices, and even the walls of our homes!). Just like technologies before it (such as telegraph, telephone, radio, and television), we will soon take the Internet for granted as it matures and eventually becomes completely entwined within the matrix of our daily lives.

My Advice to Students . . .

Unless you're interested in pursuing a career in computer science, engineering, or programming, an academic study of the inner workings of the Internet or computers will not be a requirement for a career in an Internet-based industry. However, Internet companies will have an ever-increasing demand for inventive product marketing personnel, product designers, and intellectual property attorneys.

That said, whatever career you pursue, never forget that the direction of online commerce (and the world in general) is toward more control in the hands of the individual. Adjust your career path accordingly!

Discussion Question

Jim Griffith views the online buyer as an extremely influential part of the e-commerce marketplace. Think of online purchases you have made. How did your buying decision differ from shopping locally? What factors influenced your final decision? How does the increased number of online sources for products impact the online marketplace? Do consumers have more influence over online stores than over brick-and-mortar stores? Why or why not? If you were starting a business, would you have an e-commerce presence? A brick-and-mortar presence? Both? Be prepared to discuss your position (in class, via an online class discussion group, in a class chat room, or via a class blog, depending on your instructor's directions). You may also be asked to write a short paper expressing your opinion.

>**For more information on eBay, visit www.ebay.com. For more information about e-commerce, read** *FutureShop* **by Daniel Nissanoff, and for more information about effective, safe, and successful buying or selling on eBay, refer to** *The Official eBay Bible* **by Jim "Griff" Griffith.**

6

Intellectual Property Rights and Ethics

OUTLINE

LEARNING OBJECTIVES

After completing this chapter, you will be able to do the following:

1. Understand the concept of intellectual property rights and how they relate to computer use.

2. Explain what is meant by the term "ethics."

3. Provide several examples of unethical behavior in the use of intellectual property and in computer-related matters.

4. Explain what computer hoaxes and digital manipulation are and how they relate to computer ethics.

5. Understand how ethics can impact business practices and decision making.

6. Discuss the current status of legislation related to intellectual property rights and ethics.

OVERVIEW

Like any fast-paced revolution, the computer revolution has impacted our society in more ways than could have been imagined when it first began. Computers often make daily tasks easier, but they also can make it easier to perform some types of illegal or unethical acts. For example, computers can be used to launch computer viruses, create high-quality illegal copies of software programs and music CDs, and copy information from a Web page and present it as original work. However, just because technology enables us to do something, does that make it right? Is legality the only measuring stick, or are there some acts that are legal but still morally or ethically wrong? Is there only one set of ethics, or can ethics vary from person to person? This chapter continues where Chapter 5 left off—exploring computer-related societal issues. Two important issues—intellectual property rights and ethics—are discussed in this chapter; other societal issues are included in Chapter 7.

The chapter begins with a look at a legal issue that all computer users should be aware of—intellectual property rights. The different types of intellectual property rights are discussed along with what types of property each one protects. Next is a discussion of ethics, including what they are and a variety of ethical issues surrounding computer use by individuals and businesses. Topics include the ethical use of copyrighted material, ethical uses of resources and information, unethical use of digital manipulation, ethical business practices and decision making, and the impact of cultural differences with respect to ethics and business decisions. The chapter closes with a look at legislation related to the issues discussed in this chapter. ■

PODCAST

Go to **www.course.com/uccs/ch6** to download or listen to the "Expert Insight on Systems" podcast.

INTELLECTUAL PROPERTY RIGHTS

Intellectual property rights are the legal rights to which the creators of *intellectual property*—original creative works—are entitled. Intellectual property rights indicate who has the right to use, perform, or display the creative work and what can legally be done with that work. In addition, intellectual property rights determine how long the creator retains rights to the property, if the rights can be renewed, if the property ever reverts to the public domain, and other related restrictions. Examples of intellectual property include original music compositions, music, and movies; paintings, computer graphics, and other works of art; poetry, books, and other types of written works; symbols, names, and designs used in conjunction with a business; architectural drawings; and inventions. Intellectual property can be created and the appropriate intellectual property rights claimed by individuals or by companies or other organizations. The three main types of intellectual property rights are *copyrights*, *trademarks*, and *patents*. Copyrights, trademarks, and patents are issued by individual countries and may not be recognized by other countries, depending on the type of intellectual property and the countries involved; U.S. intellectual property rights are discussed in more detail next.

>**Intellectual property rights.** The legal rights to which creators of original creative works (such as artistic or literary works, inventions, corporate logos, and more) are entitled.

BOOK COPYRIGHT NOTICES

© Red Lobster. All rights reserved.

WEB SITE COPYRIGHT NOTICES

FIGURE 6-1
Copyright statements.
Statements such as these are often included on books, Web sites, and other copyrighted works.

ONLINE VIDEO

Go to **www.course.com/uccs/ch6** to watch the "Google Book Search" video clip.

FURTHER EXPLORATION

Go to **www.course.com/uccs/ch6** for links to further information about intellectual property rights.

Copyrights

A **copyright** is a form of protection available to the creator of an original artistic, musical, or literary work, such as a book, movie, software program, musical composition, or painting. It gives the copyright holder the exclusive right to publish, reproduce, distribute, perform, or display the work. A major revision to U.S. copyright legislation was the *1976 Copyright Act*. This act extended copyright protection to nonpublished works, so, immediately after creating a work in some type of material form (such as on paper, film, videotape, or a digital storage medium), the creator automatically owns the copyright of that work. Consequently, the creator is entitled to copyright protection of that work and has the right to make a statement, such as "Copyright © 2009 John Smith. All rights reserved." Although works created in the United States after March 1, 1989 are not required to display a copyright notice to retain their copyright protection, it is wise to display this type of copyright statement on a published work (see Figure 6-1) to remind others that the work is protected by copyright law and that any use must comply with copyright law. Only the creator of a work (or his or her employer if the work is created as a *work for hire*—that is, within the scope of employment) can rightfully claim copyright. Copyrights can be registered with the *U.S. Copyright Office*. Although registration is not required for copyright protection, it does offer an advantage if the need to prove ownership of a copyright ever arises, such as during a copyright-infringement lawsuit. Most countries offer some copyright protection to works registered in other countries.

Anyone wishing to use copyrighted materials must first obtain permission from the copyright holder and pay any required fee. One exception is the legal concept of *fair use*, which permits limited duplication and use of a portion of copyrighted material for certain specific purposes, such as criticism, commentary, news reporting, teaching, and research. For example, a teacher may legally read a copyrighted poem for discussion in a poetry class, and a news photographer may take a photograph of a newly installed sculpture to show on the evening news. Copyrights apply to both published and unpublished works and last until 70 years after the creator's death. Copyrights for works registered by an organization or as anonymous works last 95 years from the date of publication or 120 years from the date of creation, whichever is shorter.

It is important to realize that purchasing a copyrighted item—such as a book, painting, or movie—does not change the copyright protection afforded to the creator of that item. Although you have purchased the right to use the item, you cannot legally duplicate it or portray it as your own creation. Some of the most widely publicized copyright-infringement issues today center around individuals illegally distributing copyright-protected music and movies via the Internet, as discussed later in this chapter.

To protect their rights, some creators of digital content such as art, music, photographs, and movies, use **digital watermarks**—a subtle alteration of digital content that is not noticeable when the work is viewed or played but that identifies the copyright holder. Digital watermarks are used with images, music, videos, TV shows, and more to identify their copyright holders, their authorized distributors, and other important information, as discussed more in the How It Works box. The market for digital watermarking technology is expected to grow from about $171 million in 2008 to nearly $600 million by 2012, according to one study. Other creators of digital content use **digital rights management (DRM) software** to control the use of the work. For instance, DRM used in conjunction

---

>**Copyright.** The legal right to sell, publish, or distribute an original artistic or literary work; is held by the creator of a work as soon as it exists in physical form. >**Digital watermark.** A subtle alteration of digital content that is not noticeable when the work is viewed or played, but that identifies the copyright holder. >**Digital rights management (DRM) software.** Software used to protect and manage the rights of creators of digital content, such as art, music, photographs, and movies.

HOW IT WORKS

Digital Watermarking

A *digital watermark* is a digital rights management (DRM) tool that can be used to identify the copyright holder of a creative work. Digital watermarks are added to works using software and are designed to be completely imperceptible to people; for example, the digital watermark for an image might consist of slight changes to the brightness of a specific pattern of pixels. Digital watermarks are easily read by software; for instance, the digital watermark for the photo shown in the accompanying figure can be viewed using a compatible image editing program (as shown in the figure) or using a Web browser with a special plug-in (the watermark shows up as an icon displayed on the photo that can be clicked to view the information contained in the watermark). The purpose of digital watermarks is to give digital content a unique identity that remains intact even if the work is copied, edited, compressed, or otherwise manipulated.

The use of digital watermarks is growing. For instance, they are currently being used to trace pirated movies and music back to the original source, such as to identify the theater in which a pirated movie was videotaped illegally; to identify and track promotional prerelease music tracks and screening copies of upcoming feature films leaked onto the Internet; to track where and when TV programs and commercials are running to help broadcasters evaluate the reach of their programming and advertisers evaluate the effectiveness of their marketing campaigns; and to identify authorized retailers for MP3 files being sold online. Future applications include using digital watermark technology with multimedia content to facilitate and enhance the legal use of that content. For example, it can be used with P2P systems to identify audio or video files that can be legally shared and with online music to enable individuals to easily download tracks of songs they hear that they would like to purchase, as well as to get local concert information or buy concert tickets for that band.

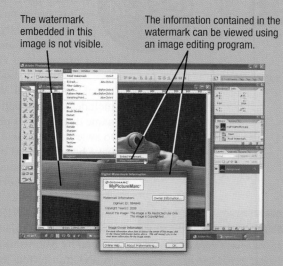

The watermark embedded in this image is not visible.

The information contained in the watermark can be viewed using an image editing program.

Digital watermarks are invisibly embedded into digital content, but the information they contain can be viewed using appropriate software.

with business documents (called *enterprise rights management*) can protect a sensitive business document by controlling usage of that document, such as who can view, print, or copy it; DRM is also used with some content (such as movies and music) downloaded from the Internet, as discussed shortly.

Trademarks

A **trademark** is a word, phrase, symbol, or design (or a combination of words, phrases, symbols, or designs) that identifies and distinguishes one product or service from another. A trademark used to identify a service is sometimes called a *service mark*. Trademarks that are claimed but not registered with the *U.S. Patent and Trademark Office (USPTO)* can use the mark ™; nonregistered service marks can use the symbol ℠. The symbol ® is reserved for registered trademarks and service marks. Trademarks for products usually appear on the product packaging with the appropriate trademark symbol; service marks are typically

>**Trademark.** A word, phrase, symbol, or design that identifies goods or services.

FIGURE 6-2
Examples of
trademarked logos.

used in the advertising of a service, since there is no product on which the mark can be printed. Trademarked words and phrases—such as iPod®, Chicken McNuggets®, Windows Vista™, and FedEx 3Day℠ Freight—are common; so are trademarked logos (see Figure 6-2). Trademark law also protects domain names that match a company's trademark, such as Amazon.com and Lego.com. Trademarks last 10 years, but can be renewed as many times as desired, as long as they are being used in commerce.

There have been a number of claims of online trademark infringement in recent years, particularly involving domain names that contain, or are similar to, a trademark. For instance, several celebrities—such as Madonna—have fought to be given the exclusive right to use what they consider their rightful domain names (Madonna.com, in this example). Other examples include Microsoft's complaint against another organization using the domain name *microsof.com* and RadioShack's objection to a private individual using *shack.com* for the Web site of his design business.

Typically, disputes such as these are brought to the registry service that registered the name or, ultimately, to the *Arbitration and Mediation Center* of the *World Intellectual Property Organization* (*WIPO*). WIPO is a specialized agency of the United Nations; the Arbitration and Mediation Center attempts to resolve international commercial disputes about intellectual property between private parties. This includes domain name disputes; in fact, WIPO received an average of 180 new domain name dispute cases per month in 2007. During the resolution process, WIPO has the power to award the disputed domain name to the most appropriate party. If the domain appears to have been acquired by someone other than the holder of the trademark for the purpose of harming the trademark holder or selling the domain name at an inflated price—an act referred to as *cybersquatting*—the trademark holder generally prevails. If the current domain name holder has a legitimate reason for using that name and does not appear to be a cybersquatter, WIPO may allow the holder to continue to use that domain name. For instance, WIPO ruled that microsof.com was confusingly similar to the trademark already owned by Microsoft and that its owner had no legitimate interest in that domain name, so WIPO transferred the disputed domain name to Microsoft Corporation. However, the owner of the design business (whose last name is Shackleton and whose nickname is "Shack") was allowed to keep the shack.com domain name because it was ruled that he had a legitimate interest in that name.

The *Anticybersquatting Consumer Protection Act*, which was signed into law in 1999, made cybersquatting illegal and it allows for penalties up to $100,000 for each willful registration of a domain name that infringes on a trademark. Sometimes, determining whether or not a domain name was registered in bad faith is a difficult judgment call. For example, a British individual registered the domain name *iTunes.co.uk* in November 2000, two months before Apple announced its iTunes service. In November 2004, Apple offered to buy the name, but the two parties could not agree on a price (Apple reportedly offered $5,000, but the individual suggested $94,000). Apple filed a formal complaint with Nominet, the British registry for Internet names, and was awarded the domain name in 2005. The reason? The individual offered to sell the domain name to Napster in late 2004 so, even though the individual may have registered the domain name without being aware of the iTunes service and without any cybersquatting intent, it was ruled that his offer to Napster showed "abusive intent," and the domain name was awarded to Apple.

Many recent cybersquatting cases deal with *typosquatting*—registering a domain name that is similar to a trademark or domain name but that is slightly misspelled. For instance, in late 2007 Dell filed a cybersquatting lawsuit against a group of domain registrars for allowing the registration of nearly 1,000 domain names that Dell considers "confusingly similar" to Dell's trademarks, such as the domain name *dellfinacncialservices.com* which is very similar to Dell's *dellfinancialservices.com* domain name used to access one of its Web sites.

Patents

Unlike copyrights (which protect artistic and literary works) and trademarks (which protect a company's logo and brand names), a **patent** protects inventions by granting exclusive rights of an invention to its inventor for a period of 20 years. A patented invention is typically a unique product, but it can also be a process or procedure that provides a new way of doing something or that offers a new technical solution to a problem. Like trademarks, U.S. patents are issued by the U.S. Patent and Trademark Office (USPTO); a recent patent issued for a new Apple portable digital media player is shown in Figure 6-3.

The number of patent applications—particularly for computer- or Internet-related products—has skyrocketed in recent years. Patents have also been granted for Internet business methods and models, such as Priceline.com's name-your-own-price business model and Amazon.com's one-click purchase procedure. When a product or business model is patented, no other organization can duplicate it without paying a royalty to the patent holder or risking prolonged patent litigation. There have been many objections to some of the Internet business model patents that have been granted and some of these patents, including Amazon's one-click patent, have been challenged. Although several of Amazon's claims to its patent were initially rejected in late 2007 by the USPTO, the final outcome of this patent dispute had not been determined at the time of this writing. There has also been a great deal of patent litigation recently surrounding computer technology. For instance, Apple has been sued in several patent infringement lawsuits since its iPhone was released, and Microsoft claimed in 2007 that Linux infringed on many of its patents and is attempting to collect royalties from vendors that use Linux in commercial products, such as with computers, networking hardware, and more.

Patents can be difficult, expensive, and time-consuming to obtain. However, patents can also be very lucrative. For instance, IBM—which has been the top patenting company for 15 consecutive years, was issued over 3,100 patents in 2007, and has over 40,000 U.S. patents—earns an estimated $2 billion per year from its patents.

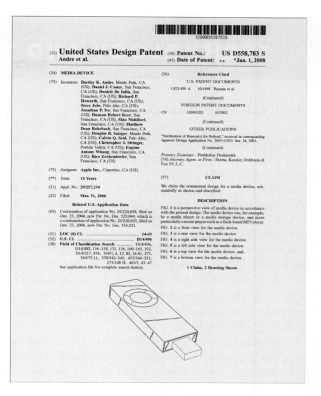

FIGURE 6-3

Patents. The patent shown here is for a new portable digital media player.

ETHICS

The term **ethics** refers to standards of moral conduct. For example, telling the truth is a matter of ethics. An unethical act is not always illegal, although it might be, but illegal acts would be viewed as unethical by most people. For example, purposely lying to a friend is unethical but usually not illegal, while perjuring oneself in a courtroom as a witness is both illegal and unethical. Whether or not criminal behavior is involved, ethics guide our behavior and play an integral role in our lives.

Much more ambiguous than the law, ethical beliefs can vary widely from one individual to another. Ethical beliefs may also vary based on one's religion, country, race, or culture. In addition, different ethical standards can apply to different areas of one's life. For example, *personal ethics* guide an individual's personal behavior and *business ethics* guide an individual's workplace behavior. Ethics with respect to the use of computers are referred to as **computer ethics**. Computer ethics have taken on more significance in recent years

---

TECHNOLOGY AND YOU

Virtual Gold and Income Taxes

While Second Life, World of Warcraft, and other virtual worlds only exist in cyberspace, there is nothing virtual about the money being made off virtual worlds and online multiplayer video games. For instance, the first virtual world millionaire (Ailin Graef, creator of Second Life resident and avatar Anshe Chung) was announced in 2006. In Second Life, Anshe buys and develops virtual real estate, owns virtual shopping malls, and performs other financial transactions for Graef; and Graef announced in late 2006 that her Second Life assets topped $1 million in U.S. dollars (virtual money in Second Life is measured in Linden dollars and has an official market driven exchange rate, approximately 265 Linden dollars per $1 U.S. at the time of this writing).

While a basic account with Second Life is free, buying land, building homes, and properly outfitting your avatar is anything but free. For instance, a pair of new sneakers costs around $0.70 U.S., a plasma TV and leather couch for your avatar's condo costs about $2.15 U.S., a furnished split level retreat costs about $225 U.S., and a region of land (16 acres) is $1,675 U.S. plus another $295 U.S. per month in land-use fees. The amount of real money exchanged in virtual worlds and online multiplayer games like World of Warcraft is staggering—one estimate is more than $1 billion U.S. per year total. In addition to buying and selling goods and services within Second Life, World of Warcraft, and other virtual entities, virtual assets (such as Linden dollars, Second Life islands, World of Warcraft gold, and so on) are listed on eBay all the time. For instance, at the time of this writing, there were 192 items listed in eBay's Second Life category with current bids or offers ranging from $0.99 to over $5,000 U.S.

With this amount of money being exchanged within virtual communities, the issue of taxability has arisen. When virtual goods are cashed out for actual cash, it's pretty clear that the profits should be reported to the IRS as taxable income. But what about taxing virtual profits that never leave the virtual world? This issue is complicated because goods or services obtained through barter or as prizes are taxable under current law and because virtual transactions have real-world value. While the IRS has not yet specifically addressed the issue of whether or not virtual income is taxable until it is exchanged for real-life money and/or for goods or services, the issue is being looked into and is the subject of a study by the Congressional Joint Economic Committee. Some analysts expect to see U.S. income taxes on virtual-only transactions within the next three years. Some countries have already made that decision, such as Australia, which implemented taxes on virtual income in late 2006, and South Korea, which implemented a value-added tax on individuals with virtual income over a certain amount. Whether the U.S. and other countries will follow suit remains to be seen.

The virtual money spent for goods and services in Second Life translates into real-world revenue for the sellers when exchanged for U.S. dollars.

because the proliferation of computers in the home and the workplace provides more opportunities for unethical acts than in the past. The Internet also makes it easy to distribute information that some would view as unethical, such as computer viruses, spam, and spyware.

Whether at home, at work, or at school, individuals encounter ethical issues every day. For example, you may need to make ethical decisions such as whether or not to accept a relative's offer of a free copy of a downloaded song or movie, whether or not to have a friend help you take an online exam, or whether or not to report as taxable income the virtual money you made in Second Life or another virtual world, as discussed in the Technology and You box. As an employee, you may need to decide whether or not to print your child's birthday party invitations on the office color printer, to correct your boss if he or she gives you credit for another employee's idea, or to sneak a look at information that you technically have access to but have no legitimate reason to view. IT employees, in particular, often face this latter ethical dilemma since they typically have both access and the technical ability to retrieve a wide variety of personal and professional information about other employees, such as their salary information, Web surfing history, and personal e-mail. Businesses also deal with a variety of ethical issues in the course of normal business activities—from determining how many computers on which a particular software program should be installed, to identifying how customer and employee information should be used, to deciding business practices. **Business ethics** are the standards of conduct that guide a business's policies, decisions, and actions.

Ethical Use of Copyrighted Material

Both businesses and individuals should be very careful when copying, sharing, or otherwise using copyrighted material to ensure that the material is used in both a legal and an ethical manner. Common types of copyrighted material encountered on a regular basis include software, books, Web-based articles, music, and movies. Software ownership rights were discussed in Chapter 2; the rest of these topics are covered next.

Books and Web-Based Articles

Print-based books, newspaper articles, e-books, Web-based articles, and other types of literary material are all protected by copyright law. Consequently, they cannot be reproduced, presented as one's own original material, or otherwise used in an unauthorized manner. Students, researchers, authors, and other writers need to be especially careful when using literary material as a resource for papers, articles, books, and so forth, to ensure the material is used appropriately and is properly credited to the original author. To present someone else's work as your own is **plagiarism**, which is both a violation of copyright law and an unethical act. It can also get you fired, as some reporters have found out the hard way after faking quotes or plagiarizing content from other newspapers. Some examples of what constitutes and what does not constitute a plagiaristic act are shown in Figure 6-4.

ONLINE VIDEO

Go to **www.course.com/uccs/ch6** to watch the "The Google Interview Process" video clip.

FIGURE 6-4

Examples of what is and what is not normally considered plagiarism.

PLAGIARISM	NOT PLAGIARISM
A student including a few sentences or a few paragraphs written by another author in his term paper without crediting the original author.	A student including a few sentences or a few paragraphs written by another author in his term paper, either indenting the quotation or placing it inside quotation marks, and crediting the original author with a citation in the text or with a footnote or endnote.
A newspaper reporter changing a few words in a sentence or paragraph written by another author and including the revised text in an article without crediting the original author.	A newspaper reporter paraphrasing a few sentences or paragraphs written by another author without changing the meaning of the text, including the revised text in an article, and crediting the original author with a proper citation.
A student copying and pasting information from various online documents to create her research paper without crediting the original authors.	A student copying and pasting information from various online documents and using those quotes in her research paper either indented or enclosed in quotation marks with the proper citations for each author.
A teacher sharing a poem with a class, leading the class to believe the poem was his original work.	A teacher sharing a poem with a class, clearly identifying the poet.

With the widespread availability of online articles and fee-based online term paper services, some students might be tempted to create their papers by copying and pasting excerpts of online content into their documents. But these students should realize that this is plagiarism, and instructors can usually tell when a paper is created in this manner. There are also online sources instructors can use to test the originality of student papers; the results of one such test are shown in Figure 6-5. Most colleges and universities have strict consequences for plagiarism, such as automatically failing the assignment or course, or being expelled from the institution; as Internet-based plagiarism continues to expand to younger and younger students, many middle schools and high schools are developing strict plagiarism policies as well.

TIP

For a review of how to cite online material properly, refer to Figure 3-17 in Chapter 3.

>**Business ethics.** Standards of moral conduct that guide a business's policies, decisions, and actions. >**Plagiarism.** Presenting someone else's work as your own.

Instructor submits electronic versions of student papers; the results are usually available online almost immediately.

The black text was correctly identified as being original.

The red text was correctly identified as being taken from a HowStuffWorks.com online article.

The green text was correctly identified as being taken from a Webopedia.com definition.

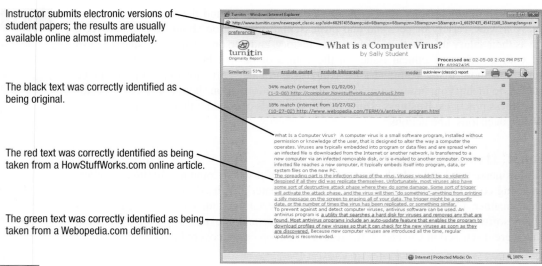

FIGURE 6-5
Results of an online originality test on an essay that contained plagiarized content.

Music

There have been many issues regarding the legal and ethical use of music over the past few years, fueled initially by the emergence and widespread use of Napster and other P2P file sharing sites to illegally download music (as discussed in Chapter 3) and later by recordable and rewritable DVD drives, downloadable movies, and portable digital media players. For instance, downloading a music file from a P2P site without compensating the artist and record label is a violation of copyright laws and an unethical act; so is transferring legally obtained songs to a storage medium to sell or give to others. Partly as a result of the Napster controversy, there are many options for legally downloading music, as discussed in detail in Chapter 3. However, illegal music exchanges are still taking place and law enforcement agencies, as well as the Recording Industry Association of America (RIAA), are pursuing individuals who violate music copyrights. For instance, the FBI's *Operation D-Elite*, which is the first criminal enforcement action targeting individuals who commit copyright infringement via P2P networks, has resulted in seven convictions to date. And the RIAA won its first lawsuit against an individual in late 2007 when a young woman was found guilty of sharing music online and was ordered to pay a total of $222,000 to record companies.

Once an MP3 file or audio CD has been obtained legally, however, most experts agree that it falls within the fair use concept for an individual to transfer those songs to a CD, PC, or portable digital media player, as long as it is for personal, noncommercial use and does not violate a user agreement. However, as discussed in the Inside the Industry box, digital rights management (DRM) tools can limit the legal actions individuals can take with downloaded music and purchased CDs.

ASK THE EXPERT

Cecily Mak, Senior Counsel Legal and Business Affairs, RealNetworks, Inc.

How can an individual know that music available for download via the Internet is legal to download?

Distribution of copyrighted works (including music) without permission from the copyright owners is illegal. The best way to determine whether music available for download is authorized is to evaluate the source—is the Web site from which you want to download the music legitimate? If the Web site has a license from the copyright owners to distribute the musical content, the copyright owner is likely being paid and the download is legal. A good test to consider is whether you have to pay for the music or view advertisements as a condition of getting the music. If the Web site is not authorized to distribute the music (often indicated by a "too good to be true" free MP3 catalog), the download is not legal and you could be held personally liable for copyright infringement. Furthermore, it is never legal to download unauthorized music from peer-to-peer (P2P) systems or pirate sites.

INSIDE THE INDUSTRY

Is Music Digital Rights Management (DRM) Dead?

As more and more intellectual property (such as movies, music, and photos) is distributed in electronic form via the Internet, the need for *digital rights management* (*DRM*)—techniques for managing or protecting the rights of digital creative works—has grown. DRM software can be used to assign usage rights (such as granting the ability to view, copy, or edit) to a creative work and to specify an expiration date after which time the content becomes inaccessible (such as assigning expiration dates for video-on-demand rentals); it may also determine what types of devices can be used to access the work (such as being able to play downloaded music files only on certain types of portable digital media players).

This latter part of DRM has met with some objections from consumers—especially when consumers are not able to transfer songs they have legally downloaded from the Internet to another device for their own personal use. For instance, some DRM systems limit the type of portable digital media players that the music files can be played on and some limit how many times a single song can be copied. In addition, the DRM software used with some subscription-based music services (that permit you to download an unlimited number of songs per month—essentially a music rental service) allows those songs to be played only on a PC or a portable digital media player (you cannot burn them to CDs), and you can play the songs only as long as you are a subscriber. Once you cancel your monthly subscription, you can no longer play the songs that were downloaded via the subscription service, unless you paid the necessary fee to purchase a permanent version of those songs.

These types of restrictions and the incompatibility of music download services have been a great inconvenience for users. In what many digital music consumers view as a step in the right direction, DRM in its current form for music appears to be on its way out. For instance, Apple and Amazon both recently eliminated DRM from songs downloaded from their music stores so the songs can be burned to an unlimited number of CDs and copied to as many portable digital media players as desired. And some digital music stores (such as AmazonMP3 and eMusic—see the accompanying illustration) now offer their songs in the universal MP3 format (instead of a more proprietary format) so they can be played on a wider range of devices.

While music piracy is still a huge issue for the music industry (a recent study estimates that global music piracy costs the U.S. economy $12.5 billion in losses and over 71,000 jobs annually), the music industry has apparently come to the conclusion that DRM, as it has existed for music, doesn't work and negatively impacts sales. While we may see new attempts at music DRM in the future (and other copyright-protection tools, such as digital watermarks, are still commonly used with downloadable music), it is hoped that any music DRM systems implemented in the future will protect the consumers' right to use purchased music as they wish, as long as it is for personal use and doesn't violate copyright laws, to ensure that consumers get the full value for their money.

Movies

Since 1984, when Disney and Universal sued Sony to stop production of the *Betamax* (the first personal VCR), concern about movie piracy has increased dramatically. Obviously, the lawsuit was eventually decided in Sony's favor—the Supreme Court upheld the consumers' rights to record shows for convenience (called *time shifting*), as long as it was for personal use. As a result of this decision, VCR use became commonplace. Interestingly, in direct contrast to the views held by the entertainment industry in 1984, videos have been credited with boosting Hollywood's revenues tremendously in past years. Nevertheless, the entertainment industry continues to be concerned about the ability of consumers to make copies of movies—especially today, since digital content can be duplicated an unlimited number of times without losing quality. The Motion Picture Association of America (MPAA) estimates that losses due to movie piracy worldwide exceed $6 billion per year.

To prevent individuals from making unauthorized copies of feature films purchased on disc or downloaded via the Internet, most of these items contain at least copy protection, if not other types of DRM. Movie pirates, however, can often circumvent copy protection with software and other tools to create illegal copies. Pirated copies of movies are also often created today by videotaping them with a camcorder during a prerelease screening or on the opening day of a movie; this practice has resulted in a vast number of movies becoming illegally available on DVDs and via the Internet at about the same time they arrive in theaters. As a result, Congress passed the *Family Entertainment and Copyright Act of 2005*, which makes transmitting or recording a movie during a performance at a U.S. movie theater illegal. To help identify and prosecute a "cammer," some movie studios now embed invisible digital watermarks in each print released to a theater. The information contained in these watermarks can be used to identify the location where the movie was recorded once a bootleg copy of a movie is discovered. To help develop other technologies essential for the fair distribution and use of digital media, several Hollywood movie studios founded *Motion Picture Laboratories Inc.* (also called *MovieLabs*). MovieLabs provides research and development resources and assistance to universities, businesses, and other entities with innovative ideas or technology to help them bring those technologies to the market.

The access to both authorized and unauthorized copies of movies via the Internet and the widespread use of digital video recorders (DVRs) create new legal and ethical dilemmas for individuals today. If one individual records a television show and then shares it with a friend via the Internet, does that go beyond the concept of fair use? If you run across a Web site from which you can download a copy of a movie not yet out on video or DVD, are you legally at risk if you make the download? What if you watch the movie once and then delete it—are you still in the wrong? What if you download a video-on-demand movie and then share it with a friend? Is that any different, legally or ethically, from sharing a movie rented from a brick-and-mortar video store with a friend before you return it? What about the *place shifting* products on the market, such as the Slingbox, that allow you to view multimedia content from your home PC or DVD at a more convenient location? If you use such a product to transfer a movie or TV show obtained through your cable or satellite TV connection to another location, are you rebroadcasting that content or simply place shifting it? What if you send the content to another individual to watch via his or her PC—is that legal?

FIGURE 6-6

The FBI Anti-Piracy seal.

While the answers to these questions have yet to be unequivocally decided, distributing bootleg copies of movies via the Internet is both illegal and unethical. There have been many local, state, and federal operations in the U.S. in recent years focusing on targeting online piracy of copyrighted software, movies, music, and games. These operations have resulted in several convictions to date, including the first conviction under the Family Entertainment and Copyright Act of 2005 for using a camcorder to make illegal copies of movies. The convicted individual—a teenager—pled guilty to making an unauthorized recording of *Bewitched* in a movie theater in mid-2005, as well as to copyright infringement (for distributing *Bewitched* and one other movie via the Internet). To help remind individuals that piracy is illegal, the FBI introduced an *FBI Anti-Piracy Warning Seal* (see Figure 6-6) that is commonly printed today on movie DVDs, music CDs, and other intellectual properties that are frequently pirated.

Movie piracy arrests are becoming more common in other countries, as well. For instance, a Hong Kong man was convicted in 2005 for distributing three Hollywood movies via a P2P service—the country's first successful action against peer-to-peer file sharing—and Australian police broke up what they believe is the largest-ever movie piracy operation in Australia when they raided a home and seized over 250,000 pirated DVDs and 100 DVD burners. In addition, China—a country where pirated movies have become commonplace in shops and on street stands—may have begun to take music and movie piracy more seriously. For instance, the first joint intellectual property rights investigation by U.S. Immigration and Customs Enforcement and Chinese authorities began in 2004, and Chinese authorities worked with U.S. agents to eventually locate and destroy three warehouses in China being used to distribute counterfeit DVDs to many countries, including the U.S. The ringleader is a U.S. citizen and, after being convicted in China and serving his 15-month prison sentence, was deported to the U.S. where he pled guilty and was sentenced to 45 additional months in U.S. prison. In 2007, a co-conspirator in this operation also pled guilty in a U.S. court and was awaiting sentencing.

The MPAA also recently began pursuing civil litigation against movie pirates. The organization is concentrating mainly on those who create illegal DVDs, but prosecution of those who upload movies to be shared via the Internet is also occurring. To catch people who are sharing movies illegally on the Internet, the MPAA uses special software that monitors file sharing networks to find copyrighted movies and then identifies the responsible individual by using the IP address of the computer being used to share the movie. The movie industry also hires special firms, such as BayTSP, that specialize in monitoring P2P networks, Web sites, and other Internet resources to identify clients' copyrighted material (such as documents, graphics, music, or movie files) being misused on the Internet. These companies typically use automated programs to scan the Web to find intellectual property that the company is charged with protecting. When a company finds a client's file that is being shared illegally, the company can issue an infringement notice to the violator via his or her ISP, and the necessary data can be collected in case the copyright holder decides to pursue legal action.

To prevent the sharing of legally downloaded movies (such as movies obtained through Movielink or another video-on-demand service), many downloaded movies include DRM controls, such as those that prevent the movie from being copied to another medium or that allow the movie to be used only for a specified period of time (such as a 24-hour period beginning when the movie first starts to play). Consumers have some objections to the current movie DRM systems, similar to the objections they have with music DRM systems, and some services (such as TiVo) have changed their systems to allow consumers to transfer video content to other devices (such as a portable computer or a portable digital media player) for convenience.

ASK THE EXPERT

Greg Weir, Webmaster, Tucows

Why should an individual or business pay for shareware?

In short, because it's the right thing to do. You are obligated to pay for shareware if you continue to use it past the end of the trial period. The fact that shareware publishers allow you to try their software on your computer at your leisure so you can be certain the software meets your needs before you pay for it is testament to their belief in the quality of their product.

There are a number of good reasons for paying for shareware beyond personal or business ethics. In some cases the title will cease to function after its trial period or will display an annoying "nag" screen every time you start the program to remind you to pay. In addition, payment allows the publisher to enhance the product, fix bugs, and provide support. Continued use of a shareware product past its trial period without paying for it should rightly be considered theft.

Ethical Use of Resources and Information

There are a variety of resources and types of information, such as school computers, company computers and equipment, and customer or employee information, which can be used in an unethical manner. For example, some employees use company computers for personal use, some students perform dishonest acts while completing assignments or taking exams, and some job applicants provide erroneous or misleading information during the application or interview process.

FIGURE 6-7
A sample code of ethics.

Ethical Use of School or Company Resources

What is considered proper and ethical use of school or company resources may vary from school to school or company to company. To explain what is allowed, many schools and businesses have policies that specify which activities are allowed and which are forbidden. Often, these policies are available as a written document—frequently called a **code of conduct**—included in a student or employee handbook; they are also often available online via an organization's intranet or Web site (a code of conduct was shown in Figure 4-1 in Chapter 4). Policies can vary from organization to organization—for example, one school may allow the use of school PCs to download software programs and another school may not, and one business may allow limited use of the office photocopier or printer for personal use while another may forbid that activity. As a result, all students and employees should make it a point to find out what is considered ethical use of resources at their school or place of business, including what types of computer and Internet activities are considered acceptable, and what personal use (if any) of resources, such as PCs, printers, photocopiers, telephones, and fax machines, is allowed. To enforce its policies, businesses may use employee monitoring techniques, such as those discussed in Chapter 5.

Another common type of code widely used by various industries and organizations is a **code of ethics**. Codes of ethics, such as the one shown in Figure 6-7, summarize the moral guidelines adopted by a particular organization (frequently a professional society) and typically address such issues as honesty, integrity, fairness, responsibility to others, proper use of intellectual property, confidentiality, and accountability. So, while codes of conduct usually address specific activities that can and cannot be performed, codes of ethics cover broader ethical standards of conduct.

Although employees are typically forbidden from revealing confidential or proprietary information to outsiders, a dilemma exists when that information is related to an illegal, an unethical, or a dangerous activity involving the business. Employees who reveal wrongdoing within an organization to the public or to authorities are referred to as *whistle-blowers*. These individuals have varying degrees of protection from retaliation, such as being fired, for whistle-blowing. The type and extent of protection depends on the kind of wrongdoing and the organization involved, as well as the state in which the company and employee are located. The *Sarbanes-Oxley Act* (also called the *Corporate Responsibility Act* and signed into law in mid-2002) provides federal protection for whistle-blowers who report alleged violations of Securities and Exchange Commission rules or any federal law relating to shareholder fraud.

Ethical Use of Employee and Customer Information

While a business may be legally bound by such restrictions as employee confidentiality laws, union contracts, and its customer privacy policy, there are gray areas inside which ethical decisions need to be made. For example, should a specific ISP comply with a request from a foreign government for customer e-mail records or the identity of a customer

FURTHER EXPLORATION

Go to **www.course.com/uccs/ch6** for links to further information about codes of ethics for a variety of industries.

>**Code of conduct.** A policy, often for a school or business, that specifies allowable use of resources, such as computers and other equipment.
>**Code of ethics.** A policy, often for an organization or industry, that specifies overall moral guidelines adopted by that organization or industry.

matching an IP address? Or, if it is legal for a business to share or sell customer information, should it do so? This latter decision is one that many businesses have struggled with, especially in challenging economic times when a quick source of revenue gained from selling customer data is tempting. Although some businesses have succumbed to this temptation and have sold their customer lists, others believe that any short-term gains achieved through ethically questionable acts will adversely affect customer loyalty and will ultimately hurt the business in the long run.

To prepare future employees for these types of decisions, most business schools incorporate business ethics into their curriculum. However, the startling number of corporate scandals in the past few years and the perceived degrading moral climate today have caused some schools to reevaluate their curriculum to see if it is sufficient. According to George Brenkert, director of the Business Ethics Institute at Georgetown University, business schools have spread the message of maximizing profit at nearly any cost for too long. He believes that businesses have to derive a profit and a return on their investments, but that they have to do it in the broader context of ethical considerations and social responsibility. The business curriculum for many schools is increasingly pushing business ethics training, and a recent study of the world's top 50 graduate business schools revealed that over half of the schools have made ethics study a graduation requirement. Corporate philosophies and employee training programs are also beginning to move in this direction by including business ethics training. For instance, in a 2007 *National Business Ethics Survey* (*NBES*) by the Ethics Resource Center, 70% of the businesses reported that their organizations have implemented ethics training. However, only 9% of the companies in the U.S. are classified as having strong ethical cultures, which is significant because the survey found that a strong enterprise-wide ethical culture dramatically decreases the risk of ethical misconduct within that organization.

Cheating and Falsifying Information

Just as computers and the Internet make it easier for individuals to plagiarize documents, computers and the Internet also make it easier for individuals to cheat on assignments or online exams, or perform other similar unethical acts.

Unfortunately, cheating by students at both the high school level and the college level is rampant today. Studies have found that 75% of all U.S. high school students cheat and 70% of students on most college campuses admit to some cheating. According to a 2005 study of over 12,000 college students by Donald L. McCabe of Rutgers University, nearly 40% of the students admitted to Internet plagiarism (such as cutting and pasting content from Internet sources without crediting the source), and 77% believe it is not a serious issue. About 25% of the students surveyed admitted to serious cheating on exams; half admitted to serious cheating on written assignments. And in a recent study of graduate business students, 56% admitted to copying another student's work, plagiarizing, or sneaking notes into an exam. Although cheating can occur with noncomputerized assignments and exams, the editing ability of a PC makes it faster and easier to cheat on assignments created on a computer, and taking online exams offsite makes it easier to cheat on those exams. In addition, the ability to take photos of exams using mobile phones; to send text messages via mobile phones or mobile devices during tests; and to store test notes in mobile phones, graphing calculators, and other electronic devices makes cheating on exams even easier than in the past.

Traditionally, it was typically weaker students who cheated to prevent failing a course or an exam. Today, according to Denise Pope, founder and director of Stanford University's SOS: Stressed-Out Students Project, the students who cheat more are the ones with the most to lose. For instance, she has found that 80% of high school honors and AP (advanced placement) students cheat on a regular basis. But whether they realize it or not, students who choose to cheat are cheating themselves of an education, as well as being unfair to honest students by possibly altering the grading curve. Widespread cheating can also have a negative impact on society, such as underprepared employees entering the workforce.

FIGURE 6-8
Academic honor codes. The honor code at the University of Denver is signed by virtually all incoming students.

To explain to students what behavior is expected of them, many schools are developing *academic honor codes*. These codes are usually published in the student handbook and on the school Web site; they may also be included in course syllabi. Research has shown that having an academic honor code effectively reduces cheating. For example, the McCabe studies have found that cheating on tests on campuses with honor codes is typically one-third to one-half less than on campuses that do not have honor codes, and the level of cheating on written assignments is one-quarter to one-third lower. To bring attention to their honor codes, some schools encourage incoming students to sign their honor codes upon admission. For instance, all incoming University of Denver students are asked to sign the school's honor code publicly (see Figure 6-8). Regardless of whether or not students choose to sign the honor code, they are required to abide by it. To remind students of this responsibility at the University of Denver, the honor code pledge "I affirm my commitment to the University of Denver Honor Code" appears on every exam blue book purchased through the university bookstore.

Like academic cheating, lying on a job application or résumé is more common than most of us may think it is. The practice of providing false information in an attempt to look more qualified for a job, sometimes referred to as *résumé padding*, is both dishonest and unethical. And it is also widespread. Recent research conducted by the *New York Times* found that almost half of hiring managers and 84% of job seekers believe that résumé padding is done by a significant number of candidates. In addition to being unethical, providing false information to a potential employer can have grave consequences. The majority of the companies surveyed in the *New York Times* study have a policy that lists termination as the appropriate action for employees who were hired based on falsified résumés or applications. Being blacklisted from an industry or being sued for breach of contract are also possibilities. Résumé writers should remember that background checks are easily available on the Web, so credentials are easy to check and verify. Regardless of whether or not they think they may get caught, applicants should not embellish their résumés or job applications to any extent because it is an unethical thing to do. Another recent ethical issue surrounding IT employees is cheating on IT certification exams. Copies of certification questions and entire certification exams are available for purchase online, and some Web sites offer the services of "gunmen" (usually located in Asia) who take certification tests for individuals at a cost of up to several thousand dollars each. In response, companies that offer IT certifications are looking at the security of their testing processes to try to put a stop to this new type of cheating.

There are also situations in personal life that tempt some individuals to provide inaccurate personal information, such as when writing personal advertisements, when participating in chat rooms, and when individuals may wish to appear differently from the person they really are. There are differing opinions about how ethical these actions are—some individuals believe that it is a person's right to portray himself or herself in any way desired; others feel that any type of dishonesty is unethical.

Computer Hoaxes and Digital Manipulation

Most people realize that information in print media can, at times, be misleading and that photos can be manipulated. Information found on the Internet may also be inaccurate, misleading, or biased. Some of this information is published on Web pages; other information is passed on via e-mail. Two types of computer-oriented misinformation include computer hoaxes and digital manipulation.

Computer Hoaxes

A **computer hoax** is an inaccurate statement or story—such as the "fact" that flesh-eating bacteria have been found in banana shipments or that antiperspirant use causes cancer—spread through the use of computers. These hoaxes are sometimes published on Web pages, but they are more commonly spread via e-mail. Common computer hoax subjects include nonexistent computer viruses, serious health risks of a particular product, impending terrorist attacks, chain letters, and free prizes or giveaways. Inaccurate information purposely posted on a Web site or wiki to be misleading can also be considered a computer hoax. E-mail hoaxes are written with the purpose of being circulated to as many people as possible. Some are started as experiments to see how fast and how far information can travel via the Internet; others originate from a joke or the desire to frighten people. Similar to spam, e-mail hoaxes can be annoying, waste people's time, bog down e-mail systems, and clog users' Inboxes. Because computer hoaxes are so common, it is a good idea to double-check any warning you receive by e-mail or read on a Web site before passing that warning on to another person, regardless of how realistic or frightening the information appears to be. One reliable source to use is the government's Hoaxbusters site shown in Figure 6-9.

Digital Manipulation

Computers make it very easy to copy or modify text, images, photographs, music, and other digital content. In addition to being a copyright concern, **digital manipulation** (digitally altering digital content) can be used to misquote individuals, repeat comments out of context, retouch photographs—even create false or misleading photographs. While there are some beneficial, ethical, noncontroversial applications of digital manipulation—such as aging photos of missing children to show what they may look like at the present time, or altering photos of wanted criminals or suspects to show possible alternate appearances for law enforcement purposes—the matter of altering photos to be published is the subject of debate. Some publications and photographers see no harm in altering photographs to remove an offending item (such as a telephone pole behind someone's head), to make someone look a little more attractive, to illustrate a point, or to increase circulation; others view any change in content as unethical and a great disservice to both the public and our history. For example, fifty years from now, will anyone know that a staged or altered photograph of a historical event was not an actual depiction of the event?

Although manipulation of photographs has occurred for quite some time in tabloids and other publications not known as being reputable news sources, there have been several incidents of more reputable news publications using digitally altered photographs in recent years. Most of these became known because the unaltered photograph was used in another publication at about the same time. One of the most widely publicized cases occurred in 1994, just following the arrest of O. J. Simpson. While *Newsweek* ran Simpson's mug shot unaltered, *TIME* magazine darkened the photograph, creating a more sinister look and

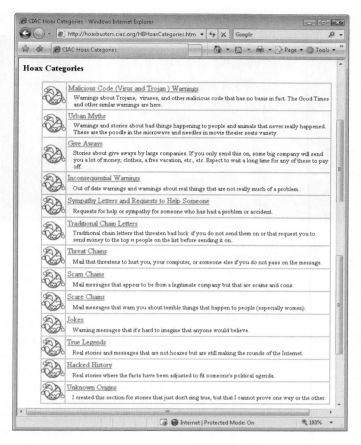

FIGURE 6-9

The Hoax Categories on the Hoaxbusters Web site.

>**Computer hoax.** An inaccurate statement or story spread through the use of computers. >**Digital manipulation.** The alteration of digital content, usually text or photographs.

Student's hat was altered.

Sign was altered.

FIGURE 6-10

Digital manipulation.
The Schundler photo
(right) is a digital
manipulation of the
Dean photo (left).

making Simpson's skin color appear darker than it actually is. This photo drew harsh criticism from Simpson supporters who felt the photograph made him appear guilty, the African-American community who viewed the alteration as an act of racial insensitivity, and news photographers who felt that the action damaged the credibility not only of that particular magazine, but also of all journalists.

Another example occurred during the 2005 New Jersey governor's race. The Web site of one of the candidates, Bret Schundler, displayed a photo showing Schundler in the foreground with a group of college students in the background (see Figure 6-10). The problem? The photo of Shundler (a Republican) was superimposed onto a photo taken at a rally for Howard Dean (a Democrat) the year before. The digital manipulation came to light when one of the college students who had attended the Dean rally recognized herself in the Schundler photo, which had been digitally altered to show her wearing a Shundler hat and holding a Shundler sign (refer again to Figure 6-10). The Shundler campaign admitted it was aware that Schundler's photo was superimposed onto a political rally photo, but they did not know it was taken at a Dean event. The photo was removed from the Web site after the issue came to light.

In a more recent example, a one-time Pulitzer Prize finalist resigned from a Toledo, Ohio newspaper in 2007 after it was discovered that he had submitted for publication nearly 80 doctored photos in just the 14 weeks prior to his resignation, including one sports photo of a basketball game with a digitally added basketball placed in midair.

Perhaps the most disturbing thing about known alterations such as these is that some may never have been noticed, and may consequently have been accepted as true representations. Adding to the problem of unethical digital manipulation is the use of digital cameras today, which virtually eliminates any concrete evidence—namely, photo negatives—that can show what photographs actually looked like at the time they were taken. Although some publications allow the use of "photo illustrations," others have strict rules about digital manipulation—especially for news photojournalists. For instance, the *LA Times* fired a staff photographer covering the war in Iraq when he combined two of his photographs into one to better convey a point.

Ethical Business Practices and Decision Making

Companies must make ethics-related business decisions, such as whether or not to sell a product or service that some may find offensive or objectionable, whether or not to install monitoring video cameras in the workplace, whether or not to release potentially misleading information, or whether or not to perform controversial research. In addition, corporate integrity, in terms of accounting practices and proper disclosure, is a business ethics topic that has come to the forefront, as a result of the many recent incidents involving corporate scandals and bankruptcies.

Fraudulent Reporting and Other Scandalous Activities

Following the large number of corporate scandals occurring since 2002, business ethics have never been quite so much in the public eye. The scandals, such as the ones surrounding executives at Enron, Tyco International, and WorldCom, involved lies, fraud, deception, and other illegal and unethical behavior. This behavior forced both Enron and WorldCom into bankruptcy proceedings. When asked to comment on the scandals, 3Com Chief Executive Officer Bruce Claflin said on CNBC, "I would argue we do not have an accounting problem—we have an ethics problem."

In reaction to the scandals, Congress passed the *Sarbanes-Oxley Act of 2002*, which includes provisions to improve the quality of financial reporting, independent audits, and accounting services for public companies; to increase penalties for corporate wrongdoing; to protect the objectivity and independence of securities analysts; and to require CEOs and CFOs to personally vouch for the truth and fairness of their company's disclosures.

Ethically Questionable Products or Services

One ethical issue a business may run into is whether or not to sell products or services that some people find objectionable. For example, the eBay Web site states that it will not allow auction listings for items that promote hate, violence, or racial intolerance. Consequently, it bans items that bear symbols of the Nazis or the Ku Klux Klan (KKK), crime scene and morgue photographs, and letters and belongings of notorious criminals, even though sellers may legally be able to sell such items elsewhere. Companies that do business in more than one country also have global considerations to address. For instance, a Brazilian court ordered YouTube in 2007 to shut down access to a racy video clip of a Brazilian celebrity and her boyfriend on the beach, even though YouTube is a U.S. company. Cultural issues such as these are discussed in more detail shortly.

Another ethical decision for businesses that allow individuals to upload content (such as wikis and video sharing sites) is how (if at all) they should monitor the content posted on their sites. For instance, YouTube relies on the user community to flag videos that might be inappropriate for some viewers (such as the Saddam Hussein execution video posted on YouTube shortly after that execution took place); all flagged videos are viewed and either removed or are left flagged so viewers need to verify that they are over 18 by logging in to their YouTube account in order to view the video. To protect children from predators, many states are pushing social networking sites, such as MySpace and Facebook, to implement age verification systems; age verification also benefits the adults who use these sites so they know they are acting appropriately with other members. Businesses that offer products or services that are inappropriate for children (such as alcohol, tobacco, adult movies and video games, pornography, online gambling, and so forth) also need to make decisions regarding access; for example, the number and types of safeguards they need to provide to ensure that children do not have access to these products and services. They also need to determine if the company is required legally, or just ethically, to provide these safeguards. This is especially significant for businesses with an e-commerce presence. In a conventional store, individuals can be asked to show an ID to prove they are of the required age before they are allowed to buy tobacco products, alcohol, pornographic materials, and other products that cannot legally be sold to minors. But, during an online transaction, it is much more difficult to verify that a buyer is the required age.

To comply with state and federal laws, as well as to protect themselves from potential litigation, Web sites selling or providing adult products and services should implement adequate age-verification procedures. Some sites require visitors to click a statement declaring they are the required age or to enter a valid credit card number before accessing or purchasing adult-only content or products. However, these precautions can be easily overcome. Requiring proof of age at delivery (see Figure 6-11) is a safer precaution and is required by law in some states for certain types of shipments. A growing trend is the use of *online age verification services*, as discussed in the Trend box.

The decisions about which products or services to offer online and offline are important—and sometimes difficult—ethical decisions for businesses to make. Typically, these decisions are based on the

 FIGURE 6-11

Ethical e-commerce. Businesses selling products or services that are inappropriate or illegal for minors should require proof of age at delivery.

Due to the alcoholic content of this gift, an adult signature is required upon delivery.

TREND

Online Age Verification Services

From e-commerce sites selling alcohol and other products that are age-restricted by law in the U.S., to social networking sites that collect and use personal information (which is prohibited by the Children's Online Privacy Protection Act (COPPA) for children under the age of 13 without parental permission), to video-on-demand and mobile TV services that may deliver movies and other content deemed inappropriate for children, opportunities for online age verification abound. While in the recent past, reliable online age verification was difficult or impossible to obtain, reliable online age verification systems are available today and they are beginning to be used by a wide variety of businesses in order to protect their reputation; guard against lawsuits, fines, or prosecution; or just because they believe it is the right thing to do.

Most online age verification systems verify an individual is of the required age for the requested Web site service or transaction by trying to match the data supplied by the customer (typically name, address or ZIP code, and date of birth—see the accompanying illustration) with the data contained in public records (such as driver's license, property, and credit records; professional and hunting licenses; voter registrations; and more). If the data matches (a process that typically takes just a few seconds), the individual is granted access to the application (such as being granted access to a site, being allowed to complete the check-out process, and so forth); if not, the access is denied.

In addition to the mandatory age verification process implemented on some Web sites, other Web sites are adding voluntary age verification systems for those individuals who wish to access certain features of those Web sites. For instance, in late 2007, Second Life introduced a new age verification system that will allow users aged 18 and older to access Second Life content flagged as "Restricted." Users who do not complete the age verification process will still be able to use the Second Life service, but they will not be able to access Restricted areas.

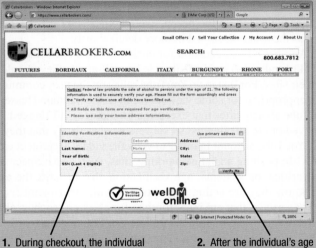

1. During checkout, the individual enters his or her official name, address, and date of birth, and the last four digits of his or her Social Security number.

2. After the individual's age is verified using a public database, the checkout procedure continues.

Example of online age verification.

company's overall corporate mission and desired public image. Consequently, some businesses may choose not to sell adult-only content at all. Others may decide to sell it via the Internet only in conjunction with a third-party age verification system, or to sell those products or services online but require an adult to sign for the items when they are delivered. Still other businesses may feel that a warning statement or similar precaution on their Web sites is all that is needed, and that it is the parents' responsibility to make sure their children do not purchase illegal or inappropriate items or view adult-only content via the Internet.

Vaporware

Vaporware is a term sometimes used to designate software and hardware products that have been announced and advertised, but are not yet—and may never be—available. Sometimes a premature announcement is not intentional, such as when a delay in production or other last-minute problem results in a late introduction. At other times, it may be an intentional act, designed to convince customers to wait for the company's upcoming product instead of buying an existing competitive product—an act some consumers are likely to view as an unethical business practice.

Workplace Monitoring

As discussed in Chapter 5, the majority of businesses monitor employees to some extent. Although U.S. businesses have the right and responsibility to ensure that employees are productive and that company resources are not being abused, many believe that businesses also have an ethical responsibility to inform employees of any monitoring that takes place. This is especially true in countries other than the U.S., such as in the European Union where companies are much more limited in what types of monitoring they can do without notifying employees. Businesses need to consider cultural differences when determining Web site content, business practices, and other global decisions, as discussed next.

Cultural Considerations

With today's global economy, businesses need to be sensitive to the ethical differences that may exist between different businesses located in the same country, as well as between businesses located in different countries. Ethics are fundamentally based on values, so when beliefs, laws, customs, and traditions vary among businesses, the ethics associated with those businesses will likely differ as well. One example is the concept of *human cloning*. There are widely differing beliefs within the United States about the ethics of human cloning—some disabled Americans look to cloning as a means of finding a medical cure to their disabilities, while other citizens and groups oppose cloning for religious or ethical reasons. Businesses need to consider cultural differences when determining Web site content, business practices, and other global decisions, as discussed next.

Ethical decisions need to be made whenever a business practice or product is legal or socially acceptable in one country, but not another. One example is copyright law. While the United States and many other countries have copyright laws, some countries do not or it is not strongly enforced. Although an individual may be able to purchase a bootleg copy of a software program, music CD, or movie in some countries (see Figure 6-12), import restrictions prevent these items from being brought legally into the United States to be sold. With the Internet, however, U.S. citizens now have the capability of buying unauthorized copies of copyrighted materials from countries in which those copies are legal or copyright law is laxly enforced. This raises the question of ethical responsibility. Is it the individual's responsibility not to make these types of unethical purchases, even if technology makes it possible? What role should the government play in preventing citizens from buying products from other countries that are illegal in its country? What legal and ethical responsibility do businesses have to ensure that customers do not have access to products or services that are illegal in their particular location?

ASK THE EXPERT

Dave Weick, Senior Vice President, Chief Information Officer, McDonald's Corporation

How important is it for a business to have a Web site today if it doesn't sell products and services online?

For McDonald's, our online presence is about extending the McDonald's experience to our customers. Mcdonalds.com allows our customers another channel to engage with our brand without ever entering a restaurant. Through our Web site, customers can find promotions and nutritional information on all of our products. On the Open for Discussion blog, customers are talking about McDonald's corporate sustainability efforts. Happymeal.com is connecting kids across the globe in fun, interactive, and uniquely McDonald's ways. Finally, customers can download podcasts about food safety.

For McDonald's, our Web site allows us the opportunity to connect with our customers on topics that are important to them in a way that they want to connect. In addition, in some parts of the world you can order off of our menu from the Web site and have it delivered to your door. As our customers demand even more convenience and control over the "ordering process," this may become even more prevalent in the future.

FIGURE 6-12

Cultural considerations. In some countries, bootleg copies of music CDs and movie DVDs are sold openly.

One incident that brought these issues into the forefront is the November 2000 French court ruling ordering the Yahoo! Auction Web site to prevent people located in France from accessing pages on the U.S. auction site containing Nazi books, daggers, uniforms, badges, and other items for sale that are illegal under French law. Although the Yahoo! France auction site did not list those items for sale, the French court order required Yahoo! to block French Web surfers from having access to these pages on its U.S. auction site. Yahoo! appealed in a U.S. court on the grounds that this order was not technologically possible without completely removing all Nazi materials from its U.S. auction site, which would violate its First Amendment rights. In a decision that may set an important precedent regarding how far foreign jurisdictions can go to impose regulations against Internet content originating within the United States, a U.S. District Court in California ruled in May 2002 that the French order could not be enforced against Yahoo! in the United States.

In addition to legal issues, organizations conducting business in other countries should also take into consideration the ethical standards prevalent in the countries with which they do business. Factors such as gender roles, religious beliefs, and cultural customs should be considered and respected when corresponding, negotiating, and otherwise interacting with businesses located in other countries. For example, some cultures may require a handshake or other ritual that is impossible to carry out online in order to close a deal. In this case, while the terms of the deal may be carried out online, the deal itself would need to be closed in person. Some cultures also move at a different pace than others, such as in India where a strong sense of hierarchy often means that immediate answers via e-mail are not possible. And, while private e-mail messages in the United States are often respected as private and not forwarded to others, group-focused cultures may feel obligated to share personal e-mails with the entire team—a potential embarrassment for individuals if they are not aware of that custom while working with businesses in those countries. Businesses should also be careful not to offend the other countries with which they do business. Some straightforward questions acceptable in the United States—such as a request to verify certain numbers or double-check a source—may be viewed as an insult in some cultures.

Several instances of poor judgment and cultural insensitivity on the part of Microsoft that cost the company millions of dollars and a great deal of foreign goodwill came to light in 2004. In one instance, Microsoft colored the disputed Kashmiri territory on a map of India in a software program a different color than that of the rest of India, implying that area was non-Indian. India promptly banned the program and required Microsoft to recall all 200,000 copies of that program sold in that country. In another case, Microsoft used chanting of the Koran in a soundtrack for a computer game, which greatly offended the Saudi Arabian government. And a poor English-to-Spanish translation of the Windows XP operating system resulted in the use of an offensive term for "female" in a prompt for which users are asked to select their gender.

To properly prepare students to succeed in our global economy, some business schools include diversity and cross-cultural training in their curriculum. Similarly, in order to avoid offending their international business partners or clients, some international organizations arrange for their employees to have such training prior to traveling out of the country. For instance, Microsoft has implemented geography training for its employees who need to have that knowledge, in order to avoid some of the mishaps of the past. Other companies are modifying products and services to appeal to a more global customer base. For example, several mobile phone models today are geared toward Muslims and include Islamic features, such as reminder alarms at prayer times, automatically switching to vibration mode during prayer times, and an automatic Qibla direction finder (showing the direction toward Mecca from the user's current position anywhere in the world).

RELATED LEGISLATION

There have been several new laws over the past few years (see Figure 6-13) attempting to revise intellectual property laws to reflect digital content and the Internet. For instance, the *Family Entertainment and Copyright Act of 2005* makes it illegal to transmit or record a movie being shown at a movie theater. Other recent laws related to intellectual property include the *U.S. Anticybersquatting Consumer Protection Act of 1999*, which makes domain name cybersquatting illegal; the *Copyright Term Extension Act*, which adds 20 years to the existing copyright terms; and the *Digital Millennium Copyright Act* (*DMCA*), which makes it illegal to circumvent antipiracy measures built into digital media and devices. Several other laws, such as to increase the penalties for illegally sharing music and movies via the Internet, are proposed on a regular basis.

Legislation regarding ethics has been more difficult to pass—or to keep as law once it has passed. For example, the *Communications Decency Act*, which was signed into law in 1996, made it a criminal offense to distribute patently indecent or offensive material online. Although the law was intended to protect children from being exposed to inappropriate Web content, the U.S. Supreme Court in 1997 declared this law unconstitutional on the basis of free speech. The courts so far have had difficulty defining what is "patently offensive" and "indecent" as well as finding a fair balance between protection and censorship. Consequently, very few ethically oriented laws have been passed in recent years. Some exceptions are the *Children's Online Privacy Protection Act* (*COPPA*), which regulates how Web sites can collect information from minors, and the *Sarbanes-Oxley Act* (*Corporate Responsibility Act*), which includes provisions to improve the quality of financial reporting and increases penalties for corporate wrongdoing.

FIGURE 6-13
Federal legislation related to intellectual property rights and ethics.

DATE	LAW AND DESCRIPTION
2005	**Family Entertainment and Copyright Act** Makes it illegal to transmit or record a movie being shown at a movie theater.
2002	**Sarbanes-Oxley Act** Requires archiving a variety of electronic records and protecting the integrity of corporate financial data. Also requires CEOs and CFOs to vouch personally for the truth and fairness of their company's disclosures.
2001	**Child Internet Protection Act (CIPA)** Requires public libraries and schools to use filtering software to block access to certain Web content in order to receive public funds.
1999	**U.S. Anticybersquatting Consumer Protection Act of 1999** Amends the Lanham Act of 1946 to extend trademark protection to domain names and makes cybersquatting illegal.
1999	**Digital Theft Deterrence and Copyright Damages Improvement Act of 1999** Amends federal copyright law to increase statutory and additional damages a court may award for copyright infringement.
1998	**Digital Millennium Copyright Act (DMCA)** Makes it illegal to circumvent antipiracy measures built into digital media and devices.
1998	**Children's Online Privacy Protection Act (COPPA)** Regulates how Web sites can collect information from minors and communicate with them.
1998	**Copyright Term Extension Act** Extends the duration of copyright in a work created on or after January 1, 1978 by 20 years
1997	**No Electronic Theft (NET) Act** Expands computer antipiracy laws to include distribution of copyrighted material over the Internet and sets penalties for willfully infringing a copyright for purposes of commercial advantage or private financial gain.
1996	**Communications Decency Act** Makes it a criminal offense to distribute patently indecent or offensive material online. Was declared unconstitutional by the U.S. Supreme Court in 1997.
1976	**Copyright Act of 1976** Gives the owner of a copyright the exclusive right to publish, reproduce, distribute, perform, or display the work.
1946	**Lanham Act (Trademark Act of 1946)** Allows the registration of trademarks for commercial purposes and prohibits the use, reproduction, or imitation of registered trademarks.

SUMMARY

INTELLECTUAL PROPERTY RIGHTS

Chapter Objective 1:
Understand the concept of intellectual property rights and how they relate to computer use.

Intellectual property rights specify how *intellectual property*, such as original music compositions, drawings, essays, software programs, symbols, and designs, may be lawfully used. **Copyrights** protect the creators of original artistic or literary works and are granted automatically once a work exists in a physical medium. A copyright can be registered, which provides additional protection should infringement occur. The copyright symbol © can be used to remind others that content is copyrighted; **digital watermarks** can be incorporated into digital content so that the copyright information can be viewed, even if the work is altered. **Digital rights management (DRM) software** can be used to protect the rights of creators and to manage digital content, such as art, music, photographs, and movies.

Trademarks are words, phrases, symbols, or designs that identify an organization's goods or services and can be either claimed (and use the symbol ™ or ℠) or registered (and use the symbol ®). In addition to logos and text-based phrases, domain names are also protected by trademark law. **Patents** grant an exclusive right to an invention for 20 years. In addition to products, processes and procedures may be patented as well.

ETHICS

Chapter Objective 2:
Explain what is meant by the term "ethics."

Ethics are standards of moral conduct. *Personal ethics* guide one's personal life, **business ethics** provide the standards of conduct guiding business decisions, and **computer ethics** provide the standards of conduct with respect to computers and computer use. Computer ethics have taken on more significance in recent years because the increased use of computers in the home, in the workplace, and at school provides more opportunities for unethical behavior than in the past.

Chapter Objective 3:
Provide several examples of unethical behavior in the use of intellectual property and in computer-related matters.

Both businesses and individuals need to make ethical decisions on a regular basis. Today one of the most important ethical concerns regarding computers is using someone else's property in an improper way. Books, music, movies, and other types of intellectual property are protected by copyright law. Presenting someone else's work as your own is referred to as **plagiarism**, which is illegal and unethical. Plagiarism can be performed by both students and employees, although it can be detected and usually has grave academic or professional consequences.

Movies and music also qualify for copyright protection. The practice of individuals sharing movies and music via the Internet has been a primary source of legal and ethical copyright debates. There has been increased prosecution against those individuals illegally distributing copyright-protected works, as well as end users, in the hopes of reducing this type of piracy. Legal alternatives, such as legal online music stores and video-on-demand (VOD) services, may help reduce illegal activity related to copyright-protected works.

It is becoming increasingly common for businesses and schools to establish **codes of conduct** to address what behavior is considered ethical and unethical at that particular organization. Students and employees should refer to these codes, if they exist, to become familiar with the behaviors viewed as ethical and unethical for that particular school or business. Some organizations and industries publish **codes of ethics** listing overall standards of conduct, such as honesty, fairness, confidentiality, and more.

Businesses need to determine how they will use employee and customer information, based on both legal and ethical guidelines. Because computers make it easier to plagiarize and cheat on assignments and exams, students need to make an ethical decision regarding their behavior. Some job applicants choose to supply erroneous or misleading information on their applications or résumés in hope of gaining an advantage. This action is unethical and can result in job termination at many organizations if this deception is later discovered.

A **computer hoax** is an inaccurate statement or story spread through the use of computers, often by e-mail. It is a good idea to make sure questionable information is not a computer hoax before passing the information on to others. **Digital manipulation** is the use of computers to modify something in digital form, usually text or a photograph. While digitally altering photographs sometimes has a positive or an ethically acceptable use—such as aging photos of missing children—the use of digital manipulation on photographs published in newspapers and magazines is more controversial and is viewed as highly unethical by many people.

Ethics are highly intertwined with determining business practices and making business decisions. Decisions, such as which financial information to publicize, which products or services to provide, which safeguards (if any) to establish with products or services that are illegal for minors or objectionable to some individuals, whether or not to promote potential *vaporware* products, and whether or not to monitor employees, all require ethical consideration.

Because ethics are fundamentally based on values, different types of businesses may have different ethics. Furthermore, ethics and moral standards may vary from country to country and from culture to culture. In addition to legal considerations, businesses with global connections should consider the prevailing ethical standards of all countries involved when making business decisions.

RELATED LEGISLATION

There are numerous laws in place to protect intellectual property. For example, there are laws relating to trademark and copyright terms, and there are a number of laws protecting various types of intellectual property, such as the *U.S. Anticybersquatting Consumer Protection Act of 1999*, which applies patent law to domain names, and the *Family Entertainment and Copyright Act of 2005*, which makes it illegal to record a movie as it is being shown in a movie theater. Because moral and ethical standards are more difficult to agree on, ethical legislation is slower in coming. However, some laws (such as the *Children's Online Privacy Protection Act* or *COPPA*) have been implemented.

Chapter Objective 4:
Explain what computer hoaxes and digital manipulation are and how they relate to computer ethics.

Chapter Objective 5:
Understand how ethics can impact business practices and decision making.

Chapter Objective 6:
Discuss the current status of legislation related to intellectual property rights and ethics.

REVIEW ACTIVITIES

KEY TERM MATCHING

Instructions: Match each key term on the left with the definition on the right that best describes it.

a. business ethics

b. computer ethics

c. computer hoax

d. copyright

e. digital manipulation

f. digital watermark

g. intellectual property rights

h. patent

i. plagiarism

j. trademark

1. _____ A form of protection that can be granted by the government for an invention; gives exclusive rights of an invention to its inventor for 20 years.

2. _____ A word, phrase, symbol, or design that identifies goods or services.

3. _____ A subtle alteration of digital content that is not noticeable when the work is viewed or played, but that identifies the copyright holder.

4. _____ An inaccurate statement or story spread through the use of computers.

5. _____ Presenting someone else's work as your own.

6. _____ Standards of moral conduct as they relate to computer use.

7. _____ The alteration of digital content, usually text or photographs.

8. _____ The legal right to sell, publish, or distribute an original artistic or literary work; is held by the creator of a work as soon as it exists in physical form.

9. _____ Standards of moral conduct that guide a business's policies, decisions, and actions.

10. _____ The rights to which creators of original creative works (such as artistic or literary works, inventions, corporate logos, and more) are entitled.

SELF-QUIZ

Instructions: Circle **T** if the statement is true, **F** if the statement is false, or write the best answer in the space provided. **Answers for the self-quiz are located in the References and Resources Guide at the end of the book.**

1.   **T   F**   All unethical acts are illegal.

2.   **T   F**   Changing the background behind a television newscaster to make it appear that he or she is reporting on location instead of from inside the television studio would be an example of digital manipulation.

3.   **T   F**   Patents are used to protect artistic works, such as music or books.

4.   **T   F**   Copying a song from a CD you own to your computer to create a custom music CD for personal use is normally considered fair use.

5.   **T   F**   Résumé padding or lying on a job application would be viewed as unethical by most employers.

6.   A software program would be protected by _____ law, while a corporate logo would be protected by _____ law.

7.   Turning in a copy of a poem you found on a Web site as your original composition for a poetry class assignment is an example of _____ .

8. _____ software is used to protect and manage the rights of creators of digital content, such as by allowing a digital music file to only be copied a limited number of times.

9. The overturning by the U.S. Supreme Court of the _____ Act, which made it illegal to distribute patently indecent or offensive material online, is considered a landmark decision for free speech advocates.

10. Match each term to its description or example and write the corresponding number in the blank to the left of each description or example.

a. _____ What the symbol © stands for.		**1.** Computer hoax
b. _____ Can vary from another's depending on his or her values, culture, and so forth.		**2.** Copyright
c. _____ A warning about a nonexistent virus spread via e-mail.		**3.** Digital manipulation
d. _____ Darkening of O.J. Simpson's photograph in the 1994 *TIME* magazine cover.		**4.** Digital watermark
e. _____ A subtle alteration of digital content that identifies the copyright holder.		**5.** Ethics

---

EXERCISES

1. For each of the following situations, write the appropriate letter—E (ethical) or U (unethical)—in the blank to the right of the situation to indicate how the act would be viewed by most individuals.

Situation — **Type of Situation**

a. A teenager rips a new CD she just bought and e-mails the MP3 files to all her friends. _____

b. An employee finds a coworker's résumé and shows it to other workers. _____

c. A photographer combines two of his photographs to create a new composite artistic piece. _____

d. A physician incorporates another doctor's research into her journal article submission, including the researcher's name and article in her submission. _____

2. Match each term with its related example and write the corresponding number in the blank to the left of each example.

a. _____ Copying and pasting Web page text.   **1.** Plagiarism

b. _____ Online age verification systems.   **2.** Intellectual property rights

c. _____ Service marks.   **3.** Ethics

3. Assume that you have created a Web site to display your favorite original photographs. Explain whether or not the site you created would be protected by copyright law. What about the photographs? If they would not be protected, explain what steps, if any, you could take to ensure they were protected.

4. Explain the difference between a copyright and a trademark.

5. When might a business need to consider cultural differences when creating a Web site? List at least two examples.

DISCUSSION QUESTION

Unarguably, the Web contains a vast amount of extremely useful information. Some content, however, is more debatable and, in fact, may be extremely harmful. For example, suicide Web sites that explain in detail how to kill oneself and Web sites broadcasting the beheadings by terrorists have received increased attention lately. And what about Web sites that explain how to build bombs and other types of weapons? If a Web site instructs visitors how to perform an illegal act, should the site's creators be criminally liable if a visitor carries out those instructions? Who, if anyone, is responsible for preventing potentially harmful information from being shared via the Web? Is there any Internet content that you believe a government has the right or obligation to censor? If so, what? Where do we draw the line between freedom of speech and national or personal safety?

BALANCING ACT

GOVERNMENT PROTECTION VS. GOVERNMENT CENSORSHIP

There has always been a delicate balance between what is viewed as government protection and what is viewed as government censorship. *Censorship*, typically defined as restricting access to materials deemed objectionable or offensive, is performed at some level by every government. Even though the United States was founded on the concept of freedom and free speech, some government censorship exists, and most of us would agree that it is necessary at a basic level. For example, public schools are not permitted to teach any particular religious viewpoint, and network television must edit out certain levels of potentially offensive language and nudity in movies before they can be aired. However, the idea of censorship gets more tricky and controversial when it is used to block access to materials and information that will offend or are inappropriate for some, but not all, citizens.

Among the most notable examples in recent years are the attempts by some groups and the government to limit access to online pornography and other Internet content that most people agree are not appropriate for children. As mentioned in the chapter, the Communications Decency Act passed in 1996 was overturned by the Supreme Court the following year, and there has been great controversy surrounding the Child Internet Protection Act (CIPA), which went into effect in 2001 and requires public libraries and schools to use filtering software to block Internet access to certain materials in order to receive public funds. Although intended to protect children, the act was fought strenuously by free speech advocacy groups and some library associations and was ruled unconstitutional by a federal court in 2002. In a six to three ruling in 2003, however, the U.S. Supreme Court reversed the lower court decision and ruled that the law was constitutional because the need for libraries to prevent minors from accessing objectionable materials outweighs the free speech rights of library patrons and Web site publishers.

YOUR TURN

Give some thought to the balance between government protection and government censorship with respect to the Internet, and form an opinion on this issue. Consider the following when forming your opinion and be prepared to discuss your position (either in class, via an online class discussion group, in a class chat room, or via a class blog) or to write a short paper expressing your opinion, depending on your instructor's directions.

- Do you think the Supreme Court was correct in overturning the Communications Decency Act and upholding the Child Internet Protection Act? Why or why not?

- One objection free speech advocates have to mandatory library filtering is based on the premise that filtering software is not perfect, and its use may block access to valuable educational material. Another is that filtering would increase the digital divide because affluent individuals with home computers would have access to Internet content that economically challenged citizens (who more often would need to use their library's free public Internet access) would not be able to access. Do you think these arguments are valid? Why or why not?

- Even if Internet filtering at schools is not required, should individual schools have the right to block access to Web content they view as inappropriate for students using school PCs? Or do students have the right to use those computers to access any content they desire, on the basis that their fees, tuition, or parents' taxes paid for that access? What about the rights of other students who do not want to see content that they find offensive displayed on computer screens as they pass by computers that other students are using? Should the ability to filter be different for public schools versus private schools? Why or why not?

PROJECTS

1. **Ethics and Virtual Worlds** As discussed in the chapter, there are a number of ethical issues surrounding virtual worlds, such as Second Life.

   For this project, consider some of the issues discussed in the chapter, such as reporting income from virtual world activities to the IRS, using online age verification systems to enable visitors to access age-restricted areas, and the ability to portray oneself differently than you really are. Select an issue and form an opinion on that issue, including what you personally think is the ethical thing to do, what you think the general public would do, and what the possible ramifications could be. Submit your opinions to your instructor in the form of a short paper, no more than one page in length.

HOT TOPICS

2. **Copyright Registration** Think of an original creation (paper, poem, photograph, or song) to which you believe you are entitled copyright protection and assume that you would like to register a copyright for your creation.

   For this project, research how you would obtain a copyright for your chosen creation. Visit the U.S. Copyright Office Web site (search for it using a search site) and determine the necessary procedure for registration, the required paperwork, and the necessary fee. Use the information located on the site to make sure your creation is entitled to copyright protection, then find the appropriate online registration form (if one is available online). If possible, open and print just one page of the form. From the site, also determine what notice you will receive once your copyright claim has been recorded and how long it will take to receive it. Prepare a short summary of your findings to submit to your instructor, stapled to the single page of the appropriate application if you were able to print it.

SHORT ANSWER/ RESEARCH

3. **Ethical Web Images** Many Web sites have free or low cost clip art, photos, or other images available for use on personal or business newsletters, reports, or other printed documents, as well as on Web pages. Use of other images located on Web page, however, may be restricted.

   For this project, use a search site to find a Web site (such as Clip-Art.com or The Free Graphics Store) that offers free images. Determine the types of images and file formats available, as well as if there are any restrictions for use. Next, use the Google Image Search feature to search for an image you might want to use on a personal Web site or MySpace page. Can you tell from the Web page on which the image is located if you are allowed to use that image? If so, is there a fee for its use? If no information is available on the Web page, is there contact information that you could use to request permission to use the image? Are similar images available for free or for a nominal fee online? If so, is the fee reasonable enough for use on a personal Web page? At the conclusion of your research, form an opinion about the availability of free or low cost images online and the ethical and legal use of Web page images and make a recommendation for individuals looking for images to use on personal Web pages. Prepare a short summary of your findings and recommendations and submit it to your instructor.

HANDS ON

WRITING ABOUT COMPUTERS

4. **Codes of Ethics** As discussed in the chapter, many industries and organizations publish codes of ethics to convey general ethical or moral standards expected to be followed by members. For instance, one well-known code of ethics in the computer industry is the Association for Computing Machinery (ACM) Code of Ethics and Professional Standards.

   For this project, locate and review at least one code of ethics issued by an organization and prepare a short summary of the document. Assuming you were a professional in this industry, do you agree with the principles involved? Do you think other professionals in this industry would agree with the ethics and principles contained in the code? Submit your findings and opinions to your instructor in the form of a short paper, no more than two pages in length.

PRESENTATION/ DEMONSTRATION

5. **Domain Hunt** As mentioned in the chapter, domain names are protected by trademark law.

   For this project, select a domain name you would like to use for a fictitious business. Visit at least two domain name registration Web sites (such as NetworkSolutions.com or Register.com) to determine how you would register your domain name and the cost. Which top-level domains would you be able to use for your Web site? For each, determine any requirements, such as length and allowable characters. Select an appropriate domain name for your business and use a lookup feature available on a registration site to see if that domain name is available. If not, keep trying variations of that name until you find an appropriate available domain name. Use a search site to try to determine if there are any Web sites or businesses with confusingly similar names to your domain name. Is there any way to determine if the domain name you selected is a trademark? Share your findings with the class in the form of a short presentation. The presentation should not exceed 10 minutes and should make use of one or more presentation aids, such as the chalkboard, handouts, overhead transparencies, or a computer-based slide presentation (your instructor may provide additional requirements). You may also be asked to submit a summary of the presentation to your instructor.

GROUP DISCUSSION

6. **Digitally Altered Photos** Today's computer and graphics software make manipulation of digital images much easier than in the past. Some acts of digital manipulation are artistic; others are designed to be misleading.

   For this project, look through magazines, newspapers, Web sites, or other media to locate two examples of digitally altered photographs. Make a photocopy of each example and indicate on each copy what manipulation you believe was performed. Is the manipulation ethical or unethical? Was the photograph altered to mislead the public? For artistic purposes? To make a statement? To entertain us? Form an opinion regarding using a computer to digitally alter photographs and be prepared to discuss your position (in class, via an online class discussion group, in a class chat room, or via a class blog, depending on your instructor's directions). You may also be asked to write a short paper expressing your opinion.

7. **Domain Tasting** When you register a domain name, there is a five-day grace period during which time you can receive a full refund. Though originally designed to protect purchasers who might make a typo and mistakenly register the wrong name, this grace period policy has led to "domain tasting"—in which millions of domain names at any given time are held for the grace period. The domain names are usually registered for the purpose of testing their marketability and/or generating income via pay-per-click ads. At the end of the grace period, the domain names that do not generate enough revenue are returned for a full refund—over 62 million domain names were tasted during the month of January 2008 alone. Do you think testing domain names in this manner is ethical? Can you think of an ethical reason for registering multiple domain names with the intention of only keeping some? Should the grace period be eliminated? ICANN, which supervises domain name registration, is considering making part of the registration fee non-refundable. Do you think this is a good solution? One twist is the practice of Network Solutions instantly registering all available domain names that match searches conducted via its Web site. It then holds each domain name for four days, during which time the name is only available for purchase via Network Solutions. A lawsuit was filed in 2008 to stop Network Solutions from this practice, but the suit has not yet been resolved. Is this practice ethical? Is domain tasting ever ethical? Like cybersquatting, should domain tasting be illegal?

   For this project, form an opinion about the ethical ramifications of domain tasting and be prepared to discuss your position (in class, via an online class discussion group, in a class chat room, or via a class blog, depending on your instructor's directions). You may also be asked to write a short paper expressing your opinion.

8. **Reservation Scalpers** There are several Web sites designed to match potential restaurant diners with individuals holding reservations they cannot use or are willing to sell. The accompanying video clip discusses one of these services used in the San Francisco area.

   Go to www.course.com/uccs/ch6 to watch the "New Web Site Allows Diners to Scalp Reservations" video clip. After watching the video, think about the impact of buying and selling restaurant reservations. Is this ethical? What if the reservation was made for the sole purpose of selling it? Are the safeguards used, such as limiting the number of reservations per individual, sufficient to keep the sites operating as they were intended (for individuals whose plans changed)? If restaurants start having more no-shows due to reservation scalpers, are they justified charging a reservation fee? Is this a good solution?

   Express your viewpoint: What is the impact of reservation scalping Web sites?

   Use the video clip and the questions previously asked as a foundation for your response. Be prepared to discuss your position (in class, via an online class discussion group, in a class chat room, or via a class blog) or to write a short paper stating and supporting your viewpoint on the issue, depending on your instructor's direction. You may also be asked to do research and provide resources to support your point of view on this issue.

Student Edition
Labs

9. **Interactive Activities** Go to www.course.com/uccs/ch6 and work the interactive **Crossword Puzzle**, listen to the **Podcasts** and watch the **Online Videos** associated with this chapter, and explore the **Further Exploration** links. In addition, work the following interactive **Student Edition Labs**.

   - Installing and Uninstalling Software
   - Working with Audio
   - Working with Graphics
   - Working with Video
   - Computer Ethics

   If you have a SAM user profile, you have access to even more interactive content. Log in to your SAM account and go to your assignments page to see what your instructor has assigned for this chapter.

10. **Test Yourself** Go to www.course.com/uccs/ch6 and review the **Online Study Guide** for Chapter 6, then test your knowledge of the terms and concepts in this chapter by completing the **Key Term Matching** exercise, the **Self-Quiz**, the **Exercises**, and the **Practice Test**.

EXPERT INSIGHT ON . . .
Systems

A conversation with **STUART FELDMAN**
President of ACM and Vice President, Engineering, Google

> **"**... as information arrives and can be examined more easily, we can do a better job of managing our health, our activities, and our personal interactions.**"**

My Background . . .

I am one of the original computer brats—I learned to program on a vacuum tube machine in the early 1960s as a kid at a summer course. I was enthralled by computer programming, and the ability to create programs that did new and surprising things.

    Throughout my computer career, I've worked as a computer science researcher at Bell Labs, a research manager and software architect at Bellcore, and as Vice President for Computer Science at IBM Research. I am now a Vice President at Google (and responsible for engineering activities at Google's offices in the eastern half of the Americas), as well as President of ACM (Association for Computing Machinery)—the largest computing society in the world. Overall, my career has been spent in research at very high-tech companies, working on the cutting edge of computing. It's fun and exciting.

It's Important to Know . . .

The world of data has shifted radically. I can remember when a megabyte was a lot of information. Today, a gigabyte fits on a thing in your pocket, a terabyte fits on an inexpensive disk, and many large companies manage petabytes—and organizations managing an exabyte of data are coming soon. The types of information to be managed are also shifting—most information today is visual, audio, or executable (not rows and columns of numbers).

Programming languages last a long time. While most programmers write in dynamic languages (such as PERL and Python) today, COBOL and FORTRAN programs are still being written and variants of C are still being born. And even more people do programming without thinking about it (such as creating or modifying word processing macros, spreadsheet formulas, and Web gadgets). We will almost certainly see a continuing expansion of the spectrum—a hard core of experts supporting basic systems and tools, and millions (perhaps billions) of people doing occasional programming and customization.

The impact of systems on society is tremendous. System capabilities have made enormous increases in efficiency possible, and have also opened new types of business and social activities. Think about how banking has changed in the last decade, and about how you look up information and find people. Also, think about how personal communication and expectations have shifted from sending letters with a stamp, to sending e-mail, to texting on a mobile device. Perhaps our attention span has shrunk, but our ability to reach out has increased. Information systems support globalization and rapid business change—sharing of information, shifting of jobs, and the creation of new jobs and whole new types of careers.

Stuart Feldman is currently the President of ACM and a Vice President of Engineering at Google. He is a member of the Board of directors of the AACSB (Association to Advance Collegiate Schools of Business), a Fellow of the IEEE, a Fellow of the ACM, and serves on a number of government advisory committees. He is a recipient of the 2003 ACM Software System Award for creating a seminal piece of software engineering known as Make, a tool for maintaining computer software. Stuart has a Ph.D. in Mathematics from MIT.

The best preparation for a long and successful career is to understand the fundamentals of computing deeply, and be able to apply them to new situations.

How I Use this Technology . . .

I spend a lot of time writing papers and presentations, so I use the Google Docs applications and the Microsoft Office suite—both complex systems that maintain data and perform reliably. I use secure, integrated financial systems when I perform online financial transactions. Of course, my favorite system "application" is the World Wide Web, which is a remarkable linkage of data servers, application providers, and communication systems. I use it many times a day for research, communications, shopping, and amusement.

What the Future Holds . . .

The cost of computing, measured in cost of instructions executed or information stored or transmitted, will continue to drop. This exponential curve will drive many of the improvements we will see in the future. In addition, the value of information and knowledge that is encapsulated in computer programs will increase—once something is in code, it can be used and replicated at low incremental cost. This will continue to drive our digitization and automation of activities.

There will also be the increasing ability to do massive amounts of computing for enormous numbers of users, and to apply computing resources to problems that were too expensive to address just a few years ago. This will be facilitated by the increased use of integration and by using available software and services in innovative ways, as well as by dynamic languages and the increased use of Web standards.

There will be new service computing models, ranging from enterprise SOA to user-based mashups to entirely new service industries like Google search tools and remote medical advice. For program development, we'll see increasing agility—shifting from waterfall and rigid development methods to more exploratory, prototype-based methods. Verification and testing will continue to be essential.

Perhaps the biggest shifts will come from our increasing dependence on information and access, the risks when things go wrong, and the possibilities of new applications that can improve our lives. For instance, as information arrives and can be examined more easily, we can do a better job of managing our health, our activities, and our personal interactions.

My Advice to Students . . .

IT jobs, computer applications, programming languages, approaches to system development, and business needs are always changing. The best preparation for a long and successful career is to understand the fundamentals of computing deeply, and be able to apply them to new situations. You need to become expert in some area—such as a programming language, a methodology, or an environment—but you also must always be prepared to learn new technologies and gain new expertise.

Discussion Question

Stuart Feldman points out how our expectations for the systems we use today have shifted, such as in terms of demands for faster communications and information retrieval. What are your expectations when you send an e-mail message or text message? Do you expect an immediate response? Are you more impatient today with personal communications than in the past? How does the instant access to communications, news, and other information affect our society today? Be prepared to discuss your position (in class, via an online class discussion group, in a class chat room, or via a class blog, depending on your instructor's directions). You may also be asked to write a short paper expressing your opinion.

>**For access to Google search tools and applications, visit www.google.com. There are some excellent papers available at research.google.com. For more information about ACM or to access the ACM Digital Library, visit www.acm.org.**

7

CHAPTER

Health, Access, and the Environment

OUTLINE

LEARNING OBJECTIVES

After completing this chapter, you will be able to do the following:

1. Understand the potential risks to physical health resulting from the use of computers.

2. Describe some possible emotional health risks associated with the use of computers.

3. Explain what is meant by the term "digital divide."

4. Discuss the impact that factors such as nationality, income, race, education, and physical disabilities may have on computer access and use.

5. List some types of assistive hardware that can be used by individuals with physical disabilities.

6. Suggest some ways computer users can practice "green computing" and properly dispose of obsolete computer equipment.

7. Discuss the current status of legislation related to health, access, and the environment in relation to computers.

Computers have unarguably changed the way many of us work and live. We typically use them at work to assist with job-related tasks; at home to shop, pay bills, correspond with others, watch TV, and more; and on the go to keep in touch with others and get the information we need at any given time. While our extensive use of computers often makes daily tasks easier, it also can cause serious health and emotional problems, and can have a negative impact on the environment. In addition, although computer use is becoming almost mandatory in our society, many believe that access to computers is not equally available to all individuals.

The chapter begins with a look at health-oriented concerns, including the impact computers may have on a user's physical and emotional health, as well as strategies individuals can use to lessen those risks. Next, we turn to the issue of equal access, including a discussion of the digital divide and how other factors—such as gender, age, and physical disabilities—may affect computer access and use. We then take a look at the potential impact of computers on our environment, and the chapter closes with a look at legislation related to the issues discussed in this chapter. ■

PODCAST

Go to **www.course.com/uccs/ch7** to download or listen to the "Expert Insight on Computers and Society" podcast.

COMPUTERS AND HEALTH

Despite their many benefits, computers can pose a threat to a user's physical and mental well-being. *Repetitive stress injuries* and other injuries related to the workplace environment are estimated to account for one-third of all serious workplace injuries and to cost employees, employers, and insurance companies over $50 billion each year in lost wages, healthcare expenses, legal costs, and worker's compensation claims. Other physical dangers, such as heat burns and hearing loss, can be associated with computers and related technology, and there are some concerns about the long-term effect of using computers and other related devices. *Stress, burnout, computer/Internet addiction*, and other emotional health problems are more difficult to quantify, although many experts believe computer-related emotional health problems are on the rise. While researchers are continuing to investigate the physical and emotional risks of computer use and are working to develop strategies for minimizing those risks, it is important for all computer users to be aware of the possible effects of computers on their health and what they can do today to stay healthy while using a computer both for personal use and while on the job.

Physical Health

Common physical conditions caused by computer use include eyestrain, blurred vision, fatigue, headaches, backaches, and wrist and finger pain. Some conditions are classified as **repetitive stress injuries** (**RSIs**), in which hand, wrist, shoulder, or neck pain is caused by performing the same physical movements over and over again. For instance, extensive

---

>**Repetitive stress injury (RSI).** A type of injury, such as carpal tunnel syndrome, that is caused by performing the same physical movements over and over again.

FURTHER EXPLORATION

Go to **www.course.com/uccs/ch7** for links to further information about computer use injuries and how they can be prevented.

keyboard and mouse use has also been associated with RSIs, although RSIs can be caused by non-computer-related activities, as well. One RSI related to the repetitive finger movements made when using a keyboard is **carpal tunnel syndrome (CTS)**—a painful and crippling condition affecting the hands and wrists. CTS occurs when the nerve in the *carpal tunnel* located on the underside of the wrist is compressed. An RSI associated with typing on the tiny keyboards and thumbpads commonly found on mobile phones and mobile devices is **DeQuervain's tendonitis**—a condition in which the tendons on the thumb side of the wrists are swollen and irritated. Another physical condition is *computer vision syndrome (CVS)*—a collection of eye and vision problems associated with computer use. The most common symptoms are eyestrain or eye fatigue, dry eyes, burning eyes, light sensitivity, blurred vision, headaches, and pain in the shoulders, neck, or back. Eyestrain is growing more common as individuals are increasingly reading content on the small displays commonly built into mobile phones and mobile devices.

Some recent physical health concerns center around heat. For instance, one study measured the peak temperature on the underside of a typical notebook PC at over 139° Fahrenheit; this means that some notebook computers are now hot enough to burn a person's legs when operated on the user's lap. Consequently, many portable PC manufacturers now warn against letting any part of the PC touch your body, and a variety of *laptop desks* (see Figure 7-1) are now available to place between the PC and your lap for those occasions when a better work surface is not available. Another growing physical health concern is noise-induced hearing loss due to headset use. The volume of today's portable digital media players can be turned up very high without audio distortion, and the earbud headsets typically used with these devices deliver sound directly into the ear. In addition, people often listen to the music stored on these devices while they are on the go and have a tendency to increase the volume in an attempt to drown out outside noise, further posing a risk to their hearing. To protect against hearing loss, experts suggest a 60/60 rule—using earbuds for only about 60 minutes per day with the volume less than 60% of the device's maximum volume. For extended use, *noise reduction headphones* that help block out external noise to allow listeners to hear music better at lower volumes can help, as can using over-the-ear-headphones instead of earbuds and using an external speaker whenever possible.

Another new danger that came into the forefront recently is text messaging while driving. There have been many cases of texting-related car accidents, including several fatalities. A survey by the the national "Drive for Life" safety initiative found that 6% of all Americans (and 32% of all drivers 16 to 20 years old) said they have read or sent a text message while driving, and one study in Great Britain found that almost 60% of people under 30 text message while they drive. Several states in the United States have made or are in the process of making talking on the phone using a handheld mobile phone illegal while driving. In order to comply with the law, drivers must place calls using hands-free devices, such as via a Bluetooth headset or a speakerphone setup (refer again to Figure 7-1). While many of these laws do not specifically include text messaging, some—such as a new law in the state of Washington—do and more states are expected to soon follow suit.

V FIGURE 7-1
Devices that can be used to increase personal safety.

LAPTOP DESKS
Help avoid getting burned from a hot notebook PC.

BLUETOOTH HEADSETS
Allow drivers to place mobile phone calls more safely while driving.

>**Carpal tunnel syndrome (CTS).** A painful and crippling condition affecting the hands and wrist that can be caused by computer use.
>**DeQuervain's tendonitis.** A condition in which the tendons on the thumb side of the wrist are swollen and irritated.

An additional health concern is the possible risks due to the radiation emitted from wireless devices, such as mobile phones, Wi-Fi and Bluetooth devices, wireless peripherals, and so forth. Mobile phones, in particular, have been studied for several decades because of their close proximity to the user's head. The results of the studies have been conflicting, with many experts believing that the possible health risks (such as cancer and brain tumors) due to wireless technology has been exaggerated, and others believing the risk is very real. A new possible health risk identified in a recent study is associated with the particles emitted from some laser printers. While more research is needed to definitively link laser printers with health risks, it is possible that the small particles released from these printers could be inhaled and cause lung problems. Until more research is performed, health experts recommend ensuring rooms with laser printers are well ventilated.

A proper work environment and good habits—a concept known as *ergonomics*—can prevent many physical problems caused by computer use and is important for anyone who works on a computer, including employees using a computer on the job, individuals using a PC at home, and children doing computer activities at home or at school.

What Is Ergonomics?

Ergonomics is the science of fitting a work environment to the people who work there. It typically focuses on making products and workspaces more comfortable and safe to use. With respect to computer use, it involves designing a safe and effective workspace, which includes properly adjusting furniture and hardware and using *ergonomic hardware* when needed. But there is more to ergonomics than just physical equipment—good user habits and procedures are important, too. These topics are discussed in the next few sections.

Workspace Design

The design of a safe and effective computer workspace—whether it is located at work, home, or school—includes the placement and adjustment of all the furniture and equipment involved, such as the user's desk, chair, keyboard, and monitor (see Figure 7-2). Workspace lighting and glare from the sun also need to be taken into consideration. Proper workspace design can result in fewer injuries, headaches, and general aches and pains for computer users. Businesses can reap economic benefits from proper workspace design, such as fewer

PODCAST

Go to **www.course.com/uccs/ch7** to download or listen to the "Ergonomics and Computer Related Injuries" podcast.

FIGURE 7-2
Workspace design. Shown here are some guidelines for designing an ergonomic workspace.

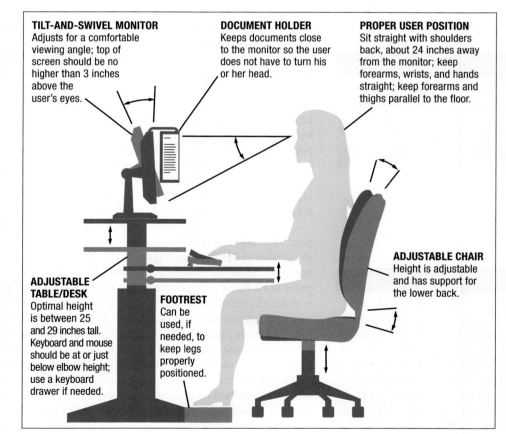

TILT-AND-SWIVEL MONITOR Adjusts for a comfortable viewing angle; top of screen should be no higher than 3 inches above the user's eyes.

DOCUMENT HOLDER Keeps documents close to the monitor so the user does not have to turn his or her head.

PROPER USER POSITION Sit straight with shoulders back, about 24 inches away from the monitor; keep forearms, wrists, and hands straight; keep forearms and thighs parallel to the floor.

ADJUSTABLE TABLE/DESK Optimal height is between 25 and 29 inches tall. Keyboard and mouse should be at or just below elbow height; use a keyboard drawer if needed.

FOOTREST Can be used, if needed, to keep legs properly positioned.

ADJUSTABLE CHAIR Height is adjustable and has support for the lower back.

> **Ergonomics.** The science of fitting a work environment to the people who work there.

absences taken by employees, higher productivity, and lower insurance costs. For example, when one government department in New Jersey installed ergonomically correct workstations in their offices, computer-related health complaints fell by 40% and doctor visits dropped by 25% in less than one year.

Proper placement and adjustment of furniture is a good place to start when evaluating a workspace from an ergonomic perspective. The desk should be placed where the sun and other sources of light cannot shine directly onto the screen or into the user's eyes. The monitor should be placed directly in front of the user about an arm's length away, and the top of the screen should be no more than 3 inches above the user's eyes once the user's chair is adjusted. The desk chair should be adjusted so that the keyboard is at, or slightly below, the height at which the user's forearms are horizontal to the floor (there are also special *ergonomic chairs* that can be used, when desired). A footrest should be used, if needed, to keep the user's feet flat on the floor once the chair height has been set. The monitor settings should be adjusted to make the screen brightness match the brightness of the room and to have a high amount of contrast. The screen should also be periodically wiped clean of dust.

When designing or evaluating a computer workspace, the type of computer work to be performed should be considered. For example, people who refer to written documents while working on their PCs should use *document holders* to keep their documents close to their monitors to avoid the repetitive motion of looking between the document and the monitor—an action that can create or aggravate neck problems. These users should also place their keyboards directly in front of them for easy access. On the other hand, for Web surfing or other computer activities (such as computer-aided design or graphics design) that require a great deal of mouse work, placement of the mouse for comfortable access should be given high priority.

The workspace design principles just discussed and illustrated in Figure 7-2 apply to users of both desktop and portable computers. However, an ergonomic workspace is more difficult to obtain when using a portable computer. To create a safer and more comfortable work environment, notebook, tablet, and UMPC users should attach and use a separate keyboard and mouse whenever possible both at home and while traveling (*travel mice* and *travel keyboards* are smaller and lighter than conventional models to make them more portable; some travel keyboards fold or roll up for easy storage). In addition to being able to position the keyboard and mouse at more comfortable positions, using a separate keyboard and mouse enables the user to elevate the screen of the portable PC to a better viewing angle. To help with this and with connecting peripheral devices to a portable PC, *docking stations* and *notebook stands* can be used.

While a keyboard, mouse, monitor, and printer can be connected to a portable PC directly, a **docking station** is a device designed to more easily connect a portable computer to peripheral devices (see Figure 7-3). They are often used in homes and offices when a notebook computer is used as a primary PC; the docking station allows the notebook computer to be easily connected and disconnected from the docking station, while the peripheral devices remain connected to the docking station. Whenever the notebook computer is connected to the docking station, the peripheral devices can be used. A **notebook stand** (also shown in Figure 7-3) is designed primarily to elevate the display screen of a notebook or tablet PC so it can be used instead of an external monitor. Some notebook stands have a built-in USB hub to connect USB peripheral devices to the notebook computer; if not, any peripheral device—such as a keyboard and mouse—used with the notebook computer while it is inserted into the notebook stand needs to be connected directly to the computer. Smaller, lightweight portable notebook stands are available to elevate a notebook's display while traveling. Notebook stands also allow air to circulate around the bottom of the

>**Docking station.** A device that connects a portable PC to conventional hardware, such as a keyboard, mouse, monitor, and printer.
>**Notebook stand.** A device that elevates the display of a notebook computer to a better viewing height; some contain USB ports to connect additional hardware.

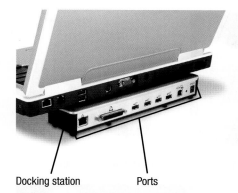

Docking station   Ports

DOCKING STATIONS
Contain a variety of ports; when the portable computer is connected to the docking station, the devices attached to these ports can be used.

Notebook stand   USB ports

NOTEBOOK STANDS
Elevate a notebook's display screen; if the notebook stand contains USB ports, devices attached to these ports can be used with the notebook while it is in the notebook stand.

FIGURE 7-3
Docking stations and notebook stands.

computer; for additional cooling, some notebook stands have a built-in cooling fan that is powered (via a USB port) by the computer. Some additional ergonomic tips for notebook users are included in Figure 7-4.

Ergonomic Hardware

In addition to the hardware (adjustable chairs and tables, footrests, notebook stands, laptop desks, and so on) already discussed that can be used to help users avoid physical problems due to extensive PC use or to help alleviate the discomfort associated with an already existing condition, there are also various types of **ergonomic hardware** specifically designed for this purpose.

FIGURE 7-4
Ergonomic tips for notebook computer users.

OCCASIONAL USERS	FULL-TIME USERS
Sit with the notebook on a table and position it for comfortable wrist posture. If no table is available, use a laptop desk as a work surface and to protect your legs from the notebook's heat.	Sit with the notebook on a desk or table and position it for comfortable wrist posture if you won't be using a separate keyboard and mouse.
Adjust the screen to a comfortable position, so you can see the screen as straight on as possible. If you have a portable notebook stand, use it to elevate the display screen for easier viewing.	Elevate the notebook so the screen is at the proper height, or connect the PC to a stand-alone monitor instead of using the notebook's built-in display; consider using a docking station or notebook stand.
Bring a travel keyboard and mouse to use with the notebook PC, whenever possible.	Use a separate keyboard and mouse, either attached directly to the PC or to a docking station or notebook stand.
When purchasing a notebook, pay close attention to the total weight of the system (PC, power supply, additional hardware, etc.) if you will be using the notebook primarily while traveling; purchase a lightweight system to avoid neck and shoulder injuries when carrying the notebook from one location to another.	When purchasing a notebook, pay close attention to the size and clarity of the monitor, unless you will be using a separate stand-alone monitor, and pay close attention to the keyboard design, unless you will be using a separate keyboard.

>**Ergonomic hardware.** Hardware, typically input and output devices, that is designed to be more ergonomically correct than its nonergonomic counterparts.

ERGONOMIC KEYBOARDS

ERGONOMIC MICE

DOCUMENT HOLDERS

ANTIGLARE SCREENS

KEYBOARD DRAWERS

WRIST SUPPORTS

COMPUTER GLOVES

FIGURE 7-5
Ergonomic devices.

Some common types of ergonomic hardware are shown in Figure 7-5 and discussed next.

▶ *Ergonomic keyboards* use a shape and key arrangement designed to lessen the strain on the hands and wrists; the keyboard shown in Figure 7-5 has keys laid out vertically to reduce the risk of an RSI.

▶ *Ergonomic mice* are shaped to be more comfortable and are designed to reduce pressure on the carpal tunnel and wrist; several (like the one shown in Figure 7-5) are designed to be used with the hand vertical, instead of horizontal, similar to the way a joystick is used. Some users find other types of pointing devices (such as a trackball) more comfortable than a mouse when extensive mouse use is required.

▶ *Document holders*—sometimes called *copy holders*—can be used to keep documents close to the monitor, enabling the user to see both the document and the monitor without turning his or her head. Document holders are available for both desktop and portable PCs.

▶ *Antiglare screens*—sometimes called *privacy filters*—that cover the monitor screen can be used to lessen glare and resulting eyestrain. Many antiglare screens double as privacy screens, preventing others sitting next to you (such as on an airplane) from reading what is displayed on your notebook screen.

▶ *Keyboard drawers* lower the keyboard, enabling the user to keep his or her forearms parallel to the floor more easily.

▶ *Wrist supports* designed to be placed next to the mouse or keyboard can be used to help keep wrists straight while those devices are being used, as well as to provide support for the wrists and forearms when the devices are not being used.

▶ *Computer gloves* support the wrist and thumb while allowing the full use of your hand and are designed to prevent and relieve wrist pain, including carpal tunnel syndrome, tendonitis, and other RSIs.

Good User Habits and Precautions
Computer users can follow a number of preventive measures while working at their PCs, in addition to establishing an ergonomic workspace. For example, finger and wrist exercises

and frequent breaks in typing are good precautions for helping to prevent repetitive hand and finger stress injuries. Using good posture and periodically taking a break to relax or stretch the body can help reduce or prevent back and neck strain. Rotating tasks—such as alternating between computer work, telephone work, and paperwork every 15 minutes or so—is also a good idea. For locations where some glare from a nearby window is unavoidable at certain times of the day, closing the curtains or blinds can help to prevent eyestrain. All computer users should refocus their eyes on an object in the distance for a minute or so on a regular basis, and mobile phone and mobile device users should increase font size and light level when viewing text on a small display screen. Eyeglass wearers should discuss any eye fatigue or blurriness during computer use with their eye doctors. Sometimes a different lens prescription or special *computer glasses* (eyeglasses that are optimized for viewing in the intermediate zone of vision where a computer monitor usually falls—that is, closer than glasses designed for driving and farther than glasses designed for reading) can be used to reduce eyestrain while working on a PC. See Figure 7-6 for list of preventive measures computer users can take.

CONDITION	PREVENTION
Wrist/arm/hand soreness and injury	▪ Use a light touch on the keyboard. ▪ Rest and gently stretch your fingers and arms every 15 minutes or so. ▪ Keep your wrists and arms relaxed and parallel to the floor when using the keyboard. ▪ When using a device with a small keyboard, type short messages, take frequent breaks, and use a separate keyboard whenever possible. ▪ Use an ergonomic keyboard, ergonomic mouse, computer glove, and other ergonomic devices if you begin to notice wrist or hand soreness.
Eyestrain	▪ Cover windows or adjust lighting to eliminate glare. ▪ Concentrate on blinking your eyes more often. ▪ Rest your eyes every 15 minutes or so by focusing on an object in the distance (at least 20 feet away) for one minute and then closing your eyes for an additional minute. ▪ Make sure your monitor's brightness and contrast settings are at an appropriate level. ▪ Use a larger text size or lower screen resolution, if needed (you should be able to read what is displayed on your monitor from three times the distance at which you normally sit).
Sore or stiff neck	▪ Use good posture. ▪ Place the monitor and any documents you need to refer to while using your PC directly in front of you. ▪ Adjust your monitor to a comfortable viewing angle with the top of the screen no higher than 3 inches above your eyes. ▪ Use a telephone headset if you spend a significant amount of time each day on the telephone.
Backache; general fatigue	▪ Use good posture and adjust your chair to support your lower back; use an ergonomic chair, if needed. ▪ Use a footrest, if needed, to keep your feet flat on the floor. ▪ Walk around or stretch briefly at least once every hour. ▪ Alternate activities frequently. ▪ When traveling with a computer, bring a lightweight computer and carry only the essentials with you.
Ringing in the ears; hearing loss	▪ Turn down the volume when using headphones (you should be able to hear other people's voices). ▪ Wear over-the-ear-headphones instead of earbuds. ▪ Intersperse listening with quiet periods. ▪ Use external speakers instead of headphones when possible.
Leg discomfort or burns	▪ Use a laptop desk or other barrier between a notebook computer and your legs when using a notebook computer on your lap.

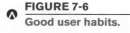

FIGURE 7-6
Good user habits.

Emotional Health

The extensive use of computers and related technology in the home and office in recent years has raised new concerns about emotional health. Factors such as financial worries, feelings of being overworked, being unable to relax, and information overload often produce emotional stress. Decades of research have linked stress to a variety of health concerns, such as heart attacks, stroke, diabetes, and weakened immune systems. Workers who report feeling stressed incur more healthcare costs—an average of $600 more per person, according to one study—than nonstressed workers. Consequently, workplace stress is expensive. According to the American Institute of Stress, it costs U.S. employers more than $300 billion each year in healthcare, missed work, and stress-reduction services provided to employees.

For many individuals, computer use or computer-related events are the cause of, or at least partially contribute to, the stress that they experience. Another emotional health concern related to computer use is *computer/Internet addiction*.

Impact of Our 24/7 Society

One benefit of our communications-oriented society is that one never has to be out of touch. With the use of mobile phones, mobile devices, and portable PCs, as well as the ability to access e-mail and company networks from virtually anywhere, individuals can be available around the clock, if needed (see Figure 7-7). Although the ability to be in touch constantly is an advantage for some people under certain conditions, it can also be a source of great stress. For example, employees who feel that they are "on call" 24/7 and cannot ever get away from work may find it difficult to relax during their downtime. Others who are used to being in touch constantly may not be able to relax when they are on vacation and supposed to be unavailable because they are afraid of missing something important that may affect their careers. In either case, these individuals may lose the distinction between personal time and work time, and so they may end up being always on the job. This can affect their personal lives, emotional health, and overall well-being. Finding a balance between work time and personal time is important for good emotional health.

FIGURE 7-7
Our 24/7 society.

FIGURE 7-8
Many jobs require computer use today.

Stress of Ever-Changing Technology

When computers were first introduced into the workplace, workers needed to learn the appropriate computer skills if their jobs required computer use. Airline agents, for example, had to learn to use computer databases. Secretaries and other office employees needed to learn to use word processing and other office-related software, and customer service representatives needed to learn how to use e-mail. Today, many people entering the workforce are aware of the computer skills they will need to perform the tasks associated with their chosen professions. However, as computers have become continually more integrated into our society, jobs that did not require the use of a computer in the recent past may very well require it today (see Figure 7-8). And, at the rapid pace that technology keeps changing, many workers must regularly learn new skills to keep up to date. For example, they may need to upgrade to a new version of a software program, learn how to use a new software program, or learn how to use a new piece of hardware. Although some find this exciting (see the Technology and You box for a look at the programming contest opportunities available to programming students), the ongoing battle to stay current with changing technology creates stress for many individuals.

UTILITY WORKERS

AIRPLANE TECHNICIANS

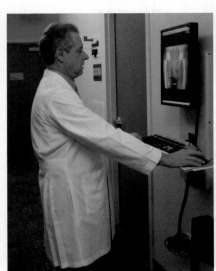

PHYSICIANS

POLICE OFFICERS

TECHNOLOGY AND YOU

Programming Contests

Think you're an awesome programmer? There are a number of contests available in which programmers can show off their stuff. One example is the *TopCoder Collegiate Challenge*, in which college students compete for bragging rights and their share of the $260,000 prize purse. Students select from five competitions (Algorithm, Software Design, Software Development, Marathon Match, and TopCoder Studio) and then compete to advance in the competition. For instance, the Algorithm Competition begins with timed online Qualification Rounds consisting of three phases. In the Coding Phase, contestants have 75 minutes to code solutions for three problems. Solutions must be each contestant's original work and can be coded in Java, C++, C#, or VB.NET. During the Challenge Phase, contestants have 15 minutes to challenge the functionality of other competitors' code. Contestants gain or lose points depending on the outcome of the challenges they make and the challenges made against them. During the System Testing Phase, an automated tester applies a set of inputs to each submitted solution and tests the code to see if the output is correct. Contestants with code deemed to be flawed lose all points previously earned for that code. Ultimately, 48 semifinalists eventually compete on site at the contest. The winners for the 2007 TopCoder Collegiate Challenge are shown in the accompanying photograph.

At any given time, TopCoder offers online competitions in software design, development, assembly, and testing, including some contests specifically for high-school students. Winning a programming contest is good for your reputation and résumé, and it can also net you some pretty decent bucks.

The 2007 TopCoder Collegiate Challenge winners.

Information Overload

Although the amount of information available through the Internet is a great asset, it can also be overwhelming at times. When you combine Internet information with TV and radio news broadcasts; newspaper, journal, and magazine articles; and telephone calls, voice mail messages, and faxes, some Americans are practically drowning in information. The amount of e-mail received each day by some individuals and organizations is almost unfathomable. For example, the U.S. Senate receives millions of e-mail messages each day, and it is estimated that workers in the United States spend an average of two hours per day dealing with e-mail messages. One strategy that can be used to avoid the stress of being continually interrupted when you are working on your computer is turning off your new e-mail alert notifier (or muting your speakers) and just checking e-mail at your convenience. Other strategies to avoid becoming completely overwhelmed by information overload are discussed next.

ASK THE EXPERT

admob

Kevin Scott, Vice President of Engineering, AdMob; Member-at-Large, ACM Council

What is the hottest IT-oriented job today? What positions do you expect to be in the most demand five years from now?

The explosive growth of networked services and the data that they create is going to continue to create huge demand for Web application developers, distributed systems and network engineers, and analytical engineers experienced in information retrieval, machine learning, natural language processing, data mining, and basic statistical techniques.

TIP

For a review of how to perform efficient and effective Internet searches, refer again to Chapter 3.

For efficiently extracting the information you need from the vast amount of information available over the Internet, good search techniques are essential. Perhaps the most important thing to keep in mind when dealing with information overload is that you cannot possibly read everything ever written on a particular subject. At some point in time when performing Internet research, the value of additional information decreases and, eventually, it is not worth your time to continue the search. Knowing when to quit a search or when to try another research approach is an important skill in avoiding information overload.

As discussed in Chapter 3, *RSS feeds* can be used to deliver on a regular basis only the Web site content you specify, which helps reduce information overload. RSS is also beginning to be used for some types of internal business communications (such as to send information to employees that they need to know about, but don't need to act on right away) to reduce the amount of internal e-mail that employees receive. *Intelligent agents*—software programs that do specified jobs based on your instructions, as discussed in Chapter 8—can also gather information for you on a regular basis, as well as perform other helpful tasks, such as notifying you when a particular Web page has been updated or a certain stock hits a specified price. Other programs can suppress those annoying pop-up ads or otherwise help you have a more efficient and pleasant Internet experience.

Efficiently managing your incoming e-mail is another way to avoid information overload. Tools for managing e-mail can help alleviate the stress of an overflowing Inbox, as well as cut down the amount of time you spend dealing with your online correspondence. As discussed in Chapter 5, e-mail filters can be used to route messages automatically into specific folders (such as suspected spam), based on criteria you set. This allows you to concentrate on the messages most important to you first and leave the others—such as the possible spam—to be sorted through and dealt with at your convenience. If you need to follow up on a message at a later time, flag it—many e-mail programs like Microsoft Outlook allow you to flag messages with a specific follow-up time (such as tomorrow or next week), as well as to add a reminder to your calendar so you will be reminded when it is time to follow up (see Figure 7-9). Some productivity training companies advise treating e-mail like physical mail and opening e-mail only a limited number of times per day. According to these companies, avoiding continually jumping back and forth between e-mail and other activities can both increase productivity and decrease stress significantly.

Click to add a flag to a message.

Flags are color-coded by follow-up time.

Reminder alarms can be set.

Items past their follow-up time are highlighted.

FIGURE 7-9
Outlook reminder flags can help you organize your Inbox.

Burnout

Our heavy use of computers, combined with information overload and 24/7 accessibility via technology, can lead to **burnout**—a state of fatigue or frustration brought about by overwork. Burnout is often born from good intentions—when, for example, hardworking people try to reach goals that, for one reason or another, become unrealistic. Early signs of burnout include a feeling of emotional and physical exhaustion, no longer caring about a project that used to be interesting or exciting, irritability, feelings of resentment about the amount of work that needs to be done, and feeling pulled in many directions at once.

When you begin to notice the symptoms of burnout, experts recommend reevaluating your schedule, priorities, and lifestyle. Sometimes, just admitting that you are feeling

>**Burnout.** A state of fatigue or frustration usually brought on by overwork.

overwhelmed is a good start to solving the problem. Taking a break or getting away for a day can help put the situation in perspective. Saying no to additional commitments and making sure that you eat properly, exercise regularly, and otherwise take good care of yourself are also important strategies for coping with and alleviating both stress and burnout.

Computer/Internet Addiction

When an individual overuses, or is unable to stop using, a computer or the Internet, it becomes a problem and is referred to as **computer/Internet addiction**—also called *computer addiction disorder (CAD)*, *Internet addiction disorder (IAD)*, and *cyberaddiction*. According to Maressa Hecht Orzack, a member of the Harvard Medical School faculty and the director of the Computer Addiction Study Center at McLean Hospital in Massachusetts, computer addiction is "an emerging disorder suffered by people who find the virtual reality on computer screens more attractive than everyday reality." She estimates that between 10% and 15% of Internet users suffer some sort of Internet dependency and the level of addiction for individuals who play online role playing games is much higher—up to 40%. In addition, as technologies improve and *massive multiplayer online role-playing games (MMORPG)* become even more sophisticated and exciting, the level of Internet addiction may increase. Addiction to online gambling, virtual worlds, and other online activities that involve real money is a growing concern, as is the increased popularity of social networking sites, which may allow individuals to divulge too much information about themselves to strangers.

Computer/Internet addiction can affect people of any age and can take a variety of forms. Some individuals become addicted to e-mailing or instant messaging. Others become compulsive online shoppers or online gamblers, or become addicted to chat room or social networking activities. Still others cannot stop playing computer or video games, or struggle with real-world relationships because of virtual world relationships. Currently, the most common forms of addictive behaviors include instant messaging, online chatting, online pornography, and online gaming. One example is a 17-year-old high school student who was addicted to instant messaging. She would immediately go online after school and would be online all day during vacations. When people did not respond immediately to her messages, she took it personally and became depressed and, eventually, suicidal. After breaking her addiction with counseling and antidepressants, she now has a healthy balance between the Internet and other activities. Another young person who is addicted to a MMORPG is not as fortunate. He has several physical problems, including seizures and lack of sleep, and has not yet graduated from high school because of these problems. In other cases of IAD, parents have lost custody of their children because they weren't taking proper care of them due to the amount of time spent online, and individuals have been fired multiple times from their jobs because they could not stop visiting pornographic or other non-work-related Web sites at work.

IAD is increasingly being tied to crime and even death in countries, such as China and South Korea, that have high levels of broadband Internet access. For instance, Internet addiction is blamed for much of the juvenile crime in China, a number of suicides, and several deaths from exhaustion by players unable to tear themselves away from marathon gaming sessions. And in one instance in 2005, an online game player in Shanghai actually stabbed and killed a fellow online gamer for selling a dragon sabre (an online sword used in the Legend of Mir 3 game) that was loaned to the victim but that the victim sold online instead of returning. The victim reportedly promised to pay the owner of the sword back, but the owner of the sword lost patience and attacked the victim in his home—the man was sentenced to life in prison for the crime.

> **TIP**
>
> View your Inbox as a temporary location only; after reading an e-mail message, immediately delete it, flag it, or file it in an e-mail folder to keep your Inbox clean.

> **Computer/Internet addiction.** The problem of overusing, or being unable to stop using, a computer and/or the Internet.

SYMPTOMS OF COMPUTER/INTERNET ADDICTION

You need to use the computer in order to experience pleasure, excitement, or relief.

You lose control when not on the computer, becoming anxious, angry, or depressed.

You have overwhelming thoughts about the computer before you power it up, while it is on, and after you have turned it off.

You crave the newest hardware or software, and you are never satisfied with what you have.

You need to spend increasing amounts of time or money on computer activities in order to get the same effect.

You lie to everybody about the amount of time spent on the computer and where you are spending that time.

You risk the loss of relationships with your family and friends because of your compulsive computer use.

You face financial trouble, or even ruin, because of excessive computer use.

You repeatedly fail at efforts to stop your compulsive computer use.

Your physical health suffers because you miss meals, do not exercise, and neglect personal hygiene.

You experience repetitive stress injuries, backaches, dry eyes, migraines, and changes in sleep patterns as a result of excessive computer use. You may even have seizures (which may require hospitalization) because of the constant motion that you experience while playing some action games.

FIGURE 7-10

Symptoms of computer addiction. You may be addicted to or dependent on your computer if you experience at least five of these symptoms.

Like other addictions, computer/Internet addiction may result in many losses, such as loss of relationships, job loss, academic failure, health problems, and suicide, and may be the result of either a mood disorder or an anxiety disorder (see Figure 7-10 for Dr. Orzack's list of computer/Internet addiction symptoms). These behaviors may result in increasing amounts of time and money spent on computers and other problems. Many experts believe computer/Internet addiction is a growing problem. A recent study from Stanford University revealed that over one-eighth of American adults exhibit at least one sign of Internet addiction, and it is estimated that about 13% of all Chinese under the age of 18 are Internet addicts and up to 30% of all South Koreans under the age of 18 are at risk for Internet addiction. Both China and South Korea have implemented military-style boot camps to treat young people identified as having Internet addiction. And the growing number of Internet-addicted youth prompted the Chinese government to ban minors from Internet cafés, as well as to issue a one-year moratorium on the opening of any new Internet cafés.

Many experts believe that while computer/Internet addiction is a growing problem, it can be treated, similar to other addictions, with therapy, support groups, and medication.

ACCESS TO TECHNOLOGY

For many, a major concern about the increased integration of computers and technology into our society is whether or not technology is accessible to all individuals. Some believe there is a distinct line dividing those who have access and those who do not. Factors such as age, gender, race, income, education, and physical abilities can all impact one's access to technology and how one uses it.

The Digital Divide

The term **digital divide** refers to the gap between those who have access to information and communications technology and those who do not—often referred to as the "haves" and "have nots." Typically, the digital divide is thought to be based on physical access to computers and other types of related technology. Some individuals, however, believe that the definition of the digital divide goes deeper than just access. For example, they classify those individuals who have physical access to technology but who do not understand how to use it or are discouraged from using it in the "have not" category. Groups and individuals trying to eliminate the digital divide are working toward providing real access to technology (including access to up-to-date hardware, software, and training) so that it can be used to improve people's lives.

> **Digital divide.** The gap between those who have access to technology and those who do not.

The digital divide can refer to the differences between individuals within a particular country, as well as to the differences between countries. Within a country, use of computers and related technology can vary based on such factors as age, race, education, and income.

The U.S. Digital Divide

Although there is disagreement among experts about the current status of the digital divide within the United States, there is an indication that it is continuing to shrink. The digital divide involves more than just Internet use—it involves the use of any type of technology necessary to succeed in our society—but the growing amount of Internet use is an encouraging sign. As discussed in Chapter 3, nearly 75% of the United States population are Internet users, using the Internet at work, home, school, or another location. Free Internet access at libraries, school, and other public locations, as well as the availability of low-cost PCs and low-cost or free Internet access in many areas today, has helped Internet use begin to approach the popularity and widespread use of telephones and TVs and become more feasible for low-income families today than in the past. In general, however, according to recent reports by the Pew Internet & American Life Project, individuals with a higher level of income or a higher level of education are more likely to go online, and younger individuals are more likely to be online than older Americans. Some overall demographic data about Internet use in the United States is shown in Figure 7-11.

Because the United States is such a technologically advanced society, reducing—and trying to eliminate—the digital divide is extremely important to ensure that all citizens have an equal chance to be successful in this country. Although there has been lots of progress in that direction, more work still remains. For instance, the Navajo Nation (a sovereign tribal nation with more than 250,000 citizens living across 27,000 square miles in New Mexico, Arizona, and Utah) is significantly behind the rest of the U.S. in terms of technology. Many schools lack computers and Internet access, many residents have no telephone, and even some government entities have dial-up or no Internet access. This may soon change as a result of the *Internet to the Hogan* project—a project to build an integrated wired and wireless network infrastructure to enable communications for government entities, as well as for individuals (via connections at community-based chapter houses) within the Navajo Nation. Once the basic infrastructure is in place, the goal is to expand to schools, medical clinics, hospitals, firehouses, and homes within a 15 to 30 mile radius of each chapter house, in order to provide additional services (such as telemedicine and distance learning) and to open up new job opportunities (such as personal Web-based businesses or telecommuting) that are not possible without high-speed Internet connectivity.

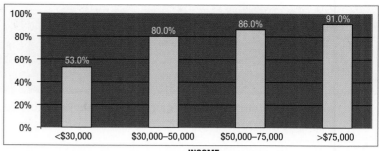

INCOME

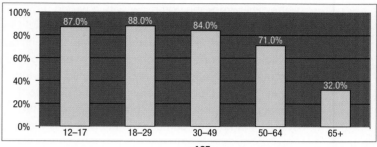

AGE

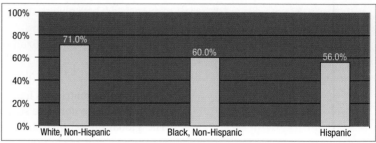

RACE

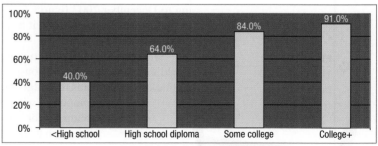

HIGHEST LEVEL OF EDUCATION OBTAINED

Source: Pew Internet & American Life Project

FIGURE 7-11
Key U.S. Internet use statistics. Shows the percent of individuals in each category who use the Internet.

ASK THE EXPERT

Sonny Rouch, Founder, Sonny's Redwoods Web site, and 88-year-old daily Internet user

Why should a senior citizen know how to use the Internet today?

To begin with, everyone should be able to operate a computer. Many seniors think they are too dumb and they will wreck the computer with a wrong move, but that's not true. And the Internet is just fantastic! Once a senior learns how to search the Web, it opens up a whole new world to explore instead of being bored at home. For instance, if you are interested in history, you can go back thousands of years and delve into the history of any country. If you are interested in the stock market, you can use the Internet to find the right company, and buying or selling stock takes but a minute. You can handle all of your finances online, and you can send e-mail to friends and receive their answers in just minutes. You can also send and receive pictures. Whether you are a senior citizen or a student, the possibilities are endless.

Many individuals view computers and the Internet as essential for all Americans today. For instance, students need access to technology and Internet resources to stay informed and be prepared for further education and careers. As already discussed, most jobs in the U.S. require some sort of computer or Internet use. And the Internet is becoming an increasingly important resource for older Americans, particularly for forming decisions about health and healthcare options. However, it is important to realize that not all individuals want to use computers or go online. Just as some people choose not to have televisions, mobile phones, or other technologies, some people—rich or poor— choose not to have a computer or go online. Sometimes this is a religious decision; at other times, it is simply a lifestyle choice.

The Global Digital Divide

While the digital divide within a country is about some individuals within a country having access to technology and others not, the global digital divide is about some countries having access to technology and others not. It is becoming increasingly important for all countries to have access to information and communications technology in order to be able to compete successfully in our global economy.

The global digital divide is perhaps more dramatic than the U.S. digital divide. It is estimated that about 1.3 billion people globally are online—only about 20% of the world's population. Overall, the United States has about 16% of the world's Internet users, according to December 2007 figures from InternetWorldStats.com. While the U.S. has the highest number of Internet users, it has fallen to sixth in the world when comparing percent of population online.

For some, it is difficult to imagine how computers and the Internet would benefit the world's hungry or the 2 billion people without access to reliable electricity. Others view technology as a means to bridge the global digital divide. For instance, mobile phones and computers with solar-rechargeable batteries can be used in developing countries for education and telemedicine. New wireless Internet projects, such as the *Wildnet* technology that is being used to extend Wi-Fi in remote areas to connect areas up to 60 miles apart, are also helping to bridge the gap. Currently deployed in several countries, Wildnets are already being used to provide Internet access to rural schools in Ghana and the Philippines, and to connect doctors in a main hospital in India with technicians in remote eye-care clinics in poor villages.

For personal computer use, new products are emerging that could help alleviate the global digital divide. Perhaps the most widely known project in this area is *One Laptop Per Child* (*OLPC*). This nonprofit organization was created to design, manufacture, and distribute affordable laptop computers to every child in the world in order to provide them with access to new channels of learning, sharing, and self-expression. The first-generation laptop from OLPC is the *XO laptop* shown in Figure 7-12. It is currently being sold to governments of developing

FIGURE 7-12
The OLPC XO laptop.

countries to be distributed to school-aged children. The cost is currently $200 per computer, though the price is expected to drop to closer to the original goal of $100 as production increases.

The XO laptop is made of thick plastic for durability with a display that can be viewed in direct sunlight. The rubber keyboard is sealed to keep out dirt and water, and the XO is very energy-efficient, consuming only one-tenth of the energy of a standard notebook computer. It can be charged via an electrical outlet, as well as from a car battery, foot pedal, or pull string. The XO is Linux-based; contains a variety of communications and connectivity capabilities, including a Wi-Fi adapter and router, USB ports, and a built-in video camera and microphone; and uses 1 GB of flash memory for storage. It also includes a touchpad, gamepad, and directional pad. According to OLPC, making it possible for students in developing countries to have a laptop will greatly impact their education, as well as society as a whole. They believe that by empowering children to educate themselves, a new generation will ultimately be better prepared to tackle the other serious problems (poverty, malnutrition, disease) facing their societies.

Assistive Technology

Research has found that people with disabilities tend to use computers and the Internet at rates below the average for a given population. Part of the reason may be that some physical conditions—such as visual impairment or limited dexterity—make it difficult to use a conventional computer system. That is where **assistive technology**—hardware and software specially designed for use by individuals with physical disabilities—fits in. While assistive technology is not currently available to help with all types of computer content (primarily streaming video and other multimedia content increasingly found on Web pages), there has been much improvement in recent years in the area of assistive technology and researchers are continuing to develop additional types of assistive technology. This growth in assistive technology is due in part to demands by disabled individuals and disability organizations for equal access to computers and Web content, as well as *Section 508* of the *Rehabilitation Act* (which requires federal agencies to make their electronic and information technology accessible to people with disabilities) and the *Americans with Disabilities Act* (*ADA*) (which requires companies with 15 or more employees to make reasonable accommodations for known physical or mental limitations of otherwise qualified individuals). In order to be accessible to users of assistive technology, Web pages need to use features like *alternative text descriptions* (text-based descriptions sometimes called *alt tags* that are assigned to Web page images) and meaningful text-based hyperlinks—such as *How to Contact Us* instead of *Click Here*.

Some states have additional accessibility laws and there has been an increase in accessibility lawsuits recently. For instance, blind employees who work for the state of Texas have filed suit against Oracle Corporation and the state of Texas because the human resources software used by the state is not accessible to these workers, as required by state law, and this causes privacy problems because blind state employees (such as HR personnel, supervisors, and any state employee needing access to his or her personnel record) who need to access the human resources software must have sighted assistance. In addition, a federal judge ruled in late 2007 that Target.com must become accessible to blind individuals under California law; there is a chance that ruling may lead to extending federal disability statutes to Web sites beyond those belonging to the federal government.

To help provide equal access to technology to individuals with physical disabilities, assistive input and output devices—such as *Braille keyboards*, specialized pointing devices, large monitors, and *screen readers*—are available, as discussed next.

>**Assistive technology.** Hardware and software specifically designed for use by individuals who have a physical disability.

BRAILLE KEYBOARDS
The keys on this keyboard contain Braille overlays.

ONE-HANDED KEYBOARDS
All keys can be reached with either the left or right hand, depending on which version of the keyboard is being used (right-handed is shown here).

HEAD-POINTING SYSTEMS WITH PUFF SWITCH
With this system, head movement controls the pointer movement, and puffs of air into the tube are used to "click" objects.

HEAD-POINTING SYSTEMS WITHOUT A SWITCH
With this system, head movement (tracked via the reflective brim of her hat) controls the pointer movement, and pointing to an object for a specified period of time "clicks" that object.

FIGURE 7-13
Assistive input devices.

Assistive Input Systems

Assistive input devices allow for input in a nontraditional manner (see Figure 7-13). For example, *Braille keyboards*, large-key keyboards, or conventional keyboards with Braille or large-print key overlays are available for visually impaired computer users. *Keyguards*—metal or plastic plates that fit over conventional keyboards—enable users with limited hand mobility to press the keys on a keyboard, using his or her fingers or a special device, without accidentally pressing other keys. *One-handed keyboards* are available for users who have the use of only one hand, and *voice input systems* (also called *voice recognition systems* and *speech recognition systems*) use special software and a microphone to input data and commands to the PC hands-free (for a look at how speech recognition works in Microsoft Word 2007, see the How It Works box). *Switches*—hardware devices that can be activated with hand, foot, finger, or face movement, or with sips and puffs of air—can be used in conjunction with a keyboard, mouse, or other input device to perform a preprogrammed set of actions, such as opening the Windows Start menu or performing a left mouse click. Some conventional input devices can also be used for assistive purposes, such as scanners, which—if they have optical character recognition (OCR) capabilities—can input printed documents into the computer as editable text.

For mouse alternatives, there are assistive pointing devices that can be used—sometimes in conjunction with a switch—to move and select items with an onscreen pointer; they can also be used to enter text-based data when used in conjunction with an onscreen keyboard. There are also *feet mice*, which are controlled by the feet, and *head pointing systems* or *head mice*, which control the onscreen pointer using head movement. For example, the head pointing systems shown in Figure 7-13 use a removable reflective dot (placed on the forehead or eyeglasses) or a special hat with a built-in tracking surface on the brim (as shown in Figure 7-13) in conjunction with a tracking camera to move an onscreen pointer based on the user's head movement. A new assistive input device under development is the *eye pointing system*, which allows users to select items onscreen using only their gaze, or, more recently, their gaze in conjunction with a special "hot key" on the keyboard to allow the user to zoom in to select an area of the screen more precisely, such as to activate a hyperlink on a Web page.

In addition to its use by disabled computer users, assistive hardware can also be used by the general population. For example, one-handed keyboards are sometimes used by people who wish to keep one hand on the mouse and one hand on the keyboard at all times; voice input systems are used by individuals who would prefer to speak input instead of type it; and head pointing systems are available for gaming and virtual reality (VR) applications.

HOW IT WORKS

Windows Vista Speech Recognition with Word 2007

Speech recognition has arrived. Surgeons use it to control surgical robotic equipment, individuals use it to dial their mobile phones, and now you can use it to control your PC.

The Speech Recognition feature built into Windows Vista allows you to use your voice to issue commands to your computer, such as to launch programs, switch to a different open program, close a window, and so forth. You can also use it in application programs—such as your e-mail program or Microsoft Word—to dictate text to the computer, as well as to edit and format already typed text.

To use Windows Speech Recognition, you need to have a microphone connected to your computer and then run through the setup process to test your microphone, adjust the volume, and so forth (choose *Ease of Access* and then *Speech Recognition Options* to start the setup process). Once Speech Recognition is set up and enabled, you will see the *Speech Recognition microphone bar* on your screen (see the accompanying illustration). When the system is "sleeping," you need to say "Start Listening" to wake it up. After that point, until you say "Stop Listening," the system will respond to your voice commands. For instance, speaking text that is not an official command will cause that text to be typed in the program in the active window. Speaking a command (such as "Undo" to undo the last change, "Select *word*" to select that word in your document, or "Correct *word*" to correct the spelling of a particular word) will carry out that command. To see a list of possible commands, say "What can I say?" and the system will display a *Speech Reference Card* on your PC.

If there are multiple possibilities for a command that you issue (such as multiple words in your document that sound alike, as in the accompanying illustration), the system displays numbered icons on the screen and waits for your selection before continuing. Similarly, if there are multiple replacement words for a correction (refer again to the accompanying illustration), the system displays a numbered list of possibilities and waits for your selection. If the system doesn't understand a command, it will display a "What was that?" message.

While there are numerous speech recognition software programs on the market, for basic dictation and voice commands, Windows' new Speech Recognition does the trick.

1. The system types your words as you talk.

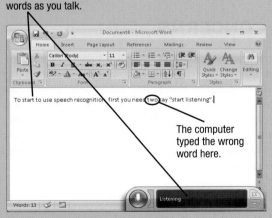

The computer typed the wrong word here.

2. After the command "Correct two" is issued, numbered icons are displayed next to each word that sounds like the word that needs to be corrected.

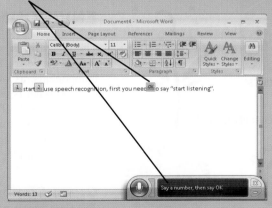

3. After the word "two" is selected for correction, possible replacement words are displayed; the proper word is selected by saying the number "3" and then "OK."

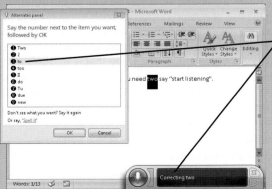

4. The correction is made.

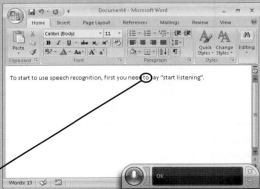

SCREEN READER SOFTWARE

BRAILLE DISPLAYS

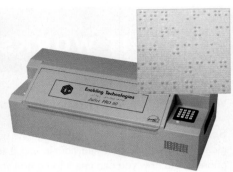

BRAILLE PRINTERS

FIGURE 7-14
Assistive output devices.

Assistive Output Systems

Once data has been input into the computer, a variety of *assistive output devices* can be used. For instance, some examples of assistive output devices that can be used by blind and other visually impaired individuals are shown in Figure 7-14. A *screen reader* is a software program that reads aloud all information displayed on the computer screen, such as instructions, menu options, documents, and Web pages. *Braille displays* are devices that can be attached to conventional computers (or built into handheld computers designed for visually-impaired individuals) and that continuously convert screen output into Braille form. *Braille printers* print embossed output in Braille format on paper instead of, or in addition to, conventional ink output.

Some operating systems also include accessibility features. For instance, Windows Vista includes a screen reader, on-screen keyboard, speech recognition, and settings that can be used to magnify the screen, change text size and color, convert audio cues into written text, and otherwise make the computer more accessible.

FIGURE 7-15
Eco-labels.

UNITED STATES

EUROPEAN UNION

KOREA

BRAZIL

GERMANY

ENVIRONMENTAL CONCERNS

The increasing use of computers in our society has caused a variety of environmental concerns. The amount of energy used to power PCs, servers, and computer components, as well as the heat generated by computing equipment, is one concern. Another is our extensive use of paper and how much of it ends up as trash in landfills (see the Trend box for one paperless alternative to paper-based coupons). The hazardous materials contained in computer equipment or generated by the production of computers and related technology, as well as the disposal of used computing products, are additional concerns.

Green Computing

The term **green computing** refers to the use of computers in an environmentally friendly manner. Minimizing the use of natural resources, such as energy and paper, is one aspect of green computing. To encourage the development of energy-saving devices, the U.S. Department of Energy and the Environmental Protection Agency (EPA) developed the **ENERGY STAR** program. Hardware that is ENERGY STAR compliant exceeds the minimum federal standards for reduced energy consumption and can display the ENERGY STAR label shown in Figure 7-15. *ENERGY STAR 4.0* requirements that went into effect in mid-2007 are even stricter than previous

TREND

Mobile Coupons

For years we have had coupons in the Sunday newspaper, and then electronic coupons became available via the Internet. The newest trend in electronic coupons is delivery to your mobile phone.

Although common in Asia and Europe for several years, electronic coupons delivered to mobile phones is relatively new to the United States. But with businesses and consumers alike now viewing the mobile phone as more than just a voice communications device, mobile phone coupon use is growing. Electronic coupons typically are delivered to mobile phones via e-mail or text message, and they can be redeemed by showing the coupon code to the cashier at the store or restaurant issuing the coupon, similar to using a paper coupon. To increase effectiveness and prevent unwanted intrusions, many mobile coupon companies require consumers to sign up or *opt-in* to coupon delivery. Some include software that can be downloaded to the phone to organize stored coupons, such as by sorting the coupons by advertiser or date received, and coupons are typically targeted to the individual based on his or her geographic location. Similar to other mobile phone applications, standard text messaging or data charges apply. Redemption rates for mobile coupons are much higher than for paper coupons—in part, because the coupons aren't forgotten at home.

What is the next step for electronic coupons expected to be? One likely possibility is sending electronic coupons to a mobile phone based on an individual's location (determined via the GPS capabilities built into many mobile phones today). For instance, an individual who walks by a Starbucks might get an electronic coupon via his or her mobile phone for 50 cents off a mocha Frappuccino. Now that's effective impulse marketing!

requirements, particularly in the area of efficiency when a computer is in standby or sleep mode. For instance, desktop power supplies must be 80% efficient and desktop PCs must consume no more than 2 watts of power in standby mode or 4 watts of power in sleep mode. Figure 7-15 also shows some **eco-labels**—environmental performance certifications—used in other countries.

With the increased cost of electricity today and the recent swell in data center energy usage, power consumption and heat generation by computers is a key concern for businesses today. Today's faster and more powerful computers tend to use more energy and run hotter than computers from just a few years ago, which leads to greater cooling costs. Servers, in particular, are power-hungry, using approximately 135 watts per processor today compared to 30 watts per processor five years ago. Consolidating servers, either alone or in conjunction with virtualization, is a common energy saving tactic used by businesses today. But energy use is still growing. In fact, the amount of electricity used to power the world's servers doubled in a five-year span due mainly to increased demand for Internet services such as music and video downloads. The estimated average utility cost for a 100,000 square-foot data center is now nearly $6 million. And, if current trends continue, the amount of power required to run servers worldwide could increase by another 40% by 2010, according to a recent report.

ONLINE VIDEO

Go to **www.course.com/uccs/ch7** to watch the "IBM's Big Green Project" video clip.

>**Eco-label.** A certification, often by a government agency, that identifies a device as meeting minimal environmental performance specifications.

In response to this growing problem, manufacturers are working to develop more energy efficient PCs, servers, microprocessors, storage systems, and other computer components. Some energy-saving features found on computer hardware today include devices (such as computers and printers) that can go into very low-power sleep mode when not in use, low-power-consumptive chips and boards, high-efficiency power supplies, energy-efficient flat-panel displays, liquid cooling systems, and CPUs that power up and down on demand. The energy savings by using more energy-efficient hardware can be significant. For instance, a typical desktop PC with a 19-inch CRT monitor consumes approximately 300 watts per hour and can raise the temperature of the room at least 5 degrees; switching to a conventional flat-panel display saves about $60 per year in electricity costs. Moving to an LED flat-panel display instead of a conventional LCD display saves around another 12% in energy consumption.

While ENERGY STAR 4.0-compliant computers are more efficient in standby and sleep mode than in the past, computers can still draw quite a bit of power when they are in these modes—particularly with a screen saver enabled. Because of this, businesses and schools are also increasingly using software to automatically shut down computers when they are not in use to save power. For instance, Seminole Community College in Florida is installing automated shutdown software on 3,500 PCs and estimates that the technology may save up to $65,000 per year in electricity costs; Cisco Systems expects to save $1 million and 8.5 million kilowatt hours of power per year by implementing power management functions on 50,000 monitors in its various offices. And mobile phone manufacturers are working to reduce the environmental impact of their products, such as displaying reminders on mobile phones to unplug them from their chargers when they are fully charged since chargers can draw up to five watts per hour even if nothing is plugged into them.

In addition to more energy-efficient hardware, other possibilities for greener computing include notebook computers and mobile phones that run on *fuel cells*, UPSs that are powered by *flywheels*, longer-lasting and more environmentally-friendly batteries (for instance, a battery that runs on sugar and last four times as long as a lithium ion battery has recently been developed and may be used to power portable devices in as little as three to five years), and portable PCs and mobile phones that use other types of alternate power. For instance, *solar power* is a growing alternative for powering electronic devices, including mobile phones and portable computers (see Figure 7-16). With solar power, *solar panels* convert sunlight into direct current (DC) electricity, which is then stored in a battery. The intensity of the sun reaching the solar panels, as well as the size and number of the panels being used, affects the amount of time needed to recharge a battery. If the solar system being used is powerful enough to charge the battery in your computer or other device being used at the same rate as you use it, the device's battery will never run down. However, even if the solar power system is not powerful enough to keep up with the rate of battery consumption, it can still greatly extend the amount of time your device can operate without recharging its batteries. PCs and other devices can also be charged via solar power when they are not being used

FIGURE 7-16

Alternate power.
Solar and hand power can be used to power mobile phones, portable digital media players, GPS devices, portable PCs, and other devices.

Mobile phone is being powered by the backpack.

Solar panels are built into the backpack.

SOLAR BACKPACKS

Solar panels

SOLAR-POWERED CHARGERS

HAND-POWERED CHARGERS

The PC uses a low power processor and chipset and includes additional cooling features.

A custom BIOS helps manage power and sleep settings of the PC and monitor more efficiently.

The external case is bromine-free and the chassis uses less painted metal, making the PC easier to recycle.

The plastic components are made out of recycled materials and at least 90% of the materials used in the PC are reusable or recyclable.

FIGURE 7-17
An environmentally friendly PC.

to prepare them for the next use. As solar technology improves, solar panels will likely become integrated into a wider variety of products. Already solar panels are being designed to be built into the covers of notebook computers and both solar-powered and hand-powered chargers (refer again to Figure 7-16) are available for use with portable PCs, mobile phones, and other small portable devices. These devices can be used wherever dependable electricity is not available, such as in developing countries and while outdoors. And solar power can be used to power more permanent computer set-ups, as well. For instance, there are at least two Web hosting companies in the U.S. that are 100% solar powered. Solar power plants are also being developed, and some experts predict that many buildings in the future will be *solar buildings* with solar cells integrated into the rooftop, walls, and windows of the building to generate electricity.

In addition to being more energy-efficient, computers today are being built to run quieter and cooler, and they are using more recyclable hardware. Many PC manufacturers are also reducing the amount of toxic chemicals being used in PCs. For instance, Dell bars the use of some hazardous chemicals, such as cadmium and mercury; has reduced the amount of lead used in several desktop computers; and meets the European Union requirement of being completely lead-free for all electronics shipped to the EU. All professional PCs made by Fujitsu Siemens computers also comply with the EU requirements. And Hewlett-Packard has announced that all its business desktop PCs meet ENERGY STAR 4.0 requirements and that switching to one of these desktop systems can reduce power consumption by up to 52%, for a cost savings of $6 to $58 per computer. The HP desktop computer shown in Figure 7-17 meets ENERGY STAR 4.0 standards, uses at least 10% post-consumer waste plastics, uses bromine-free external case parts and less painted metal on the chassis, is 90% recyclable (including at least 90% of the product packaging), is designed to have a five-year lifecycle, and costs about $6 a year in electricity to operate.

Another environmental concern stemming from the use of computers and computing equipment is paper use and paper waste. It now appears that the so-called *paperless office* that many visionaries predicted would arrive is largely a myth. Instead, research indicates that global paper use has grown more than sixfold since 1950, and one-fifth of all wood harvested in the world today ends up as paper. According to a Gartner study, Web users alone print an average of 28 pages per day. The estimated number of pages generated by computer printers worldwide is almost one-half billion a year—an amount that would stack more than 25,000 miles high. One possible solution for the future—electronic paper—is discussed in the Inside the Industry box.

Recycling and Disposal of Computing Equipment

Another environmental concern is the amount of trash—and sometimes toxic trash—generated by computer use. In addition to paper-based trash, computing refuse includes used toner cartridges, obsolete or broken hardware, and discarded CDs, DVDs, and other storage media. Mobile phones that are discarded when individuals switch providers—as well as new disposable consumer products, such as disposable digital cameras—also add

INSIDE THE INDUSTRY

E-Paper

Electronic paper (*e-paper*) consists of a display device on which written content is displayed in electronic form, but the display is thinner and more paper-like than other types of display devices. E-paper devices display content in high contrast, so they can be viewed in direct sunlight. E-paper devices also require much less electricity than other types of displays, since they don't require a backlight and they don't require power to maintain the content shown on the display—they only require power to change the content. The purpose of e-paper displays is to give the user the experience of reading from paper, while providing them with the ability to electronically update the information shown on the device. Practical applications for e-paper from an environmental standpoint include any document that only needs to be kept for a short time; e-paper versions of these documents could be erased and then reused instead of being discarded when their useful life has ended.

For instance, one of the first areas in which e-paper has been applied is retail signs, such as those found in department stores and other retail establishments, as well as hotels, conference centers, schools, hospitals, and more. These *e-signs* look like ordinary paper signs, but their text can be changed wirelessly. Consequently, instead of continually having to print new paper signs, e-signs can be reused since they can be changed electronically, which saves the time and expense of printing, delivering, and setting up new signs, as well as the time, cost, and waste associated with disposing of the old ones. Their low power consumption means that e-signs can run off battery power for an extended period of time. Some e-paper signs (such as the ones using *Ink-In-Motion* technology developed by E Ink Corporation) can even include moving content. Because of their low power consumption, even moving e-ink signs can be used in locations without electricity since a typical postcard-sized Ink-In-Motion display is capable of running on just 2 AA batteries for up to 6 months.

Other retail applications currently on the market include e-paper shelf price tags that can electronically communicate with the store's database to always display the current price, e-ink displays on wristwatches and USB flash drives, destination displays on German trains, e-paper-based *e-book readers* (which are used to display electronic versions of books), and e-paper newspapers that can be updated periodically during the day to reflect the latest news (see the accompanying photograph). For instance, in late 2007, the French newspaper *Les Echos* announced an electronic paper edition. This e-newspaper is delivered automatically to subscribers via a Wi-Fi connection (no PC is needed) and it is updated every hour during the day on weekdays.

So how does e-paper work? It is based on *electronic ink* or *e-ink*, which is millions of tiny beads or *microcapsules* about the diameter of a human hair. These beads contain positively charged white particles and negatively charged black particles suspended in a clear fluid. When electronic signals are applied to the beads, either the white or the black particles rise to the top and the opposite colored particles are pulled to the bottom of the bead, depending on the type of charge applied. Consequently, the bead appears to be either white or black (see the accompanying illustration).

To make an e-ink display, e-ink is printed onto a sheet of plastic film that is laminated to a layer of circuitry. The circuitry creates a grid of pixels that can be used to display images. The color of the beads in each pixel is determined by electronic signals that are sent to the display, usually via a wireless transmission. Based on the electronic signals, the beads display either black or white in order to form the proper text and images, similar to the way pixels are used to display images on a monitor. The content remains displayed until another transmission changes the pattern. Current e-paper products can be written to and erased electronically thousands of times, but in the near future that number is expected to increase to several million times.

Improvements that need to be made before e-paper and other e-ink applications become more commonplace include color capabilities, lower cost, and increased life span. Future possibilities for e-ink include its use on billboards, T-shirts, and even paint for easy redecorating, as well as regular-sized e-paper that can be inserted into a special computer printer to be printed electronically and then reused over and over again. *Conductive e-ink*, which is currently in development, can carry electricity after it is printed; conductive e-ink will potentially enable keyboards to be printed onto military uniform sleeves, light switches to be printed onto wallpaper, and radio circuitry and controls to be printed onto clothing and other everyday objects.

The white particles are at the top, so this pixel appears white.

AN E-PAPER NEWSPAPER   **AN E-INK MICROCAPSULE**

to the amount of electronic trash (also called **e-trash** or *e-waste*). In fact, the Silicon Valley Toxics Coalition estimates that there are 500 million obsolete computers and 130 million mobile phones discarded every year in the U.S. A surge in discarded televisions is also expected as TV signals make the mandatory switch from analog to digital, prices of plasma TVs continue to decrease, and many consumers replace their older TVs with flat-screen displays and TVs that support HDTV.

Compounding the problem of the amount of e-trash generated today is the fact that PCs, mobile phones, and related hardware contain a variety of toxic and hazardous materials. For instance, the average CRT monitor alone contains about eight pounds of lead, and a single computer may contain up to 700 different chemical elements and compounds, many of which (such as arsenic, lead, mercury, and cadmium) are hazardous and expensive to dispose of properly. Conventional computers may also be constructed out of material that is difficult to recycle.

A global concern regarding e-trash is where it all eventually ends up. The majority of all discarded computer equipment (at least 70%, according to most estimates) ends up in landfills and in countries with lower recycling costs, cheaper labor, and laxer environmental standards than the United States, such as China, India, and Nigeria. Much of the e-trash exported to these countries is simply dumped into fields and other informal dumping areas. Unaware of the potential danger of these components, rural villagers often sort through and dismantle discarded electronics parts looking for precious metals and other sources of revenue (see Figure 7-18)—potentially endangering their health as well as polluting nearby rivers, ponds, and other water sources. Compounding the problem, the remaining waste is often burned, generating huge clouds of potentially toxic smoke. Activists believe unchecked dumping by the United States and other countries—such as England, Japan, Australia, and Singapore—has been going on for at least 10 years. The primary reason for exporting e-trash is expense—proper disposal of a computer in the United States normally costs between $5 and $10, compared to $1 or less in third-world countries. Another reason is that some states in the United States are beginning to ban the most dangerous computing equipment—such as CRT monitors—from landfills.

While it is difficult—or, perhaps, impossible—to correct the damage that has already occurred from e-waste, many organizations are working on ways to protect people and the environment from future contamination. For instance, the *Climate Savers Computing Initiative* is an industry group started by Google and Intel in 2007 that is dedicated to reducing greenhouse-gas emissions, and the *Green Grid Alliance* is a global consortium dedicated to advancing energy efficiency in data centers and business computing. There are also some environmental regulations (such as California's *Electronic Waste Recycling Act* and Europe's *Restrictions on Hazardous Substances Directive*) that prohibit throwing away some types of computer components. For instance, California does not allow computer monitors to be thrown out as trash and has implemented mandatory fees of $6 to $10 on all TV and computer monitor purchases to be used to recycle and properly dispose of discarded TVs and monitors. In the United States, PC manufacturers are beginning to produce more environmentally friendly components, such as system units made from recyclable plastic, nontoxic flame-retardant coatings, and lead-free solder on the motherboard.

Even though recycling computer equipment is difficult because of the materials currently being used, proper disposal is essential to avoid pollution and health hazards. Some recycling centers will accept computer equipment, but many charge a fee for this service. Many computer manufacturers have recycling programs that will accept obsolete or broken computer equipment from consumers, typically for a fee of about $15 to $30 per unit.

FIGURE 7-18
E-trash.

ONLINE VIDEO

Go to **www.course.com/uccs/ch7** to watch the "Climate Savers Computing Initiative" video clip.

>**E-trash.** Electronic trash, such as discarded computers, toner cartridges, storage media, and more.

ASK THE EXPERT

Lauren Ornelas, Campaign Director, Silicon Valley Toxics Coalition

What impact does U.S. e-waste have on other countries?

According to the California Department of Toxic Substances Control report that was released in 2007, roughly 20 million pounds of e-waste were shipped out of California alone in 2006 to places such as Brazil, China, India, South Korea, Malaysia, Mexico, and Vietnam. For some countries, we have some idea of the impact. In China, for instance, workers dismantle electronics without adequate protection for themselves or the environment. Consequently, workers are exposed to lead and other hazardous substances and hazardous chemicals get into the water and air. In some areas, the water is so polluted they can no longer drink from it. Nigeria has become a place where our e-waste is essentially just dumped without the pretense of it being recycled. While many electronic products are shipped under the guise of reuse, up to 75% of what is being shipped to that country cannot be repaired or recycled.

Expired toner cartridges and ink cartridges can sometimes be returned to the manufacturer (using the supplied shipping label included with some cartridges) or exchanged when ordering new cartridges; the cartridges are then *recharged* (refilled) and resold. Cartridges that cannot be refilled can be sent to a recycling facility. In addition to helping to reduce e-trash in landfills, using recharged printer cartridges saves the consumer money since they are less expensive than new cartridges. Other computer components—such as CDs, DVDs, and hard drives—can also be recycled through some organizations, such as the GreenDisk group that accepts shipments of these items (plus printer cartridges, mobile phones, mobile devices, notebook computers, power cords, and more) for a modest charge (such as $6.95 for 20 pounds of items if you ship them yourself) and then reuses salvageable items and recycles the rest. There are also a number of recycling programs specifically designed for discarded mobile phones. These programs typically refurbish and sell the phones; many organizations donate a portion of the proceeds to nonprofit organizations.

In lieu of recycling, older equipment that is still functioning can be donated to schools and nonprofit groups. Some organizations accept and repair donated equipment and then distribute it to disadvantaged groups. For example, the organization Computers for Africa (see Figure 7-19) refurbishes used computers, networks them, and then ships ready-to-set-up labs to nonprofit organizations in Africa. In the United States, Operation Homelink refurbishes donated PCs and sends them free of charge to families of U.S. military personnel deployed overseas, who use the PCs to communicate with the soldiers via e-mail (refer again to Figure 7-19).

For security and privacy purposes, data stored on all computing equipment should be completely removed before disposing of that equipment so the data cannot be recovered by someone else. Hard drives should be wiped clean (not just erased) using special software that overwrites the data on the drive several times to ensure it is completely destroyed; storage media that cannot be wiped (such as DVD+R discs) or that contain very sensitive data (such as business hard drives being discarded, as discussed in the Chapter 5 Inside the Industry box) should be shredded. The shredded media is then typically recycled.

Consumers and companies alike are recognizing the need for green computing. A growing number of computing equipment manufacturers are announcing that they are committed to environmental responsibility. Support for a nationwide recycling program is growing, and new classifications from the EPA are expected to encourage recycling of an even greater number of computer components. So, even though computer manufacturing and recycling have a long way to go before computing equipment stops being an environmental and health hazard, it is encouraging that the trend is moving toward creating a safer and less wasteful environment.

FURTHER EXPLORATION

Go to **www.course.com/uccs/ch7** for links to further information about green computing.

COMPUTERS FOR AFRICA
Sends computer labs consisting of refurbished, donated PCs to nonprofit organizations in Africa.

OPERATION HOMELINK
Sends donated PCs to families of soldiers stationed overseas so they can communicate with their loved ones, such as with this soldier in Iraq.

FIGURE 7-19

Donating PCs. You can donate computer equipment to nonprofit organizations so it can be given to others who can use it.

RELATED LEGISLATION

There has been some legislation related to health, access, and the environment in the past few years. For instance, many states make it illegal to use a mobile phone without a hands-free system while driving in an attempt to cut down on the number of accidents due to distracted drivers. The most significant recent legislation regarding accessibility has been the 1998 amendment to the *Rehabilitation Act* requiring federal agencies to make their electronic and information technology accessible to people with disabilities. This act applies to all federal Web sites, as well, creating a trend of Web sites that are *Section 508 compliant*. While there are currently no federal computer recycling laws in the U.S., one (the *National Computer Recycling Act*) has been under consideration since 2005. In addition, federal agencies are required to purchase energy-efficient electronic products, some federal laws (such as the Sarbanes-Oxley Act and HIPAA) have established privacy and data protection standards for companies disposing of computer hardware that contained specific types of data, and some states have implemented laws related to electronic waste.

SUMMARY

COMPUTERS AND HEALTH

Chapter Objective 1:
Understand the potential risks to physical health resulting from the use of computers.

Since the entry of computers into the workplace and their increased use in our society, they have been blamed for a variety of physical ailments. **Carpal tunnel syndrome (CTS)**, **DeQuervain's tendonitis**, and other types of **repetitive stress injuries (RSIs)** are common physical ailments related to computer use; *computer vision syndrome (CVS)*, eyestrain, fatigue, backaches, and headaches are additional possible physical risks.

Ergonomics is the science of how to make the computer workspace, hardware, and environment fit the individual using it. Using an ergonomically correct workspace and **ergonomic hardware** (such as *ergonomic keyboards*, *ergonomic mice*, *document holders*, *antiglare screens*, *keyboard drawers*, *wrist supports*, and *computer gloves*) can help avoid or lessen the pain associated with some RSIs. In addition, all users should use good posture, take rest breaks, alternate tasks, and take other common-sense precautions. For portable PCs, **docking stations** can be used to allow easy connections to more ergonomically correct hardware, and **notebook stands** can be used to elevate a notebook PC so its display screen can be set at an ergonomically correct height.

Chapter Objective 2:
Describe some possible emotional health risks associated with the use of computers.

In addition to physical health issues, the extensive use of computers and related technology in the home and office has raised concerns about emotional side effects of computer use. The *stress* of keeping up with ever-changing technology, layoffs, always being in touch, fear of being out of touch, information overload, and **burnout** are all possible emotional problems related to computer use. Taking a break, reevaluating your schedule, and taking good care of yourself can help you avoid or reduce the stress that these problems may cause. To manage all the digital information you encounter, good search techniques, *RSS feeds*, and e-mail filters can be used.

Computer/Internet addiction (also referred to as *computer addiction disorder (CAD)*, *Internet addiction disorder (IAD)*, and *cyberaddiction*) refers to not being able to stop using computers or the Internet, or to the problems that their use creates in a user's personal or professional life. Many experts believe it is a growing problem and is most prominent in countries with high levels of broadband Internet access. It can affect users of any age and is treated similarly to other addictions.

ACCESS TO TECHNOLOGY

Chapter Objective 3:
Explain what is meant by the term "digital divide."

The term **digital divide** refers to the gap between those who have access to computers and communications technology and those who do not. Although the digital divide normally refers to physical access to technology, its "have not" category is sometimes thought to include not only those who do not have access to technology but also those who have physical access to technology but who do not understand it or are discouraged from using it. There can be a digital divide within a country or between countries. Globally, the digital divide separates countries with access to technology from those without access to technology.

In the United States, studies show that the digital divide may be lessening, as people of every income, education, race, ethnicity, and gender continue to go online at increased rates. However, individuals living in low-income households or having little education still trail the national average for computer use.

Globally, the digital divide separates countries with access to technology from those without access to technology. The United States has a high number of Internet users, though it is only sixth in the world when comparing the percent of population online. There are several programs designed to bring computers, Internet access, and technology to developing countries, such as the *One Laptop Per Child (OLPC) project*.

Research suggests that people with disabilities tend to use computers and the Internet at rates lower than the average population. Part of the reason may be because some types of conventional hardware—such as keyboards and monitors—are difficult to use with some types of physical conditions. **Assistive technology** includes hardware and software that makes conventional PC systems easier for users with disabilities to use.

Examples of assistive input devices include *Braille keyboards*, *keyguards*, *voice input systems*, *switches*, *feet mice*, and *head pointing systems*. *Assistive output devices* include *screen readers*, *Braille displays*, and *Braille printers*. In order to be compatible with screen readers and other assistive devices, Web pages need to use features, such as *alternative* text descriptions for Web page images and descriptive text-based hyperlinks.

Chapter Objective 4:
Discuss the impact that factors such as nationality, income, race, education, and physical disabilities may have on computer access and use.

Chapter Objective 5:
List some types of assistive hardware that can be used by individuals with physical disabilities.

ENVIRONMENTAL CONCERNS

Many people worry about the environmental issues related to computer use, such as high energy use and the massive amount of paper computer users consume. The term **green computing** refers to using computers in an environmentally friendly manner. It can include using environmentally friendly hardware (such as devices approved by an **eco-label** system like the **ENERGY STAR** certification used in the United States), as well as using procedures (such as consolidating servers and using power management features to place devices into standby or sleep mode when not in use) to reduce energy consumption. Environmentally friendly computers are just starting to come on the market, and alternate-powered hardware is beginning to become available.

In addition to practicing green computing when buying and using computer equipment, discarded equipment should be reused whenever possible. Computer equipment that is still functioning may be able to be donated and refurbished for additional use, and toner and ink cartridges can often be refilled and reused. Hardware that cannot be reused should be recycled if possible, or properly disposed of if not recyclable so that it does not end up as hazardous **e-trash** in landfills. Recycling programs and initiatives may help obsolete products be disposed of in a more environmentally friendly manner.

For security and privacy purposes, storage media containing personal or sensitive data should be disposed of properly, such as wiped or shredded before being reused or recycled.

Chapter Objective 6:
Suggest some ways computer users can practice "green computing" and properly dispose of obsolete computer equipment.

RELATED LEGISLATION

There are some laws in place to help protect our health, access to technology, and the environment. The most significant legislation regarding accessibility is the 1998 amendment to the *Rehabilitation Act* requiring federal agencies to make their electronic and information technology accessible to people with disabilities. In the U.S., some federal regulations and state laws impact the disposal of computer hardware.

Chapter Objective 7:
Discuss the current status of legislation related to health, access, and the environment in relation to computers.

REVIEW ACTIVITIES

KEY TERM MATCHING

Instructions: Match each key term on the left with the definition on the right that best describes it.

a. assistive technology

b. carpal tunnel syndrome (CTS)

c. computer/Internet addiction

d. DeQuervain's tendonitis

e. digital divide

f. docking station

g. eco-label

h. ergonomic hardware

i. green computing

j. notebook stand

1. _____ A certification, often by a government agency, that identifies a device as meeting minimal environmental performance specifications.

2. _____ A condition in which the tendons on the thumb side of the wrist are swollen and irritated.

3. _____ A device that connects a portable PC to conventional hardware, such as a keyboard, mouse, monitor, and printer.

4. _____ A device that elevates the display of a notebook computer to a better viewing height; some contain USB ports to connect additional hardware.

5. _____ A painful and crippling condition affecting the hands and wrist that can be caused by computer use.

6. _____ Hardware and software specifically designed for use by individuals with physical disabilities.

7. _____ Hardware, typically input and output devices, that is designed to be more ergonomically correct than its nonergonomic counterparts.

8. _____ The gap between those who have access to technology and those who do not.

9. _____ The problem of overusing, or being unable to stop using, the Internet.

10. _____ The use of computers in an environmentally friendly manner.

SELF-QUIZ

Instructions: Circle **T** if the statement is true, **F** if the statement is false, or write the best answer in the space provided. **Answers for the self-quiz are located in the References and Resources Guide at the end of the book.**

1. **T** **F** A repetitive stress injury is related to the emotional health issue of stress.

2. **T** **F** The ENERGY STAR program is an energy conservation program developed by the United States government.

3. **T** **F** Carpal tunnel syndrome can be caused by using a computer keyboard.

4. **T** **F** As computer use has become more common, the potential for stress related to computer use has decreased.

5. **T** **F** Assistive technology is hardware and software designed to help all beginning computer users learn how to use a computer.

6. The science of fitting a work environment to the people who work there is called _____

7. A state of fatigue or frustration usually brought on by overwork is referred to as _____ .

8. Craving more and more time at the computer can be an indicator of _____.

9. The _____ can be used to describe discrepancies in access to technology by individuals within a country, as well as to compare access from country to country.

10. _____ power refers to electricity generated by the sun.

---

1. For each of the following situations, write the appropriate letter—Y (yes) or N (no)—in the blank to the right of the situation to indicate if the act is an example of green computing.

Situation   **Type of Situation**
a. You adjust the power settings on your PC to never go into sleep mode.   _____
b. Your boss requires you to print all of his e-mail messages so he can read them on paper.   _____
c. You exchange your CRT monitor for a flat-panel monitor.   _____
d. You drop your old mobile phone off in a recycling box instead of throwing it in the trash.   _____

2. Match each term with its related example and write the corresponding number in the blank to the left of each example.

a. _____ Assistive hardware.   **1.** Green computing
b. _____ Server consolidation.   **2.** Ergonomics
c. _____ Docking stations.   **3.** Digital divide
d. _____ E-mail filters and flags.   **4.** Information overload

3. List at least two assistive input or output devices designed for individuals with a visual impairment and explain the function of each.

4. List three possible negative physical effects that can result from computer use and describe one way to lessen each effect.

5. List three possible negative effects on the environment that can result from computer use and describe one way to lessen each effect.

It is becoming increasingly common for biometric devices to be used to grant or deny access to corporate and government facilities. They are also beginning to be used to identify consumers for financial transactions, such as making ATM withdrawals or cashing checks. While biometric systems can benefit some secure transactions by speeding up identification verification and providing a greater level of security than other systems, do they have societal benefits as well? For instance, are they easier to use by individuals who are not comfortable using a computer or have a physical disability? Can using biometric identification, voice recognition systems, and other systems that require less actual use of the computer by individuals help to lessen the digital divide? If, for instance, the norm for controlling a PC was the voice, would that level the technological playing field for all individuals? Why or why not?

BALANCING ACT

INTERNET ACCESS: LUXURY OR NECESSITY?

A luxury can be defined as something that is an indulgence, rather than a necessity. Most people in the world would view items such as food, shelter, and water as necessities. In the United States, many would likely add electricity, indoor plumbing, and, possibly, telephone service to that list. But about 2.5 billion people in the world have no access to electricity, let alone indoor plumbing or telephone service. This opens up an interesting question: How can one item—such as electricity—be a luxury for some and a necessity for others? The answer lies in the fact that what society views as a luxury tends to evolve into a necessity as access to that item improves over time. For example, think of telephone use in the United States. One century ago, it was rare to have a telephone. Fifty years ago, many people had party lines. A decade or two ago it was uncommon to meet someone who did not have a telephone. Now it is quite rare.

One reason for these types of transitions is access—that is, when an item becomes available at an affordable cost, its status tends to change from that of a luxury to that of a necessity. Another contributing factor seems to be the way an item is integrated into society. If an item becomes critical to the daily tasks of the general public, then it changes from being viewed as a luxury item to being thought of as a necessity. For example, Internet use has expanded dramatically in the United States in recent years, with the majority of the population now online. As a result, many individuals are beginning to view mobile phones, handheld PCs, and Internet connections as necessities. But while most people would agree that the Internet offers many conveniences, the question remains: Is it a necessity—that is, is it essential for existence? For instance, are there activities that must be performed online? If so, what about the people that do not have Internet access? How does this lack of Internet access affect them?

YOUR TURN

Give some thought to whether or not Internet access is a luxury or necessity in the United States, and form an opinion on this issue. Consider the following when forming your opinion and be prepared to discuss your position (either in class, via an online class discussion group, in a class chat room, or via a class blog) or to write a short paper expressing your opinion, depending on your instructor's directions.

- What technology products or services do you view as necessities? Did you include computers or Internet access? If not, do you think you might list these as necessities five years from now? Why or why not?

- In order for Internet access to be viewed as a necessity, must there be activities that can only be performed online? Or can Internet access be viewed as a necessity even if there are alternative methods for accomplishing the same tasks you might accomplish using the Internet? Why or why not?

- Research indicates that people who have low incomes, less education, or disabilities are less likely to have Internet access. If Internet access becomes mandatory for certain activities—such as voting or taking college classes—whose responsibility is it to get those individuals who do not have Internet access online? Should the government subsidize Internet access, as with telephone and electricity services today, or is it each American's responsibility to gain access to products deemed necessary in our country? Explain.

- There will likely always be some individuals who will never use a computer or the Internet, just as there are some individuals in this country who choose to live without electricity or indoor plumbing. How is the necessity status of a product or service affected if some individuals choose to live without it?

PROJECTS

---

1. **E-Paper** The chapter Inside the Industry box discusses e-paper—an erasable, reusable alternative to traditional paper and ink for computer output. Although currently in its early stages, some experts predict that it will become a viable product for many personal applications in the very near future. The obvious benefit of e-paper is reducing the use of traditional paper and ink and the resources needed to create and dispose of paper and ink. Two disadvantages at the current time are longevity (the medium is not designed to display an image for long periods of time) and expense.

   For this project, research the current state of e-paper. What products are available now and what products are due out soon? Do you think businesses or individuals will choose to use e-paper products if the only incentive is a cleaner environment? Or will there need to be an economic incentive, such as savings on paper and ink surpassing the cost of e-paper? What applications do you think are the most appropriate for the use of e-paper technology? At the conclusion of your research, prepare a one-page summary of your findings and submit it to your instructor.

HOT TOPICS

---

2. **Section 508** As discussed in the chapter, Section 508 is a section in the U.S. Code that refers to requirements for making electronic and information technology accessible to people with disabilities.

   For this project, research Section 508 and the Rehabilitation Act in general to see how the law applies to Web site design and to whom the law applies. If you were to set up a personal or small business Web site, would you be legally obligated to conform to Section 508 regulations? If not, what would be the advantages and disadvantages of conforming anyway? What types of features or modifications does a Web site need to include to be Section 508 compliant? How would one go about testing to see if a Web site was Section 508 compliant? Are there any Web sites available to help you check to see if your Web site is Section 508 compliant? Prepare a one-page summary of your findings and submit it to your instructor.

SHORT ANSWER/ RESEARCH

---

3. **Ergonomic Workspaces** Some aspects of an ergonomic workspace, such as a comfortable chair and nonglaring light, may feel good right from the beginning. Others, such as using an ergonomic keyboard or wrist rest, may take a little getting used to.

   For this project, find at least one local store that has some type of ergonomic equipment—such as adjustable office chairs, desks with keyboard drawers, ergonomic keyboards, or notebook stands—on display that you can try out. Test each piece, adjusting it as needed, and evaluate how comfortable it seems. Next, evaluate your usual computer workspace. Are there any adjustments you should make or any new equipment you would need to acquire to make your workspace setup more comfortable? Make a note of any changes you could make for free, as well as a list of items you would need to purchase and the estimated cost. Prepare a short summary of your findings to submit to your instructor. If you made any adjustments to your regular workspace during this project, be sure to include a comment regarding whether or not you think it increased your comfort.

HANDS ON

WRITING ABOUT COMPUTERS

4. **Assistive Computing** In addition to the conventional input and output hardware mentioned in the chapter, there are a variety of assistive input and output devices that physically challenged individuals can use to make computing easier and more efficient.

   For this project, select one type of disability, such as being blind, deaf, paraplegic, quadriplegic, or having the use of only one arm or hand. Make a list of potential limitations of any standard PC hardware for a person with that disability. Research the hardware and software options that could be used with a new PC for someone with the selected disability. Research each assistive option, comparing the ease of use, cost, and availability, and then prepare a recommendation for the best computer system for your selected hypothetical situation. Summarize your findings in a two- to three-page paper.

PRESENTATION/ DEMONSTRATION

5. **Recycle or Trash?** As mentioned in the chapter, a great deal of obsolete computer equipment eventually ends up in a landfill, although there may be alternative actions that could be taken instead.

   For this project, research what options would be available to discard the following: (1) a 10-year-old computer that is no longer functioning, (2) a 4-year-old computer that still works but is too slow for your needs, and (3) a used-up toner cartridge for a laser printer. Check with your local schools and charitable organizations to see if they would accept any of these items. Check with at least one computer manufacturer and one recycling company to see if they would accept the computers, and, if so, what the procedure and cost would be. Check with at least one vendor selling recharged toner cartridges to see if it buys old cartridges or requires a trade-in with an order. Share your findings with the class in the form of a short presentation. Be sure to include any costs associated with the disposal options you found, as well as your recommendation for each disposal situation. The presentation should not exceed 10 minutes and should make use of one or more presentation aids, such as the chalkboard, handouts, overhead transparencies, or a computer-based slide presentation (your instructor may provide additional requirements). You may also be asked to submit a summary of the presentation to your instructor.

GROUP DISCUSSION

6. **Toxic PCs** As discussed in the chapter, computer hardware contains a variety of toxic and hazardous materials which brings up a number of important issues. Whose responsibility is it to correct this problem? Is the U.S. at fault for allowing the exportation of our e-waste? Should PC manufacturers be allowed to continue to use hazardous materials, or should they be forced to find alternatives? What if a restriction on these compounds severely limited the types of computer equipment that could be manufactured or significantly increased the price? Are landfills full of discarded equipment just the price we pay for being a technological society? What efforts should be made to recycle discarded PCs? Who should bear the cost of the recycling—the manufacturers, the consumers, or the government?

   For this project, form an opinion about the impact of e-waste on our society and who (if anyone) is responsible for reducing the amount of e-waste being generated. Be prepared to discuss your position (in class, via an online class discussion group, in a class chat room, or via a class blog, depending on your instructor's directions). You may also be asked to write a short paper expressing your opinion.

7. **Net Neutrality and Your ISP** The chapter talks about equal access to the Internet, but what if it is your ISP that is interfering with your Internet access? Such is the case in a recent controversy surrounding the cable giant Comcast. According to complaints by customers, Comcast has been blocking the use of P2P sites like BitTorrent to download movies, music, and other large files. Comcast, like most ISPs, includes a statement related to being able to use tools to "efficiently manage their networks" in their terms of service, in order to prevent those customers using a higher than normal level of bandwidth from interfering with the access of other customers. However, the Comcast issue was considered by many to be a blatant net neutrality issue—blocking access to multimedia from sources other than its own cable sources. Do you think the actions taken by Comcast were ethical? Does an ISP have a right to block selected Internet traffic? Why or why not? Was there a more ethical way Comcast could have handled the problem of some users consuming a higher than normal level of bandwidth?

   For this project, form an opinion about the ethical ramifications of ISPs blocking selected Internet traffic and be prepared to discuss your position (in class, via an online class discussion group, in a class chat room, or via a class blog, depending on your instructor's directions). You may also be asked to write a short paper expressing your opinion.

ETHICS IN ACTION

8. **"Wii" habilitation** While designed for entertainment, the Nintendo Wii is also becoming a staple in physical therapy programs. Referred to as "wiihabilitation," Wii games, such as bowling, tennis, and golf, are proving useful for patients recovering from strokes, broken bones, and even combat injuries. One of the biggest advantages over traditional therapy is that it is enjoyable. The accompanying video clip discusses the use of the Wii in one rehab hospital.

   Go to www.course.com/uccs/ch7 to watch the "Craig Hospital Uses Wii for Rehabilitation" video clip. After watching the video, think about the impact of using technology for purposes other than it was intended. Rehab hospitals are seeing impressive results with the Wii and view it as a useful rehabilitation tool. But the Wii has not been studied in a medical setting and extensive Wii playing can cause physical injuries due to repetitive motions. Is there a risk to using entertainment devices for medical treatment without official studies? Some worry that rehab patients will overdo their activities because the Wii is fun. Is this a valid concern? Are hospitals at risk using technology in innovative ways or should they be congratulated for making rehab more pleasurable? What if a patient develops an addiction to the Wii? Who is responsible?

   Express your viewpoint: What is the impact of using technology for purposes other than it was intended?

   Use the video clip and the questions previously asked as a foundation for your response. Be prepared to discuss your position (in class, via an online class discussion group, in a class chat room, or via a class blog) or to write a short paper stating and supporting your viewpoint on the issue, depending on your instructor's direction. You may also be asked to do research and provide resources to support your point of view on this issue.

VIDEO VIEWPOINT

9. **Interactive Activities** Go to www.course.com/uccs/ch7 and work the interactive **Crossword Puzzle**, listen to the **Podcasts** and watch the **Online Videos** associated with this chapter, and explore the **Further Exploration** links. In addition, work the following interactive **Student Edition Labs**.

   • Web Design Principles   • Creating Web Pages

   If you have a SAM user profile, you have access to even more interactive content. Log in to your SAM account and go to your assignments page to see what your instructor has assigned for this chapter.

WEB ACTIVITIES

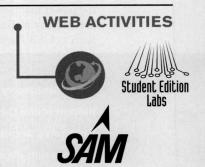

Student Edition Labs

SAM

10. **Test Yourself** Go to www.course.com/uccs/ch7 and review the **Online Study Guide** for Chapter 7, then test your knowledge of the terms and concepts in this chapter by completing the **Key Term Matching** exercise, the **Self-Quiz**, the **Exercises**, and the **Practice Test**.

EXPERT INSIGHT ON . . .
Computers and Society

A conversation with **FRANK MOLSBERRY**
Technologist for Dell Inc.

My Background . . .

I've been in the field of computer software and hardware development for over 25 years. I joined Dell in 1998 after working at IBM for 15 years. I am currently a Technologist in the Office of the CTO. My focus area is on Security Architecture and Technology. In that role I support the current engineering efforts for incorporating security hardware and software into Dell products, work with the various security technology companies to evaluate and influence current and planned offerings, and participate with standards organizations, such as the Trusted Computing Group (TCG), in the definition of future security standards.

In many cases the subjects we focus on now (such as security) are not about stand-alone systems anymore, but instead involve an entire ecosystem of hardware devices, software applications, and the infrastructure connecting them. Because this can entail a great deal of breadth and depth of knowledge, I've found that it is important to have a "big-picture" vision and the ability to rapidly drill into the details as needed, but only to the level needed to answer the questions in front of you.

> **The products and services you provide must ... satisfy the varying customs, rules, and requirements of a global economy.**

It's Important to Know . . .

The recommendations presented in these chapters are not one time things. Managing your security and privacy needs to be a regular routine—like brushing your teeth.

Technology is a double-edged sword and can always have a dark side. As you develop new and innovative hardware or software applications, you must always look at the threats that can be brought against it and, more importantly, how the technology could be misused beyond its intended purpose. By stepping back and identifying these issues up front, the developers and users of the technology can be better prepared to combat it. Security is a mindset. In the same way you look at the features, usability, and performance of a solution, you need to specifically look at the security characteristics, as well.

We now have a global economy. The products and services you provide must consider a global culture and have the flexibility to satisfy the varying customs, rules, and requirements of a global economy.

How I Use this Technology . . .

I use all the standard precautions on my personal computer—such as antivirus software, antispyware software, and backing up my data—to avoid data loss. I keep my systems on a UPS/surge protector and have the power management features configured. When traveling, I use a privacy screen to prevent others from viewing my work and I use data encryption software to protect the data on my system and portable media, such as USB flash drives.

Frank Molsberry is a Technologist in Dell's Office of the CTO. Prior to his current position, he helped found Dell's Workstation Architecture and Development team and, more recently, the Enterprise Architecture and Technology Group. In all, he has over 25 years of management and engineering experience in advanced system software development and PC system architectures. Frank has a Bachelor's degree in Computer Science and has several patents in the area of computer security. He does regular customer briefings on emerging technology trends.

Security is a mindset. In the same way you look at the features, usability, and performance of a solution, you need to specifically look at the security characteristics, as well.

What the Future Holds . . .

The next big thing is not usually a revolution as much as it is a continued progression that, when looked at over a long window of a time, shows up as a major change in technology or use model. So the trends of faster, smaller, cheaper will continue for the next decade.

The impact of security and privacy technology on society is huge, but it is not yet well understood. One of the biggest issues is identity theft and the tremendous effort it takes to recover from it. Tasks like shredding papers and monitoring your credit report activity can help prevent identity theft or alert you to suspicious activity. Patent reform is also getting significant attention right now, as many individuals feel that the focus on patent quantity over quality has increased litigation and decreased innovation in the industry. This is a global problem as patent rules can vary significantly from country to country.

For the impact of technology on the environment, the activities in place already will continue and expand. Major manufacturers like Dell have implemented initiatives to reduce or eliminate things like lead from their systems. There are now major programs for system recycling and for returning consumables, such as printer cartridges. Another development is the trend to move toward more modular architectures in the future, allowing the average user to easily change or upgrade the capabilities of a computer, TV, or printer without having to purchase an entirely new system.

In terms of the digital divide, it's important to realize that the digital divide is not new. It has always existed when each new method of information communication was developed, such as with the introduction of radio and television. We focus on it more now because of the volume of information available via the Internet and the bidirectional nature of electronic communications. The continued decreases in the cost of computing and the increases in wireless connectivity will continue the closing of this divide, but there may be new digital divides in the future. For this divide, we must not lose sight of where information communication fits in the hierarchy of needs. For those populations where the basic needs of food, clothing, and shelter are not being met, access to computing resources must first focus on enabling solutions to those problems. Another key is connectivity. It does little good to have a PC today without Internet access. Advancements in broad reach wireless communication like WiMAX are crucial.

My Advice to Students . . .

Computers and the ever changing technology they are based on are just tools. It is important not to just focus on the "coolness" of something new, but the problem it is trying to solve, the user experience, and the barriers to adoption.

Discussion Question

Frank Molsberry views technology as a double-edge sword and believes that hardware and software developers must look at how new products could be misused. Think about a few recent new technologies or products. Have they been used in an illegal or unethical manner? If so, did the manufacturer build in controls to prevent this misuse? If not, should they have? What responsibility, if any, does a developer have if its product or service is used inappropriately? Be prepared to discuss your position (in class, via an online class discussion group, in a class chat room, or via a class blog, depending on your instructor's directions). You may also be asked to write a short paper expressing your opinion.

>**For more information on Dell, visit www.dell.com and www.dell.com/innovation. For security information, visit www.trustedcomputing.org and searchsecurity.techtarget.com. For a summary of many online tech news sites, visit www.dailyrotation.com.**

8

CHAPTER

Emerging Technologies

OUTLINE

LEARNING OBJECTIVES

After completing this chapter, you will be able to do the following:

1. Describe what the PC of the future might look like, including some examples of emerging types of hardware.

2. Understand the effect that emerging computer technologies, such as nanotechnology, quantum computers, and optical computers, may have on the PC of the future.

3. Name some emerging wired and wireless networking technologies.

4. Explain what is meant by the term "artificial intelligence" (AI) and list some AI applications.

5. List some new and upcoming technological advances in medicine.

6. Name some new and upcoming technological advances in the military.

7. Discuss potential societal implications of emerging technologies.

OVERVIEW

No study of computers would be complete without a look to the future. The rapid technological advancements that we've seen in the last few decades have been extraordinary, but some believe the best is yet to come. New advances are being made all the time in areas such as computer hardware and networking technologies. In general, technology is continuing to become more user-friendly and more integrated into our daily lives, and that trend is expected to continue. For instance, imagine the following scenario: You walk up to your locked front door and gain access simply by touching the doorknob or speaking your name. When you enter a room, the lights, stereo system, and digital artwork on the walls change automatically to reflect your preferences. Your refrigerator and pantry keep up-to-the-moment inventories of their contents, and your closet automatically selects outfits for you based on the weather and your schedule for the day. Sounds like something out of a science fiction movie, doesn't it? Yet, all the technologies just mentioned are either available or in development.

Many of us are excited to see what new applications and technological improvements the future will bring, as well as how computers, the Internet, and other technologies will evolve. However, our enthusiasm for this progress should be balanced with the understanding that some future applications may not turn out the way we expect or may actually have a negative impact on society. One of the biggest challenges in an era of rapidly changing technologies is evaluating the potential impact of new technology and trying to ensure that new products and services do not adversely affect our security, privacy, and safety.

This chapter focuses on some of the emerging technologies that are already beginning to impact our lives. Topics include the PC of the future, emerging networking technologies, artificial intelligence (AI), and technological advances in medicine and in the military. The chapter closes with a discussion of the societal implications of emerging technologies. ∎

TIP

Be sure to look at the References and Resources Guide immediately following this chapter—it contains a variety of useful information.

THE PC OF THE FUTURE

While the exact makeup of future PCs is anyone's guess, it is expected that they will keep getting smaller, faster, more powerful, and more user-friendly, and that they will eventually be driven primarily by voice-input and gesture/touch interfaces. Portable PCs will continue to grow closer in capabilities to conventional desktop PCs and will continue to be used for additional purposes. Tomorrow's home and business PCs will likely not even look like today's PCs—instead they may be built into walls, desks, appliances, and perhaps even clothing. In addition to their changing appearance, computers are expected to keep converging with other devices and continue to take on multiple roles to serve our personal needs, as well as to control our household or office environment. Computers in the future may also be able to offer multisensory output—enabling users to see, hear, feel, taste, and smell output—and will likely become even more environmentally friendly.

Some examples of new hardware beginning to become available are discussed next, followed by a discussion of some technologies that may change the overall makeup of computers in the future—*nanotechnology*, *quantum computers*, and *optical computers*.

ONLINE VIDEO

Go to **www.course.com/uccs/ch8** to watch the "Demo of the Android Software Development Kit for Mobile Phones" video clip.

ASK THE EXPERT

Martin Smekal, President and Founder, TabletKiosk

What do you expect to be the optimal input device of the future?

Right now, touch screens are gaining major momentum in the enterprise business communities. Companies are recognizing how touch screen applications can increase productivity, and the mode of input is extremely intuitive. Ideally, the optimal device for mobile computing would incorporate both touch screen and digital ink capabilities. The touch function would be used for menu-driven applications like restaurant point-of-sale systems and multiple choice survey questionnaires, and the inking capabilities would be used for handwriting recognition.

Emerging Hardware

The overall size and appearance of PCs seem to change on a continual basis. We now have fully functioning PCs that are small enough to fit in a pocket or be worn on the body. Technologies are continuing to be developed to make computers and computer components smaller, faster, and more capable. Some of the exciting emerging input, processing, output, and storage hardware and technologies are discussed next.

Emerging Input Devices

While voice input is expected to gain even more prominence in the future, other more touch-based input options are emerging. One is the **virtual keyboard**. A virtual keyboard uses a projector and camera—the projector projects a keyboard image onto a flat surface and the camera translates motion on that projected image back to the computer as input (see Figure 8-1). Virtual keyboard capabilities are expected to be built into mobile phones, portable PCs, and other portable devices soon in order to allow input via a standard keyboard layout without requiring actual keyboard hardware. A related emerging application is the use of projected images for consumer kiosks. Instead of requiring floor space, kiosk images are displayed on a wall or the floor using a wall- or ceiling-mounted projector; a camera tracks the user's interactions with the projected images as input. Game interfaces can also be projected on the floor for entertainment applications.

Input devices that support *gestures* (similar to the Nintendo Wii remote control and other gesture-oriented gaming controllers) are also expected to become more prominent in the future. Mice that can be held in the air and moved to control onscreen activity, such as gesturing to the right in order to skip to the next song on a CD that is playing, are beginning to become available, and the Apple iPhone supports the use of some gestures on its touch screen. In addition, complete noncontact gesture interfaces, similar to the one used

FIGURE 8-1
Examples of emerging input devices.

VIRTUAL KEYBOARDS

RFID CHECKOUT SYSTEMS

NFC MOBILE PAYMENT SYSTEMS

>**Virtual keyboard.** A device that projects a keyboard image onto any flat surface and translates finger motion on the projected image back to the computer as input.

TREND

Microsoft Surface and Other New Input Possibilities

There is an ongoing trend to continue to make input methods and devices easier and more natural to use. Voice recognition is one option that is already here. Other possibilities include more *virtual*, less physical, devices that use projections or gestures instead of more conventional methods of input.

One possibility—the virtual keyboard—is shown in Figure 8-1. Another option being developed by Microsoft is called *Surface*. This product (essentially a Windows Vista PC built into a table as shown in the accompanying photograph) uses built-in cameras and software to detect human gestures made on the Surface tabletop, as well as to detect objects and other devices placed on the table's surface and use them as input. For instance, photos can be wirelessly transferred to the Surface device by simply placing a digital camera on the table. Individuals can move through menus and select objects with the flick of a finger and, unlike conventional touch screens, Surface can recognize input from multiple sources simultaneously. While originally being targeted to a select group of retail partners, such as T-Mobile and Harrah's Casinos, it is possible that Surface or a similar technology might reach the home market in five years or so.

Related gesture-based input devices include the *EyeToy* system used with some Sony PlayStation games, the Nintendo Wii controller, and new gesture-enabled mobile phones that allow users to tilt or wave the device to navigate

Web sites and play games. One emerging interface even enables users to "write" in the air with a mobile phone and have the phone recognize and input the letters or numbers being written. These and other touch- and gesture-based input technologies are expected to be included in the PC of the future.

Microsoft Surface.

by Tom Cruise's character in the movie *Minority Report* to change the images on the display by simply gesturing with his hands, are beginning to be available. For instance, the CNN *Magic Wall* uses an interface that works similarly to the one in that movie and allows newscasters to display and change content on the Magic Wall by tapping and/or gesturing on its surface. For a look at the new *Microsoft Surface* input system and other emerging input devices, see the Trend box.

For making electronic payments while on the go, use of the radio frequency identification (RFID) and Near Field Communication (NFC) technologies discussed in Chapter 2 are expected to continue to grow. To use RFID as a replacement for the barcodes found on end products in retail stores, a unique identifying product code referred to as an *Electronic Product Code (EPC)* is typically assigned to each product and stored in its RFID tag. The EPC code can be used in conjunction with a database to determine additional product information, such as pricing information, when the RFID tag is read at the checkout using an appropriate reader. Because RFID technology can read numerous items at one time, it is possible that, someday, RFID will allow consumers to perform self-checkout at a retail store by just pushing their carts filled with items through a portal RFID reader (see Figure 8-1) to ring up all of their items at one time. And as RFID and NFC capabilities continue to be integrated into credit cards and mobile phones (the research firm In-Stat predicts as many as 25 million NFC-enabled phones will be in use in the United States by 2011), it is expected that these devices will be increasingly used to quickly pay for goods and services by waving the card or phone in front of the appropriate reader (refer again to Figure 8-1). For security purposes, *high-frequency RFID chips* are used in electronic payment applications, so the device has to be within an inch or so of the reader in order to be read.

FIGURE 8-2
Flexible processors.

Emerging Processing Technologies

Computer and CPU manufacturers are continually working to develop ways to make computers work better, faster, more reliably, and more efficiently. For example, new designs for motherboards and CPUs are being developed, the number of cores used with multi-core CPUs is growing, new materials are being used, and new technologies are being developed on a continual basis. For instance, the upcoming *USB 3.0* standard will allow peripheral devices to communicate with a computer at more than 10 times the speed of USB 2.0. And, for integrating CPUs and other computer components into clothing and other flexible materials, a number of companies are developing flexible electronic components, such as the flexible processor shown in Figure 8-2. In addition to the ability to be bent without damaging the circuitry, flexible processors are thinner, lighter, generate little heat, and consume significantly less energy than conventional processors.

As demand by consumers and businesses for online software, services, and media-rich experiences continues to increase, some experts predict that *terascale computing*—the ability of computers to process at least one trillion floating-point operations per second (one *teraflop*)—will eventually be needed. Terascale research is currently focusing on multi-core processors used in conjunction with other hardware and special software to increase the number of tasks that can be processed at the same time. It also includes working to develop higher-speed communications between computers, such as between Web servers and high-performance mobile devices or PCs. Intel, one of the leaders in terascale research, has created a *teraflop processor* that contains 80 cores to test strategies for rapidly moving terabytes of data from core to core and between cores and memory. It has also developed a 20-megabyte memory chip that is attached directly to the processor in order to speed up communication between processors and memory. This design allows thousands of interconnections, which enable data to travel at more than one *terabyte per second* (*TBps*) between memory and the processor cores. It is expected that this speed will be needed to handle the terabytes of data used by applications in the near future.

For packing an increasing number of components onto small chips, the use of *three-dimensional (3D) chips* is one emerging possibility. With 3D chips, the components are layered, which cuts down on the surface area required. Typically, 3D chips are created by layering individual silicon wafers on top of one another with a special machine that uses cameras to align the wafers properly. Researchers at the University of Southampton, UK, however, have recently developed wafers that contain matching sets of pegs and holes, similar to the way Lego bricks fit together. In preliminary tests, the researchers lined up the edges of two chips by hand and pressed them together—images taken with an electron microscope show that the two chips aligned roughly five times better than with the camera-based technique. While still in the research stage, the researchers believe that this new design could aid the development of 3D electronics. 3D chips are now available for some applications—such as video cards—and are expected to be used for other multimedia applications in the near future.

For memory improvements, several forms of **nonvolatile RAM (NVRAM)** are becoming available or under development. One of the most promising types of nonvolatile RAM is *MRAM* (*magnetic*, or, more precisely, *magnetoresistive RAM*). MRAM uses *magnetic polarization* rather than an electrical charge to store data. The magnetic polarization cannot leak away over time and does not require a constant stream of electricity to

INSIDE THE INDUSTRY

Memory Spots: Embedded Video for the Future

A recent development by HP may soon link the digital and physical worlds. How? Via a new miniature wireless data chip that can be attached to end products and other physical items to provide access to digital content related to that item.

Referred to as *Memory Spots*, these chips are about the size of a grain of rice and have a built-in antenna. They have a relatively fast (10 MBps) data transfer rate and are expected to store up to one-half MB of video, audio, photo, or text-based data, such as a very short video or audio clip, several images, or dozens of pages of text. The chips are small enough to be embedded in a sheet of paper or stuck to any surface. Information stored in a Memory Spot is expected to be accessed by readers incorporated into mobile phones, handheld computers, digital cameras, printers, and other devices.

Some potential applications include storing medical records on a hospital patient's wristband; adding security information to passports and other types of identity documents; tracking the history of, or facilitating the photocopying of, business documents; and adding video and sound to books, postcards, magazine ads and articles, and other printed items. For example, individuals with mobile phones or portable PCs with Memory Spot readers built in could view a trailer for an upcoming movie by placing their phone or PC close to a Memory Spot incorporated into a movie poster or an ad in a magazine or newspaper. Similarly, Memory Spots can be added to post cards, books (see the accompanying photograph), and other printed items in order to enable individuals to play audio or video content related to the printed content.

retain data. Consequently, MRAM is nonvolatile. MRAM chips are expected to eventually have greater storage capacity, faster access times, and lower power consumption than conventional memory chips. The most common applications for MRAM today include storing critical data for enterprise systems as they operate, in order to guard against data loss, and saving the data necessary to help industrial automation and robotics systems recover quickly from a power loss. Another emerging type of nonvolatile memory is *PRAM* (*phase-change random access memory*). PRAM chips have a special coating that changes its physical state when heat is applied. This change is used to represent data 1s and 0s, similar to the *phase-change technology* used to record data on recordable CDs and DVDs. With PRAM, an electrical charge is used to store data and a probe is used to read data. Another possibility for nonvolatile memory is *NRAM* (*Nanotube-based/Nonvolatile RAM*) being developed by Nantero, Inc. NRAM is considerably faster and denser than conventional RAM, uses less power, and is highly resistant to environmental forces such as heat and cold. All three of these types of nonvolatile RAM guard against data loss and enable "instant-on" capabilities for PCs and other devices, so it is expected that, eventually, nonvolatile RAM may replace *SDRAM* as the main memory for a computer. It is even possible that a type of nonvolatile memory could replace all memory and storage in a PC. For a look at an emerging use for nonvolatile memory chips—incorporating video or other multimedia into end products—see the Inside the Industry box.

One byproduct of packing an increasing amount of technology in a smaller system unit is heat, an ongoing problem for CPU and computer manufacturers. Since heat can damage components and cooler chips can run faster, virtually all computers today employ *fans*, *heat sinks* (small components typically made out of aluminum with fins that help to dissipate heat), or other methods to cool the CPU and system unit. For instance, PCs today typically include several fans, such as one fan on the power supply that can be seen on the

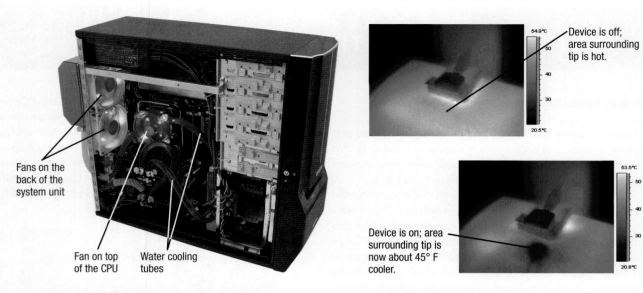

Device is off; area surrounding tip is hot.

Device is on; area surrounding tip is now about 45° F cooler.

Fans on the back of the system unit

Fan on top of the CPU

Water cooling tubes

FANS AND WATER COOLING SYSTEMS
These cooling methods and heat sinks are used with computers today.

ION PUMP COOLING SYSTEM
This cooling method may be used with computers in the future.

FIGURE 8-3

New and emerging computer cooling methods.

back of the PC and one fan and a heat sink on top of the CPU. One of the newest cooling methods being used with PCs consists of liquid-filled tubes that act as radiators to draw heat away from processors. Although initially expensive, difficult to install, and complicated to use, these *water cooling systems* are now available in simpler and less expensive formats. An added bonus of water-cooled PCs is that they are quieter than conventional systems. As shown in Figure 8-3, some PCs today use a combination of fans and water cooling systems; water cooling systems are expected to be more prominent in the near future.

One possibility for the future is a new *ion pump* cooling system being developed by researchers from the University of Washington. This tiny silicon-based cooling system uses ionized air and an electric field to cool the surface. The system has no moving parts and uses minimal energy consumption. To cool a CPU or other component located close to the cooling system, an electrode tip is set to a high voltage—creating a high electric field that strips electrons from molecules of oxygen and nitrogen in the air, ionizing them. These positively charged ions then flow from the electrode tip to a negatively charged collector electrode. As the ions move toward the collector electrode, they drag the surrounding air with them, creating a net flow of air to cool the area beneath the collector electrode (refer again to Figure 8-3). The voltage being applied to the electrode tip can be modified to cool the area to different temperatures and, since the device is made of silicon, it could eventually be integrated into CPUs and other computer components during manufacturing. While just in the prototype stage at the moment, researchers estimate that a commercial product based on this technology may reach the market by 2010.

Emerging Output Devices

Some of the most recent improvements in display technology center on more versatile output devices and new flat-screen technologies. For instance, *3D display screens* that use filters, prisms, multiple lenses, and other technologies built into the display screen to create the 3D effect are becoming available to allow users to view 3D images without the use of special glasses. In addition to their appeal for games, movies, and other consumer PC applications, 3D displays are an important improvement for scientists, physicians, architects, and other professionals who routinely view detailed graphics or diagrams in the course of their work. Another emerging display option is the *wearable personal display*, such as the one shown in Figure 8-4. Similar to the *head-mounted displays* used by soldiers, surgeons, and other individuals who require a hands-free display while working, wearable personal displays project the image from a PC or other device (such as a digital camera, portable DVD player, or handheld gaming device) to a display screen built into the glasses, but they are designed for personal use. The display screen is located close to the eye, but the technology allows the user to see the image as if it is on a distant large screen display.

3D projectors, such as those used to display *holograms* (three-dimensional projected images), are also in the works. For instance, researchers at Tokyo University have developed a holographic device that uses a 360-degree digital camera to scan a person's head and then that data can be sent over communications media to a special display device that projects a 3D image of the person, and the U.S. military is developing a six-foot-wide display that can produce sharp, color, realistic holograms. Another emerging projector application is a tiny projector designed to be placed inside a mobile phone (see Figure 8-4), digital camera, portable digital media player, portable PC, or other device, allowing the device to project an image (such as a document, presentation, or movie) onto a wall or other flat surface from up to 12 feet away, creating a display up to 10 feet wide. Projector-equipped phones are expected to be available by 2009; stand-alone portable projectors using the same technology are expected about the same time.

For display screens used with computers, mobile devices, and other electronic devices, there are a number of technologies under development designed to create displays that are more visible, while at the same time using less energy. Some of these technologies are based on *organic light emitting diode (OLED)* technology. **Organic light emitting diode (OLED) displays** use a layer of organic material which, when electric current is applied, emits a visible light. While conventional flat panel displays based on *LCD (liquid crystal display)* technology are *nonemissive* (which means they do not produce light and so they require *backlighting*), OLEDs emit a visible light and, therefore, do not use backlighting. This characteristic makes OLEDs more energy efficient and lengthens the battery life of portable devices using OLED displays. Other advantages of OLEDs over LCDs include the fact that OLEDs are even thinner than LCDs, they have a wider viewing angle and so are visible from virtually all directions, and their images are brighter and sharper. OLED computer displays and televisions are just beginning to become available and OLED displays are beginning to be incorporated into digital cameras, mobile phones, portable digital media players, and other consumer devices.

In addition to the overall advantages of using OLED technology, some special types of OLEDs support applications not possible with CRT or LCD technology. For instance, *flexible OLED (FOLED)* displays—a technology developed by Universal Display Corporation—are OLED displays built on flexible surfaces, such as plastic or metallic foil. Flexible displays using FOLED technology—such as displays that can

WEARABLE PERSONAL DISPLAY
The glasses shown here display images close to the user's eyes, but the image appears as if it is on a distant large screen display.

INTEGRATED PORTABLE PROJECTORS
Images displayed on the device (such as the mobile phone shown here) are projected onto any surface.

FIGURE 8-4
Examples of emerging output devices.

FURTHER EXPLORATION

Go to **www.course.com/uccs/ch8**
for links to further information about display device technologies.

> **Organic light emitting diode (OLED) display.** A type of flat-panel display that uses emissive organic material to display brighter and sharper images.

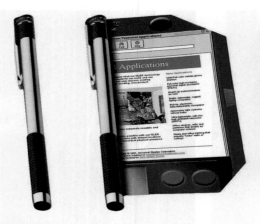

FOLEDS
Used to create flexible displays on plastic or another type of flexible material.

TOLEDS
Used to create transparent displays.

IMODS
Display is bright and readable, even in direct sunlight.

FIGURE 8-5
Examples of emerging display technologies.

FIGURE 8-6
Emerging types of USB flash drives.

USB FLASH DRIVE BUILT INTO NECKLACE

USB FLASH DRIVE WATCH

roll up when not in use—are being developed by several companies. This technology may result in pullout displays (see Figure 8-5) that can be used in conjunction with handheld PCs and mobile devices, displays integrated into military uniform sleeves, and retractable wall-mounted big screen televisions and monitors. Another form of OLED developed by Universal Display Corporation is *transparent OLED* (*TOLED*). TOLED displays are transparent; the portion of the display that does not currently have an image displayed (and the entire display device when it is off) is nearly as transparent as glass, so the user can see through the screen (refer again to Figure 8-5). TOLEDs open up the possibility of displays on home windows, car windshields, helmet face shields, and other transparent items.

Another emerging display technology is *interferometric modulator* (*IMOD*) *displays*. Designed initially for mobile phones and other portable devices, an IMOD screen is essentially a complex mirror that uses external light—such as from the sun or artificial light inside a building—to display images. Because IMOD displays are utilizing light instead of fighting it the way LCD displays do, images are bright and clear (see Figure 8-5) even in direct sunlight. And because backlighting isn't used, power consumption is much less than what is needed for LCD displays. In fact, devices using IMOD screens use no power unless the image changes, so they can remain on at all times without draining the device's battery. Expected to be used initially with mobile devices, IMODs could eventually be used for outdoor television screens, large digital signs, and other outdoor display devices that normally consume a great deal of power.

For a look at the secondary displays beginning to be built into notebook covers and other objects, see the Technology and You box.

Emerging Storage Devices

Many emerging storage devices today are focused on creating even more convenient portable personal storage or packing an increasing amount of data on an optical disc or similar storage medium. For portable personal storage, USB flash drives are continuing to be built into a variety of everyday items, such as watches, sunglasses, Swiss Army knives—even jewelry (see Figure 8-6). In addition to providing an increasing amount of portable data storage, USB flash drives are also continuing to provide additional capabilities, such as to recreate the user's primary PC environment (including appearance, e-mail, contact lists, calendar, browser favorites, documents, and other designated files) on any PC to which the USB flash drive is connected or to lock a PC or protect the data stored on the USB flash drive by using a fingerprint reader built into the drive.

TECHNOLOGY AND YOU

Smart Notebook Covers

Ever want to change the cover of your PC to reflect your mood or check your e-mail when your notebook PC is closed? Well, the solution is just about here. Because of the progress being made in the area of flexible electronics, experts predict that soon a variety of images and information will be able to be displayed on the cover of portable PCs, even if the PC is turned off. Possibilities include displaying images for decorative purposes, as well as usable content from the PC. While this feature has yet to materialize on the entire notebook cover, Windows Vista does include support for a secondary display device located on the cover of a portable PC. The new technology, called *SideShow*, allows users to access content—such as e-mail messages, schedules, maps, flight information, address books, Wi-Fi connectivity information, digital music, and more—located on the portable primary PC and display that information on the secondary display (see the accompanying photo). This display, technically a tiny computer, can be left on continually since it uses minimal power, and it can be set up to access information on the portable PC to update the SideShow device on a regular basis.

SideShow devices typically connect to their respective PCs via a wireless networking connection and users determine the information they would like displayed by installing *gadgets*—small programs—on the SideShow device. SideShow technology also allows hardware manufacturers to build auxiliary displays into peripheral devices (such as keyboards, LCD monitors, laptop bags, remote controls, digital picture frames, and mobile phones), which can then display information received from a Windows Vista-based PC. For example, a SideShow-enabled remote control can be used to retrieve program listing information from a Media Center PC, and a SideShow-enabled digital picture frame can be used to display e-mail messages, flight information, and other information, in addition to displaying digital photos.

Secondary display is built into the notebook cover.

Display has its own directional and selection controls.

Content, such as new e-mail messages, maps, or schedule information, is displayed here.

Windows SideShow enables notebook PCs to display information on a secondary display.

Another storage possibility that is finally a reality after many years of research and development is **holographic storage**. To record data, holographic storage systems split the light from a blue laser beam into two beams (a *reference beam* whose angle determines the address used to store data at that particular location on the storage medium and a *signal beam* that contains the data). The signal beam passes through a device called a *spatial light modulator* (*SLM*) which translates the data's 0s and 1s into a hologram—a three-dimensional representation of data in the form of a checkerboard pattern of light and dark pixels. The two beams intersect within the recording medium to store the hologram at that location (see Figure 8-7) by changing the optical density of the medium. Over one million bits of data can be stored at one time in a single flash of light, so holographic storage systems are very fast. And, because the hologram goes through the entire thickness of the medium, much more data can be stored on a holographic disc than on a CD or DVD of the same physical size. In fact, hundreds of holograms can be stored in an overlapping manner in the same area of the medium—a different reference beam angle or

>**Holographic storage.** A type of storage technology that uses multiple blue laser beams to store data in three dimensions.

HOW HOLOGRAPHIC STORAGE WORKS

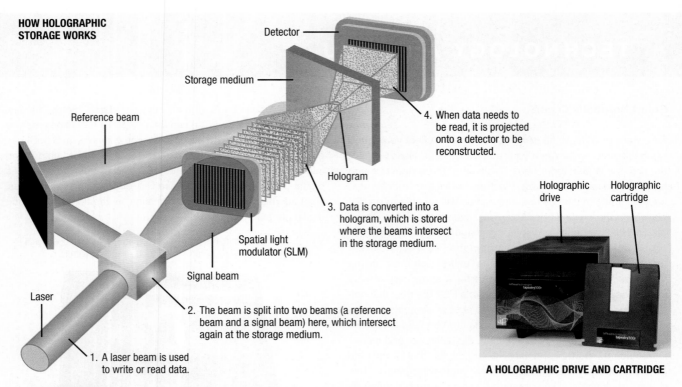

Detector

Storage medium

Reference beam

4. When data needs to be read, it is projected onto a detector to be reconstructed.

Hologram

3. Data is converted into a hologram, which is stored where the beams intersect in the storage medium.

Spatial light modulator (SLM)

Signal beam

2. The beam is split into two beams (a reference beam and a signal beam) here, which intersect again at the storage medium.

Laser

1. A laser beam is used to write or read data.

Holographic drive   Holographic cartridge

A HOLOGRAPHIC DRIVE AND CARTRIDGE

FIGURE 8-7
Holographic storage. Holographic drives store up to one million bits of data in a single flash of light.

ONLINE VIDEO

Go to **www.course.com/uccs/ch8** to watch the "Holographic Storage: Data at the Speed of Light" video clip.

media position is used for each hologram so it can be uniquely stored and retrieved when needed. To read data, the reference beam projects the hologram containing the requested data onto to a *detector* that reads the entire data page at one time. Today's holographic storage systems typically consist of a *holographic drive* and removable recordable *holographic media cartridges*; current capacity is 300 GB per cartridge with 1.6 TB cartridges expected by 2009. Holographic data storage systems are particularly suited to applications in which large amounts of data need to be stored or retrieved quickly, but rarely changed, such as for business data archiving, high-speed digital video delivery, and image processing for medical, video, and military purposes. Rewritable holographic drives and media are currently in the development stage and are expected to be available by 2009.

One emerging possibility for high-capacity business data storage applications is *Ultra Density Optical (UDO)* discs. UDO drives and media use phase-change and blue laser technology similar to some DVD discs, but they are optimized for data storage, instead of for movies and other home entertainment applications. They can also hold a larger amount of data per disc. Currently, UDO discs hold either 30 GB or 60 GB, with 240 GB discs expected by 2010. And a new *2-photon* 3D technology being developed by one company enables 1 TB to be stored on a standard-sized optical disc. Discs based on this technology are expected to be on the market in less than five years.

The Impact of Nanotechnology

Although there are varying definitions, most agree that **nanotechnology** involves creating computer components, machines, and other structures that are less than 100 nanometers in size (one *nanometer (nm)* is one-billionth of a meter). Today's CPUs—which are formed using a process called *lithography* that imprints patterns on semiconductor materials—

>**Nanotechnology.** The science of creating tiny computers and components by working at the individual atomic and molecular levels.

typically contain *transistors* (switches that control the flow of electrons) that are 65 *nanometers* (*nm*) or less in size (45 nm chips are due out in 2008), so they contain components that technically fit the definition of nanotechnology. But some experts believe that, eventually, current technology will reach its limits. At that point, transistors and other computer components may need to be built at the atomic and molecular level—starting with single atoms or molecules to construct the components. Prototypes of computer products built in this fashion include a single switch that can be turned on and off like a transistor but is made from a single organic molecule and tiny nickel-based *nanodots* that would, theoretically, allow about 5 TB of data to be stored on a hard drive roughly the size of a postage stamp. In another nanotechnology development, researchers at the University of Arizona recently discovered how to turn single molecules into working transistors and created transistors as small as a single nanometer. While still in the experimental stage, this discovery may significantly impact computing technologies in the future.

But nanotechnology is impacting more than just computers. One nanotechnology development that is already being used in a variety of products available today is **carbon nanotubes**—tiny, hollow tubes made up of carbon atoms. The wall of a single-walled carbon nanotube is only one carbon atom thick and the tube diameter is approximately 100,000 times smaller than a human hair. Lithium ion batteries that use nanotubes are currently on the market, Samsung has created a 15-inch prototype display screen that uses carbon nanotubes to illuminate images on the screen, and NRAM—a new type of fast, nonvolatile memory discussed earlier in this chapter—is nanotube-based and is scheduled to begin shipping soon. Because of their strength and lightness for their size, carbon nanotubes are also being integrated into nonelectronic products, such as automobile panels and racing bikes. In fact, the frame of the bike that Floyd Landis rode in the 2006 Tour de France is built with carbon nanotubes (see Figure 8-8)—the entire bike frame weighs less than one kilogram (2.2 pounds).

FIGURE 8-8
Carbon nanotubes make this bike frame very strong, but light.

One new environmental application for nanotechnology is cleaning up contaminated water. Several products are coming on the market, such as powders containing *nanoparticles* that form chemical bonds with contaminants (including mercury, arsenic, and lead) in order to remove those contaminants from water sources, and ceramic filters that contain tiny holes lined with highly absorbent *nanocrystals*. In the future, nanotechnology may help to solve much of the toxic waste problem associated with *e-trash* (electronic waste, such as old computer equipment, as discussed in Chapter 7) by rearranging dangerous components, at the atomic level, into inert substances. Other possible future applications of nanotechnology include improved military uniforms that protect soldiers from bullets and germ warfare, microscopic devices that can enter the bloodstream and perform tests or irradiate cancerous tumors, and computers and sensors that are small enough to be woven into the fibers of clothing or embedded into paint and other materials. Some of the devices generated by nanotechnology research may contain or be constructed out of organic material. Complete *organic computers* (discussed next) are a long way off in the future, but researchers have already created biological computing devices—such as the *MAYA-II* computer that uses strands of DNA to perform computations. Although very slow and only programmed to play tic-tac-toe, the computer has never lost at that game.

>**Carbon nanotube.** A tiny, hollow tube made up of carbon atoms; used as part of a variety of products today.

Quantum and Optical Computers

Computers a few decades from now will likely use technology that is very different from the silicon chips and electronic bits and bytes we are accustomed to today. In addition to being miniature—based on nanotechnology—and likely incorporated into a variety of everyday devices, computers in the future may be *quantum* or *optical computers*.

Quantum Computing

The idea of **quantum computing** emerged in the 1970s, but it has received renewed interest lately. Quantum computing applies the principles of quantum physics and quantum mechanics to computers, going beyond traditional physics to work at the subatomic level. Quantum computers differ from conventional computers in that they utilize atoms or nuclei working together as quantum bits or *qubits*. Qubits function simultaneously as both the computer's processor and memory, and each qubit can represent more than just the two states (one and zero) used with today's electronic bits; a qubit can even represent many states at one time. Quantum computers can perform computations on many numbers at one time, making them, theoretically, exponentially faster than conventional computers. Physically, quantum computers in the future might consist of a thimbleful of liquid whose atoms are used to perform calculations as instructed by an external device.

FIGURE 8-9

Quantum computers.
The vial of liquid shown here contains the 7-qubit computer used by IBM researchers in 2001 to perform the most complicated computation by a quantum computer to date—factoring the number 15.

While quantum computers are still in the pioneering stage, working quantum computers do exist. For instance, in 2001 the researchers at IBM's Almaden Research Center created a 7-qubit quantum computer (see Figure 8-9) composed of the nuclei of seven atoms that can interact with each other and be programmed by radio frequency pulses. This quantum computer successfully factored the number 15—not a complicated computation for a conventional computer, but the fact that a quantum computer was able to understand the problem and compute the correct answer is viewed as a highly significant event in the area of quantum computer research. In addition, Hewlett-Packard scientists have developed a *crossbar latch*—a switch just a single molecule thick that can store binary data and might one day function as a transistor in a quantum computer.

Quantum computing is not well suited for general computing tasks but is ideal for, and expected to be widely used in, the areas of encryption and code breaking.

Optical Computing

Optical chips, which use light waves to transmit data, are also currently in development. A possibility for the future is the **optical computer**—a computer that uses light, such as from laser beams or infrared beams—to perform digital computations. Because light beams do not interfere with each other, optical computers can be much smaller and faster than electronic PCs. For instance, according to one NASA senior research scientist, an optical computer could solve a problem in one hour that would take an electronic computer 11 years to solve. While some researchers are working on developing an all-optical computer, others believe that a mix of optical and electronic components—or an *opto-electronic computer*—may be the best bet for the future. Opto-electronic technology is already being used to improve long-distance fiber-optic communications. Initial opto-electronic PC applications are expected to be used for speeding up communications between PCs and other devices, as well as between PC components. In fact, prototypes of chips that have both optical and electrical functions combined on a single silicon chip—a feat that was

>**Quantum computing.** A technology that applies the principles of quantum physics and quantum mechanics to computers to direct atoms or nuclei to work together as quantum bits (qubits), which function simultaneously as the computer's processor and memory. >**Optical computer.** A computer that uses light, such as from laser beams or infrared beams, to perform digital computations.

thought to be impossible until recently—already exist. It is generally expected that optical computers won't become mainstream for at least another decade.

EMERGING NETWORKING TECHNOLOGIES

Improvements are being made on a continual basis to both wired and wireless networking technologies to increase speed and connectivity options for both *local area networks* (*LANs*) and Internet connections, as well as to support the continued growth in Internet-based multimedia and communications applications used with PCs and mobile devices that require fast, dependable connections, such as Voice over IP (VoIP), video-on-demand (VOD), mobile TV, and teleconferencing. For instance, one new improvement to videoconferencing technology to make it more closely mimic a real-time meeting environment is *telepresence videoconferencing*. Telepresence videoconferencing systems typically allow participants in different physical locations to see high-quality, life-sized video images of each other in real time (see Figure 8-10); the corresponding audio even appears to be coming from the appropriate individual. Some systems also allow the use of a shared display so that all participants can see the same data (such as documents or presentations stored on a computer, or a live high-definition video feed of a product prototype or other item that is located in one of the conference rooms). Although telepresence videoconferencing setups are expensive, with travel becoming increasingly more expensive and time-consuming, many businesses are looking to videoconferencing as a viable replacement for face-to-face meetings. Some specific improvements to wired and wireless networking that are on the horizon are discussed next.

Life-size video images of remote participants appear on the display screen.

FIGURE 8-10
Telepresence videoconferencing.

Wired Networking Improvements

Ethernet is the most widely used wired networking protocol. Ethernet was invented in the mid-1970s and has continued to evolve over the years to support faster speeds. The most common Ethernet standards for LANs today are *Fast Ethernet*, which supports data transfer rates of up to 100 Mbps, and *Gigabit Ethernet*, which is even faster at 1,000 Mbps (1 Gbps); the newer *10 Gigabit Ethernet* standard supports data transfer rates of 10 Gbps. For the future, standards for *40 Gigabit Ethernet* and *100 Gigabit Ethernet* supporting transfer rates of 40 Gbps and 100 Gbps, respectively, are under development and are expected to be approved in 2010. 100 Gigabit Ethernet is expected to be used for transmitting video; digital MRIs, X-rays, and other types of digital medical images; and other high-speed, bandwidth-intensive Internet applications.

A recent Ethernet development with potential for future business networking applications is **Power over Ethernet (PoE)**. PoE allows both electrical power and data to be sent over standard Ethernet cables (see Figure 8-11). Consequently, the Ethernet cable, in addition to sending data, can be used to supply power to the devices on a network. PoE is most often used in business networks with remote wired devices (such as outdoor networking hardware, security cameras, and other devices) that are not located near a power

---

>**Ethernet.** A widely used LAN communications protocol. >**Power over Ethernet (PoE).** A wired networking standard that allows electrical power to be sent along with data over standard Ethernet cables.

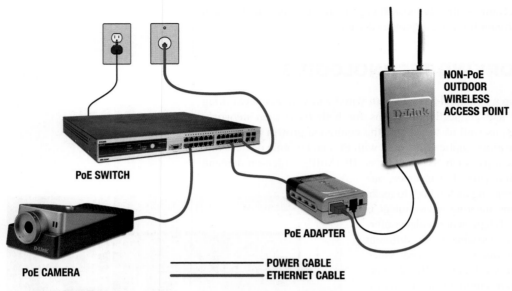

PoE SWITCH

PoE CAMERA

NON-PoE OUTDOOR WIRELESS ACCESS POINT

PoE ADAPTER

——— **POWER CABLE**
——— **ETHERNET CABLE**

FIGURE 8-11
With Power over Ethernet (PoE), devices are powered through the Ethernet connection.

outlet, as well as to place devices near ceilings or other locations where a nearby power outlet may not be available. Using PoE requires special hardware and devices designed for PoE but it eliminates the need for access to power outlets for that portion of the network. Regular Ethernet-enabled devices can be powered via PoE if a special *PoE adapter* is used.

For easily creating wired home networks, both the *Phoneline* (more officially called the *Home Phoneline Networking Association* or *HomePNA*) standard (that allows computers to be networked through ordinary telephone wiring and telephone jacks, without interfering with voice telephone calls) and the *Powerline* standard (that allows PCs to be networked over existing power lines using conventional electrical outlets) are also continuing to emerge to support faster speeds. The newest version of the Phoneline standard—*HomePNA 3.0*—supports speeds up to 320 Mbps and is designed to network the computers, as well as the home entertainment devices, within a home. Powerline networks are expected to soon operate as fast as 200 Mbps and, similar to the newest Phoneline standard, the newest Powerline standard—named *HomePlug AV*—can be used to network home entertainment devices, in addition to PCs.

An emerging technology based on the Powerline standard is **broadband over power lines** (**BPL**). BPL allows data (at the moment, primarily Internet data) to be sent over the existing power-pole infrastructure (with the addition of some new hardware at the power poles) and a building's regular power lines. The data does not interfere with the electrical signals because electrical current and digital data use different frequencies. Although only available in limited areas at the moment, BPL has great potential for delivering broadband Internet access to virtually any home or business that has access to electricity.

Wireless Networking Improvements

Developed in the late 1990s, **Wi-Fi** (for *wireless fidelity*) is a family of wireless networking standards that use the IEEE standard **802.11**. Wi-Fi is the current standard for wireless networks in the home or office, as well as for stationary wireless access to the Internet in public locations. Like Ethernet, the Wi-Fi standard is continually evolving to support increased speed and other capabilities. The speed and distance of a Wi-Fi network depends on a variety of factors, such as the particular Wi-Fi standard and hardware being used, the number of solid objects (such as walls, trees, or buildings) between the access point and the PC or other device being used, and possible interference from cordless phones, baby monitors, microwave ovens, and other devices that also operate on the same radio frequency as Wi-Fi (usually 2.4 GHz). In general, Wi-Fi is designed for medium-range data transfers—typically between 100 and 300 feet indoors and 300 to 900 feet outdoors.

>**Broadband over power lines (BPL).** A type of Internet connection that uses a building's regular power lines to access the Internet. >**Wi-Fi (802.11).** A widely used communications protocol for wireless networks.

There are a number of different versions of the 802.11 standard; the *802.11g* standard is the norm today. It uses the 2.4 GHz frequency, supports speeds up to 54 Mbps, and has an approximate range of 100 to 200 feet indoors. Newer—sometimes called *enhanced G*— 802.11g products are faster and have a further range than is possible with earlier 802.11g products. Enhanced G products use newer technology, such as *MIMO (multiple in, multiple out) antennas* that use multiple antennas to transfer multiple streams of data at one time in order to increase *throughput*—the amount of data that can be transferred over a communications medium during a given period of time. The newest Wi-Fi standard under development is *802.11n*. While the standard is not expected to be ratified until 2009, *Draft-N* hardware (hardware based on the draft standards of 802.11n) is available and use of Draft-N products is growing rapidly. *Draft-N* hardware uses MIMO antennas and other improvements that allow for faster transmissions (about five times as fast as 802.11g) and about twice the range. Draft-N devices can operate using either the 2.4 GHz frequency or the less crowded 5 GHz frequency. Typically, 802.11b, 802.11g, and 802.11n products can all be used on the same network—these products are typically identified as *802.11n/g/b compatible*.

Because the range of Wi-Fi networks is still fairly limited, a number of newer wireless networking technologies are currently in development and are designed to be used in conjunction with, or instead of, Wi-Fi to extend the range of wireless networks or to create wireless home multimedia networks, as discussed next. For a look at a new wireless networking application that you may encounter in a restaurant, see the How It Works box.

ONLINE VIDEO

Go to **www.course.com/uccs/ch8** to watch the "WiMAX vs. Wi-Fi" video clip.

WiMAX

An emerging new wireless networking option is **WiMAX** (*Worldwide Interoperability for Microwave Access*, also known as *802.16*). WiMAX is a series of standards designed for longer range wireless networking connections—up to 70 Mbps over a distance of up to 30 miles or so. WiMAX does not require line of sight (although the range drops to about 6 miles without line of sight) and so can be used in areas containing buildings and trees. Similar to Wi-Fi, WiMAX is designed to provide Internet access to fixed locations, but the coverage is significantly larger. While *802.16a* is designed to deliver broadband Internet to homes, businesses, and other fixed locations, the mobile version of this standard—**mobile WiMAX (802.16e)**— is designed to deliver broadband Internet to mobile users via a mobile phone, portable PC, or other WiMAX-enabled device. At the moment, the primary use for WiMAX is to provide Internet access to rural areas; it is also beginning to be used by businesses and schools to create fast, private, large LANs. However, at least one mobile WiMAX (802.16e) network is currently in development and is expected to begin offering services sometime in 2008. Research firm Yankee Group predicts there will be 28 million WiMAX subscribers by 2011. WiMAX capabilities are expected to be built into PCs, portable gaming devices, mobile phones, and digital cameras by the end of 2008, and

ASK THE EXPERT

Debra Jensen, Vice President and Chief Information Officer, Jack in the Box Inc.

How long will it be until paying for fast-food purchases by mobile phone is the norm?

The technology exists today to allow for the payment of fast-food purchases by mobile phone and it's being used in Europe and Japan. Though it's being tested in the United States, there are still some hurdles, primarily the adoption of the technology by cell phone providers and retailers, and consumers' willingness to use it. Another hurdle is consumers' concerns about the technology being secure. It will likely be 2011 before there is widespread use.

>**WiMAX.** A wireless networking standard that is faster and has a greater range than Wi-Fi. >**Mobile WiMAX (802.16e).** A version of WiMAX designed to be used with mobile phones.

HOW IT WORKS

Wireless Waiters

Ever wait an eternity in a restaurant to get a drink refill or your check? Well, wait no more. . .if your waiter has *ESP*.

This new system, developed by ESP Systems and already being deployed in numerous restaurants including Applebee's, T.G.I. Friday's, and Fatz Cafe, uses RF technology to connect everyone inside the restaurant—the customer, host, bus people, servers, bartenders, and kitchen staff. ESP streamlines the service process by keeping track of the real-time status of each table and customer, including when each table is ready for customers, is seated with customers, or needs bussing; when a drink or food order is ready for delivery; and—most importantly—when a customer needs his or her server. The goal of ESP is to increase guest loyalty and satisfaction by giving guests control over and the ability to customize their own dining experience, as well as to give servers the real-time information they need to better do their jobs while increasing productivity. Here's how it works (see the accompanying illustration).

Each table has a wireless device called an *ESP Hub*. This device keeps track of the status of that table, which is reflected on a display at the host station at the front of the restaurant. Using this display, hosts can determine available tables and seat guests without looking around the restaurant for an empty table.

When a guest is seated, the host "shoots" a signal at the ESP hub to turn the table status to "Dining." The server assigned to that table is then immediately notified via his or her *ESP Watch* that customers are seated.

The server then greets the guests and explains that they can press the ESP Hub at any time to call the server to the table. Orders are taken and, when a drink or food order is ready, a device in the bar or kitchen is used to "ESP" or instantly notify the server that those items are ready for delivery. Guests at any time can press the ESP Hub to ESP their servers, as well.

After a guest leaves, the table status is changed to "Bussing" and the appropriate bus person is notified. After the table is cleaned, the bus person uses his or her ESP Watch to change the status of the table back to "Ready."

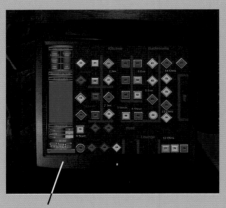

A display at the host station shows the current status of each table in the restaurant (Ready, Dining, or Bussing).

A device in the kitchen and bar is used to immediately notify a server that an order is ready for pickup.

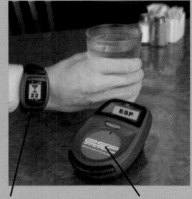

The server's watch buzzes and shows the appropriate table number when an order is ready or a guest ESPs.

Guests can press the ESP Hub at any time to ESP their servers.

WiMAX is expected to be the basis for at least some *fourth-generation* (*4G*) cellular standards used with mobile phones in the future. For a comparison of WiMAX to other widely used wireless networking standards that are discussed next, see Figure 8-12.

Mobile-Fi

Mobile-Fi, also known as *802.20* and *MBWA* (*Mobile Broadband Wireless Access*), is another standard currently in development for providing high-speed mobile Internet access. Unlike mobile WiMAX, Mobile-Fi was originally designed to be used while in cars or while traveling in other vehicles, such as trains, which are moving at up to 180 miles per hour. Mobile-Fi has a range of about two miles. While somewhat of a competitor of mobile

WiMAX at the moment, Mobile-Fi is expected to be compatible and used in conjunction with WiMAX. Some experts predict that WiMAX will be used to create large hotspots to provide access to stationary users and users moving around within a limited geographic area, and Mobile-Fi will be used for broader coverage and in high-speed mobile situations, such as to provide Internet access for individuals who commute to work via train.

Ultra Wideband (UWB) and Wireless USB

A wireless technology being developed for short-range wireless connections is **Ultra Wideband** (**UWB**). UWB (also referred to as *WiMedia*) was originally developed for the military in the 1960s to locate tanks, enemies, and other objects hidden behind walls or in foliage, but it is now used to wirelessly network consumer multimedia devices. UWB can be used to wirelessly deliver multimedia content—such as video, music, and photos—stored on a computer or DVR to other devices that are within range (about 100 feet away or less). The speed of UWB at the present time depends on the distance between the devices being used, but at 100 Mbps at 10 meters (about 33 feet) or 480 Mbps at 2 meters (about 6.5 feet), UWB is significantly faster than *Bluetooth* and has a greater range. The UWB standard is still evolving, but it is expected to be used primarily for high-speed transfers over short distances.

One development related to UWB is the announcement that upcoming Bluetooth standards will incorporate UWB technology to speed up connections between Bluetooth devices for transferring large quantities of data, such as to transfer music or video files from a PC to a mobile phone. Another development is the emerging **wireless USB** standard. Backed by Intel and based on UWB, wireless USB is designed to connect peripheral devices to a PC, similar to Bluetooth, but transfers data at UWB speeds and distances. It is expected that UWB will be used to connect home entertainment devices and wireless USB will be used to connect PC hardware, while Bluetooth will continue to be used with portable PCs and mobile devices. One of the first wireless USB products to come on the market is the *wireless USB hub*. As shown in Figure 8-13, USB peripheral devices are plugged into the wireless USB hub and the hub is connected to the PC via a wireless connection and a *wireless USB adapter* plugged into a USB port on the PC.

WIRELESS STANDARD	INTENDED PURPOSE	APPROXIMATE RANGE
WiMAX (802.16)	Long-range wireless networking, such as to provide Internet access to a particular geographic area	30 miles (line of sight); 6 miles (non-line of sight)
Mobile-Fi (802.20)	High-speed mobile networking, such as to access the Internet via a PC or mobile device while on the go	2 miles
Wi-Fi (802.11)	Short-range wireless networking, such as to network PCs within a building	100–300 feet indoors and 300–900 feet outdoors, depending on the Wi-Fi standard being used
Bluetooth	Very-short-range wireless networking, such as to connect an individual's personal devices	30 feet
Ultra Wideband (UWB)	High-speed short-range data transfers between consumer multimedia devices.	100 feet
Wireless HD	High-speed short-range data transfers between consumer multimedia devices.	30 feet

FIGURE 8-12
Comparison of WiMAX to other wireless networking standards.

FIGURE 8-13
Wireless USB.

WIRELESS USB ADAPTER
Plugs into the PC's USB port to connect the wireless USB hub to the PC.

WIRELESS USB HUB
Wirelessly connects all devices plugged into the hub to the PC.

WirelessHD (WiHD)

Another wireless standard in development that may be used to easily connect a variety of home consumer electronic devices (such as high-definition TVs, set-top boxes, gaming consoles, and DVD players) in the future is **WirelessHD** (**WiHD**). Backed by seven major

>**Ultra Wideband (UWB).** A wireless technology being developed for short-range wireless connections, such as to wirelessly network consumer multimedia devices. >**Wireless USB.** A form of USB that is based on UWB and enables peripheral devices to be connected wirelessly to a PC.
>**WirelessHD (WiHD).** A wireless networking specification designed for connecting home consumer devices.

FURTHER EXPLORATION

Go to **www.course.com/uccs/ch8** for links to further information about wireless networking protocols.

electronics companies, WirelessHD is designed to transfer full-quality uncompressed high-definition audio, video, and data within a single room and is expected to hit the market by the end of 2008. The first WiHD standard supports speeds up to 4 Gbps at a range of 10 meters; eventual speeds of up to 25 Gbps are expected. WiHD operates at 60 GHz and incorporates smart antenna systems that allow the system to steer the transmission, allowing for non-line of sight communications. WiHD aims to help users create an easy to manage wireless video network with a universal remote control; it also includes content protection mechanisms to secure data.

ZigBee and Wireless Sensor Networks

An emerging networking standard designed for inexpensive and simple short-range networking is *ZigBee (802.15)*. ZigBee is intended for applications that require low data transfer rates and several years of battery life. For instance, ZigBee can be used for home and commercial building automation to connect a wide variety of devices (such as appliances and lighting, heating, cooling, water, filtration, and security systems), and allows for their control from anywhere in the world. ZigBee is also used in industrial plant manufacturing, personal home healthcare, device tracking, and telecommunications. ZigBee is designed to accommodate more than 65,000 devices on a single network and supports speeds from 20 Kbps to 250 Kbps, depending on the frequency being used (several different frequencies are available for ZigBee networks). ZigBee has a range of 10 to 100 meters (about 32 to 328 feet) between devices, depending on power output and environmental characteristics.

ZigBee can also be used in *wireless sensor networks*—a network of *sensors* that can respond to a stimulus (such as heat, light, or pressure) and generate an electrical signal that can be measured or interpreted. Other wireless sensor networks are comprised of individual wireless sensor nodes known as *motes*. A mote (see Figure 8-14) is a tiny computer connected to one or more sensors that is powered by a battery and can communicate with other motes via miniscule radio transmitters. The sensors can perform a variety of measurements (such as assessing temperature, light, sound, position, acceleration, weight, and humidity), and the motes work together to transmit data about their environment. Some current applications for wireless sensor networks are to monitor critical processes within manufacturing plants in a broad range of industries, such as taking real-time temperature readings of moving railcars transporting chemicals to ensure the contents are kept within the temperature ranges needed to ensure safe transport, monitoring temperature and relative humidity in the drug development process at pharmaceutical plants, and monitoring mission critical heating, cooling, and processing activities in steel factories and power plants. In the future, motes could be embedded into concrete foundations on bridges to take and relay periodic structural and salt readings to detect possible problems with structural damage due to salt or other factors. They could also be attached to power meters and water meters in businesses and homes to transmit readings to the utility company on a regular basis, and they could be scattered in vineyards, orange groves, and other agricultural fields to relay temperature and moisture settings to the farmer.

▼ FIGURE 8-14

Motes. Motes contain sensors to collect data and an antenna to transmit the data to the other motes on the network.

DN2510 Mote-on-Chip (MoC)
12x12mm LGA
System-in-Package (SiP)

ARTIFICIAL INTELLIGENCE (AI)

Computers are continually becoming faster and smarter. Although they cannot yet think completely on their own, computers and software programs have become more sophisticated, and computers are being programmed to act in an increasingly intelligent manner.

What Is Artificial Intelligence (AI)?

According to John McCarthy, who coined the term **artificial intelligence** (**AI**) in 1956 and is considered by many to be one of its fathers, AI is "the science and engineering of making intelligent machines." In other words, AI researchers are working to create intelligent devices controlled by intelligent software programs; in essence, machines that think and act like people and that perform in ways that would be considered intelligent if observed in humans. In 1950, Alan Turing—one of the first AI researchers—argued that if a machine could successfully appear to be human to a knowledgeable observer, then it should be considered intelligent. To illustrate this idea, Turing developed a test—later called the *Turing Test*—in which one observer interacts electronically with both a computer and a person. During the test, the observer submits written questions electronically to both the computer and the person, evaluates the typed responses, and tries to identify which answers came from the computer and which came from the person. Turing argued that if the computer could repeatedly fool the observer into thinking it was human, then it should be viewed as intelligent.

FIGURE 8-15
The Loebner Prize gold medal has yet to be awarded.

Many Turing Test contests have been held over the years, and in 1990, Dr. Hugh Loebner initiated the Loebner Prize, pledging a grand prize of $100,000 and a solid gold medal (see Figure 8-15) for the developer of the first computer whose responses to a Turing Test were indistinguishable from that of a human's responses. A contest is held every year, awarding a prize of $2,000 and a bronze medal to the developer of the most human computer, but so far the gold medal has not been awarded. Although the Turing Test is interesting and is still providing grounds for research today, many experts believe that the Turing Test provides only one possible test of computer intelligence. These experts argue that there could be different definitions of intelligence, and a machine could still be considered intelligent without knowing enough about humans to imitate one.

Some of the initial advances in AI were made in the area of game playing—namely, chess. Early chess-playing programs were easily defeated by amateur chess players. But, as computers became more powerful and AI software became more sophisticated, chess-playing programs improved. In 1996, IBM's Deep Blue computer won two of six games in a chess match against then world chess champion Garry Kasparov. A landmark moment in AI history occurred in 1997 when Deep Blue beat Kasparov in a rematch, winning the match 3½ to 2½ (three of the six games ended in a draw). In late 2003, Kasparov played a chess match against a 3D chess program called *X3D Fritz*. The match was played on a virtual chessboard and

FIGURE 8-16
AI and chess playing.

ended in a draw of 2 to 2. *Deep Fritz*, a newer version of Fritz, played a match against world chess champion Vladimir Kramnik in late 2006 (see Figure 8-16). Deep Fritz won the match 4 to 2. As some of these chess matches have revealed, one disadvantage of playing against a computer is that once the human player makes a mistake, there is no hope (as there would be with a human opponent) that the computer opponent will make its own mistake at a later time to level the playing field in that game.

KRAMNIK VS. DEEP FRITZ
Shown here are images from the match in 2006 where the Deep Fritz chess program beat world champion Vladimir Kramnik 4 games to 2.

>**Artificial intelligence (AI).** When a computer performs actions that are characteristic of human intelligence.

AI Applications

Today's AI applications contain some aspect of artificial intelligence, although they tend to mimic human intelligence rather than display pure intelligence. Technological advances will undoubtedly help AI applications continue to evolve and become more intelligent and sophisticated in the future. While many welcome the idea of more intelligent computers to help people, some foresee a future in which people and computers may eventually merge. Not surprisingly, that scenario is frightening and objectionable to some. Just as the debate about what constitutes intelligence in nonhumans will continue, so will the debate about how far we as a society should delve into the area of artificial intelligence. AI applications that exist in some form today include *intelligent agents*, *expert systems*, *neural networks*, and *robotics*.

Intelligent Agents

Intelligent agents are programs that perform specific tasks to help make a user's work environment more efficient or entertaining. Typically, the tasks are small and specific and the agent program runs in the background until it is time for the agent to perform an action. Intelligent agents can often modify their behavior based on the user's actions, and they are used extensively on Web sites in addition to being built into operating systems, e-mail programs, Web browsers, application programs, and other products. Some specific types of intelligent agents include the following:

- ► *Application assistants*—provide help or assistance for a particular application program. Some can detect when the user might be having trouble with the program and automatically offer appropriate advice.

- ► *Search agents*—search for specified information on the Web, such as regularly gathering news articles and other information on specified subjects.

- ► *Shopping bots*—search online stores to find the best overall prices for specified products.

- ► *Entertainment bots*—provide entertainment, such as a virtual pet to take care of or an animated character to play games with.

- ► *Chatterbots*—carry on written "conversations" with people in a *natural language* (such as English, Spanish, French, or Japanese). Chatterbots are often represented by an animated character and typically respond both verbally and with appropriate physical gestures to create the illusion that the exchange is taking place between two thinking, living entities (see Figure 8-17).

FIGURE 8-17
A Web page chatterbot.

Expert Systems

Expert systems are software programs that can make decisions and draw conclusions, similar to a human expert. To do this, expert systems have two main components: a *knowledge base* and an *inference engine*. The *knowledge base* is a database that contains facts provided by a human expert and rules that the expert system should use to make decisions based on those facts. For instance, an expert system used to authorize credit for credit card customers would have in its knowledge base facts about customers, as well as rules, such as "Do not automatically authorize purchase if the customer has exceeded his or her credit limit." The *inference engine* is a software program that applies the rules to the data stored in the knowledge base in order to reach decisions. Figure 8-18 shows a simplified example of an expert system.

>**Intelligent agent.** A program that performs specific tasks to help to make a user's work environment more efficient or entertaining and that typically modifies its behavior based on the user's actions. >**Expert system.** A computer system that provides the type of advice that would be expected from a human expert.

Expert systems are widely used for tasks such as diagnosing illnesses, making financial forecasts, scheduling routes for delivery vehicles, diagnosing mechanical problems, and performing credit authorizations. Some expert systems are designed to take the place of human experts, while others are designed to assist them. For instance, medical expert systems, which incorporate the knowledge and decision making guidelines of some of the world's best physicians, are used to assist physicians with patient diagnoses. To use such a system, the symptoms exhibited by a patient are entered into the expert system. The program then asks the attending healthcare provider questions and compares the provided data to a large database of successfully diagnosed cases, in order to suggest one or more possible diagnoses. Because the expert system has access to an extensive knowledge base, the expert system may provide more possible diagnoses than the ones offered by the attending physician.

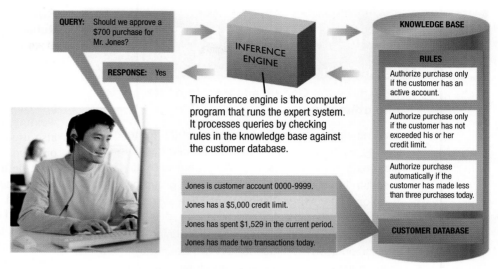

The inference engine is the computer program that runs the expert system. It processes queries by checking rules in the knowledge base against the customer database.

FIGURE 8-18
An expert system at work.

Expert systems can be built from scratch or by using an *expert system shell*—a skeletal system that needs to be supplied with the expert knowledge and rules to be used in the system. Regardless of how an expert system is created, it is important to realize that the conclusions of an expert system are based on the data and rules stored in its knowledge base, as well as the information provided by the users. If the expert knowledge is correct, the inference engine program is written correctly, and the user supplies accurate information in response to the questions posed by the expert system, the system will draw correct conclusions; if the knowledge base is wrong, the inference engine is faulty, or the user provides inaccurate input, the system will not work correctly.

Neural Networks

Artificial intelligence systems that attempt to imitate the way a human brain works are called **neural networks**. Neural networks (also called *neural nets*) are networks of processors that are connected together in a manner similar to the way the neurons in a human brain are connected. Neural networks can learn by observation, as well as by trial and error. They are designed to emulate the brain's pattern-recognition process in order to recognize patterns in data and make more progressive leaps in associations and predictions than conventional computer systems. Neural networks are used in areas such as handwriting, speech, and image recognition; geographical mapping; medical imaging; crime analysis; and biometric identification (see Figure 8-19). They are also increasingly being used in *vision systems*, in which cameras are used in conjunction with a neural network to inspect objects and make determinations—for example, the systems that check products for defects at manufacturing plants or that recognize stamps during postal processing.

FIGURE 8-19
Neural networks.
Often used in biometric identification systems, such as to analyze fingerprints.

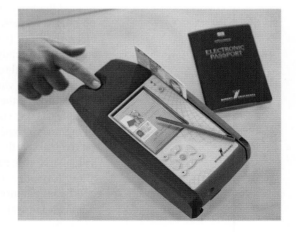

> **Neural network.** An expert system in which the human brain's pattern-recognition process is emulated by the computer system.

ASK THE EXPERT

Google

Rajen Sheth, Product Manager, Google Enterprise

How does the Google site translate Web pages into other languages?

Our translation is produced by state-of-the-art technology, without the intervention of human translators. Automatic translation is also often referred to as machine translation. Google's research group has developed its own statistical translation system for several language pairs.

Most state-of-the-art, commercial machine-translation systems in use today have been developed using a rules-based approach, and they require a lot of work by linguists to define vocabularies and grammars. Our system takes a different approach: we feed the computer billions of words of text, both monolingual text in the target language and aligned text consisting of examples of human translations between the languages. We then apply statistical learning techniques to build a translation model. We've achieved very good results in research evaluations.

ONLINE VIDEO

Go to **www.course.com/uccs/ch8** to watch the "IBM Speech Translation" video clip.

Robotics

Robotics is the field devoted to the study of **robots**—devices, controlled by a person or a computer, that can move and react to sensory input. Robots are currently used in factories to perform high-precision but monotonous jobs, such as welding, riveting, and painting. They are also used in situations that are dangerous or impossible for people, such as mining coal, defusing bombs, exploring the bottom of the ocean, repairing oil rigs, locating land mines, locating survivors in collapsed mines and buildings, and photographing the surface of Mars. Robots used for medical and military applications are discussed shortly; some other types of robots are discussed next.

Business or *industrial robots* can be used to perform business-oriented tasks, such as monitoring facilities for security purposes (looking for intruders, gas leaks, and other hazards, for instance) or facilitating videoconferencing by sitting in for a participant. With videoconferencing, the robot relays video and audio images to and from the participant, who is at a remote location, during the meeting. Business robots can also be used in search and rescue missions, for firefighting, and for manufacturing.

There are also a number of *personal robots* (also called *service robots*) available or in development to assist with personal tasks. Some, like the *RS robot* shown in Figure 8-20, are primarily entertainment robots. Using sensors, cameras, and microphones to input data about their current surroundings, these robots can typically recite phrases to make small talk with people, deliver messages, take photos or video, sing and dance, play games, and more. Other personal robots (such as the *Pleo robot* shown in Figure 8-20) are designed to be treated as pets. Still others are designed for household tasks, such as to mow the lawn, clean the floor (refer again to Figure 8-20), or clean the pool. One new type of personal robot almost ready to come on the market is designed to facilitate *virtual visiting*—essentially a personal teleconferencing robot designed to allow distant grandparents or traveling parents to visit with children, vacationing families to check on their pets, and so forth.

A little further in the future are household robots that can assist individuals with more complex tasks, such as putting away the dishes or picking up toys before vacuuming the living room. Expected to have a more *humanoid* form than the household robots currently on the market, these robots could be used to assist the elderly and wheelchair bound individuals. Newer robots will likely have improved vision and sensor systems, which will allow for better navigation, and be better at physical manipulation. Artificial intelligence and facial emotions will make humanoid robots appear even more lifelike, and their communications systems will continue to improve. Household robots in the future are expected to be networked to work together, instead of acting independently, as well as to be the

---

>**Robotics.** The study of robot technology. >**Robot.** A device, controlled by a human operator or a computer, that can move and react to sensory input.

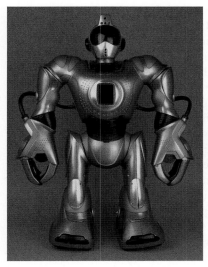

RS
Can recognize faces, follow voice commands, wake you up, read aloud the weather forecast and headlines, relay phone and e-mail messages, and perform other personal tasks.

PLEO
Can convey emotions and evolves from a hatchling to a juvenile dinosaur as he interacts with and is nurtured by his owner.

SCOOBA
Can prep, wash, scrub, and dry hard floors in a single pass.

FIGURE 8-20
Personal robots.

centerpiece of home maintenance, security, and communications. As new robotic applications are developed and as the prices come down, robots are expected to be used increasingly in both homes and businesses. In fact, it has been reported that the South Korean government expects to have at least one robot in every South Korean household by 2020.

Many would agree that the use of robots has numerous benefits to society—such as adding convenience to our lives, replacing people in dangerous situations, and, potentially, monitoring and assisting the disabled and the elderly. But some individuals are concerned that, as true artificial intelligence becomes closer to reality, a class of robots with the potential for great harm could be created. In response, several organizations—including the South Korean government and the European Robotics Research Network—are in the process of developing standards for robots, users, and manufacturers concerning the appropriate use and development of robots. Regardless, the issue of the role robots should take in our society is likely to continue to be debated for quite some time.

TECHNOLOGICAL ADVANCES IN MEDICINE

Technological advances in the area of medicine in the past several years include computers that can analyze test results to identify precancerous cells too small for a person to see, implanted devices that enhance the functions of a current organ (such as cochlear implants that can restore hearing), electronic monitors that detect potentially dangerous medical conditions, and digital cameras the size of a pill that are swallowed to photograph the patient's digestive tract. Other topics in the forefront of medical technology research include *electronic monitoring* and *electronic implants*, as well as *telemedicine* and *telesurgery*.

Electronic Monitoring and Electronic Implants

There are a number of *electronic monitoring systems* in use today. Some use radio frequency identification (RFID)—when used in conjunction with a communications network, RFID technology can locate the objects to which the RFID tags are attached. In hospitals, RFID systems are beginning to be used for patient identification, medical equipment asset tracking, and prescription drug identification.

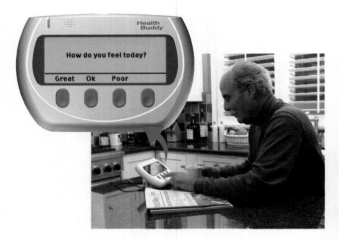

FIGURE 8-21

Home medical monitoring systems.

FIGURE 8-22

A VeriChip being tested with a reader before the VeriChip is implanted into an individual.

Another area of growth in electronic monitoring systems is home healthcare. With the U.S. population aging, there are a variety of home medical monitoring systems available to monitor elderly or infirm individuals and notify someone if a possible problem is detected. For instance, electronic *medical monitors* (see Figure 8-21) are available that take the vital signs of an individual (such as weight, blood-sugar readings, or blood pressure) or prompt an individual to answer questions (such as if he or she ate yet that day, took prescribed medication, or feels well) and then transmit that information to a healthcare professional for evaluation and feedback. Other medical monitoring systems use pressure pads and motion sensors to track an individual's movement within his or her home, and electronic pill dispensers automatically dispense the proper medication at the proper time. These devices usually transfer readings and the individual's responses to questions to a healthcare provider automatically via the Internet or a telephone network so that potential problems can be detected early. Some also include a built-in communications system so the individual being monitored can immediately contact someone if they don't feel well or otherwise need medical attention.

While many electronic medical monitoring devices are external, some are implanted inside the individual. One example is an implanted cardiac device that continually monitors the heart rhythms, and records the rhythms for a set period of time in order to replay that information to the attending physician if the patient faints or otherwise does not feel well. Another example is the **VeriChip**—a tiny RFID chip about the size of a grain of rice (see Figure 8-22) that is implanted under a person's skin (usually on the hand or arm) and is used for identification purposes. Like the chips used to identify pets and to track the migration habits of animals, each VeriChip contains a unique verification number that can be read when a proprietary scanner is passed over the implanted chip. Although the VeriChip itself does not contain any personal data, it is designed to be used in conjunction with a database to access personal data, as needed, such as to provide hospital emergency room personnel with health information about an unconscious patient. A version of the VeriChip under development will be able to continuously monitor the glucose levels of a diabetic without a blood sample. The VeriChip also has nonmedical applications, such as access control to government installations, nuclear power plants, and other highly secure facilities; identity verification for airport security purposes and financial transactions; and access control for personal computers, cars, homes, and other personal security applications. Versions of the VeriChip with GPS capabilities could also be used to find missing individuals, such as kidnap victims and lost Alzheimer's patients, like the clip-on and wristwatch monitoring systems available today that allow location information to be broadcast continuously to a proprietary receiver. Although privacy-rights advocates worry that a chip like the VeriChip could someday be used by the government to track citizens, others view it as no different from a medical ID bracelet and are not concerned because it is available on a purely voluntary basis.

An emerging possibility is *brain-to-computer interfacing* (*BCI*)—the process of connecting the brain with a computer, such as implanting electrodes directly into the brain to restore lost functionality to or facilitate the communications of severely disabled individuals. For instance, a severely paralyzed individual implanted with such a device can, after training, move a mouse, click it to type text, and perform other computer-related tasks using only his or her thoughts. In BCI experiments conducted with monkeys, the monkeys were able to control both a cursor and a robotic arm with their thoughts—raising the

>**VeriChip.** A tiny RFID chip about the size of a grain of rice that is implanted under a person's skin for identification purposes.

possibility that paralyzed individuals will someday be able to control robot assistants with their thoughts. Despite the potential benefits of brain implants, there is the concern that this technology could be misused. Medical ethicists are currently working on setting up standards and criteria to ensure that brain implant devices allow, according to medical ethicist Joseph Fins of Cornell University, "...patients to have control, not be under control." Currently the focus of brain implants and thought-controlled computers is bringing communications capabilities to the severely disabled. Some researchers, however, foresee the technology someday becoming mainstream—viewing brainwave input as the next step in the evolution of the human-computer input interface.

Telemedicine and Telesurgery

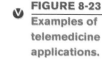

FIGURE 8-23
Examples of telemedicine applications.

Telemedicine is the use of communications technology to provide medical information and services. In addition to the remote medical monitoring systems already discussed, some physicians offer additional telemedicine services, such as e-mail consultations and Web-based appointment scheduling. Videoconferencing can be used to allow physicians to communicate with other physicians or with hospitalized patients (see Figure 8-23); it is also being expanded to include language interpreting. Because they are unable to provide translators for the wide variety of non-English speaking patients that are treated today, some hospitals are using videoconferencing to share a staff of interpreters with a network of hospitals. Unlike telephone interpreting services, which require handing the phone back and forth and are not compatible with nonverbal languages (such as American Sign Language), videoconferencing interpreting systems allow patients to more easily and effectively communicate with their healthcare providers.

One of the biggest advantages of telemedicine is the ability to provide care remotely to individuals who may not otherwise have access to that care, such as allowing individuals living in remote areas to consult with a specialist. It can be used to perform remote diagnosis of patients (in which local healthcare workers at rural locations, childcare facilities, and other locations with telemedicine equipment use video cameras, electronic stethoscopes, and other tools to send images and vital statistics of a patient to a physician located at a medical facility), as well as to perform *telesurgery* (refer again to Figure 8-23).

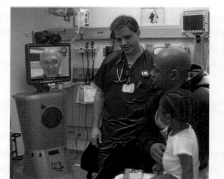

REMOTE CONSULTATIONS
Using remote-controlled teleconferencing robots, physicians can "virtually" consult with patients or other physicians in a different physical location (left); the robot transmits video images and audio to and from the doctor (via his or her PC) in real time (right).

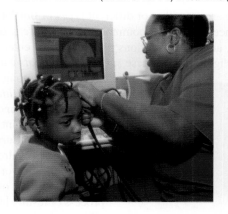

REMOTE DIAGNOSIS
At remote locations, such as the New York childcare center shown here, trained employees provide physicians with the real-time data (sent via the Internet) they need to make a diagnosis.

TELESURGERY
Using voice or computer commands, surgeons can now perform operations via the Internet; a robotic system uses the surgeon's commands to operate on the patient.

>**Telemedicine.** The use of communications technology to provide medical information and services.

Telesurgery is a form of *robot-assisted surgery*, in which a robot controlled by a physician operates on the patient. Robot-assisted surgery systems typically use cameras to give the human surgeon an extremely close view of the surgical area. In addition, these systems are typically more precise and make smaller incisions than human surgeons, allowing for less invasive surgery (for example, not having to crack through the rib cage to access the heart) and resulting in less pain for the patient, a faster recovery time, and fewer potential complications. Some robot-assisted surgery takes place with the doctor, patient, and robotic device in the same operating room; with telesurgery, at least one of the surgeons performs the operation by controlling the robot remotely, such as over the Internet. In general, telemedicine has enormous potential for providing quality care to individuals who live in rural or underdeveloped areas and who do not have access to sufficient medical care. Telemedicine will also be necessary for future long-term space explorations—such as a trip to Mars and back that may take three years or more—since astronauts will undoubtedly need medical care while on the journey. In fact, NASA astronauts and physicians recently performed telesurgery experiments in the Aquarius Undersea Laboratory 50 feet below the ocean surface to help eventually develop a robotic unit that will allow physicians to perform surgery remotely on patients who are in outer space. Some individuals envision the eventual use of portable robot-assisted telesurgery units in space, war zones, and other environments where access to surgeons is extremely limited.

TECHNOLOGICAL ADVANCES IN THE MILITARY

The U.S. military works on a continual basis with technological and research organizations to improve military equipment, such as weapons, protective gear for soldiers, and surveillance tools. The military is also involved in researching many of the other emerging technologies already discussed, such as nanotechnology and artificial intelligence. Two specific areas of research related to the military—*battlefield robots* and *exoskeleton systems*—are discussed next.

FIGURE 8-24

Battlefield robots.
This robot, PackBot Explorer, is designed to investigate hostile and inaccessible areas prior to human entry.

Battlefield Robots

There are a number of different types of **battlefield robots** used by the U.S. military. For instance, robots are commonly used in areas of conflict to investigate caves, buildings, trails, and other locations before soldiers enter them to make sure the locations are safe (see Figure 8-24). These *surveillance robots* can also be used to locate snipers and otherwise find the point of hostile gunfire. Robots with *explosive detection capabilities* are used to help soldiers locate and dispose of bombs, landmines, and other explosive devices in the field, at checkpoints, and at other locations where explosives are suspected. Currently, both of these types of battlefield robots are controlled remotely by soldiers, although researchers are working on more *autonomous robots* that can navigate on their own. For instance, the U.S. Army is in the process of testing larger unmanned robotic vehicles to eventually accompany soldiers into combat. These vehicles will carry machine guns and missiles and use an integrated *Autonomous Navigation System* (*ANS*) to perceive obstacles and determine their course without continuous directions from a human operator. Another autonomous robot in

---

>**Telesurgery.** A form of robot-assisted surgery in which the doctor's physical location is different from the patient's physical location and the doctor controls the robot remotely over the Internet or another communications medium. >**Battlefield robot.** A robot used by the military to ensure that locations are safe prior to sending in soldiers.

development is *BigDog*—a robotic pack animal that resembles a dog and is designed to carry hundreds of pounds of gear for soldiers. A future version, able to read terrain, spot obstacles, and determine its course without human intervention is expected to be ready for use in combat by 2015.

Exoskeleton Systems

An emerging military robotic application is the **exoskeleton suit**, whose name is derived from the term "exoskeleton," which refers to a hard protective or supportive outer structure. Currently being researched and developed by several organizations under grants from the Defense Advanced Research Projects Agency (DARPA), exoskeleton suits are wearable robotic systems designed to give an individual additional physical capabilities and protection. For instance, an exoskeleton suit can give a soldier the ability to run faster and carry heavier items than he or she could without the suit. The exoskeleton suits that are expected to be used eventually by the military will likely be made of light, protective material that will be bulletproof and may be able to solidify on demand to form a shield or turn into a medical cast if a soldier is injured. Other possible features include changing its color automatically for camouflage purposes; relaying information via sensors about a soldier's health, injuries, and location to field headquarters; and administering painkillers or applying pressure to a wound when directed by a physician.

Although they hope to deliver some usable exoskeleton components within the next five years, most researchers project that a true exoskeleton suit is many years from reality. In addition to the military possibilities, exoskeleton suits may eventually lead to stronger and safer search and rescue workers, be used to give the elderly back their youthful physical abilities, or provide paralyzed people with a means of mobility. For instance, the *Robot Suit HAL* (*Hybrid Assisted Limb*) developed in Japan that is designed to expand and improve the physical capability of individuals is shown in Figure 8-25. This suit uses sensors on the surface of the skin to interpret the signals sent from the brain to the muscles when a person attempts to move and the suit moves accordingly, giving individuals close to twice their normal strength.

SOCIETAL IMPLICATIONS OF EMERGING TECHNOLOGY

A new computing technology usually provides many benefits, since it normally would not become widely available for consumers if it was not designed to solve a problem or add convenience to our lives. However, not all advances are embraced by all individuals. For instance, security and privacy issues are areas of continual concern with emerging technologies. Potential dangers include trusting "intelligent" computers and robots so much that they become a personal safety hazard, allowing medical technology to enable people to be controlled by others, and spending resources on some areas of research and development that might be better spent elsewhere. Some people also worry that technology is advancing at such a rapid pace that we cannot possibly envision all the potential repercussions until it is too late. It is important to evaluate new and emerging technologies in terms of the entire picture—their benefits, as well as their possible risks and societal implications.

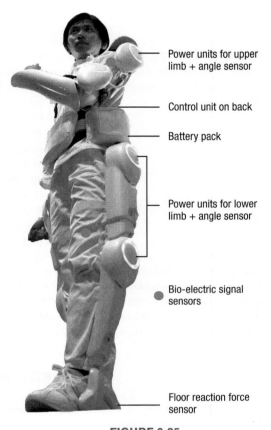

Power units for upper limb + angle sensor

Control unit on back

Battery pack

Power units for lower limb + angle sensor

Bio-electric signal sensors

Floor reaction force sensor

FIGURE 8-25
Exoskeleton suits are designed to increase the physical abilities of individuals.

>**Exoskeleton suit.** A wearable robotic system designed to give an individual additional physical capabilities and protection.

SUMMARY

THE PC OF THE FUTURE

Chapter Objective 1:
Describe what the PC of the future might look like, including some examples of emerging types of hardware.

While the exact makeup of future PCs is not certain, they will likely continue to get smaller, smarter, and more user-friendly. Portable PCs will continue to grow more powerful and useful, and home and business PCs may be built into furniture, walls, desks, and other objects. Emerging input devices include **virtual keyboards**, gesture-based devices, and a variety of RFID systems. CPU technology is continuing to evolve and it is possible that a form of **nonvolatile RAM** (**NVRAM**) may eventually replace the RAM we know today. PCs of the future will also likely contain improved cooling devices, such as the *ion pump* system in development. Emerging output devices include *3D display screens*, *3D projectors*, *wearable personal displays*, and displays based on variations of **organic light emitting diode** (**OLED**) **display** technology; *interferometric modulator* (*IMOD*) *displays* are another possibility for the future for mobile devices. For storage, new types of USB flash memory drives are emerging, **holographic storage** has finally arrived, and higher-capacity optical formats—such as *Ultra Density Optical* (*UDO*) discs—are being developed.

Future computers will likely be influenced by **nanotechnology** research, which focuses on building computer components at the individual atomic and molecular levels. Both computing and noncomputing products that use **carbon nanotubes** are being developed. **Quantum computing** (which use atoms or nuclei working together as quantum bits or *qubits*) and **optical computers** (which perform operations using light instead of electrical current) are in the early stages of development.

Chapter Objective 2:
Understand the effect that emerging computer technologies, such as nanotechnology, quantum computers, and optical computers, may have on the PC of the future.

EMERGING NETWORKING TECHNOLOGIES

Chapter Objective 3:
Name some emerging wired and wireless networking technologies.

Improvements are being made on a continual basis to wired and wireless networking to increase speed and connectivity options. Faster versions of the **Ethernet** standard are under development, and **Power over Ethernet** (**PoE**)—which sends both electrical power and data over Ethernet cables—is a new option for business networks. For easy home networks, the *Phoneline* or *Powerline* standards can be used; an emerging standard for delivering Internet over existing power lines is **broadband over power lines** (**BPL**).

New versions of the **Wi-Fi** (**802.11**) standard for wireless networks (such as the emerging *802.11n* standard) are being developed on a regular basis. **WiMAX** is an emerging wireless standard with a larger range than Wi-Fi, **mobile WiMAX** (**802.16e**) is a version of WiMAX designed for use while on the go, and *Mobile-Fi* is a standard for high-speed mobile Internet access. **Ultra Wideband** (**UWB**) is an emerging standard for short-range wireless connections that is faster and has a longer range than *Bluetooth*, the **wireless USB** standard is a new option for connecting peripheral devices to a PC, and **WirelessHD** (**WiHD**) is designed for networking home consumer devices. *ZigBee* (*802.15*) is one wireless networking standard used to create *wireless sensor networks*.

ARTIFICIAL INTELLIGENCE (AI)

Chapter Objective 4:
Explain what is meant by the term "artificial intelligence" (AI) and list some AI applications.

When a computer performs in ways that would be considered intelligent if observed in people, this is referred to as **artificial intelligence** (**AI**). Some of the earliest advances in AI were in the area of chess; the most common test for AI is the *Turning Test*. One AI application is the **intelligent agent**. Examples include *application assistants*, *search* *agents*, *shopping bots*, *entertainment bots*, and *chatterbots*. Intelligent agents typically act as *virtual assistants* and modify their behavior based on the user's actions. They are frequently built into application programs and operating systems and are beginning to be used on Web pages. Some—like many chatterbots—use a *natural language interface*.

Expert systems perform tasks that would otherwise be performed by a human expert, such as diagnosing medical conditions, making financial forecasts, and performing credit authorizations. Expert systems use a *knowledge base* (a database containing specific facts and rules about the expert area) and an *inference engine* (a software program used to apply rules to the data stored in the knowledge base to reach decisions).

Neural networks and *robotics* are two other areas of artificial intelligence. A neural network is an AI system that tries to imitate the way the human brain works and is typically used for pattern recognition, such as speech analysis, crime analysis, and biometric identification. **Robotics** is the study of **robots**—devices, controlled by a person or a computer, that can move and react to sensory input. Robots are commonly used for repetitive and dangerous tasks; they are also being used for household tasks, for entertainment purposes, and to assist with business and personal tasks.

TECHNOLOGICAL ADVANCES IN MEDICINE

Technological advances in recent years include computers that analyze test results, implanted devices that assist an organ's functioning, and digital cameras that can be ingested to record images of a person's digestive tract. *Electronic monitoring* can take the form of internal or external monitors. Certain electronic implant applications—such as the **VeriChip** used for identification purposes and electrodes implanted in the brain—are embraced by some, but are not without controversy.

Telemedicine is the use of communications technology to provide medical information and services and can take a variety of forms. One application is **telesurgery**—a form of *robot-assisted surgery* where a robot (controlled by a physician) operates on a patient. With telesurgery, the robot is controlled remotely, such as over the Internet. Robots can use smaller incisions in some types of surgeries, which results in less pain for the patient and a faster recovery period. Other forms of telemedicine include remote professional consultations and diagnosis, such as via a videoconferencing system or a system set up at a remote facility.

Chapter Objective 5:
List some new and upcoming technological advances in medicine.

TECHNOLOGICAL ADVANCES IN THE MILITARY

Recent and expected future technological advances in the military include newly designed weapons, protective gear, and surveillance tools. Surveillance tools in the future may include an increased use of **battlefield robots** and unmanned air and ground vehicles and devices. The uniform of the future may include an **exoskeleton suit**—a wearable robotic system that not only protects the user, but gives him or her additional physical capabilities.

Chapter Objective 6:
Name some new and upcoming technological advances in the military.

SOCIETAL IMPLICATIONS OF EMERGING TECHNOLOGY

There are many potential societal implications associated with emerging technologies, such as unexpected results, trusting "intelligent" computers and robots so much that they become a personal safety hazard, and allowing medical technology to enable people to be controlled by others. Since virtually any new technology could be used for both good and evil, we need to weigh the societal risks and benefits of emerging technologies in order to make educated and informed decisions about what we would like our lives and society to be like.

Chapter Objective 7:
Discuss potential societal implications of emerging technologies.

REVIEW ACTIVITIES

KEY TERM MATCHING

Instructions: Match each key term on the left with the definition on the right that best describes it.

a. artificial intelligence (AI)

b. exoskeleton suit

c. expert system

d. nanotechnology

e. neural network

f. optical computer

g. robot

h. telemedicine

i. Ultra Wideband (UWB)

j. virtual keyboard

1. _____ A computer system that provides the type of advice that would be expected from a human expert.

2. _____ A computer that uses light, such as from laser beams or infrared beams, to perform digital computations.

3. _____ A device, controlled by a human operator or a computer, that can move and react to sensory input.

4. _____ A device that projects a keyboard image onto any flat surface and translates finger motion on the projected image back to the computer as input.

5. _____ An expert system in which the human brain's pattern-recognition process is emulated by the computer system.

6. _____ A wearable robotic system designed to give an individual additional physical capabilities and protection.

7. _____ A wireless technology being developed for short-range wireless connections, such as to wirelessly network consumer multimedia devices.

8. _____ The science of creating tiny computers and components by working at the individual atomic and molecular levels.

9. _____ The use of communications technology to provide medical information and services.

10. _____ When a computer performs actions that are characteristic of human intelligence.

SELF-QUIZ

Instructions: Circle **T** if the statement is true, **F** if the statement is false, or write the best answer in the space provided. **Answers for the self-quiz are located in the References and Resources Guide at the end of the book.**

1. **T** **F** A virtual keyboard is used only via the Internet.

2. **T** **F** Nonvolatile RAM (NVRAM) chips do not lose their contents when the power to the computer is turned off.

3. **T** **F** Computers that process data with light are referred to as quantum computers.

4. **T** **F** Diagnosing a patient from a distance is referred to as telesurgery.

5. **T** **F** One advantage of robot-assisted surgery is faster recovery time.

6. In quantum computing, _____—which can represent more than two possible states—are used instead of electronic bits.

7. _____ is an emerging wireless networking standard that is faster and has a greater range than Wi-Fi—up to 30 miles.

8. The _____ is an RFID chip approved to be implanted under a person's skin for identification purposes.

9. RS, Pleo, and Scooba are examples of personal _____.

10. Many products today use carbon _____, a byproduct of nanotechnology research.

EXERCISES

1. For the following list of abbreviated emerging devices or technologies, write the appropriate letter (I, P, O, S, or C) in the space provided to indicate whether each device or technology is used for input (I), output (O), processing (P), storage (S), or communications (C).

   a. _____ WiHD   d. _____ OLED
   b. _____ BPL   e. _____ NRAM
   c. _____ UDO   f. _____ IMOD

2. Supply the missing words to complete the following statements.

   a. _____ storage systems use multiple blue laser beams to store data in three dimensions.
   b. _____ is a form of robot-assisted surgery in which the doctor's physical location is different from the patient's physical location, and the doctor controls the robot remotely over the Internet or another communications medium.
   c. A(n) _____ robot is used by the military to ensure that locations are safe prior to sending in soldiers.

3. Write the number of the networking protocol that best matches each of the following descriptions in the blank to the left of each description.

   a. _____ Used to wirelessly connect home multimedia devices.   1. PoE
   b. _____ Used to create a home network via existing telephone jacks.   2. BPL
   c. _____ Used to send power along with data over networking cables.   3. UWB
   d. _____ Used to connect a building to the Internet over existing power lines.   4. HomePNA

4. Would an OLED display or an LCD display use more battery power? Explain why.

5. Would Wi-Fi or WirelessHD be better for creating a wireless network for the computers located within a home? Explain.

DISCUSSION QUESTION

More and more everyday devices—including cars and other vehicles—are being controlled by computers. Even large transportation systems, such as subway trains, are increasingly becoming automated. There are advantages, such as avoiding possible driver errors and the ability to change the speed of or reroute trains to avoid collisions or to run the system more efficiently. But are there potential risks, as well? For example, Thailand's Finance Minister once had to be rescued from inside his limousine after the onboard computer malfunctioned, leaving the vehicle immobilized. With the door locks, power windows, and air conditioning not functioning, the Minister and his driver were in growing danger until a guard freed them 10 minutes later by smashing one of the vehicle's windows with a sledgehammer. Do you think the benefits of increased automation of devices that could put us in danger if they malfunction outweigh the risks? What types of safeguards do you think should be incorporated into computer-controlled cars, subway trains, and other automated vehicles? What about medication dispensers and other automated medical devices?

BALANCING ACT

UBIQUITOUS COMPUTING VS. BIG BROTHER

Ubiquitous computing—also known as pervasive computing—suggests a future in which few aspects of daily life will remain untouched by computers and computer technology. Computers and related technology will become embedded into more and more devices, and people will depend on computing technology for an ever-increasing number of everyday activities. All of the devices in our lives are expected eventually to communicate wirelessly with each other and to do their jobs so invisibly that we do not even pay attention to them anymore.

That is the part that really bothers some people. If all of the electronic devices in our lives can communicate with one another automatically, how can we control what they say and whom they say it to? Will these devices be used to track our movements so that the government will always know where we are? Will there really be a "Big Brother" computer that knows everything about everybody? What about personal privacy? How will it be protected?

The big challenge for ubiquitous computing is making it work while still giving us control over what it does. That is difficult to accomplish, since the idea is that the computing devices in our lives will become invisible. If we do not need to instruct these devices on a regular basis, and if we can just forget about them, it becomes much more difficult for us to realize what the devices are doing, which device is controlling which function, where information about us is going and how it is being used, which systems are not functioning, and what the consequences of any given action (such as walking into a room, making a telephone call, or placing an order over the Internet) might be. Balancing simplicity and control is one of the biggest issues facing ubiquitous computing research.

YOUR TURN

Give some thought to the potential impact of ubiquitous computing and form an opinion on this issue. Consider the following when forming your opinion and be prepared to discuss your position (in class, via an online class discussion group, in a class chat room, or via a class blog) or to write a short paper expressing your opinion, depending on your instructor's directions.

- Does the idea of ubiquitous computing concern you or interest you? Is it something that you would like to see become a reality in the near future? Why or why not?

- Some aspects of ubiquitous computing at work are intriguing. For example, as you move from place to place within your office building, computers would recognize you and adjust to reflect your PC settings automatically. As you approached any computer not being used by someone else, it would display the desktop exactly as it is usually displayed on your PC and unlock your files to allow you to use the computer as if it were your own. What are some other advantages and some disadvantages of ubiquitous computing at work?

- If ubiquitous computing becomes the norm, how easy do you think it will be for an individual who strongly objects to the concept to choose not to participate? Do you think people should have the right to make that decision? If some people opt out of participating, what might be the consequences for them and for the rest of society?

PROJECTS

---

1. **WiMAX vs. Wi-Fi** As discussed in the chapter, WiMAX and Wi-Fi are both wireless networking standards. Although they have some similar features, these two technologies are
designed for different purposes.

    For this project, research WiMAX and Wi-Fi to determine their current status and the dif-
ferences between the two standards. What is the purpose of each technology and how do the
two technologies differ? Explain. How are they being used today? Do you think the standards
will coexist in the future, or will one eventually replace the other? At the conclusion of your
research, prepare a one-page summary of your findings and submit it to your instructor.

HOT TOPICS

---

2. **Today's Robots** As discussed in the chapter, there are a variety of robots on the market today
that can be used for a multitude of purposes in the home. There are also robots specifically
designed for business and military applications.

    For this project, select one type of robotic device on the market today—for instance, a
robotic toy, vacuum cleaner, or lawn mower; a security or manufacturing robot; a robot used
by the military or NASA; or a robotic personal assistant—and research it. Find out what the
product does, what it costs, how it is powered and controlled, and if it can be reprogrammed.
What makes this a robotic device? What are the advantages of adding robotics technology to
the product? Do you think this is a worthwhile or beneficial product? What type of nonrobotic
product (if any) is this product designed to replace? Would you prefer to use the nonrobotic or
the robotic product? Why? At the conclusion of your research, prepare a one- to two-page
summary of your findings and submit it to your instructor.

**SHORT ANSWER/
RESEARCH**

---

3. **Chatterbots** As discussed in the chapter, a chatterbot is a program that attempts to simulate
the "chat" of another human.

    For this project, find a chatterbot on a Web page (either Cybelle on the Agentland.com
Web site shown in Figure 8-17 or another you find using a search site) and have a conversation
with the chatterbot. Form an opinion about how humanlike the exchange was. Do you think
the chatterbot responded to your comments in a humanlike fashion? Was it able to answer your
questions? If not, what did it do when it could not answer a question? Do you think chatterbots
can be a worthwhile addition to a Web site? Would you prefer to chat in real time with a customer service chatterbot if it could answer your questions correctly, or would you rather wait
for a human customer service representative? Explain. At the conclusion of your research, prepare a one-page summary of your experience and submit it to your instructor.

HANDS ON

WRITING ABOUT COMPUTERS

4. Who's to Blame? As computers become continually integrated into our daily lives, the risk of problems due to those computers or computer components increases. When humans and computers are both involved in accomplishing a task and something goes wrong, we tend to blame the computer. There is little question about the existence of software bugs, but can all errors we read about in the newspapers or see on the television be attributed to the software program?

For this project, investigate at least two publicized problems in which a computer was involved (such as an erroneous bank transaction, a military training incident, a mistaken identity, or a privacy breach) and determine if the fault of the incident rests with a human, the computer, or both. Write a short essay summarizing the events and expressing your opinion about who or what was responsible. Do you think it is more likely that a computer or a human being would be responsible for a serious system problem? Why? Submit this project to your instructor in the form of a short paper, not more than two pages in length.

PRESENTATION/ DEMONSTRATION

5. Emerging Technologies Many new and emerging technologies were discussed in this chapter, and more are announced virtually every day.

For this project, identify and research one type of emerging technology. It could be one that was mentioned in this chapter or a brand new product or technology just announced. After you select a technology, investigate it to determine how it works, what it is used for, and if alternate products or technologies are available. Try to locate an illustration of your chosen technology or a photo of a resulting product to share with the class. Be sure to find out when products or services based on that technology are expected to become commercially available, who will use them, and how much they are expected to cost. Form an opinion about the usefulness of your selected technology. Share your findings with the class in the form of a short presentation, including the products that you found and their specifications, as well as your opinion regarding the usefulness of the technology. The presentation should not exceed 10 minutes and should make use of one or more presentation aids, such as the chalkboard, handouts, overhead transparencies, or a computer-based slide presentation (your instructor may provide additional requirements). You may also be asked to submit a summary of the presentation to your instructor.

GROUP DISCUSSION

6. NASA Robot Crews Robotics research is continuing to make smarter and more capable robots. For instance, NASA researchers have developed a way to make a crew of robots work together to grasp, lift, and move heavy loads across rough, varied terrain. The software allows the robots to "share a brain" so that each robot knows what the rest are doing and enables the robots to work together to develop plans, such as how to maneuver around a rock or other obstacle the crew may encounter. Some might worry that this technology also provides the potential for a "super robot" in the future, such as the Borg enemy portrayed in the *Star Trek: The Next Generation* television show. Can robots get too smart? What steps should our society take to ensure that robots cannot become physically dangerous? What is the potential implication of replacing human laborers with robots? Will the continued use of robots adversely affect our economy, or will human workers automatically be able to evolve to more advanced positions? Would you feel comfortable being in physical proximity to a group of robots capable of working together on tasks?

For this project, form an opinion about the potential impact of continuing to make smarter and more capable robots and be prepared to discuss your position (in class, via an online class discussion group, in a class chat room, or via a class blog, depending on your instructor's directions). You may also be asked to write a short paper expressing your opinion.

7. **People Chips** As discussed in the chapter, the VeriChip is a tiny chip that is designed to be implanted under a person's skin, such as on the forearm. Currently, VeriChips are used primarily for identification purposes—the unique number contained in a VeriChip can be read by a proprietary scanner and used in conjunction with a database, such as to provide hospital emergency room personnel with health information about an unconscious patient. However, implanted chips can also be used to control access to secure areas and for electronic payment purposes. What do you think of implanted devices, such as the VeriChip, being used for access control (such as for government buildings or highly-secure facilities), for expediting passage through security check points (such as at airports), or for making electronic payments (such as at a grocery store)? Would you be willing to be "chipped" if it made some tasks (such as unlocking your home or car) easier or some types of transactions (such as ATM withdrawals) more secure? Is it ethical for a government to require its citizens to be chipped, similar to a national ID card? Is it ethical for a business to request that its employees be chipped for security purposes? Should businesses be allowed to require chipping as a condition of employment?

   For this project, form an opinion about the ethical use and ramifications of human-implantable chips, and be prepared to discuss your position (in class, via an online class discussion group, in a class chat room, or via a class blog, depending on your instructor's directions). You may also be asked to write a short paper expressing your opinion.

8. **Robot Rights** We have ethical codes for students, businesspeople, physicians, and other individuals. But an ethical code for robots? As discussed in the accompanying video clip, South Korea is in the process of creating an ethical code to protect humans from harm and robots from abuse.

   Go to www.course.com/uccs/ch8 to watch the "Robot Rules" video clip. After watching the video, think about the impact of robots in our society and the need for regulations. Is an ethical code needed for robot developers to ensure robots are created for valid purposes? Should robot developers be required to build in safeguards, such as not harming humans or always obeying humans, into the robot's programming? Is regulation needed for robot users to ensure robots are treated appropriately and not abused? Do you think ethical codes, such as the one under development in South Korea, will be needed in the U.S. and other countries as robot use grows? What other legal or ethical areas might the increased use of robots in our society affect? Will the increased use of robots create new risks that will need to be addressed?

   Express your viewpoint: What is the impact of increased use in our society and how, if at all, should that use by regulated?

   Use the video clip and the questions previously asked as a foundation for your response. Be prepared to discuss your position (in class, via an online class discussion group, in a class chat room, or via a class blog) or to write a short paper stating and supporting your viewpoint on the issue, depending on your instructor's direction. You may also be asked to do research and provide resources to support your point of view on this issue.

9. **Interactive Activities** Go to www.course.com/uccs/ch8 and work the interactive **Crossword Puzzle**, listen to the **Podcasts** and watch the **Online Videos** associated with this chapter, and explore the **Further Exploration** links. In addition, work the following interactive **Student Edition Labs**.

   • Project Management   • Visual Programming   • Advanced Spreadsheets

   If you have a SAM user profile, you have access to even more interactive content. Log in to your SAM account and go to your assignments page to see what your instructor has assigned for this chapter.

10. **Test Yourself** Go to www.course.com/uccs/ch8 and review the **Online Study Guide** for Chapter 8, then test your knowledge of the terms and concepts in this chapter by completing the **Key Term Matching** exercise, the **Self-Quiz**, the **Exercises**, and the **Practice Test**.

REFERENCES AND RESOURCES *GUIDE*

INTRODUCTION

When working on a PC, you often need to look up information related to computers. For instance, you may need to find out when the IBM PC was first invented, you may want tips about what to consider when buying a PC, or you may want to find out more about how numbering systems work. To help you with the tasks just mentioned and more, this References and Resources Guide brings together in one convenient location a collection of computer-related references and resources. Some of the resources are located in this handy section; these resources plus additional resources (such as a variety of interactive activities and study tools, and a Web Guide containing URLs for useful Web resources) are located on the Web site that accompanies this textbook, which is located at www.course.com/uccs.

OUTLINE

The earliest recorded calculating device, the abacus, is believed to have been invented by the Babylonians sometime between 500 B.C. and 100 B.C. It and similar types of counting boards were used solely for counting.

Blaise Pascal invented the first mechanical calculator, called the Pascaline Arithmetic Machine. It had the capacity for eight digits and could add and subtract.

Dr. John V. Atanasoff and Clifford Berry designed and built ABC (for Atanasoff-Berry Computer), the world's first electronic computer.

500 B.C.   1642   1937

Precomputers and Early Computers

1621   1804   1944

French silk weaver Joseph-Marie Jacquard built a loom that read holes punched on a series of small sheets of hardwood to control the weave of the pattern. This automated machine introduced the use of punch cards and showed that they could be used to convey a series of instructions.

The Mark I, considered to be the first digital computer, was introduced by IBM. It was developed in cooperation with Harvard University, was more than 50 feet long, weighed almost five tons, and used electromechanical relays to solve addition problems in less than a second; multiplication and division took about six and twelve seconds, respectively.

The slide rule, a precursor to the electronic calculator, was invented. Used primarily to perform multiplication, division, square roots, and the calculation of logarithms, its wide-spread use continued until the 1970s.

Precomputers and Early Computers (before approximately 1945)
Most precomputers and early computers were mechanical machines that worked with gears and levers. Electromechanical devices (using both electricity and gears and levers) were developed toward the end of this era.

First Generation (approximately 1946–1957)
Powered by vacuum tubes, these computers were faster than electromechanical machines, but they were large and bulky, generated excessive heat, and had to be physically wired and reset to run programs. Input was primarily on punch cards; output was on punch cards or paper. Machine and assembly languages were used to program these computers.

The UNIVAC 1, the first computer to be mass produced for general use, was introduced by Remington Rand. In 1952, it was used to analyze votes in the U.S. presidential election and correctly predicted that Dwight D. Eisenhower would be the victor only 45 minutes after the polls closed, though the results were not aired immediately because they weren't trusted.

The COBOL programming language was developed by a committee headed by Dr. Grace Hopper.

The first floppy disk (8 inches in diameter) was introduced.

UNIX was developed at AT&T's Bell Laboratories; Advanced Micro Devices (AMD) was formed; and ARPANET (the predecessor of today's Internet) was established.

BUSINESS INTERNATIONAL MACHINES

IBM unbundled some of its hardware and software and began selling them separately, allowing other software companies to emerge.

1951 1960 1967 1969

First Generation **Second Generation** **Third Generation**

1947 1957 1964 1968

The FORTRAN programming language was introduced.

Robert Noyce and Gordon Moore founded the Intel Corporation.

John Bardeen, Walter Brattain, and William Shockley invented the transistor, which had the same capabilities as a vacuum tube but was faster, broke less often, used less power, and created less heat. They won a Nobel Prize for their invention in 1956 and computers began to be built with transistors shortly afterwards.

The first mouse was invented by Doug Engelbart.

The IBM System/360 computer was introduced. Unlike previous computers, System/360 contained a full line of compatible computers, making upgrading easier.

Second Generation (approximately 1958–1963)
Second-generation computers used transistors instead of vacuum tubes. They allowed the computer to be physically smaller, more powerful, more reliable, and faster than before. Input was primarily on punch cards and magnetic tape; output was on punch cards and paper; and magnetic tape and disks were used for storage. High-level programming languages were used with these computers.

Third Generation (approximately 1964–1970)
The third generation of computers evolved when integrated circuits (IC)—computer chips—began being used instead of conventional transistors. Computers became even smaller and more reliable. Keyboards and monitors were introduced for input and output; magnetic disks used for storage. The emergence of the operating system meant that operators no longer had to manually reset relays and wiring.

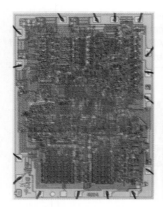

The first microprocessor, the Intel 4004, was designed by Ted Hoff. The single processor contained 2,250 transistors and could execute 60,000 operations per second.

1971

Bill Gates and Paul Allen wrote a version of BASIC for the Altair, the first computer programming language designed for a personal computer. Bill Gates dropped out of Harvard to form Microsoft with Paul Allen.

1975

Hailed as the first "personal computer," the Altair—allegedly named for a destination of the Starship Enterprise from a Star Trek TV episode—began to be sold as a kit for $395. Within months, tens of thousands were ordered.

Software Arts Inc.'s Visi-Calc, the first electronic spreadsheet and business program for PCs, was released. This program is seen as one of the reasons PCs first became widely accepted in the business world.

1979

Fourth Generation

1972

The C programming language was developed by Dennis Ritchie at Bell Labs.

Seymour Cray, called the "father of supercomputing," founded Cray Research, which would go on to build some of the fastest computers in the world.

1976

Steve Wozniak and Steve Jobs' founded Apple computer and released the Apple I (a single-board computer), followed by the Apple II (a complete PC that became an instant success in 1977). They originally ran the company out of Jobs' garage.

1980

Sony Electronics introduced the 3.5-inch floppy disk and drive.

Seagate Technology announced the first Winchester 5.25-inch hard disk drive, revolutionizing PC storage.

IBM chose Microsoft to develop the operating system for its upcoming PC. That operating system was PC-DOS.

Fourth Generation (approximately 1971–present)

The fourth generation of computers began with large-scale integration (LSI), which resulted in chips that could contain thousands of transistors. Very large-scale integration (VLSI) resulted in the microprocessor and the resulting microcomputers. The keyboard and mouse are predominant input devices, though many other types of input devices are now available; monitors and printers provide output; storage is obtained with magnetic disks, optical discs, and memory chips.

IBM introduced the IBM PC. This DOS-based PC used a 4.77 MHz 8088 CPU with 64 KB of RAM and quickly became the standard for business PCs.

The first general-interest CD-ROM product (*Grolier's Electronic Encyclopedia*) was released, and computer and electronics companies worked together to develop a universal CD-ROM standard.

Intel introduced the Intel386 CPU.

Tim Berners-Lee of CERN invented the World Wide Web.

Compaq Corporation released the first IBM-compatible PC that ran the same software as the IBM PC, marking the beginning of the huge PC-compatible industry.

Quantum Computer Services was founded; this company became AOL.

Intel introduced the Intel486 chip, the world's first million transistor CPU.

1981   1983   1985   1989

1982   1984   1986   1993

Intel introduced the 80286 CPU.

The first version of Microsoft Windows, a graphical environment, was released.

The Apple Macintosh debuted. It featured a simple, graphical user interface, used an 8 MHz, 32-bit Motorola 68000 CPU, and had a built-in 9-inch black and white screen.

Microsoft was listed on the New York Stock Exchange and began to sell shares to the public; Bill Gates became one of the world's youngest billionaires.

Marc Andreessen and James H. Clark founded Netscape Communications and released Netscape Navigator, a graphical Web browser based on the Mosaic browser Andreessen had created the previous year.

Apple's Steve Jobs founded Pixar.

TIME magazine named the computer its "Machine of the Year" for 1982, emphasizing the importance the computer had already reached in our society at that time.

Intel introduced the Pentium CPU.

Linus Torvalds created Linux, which launched the open source revolution. The penguin logo/mascot soon followed.

The first DVD players used for playing movies stored on DVD discs were sold.

After winning 2 of 6 games in their first contest in 1996, the IBM computer Deep Blue beat chess master Garry Kasparov in a chess match.

The Intel Pentium II was introduced.

Shawn Fanning, 19, wrote the software to drive his Napster P2P service and began the debate about P2P filesharing and online music.

Palm released the Palm VII, its first handheld PC with wireless Internet access.

The Intel Pentium III CPU was introduced.

1994

1997

1999

1995

1998

2000

Windows 95 was released and sold more than one million copies in four days.

Both eBay and Amazon.com were founded.

Sun Microsystems released Java, which is still one of the most popular Web programming languages.

Microsoft shipped Windows 98.

Apple released the iMac, a modernized version of the Macintosh computer. Its futuristic design helped to make this computer immensely popular.

Microsoft released the Windows 2000 Professional Server business operating systems and Windows ME for home users.

E-commerce skyrocketed, but unprofitable dot-com companies began going out of business at a record pace.

Intel introduced its Pentium 4 CPU chip. A popular advertising campaign, launched in 2001, featured the Blue Man Group.

The first USB flash drives were released.

Intel's first 64-bit CPU, the Itanium, was introduced.

Microsoft released its XP line of products, including Windows XP and Office XP.

The Internet and wireless networks enabled people to work and communicate with others while on the go.

Spyware became a major problem; some studies indicated that over 80% of computers had spyware installed.

Delivery of TV shows and other media to mobile phones became more common.

New Internet-enabled gaming consoles, like the Wii shown here, were released.

Blu-ray Disc and HD-DVD movies, discs, and players became available in the U.S.

Broadband Internet access approached the norm and improvements to wireless networking (such as WiMAX) continued to be developed.

Use of the Internet for online shopping, as well as downloads of music, movies, games, and television shows, continued to grow.

2001

2004

2006

2003

2005

2007

Digital camera sales in the United States exceeded 14 million, surpassing film camera sales for the first time.

AMD released the 64-bit Opteron server microprocessor and the Athlon 64, the first 64-bit CPU designed for desktop PC use.

Microsoft shipped the Office 2003 editions of its Microsoft Office System.

Phishing and identity theft became household words as an increasing number of individuals fell victim to these Internet scams.

The capabilities of mobile devices continued to grow; Palm's LifeDrive came with a 4 GB hard drive and built-in Wi-Fi and Bluetooth support.

Portable media players, such as the iPod, were common; digital music capabilities were built into a growing number of objects and devices, such as the Oakley THUMP sunglasses shown here.

Intel and AMD both released their first dual-core CPUs.

Dual-mode phones that can make calls via both a cellular and a Wi-Fi network became available.

Microsoft released Windows Vista and Office 2007.

Quad-core CPUs were released by both Intel and AMD.

Before buying a new PC, it is important to give some thought to what your needs are, including what software programs you wish to run, any other computers with which you need to be compatible, how you might want to connect to the Internet, and whether or not portability is important. This section of the References and Resources Guide explores topics related to buying a new PC. ■

Analyzing Needs

When referring to a computer system, a need refers to a functional requirement that the computer system must be able to meet. For example, at a video rental store, a computer system must be able to enter barcodes automatically from videos or DVDs being checked in and out, identify customers with overdue movies, manage movie inventories, and do routine accounting operations. Portability is another example of a possible need. For example, if you need to take your computer with you as you travel or work out of the office, you will need a portable computer instead of a desktop computer.

Selecting a PC for home or business use must begin with the all-important question "What do I want the system to do?" Once you have determined what tasks the system will be used for, you can choose among the software and hardware alternatives available. Making a list of your needs in areas discussed in the next few sections can help you get a picture of what type of system you are shopping for. If you are not really sure what you want a system to do, you should think twice about buying one yet—you can easily make expensive mistakes if you are uncertain about what you want a system to do. Some common decision categories are discussed next; Figure R-1 provides a list of questions that can help you define the type of computer that will meet your needs.

▼ FIGURE R-1
Questions to consider when getting ready to buy a PC.

POSSIBLE QUESTIONS

What tasks will I be using the computer for (writing papers, accessing the Internet, watching TV, making telephone calls, composing music, playing games, etc.)?

Do I prefer a Mac or a PC-compatible? Are there any other computers I need my documents and storage media to be compatible with?

How fast do I need the system to be?

Do I need portability? If so, do I need the features of a conventional PC (notebook or tablet) or can I use a handheld PC?

What size and type of screen do I need?

What removable storage media will I need to use in the PC (such as CDs, DVDs, flash memory cards, or a USB flash drive)?

Do I need to be able to connect the PC to the Internet? If so, what type of Internet access will I be using (such as conventional dial-up, DSL, cable, satellite, or mobile wireless)?

Do I need to be able to connect the PC to a network? If so, is it a wired or wireless network and what type of network adapter is needed to connect to that network?

What additional hardware do I need (scanner, printer, or digital camera, for example)?

When do I need the computer?

Do I want to pay extra for a better warranty (such as a longer time period, more comprehensive coverage, or on-site service)?

Operating Systems and Application Software

Determining what functions you want the system to perform will help you decide which application software is needed. Most users start with an application suite containing a word processor, spreadsheet, and other programs. In addition, specialty programs, such as tax preparation, drawing, home publishing, reference software, games, and more may be needed or desired.

Not all software is available for all operating systems. Consequently, if a specific piece of software is needed, that choice may determine which operating system you need to use. In addition, your operating system decision may already be made for you if your documents need to be compatible with those of another computer (such as other office computers or between a home and an office PC). The most widely used PC operating systems are Windows, Mac OS, and Linux.

Platforms and Configuration Options

If your operating system has already been determined, that is a good start in deciding the overall platform you will be looking for—most users will choose between the PC-compatible and Apple Macintosh platform. PC-compatible computers usually run either Windows or Linux; Apple computers almost always use Mac OS.

Configuration decisions initially involve determining the size of the machine desired. For nonportable systems, you have the choice between tower, desktop, or all-in-one configurations; in addition, the monitor size and type (CRT or flat-screen) needs to be determined. Portable, fully functioning PCs can be notebook or tablet PCs. For tablet PCs, you need to decide if you will require keyboard use on a regular basis; if so, a convertible tablet PC would be the best choice. If a powerful fully functioning PC is not required, you may decide to go with a more portable option, such as a handheld PC or UMPC.

You should also consider any other specifications that are important to you, such as the size of the hard drive, types of other storage devices needed, amount of memory required, and so forth. As discussed in the next section, these decisions often require reconciling the features you want with the amount of money you are willing to spend.

Power vs. Budget Requirements

As part of the needs analysis, you should look closely at your need for a powerful system versus your budgetary constraints. Most users do not need a state-of-the-art system. Those who do should expect to pay more than the average user. A PC that was top of the line six months or a year ago is usually reasonably priced and more than adequate for most users' needs. Individuals who just want a PC for basic tasks, such as using the Internet and word processing, can likely get by with an inexpensive PC designed for home use.

When determining your requirements, be sure to identify the features and functions that are absolutely essential for your primary PC tasks (such as a large hard drive and lots of memory for multimedia applications, a fast video card for gaming, a fast Internet connection, a TV tuner card for individuals who wish to use the PC as a TV set, and so forth). After you have the minimum configuration determined, you can add optional or desirable components, as your budget allows.

Listing Alternatives

After you consider your needs and the questions mentioned in Figure R-1, you should have a pretty good idea of the hardware and software you will need. You will also know what purchasing options are available to you, depending on your time frame (while some retail stores have systems that can be purchased and brought home the same day, special orders or some systems purchased over the Internet may take a few weeks to arrive). The next step is to get enough information from possible vendors to compare and contrast a few alternative systems that satisfy your stated needs. Most often, these vendors are local stores (such as computer stores, warehouse clubs, and electronic stores) and/or online stores (such as manufacturer Web sites and *e-tailers*—online retailers). To compare prices and specifications for possible computer systems, find at least three systems that meet or exceed your needs by looking through newspaper advertisements, configuring systems online via manufacturer and e-tailer Web sites, or calling or visiting local stores. A comparison sheet listing your criteria and the systems you are considering, such as the one in Figure R-2, can help you summarize your options. Although it is sometimes very difficult to compare the prices of systems since they typically have somewhat different configurations and some components (such as CPUs) are difficult to compare, you can assign an approximate dollar value to each extra feature a system has (such as $50 for an included printer or a larger hard drive). Be sure to also include any sales tax and shipping charges when you compare the prices of each total system.

If your budget is limited, you will have to balance the system you need with extra features you may want. But do not skimp on memory or hard drive space because sufficient memory can help your programs to run faster and with fewer problems and hard drive space is consumed quickly. Often for just a few extra dollars, you can get additional memory, a

COMPONENT	EXAMPLE OF DESIRED SPECIFICATIONS	SYSTEM #1 VENDOR:	SYSTEM #2 VENDOR:	SYSTEM #3 VENDOR:
Operating System	*Windows Vista Home Premium*			
Manufacturer	*HP or Dell*			
Style	*Notebook*			
CPU	*Intel dual core*			
RAM	*2 GB or higher*			
Hard drive	*300 GB or higher*			
Removable storage	*8-in-1 and flash memory card reader*			
Optical drive	*DVD-RW*			
Monitor	*Widescreen 15.4" minimum*			
Video card and video RAM	*Prefer dedicated video RAM*			
Keyboard	*Prefer speaker control keys*			
Mouse	*Portable USB with scroll wheel*			
Sound card/speakers	*No preference*			
Modem	*Conventional dial-up*			
Network card	*Wi-Fi (802.11n)*			
Printer	*Ink-jet if get deal on price with complete system*			
Scanner	*Don't need*			
Included software	*Microsoft Office*			
Warranty	*3 years min. (1 year onsite if not a local store)*			
Other features	*3 USB ports minimum; TV tuner ExpressCard module*			
Price				
Tax				
Shipping				
TOTAL COST				

FIGURE R-2
Comparing PC alternatives. A checklist such as this one can help to organize your desired criteria and evaluate possible systems.

faster CPU, or a larger hard drive—significantly cheaper than trying to upgrade any of those features later. A good rule of thumb is to try to buy a little more computer than you think you need. On the other hand, do not buy a top-of-the-line system, unless you fall into the power user category and really need it. Generally, the second or third system down from the top of the line is a very good system for a much more reasonable price. Some guidelines for minimum requirements for desktop PCs for most home users are as follows:

▶ A relatively fast CPU, such as the Intel Core 2 Duo (generally, any CPU currently being sold today is fast enough for most users).

▶ 1 GB or more of memory (RAM).

▶ 320 GB or more hard drive space.

▶ Recordable or rewritable DVD drive.

▶ Conventional dial-up modem plus a special modem, if needed, for an alternative type of Internet access.

▶ Sound card and external speakers.

▶ At least 4 USB ports.

▶ A built-in flash memory media reader.

As discussed in Chapter 2 of this text, a numbering system is a way of representing numbers. People generally use the *decimal numbering system* explained in Chapter 2 and reviewed next; computers process data using the *binary numbering system*. Another numbering system related to computer use is the *hexadecimal numbering system*, which can be used to represent long strings of binary numbers in a manner more understandable to people than the binary numbering system. Following a discussion of these three numbering systems, we take a look at conversions between numbering systems and principles of computer arithmetic, and then close with a look at how to perform conversions using a scientific calculator. ■

The Decimal and Binary Numbering System

The *decimal (base 10)* numbering system uses 10 symbols—the digits 0, 1, 2, 3, 4, 5, 6, 7, 8, and 9—to represent all possible numbers and is the numbering system people use most often. The *binary (base 2)* numbering system is used extensively by computers to represent numbers and other characters. This system uses only two digits—0 and 1. As mentioned in Chapter 2, the place values (columns) in the binary numbering system are different from those used in the decimal system.

The Hexadecimal Numbering System

Computers often output diagnostic and memory-management messages and identify network adapters and other hardware in *hexadecimal (hex)* notation. Hexadecimal notation is a shorthand method for representing the binary digits stored in a computer. Because large binary numbers—for example, 1010100010011101—can easily be misread by people, hexadecimal notation groups binary digits into units of four, which, in turn, are represented by other symbols.

The hexadecimal numbering system is also called the *base 16 numbering system* because it uses 16 different symbols. Since there are only 10 possible numeric digits, hexadecimal uses letters instead of numbers for the additional 6 symbols. The 16 hexadecimal symbols and their decimal and binary counterparts are shown in Figure R-3.

Hexadecimal is not itself a code that the computer uses to perform computations or to communicate with other machines. This numbering system does, however, have a special relationship to the 8-bit bytes of ASCII and EBCDIC that makes it ideal for displaying addresses and other data quickly. As you can see in Figure R-3, each hex character has a 4-bit binary counterpart, so any combination of 8 bits can be represented by exactly two hexadecimal characters. For example, the letter N (represented in ASCII by 01001110) has a hex representation of *4E* (see the Binary Equivalent column in Figure R-3).

FIGURE R-3
Hexadecimal characters and their decimal and binary equivalents.

HEXADECIMAL CHARACTER	DECIMAL EQUIVALENT	BINARY EQUIVALENT
0	0	0000
1	1	0001
2	2	0010
3	3	0011
4	4	0100
5	5	0101
6	6	0110
7	7	0111
8	8	1000
9	9	1001
A	10	1010
B	11	1011
C	12	1100
D	13	1101
E	14	1110
F	15	1111

Converting Between Numbering Systems

The concept of interpreting binary numbers was discussed in Chapter 2. Specifically, to convert from binary to decimal you need to multiply each digit of the binary number by the appropriate power of 2 for that place value, such as by 2^0 or 1 for the right-most digit, 2^1 or 2 for the next digit, and so forth, and then add those products together. Three other types of conversions are discussed next.

Hexadecimal to Decimal

As shown in Figure R-4, the process for converting a hexadecimal number to its decimal equivalent is similar to converting a binary number to its decimal equivalent, except the base number is 16 instead of 2. To determine the decimal equivalent of a hexadecimal number (such as 4F6A, as shown in Figure R-4), multiply the decimal equivalent of each individual hex character (determined by using the table in Figure R-3) by the appropriate power of 16 and then add the results to obtain the decimal equivalent of that hex number.

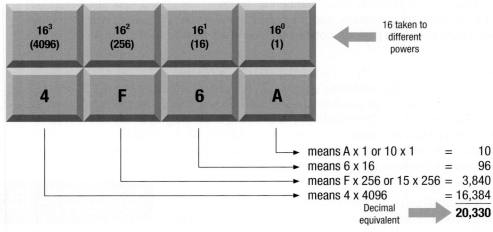

FIGURE R-4
The hexadecimal (base 16) numbering system. Each digit in a hexadecimal number represents 16 taken to a different power.

Hexadecimal to Binary and Binary to Hexadecimal

To convert from hexadecimal to binary, we convert each hexadecimal digit separately to 4 binary digits (using the table in Figure R-3). For example, to convert F6A9 to binary, we get

F	6	A	9
1111	0110	1010	1001

or 1111011010101001 in binary representation. To convert from binary to hexadecimal, we go through the reverse process. If the number of digits in the binary number is not divisible by 4, we add leading zeros to the binary number to force an even division. For example, to convert the binary number 1101101010011 to hexadecimal, we get

0001	1011	0101	0011
1	B	5	3

or lB53 in hexadecimal representation. Note that three leading zeros were added to change the initial 1 to 0001 before making the conversion.

Decimal to Binary and Decimal to Hexadecimal

To convert from decimal to either binary or hexadecimal, we can use the *remainder method*. To use the remainder method, the decimal number is divided by 2 (to convert to a binary number) or 16 (to convert to a hexadecimal number). The *remainder* of the division operation is recorded and the division process is repeated using the *quotient* as the next dividend, until the quotient becomes 0. At that point, the collective remainders (written backwards) represent the equivalent binary or hexadecimal number (see Figure R-5).

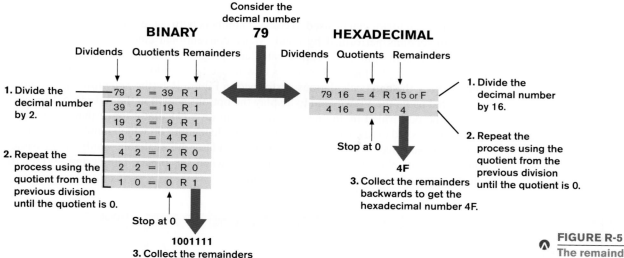

FIGURE R-5
The remainder method. The remainder method can be used to convert decimal numbers to binary or hex format.

A table summarizing all the numbering system conversion procedures covered in this text is provided in Figure R-6.

FROM BASE	TO BASE		
	2	10	16
2		Starting at the right-most digit, multiply binary digits by 2^0, 2^1, 2^2, etc., respectively and then add products.	Starting at the right-most digit, convert each group of four binary digits to a hex digit.
10	Divide repeatedly by 2 using each quotient as the next dividend until the quotient becomes 0, and then collect the remainders in reverse order.		Divide repeatedly by 16 using each quotient as the next dividend until the quotient becomes 0, and then collect the remainders in reverse order.
16	Convert each hex digit to four binary digits.	Starting at right-most digit, multiply hex digits by 16^0, 16^1, 16^2, etc., respectively. Then add products.	

FIGURE R-6
Summary of conversions.

Computer Arithmetic

To most people, decimal arithmetic is second nature. Addition and subtraction using binary and hexadecimal numbers is not much different than the same operations with decimal numbers—just the number of symbols used in each system varies. For instance, the digits in each column are added or subtracted and you carry to and borrow from the column to the left as needed as you move from right to left. Instead of carrying or borrowing 10, however—as you would in the decimal system—you carry or borrow 2 (binary) or 16 (hexadecimal).

Figure R-7 provides an example of addition and subtraction with decimal, binary, and hexadecimal numbers.

FIGURE R-7
Adding and subtracting with the decimal, binary, and hexadecimal numbering systems.

	DECIMAL	BINARY	HEXADECIMAL
Addition	144 + 27 171	100101 + 10011 111000	8E + 2F BD
Subtraction	144 - 27 117	100101 - 10011 10010	8E - 2F 5F

Using a Scientific Calculator

A scientific calculator can be used to convert numbers between numbering systems, or to check conversions performed by hand. Many conventional calculators have different numbering system options; scientific calculator programs can be used for this purpose, as well. For example, Figure R-8 shows how to use the Windows Calculator program to double-check the hand calculations performed in Figure R-5 (the *Scientific* option must be selected using the View menu to display the options shown in the figure). Arithmetic can also be performed in any numbering system on a calculator, once that numbering system is selected on the calculator. Notice that, depending on which numbering system is currently selected, not all numbers on the calculator are available—only the possible numbers are displayed, such as only 0 and 1 when the binary numbering system is selected, as in the bottom screen in the figure.

FIGURE R-8

Using a scientific calculator. A physical calculator or calculator program can be used to convert between numbering systems, as well as to perform arithmetic in different numbering systems.

WINDOWS CALCULATOR
The Calculator program is typically located under Accessories on the Windows Start menu; select the *Scientific* option using the Calculator's View menu.

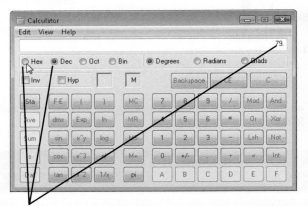

1. After entering a number (such as the decimal number 79 with the decimal numbering system selected shown here), select the numbering system to which the number should be converted (hex in this example).

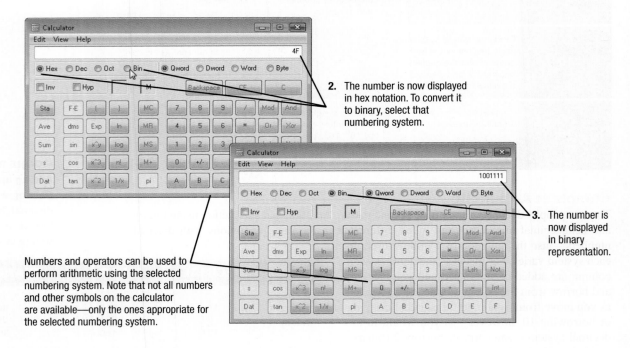

2. The number is now displayed in hex notation. To convert it to binary, select that numbering system.

3. The number is now displayed in binary representation.

Numbers and operators can be used to perform arithmetic using the selected numbering system. Note that not all numbers and other symbols on the calculator are available—only the ones appropriate for the selected numbering system.

CODING CHARTS

As discussed in Chapter 2 of this text, coding systems for text-based data include ASCII and Unicode; *EBCDIC* (*Extended Binary-Coded Decimal Interchange Code*) is another coding system for text-based data that was developed primarily for use with mainframes. ∎

FIGURE R-9
ASCII and EBCDIC binary codes for typical keyboard symbols.

ASCII and EBCDIC

Figure R-9 provides a chart listing the 8-digit ASCII and EBCDIC representations (in binary) for most of the symbols found on a typical keyboard.

SYMBOL	ASCII	EBCDIC	SYMBOL	ASCII	EBCDIC	SYMBOL	ASCII	EBCDIC
A	0100 0001	1100 0001	e	0110 0101	1000 0101	8	0011 1000	1111 1000
B	0100 0010	1100 0010	f	0110 0110	1000 0110	9	0011 1001	1111 1001
C	0100 0011	1100 0011	g	0110 0111	1000 0111	(	0010 1000	0100 1101
D	0100 0100	1100 0100	h	0110 1000	1000 1000	)	0010 1001	0101 1101
E	0100 0101	1100 0101	i	0110 1001	1000 1001	/	0010 1111	0110 0001
F	0100 0110	1100 0110	j	0110 1010	1001 0001	-	0010 1101	0110 0000
G	0100 0111	1100 0111	k	0110 1011	1001 0010	*	0010 1010	0101 1100
H	0100 1000	1100 1000	l	0110 1100	1001 0011	+	0010 1011	0100 1110
I	0100 1001	1100 1001	m	0110 1101	1001 0100	,	0010 1100	0110 1011
J	0100 1010	1101 0001	n	0110 1110	1001 0101	.	0010 1110	0100 1011
K	0100 1011	1101 0010	o	0110 1111	1001 0110	:	0011 1010	0111 1010
L	0100 1100	1101 0011	p	0111 0000	1001 0111	;	0011 1011	0101 1110
M	0100 1101	1101 0100	q	0111 0001	1001 1000	&	0010 0110	0101 0000
N	0100 1110	1101 0101	r	0111 0010	1001 1001	\	0101 1100	1110 0000
O	0100 1111	1101 0110	s	0111 0011	1010 0010	$	0010 0100	0101 1011
P	0101 0000	1101 0111	t	0111 0100	1010 0011	%	0010 0101	0110 1100
Q	0101 0001	1101 1000	u	0111 0101	1010 0100	=	0011 1101	0111 1110
R	0101 0010	1101 1001	v	0111 0110	1010 0101	>	0011 1110	0110 1110
S	0101 0011	1110 0010	w	0111 0111	1010 0110	<	0011 1100	0100 1100
T	0101 0100	1110 0011	x	0111 1000	1010 0111	!	0010 0001	0101 1010
U	0101 0101	1110 0100	y	0111 1001	1010 1000			0111 1100	0110 1010
V	0101 0110	1110 0101	z	0111 1010	1010 1001	?	0011 1111	0110 1111
W	0101 0111	1110 0110	0	0011 0000	1111 0000	@	0100 0000	0111 1100
X	0101 1000	1110 0111	1	0011 0001	1111 0001	_	0101 1111	0110 1101
Y	0101 1001	1110 1000	2	0011 0010	1111 0010	`	0110 0000	1011 1001
Z	0101 1010	1110 1001	3	0011 0011	1111 0011	{	0111 1011	1100 0000
a	0110 0001	1000 0001	4	0011 0100	1111 0100	}	0111 1101	1101 0000
b	0110 0010	1000 0010	5	0011 0101	1111 0101	~	0111 1110	1010 0001
c	0110 0011	1000 0011	6	0011 0110	1111 0110	[	0101 1011	0100 1010
d	0110 0100	1000 0100	7	0011 0111	1111 0111	]	0101 1101	0101 1010

A 0041	N 004E	a 0061	n 006E	0 0030	{ 007B	* 002A	■ 25A0	অ 0985
B 0042	O 004F	b 0062	o 006F	1 0031	| 007C	+ 002B	□ 25A1	গ 0997
C 0043	P 0050	c 0063	p 0070	2 0032	} 007D	, 002C	▲ 25B2	ে 09C7
D 0044	Q 0051	d 0064	q 0071	3 0033	~ 007E	- 002D	% 2105	য 09F6
E 0045	R 0052	e 0065	r 0072	4 0034	! 0021	. 002E	℞ 211E	č 0685
F 0046	S 0053	f 0066	s 0073	5 0035	" 0022	/ 002F	⅓ 2153	ڴ 06B4
G 0047	T 0054	g 0067	t 0074	6 0036	# 0023	£ 20A4	⅔ 2154	ڪ 06AA
H 0048	U 0055	h 0068	u 0075	7 0037	$ 0024	Σ 2211	♛ 2655	α 03B1
I 0049	V 0056	i 0069	v 0076	8 0038	% 0025	∅ 2205	☂ 2602	β 03B2
J 004A	W 0057	j 006A	w 0077	9 0039	& 0026	√ 221A	❑ 2750	Δ 0394
K 004B	X 0058	k 006B	x 0078	[005B	' 0027	∞ 221E	☀ 2742	φ 03A6
L 004C	Y 0059	l 006C	y 0079	\ 005C	(0028	≤ 2264	❂ 27B2	Ω 03A9
M 004D	Z 005A	m 006D	z 007A	] 005D	) 0029	≥ 2265	♥ 2665	Ÿ 03AB

FIGURE R-10
Selected Unicode codes.

Unicode

Since consistent worldwide representation of symbols is increasingly needed today, use of Unicode is growing rapidly. Unicode can be used to represent every written language, as well as a variety of other symbols. Unicode codes are typically listed in hexadecimal notation—a sampling of Unicode is shown in Figure R-10.

The capability to display characters and other symbols using Unicode coding is incorporated into many programs. For instance, when the Symbol dialog box is opened using the Insert menu in Microsoft Office Word, the Unicode representation (as well as the corresponding ASCII code in either decimal or hexadecimal representation) can be viewed (see Figure R-11). Some programs allow you to enter a Unicode symbol using its Unicode hexadecimal value. For instance, in Microsoft Office programs you can use the Alt+X command when the insertion point is just to the right of a Unicode hex value to convert that hex value into the corresponding symbol. For example, the keystrokes

2264Alt+X

result in the symbol corresponding to the Unicode code 2264 (the less than or equal sign ≤) being inserted into the document; entering 03A3 and then pressing Alt+X inserts the symbol shown in the Word screen in Figure R-11.

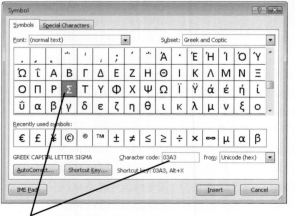

Unicode representation for Greek capital letter sigma Σ symbol.

FIGURE R-11
Using Unicode.

INSERTING SYMBOLS USING UNICODE
In Microsoft Office programs, typing the hexadecimal Unicode code for a symbol and then pressing Alt+X displays the corresponding symbol.

UNICODE REPRESENTATION
The Symbol dialog box shown here lists the Unicode representation of each symbol as it is selected. If preferred, the ASCII representation can be displayed.

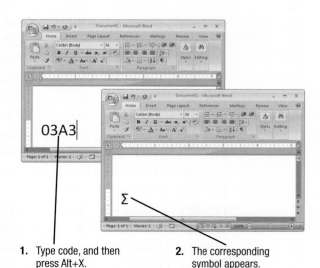

1. Type code, and then press Alt+X.

2. The corresponding symbol appears.

ANSWERS TO SELF-QUIZ

Chapter 1
  1. T **2.** F **3.** F **4.** F **5.** T **6.** Input **7.** tablet **8.** hyperlinks **9.** electronic mail or e-mail **10. a.** 4 **b.** 2 **c.** 1 **d.** 3

Chapter 2
  1. F **2.** T **3.** F **4.** F **5.** T **6.** scanner, optical scanner, flatbed scanner, or handheld scanner **7.** quad-core **8.** flash memory
  9. folders **10. a.** 3 **b.** 2 **c.** 5 **d.** 4 **e.** 1

Chapter 3
  1. F **2.** F **3.** T **4.** T **5.** F **6.** Digital Subscriber Line or DSL **7.** keyword; directory **8.** instant messaging or IM **9.** online
  auction **10. a.** 2 **b.** 5 **c.** 3 **d.** 1 **e.** 6 **f.** 4

Chapter 4
  1. F **2.** T **3.** F **4.** T **5.** F **6.** war driving **7.** Biometric **8.** firewall **9.** digital signature **10. a.** 4 **b.** 3 **c.** 6 **d.** 1 **e.** 5 **f.** 2

Chapter 5
  1. F **2.** T **3.** T **4.** F **5.** F **6.** disaster recovery **7.** digital counterfeiting **8.** filter **9.** opt out; opt in **10. a.** 4 **b.** 5 **c.** 2
  d. 3 **e.** 1

Chapter 6
  1. F **2.** T **3.** F **4.** T **5.** T **6.** copyright; trademark **7.** plagiarism **8.** Digital rights management (DRM)
  9. Communications Decency **10. a.** 2 **b.** 5 **c.** 1 **d.** 3 **e.** 4

Chapter 7
  1. F **2.** T **3.** T **4.** F **5.** F **6.** ergonomics **7.** burnout **8.** computer/Internet addiction **9.** digital divide **10.** Solar

Chapter 8
  1. F **2.** T **3.** F **4.** F **5.** T **6.** qubits **7.** WiMAX **8.** VeriChip **9.** robots **10.** nanotubes

CREDITS

Throughout the chapters: Screen shots of Microsoft Access®, Excel®, Paint®, PowerPoint®, Word®, and Windows® reprinted with permission from Microsoft Corporation. Copyright © Microsoft Explorer® reprinted with permission from Microsoft Corporation.

Chapter 1

Figure 1-1a, Photo courtesy of Nokia. Copyright © 2007 Nokia. All rights reserved. Nokia and Nokia Connecting People are registered trademarks of Nokia Corporation.; **Figure 1-1b**, Courtesy, Hewlett-Packard Company; **Figure 1-2a**, Courtesy, Hewlett-Packard Company; **Figure 1-2b**, © Flying Colours Ltd/Getty Images; **Figure 1-2c**, Courtesy of Nintendo; **Figure 1-2d**, Courtesy TMIO, Inc.; **Figure 1-2e**, Courtesy T-Mobile USA, Inc.; **Figure 1-3a**, Photo provided courtesy of the Wi-Fi Alliance; **Figure 1-3b**, Copyright 2001-2007 SMART Technologies Inc. All rights reserved.; **Figure 1-3c**, Courtesy General Dynamics Itronix; **Figure 1-3d**, Courtesy U.S. Navy; **Figure 1-4a**, Courtesy of Gateway, Inc.; **Figure 1-4b**, Courtesy General Dynamics Itronix; **Figure 1-4c**, Courtesy NEC Display Solutions; **Figure 1-4d**, Courtesy Motion Computing; **Figure 1-4e**, Courtesy of Motorola; **Figure 1-4f**, Courtesy Ingersoll Rand Security Technologies; **Figure 1-5a**, Courtesy Intel Corporation; **Figure 1-5b**, Courtesy 3M Touch Systems; **Figure 1-5c**, Courtesy of NCR Corporation; **Figure 1-5d**, Courtesy MasterCard Worldwide; **Figure 1-5e**, Courtesy Ingersoll Rand Security Technologies; **Figure 1-5f**, Courtesy of Garmin Ltd. or its subsidiaries; **Figure Chapter 1 Trend**, Courtesy MobiTV, Inc.; **Figure 1-7ace**, Courtesy IBM Corporate Archives; **Figure 1-7b**, Courtesy U.S. Army; **Figure 1-7d**, Courtesy, Hewlett-Packard Company; **Figure 1-8a**, Courtesy of Gateway, Inc.; **Figure 1-8b**, Courtesy, Hewlett-Packard Company; **Figure 1-8c**, © Logitech. All rights reserved. Images/materials on page 14 used with permission from Logitech; **Figure 1-8d**, Courtesy SanDisk Corporation; **Figure 1-8e**, Courtesy Imation; **Figure 1-12e**, Courtesy RedLobster.com; **Figure 1-13**, Courtesy Volvo Cars of North America; **Figure 1-14**, Photo courtesy of Nokia. Copyright © 2007 Nokia. All rights reserved. Nokia and Nokia Connecting People are registered trademarks of Nokia Corporation.; **You box**, Courtesy PumpOne.com; **Figure 1-15a**, © 2007 Dell Inc. All Rights Reserved.; **Figure 1-15b**, Courtesy of Apple Inc.; **Figure 1-16a**, Courtesy Acer America; **Figure 1-16b**, Photo courtesy of TabletKiosk; **Figure 1-16cde**, Courtesy of Gateway, Inc.; **Figure 1-17a**, Courtesy, Hewlett-Packard Company; **Figure 1-17b**, © 2007 OQO, Inc.; **Figure 1-18a**, Courtesy Bluetooth SIG; **Figure 1-18b**, © 2007 OQO, Inc.; **Figure 1-19a**, Photo by Dom Miguel Photography for Seaport; **Figure 1-19b**, MSN TV Set Top Box from Microsoft; **Figure 1-19c**, Courtesy Sony Electronics Inc.; **Figure 1-19d**, Courtesy of Nintendo; **Figure 1-20a**, Courtesy Sutter Gould Medical Foundation; **Figure 1-20b**, Courtesy of Gateway, Inc.; **Figure 1-21**, Courtesy of IBM; **Figure 1-22**, Courtesy of IBM; **Inside b**, Courtesy of Gateway, Inc.; **Figure 1-23a**, Courtesy of Gateway, Inc.; **Figure 1-23bcd**, Courtesy Acer America; **Figure 1-23e**, Courtesy, Hewlett-Packard Company; **Figure 1-24b**, MapQuest and the MapQuest logo are registered trademarks of MapQuest, Inc. Map content © 2007 by MapQuest, Inc. and its respective copyright holders. Used with permission.; **Figure 1-24c**, Courtesy WHAT THE BUCK and YouTube; **Figure 1-24f**, Gmail screenshot © Google Inc. and used with permission.; **Figure 1-27a**, Courtesy of Gateway, Inc.; **Figure 1-27b**, ARTHUR Web site © 2007 WGBH; underlying ARTHUR TM/© Marc Brown.; **How box**, Courtesy e2Campus by Omnilert, LLC; **Figure 1-29**, Courtesy of Stanford University; **Figure 1-30**, Google screenshot © Google Inc. and used with permission.; **Figure 1-31a**, Courtesy of Gateway, Inc.; **Figure 1-31b**, Courtesy Acer America; **Figure 1-32**, The Survivor: China Logo is a registered trademark of Survivor Productions, LLC. CBS.com website contents © CBS Broadcasting Inc. Used by permission. CBS and the CBS Eye are registered trademarks of CBS Broadcasting Inc.; **Figure 1-33**, Courtesy of Symantec; **Ask the Expert 1**, Courtesy Strike Fighter Weapons School Pacific, NAS Lemoore; **Ask the Expert 2**, Photo courtesy of TabletKiosk; **Ask the Expert 3**, Courtesy Igel; **Expert Insight**, Photo courtesy of Nokia. Copyright © 2007 Nokia. All rights reserved. Nokia and Nokia Connecting People are registered trademarks of Nokia Corporation.

Chapter 2

Figure 2-4, Courtesy HTC; **Figure 2-5**, © Logitech. All rights reserved. Images/materials on page 58 used with permission from Logitech; **Figure 2-6a**, Courtesy Kensington Computer Products Group; **Figure 2-6b**, © Logitech. All rights reserved. Images/materials on page 59 used with permission from Logitech; **Figure 2-6c**, Courtesy Acer America; **Figure 2-7a**, Photo courtesy of Nokia. Copyright © 2007 Nokia. All rights reserved. Nokia and Nokia Connecting People are registered trademarks of Nokia Corporation.; **Figure 2-7b**, Courtesy Wacom Technology Corp.; **Figure 2-7c**, Courtesy of Hand Held Products, Inc.; **Figure 2-8a**, Courtesy, Hewlett-Packard Company; **Figure 2-8b**, © Logitech. All rights reserved. Images/materials on page 60 used with permission from Logitech; **Figure 2-8c**, Courtesy of Apple Inc.; **Figure 2-8d**, © Fujitsu Siemens Computers; **Figure 2-9a**, Courtesy, Hewlett-Packard Company; **Figure 2-9b**, Courtesy of Motorola; **Figure 2-9c**, Courtesy of NCR Corporation; **Figure 2-9d**, Courtesy Ingersoll Rand Security Technologies; **Trend box**, Courtesy Philips Electronics; **Figure 2-10**, Courtesy of Sony Electronics Inc.; **Figure 2-13a**, Courtesy of Intel Corporation; **Figure 2-13b**, © 2003, 2005, 2007 Advanced Micro Devices, Inc., Reprinted with permission. AMD, and combinations thereof as well as certain other marks listed at http://www.amd.com/legal/trademarks.html are trademarks of Advanced Micro Devices, Inc.; **How box**, Courtesy, Hewlett-Packard Company; **Figure 2-14**, Courtesy Kingston Technology; **Figure 2-15**, Courtesy © 2007 Sony Computer Entertainment America Inc. All Rights Reserved. "PlayStation", "PLAYSTATION", "PS" Family logo and "PSP" are registered trademarks of Sony Computer Entertainment Inc.; **Figure 2-16**, Courtesy Acer America; **Figure 2-18b**, Courtesy, Hewlett-Packard Company; **Figure 2-18c**, Courtesy, Hewlett-Packard Company; **Figure 2-19**, © Fujitsu Siemens Computers; **Figure 2-20**, Copyright © Iomega Corporation. All Rights Reserved. Iomega, the stylized "i" logo and all product images are property of Iomega Corporation in the United States and/or other countries. Zip and REV are registered trademarks of Iomega Corporation in the United States and/or other countries.; **Figure 2-22a**, Courtesy Western Digital; **Figure 2-22b**, Courtesy of Fabrik; **Figure 2-23**, Copyright © Iomega Corporation. All Rights Reserved. Iomega, the stylized "i" logo and all product images are property of Iomega Corporation in the United States and/or other countries. Zip and REV are registered trademarks of Iomega Corporation in the United States and/or other countries.; **Inside box**, Courtesy of DriveSavers, Inc. www.drivesavers.com; **Figure 2-25a**, Courtesy, Hewlett-Packard Company; **Figure 2-25b**, Courtesy Memorex Products, Inc.; **Figure 2-25c**, Courtesy CD Digital Card www.cddigitalcard.com; **Figure 2-26**, Courtesy LaCie USA; **Figure 2-27a**, Courtesy Oakley Inc.; **Figure 2-27c**, Courtesy Imation; **Figure 2-27d**, Courtesy Transcend Information, Inc.; **Figure 2-28**, Courtesy of Seagate Technology LLC; **Figure 2-29b**, © 2007 Xdrive LLC. All Rights Reserved. Used with permission.; **Figure 2-30**, Photo by HID Global Corporation; **Figure 2-31abef**, Courtesy D-Link Systems; **Figure 2-31c**, Courtesy of Belkin International, Inc.; **Figure 2-31d**, Courtesy of Linksys; **Ask the Expert 1**, AMD, the AMD Arrow logo and combinations thereof are trademarks of Advanced Micro Devices, Inc.; **Ask the Expert 2**, Courtesy Kingston Technology; **Ask the Expert 3**, Courtesy McDonald's Corporation; **Expert Insight**, Courtesy, Hewlett-Packard Company.

Chapter 3

Figure 3-1a, Courtesy of Gateway, Inc.; **Figure 3-1b**, The Survivor: China Logo is a registered trademark of Survivor Productions, LLC. CBS.com website contents © CBS Broadcasting Inc. Used by permission. CBS and the CBS Eye are registered trademarks of CBS Broadcasting Inc.; **Figure 3-2a**, Courtesy of Verizon Communications; **Figure 3-2b**, Courtesy Road Runner; **Figure 3-2c**, AOL and the triangle logo are registered trademarks of AOL LLC.; **Figure 3-2d**, Use of the AT&T logo is granted under permission by AT&T Intellectual Property.; **Figure 3-2e**, Photo(s) courtesy of Hughes Network Systems, LLC.; **Figure 3-2f**, Courtesy Clearwire; **Figure 3-5**, Courtesy CoreFTP.com; **Figure 3-6a**, Courtesy Acer America; **Figure 3-6b**, Courtesy T-Mobile USA, Inc.; **Figure 3-6c**, Courtesy © 2007 Sony Computer Entertainment America Inc. All Rights Reserved. "PlayStation", "PLAYSTATION", "PS" Family logo and "PSP" are registered trademarks of Sony Computer Entertainment Inc.; **Figure 3-9ab**, Photo provided courtesy of the Wi-Fi Alliance; **Figure 3-9c**, Courtesy Intel Corporation; **Figure 3-9d**, Courtesy Bluetooth SIG; **Figure 3-11ab**, Google screenshot © Google Inc. and used with permission.; **Figure 3-12a**, 2007 InfoSpace, Inc. All rights reserved.; **Figure 3-12b**, Reproduced with permission from Ask.com, a division of IAC Search & Media, Inc.; **Figure 3-13b**, Google screenshot © Google Inc. and used with permission.; **Figure 3-19a**, Courtesy SIPphone; **Figure 3-19bc**, Courtesy Vonage; **Figure 3-19d**, Courtesy D-Link; **Figure 3-20b**, © Logitech. All rights reserved. Images/materials on page 126 used with permission from Logitech; **Figure 3-21a**, Courtesy Facebook; **Figure 3-21b**, Courtesy Fotki, Inc.; **Figure 3-21c**, Courtesy LinkedIn; **Figure 3-21d**, Courtesy Cozi Central; **Figure 3-22b**, These materials have been reproduced with the permission of eBay Inc. COPYRIGHT © EBAY INC. ALL RIGHTS RESERVED.; **Figure 3-23a**, Used by Permission of Clear Channel Radio.; **Figure 3-23b**, The Survivor: China Logo is a registered trademark of Survivor Productions, LLC. CBS.com website contents © CBS Broadcasting Inc. Used by permission. CBS and the CBS Eye are registered trademarks of CBS Broadcasting Inc.; **Figure 3-23c**, © CinemaNow. All Rights Reserved.; **Figure 3-23d**, Courtesy of IGN.com; **You box**, Napster logo and marks reprinted with the permission of Napster, LLC.; **Figure 3-24b**, MapQuest and the MapQuest logo are registered trademarks of MapQuest, Inc. Map content © 2007 by MapQuest, Inc. and its respective copyright holders. Used with permission.; **Figure 3-25**, iGoogle screenshot © Google Inc. and used with permission. **How box ab**, "Audacity" is a trademark of Dominic Mazzoni; **Figure 3-26b**, Courtesy of SCOTTeVEST, www.scottevest.com; **Figure 3-28**, Courtesy Software Secure, Inc.; **Ask the Expert 1**, Courtesy NuNomad; **Ask the Expert 2**, Citrix, Citrix Online and GoToMyPC are registered trademarks of Citrix Systems, Inc.; **Ask the Expert 3**, Courtesy Throw the Fight www.myspace.com/throwthefight, www.throwthefight.com; **Expert Insight**, Courtesy Microsoft, Inc.

Chapter 4

Figure 4-2, Courtesy JiWire, Inc.; **Figure 4-3a**, Courtesy Acer America; **Figure 4-3b**, Courtesy of Gateway, Inc.; **Figure 4-3c**, Courtesy Kingston Technology; **Figure 4-4**, Courtesy Acer America; **Figure 4-7a**, Courtesy Innovative Card Technologies; **Figure 4-7b**, Courtesy Passfaces Corporation; **Inside box**, Courtesy SafeNet Inc.; **Figure 4-8**, Courtesy ActivIdentity; **You box**, Joseph Mehling, Dartmouth College; **Figure 4-9ac**, Copyright © 2007 L-1 Identity Solutions Operating Company. All rights reserved. Used with permission.; **Figure 4-9b**, Courtesy Ingersoll Rand Security Technologies; **Figure 4-9d**, DoD photo by Staff Sgt. Jonathan C. Knauth, U.S. Marine Corps.; **Figure 4-10a**, Courtesy D-Link; **Figure 4-12**, Courtesy of Symantec; **Trend box**, Courtesy JiWire, Inc.; **Figure 4-14**, Courtesy of Symantec; **Figure 4-17**, Courtesy Centennial Software Limited; **Figure 4-21**, These materials have been reproduced with the permission of eBay Inc. COPYRIGHT © EBAY INC. ALL RIGHTS RESERVED.; **Figure 4-23**, Courtesy Lavasoft AB; **Ask the Expert 1**, Courtesy ACM; **Ask the Expert 2**, Courtesy of Symantec; **Ask the Expert 3**, Courtesy of Symantec; **Expert Insight**, Courtesy of Symantec.

Chapter 5

Figure 5-1, Courtesy of Verizon Communications; **Figure 5-2**, Courtesy Kensington Computer Products Group; **Figure 5-3**, Courtesy Trekstor USA Inc.; **How box**, Courtesy Absolute Software Corporation; **Figure 5-4**, Courtesy NTT DoCoMo, Inc.; **Trend box a**, Courtesy of DataDotDNA; **Trend box b**, Photo courtesy of Nokia. Copyright © 2007 Nokia. All rights reserved. Nokia and Nokia Connecting People are registered trademarks of Nokia Corporation.; **Figure 5-6**, Courtesy General Dynamics Itronix; **Figure 5-7**, Courtesy APC; **Figure 5-8**, Courtesy Getac Inc.; **Figure 5-10**, Photo courtesy of United States Secret Service; **Figure 5-11**, Photo courtesy of United

GLOSSARY/INDEX

A

abacus, 12, R-2

ABC. *See* Atanasoff-Berry Computer (ABC)

academic honor code, 270

access control system, 168–175

biometric access systems, 172–173

possessed knowledge access system, 169–171

possessed object access system, 171–172

wireless networks, 174–175

access mechanism, hard disk drive, 76

access to technology, 300–306

assistive technology, 303–306

digital divide, 300–303

acronym, online communications, 42

Active Server Pages, 34

ActiveX, 176

adaptive cruise control system, 20

adaptive input device, 64

Ad-Aware, 194, 220

Add Tab Group to Favorites option, Add to Favorites button, 38

Add to Favorites button, 38

Add to Favorites option, Add to Favorites button, 38

addiction to Internet, 136

address

communications port, 176

e-mail. *See* e-mail address

Internet, 33, 35

IP, 33

MAC, 175

URLs, 34–35, 37

Address bar, browser, 37

Advanced Encryption Standard (AES), 177

Advanced Micro Devices (AMD), 66, 67, R-3, R-7

Advanced Research Projects Agency (ARPA), 102

Advanced Search option, 120

advertising

pop-under ads, 230–231

pop-up ads, 230–231

adware, 147

Aero (Vista), 224

AES. *See* Advanced Encryption Standard (AES)

age verification service, online, 273, 274

AI. *See* artificial intelligence (AI); artificial intelligence (AI) system

AIM. *See* AOL Instant Messenger (AIM)

Allen, Paul, R-4

all-in-one. *See* multifunction device (MFD)

all-in-one case, 22

all-in-one printer, 71

alt tag, 303

Altair, R-4

Alternate key, 58

alternative text description, 303

ALU. *See* arithmetic/logic unit (ALU)

always-on connection, 32, 110, 112

Amazon, 261, 265

Amazon Unbox, 134

AMD. *See* Advanced Micro Devices (AMD)

America Online (AOL), 30

American Psychological Association (APA), 122

American Standard Code for Information Interchange. *See* ASCII (American Standard Code for Information Interchange)

Americans with Disabilities Act (ADA), 303

analog camcorder, 64

Andreessen, Marc, R-5

anonymity of online communications, 43

Anonymizer, 43, 232, 233

anonymous e-mail service, 232

Anonymous Surfing, 233

anonymous Web surfing program, 233

ANS. *See* Autonomous Navigation System (ANS)

antenna A device used for receiving or sending radio signals. 85

Anticybersquatting Consumer Protection Act, 260

antiglare screen, 294

antispam appliance, 234

antispyware program, 147, 168, 194, 220, 243

antivirus software Software used to detect and eliminate computer viruses and other types of malware. 16, 41, 167, 168, 176, 181–182, 220

AOL (America Online), 30

AOL Instant Messenger (AIM), 123

AOL Mail, 39, 231

Apple Computer, 265, R-4, R-6

Apple Macintosh, 12, 13, R-5

Apple TV, 135

application assistant, 344

application service provider (ASP) A company that manages and distributes software-based services over the Internet. 106

application software Programs that enable users to perform specific tasks on a computer, such as writing a letter or playing a game. 15, 17–18. *See also specific types of application software*

Arbitration and Mediation Center, 260

archiving e-mail messages, 147

arithmetic/logic unit (ALU), 66

arm soreness/injury, prevention, 295

ARPA. *See* Advanced Research Projects Agency (ARPA)

ARPANET The predecessor of the Internet, named after the Advanced Research Projects Agency (ARPA), which sponsored its development. 102, R-3

arrow key, 58

artificial intelligence (AI) When a computer performs actions that are characteristic of human intelligence. 12, 13

artificial intelligence (AI) system A system in which a computer performs actions that are characteristic of human intelligence. 342–347

expert systems, 344–345

intelligent agents, 344

neural networks, 345

robotics, 346–347

ASCII (American Standard Code for Information Interchange) A fixed-length, binary coding system widely used to represent text-based data for computer processing on many types of computers. 56

coding chart, R-16

ASP. *See* application service provider (ASP)

.asp file extension, 34

assistive input device, 304–305

assistive output device, 306

assistive technology Hardware and software specifically designed for use by individuals who have a physical disability. 303–306

asymmetric key encryption. *See* public key encryption

Atanasoff, John V. R-2

Atanasoff-Berry Computer (ABC), R-2

Athlon 64, 66, 67, R-7

Athlon 64 X2, 66, 67

AT&T, 232

auction, online, 131–132

Audacity, 138

audio, 11

denial of service (DoS) attack An act of sabotage that attempts to flood a network server or a Web server with so much activity that it is unable to function. 163, 164, 167–168

DeQuervain's tendonitis A condition in which the tendons on the thumb side of the wrist are swollen and irritated. 290

desktop case, 22

desktop PC A personal computer designed to fit on or next to a desk. 19, 22
Internet use, 109

desktop virtualization, 29

detector, 334

dialing program, 32

dialog box A window that requires the user to supply additional information. 16, 17

dial-up connection A type of Internet connection in which the PC or other device must dial up and connect to a service provider's computer via telephone lines before being connected to the Internet. 32, 110, 111–112

Digg collaborative news community, 128

digital camcorder, 64

digital camera An input device that takes pictures and records them as digital data (instead of film or video-taped) images. 14, 15, 60, 62–64, R-7
mobile phones, 240
still, 62–64
video, 62, 64

digital cash, 83

digital certificate A group of electronic data, such as encryption key pairs and a digital signature, that can be used to verify the identity of a person or organization. 194, 195–196

digital computer, 55

digital counterfeiting The use of computers or other types of digital equipment to make illegal copies of currency, checks, collectibles, and other items. 222–223
prevention, 224–225

digital data representation, 55–57

digital divide The gap between those who have access to technology and those who do not. 300–303
global, 302–303
U.S. 301–302

digital manipulation The alteration of digital content, usually text or photographs. 271–272

digital media receiver, 135

Digital Millennium Corporation Act (DMCA), 277

digital pen. *See* electronic pen

digital phone. *See* Voice over Internet Protocol (VoIP)

digital projector. *See* data projector

digital rights management (DRM), 264, 265, 266

digital rights management (DRM) software Software used to protect and manage the rights of creators of digital content, such as art, music, photographs, and movies. 258–259

digital signature A unique digital code that can be attached to a file or an e-mail message to verify the identity of the sender and guarantee the file or message has not been changed since it was signed. 194–195

Digital Subscriber Line. *See* DSL (Digital Subscriber Line) Internet access

digital tape cartridge, 62

Digital Theft Deterrence and Copyright Damages Improvement Act of 1999, 277

digital video disc. *See* DVD (digital video disc)

digital video recorder (DVR), 5

digital watermark A subtle alteration of digital content that is not noticeable when the work is viewed or played, but that identifies the copyright holder. 225, 258, 259
movies, 266

digital writing, 59

digitizing tablet. *See* graphics tablet

direct connection An always-on type of Internet connection in which the PC or other device is continually connected to the Internet. 32, 110, 112

directory. *See* folder

directory search A type of Internet search in which categories are selected to locate information on the Internet. 117, 118

disaster recovery plan A written plan that describes the steps a company will take following the occurrence of a disaster. 221

discussion group A type of Internet communications that enables individuals to post messages on a particular topic for others to read and respond to. 36, 126–127

disk
floppy. *See* floppy disk
hard. *See* hard disk drive (HDD)

disk-erasing, 236

diskette. *See* floppy disk

disk-wiping, 236

Disney, 265

display device An output device that contains a viewing screen. 70–71. *See also specific devices*
Braille, 306
color, 70
CRT monitor, 70
data and multimedia projectors, 70
flat-panel, 70
HDTV, 70
monochrome, 70

display screen A display device built into a notebook computer, handheld PC, or other device. 70–71

disposable e-mail address. *See* throw-away e-mail address

disposal
data, 236–237
hardware, 236, 309, 311–313

distance learning A learning environment in which the student is physically located away from the instructor and other students; commonly, instruction and communications take place via the Internet. 6, 139, 140–141

distance learning program, accreditation, 270

distributed denial of service (DDoS) attack, 167

DMCA. *See* Digital Millennium Corporation Act (DMCA)

DNS. *See* domain name system (DNS)

DNS poisoning, 190

DNS server, 190

Do Not Call Implementation Act, 245

Do Not E-Mail Registry, 236

docking station A device that connects a portable PC to conventional hardware, such as a keyboard, mouse, monitor, and printer. 25, 292, 293

document. *See also* file
editing, 89
formatting, 89
word processing software. *See* word processing software

document formatting, 89

document holder, 291, 292, 294

Document Workspaces, 243

domain name A text-based Internet address used to uniquely identify a computer on the Internet. 33

domain name system (DNS), 33
DNS poisoning, 190
DNS server, 190

DomainKeys, 195

donating computer equipment, 312–313

DoS. *See* denial of service (DoS) attack

dot con A fraud or scam carried out through the Internet. 185
protecting against, 192–194

dot-com crash, R-6

dot-matrix printer, 71

dots per inch (dpi), 61, 71

double-layer disc, 79

double-sided disc, 79

downward-compatible optical drive, 80

Draft-N hardware, 339

drive
DVD, 15
flash. *See* flash memory *entries*
hard. *See* hard disk drive (HDD); hard drive